INTER/MEDIA

INTER/MEDIA

Interpersonal Communication in a Media World

SECOND EDITION

Edited by
GARY GUMPERT and ROBERT CATHCART
Queens College of the City University of New York

New York / Oxford
OXFORD UNIVERSITY PRESS
1982

Library of Congress Cataloging in Publication Data
Main entry under title:
Inter/media: interpersonal communication in a media
  world.
  Bibliography: p.
  1. Mass media—Addresses, essays, lectures.
2. Interpersonal communication—Addresses, essays,
lectures. I. Gumpert, Gary. II. Cathcart, Robert S.
P91.25.I48 1982   302.2'34   82-10602   ISBN 0-19-503078-8

Printing (last digit): 9 8 7 6 5 4 3 2 1

Printed in the United States of America

Preface to the Second Edition

In the first edition of *Inter/Media* we presented a collection of essays based on a thesis neglected by most communication scholars—that our interpersonal communication is deeply interwoven with our universal involvement with and dependence on the media of communication. Apparently the time and topic were right for that publication, and we have been gratified by the supportive reactions of students and colleagues. The second edition is a response to dynamic changes in this field reflected in scholarly convention programs, research papers, new courses, and a tremendous growth of interest in the subject matter.

In the five years since we prepared the original edition, the scholarly void has been alleviated somewhat by this growing interest among scholars and media experts who grapple with the intricacies of the interpersonal communication/media world. Whereas our earlier edition had to make the connection by juxtaposing disparate views, our editorial function of guiding the reader has since been made easier as more writers have dealt directly with the media/interpersonal relationship.

We have capitalized on this increased interest and concern by selecting the best of the available research and insights published since the appearance of the first edition. In addition, we sought the advice and criticism of our colleagues to identify those elements that could be eliminated, altered, or replaced in our search for a more satisfying revision. The decision to eliminate old essays and substitute new ones was often difficult, but we tried, whenever possible, to provide current essays dealing directly with the theme of this book. Moreover, we have the pleasure of presenting eight original essays written especially for this edition. That eight leading scholars in the field have contributed their ideas and insights to *Inter/Media* indicates the growing importance of the study of media and interpersonal communication and leads us to believe that the approach is a viable one. We wish to thank Robert K. Avery and Thomas A. McCain, Nancy Bliese, James W. Chesebro and John D. Glenn, Jeffrey Ian Cole, Paul Messaris, Gerald R. Miller, and Lance Strate as well as George Lellis and Joshua Meyrowitz (who wrote original essays for the first edition) for their valuable contributions to this new edition.

It is our hope that this volume contributes to and stimulates a body of communication literature that will allow each of us to better understand our relationships with our fellow human beings and the media that facilitate human interaction.

Flushing, N.Y.   G.G.
July 1982   R.S.C.

Preface to the First Edition

This volume is the result of a ten-year academic and personal relationship. During that period the editors learned a great deal about each other's particular area of scholarship: media and interpersonal communication. At the same time we each began to alter our perspective regarding the limits or boundaries that defined our respective areas. Eventually the boundaries began to blur and overlap; we learned that media are manifested in every facet of human communication and that interpersonal communication has important effects on media. We now assume a holistic approach to media events and the communication process while preserving our own particular research orientation. We believe that it is misleading to study interpersonal communication and pretend that media do not influence the nature of the phenomenon. It is equally misleading to represent the media world as one disconnected from our interpersonal relations.

This volume emphasizes the point of view that each of us ought to be conscious of the influences that guide and structure our communication relationships. Its purpose is to provide insights into and awareness of the role of media in our daily environment. We do not seek to judge the media as corrupting or ameliorating, but seek to provide the bases for analyzing and evaluating our own communication in relation to media and others. We do not suggest a hierarchy in which one medium is considered better or worse than another, but ask the reader to be aware of individual needs and the meeting of those needs through both interpersonal and mediated communication. To this end we have organized the readings in two ways: the first according to a media perspective, and the second according to an interpersonal perspective.

This book is intended for both the liberal arts student and the communication specialist. It is vital that individuals understand the technological forces that influence them, no matter what profession they will enter. No one is exempt from the impact of media. The specialists in communication, those who will control the form and content of media, need also be aware of the impact and consequences of technological innovation and artistry on individuals and society.

We are indebted to a number of individuals who were instrumental in the process of publication. We are grateful to all the authors whose ideas had previously appeared in a different context, but who have contributed immensely to an understanding of the important relationship of media and interpersonal communication. Particularly, we are obliged to the six authors who wrote original essays especially for this volume. We want to thank Robert K. Avery and Donald G. Ellis, Bert Cowlan, James W. Chesebro, George Lellis, and Joshua Meyrowitz for their effort and unique contribution. And finally, we are indebted to John Wright, our editor, for exceptional support of a project that offers a new and different approach to the study of media and interpersonal communication.

Flushing, N.Y.   G.G.
January 1979   R.S.C.

Contents

Alternate Table of Contents
Source–Message–Channel–Receiver

3. Channel

INTER/MEDIA

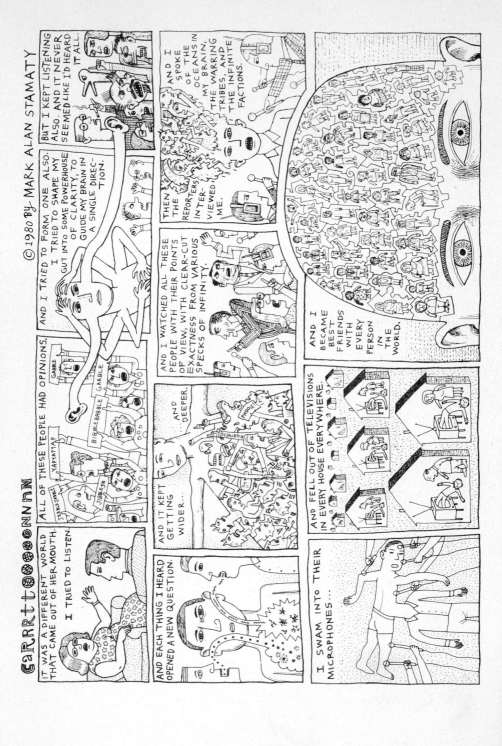

Good Morning

The television screen showed an orange sun rising slowly above an expanse of serene and empty farmland. There was a scene of horses frisking about a dewy paddock. A freight train rushed silently across a desert.

"I can't find my shirt anywhere," said Father.

"Here's your orange juice," said Mother.

"Good morning, I'm Bill Beutel," said Bill Beutel, his jacket flickering in alternating shades of green and yellow. "The Westminster Kennel Club Show is opening in New York, and in a few moments we're going to be talking to you about that."

"Don't you want your orange juice?" Mother said.

Father took the glass of orange juice and held it in his hand, and then put it down on the kitchen counter.

"I saw it in the closet only last night," he said. "Joey, you leave the set alone. The color's automatic."

"Joey, go get your juice," said Mother.

Stephanie Edwards said, "I'm really looking forward to hearing about that dog show, Bill, but right now we're going to have a report on the unemployment picture that's been causing such widespread distress across the nation."

"Mom, did you see my homework anywhere?" said Clarice. "Hi, Dad. That looks real cool without a shirt."

Peter Jennings, in Washington, said, "President Ford's top economist, Alan Greenspan, testified yesterday on Capitol Hill that the country will just have to reconcile itself to 8 percent unemployment through 1976." Alan Greenspan said, "As I evaluate the current trade-off between stimulus and unemployment, I do not give great credence to the idea that a sig-

From Michael J. Arlen *The View From Highway I.* (New York: Farrar, Straus & Giroux, 1976). Copyright © 1974, 1975, 1976 by Michael J. Arlen. This selection appeared originally in *The New Yorker.* Reprinted by permission of the publisher.

nificant reduction will be caused by a stimulus greater than that proposed by the President."

"It was the white shirt," Father said. "The one with the shoe polish on the cuff. Is that coffee ready?"

"I'll get the coffee, Dad," said Clarice.

"Clarice, you do the toast," said Mother.

"Mother, I have all this *homework*. I have a quiz in social studies."

Bill Beutel said, "Johnny Miller's 69 keeps him out front in the Bob Hope Desert Classic. As of this moment, it looks as if the women are going to boycott Wimbledon."

Father switched channels. Frank Blair said, "Yesterday, in Cambodia, a direct hit was scored upon this school in Phnom Penh."

Father said, "I guess I'll go look for it myself."

Frank Blair said, "Repercussions from yesterday's rioting in Lima, Peru, are still being felt today in that strife-torn capital." There are scenes of tanks driving down a city street.

"Clarice, remember the left side of the toaster doesn't work," said Mother.

"Mother, I *know*," said Clarice.

Frank Blair said, "North Dakota has an advisory for snow. Pacific Ocean storms are moving toward the Pacific Coast."

The telephone rang. Father reappeared, holding his shoes and a towel. He picked up the phone. "No, there isn't any Lisa here," he said, and started to put the phone back. "Oh, Dad, is that *Lisa?*" Clarice screamed. Father handed her the phone.

On the television screen, soldiers were now walking slowly down a country road. "Patrols fan out from the city, looking for insurgents," said a voice.

Mother said, "Joey, you finish the toast."

Joey said, "How come I have to do the toast when I don't eat toast?"

"Do you think it might be in the laundry?" Father said. "It might have fallen to the floor of the closet, and somebody might have put it in the laundry." Father passed by Clarice on his way out of the kitchen. "Don't talk all day on the phone, Clarice," he said. Clarice rolled her eyes at the ceiling.

Frank Blair said, "Scattered fighting continued until well toward evening." There were scenes of more tanks speeding three abreast down a road.

"Here's your coffee," Mother said. "Now, where did he go?"

Frank Blair said, "Armored cars and Russian-made tanks broke up the disorder. A curfew and a state of national emergency have been proclaimed."

There was the sound of a crash from the back of the house.

"Eggs are ready, everyone!" Mother said. On the television screen, two tanks were firing into a brick wall. "Fix the set. That's too loud, Joey," she said. "Everyone! The eggs are getting cold."

Father came back into the kitchen, with a blue shirt hanging partly out of his trousers, and clutching one of his fingers, from which a small drop of blood appeared. "Goddamn towel rack," he said.

"Here are your eggs," Mother said. "I thought you were going to get it fixed."

"I think I may have hurt myself," Father said.

On the television set, Fred Flintstone was rolling a stone wheel down a long hill. Father looked at the stone as it sped down the hill. At the bottom of the hill, there was a dinosaur sleeping. Father watched as the wheel rolled down the hill and then along the back of the dinosaur until it hit him on the head. "Who turned this on?" Father asked.

"Mom asked me to," said Joey.

"I did no such thing, Joey," said Mother. "Eat your eggs before they're cold. Clarice, come eat your eggs!"

Father switched channels. Stephanie Edwards said, "Nearly the entire central part of the country is in the grip of a cold-air mass. In Oklahoma City, the high today will be thirty-seven, the low around twenty."

"Did you know that thirty-two degrees is freezing, Mom?" said Joey.

"I don't like it when it gets that cold," said Mother.

"That was Oklahoma City," Father said. "Oklahoma City, Oklahoma."

"Clarice, you get off the phone this instant," Mother said.

Bill Beutel said, "In a little while, we're going to be talking about that Westminster Kennel Club Show, but right now we're going to Washington to visit with sociologist Donald Warren, who has been in the nation's capitol all week examining the way that unemployed workers handle stress." Peter Jennings, in Washington, said, "Professor Warren, I understand that you're here in the nation's capitol trying to find out more about how the unemployed react in times of stress. Is that correct?" Professor Warren said, "Yes, that's fundamentally correct, Peter. We've been following people through a series of crises, and these have been difficult times."

Mother said, "I ought to check at Garfields and see if they got in any of those new bird feeders yet. How come you're eating with your hand all bent like that?"

"Can't you see my finger is bleeding?" said Father.

"You're supposed to hold it above your head, Dad," said Joey. "If you hold it above your head, then gravity stops the blood from spurting up through your arm and sloshing all over everything."

"That's the most *disgusting* thing I ever heard," said Clarice, sitting down at the table. Clarice spread butter over a piece of toast and began to eat it.

"The fact is our formal institutions lie to us. They do not and are not able to give us the true picture of the crime rates and issues which confront people," said Professor Warren.

Clarice got to her feet. "Mom, I have to run."

"Eat your eggs, Clarice," said Joey.

"Where do you have to run to, young lady?" said Father. He reached forward and changed the channel again. Jim Hartz said, "In a moment, we'll be talking to a United Nations official who says that five hundred million people in the world aren't getting enough to eat. Here is Mr. Eric Ojala, head of the United Nations food program. Mr. Ojala, I understand that the United Nations has been developing an early-warning system for the world food situation."

The telephone rang. Father answered it. "Lisa?" he said. "I thought you just called."

"Oh, *Dad,*" Clarice said, taking the phone.

The doorbell rang. Mr. Ojala said, "We receive reports nowadays from all member countries."

A door slammed, and a boy's voice bellowed, "Joey!"

"Why, good morning, Gordon," Mother said.

Mr. Ojala said, "Although this system is still in its early stages, nonetheless it gives us time to anticipate where certain crops may fail." Jim Hartz said, "Mr. Ojala, do these reports have to do with crops as well as weather?"

Father suddenly got to his feet. "Have you seen the car insurance papers?" he said.

"I can't imagine where," said Mother. "I thought you always kept them in the envelope with the stereo warranty."

Mr. Ojala said, "It's true that fertilizer has been in short supply all during the year, but I don't believe it is fair to blame this shortage on the petroleum industry."

Father came back in. "I can't find the stereo warranty, either," he said.

"Are we getting a new stereo?" asked Clarice, still on the phone.

"Don't bother your father," said Mother.

Joey changed the channel.

"You'll be late for the bus," said Mother. Clarice hung up the phone. "Who put this *disgusting* sticker on my notebook?" she screamed.

Bill Beutel said, "Now we're going to see three very unusual species of the canine family. This aristocratic pooch, I think, is called a Pharaoh hound, and I gather they're supposed to smile when they're happy, and they're supposed to blush."

Clarice said, "Joey, someday I'm going to kill you. Honestly, I am going to *kill* you. Mother, I'm going to Modern Dance this afternoon with Lisa."

Father reappeared, wearing an overcoat and holding a white shirt. "I found the white shirt," he said.

"Dad, you've got shaving cream on your ear," said Clarice.

Bill Beutel said, "Miss Laventhall, would you say he is blushing now?" Miss Laventhall said, "Oh, definitely. He is definitely blushing."

"I wouldn't feel safe with a dog like that," said Mother.

"I'll call you from the office," said Father.

"Can Lisa come overnight Thursday?" asked Clarice.

"Now, this is an extremely rare breed of Chinese dog. Two thousand years ago in China, it was the pet of the aristocratic set," said Bill Beutel.

"Don't forget to stop by Windsor Supply on your way home," said Mother.

"How come Clarice always has overnights?" said Joey.

"Can I have some ice cream?" asked Gordon.

"You run along now, boys," said Mother.

There was the sound of the storm door slamming, then reopening, then slamming. Mother changed the channel on the television set and started collecting the dishes. The door opened again. "Somebody left roller skates in the car," Father said. The door closed again. A car engine started, missed, started, missed, then started. Mother stood before the sink, rinsing dishes. On the set behind her, Barbara Walters said to Charles Colson, "Tell us about that prison experience, will you. Tell us about the first night." Charles Colson said, "Well, I think, Barbara, from my standpoint, it was just one of the most revealing experiences of my life." Mother put the dishes one by one into the dishwasher and turned the switch. Outside the window, two robins padded on the snow. The rumble of the dishwasher filled the room. Mother sprayed the skillet with a jet of hot water. Charles Colson said, "There was certain information of that nature which was passed to us in the White House in 1972." The refrigerator clicked on. The dishwasher churned. The telephone began to ring. "Hi, Beth," Mother said. "Wait a minute while I turn the TV down. We were just listening to the morning news."

Introduction

This book, like Michael Arlen's amusing vignette, is about people like you and us, and our instruments of communication like the TV, the telephone, and the stereo. Like the vignette, it is about the way we communicate with each other face to face, while at the same time being influenced by the media. It is a book about the inextricable relationship between media and interpersonal communication.

The book grew out of our experience over the years, trying to learn and teach about the mass media and about the uses and functions of interpersonal communication. We became concerned that our students were not being exposed to the larger, truer picture of the human communication process, and began to assemble the kinds of articles and research studies which would reveal how interpersonal and media worlds are intertwined. We present them to you along with our ideas about the significance of this relationship for human communication.

The Impact of Media

We begin this exploration with the belief that the acceleration of media (technological innovation) has had an impact on all our relationships. The new media have altered our patterns of communication just as surely as the Ice Age changed the contours of the land. When we can be there as Egyptian President Anwar Sadat steps from an airplane and shakes hands with Israeli Prime Minister Menachem Begin; when an astronaut walking on the moon can converse with us across 180,000 miles as easily as talking with a next-door neighbor; when we can telephone a friend or relative in Australia via a communication satellite, our world has been changed and so have we. Time and space, man's age old barriers, have been erased and each of us lives with this new reality. When our concepts of time and space are altered, our perception of reality shifts. Knowledge and truth take on different dimensions. Our symbols have new or added meanings. And, our notions of self and other are affected. The very stuff of human communication is changed.

The modern electronic media have affected what we know, who and what we talk about, who talks to us, and who listens. Our knowledge and store of information have been immeasurably increased. The most rural, isolated coal miner can speak knowledgeably about cancer or the Russian Flu, certainly knows what goes on inside a modern hospital, and knows what Rome looks like from the steps of the Vatican. Our ability to sustain communication is almost unlimited. Every member of our family is only seven touch tones and fifteen seconds away. Every driver on the road within eight miles is a "good buddy." Any doctor, nurse, or repairperson is in continual contact with his or her home base through an electronic umbilical carried on the belt. Our ability to consume communication is awesome. On a given weekday afternoon, three hundred and eighty thousand women and men in New York City alone consume *Ryan's Hope*. On Superbowl Sunday almost seventy million Americans watch this pageant of masculine violence. In any given month, almost every man, woman, and child in the United States will be exposed to a "Big Mac" commercial. Let there be a skyjacking in Italy or a riot in Soweto, South Africa, and within minutes half of the world's population will be tuned in. It must follow that our notions of self and other, source and receiver, channel and message have been affected.

The Media-Interpersonal Gap

It is our intention, through this collection of readings and original essays, to begin to bridge the gap that has existed in the study of mediated communication and interpersonal communication. We have tended in the past to treat the mass media as isolated phenomena having little to do directly with interpersonal communication, and we have dealt with interpersonal communication as though mass media did not exist. Too often the study of mass media has been from a commercial and technological viewpoint having little or nothing to do with the whole process of human communication. To a large extent, the study of interpersonal communication has concentrated on the relationship between two persons without regard for the media environment which contains that relationship.

This is understandable when we see how the academic study of human communication has evolved over the past seventy-five years. There have been created a number of separate disciplines such as journalism, public speaking, broadcasting, group dynamics, film theory, rhetoric, each dealing with particular aspects of human communication. This artificial division was necessary in order to deal with the complexities of communication and to identify suitable areas for research and training. What has been lost in this quest for territory and identity are the inherent connections which make human communication an on-going process. For example, the nexus of media and interpersonal communication has been overlooked. We have come to know and understand the technology of media, the art of media as performance, the regulatory problems of the media and the public, the economics of the mass media, and the professional possibilities for employment in the media. We have explored the relationship of self and other, of verbal and nonverbal communication, of personal and social space, of disclosure and feedback in interpersonal encounters. What has been underemphasized is the whole of the communication process: a process in which each part affects the other part and no one part can be fully understood apart from the whole. It is our intent in this book to emphasize the connections; to restore a perspective that has been overlooked in the acceleration of technology and the collision with face-to-face communication.

We want to make clear at the outset that it is not our purpose to suggest another, newly demarcated territory for communication study replete with its own experts. We firmly believe that the social scientist, the historian, the philosopher, the dramatist have all contributed immensely to our understanding of the communication process. We have found that there exists a great reservoir of materials that provide insights into the significant relationship of media and interpersonal behavior. From this vast array of writings and research we have selected a number of readings which we believe will help you understand and more accurately assess your communicative behavior in this media world. Our purpose has been to select from the widest range of disciplines in order to juxtapose ideas that reveal processes and that enable us to appreciate the ambiguities and subtleties that characterize our mediated relationships.

This volume asks you to examine your interpersonal relationships as reflected and infected by the media of mass communication. We are concerned with more than the media of television, although there is no escaping the fact that television is now the dominant influence in our lives. We want you to think about all the media you are dependent on and all the ways you use and are used by media. More specifically, we are asking you to attempt to look critically at yourself and your interpersonal relationships, while analyzing the communications media that surround you, and to make connections with your intrapersonal and interpersonal behavior.

The Reflexive Problem

We are all somewhat defensive about our media habits because there has always been a great deal of negativism associated with the advent of each medium. You can hear the negative comments all around you: Popular music can corrupt you! Newspapers, books, and magazines can arouse you! Films can give you unreal expectations! Television can turn your brain to jello!

It has been fashionable to blame the mass media for the ailments of our society. You have been told that the media are to blame for the growth of pornography and violence. Political parties blame the media when they lose an election. There may be, of course, some truth to these charges. But the point is that the media do receive a great deal of criticism and we all feel somewhat guilty about our dependence on media. It is hard, for example, not to be concerned about television viewing when Marie Winn writes in *The Plug-in Drug:*

> Its use and overuse may be seen as symptoms of other modern ills: alienation, de-humanization, apathy, moral vacuum. Or one can regard the television set as a pathogen, a source of such symptoms. [1]

In 1938 it was a different medium that we were warned about:

> This passive state is increasing because people are depending more and more on the radio, etc., for their entertainment and knowledge of world affairs. They are becoming too passive and being passive they will be more easily led. Where they will be led depends on the viewpoint of those who control the channels of information. If people neglect to see for themselves they will be unable to cure the evils they see. [2]

Despite doubts and warnings, no medium has been eliminated and we have all adjusted our lives, or have had them adjusted, to functioning with each medium while still harboring some doubts about its effects.

While we may enjoy hearing and making our own criticism of media content and effects, criticism of our personal utilization of media is much more threatening. We can all judge various media performances: "I don't like the record;" "The film was great," "She's a terrific comedian." It is more difficult to admit we really enjoy watching *Family Feud;* that we want to see closeups of violence on TV and in films; that some of our attitudes about sex have been formed by the media; that we would rather listen to our favorite DJ than talk with someone riding in the car with us.

The task of looking at ourselves objectively while we are in the midst of the very circumstances we are examining presents great problems. Can we be thoughtful and analytical about how we are being manipulated by the media *while* we are being manipulated? It is difficult to be reflective about an activity while we are part of that activity because we lack psychological space in which to make an examination. When asked to look at ourselves, particularly in reference to our media activities, we tend to become protective of our behavior and attitudes even though we do have a vague sense of dissatisfaction.

Some degree of psychological distance is necessary if we are to become critics of our face-to-face and media behaviors. Detachment can be developed only to the degree that we can gain perspective on, as well as gain some knowledge about, the process in which we are enmeshed. Perhaps an analogy would be helpful. An actor on the stage must engage in real, interpersonal communication as the character being portrayed. The actor must put himself into this role completely, without reservations, and interact with the other characters in a truly involved way if the play is to be effective. Yet, to understand what is happening in a play as it develops its own life, the actor must maintain some detachment or distance from the role he is playing. Actors learn to do this through years of training, but they can also stop the play or step into the wings and look at it from a "real world" perspective. And when the play is finished, they can leave the reality of make-believe and return to the reality of everyday existence. It would be easier if we, like the actor, could stop the media world and reflect on it and ourselves; but we can't. We have to learn how to look at ourselves and our relationships while we are interacting with others. This book is designed to help you step back and look— to help you gain some psychological space for a perspective on yourself and the media that connects you to the world and to others.

The Media, the Mass, and the Individual

You may think perhaps that we are overstating the case with regard to the pervasiveness of media influence on ourselves and our interactions with others. Try the following nonscientific experiment: meet a friend and interact with that person in your usual manner, but keep a part of yourself detached. Maintain a sense of objectivity. Answer the following questions: (1) How many times did some media language get into the conversation? ("That turns me off.") (2) How many media intrusions occurred during the conversation? (Posters and neon signs across the street, someone walking by playing a radio or tape recorder.) (3) How dependent was your interaction on media? ("I'll phone you right after *Dick Cavett*.") (4) How much media content was fed into your exchanges? ("He's an Archie Bunker if ever I saw one.")

We could go on, but you get the idea. Self-identity is formed by the media as well as by interpersonal acts. As explained earlier, one reason for this is that we have been conditioned to think negatively about the impact of media, just as we have been trained to take very seriously our face-to-face relationships with parents, teachers, friends, and coworkers. Another, and perhaps more subtle, reason is related to how we define the media and how we define ourselves. Most textbook definitions of the media explain them as a means of transmission: a channel for carrying a message to an audience. The definition usually carries with it the concept of a mechanism of impersonal reproduction that intervenes between the source and a mass audience. The term "mass," however, is not intrinsic to media. It is a characteristic of only some media, such as the electronic media, that are extremely efficient delivery systems for bringing messages to huge, undifferentiated audiences. Any of today's "mass" media could be utilized for "non-mass" purposes, such as point-to-point communication, e.g., a "ham" radio operator talking to a friend on the other side of the world. Because they are efficient, cheap, and relatively unrestricted means of reaching a great number of people quickly, the electronic media and the daily newspapers of the United States have come to be thought of as mass media. In this case, mass media are those complex institutions that distribute content to potential customers as a means of economic gain. While it might be interesting to debate the values of American institutions of media versus those of other nations, it is more important to recognize what this has meant for our attitudes toward mass media and what influence it has had on mass culture.

There is also a reluctance to examine our relationship to the mass media due in part to our negative attitude toward mass culture. Fostered by those who claim that the masses enjoy (or consume) a culture significantly different from that enjoyed now or in the past by the elite members of society, the feeling is that the culture made available to the masses is poorer in both the content and quality. When cultural objects are transmitted and diffused through the mass media, they are thought to be affected by this act of transmission, by their marketability, and by the size of the market. This attitude toward mass culture has influenced all of us. We don't like to think that we enjoy things that are low class—that we are being herded into a mass audience just to be sold a product. We have been taught that we are individuals; that we make our own decisions about whom to associate with and about how to spend our money. We never think of ourselves or our friends as part of the "mass." To be involved with the mass media is to be faceless, to be part of the herd. We want to think of ourselves as unique individuals and we want to be perceived on that level. Ironically, the mass media never address the mass. Rather, they appeal to numerous individuals, none of whom see themselves as part of the mass. Most of us prefer the romantic version of life where we alone control our destinies, choose our relationships, decide for ourselves what we want to hear and see, and above all, where we each create a life full of warm and affectionate personal relationships. The romantic vision says that all these "true" and "real" relationships exist outside the realm of media. The reality is that our relationships coexist and interact with the media as well as with others on a face-to-face basis. While we worship face-to-face interaction, it is very probable that everyone who reads this has a telephone, and would be quite unhappy without that instrument, which has done so much to alter face-to-face relationships. Think about the actuality of our family relationships when the TV set is on for a period of six-and-a-half hours each day. What used to occur during that time in pre-TV days? You probably have your own radio and your own stereo. Your car undoubtedly has a radio, maybe even a tape deck and a CB. If you made a media inventory you would discover that an extraordinary amount of time each day is taken up with mediated communication. Just the time alone that we devote to media must have a profound effect on our interpersonal relationships. Moreover, the process is cyclical. The media are dependent on us to alter our relationships to accommodate the media, and the media in turn present us with a picture of our altered relationships. The media-interpersonal helix reverberates throughout our society. We cannot help but dwell upon our own images. We must learn how to develop enough psychological space to see which image is which.

The Uses of This Book

We have just pointed out the complexities, difficulties, and threatening aspects of examining our own interpersonal behavior in a media world. We believe, however, that there are ways to develop an awareness and an understanding of the processes of mediated communication and their effects on us.

First, it is necessary to juxtapose appropriate interpersonal concepts with media concepts. To do this we have divided our study into four sections—"The Interpersonal and Media Connection," which presents the framework for the interpersonal and media interface and the research that supports it; "Media and Interpersonal Intimacy," which considers the technological identities of the media and relates those properties to our search for intimate contacts; "Reality and Media Perception," which shows how the intrinsic nature of media influences the way we perceive ourselves and our environment; "Media Values and Interpersonal Roles," which examines the connection among roles, values, and media.

An essay introduces each section to provide a perspective from which to view and relate the readings in the section. Each essay should provide you with (1) an understanding of the linkage between the two concepts being examined; (2) a construct in which to fit the significant ideas from each reading; and (3) a stimulus to an analysis of your own interpersonal behavior and media involvements.

Finally, the readings are arranged in each section so that they can unfold a view of media as part of our personal world of communication. In addition, we provide an alternate table of contents that groups the readings according to a source-message-channel-receiver model of communication. This arrangement emphasizes the interaction of media with each component of the communication process. The readings in their original presentations were not necessarily used to reveal the relationships that we are trying to uncover, but in each case the author of the reading recognized (either explicitly or implicitly) the interconnectedness of media and interpersonal behavior. Not all the pieces take the same approach. Some present a unique perspective on media, while others reveal unique aspects of a particular medium. In every reading, however, there is something to make us more aware and self-critical. At the end of the book is an extensive list of references that will guide you to other books, articles, and research reports pertinent to the study of media and interpersonal communication.

The arrangement of essays reflects the authors' attempt at providing a structure or pattern that will give some perspective on the complexities of our modern media world. The forty pieces here are not a continuum nor do they neatly explain the authors' point of view as an introductory textbook might. Some are theoretical, some are reports of social scientific research, some are anecdotal, and others are polemical. Some touch lightly on the issues while others explore deep sociological problems. What all of them have in common is a fundamental awareness that media are pervasive and inseparable from our personal worlds. Each essay offers some insight into the ways our notions of self, other, family, community and environment are being altered by our interactions with the media. Most importantly, none accept that the media are simply a vast entertainment industry with little import for the tasks and crises that fill our personal worlds.

Readers' interests and needs may dictate other arrangements of these essays. Some may want to read as a unit all those essays dealing with the impact of television; others may wish to concentrate on those essays that reveal the information functions of media. The four groupings we have are not unique nor does each essay fit neatly into a category like "values" or "reality," but taken as a whole they all reveal the importance of our media connections and the inevitability of interpersonal and media interactions.

In reading these essays, what is important is not that a select group of them tells you something about the affects of media on interpersonal intimacy or societal values, but rather that you read them with the kind of psychological distance that will enable you to see new relationships with the media and altered patterns of socialization. We caution you not to fall into the trap of believing that television is the only medium with which to be concerned. Accept that you are a participant in a vast and varied media-communication system. You are not exempt from the influences of the media even if you tell yourself that you use the media only for entertainment. Nor is it helpful to think of the media as some gigantic monster forcing people to believe and act in ways they do not want. Bell Telephone might be a huge, impersonal conglomerate, but it does not make you use the telephone to talk over the latest soap opera episode with your friends. We are suggesting that you accept what is patently true; that we all make use of media technology to facilitate daily living and that the media serve a variety of functions in our society. We recommend that you use these readings to better understand the functions of media and the uses that we all make of them. We hope that you will become more aware that as we make increased use of the media, our interpersonal relationships are changed just as surely as our use of the automobile and electric light changed our homes, our architecture, our industries, and our cities. It is not necessary to begin this book at the beginning. We are using the print form to examine events, concepts, and processes that are not linear. Enter the book through any section that interests you and continue until you return to where you began.

Notes

1. Marie Winn, *The Plug-in Drug: Television, Children and the Family* (New York: The Viking Press, 1977), p. 215.
2. Tim Madden, "The Passive State," *The Weekly Review* (May 5, 1938), p. 147.

1
The Interpersonal and Media Connection

Traditionally human communication has been viewed as a speaker saying something to a listener. Even though there have been tremendous variations on this simple theme of sender-message-receiver, it has served throughout the centuries as our basic communication model. In classical antiquity Socrates presented the dialogue—questioner, answerer—as the ideal way to advance learning and thought. Aristotle utilized the speaker-message-audience or actor-performance-audience model in all his writings about the uses and effects of human communication. With the development of the alphabet and systems of writing, there was applied this same configuration—writer, message, reader. Even with the development of the printing press, radio, film and television, we have continued to look upon human communication as basically one human being directing words and gestures at another human being.

There have been more intricate models of human communication developed, especially in this century, but all serve similar functions: (1) they permit us to make predictions based upon a description of the communication process, (2) they indicate the relationships of components found within the process, (3) they facilitate our understanding, and (4) they generate research. Some of the more well-known models are the Shannon and Weaver mathematical model (encoder-transmitter-noise-receiver-decoder), which is concerned with how information is sent and received; the Berlo model (sender-message-channel-receiver), which is concerned with the makeup and relationship of each element in the process; the Westley-MacLean model (A transmits something about an object X through C to B), which focuses on the gatekeeping aspect of C as well as the nonpurposiveness of some of A's messages; and the Lasswell model (who says what through which channels to whom with what effects), which is concerned with how effects are produced and controlled. All models and all theories of human communication begin with an acceptance of the basic act and process whereby two human beings are able to symbolize internal and external states and transmit and receive signs and signals of those states. No matter whether the model and its theory concentrate on the nature of the symbolizing process, or the means by which

I AM LOVED.

PEOPLE NEED ME, WORSHIP
ME, CAN'T LIVE WITHOUT ME

I DRAIN EMPTINESS
FROM LIVES. FILL THE
VOID WITH JUNK. PEOPLE
ARE GRATEFUL.

I AM THE GIVER OF
NEWS. OPINIONS DON'T
EXIST WITHOUT ME.

11-28

signs are transmitted, or how symbols affect and are affected by the human senses, it is assumed that the "simple" face-to-face communicative act is *the* act of communication and contains all the necessary elements of human communication.

To engage in face-to-face communication requires: a language; a set of meanings; a process of encoding and decoding signals; a means of transmitting and receiving symbols; a channel or medium to carry the signals from one individual to another; an understanding of the rules or grammar entailed; awareness of the social norms and psychological states involved in such an act; and an implicit agreement about behaviors appropriate to the communication act. In other words, everything that is necessary to communicate can be found in the face-to-face or interpersonal communication model. Furthermore, more complex acts of human communication such as group communication, or a speaker addressing an audience, or an

GO CRAZY WHEN I DON'T
COME ACROSS WITH WHAT
THEY WANT.

I SHAPE LIVES. I TEACH:
HOW TO SHOOT. WHAT
TO BUY.

I AM THE INSIDES
OF YOUR HEAD.

IF YOU WANTED A GROSS
NATIONAL PRODUCT, YOU GOT IT.

editor writing a magazine article, are only variations of this basic process and not different in kind. When people talk with each other in groups they are still communicating face-to-face in dyads, but with added rules governing the flow of conversation and with more complicated feedback procedures. The public speaker addressing a large audience makes use of all the same processes of language and gesture, of grammar and syntax as does the interpersonal communicator, but is limited in the amount and type of feedback that can be received; the audience is limited in what it can hear and see, and how it can respond. Nevertheless, all parties, especially the speaker, attempt to make the communicative act as similar as possible to the interpersonal one by compensating for the limitations such as speaking more slowly, projecting more, using enlarged gestures, etc. The writer writing a magazine article faces even greater limitations because of the lack of direct and immediate feedback, because of the added effort of reading and translating alphabetic symbols, because of the lack of vocal cues, and because of the lack of control over the setting in which the communication act is completed. But even in the case in which the receiver may not be physically present, every effort is made within the limits of written communication to make the communicative act as close an imitation as possible of the face-to-face one. Alphabetic letters which approximate spoken sounds are employed, as are punctuation marks which substitute for vocal pauses and inflections, styles of writing which reveal the persona of the communicator are employed, and language which can make the communication seem more or less intimate. All these make the written communication a derivation of face-to-face communication.

Every type of human communication, from face-to-face to mass communication, is still basically an interpersonal communicative act. This does not mean there is no need to study or understand communicative acts other than interpersonal, but rather that all human communication is, in the final analysis, interpersonal. Also, we do not mean to imply that all human communication is simple or just like ordinary conversation, but that all the necessary components as well as complexities of communication exist in the interpersonal communicative act and as such provide a touchstone for measuring all communication. Whatever communication does to relate us to our universe—to relate individual to individual, and to produce the "humanizing" process—must in some way be related to that basic communicative act in which one human interacts with another.

Mediated Interpersonal Communication

The great technological advances of the nineteenth and twentieth centuries brought about what has now come to be known as "mass communication." With the invention of the telegraph, the telephone, the gramophone, the camera, and finally radio, television, and film, human beings have been able to expand the fundamental interpersonal communicative act into an instantaneous, public dissemination of messages on an almost unlimited scale. Never before has a speaker or source of a message been able to reach so many receivers with so many sense modalities as can now be achieved by the use of the electronic media. Today a speaker can instantly engage in several million interpersonal communicative acts simultaneously through electronic channels. The only component missing from the traditional dyadic model is instant feedback. (Feedback here includes smell, touch, and body heat.)

That a communicator can reach a mass audience over time and space is not new. Marshall McLuhan refers to the invention of the printing press in 1450 as the beginning of mass communication, but man's attempt to extend the senses and bridge time and space with his communications began long ago in prehistory. The use of smoke signals and the beating of drums have long been utilized as ways of extending the "voice" of the communicator over distance. Cave paintings and hieroglyphic writings were early attempts at bridging time so that messages could be preserved and the voice of the sender could be heard by later generations. In other words, human beings have always engaged in the activity of extending and expanding the simple face-to-face communicative act. It is only in the last hundred years that technology has been developed to almost perfectly replicate the interpersonal dyadic communicative act over time and space. This phenomenal extension of communicative potential has naturally produced great changes in our use of media and in the effects that can be achieved. We have now an overwhelming communications industry and have produced an explosion of information. These changes have not only produced jobs and commerce, they have also created questions about the meaning and impact of mass communication. Scholars and researchers have attempted to answer those questions. New theories of communication have been forthcoming and new communication models have been developed to account for these extensions. In the last fifty years, mass communication has emerged as a discipline within the academic community.

Stages in the Growth of Mass Media
General interest in the media of mass communication has followed a pattern similar to that of other types of technological advances. First, the new medium (telegraph, photograph, motion picture) is viewed as a toy—something to be played with or owned by the rich or the eccentric—something that society could get along just as well without. At that stage, the medium is not taken seriously by scholars and researchers, nor is it considered to have social or political significance by the general public. There are, of course, those who make "wild" and sometimes accurate predictions about the future impact of the medium, as well as those individuals who point out what foolishness it is. A common source of jokes about photography in the nineteenth century was the discomfort it caused the subject to sit still for so long and the flash powder that frightened the horses.

The next stage of interest and involvement is concerned with the techniques of the phenomenon. People want to know how it works and they marvel at how its effects are achieved. The early days of radio and television were marked by public displays and demonstrations showing the workings of a microphone, the inside of a vacuum tube, the parts of a TV camera. Now the medium has become "commercialized"; that is, it has developed to where it can be an aid in promoting commerce both in terms of selling the medium to the public and using the medium to sell products. At this stage, "schools" are created to train technicians to make the necessary components of the camera, transmitter, receiver, etc., and to train the personnel who will produce for the medium—cameramen, programmers, directors, scriptwriters, and support personnel. This is usually a stage of accelerated growth, and as a result of that growth, business leaders and politicians become concerned with the advantages groups might gain through the use of the medium. They begin to devise ways to control its growth and use, usually in the name of protecting the public who are viewed as helpless victims ensnared by the magic of the new medium. The media of the nineteenth and twentieth centuries introduced the need for governmental or self-regulation because of the public's "interest, convenience, and necessity" (a phrase later incorporated into the 1934 Federal Communication Commission Act). The desire to regulate leads to questions about how the medium affects the general public and what the role of the innovation should be. This in turn produces experts who study and predict the effects of the media. The results of these studies feed public debate, which usually centers around whether the new medium will destroy established institutions and corrupt the nation's youth. Well into the 1930s numbers of preachers argued that it was a sin to see a motion picture. In the 1920s there were cartoons that depicted radio listeners with enlarged ears and atrophied eyes. In the 1970s public officials cited television as the main cause of violence in our society.

The third stage of media usage and involvement can be labeled the "artistic" stage. At this point the medium has been institutionalized, has survived its critics, and has legitimized its functions. Award systems are established by the institution in recognition of its own contributions to society. Distinctions are made among schools that train technicians of the media and those that instruct the future performers and directors of the media in its proper use. To do the latter requires that the medium have a history or tradition, agreed-upon standards of excellence, and a secure place in the shaping of attitudes, beliefs, and values. By this stage, the public, the business sector, and the politicians have accepted the medium as an unquestioned part of the system and have usually forgotten the earlier predictions of doom and gloom. It is characteristic of young people at this stage to assume that the particular medium has always been present and that there is no choice about whether to use it or not. Furthermore, it is characteristic of academicians at this stage to argue whether the medium is a social science, a fine art, or a practical art; and to study it and teach about it accordingly.

There is a fourth stage in the development of most media and that is the one where the medium has become so much a part of the scheme of things that much of the public is unaware of how dependent it is. The medium comes to be accepted as "natural" as running water, electricity, and automobiles, and it fulfills a need that the medium itself helps to create. People no longer consider whether they need the medium, but the fear of being disconnected from the medium becomes a major concern, as when the telephone goes dead or the television set is in the repair shop.

At this stage people begin to anticipate the next technological advance in the life of the medium, like those now who are concerned with two-way television where the viewer can respond directly to the TV performer, or the videophone where communicators can be seen as well as heard. It is a time when scholars begin to look at the medium as an integral part of human activity and try to develop models and theories which incorporate the medium into whatever "system" they are studying, e.g. sociology, psychology, history, communication. Researchers no longer consider the medium as something separate or alien to be examined as though it were from another universe, but view it as part of the human condition. This book is part of that fourth stage.

Theories and Models of Mass Communication

It should not be necessary to point out that the four stages discussed are not mutually exclusive. It is possible that one stage continues long after the advent of the next stage. There are probably some people who still consider TV a luxury toy having nothing to do with the important aspects of life, just as there are people who are still enamored of its techniques and wonder how, and with grave suspicion, a "live" picture can be transported over thousands of miles of space into someone's home. There are also academicians who believe that the study of mass communications has little or nothing to do with the way human beings organize or think or how they talk to each other.

While we have suggested four stages in the evolution of a medium, the total picture is far more complex because media do not exist alone but in association with other media. No one medium develops separately, but in conjunction with its audiences and with other media as well. The interaction of media, audience, and society creates a complexity in which the four stages of evolution are sometimes hidden.

Early studies, particularly of the broadcasting media, concentrated on how the media shaped or influenced the response of its listeners and viewers without recognizing the various stages of development of a given medium or the milieu in which that medium arose. Researchers tended to look at the mass media as singular sources sending forth messages to a passive mass of individual receivers who were directly manipulated by the message. Their investigations focused on persuasive strategies utilized in media messages, on the numbers of audience members reached by the message, and on the resultant change in attitudes and beliefs. This resulted in a one-step model of mass communication where there were no recognized intervening variables between the medium and the individual receiver. It was held that if the media employed the correct persuasive strategies and controlled the exposure situation, then the individual receiver could be manipulated by the message. There was little regard for social structure, group influence, peer pressure, or other sources of information and influence. In these studies it was assumed that mass communication had little or nothing to do with interpersonal communication and vice versa.

When media became institutionalized, the research became more sophisticated and concentrated on the behavior of persons exposed to the mass media. It was discovered that individual audience members were influenced simultaneously by a variety of media and by opinion leaders who frequently relayed, reinforced, and interpreted the media content. The resultant two-step flow model of mass communication effects was very useful in bringing to media theory the important role of face-to-face communication. It was no longer assumed that the media audience was either passive or an undifferentiated mass, but that it was made up of groups of interacting people dependent on opinion leaders for much of their response to mass media messages. There was, at this point, the recognition of a direct connection between interpersonal communication and mass communication.

Further research along this line led to the "multi-step" flow model which included sequential effects of messages over time, gatekeeping, opinion leadership, and interpersonal communication. It was found that communication flowed not only from opinion leaders to followers, but from followers to leaders, and from followers to followers, all of which has to be accounted for in explaining media effect. Much of the media industry itself, however, has continued to rely on linear models of mass communication flow. The usual industry model holds that the most effective media message is the one that reaches the largest number of persons with minimum delay and holds them long enough to be manipulated by the advertisement. Some experts in the media industry have recognized a different version of the two-step model. In this model, the first step in selling a product is to capture the largest number of receivers available through the vehicle of entertainment or news. The second step is to deliver a direct and appealing pitch for the advertiser's product. Many in the media industry have yet to recognize the complexities of mass communication and the relationship with interpersonal communication.

A Systematic Model of Mass and Interpersonal Communication
Those in the fourth stage of media involvement have begun to look at the mass media as part of a *total system,* a system which includes all the ways that human beings receive and process information; symbolize thoughts, feelings, and experiences, encode messages; send, retrieve, and preserve messages; and the ways these functions relate to the sociocultural context. In a systems model, mass communication cannot be viewed as an external force manipulating passive receivers, nor can interpersonal communication be examined apart from the mediated communication that surrounds and involves each individual in the social environment. A systems theory of human communication assumes that all message inputs—verbal, nonverbal, firsthand

or mediated, and purposeful or accidental—affect the internal states of the individual and help shape the message outputs from the individual to others (interpersonal behaviors) as well as the messages one sends to oneself (intrapersonal behaviors).

A systems model of communication shifts attention away from concern primarily with how the source manipulates messages or controls the effects, as in the speaker-message-receiver model. It goes beyond a multi-step or gatekeeper model, with its focus on channels of communication and diffusion of information, to focusing attention on how each component of the model *functions* in making the entire communicative system work. Receivers or audiences are considered an active part of the system, utilizing all the channels, mediated as well as interpersonal, to meet individual and societal needs. In turn, receivers influence the entire system by their messages and behaviors that become part of the inputs that influence attitudes and behaviors of those who create messages for the mass media. It requires that media and channels of communication be viewed as having distinct forms and structures which shape the messages carried and in turn influence those who produce the mediated messages as well as those who receive them. A systems theory looks at human communication as an ongoing process interacting with all the other elements in human existence, ever changing to meet the needs of human beings who must by nature communicate with each other and respond to changes in their environment. A systems approach does not seek to "blame" one component of the communication system for the effects produced, nor does it resist or reject innovation in human communication. Rather it attempts to explain how the system functions. In such an approach the mass media cannot be considered a technical monster manipulating helpless human beings, nor can it be pretended that human beings can communicate in face-to-face situations without being influenced by the mass media which surround them. We contend that mass communication and interpersonal communication are of a piece, and that we have a great deal at stake in learning how these two important aspects of human communication interrelate.

In the readings that follow, a number of leading theorists of mass media and interpersonal communication examine the connections in the human communicative system. Each one is saying something about how we use and become dependent on our media of communication. They explore the reasons for the supposed dichotomy between "real" and "pseudo" communication, i.e., face-to-face conversation and interposed media conversation. They explain that although communication stimuli are processed as information by the human individual, that what we bring to this process, the context in which we receive it, and the form that it takes, produces different results. Walter Ong, like Marshall McLuhan, believes that the change in technologies of communication, such as the shift from print channels of information to electronic channels, alters the way we think about the world and see our place in it. As the information flow increases, we have to change the way we organize and respond to that information. We now see and hear hundreds of mediated images a day, but we also see and hear the images of our immediate, directly sensed environment. What do we do with all this information? How do the amount and form of this new media information, along with the traditional information, influence what we talk about and with whom we interact? Professors Avery and McCain, Chaffee, Miller, and Thayer address themselves to these questions. They explain how we make use of all sources of information to help us in our daily lives and that the uses we make of it shape our intra- and interpersonal communications. What emerges is a theory that contends that mass media and interpersonal communication are part of a dynamic interactive system, no part of which can be separated or removed from the other. This theory can be cast in the form of a model that relates our social system to our media of communication and our individual uses of media to our need for socialization.

ROBERT K. AVERY and THOMAS A. McCAIN

Interpersonal and Mediated Encounters: A Reorientation to the Mass Communication Process

What are the differences between an interpersonal encounter and a media-person encounter? Are these communication interactions basically the same? Is the only real difference the lack of immediate feedback? Although many scholars hold that the introduction of a medium only slightly alters the communication process, Robert Avery and Thomas McCain contend that media-person encounters are inherently different from interpersonal ones. They rest their case on the differences found in sensory potential, control over the exchange, and knowledge of the source. To demonstrate these differences they examined talk-radio call-in shows, which seem like interpersonal encounters but actually are a unique media phenomenon.

It was a typical family room: television set blaring in the corner, homework strewn this way and that, Dad reading the newspaper and trying to share every tidbit with a noncaptive audience. Kids watching—playing, not watching or listening—listening—arguing—watching but not listening—Dad talking to kids—kids not listening—Dad reads—Dad goes to the TV, turns it off.

DAD: "What do you want to do anyway, watch TV or communicate?"

SON: "You mean watching TV isn't communication?"

DAD: "No, it's not the same."

SON: "I guess you're right. I'd rather watch TV now, OK?"

People who watch television and read newspapers generally view these forms of communication differently than they do talking to someone. Why and how mass communication and interpersonal communication are different is a more complicated issue than would appear at first glance.

The purpose of this essay is to explore these differences between interpersonal transactions (those people have with one another) and transactions people have with the mass media. The perspective of the essay is receiver oriented; that is, it seeks to define some differences between the interpersonal communication process and the media-person process, from

This article was written expressly for the present volume. Copyright © 1982 by Robert K. Avery and Thomas A. McCain.

the vantage point of the viewer, listener, or reader. Further, it argues that there are a host of factors in this media-person encounter that may inherently prohibit the audience member from forming a transactional relationship with a media source. As the dialogue between Dad and Son suggests, we can have transactional relationships with our fathers, but never with a television set.

The first portion of the essay addresses an orientation held by many communication scholars (including at one time the authors of this piece) that the differences between the process of mass communication and interpersonal communication are but differences in degree. Schramm's position is typical: "On the whole the similarities between the processes of mass and interpersonal communication are far greater than the differences." [1] By narrowly focusing on a single aspect of the mass communication process, the media-person encounter, it is hoped that continued thinking on this topic will be stimulated, as we believe it is an important issue. Three factors that are related to distinguishing media-person encounters from interpersonal encounters must be addressed from the perspective of the receiver: technology and sensory integration, receiver control of the source, and receiver knowledge of the source. Each of these three factors should be viewed as a dimension of a larger process; in many cases they operate independently of one another. It is our position that the placement of intrapersonal communication and mass communication at opposite ends of a single continuum has resulted in masking the multifaceted nature of the differences among types of communicative encounters. The following three propositions will be dealt with individually: (1) The technology of mass media messages inherently limits the sensory integration potential for receivers; (2) Receivers of mass media have no functional control over media sources; (3) Receivers of mass media messages have only limited or imaginary knowledge of media sources. Finally, the process of talk radio is examined as an example of why we need to study media-person encounters carefully from new perspectives.

I. The Technology of Mass Media Messages Inherently Limits the Sensory Integration Potential for Receivers. The human system is a homeokinetic one; that is, it is self-stimulating and self-perpetuating. Human sensory modalities are not dormant sensors waiting to be stimulated and affected by objects in the environment. Instead, the perceptual systems of the human body are searching systems, actively and constantly scanning the environment for information appropriate to the needs of the information processor.[2]

Seven modalities are of particular importance to those interested in the process of communication. These modalities are important because they have been isolated as systems that are handled by the brain in differential fashion according to their unique attributes. They have been labeled *audio verbal, audio nonverbal, visual verbal, visual pictoral, olfactory, tactile* and *taste.* One of the objectives of the human information processor is to achieve sensory integration from and between the various modalities; to gain an understanding of a phenomenon by receiving complimentary information about the perceived object from varying modalities. As Travers notes, "the full *experience* of the environment requires that redundant information be experienced through the different perceptual systems."[3] When an object is perceived that is lacking in information from one of the modalities, past experience from similar objects is used by the human system in order to gain a more complete understanding of the object. For example, if all a person knows about a particular object in the environment is the word "cat" spoken by someone (audio verbal), a vague picture as to the nature of that feline is brought to mind. If he or she hears the word cat and can hear the animal purr or meow (audio nonverbal), the receiver has a more complete idea as to the nature of the animal. If a person could see the cat in all its furriness (visual pictoral) and see C-A-T spelled out, along with the purr and the spoken word, the complimentarity of the modalities begins to reduce even more uncertainty as to the nature of the animal. To really understand the cat, however, you would need to touch its fur (tactile), smell its litter box (olfactory), and perhaps lick its coat (taste). Then you would have even more complete sensory integration, and significantly less uncertainty as to what the cat is all about.

Interpersonal encounters can provide the maximum of sensory integration potential, for the participants afford interaction among living organisms that move, speak, emit paralinguistic cues, have texture, odor, and taste. The modalities of the receiver constantly scan the other participant in an interpersonal encounter, seeking to integrate information from the varying sensory sources. This is simply not possible when listening to the radio, watching television, or reading the newspaper. The media-person encounter is inherently a different phenomenon.

Media are the result of technology. It may be useful to define media as unique combinations of potential sensory integration constrained by their technology. Technology has enabled the combining of potential cross modality checking with definite limiting parameters. Each of the media includes in every message the potential use of a specific number of modality stimuli. For example, of the seven sensory modalities individuals use to scan the environment and reduce uncertainty, newspapers offer information that can be processed by only two modalities—visual verbal and visual pictoral. These are the only modalities manipulable by a newspaper source. Radio offers audio verbal and audio nonverbal stimulation, while television holds the potential for providing four sensory stimuli—visual verbal, visual pictoral, audio verbal and audio nonverbal. Television and film offer more potential for sensory integration than either newspapers or radio, due to the technologies of each medium. However, all media generally have less potential for sensory integration than does an interpersonal encounter.

The technological constraints on sensory integration potential result in a different task for the information processor in a media encounter than he or she finds in the interpersonal setting. People must either supply the missing sensory data from their past experience or "know" the object in question based on "incomplete" sensory data. While interpersonal encounters are often lacking in sensory integration as well, it is the participants and the social situation that determine and constrain the extent of sensory data available. In short, the potential for total integration is always present in the interpersonal setting, but in the media-person encounter, technology inherently inhibits this potential.

II. Receivers of Mass Media Messages Have Little or no Functional Control over Media Sources. Feedback is an element in almost every communication model. It is a concept borrowed from cybernetics and engineering to help describe the human communication process. What is critical to our understanding of this element is that, functionally, feedback serves as a control device. Positive and negative feedback (in a cybernetic sense) provide information to the system as to how the system is reaching its goal. Feedback in a human communication sense is traditionally defined as the responses of a receiver to a source's message. This element is critical for human communication because feedback tells the source how his or her message is being processed. Most writers of human communication would have little problem with Burgoon and Ruffner's delineation of feedback:

> The receiver may smile, frown, sigh, yawn, wiggle, nod the head in disagreement, and make a variety of verbal answers. These cues let the source know whether his or her message is being received; *they are one of the most powerful means of control the receiver has.*[4] (emphasis added)

In order to understand the transactional nature of communication, we must recognize the extent to which participants can control the communicative situation. Some people refer to this as reciprocity. Feedback enables participants (both source and receiver) to adjust and change in order to fit the needs of self and coparticipants. Feedback is important to the extent that change in the message encoding and decoding process is facilitated. It is feedback that informs the participants in a communicative transaction whether a genuine sharing of personal experience is taking place. The functional consequences of this constrained feedback in the media-person encounter constitute the critical factor that distinguishes it from interpersonal communication.

Audience members learn quickly in their media-person encounters that they are unable to control the sources of mass media messages. No matter how much the mass media audience members wiggle, talk, frown, or smile, the media message does not adjust or change. Mass media technology limits an audience member's direct interaction with a media source in the vast majority of encounters with the media. This is a phenomenon substantially different from the experiences of interpersonal encounters that people have with one another. Letter writing, phone calling, or turning the TV set off are not the same as nonverbally or verbally *correcting* or *guiding* other participants in a transaction.

In order for media transactions to be more similar to interpersonal transactions, the audience member must perceive an opportunity to control what he or she sees and hears during the transaction itself. Without this opportunity the audience member can only use media messages as a source of information and as topics for communicative transactions with others over whom they can exercise some control. New technology, especially interactive cable, may change this. When audience members are able to interact and correct or change the course of the media message during the transmission, then an interpersonal encounter may be approximated.

The fact that audience members have little or no functional control over the nature of the communicative transaction due to technology and the structure of mass media industries, makes mass media encounters substantially different from encounters people have with each other.

III. Receivers of Mass Media Messages Have only Limited or "Imaginary" Knowledge of Media Sources. A receiver in any communicative transaction brings to the encounter two kinds of orientations or predispositions. The first is an orientation toward the topic or subject of the transaction. Every individual orients to topics with varying degrees of prior knowledge, experience, and attitudes. These predispositions are the result of past experience the participants have had with the topic under consideration. The second orientation is, of course, toward the other participant, or source. The perceived credibility of the other involved in any transaction is similarly based on past experiences in communicative encounters. Some communication scholars refer to the process a person goes through during the communicative enterprise as "co-orientation." They argue that a person interprets messages and carries on a communicative transaction by continually co-orienting, or adjusting, to both topic and other.

A number of factors concerning receivers' orientations toward media sources make the co-orientations toward media sources unique and substantially different from the interpersonal encounters people have with one another.

1. The concept of media source is vague and highly variant to most receivers. Viewers of television programs or readers of newspapers have at best a vague notion as to the source or originator of these messages. Is the source the producer, editor, writer, actor, television station, network, the newspaper owner? Perhaps it is all of them. People engaged in media encounters perceive media sources in a highly varied manner. Some viewers of "Dallas" think J.R. is the source and orient to the character. Others may orient to Larry Hagman the actor; some may consider the series producer to be the source, while others might perceive it to be the local network affiliate. The important point is that in media encounters the receiver is faced with far more variation as to the possible source of the message than in interpersonal encounters. Interpersonally, people have fewer choices in perceiving who the source of the message "really" is.

2. Technology limits the kinds of sensory data people may obtain about media sources. People do not know media sources as the result of total sensory integration. Receivers can only imagine or project how Dan Rather feels, smells, or tastes. These sensory data are not available to them. It is even more constrained for newspaper readers and radio listeners. All sorts of missing sensory data demand that people compensate for this lack in a variety of ways. For instance, millions of people attend rock concerts in order to see the stars perform. Even though the audio is often inferior to that available on a good stereo, the experience of seeing the performers, feeling the vibrations, and smelling the array of human odors, all contribute to a more complete and usually more satisfying understanding of the music. Generally speaking, fans frequently appreciate artists' records more if they have "seen" them perform. In other words, people desire maximum sensory integration in order to co-orient to both topic and source

(music and performer). Technology inherently limits the information people have about media sources. This is in sharp contrast to the kinds of sensory data available in the interpersonal encounter.

3. Receivers of media messages tend to be functionally illiterate as to how media sources manipulate their credibility. It is not our intent to summarize how perceived credibility can be controlled by a source. What is important to recognize is that the presentation of media sources requires message forms decidedly different from interpersonal message forms. Television requires that camera shots be taken to represent the "reality" of the source. Newspapers print in varying type faces and sizes. The media industries encode their thinking in a stylized and limiting form in order to present to potential receivers, sources of varying credibility. For example, research has shown that such things as camera angle and image size effect the perceived credibility and attractiveness of media sources.[5]

Most television viewers have little difficulty in determining the good guys from the bad guys. This is true (though more difficult) even when the sound is turned off and only the pictures are present. And yet audience members are often at a loss as to *how* they know who's good and bad. The conventions and methods employed by media sources to manipulate and control the projected images requires specialized knowledge about such things as lenses, editing, lighting, image size, music, camera movement, color, and a host of other technical and esthetic factors. Most participants in media encounters are functionally illiterate when it comes to decoding the grammar of visualization and presentation. Because of this, the knowledge people have of media sources is often based on experiences and forms that are importantly different from those used by interpersonal sources to present themselves.

4. Media sources are assigned status by receivers due to their mere appearance in the media. Lazarsfeld and Merton referred to this phenomenon as status conferal.[6] People who appear in the media tend to enjoy higher credibility and status because they have been "chosen" to appear before large numbers of people. This credibility bestowed on media sources confounds the relationship in the co-orientation process people have in the media-person encounter.

While there may be other factors that influence the knowledge receivers have of media sources compared with interpersonal sources, these four, collectively, appear to make these differences substantial.

We have argued here that media-person encounters differ substantially from interpersonal encounters along three dimensions. First, interpersonal encounters allow for more sensory integration potential than any of the mass media. Second, because receivers in media encounters have no functional control of media sources like that which is available in interpersonal encounters, the concept of feedback in the two contexts is more than a difference of degree. Finally, the knowledge a receiver may have of a media source is inherently limited by technology and ranges of experience. This renders the co-orientation people have with topic and source to be different for media encounters than it is for interpersonal ones.

IV. Implications for Understanding the Mass Communication Process. Our argument for a conceptual reorientation to the media-person encounter is supported by contemporary social scientists who are calling into question the American norm for judging successful interpersonal communication. According to communication educators, and any one of a host of interpersonal communication texts, effective interpersonal communication has a number of "universal" characteristics. These elements of good conversation have been described in a variety of ways, but sociologist Michael Schudson has summarized the American "conversation ideal" in the following five statements:

(1) continuous feedback between two people in a face-to-face setting;
(2) multichannel communications: one not only hears the conversational partner but sees and touches him or her;
(3) spontaneous utterance: the content of the conversation is unique and created on the spot;
(4) the same person acts at once as sender and receiver of messages;
(5) the norms of the conversation are egalitarian: whatever rules of speaking (like alternation of speakers) govern one govern the other.[7]

Just as Schudson and his colleagues effectively argue that these characteristics have no universal significance across cultures, it is our position that in order to better understand mass communication we should abandon this set of characteristics as the basis for describing and evaluating the media-person interaction.

By developing an entirely new "communication ideal" for the media-person encounter which is based upon the technological and functional realities of the mass media, we can begin to understand mass communication within the context of its own norms and standards, rather than those imposed by demarcations along a single continuum. To assume that an interpersonal paradigm provides an appropriate framework for the understanding of mass communication forces us to accept the basic premise that for many kinds of human interaction, the mass media are simply inferior. However, if our conceptual orientation focuses on the realities of the media-person interaction, we begin to recognize new functional alternatives that may have been previously hidden by the standards and ideals of the interpersonal perspective.

One line of inquiry that has provided new insights into the media-person encounter is research dealing with two-way or talk radio.[8] The very fact that the interaction between call-in listeners and talk radio hosts more closely approximates the characteristics generally attributed to interpersonal communication enables us to begin bridging the gap in our understanding of face-to-face and media-person encounters.

Consistent with our growing dependence on mediated information, there exists today a general feeling among many individuals that we are becoming less and less informed about matters of central importance to our daily lives. Of equal concern to many is the belief that we are frequently unable to express our own opinions to those people who are in positions of authority and decision-making power. Individuals who face additional barriers to interpersonal relationships due to poor health, physical disability, or geographic isolation have an even greater need to seek out alternative communication channels, especially those created by the electronic media.

Within this context, the interpersonal character of talk radio is especially significant. Talk radio is one of the few public media that allow for spontaneous interaction between two or more people. The exchange of messages between a call-in listener and a talk radio host creates a pattern of talk that defines a symbol system for the interactants. That is, social reality is uniquely defined by the interactants, and hence becomes significant to the communication process.

After reviewing the results of several talk radio studies, one might easily come to the conclusion that although the communication patterns between a call-in listener and a talk radio host reveal numerous similarities to the face-to-face encounter, the unique characteristics imposed by this communication setting afford a special context that needs to be considered in order to develop a complete understanding of this particular media-person transaction.

The on-air presence of the talk radio host on a regular basis permits the listener to form a variety of opinions about this person who is known only by his/her voice. The opportunity to witness the interaction patterns between the host and other callers without any personal threat to the listener enables him/her to prepare for a future media-person encounter. Even before the listener makes the conscious decision to initiate contact with the host, the impersonality of the medium allows the listener to use the information gleaned from the medium to facilitate interaction with others, or to simply reinforce or expand existing ideas.

One of the reasons that the two-way format has proved more successful on radio than television is that the interaction is enhanced by the absence of the visual pictoral and visual verbal modalities. What might be considered by some as a technological limitation of the radio medium actually contributes to this form of media-person interaction. In-depth interviews with selected call-in listeners revealed that not being able to see or even know what the host looked like (and vice versa) contributed greatly to the listener's level of relaxation and satisfaction with the media encounter.

Although the listening patterns of those who follow talk radio reveal a fairly faithful allegiance throughout the broadcast day, the vast majority of call-in listeners communicate directly with only one or two of the half-dozen hosts employed by a station. Analysis of the interaction patterns between caller and host revealed that the majority of the conversations are spent reinforcing the opinions or positions of the interactants. The conclusion drawn from these findings is that talk radio functions to expose listeners to a variety of opinions and issues, but listeners are seldom willing to engage in interaction with hosts who hold a competing position. Even though callers selected hosts who shared a common perspective, interviewees frequently noted that they never forgot who was in control of the interaction. For some, being cut off for whatever reason represented a form of chastisement and humiliation that they found difficult to accept.

We hope that these examples drawn from talk radio research will serve to support the position that media-person encounters differ significantly from interpersonal encounters, even in the case of a highly specialized mass medium that embodies many of the characteristics of personal conversation. The talk radio listener is both constrained and aided by the technology of radio broadcasting and telephonic communications. When a listener initiates contact with the talk radio host, he/she must remember that the interaction remains completely under the control of the host, who can terminate the conversation at any time. Similarly, the caller's knowledge and understanding of the talk host and the radio station he/she represents are generally limited to the level of information that has been transmitted by the station to its listening audience.

The suggestion that we need to reconsider a media-person paradigm for understanding the mass communication process is not offered at the expense of the well-established interpersonal model. The early two-step flow and subsequent multi-step flow theories of information diffusion provide ample support for the critical importance of an interpersonal orientation to some aspects of the mass communication process. Rather than discard one conceptualization in favor of the other, the interpersonal and media-person models should be viewed as companion orientations. One cannot fully understand the meaning of the media without recognizing that media-person encounters are but one aspect of a much larger process. People's subsequent talk about the media, as well as their conversation with others during media encounters, must obviously be taken into account.

One final issue regarding this broad topic needs to be raised. Do receivers use an interpersonal model of communicative expectations when they encounter the media? Do people use a media model of communicative expectation when they engage in interpersonal transactions? Or, do people have one model of expectations for media encounters and another for interpersonal ones? Part of the answer to these questions may be uncovered in terms of age and differential experiences with the media. It may well be the case that people who developed their communicative style and expectations in a pre-television and pre-technological time approach media encounters and interpersonal encounters far differently than do those born in the television and technology milieu of today. Because of this, the examination of interpersonal and media encounters must continue. Research on personal junctures with media and others needs careful description and understanding.

"So what do you want to do anyway, watch TV or communicate?"

Notes

1. W. Schramm, "The Nature of Communication Between Humans," in *The Process and Effects of Mass Communication*, eds. W. Schramm and D. Roberts (Urbana: University of Illinois Press, 1971), p. 50.
2. J. Gibson, *The Senses Considered as Perceptual Systems.* (Boston: Houghton Mifflin, 1966).
3. R. M. W. Travers, *Man's Information System.* (Scranton: Chandler Publishing Company, 1970), p. 9.
4. M. Burgoon and M. Ruffner, *Human Communication.* (New York: Holt, Rinehart and Winston, 1977), p. 82.
5. T. A. McCain, J. C. Chilberg, and J. J. Wakshlag, "The Effect of Camera Angle on Source Credibility and Attraction," *Journal of Broadcasting*, 21:35–46 (Winter 1977).
6. P. F. Lazarfeld and R. K. Merton, "Mass Communication, Popular Taste, and

Organized Social Action," in *The Communication of Ideas*, ed. T. Bryson (New York: Harper, 1948).

7. M. Schudson, "The Ideal of Conversation in the Study of Mass Media," *Communication Research*, 5:320–329 (July 1978).

8. R. K. Avery, D. G. Ellis, and T. W. Glover, "Patterns of Communication on Talk Radio," *Journal of Broadcasting*, 22:5–17 (Winter 1978).

MICHAEL SCHUDSON

The Ideal of Conversation in the Study of Mass Media

In this essay Michael Schudson questions the common belief that face-to-face conversation is always preferable to mass media interaction. He light-heartedly but seriously points out that much of our conversation is trivial, stereotypical, and of little social use. He argues that what we have in actuality is a "conversational ideal" that is seldom achieved, and yet has become the model for evaluation of the media. Furthermore, he claims that the mass media have helped establish what is ideal conversation by expanding the content of conversation and making it more egalitarian. For Schudson it is not a matter of interpersonal conversation versus the mass media, but rather how each helps shape our notion of what is ideal.

American social thinkers in the 1920s spoke with great sympathy of the mass media. Dewey (1920: 686), Mead (1926: 382–393), Park (1923: 273–289) all wrote of newspapers with considerable affection. Social scientists and social philosophers since then have praised the mass media or blamed the mass media but rarely demonstrated anything we could call affection. They seem to feel that the mass media have not provided new ways to communicate so much as interrupted the old way of face-to-face, interpersonal conversation. It is a stock image in cartoons—the husband at breakfast with his face buried in the newspaper while his wife tries vainly to talk to him.[1]

The distinction between mass media and face-to-face communication seems to be invidious. For instance, typical lists of the characteristics of "interpersonal" channels of communication and "mass media" channels emphasize that the "message flow" in interpersonal channels is two-way, the message flow in the mass media one-way. In interpersonal channels there is a high amount of feedback readily available, while in mass media channels the amount is low. Given the cultural assumptions of a democratic society, this contrast is necessarily to the disadvantage of the mass

From *Communication Research*, Vol 5, No 3 (July 1978). © 1978 Sage Publications, Inc. Reprinted by permission of the publisher and the author.

Author's Note: *I would like to thank Paul Hirsch, Susan Noakes, and David Riesman for comments on an earlier draft of this paper.*

media. Who could approve of one-way over two-way message flow? Or low rather than high possibilities for immediate feedback?

But while it is true that ordinarily messages in the mass media move in one direction with little opportunity for feedback, it is *not* true that ordinarily messages in face-to-face conversation move in two directions with great opportunity for feedback. There is an unspoken sense among students of the mass media that the world of face-to-face communication is the world of rich and complicated interaction that would be possible if the cartoon husband put down his morning paper and talked to his cartoon wife.

But what would that conversation actually be like? As an example, take the opening scene in Pinter's (1962) play, "A Slight Ache." Flora and Edward are at breakfast. As the scene opens, Edward, as we might expect, is reading the paper, but Flora manages to engage him in conversation:

Flora: Have you noticed the honeysuckle this morning?
Edward: The what?
Flora: The honeysuckle?
Edward: Honeysuckle? Where?
Flora: By the back gate, Edward.
Edward: Is that honeysuckle? I thought it was . . . convolvulus, or something.
Flora: But you know it's honeysuckle.
Edward: I tell you I thought it was convolvulus.
    [Pause.]
Flora: It's in wonderful flower.
Edward: I must look.
Flora: The whole garden's in flower in this morning. The clematis. The convolvulus. Everything. I was out at seven. I stood by the pool.
Edward: Did you say—that the convolvulus was in flower?
Flora: Yes.
Edward: But good God, you just denied there was any.
Flora: I was talking about the honeysuckle.
Edward: About the what?
Flora [calmly]: Edward—you know that shrub outside the toolshed . . .
Edward: Yes, yes.
Flora: That's convolvulus.
Edward: That?
Flora: Yes.
Edward: Oh.
    [Pause.]
    I thought it was japonica.
Flora: Oh, good Lord no.
Edward: Pass the teapot, please.

And so on, for pages. Is this the communication the mass media interfere with? Pinter's dialogue has a touch of the cynical, even the sinister, but there is no doubt that we recognize the speech he captures.

Another culture, another breakfast. In a Tunisian village, Nawa's husband Muhammed comes into the room to eat. He says to his wife, "May Allah grant you a long life, and may he let us stay long together." Nawa and her daughter reply, "May light shine upon your day." Every morning the same words, and few words if any beyond them. The sociologist Duvignaud writes:

> No one attaches any importance to these words, but they must be spoken. There would be a catch in the throat and an uncomfortable feeling in the whole body if they were not mumbled every morning. Actually Muhammed and Nawa have rarely said a word to each other, since the time when the children were very small and one or the other was ill. Now, except when they are harassed by an unpaid debt, they have nothing to talk about [1970: 10].

This is common: first, that silence rather than conversation is usual between people, even intimates in a family, and second, that where silence is broken, it is broken by ritual or stereotypic utterances. It is not only in Tunisian villages that children are supposed to be seen and not heard or that women are supposed to know their place. Our model of ideal conversation may be that of two lovers or of husband and wife over coffee after the kids are in bed. But in the Tunisian village, most conversation is segregated by sex—men talking to other men in front of the grocer's shop or women talking to women while they do the laundry. Our own urban and corporate villages are different, but not so different as we might like to imagine—at least, not before the advent of the mass media.

When we criticize the reality of the mass media, we do so by opposing it to an ideal of conversation which we are not inclined to examine. We are not really interested in what face-to-face communication is like: rather, we have developed a notion that all communication *should* be like a certain model of conversation, whether that model really exists or not. The "conversational ideal" of communication, as I will call it, includes the following characteristics:

(1) continuous feedback between two people in a face-to-face setting;
(2) multichannel communications; one not only hears the conversational partner but sees and touches him or her;
(3) spontaneous utterance: the content of the conversation is unique and created on the spot.

(4) the same person acts at once as sender and receiver of messages;

(5) the norms of the conversation are egalitarian: whatever rules of speaking (like alternation of speakers) govern one govern the other.

This ideal is not one concocted by social scientists. Rather, it is a widely shared ideal in contemporary American culture which social science has uncritically adopted. It is by no means an ideal of universal significance. The ideal of conversation in contemporary Antigua, for example, does not presume that the utterances of different people in a conversation are or should be oriented to one another and shaped as responses to what others have just said—"continuous feedback" is not a criterion of good conversation. In Antigua, on the contrary, as anthropologist Reisman (1974) suggests, there is "no sense of interruption, or need to fit carefully into an ongoing pattern of conversation." Reisman (1974: 115) concludes that in Antigua "the impulse to speak is not cued by the external situation but comes from within the speaker." Without the "norm of interruption" customary in our own conversational ideal, it is quite acceptable in Antiguan conversation for several people to speak simultaneously.

> [T]he fact that one is not heard does not mean one has to stop. One can go right on with perhaps one listener, or perhaps none. On some occasions, perhaps more serious, or particularly in more formal settings as part of an almost ritualized debate between sets of conventions, someone will be told to "have some behavior" or "let the man speak." In many conversations, however, several participants already involved may feel that the point they are making is not receiving sufficient attention and will each of them continue speaking, repeating the point they are making—so that several people are speaking at once [1974: 114].

In any society, people try to abide by norms of conversational practice and will feel disoriented when they are violated. In mainstream American culture, when an element of the conversational ideal described above is missing, people feel uncomfortable. It can be distressing, for instance, to pass an acquaintance in the street where there is opportunity only for a ritual exchange of greetings rather than for a spontaneous conversation. It is equally awkward when the same person is not sender and receiver—for instance, one person will not stop talking (something that would be taken as normal in Antigua) or else, when one person pauses for the other person's response, there is no response. Or suppose a channel of communication has been cut off. Recently I talked to a man whose face was altogether impassive—everything I said sunk into it as if it were a black hole. This was most disconcerting. Or take the familiar case where the rules of speaking do not apply equally. When people who are unequal in status talk, there are special rules—for instance, that the person of higher status should be the one to signal the close of the conversation. In some cases the person of inferior status, feeling disarmed in conversation with superiors, will choose where possible some less intimate means of communication. A woman of my acquaintance who does research in libraries in Europe prefers to have a calling card to announce her appearance to a curator or librarian because this puts her on a more equal footing with the official than does her personal arrival in a world of men.

The characteristic of "spontaneous utterance" deserves further comment. It suggests the expression of authentic or true feelings. This is a modern view of conversation. If one looks in the card catalog under "conversation," what one finds are eighteenth century guides to the "art of conversation" which had nothing at all to do with authenticity. Conversation was a social grace for people of leisure, like playing the piano, and was cultivated as a highly artificial pursuit (see Sennett, 1977: 82). We still recognize that conversation can be artful or even artificial in the notion of a "conversation piece" or in the grudging recognition of some people who are especially skilled at cocktail-party talk.

Sometimes the ideal of conversation is violated and it does not disturb us. It is as if we have some tacit understanding that talk comes in different forms, each with its own rules. In the ideal situation, conversation is a constantly evolving social contract determined by the two parties and the two parties alone. But in fact, there are ordinarily many constraints which direct or almost determine the outcome, reducing the possibility of spontaneous utterance. Talk with the store clerk or the bank teller is ordinarily stereotypic—indeed, bank tellers can be replaced by computers, candy store owners by vending machines, corner newsstand operators by newsboxes, and most interaction with sales people by self-service stores. When we do talk to a sales person, the stereotypic character of the talk may not disturb us—indeed, too much spontaneity might. The dental hygienist will want to talk to the patient in the chair to establish rapport, but if this leads the two to get into a conversation—note how the ideal is presumed in that phrase—the hygienist will withdraw to get on with the work.

We have, then, an ideal of what is the best kind of communication. We may not want to give it up, but we should be aware that it is an ideal, one that most communication, including most conversation, rarely achieves. It is notable that we do not have a separate ideal of what good *mass* communication might be. Not that we do not have good examples of it: Shakespeare in theater, Tolstoy in the novel, Bergman in film. There are outstanding instances of newspaper correspondence. Television has had outstanding moments, though there is not yet consensus on what these have been. But implicit in studies of the mass media in the social sciences is the old ideal of perfect communication in the face-to-face conversation. By this standard, the mass media are judged and found wanting.

One might conclude that for most decent human purposes the mass media are inferior to conversation, but that is not something to assume from the outset. Indeed, I would go further to suggest that the conversational ideal we now subscribe to has developed only in a world shaped by the mass media. Both the ideal of conversation, and its occasional realization, are in part a consequence of mass media.

This is so in at least two respects. First, the mass media have contributed to making the "egalitarian" criterion of ideal communication more prominent and more possible to realize. In the United States in the late nineteenth century, for instance, not only were women agitating for formal access to the political system through suffrage, but they were achieving a certain amount of political competence through newspaper reading. Newspapers, before the 1830s, were generally read only by males at offices or clubs. Papers were more widely available thereafter. The major increase in circulation after 1880, the heyday of newspaper growth, came in evening papers the man read at home rather than on the way to work or at work—and so his wife read too.[2] Television, even more than the evening paper, has made political and cultural information available to large numbers of women as never before. It seems reasonable to assume that this has changed the possibilities for conversation between men and women and, for that matter, between women and children. Sociologist Iwanska observed in her study of a rural community in Washington in the early 1950s that women had more time for television than men and, thanks to the tube, gained more knowledge of the outside world than their husbands. The result was significant: "It is more likely today that a child will go to the mother than to the father to ask about foreign countries or about the United Nations" (Iwanska, 1958: 29).

The mass media helped democratize conversation between the sexes. It has democratized conversation between age groups, as well. Film and television have made a common culture available to children who partake of it as equals with adults. Indeed, children are often well ahead of adults in their knowledge of the culture of the mass media. This surely has hastened the demise of the rule that children are to be seen and not heard. Children are simply more competent than they once were to participate in many of the conversations adults enjoy.[3]

The mass media have had a second effect in making the conversational ideal more frequently realizable. They have made spontaneous utterance more possible. Of course, we are familiar with the ways in which one can parrot a book or film or television in conversation. But, even then, the mass media bring into conversation a third party, a topic of discourse outside the immediacy of what-I-did-today-what-did-you-do-today. This expands the grammatical possibilities of discourse—not just the first and second person but the third person is involved. This adds to the complexity, the thickness of conversation.

But couldn't the "third person" be, in fact, a third person? A real human being rather than a mass media message? Certainly. Nevertheless, the mass media have an advantage here. If one person in the conversation recounts something a third person did or said, the burden of putting the third person's words or deeds into some *form,* a story which can be communicated, is still on the first person. However, if that person recounts something heard or seen or read in the mass media, it is more likely that the thing recounted will already have a form of its own. Of course, the message from the mass media will also be selectively perceived and retold in the conversationalist's frame of reference, but it will be relatively more resistant to distortion. The mass media message has a better chance of being a genuinely "third person" in the conversation than an actual third person.

This will not always be true. Research on the "two-step flow" of communication suggests that mass media messages have most power in influencing attitudes when they are mediated by a person. Even if that is the case, there may still be another kind of "two-step" in which another person's message gains power only when mediated or *legitimated* by the mass media. For instance, a neighbor may tell us that he has traced his ancestry. But will that message register? Will we take it seriously as a communication *to* us rather than as an additional quirky item about the neighbor? Very likely not—unless, of course, we have watched or talked about the television series, "Roots." Then the neighbor's quirk gains a context, a salience, a place in a wider realm of culture and meaning. We make meaning collectively, but we often do not know "what to make of" the information around us until it has a setting. The mass media, I think, will as often provide the setting for a message from an acquaintance as the acquaintance will offer an authoritative interpretation for a message from the mass media.

None of this is meant to diminish the supreme importance of talk in human life. Conversation holds a primary place in our lives and our sense of reality which neither novels nor newspapers nor film nor television can match. Dewey (1948: 2) wrote, with hunting and gathering societies in mind, "the conscious and truly human experience of the chase comes when it is talked over and re-enacted by the camp fire." One can believe this and still admit that the chase will often have been uneventful and the talk about it trivial. Even around the camp fire, talk is likely to be of convolvulus and honeysuckle.[4]

There is nothing wrong with that. But to recognize it should make us more realistic in what we expect from the mass media. We should be more aware of the irony in condemning the mass media for failing to live up to a standard, the conversational ideal, which the mass media have helped make conceivable.

Notes

1. Why is it always the husband and so rarely the wife who reads the morning paper in this stock scene? The different patterns of both conversation and orientation to the mass media of men and women is a topic of great importance, I think. It deserves more systematic attention. On conversation see Keenan (1974: 125–143).

2. On the rise of evening papers, see Emery (1972: 292); on the orientation of newspapers in the 1880s to a female readership, see Juergens (1966) and Schudson (1978).

3. The mass media also can democratize social relations by substituting for conversation between people unequal in status. For instance, one study indicates that college-educated parents rely more on direct personal contact with school officials to learn about local schools, while parents without college education prefer newspapers as a source of information. The study holds that "the mass media seem to be relatively more useful channels for that large segment of the citizenry that is less educated than are school personnel. One might even describe the media as the least 'elitist' of the several potential sources of public information about schools" (Chaffee, 1967: 732).

4. Marshall, for instance, reports that the !Kung bushmen are an especially loquacious people—particularly the males. They talk frequently, generally about food. They do not generally speak openly of sexual matters or of the gods. They do not tell myths. They do not invent stories: "They said they had no interest in hearing things that are not true and wonder why anybody has" (Marshall, 1968: 179–184).

GERALD R. MILLER

A Neglected Connection: Mass Media Exposure and Interpersonal Communicative Competency

All of us need information to communicate effectively. We need information to understand other people's attitudes and outlooks, likes and dislikes, interests and motivations, if we are to interact and communicate successfully. Where do we obtain this needed information and how do we process it? Quite obviously we acquire it through personal interaction and the mass media. How we process and use it depends on whether the information is cultural, sociological, or psychological. Gerald Miller explains what each type of information does to help us better predict the outcomes of our communication efforts. He examines the essential function of psychological information in interpersonal communication and contrasts this with media's overwhelming reliance on cultural and sociological information. Miller argues that heavy doses of media messages may inhibit our ability to relate interpersonally.

Communication researchers are certainly no strangers to issues concerning the interface between the mass media and interpersonal communication. The "two-step flow" studies of Lazarsfeld, Katz, and their associates (e.g., Katz and Lazarsfeld, 1955; Lazarsfeld, Berelson, and Gaudet, 1944) are of ancient vintage, and almost all students of communication are aware that media influence is not injected directly into the cognitive and affective veins of message recipients but rather is administered in oral doses by opinion leaders plying their trade in interpersonal settings. Turning from issues involving social influence per se to the question of why persons expose themselves selectively to media content, the uses and gratifications approach to media consumption (Blumler and Katz, 1974) emphasizes that media communications can be used for such purposes as achieving social contact (Nordenstreng, 1970) or acquiring information to be used in interpersonal transactions (Katz, Guervitch, and Haas, 1973). Unquestionably, much of the conversational grist for interpersonal dialogues is ground at the media mill, with such dialogues ranging in sophistication from the disjointed exchanges of several teenagers debating the relative merits of currently popular punk rock groups to the studied analyses of a particular

New York Times editorial or CBS public affairs program performed by two or more like-minded members of the intellectual community.

Though these previously established relationships are of substantial import, I will argue in this chapter that mass communication messages potentially affect interpersonal relationships in even more fundamental, pervasive ways which at this writing have received relatively little research attention. Specifically, I will propose that the media often: (1) exert a powerful impact on people's initial perceptions of other interpersonal transactants; (2) influence the manner in which information about other transactants is processed and interpreted; and in many cases (3) distract persons from gathering the kind of information they need to relate effectively in interpersonal settings. While my position falls somewhat short of McLuhan's (1964) cryptic "the medium is the message," at least as I understand this dictum, it does posit that consumption of media messages and expectations regarding interpersonal relationships are woven together in a complex relational fabric.

Some Conceptual Groundwork

A conceptualization of interpersonal communication developed by Mark Steinberg and me (Miller and Steinberg, 1975; Miller and Sunnafrank, 1982) provides the grounds for my argument. We began with the assumption that whenever people communicate with each other, they make predictions about the possible consequences, or outcomes, of their messages. Stated differently, message making does not occur haphazardly; rather, communicators purposively weigh the available message alternatives, including the option of sending no message, and select the alternative or alternatives expected to yield the most favorable outcomes. Naturally, the degree of cognitive involvement in prediction making varies from one situation to another: in certain situations, such as job interviews or oral examinations for graduate degrees, much conscious rehearsal and evaluation occurs; in other situations, such as greeting or leave-taking exchanges, prediction may occur at such a low level of awareness as to be almost synonymous with perception. Nevertheless, predictions are made in the latter situations, a fact that is most vividly underscored on those rare occasions when the predictions are disconfirmed.

Unless a random decision process is assumed—and in a few cases, this assumption may be justified because of the complete absence of relevant data; e.g., people sometimes speculate how they would communicate with aliens from other planets—prediction making requires information. Three types of information assist communicators in determining the probable outcomes of their messages.

First, a communicator's predictions about probable message outcomes may be grounded in *cultural information.* Knowledge about people's culture—its language, dominant values, myths, and prevailing ideology—often permits prediction of probable responses to certain messages. To illustrate this process, consider a widely aired perfume advertisement of several years ago. The commercial stressed that this particular perfume "interacts with normal body chemistry" to produce a unique fragrance for each wearer. The advertisement's potential appeal—in marketplace parlance, its effectiveness in persuading viewers to buy perfume—rested on the premise that members of our society assign a high value to individuality. Thus, the commercial sought to curry product conformity by focusing on individuality and uniqueness, a logical absurdity yet a potentially persuasive message based largely on cultural-level prediction making.

Sociological information may also provide the primary grounds for prediction making. Knowledge of others' membership groups, as well as the reference groups to which they aspire, allows communicators to make predictions about probable responses to numerous messages. Again, media advertising abounds with messages relying heavily on sociological information. The once popular practice of adorning patent medicine commercials with actors garbed in white medical coats sought to capitalize on the credibility conferred by many persons on this particular professional group. Advertisements for life insurance, toothpaste, and numerous other products and services rest on sociological-level predictions associated with the amorphous membership groups labeled "parents" and "spouses." Examples of messages grounded in sociological predictions are numerous; in fact, of the three types of information discussed herein, sociological information is probably used most frequently in arriving at predictions about message outcomes.

Predictions derived from both cultural and sociological information are founded on a process of *stimulus generalization;* i.e., the communicator abstracts a set of characteristics common to most members of a group and then assumes that any given individual or individuals belonging to that group will manifest these characteristics. As a result, cultural and sociological predictions are inevitably subject to error, since some individuals are certain to deviate from the majority of the group. All Americans do not value individuality and all parents do not place a high premium on their children's dental health or their family's economic security.

The third type of information used in prediction making differs markedly from the two types discussed thus far. Though our usage is more restricted than is typically the case, Steinberg and I call the third type *psychological information*. Such information departs drastically from sociological and cultural information because it directs attention at another person's prior learning history, particularly as it *varies* from the learning histories of other persons. To put it differently, cultural and sociological predictions rest on a view of individuals as undifferentiated role occupants, whereas psychological prediction treats people as individuals (Berger, Gardner, Parks, Schulman and Miller, 1976). Moreover, predictions based on psychological information are akin to a process of *stimulus discrimination;* i.e., the communicator seeks to determine how particular persons differ from others of common cultural and sociological lineage. Such an approach can, in principle, produce error-free prediction; though as a matter of fact, predictive perfection probably occurs seldom, if ever, since communicators need considerable personal information to make totally accurate psychological predictions.

Steinberg and I posit that interpersonal communication is characterized by frequent reliance on psychological prediction-making. Initial transactions are, perforce, largely impersonal, relying primarily on cultural and sociological information as guides to message making. *If* the transactants continue the relationship, *if* they are motivated to seek psychological information, and *if* they have the needed skills to acquire it, the relationship becomes increasingly interpersonal. Thus, the crux of our conceptualization of interpersonal communication can be stated as follows: *when predictions about communicative outcomes rely heavily on cultural and/or sociological information, the communicators are engaged in impersonal communication; when predictions are heavily grounded in psychological information, the communicators are engaged in interpersonal communication.*

Implications for the Media/Interpersonal Interface

Both the nature of the three types of information and my previous examples underscore the fact that mass media transactions are impersonal. In seeking to appeal to large, heterogeneous audiences, media communicators necessarily rely on cultural and sociological information when selecting among message alternatives. Some predictive error is inevitable and expected; no media message can ever hope to be effective with every potential recipient. In a sense, the hallowed ratings provide a quantitative index of success in predictive accuracy and relative reduction of error. Furthermore, while my prior examples were drawn from media advertising appeals, it should be obvious that the same strategy of prediction underlies all media messages. Characters in television or radio dramas are cultural and sociological stereotypes designed to appeal to the majority of viewers: though they differ in skin pigmentation, George Jefferson and Archie Bunker, Bill Russell and Rick Barry,[1] or Lea Thornton and Jessica Savitch,[2] are highly similar cultural and sociological creations who embody a number of widely shared American values and reflect commonly held stereotypes about certain membership and reference groups. Phrases such as, "All the news that's fit to print," or, "And that's the way it is, Monday, November 12, 1979," are most accurately translated to mean, "Based on cultural and sociological predictions, these are the items of news expected to appeal to, or capture the interest of, the reading and viewing public." Thus, though this chapter may be of considerable interest to some of this book's readers, it can safely be predicted that the effort I have devoted to it today will not be mentioned on tonight's CBS News or in tomorrow's *New York Times*—unless, of course, something quite dramatic and totally unexpected occurs while I am working on it.

Given their communicative objectives, the media's approach to prediction making is perfectly sensible. Still, it can be asked how consumption of media messages influences people's perceptions of others as well as their habitual ways of processing and interpreting information in face-to-face settings. Assuming the validity of such learning theory constructs as *transfer* and the previously mentioned *stimulus generalization*, the following fundamental proposition seems quite defensible: *extensive exposure to media messages predisposes persons to view other people as undifferentiated role occupants—simplistic cultural and sociological caricatures—rather than individuals.* This proposition stems from the likelihood that heavy doses of media messages contribute to the development of cognitively simple information processors who are conditioned to think in terms of stimulus generalization rather than stimulus discrimination. Hence, I am not primarily concerned with the persuasive impact of the media—except in its broadest, most pervasive sense—nor am I preoccupied with whether or not mass media make us more violent or more licentious creatures. Rather,

I am disturbed by the possibility that the mass media inhibit our ability to relate interpersonally to each other; that they create sets, expectations, and thinking habits which hinder us in dealing with others in our daily environment *as individuals.*

It should be stressed that, depending on how broadly the term is defined, not all media are equally guilty of encouraging simplistic cultural and sociological stereotyping. Great novels and plays are often treasured because of their intricate, insightful, and individualistic character development: Captain Ahab is much more than just the commanding officer of a merchant whaling ship and Willy Loman is certainly not just another traveling salesman. Even in these cases, however, the notion that great drama and literature reveal identifiable universals of temperament and behavior suggests that the major goal of the author is to stimulate her or his readers or viewers to engage in stimulus generalization—to lump people together in terms of one or two general characteristics. Upon turning to the typical dramatic fare served up by television and popular magazines, any semblance of careful development of individual traits and personality attributes vanishes; rather, as mentioned earlier, viewers and readers are served a diet of uncomplicated cultural and sociological caricatures.

Numerous research questions are suggested by the position I have outlined above. For example, my viewpoint suggests that an inverse relationship exists between frequency of media exposure and the number of attributes assigned to others in one's personal environment; i.e., it implies that heavy media exposure inhibits the development of cognitively complex information processors. This possibility could be tested by employing a measure of cognitive complexity, such as Kelly's (1955) Rep Test, and correlating scores with reports of amount of time spent attending to media messages. Or alternatively, since problems associated with inferring causality can be raised regarding the preceding approach, measures of cognitive complexity could be obtained from individuals following varying amounts of media exposure, an experimental procedure which permits less ambiguous interpretation of causal linkages.

In a similar vein, it can also be hypothesized that frequency of media exposure is inversely related to the ability to make psychological-level predictions. Recently, several colleagues at Michigan State University (e.g., Bundens, 1980) have commenced developing procedures that permit tests of people's ability to use cultural, sociological, and psychological information in arriving at predictions about others' responses. Presently, Mark deTurck and I (1981) are devising a paper-and-pencil test designed to tap respondents' relative predilections to think in terms of stimulus generalization or stimulus discrimination. By taking advantage of these procedures and measurement tools, a variety of studies dealing with possible relationships between amount of media exposure and interpersonal communicative competency can be carried out.

Apart from possible influences of actual media content, I would suggest that the time spent consuming media messages detracts from people's opportunities and abilities to move their relationships to a more interpersonal plane. As the conceptualization developed herein implies, gathering psychological information demands considerable time and energy. When the television set, the radio, or the print media consistently intrude on people's chances for face-to-face dialogue, the likelihood of obtaining the necessary data base for psychological-level predictions is slim. Research that examines the abilities of relational partners with varying amounts of media consumption to make accurate predictions about each other's message responses should permit increased understanding of the possible intrusion of media on interpersonal relationships.

I have painted an extensive picture for future research in very broad brush strokes. Permit me a final observation about the potential utility of my conceptual perspective. It has always seemed to me that much research on media effects suffers from being pitched at too low a level of abstraction: interest is typically directed at isolating the effects of some particular kind of media message content, rather than identifying a set of overarching propositions or constructs capable of embracing diverse media content areas. My perspective posits that all media messages, whether a thirty-second advertisement on network television, a pornographic movie, a violent episode of "Hill Street Blues," or a 6:30 network news item, share a primary reliance on cultural and sociological information and prediction making. If it can be shown that differences in the extent to which persons are exposed to this common antecedent result in systematic variations in person perception and processing of personal information, we will be in a position to make wider generalizations about the impact of the media on face-to-face relationships.

As my remarks in this chapter clearly emphasize, I believe that mass media and interpersonal communication are psychologically interconnected in very fundamental ways, that the influence of one domain pervades communicative activities in the other. To avoid misunderstanding, I must stress that I see nothing inherently insidious or threatening about the mass media: they are designed to fulfill consensually agreed upon societal functions and they generally accomplish this goal admirably. Still, if we are to recognize the oft-endorsed objective of improving the quality of our interpersonal relationships, we must understand the impact of the media on the interpersonal arena. My concern is best captured by this statement from one of my earlier papers:

> The most calamitous possible effect of increased reliance on mediated communication lies in people's diminished ability to function and relate as individuals, and even more important, in their subsequent failure to satisfy basic human needs that are served by interpersonal contact. To say this in no way demeans the important gains that can be realized by improved and expanded communication technology; rather, it underscores the necessity of maintaining a balanced perspective between the social benefits to be reaped from advances in mediated communication systems and the individual rewards gained from face-to-face encounters. (Miller, 1977, 190).

Notes

1. Indeed, while this chapter was being written, an unfortunate cultural-level prediction has clouded the future effectiveness of the Russell and Barry sports broadcasting team. I refer, of course, to the incident in which Barry responded to a picture of Russell by asserting that he could immediately recognize him because of his "watermelon grin," a vivid example not only of failure to use psychological information in prediction making but also an illustration of inept cultural-level prediction.

2. A recent amusing story appearing in the *Detroit Free Press* contends that the esoteric, sophisticated names used by most women network reporters—"Jessica," "Lea," "Leslie," "Andrea," etc.—represent an instance of poor prediction making. The writer argues that most viewers prefer the "old shoe" names of male reporters—"Walter," "John," "Dan," "Bob," etc.—and contends there will never be a successful woman anchor person until she adopts a name such as "Nellie" or "Martha." Whether accurate or not, the story again underscores the centrality of cultural and sociological prediction to the enterprise of creating media messages.

STEVEN H. CHAFFEE

Mass Media and Interpersonal Channels: Competitive, Convergent, or Complementary?

Which would you prefer? A first-hand account of an event from a friend or media coverage of the event? If you needed advice about an overcharge on an automobile repair bill would you ask an acquaintance or call the consumer reporter at the television station? Are Ann Landers and Abigail better sources of information about personal problems than members of your family? Steven Chaffee is concerned with answers to such questions and what they reveal about our reliance on mass and interpersonal channels of information. He finds that there has been created a false competition between mass and interpersonal channels wherein we are led to believe that most people prefer interpersonal to media information. His thorough review of research and his careful analysis reveals that no such polarity exists. Rather, the accessibility of a channel and the likelihood of finding desired information through it are the main determinants for our choice of source of information.

An act of communication is a transaction between persons and can be described from either's point of view. Different questions and different answers are produced from each perspective. Compare:

Who (source)	Who (receiver)
Says what	Hears what
To whom (receiver)	From whom (source)
Via which channel	Via what channels
With what effect?	For what purpose?

The first of these models is the classic formulation of communication research by Harold Lasswell.[1] It envisions the act of communication from the viewpoint of the source of a message, and the questions for study unfold in sequence. The source creates a message, which is sent through some channel to an audience upon which it may exercise some effect. The second model examines the process from the other end. The initial "Who" in this formulation is the audience member, or receiver. The emphasis is on what is received (rather than what was sent), and the ultimate question concerns the purposes the information serves for the person (rather than its influence imposed on him). This is the general approach taken in the study of information-seeking, and of needs and gratifications served by the mass media.[2]

Neither model is the "correct" one, and even both models taken together fail to state many important questions we might ask about communication. This paper will focus on an element that is common to both models, the question of communication channels. In the first model, the source confronts a choice among a number of ways of conveying the message. It may be written or printed and delivered on paper, or spoken and sent via electronic means, or stated directly to the intended audience. These are commonly referred to as print, electronic, and interpersonal channels; print and electronic transmission are usually studied as mass media, although they can also be used in one-to-one communication, as in the case of a letter or telephone call. Specific questions about channel selection are often conceived from the source's point of view: "Can we most effectively reach our audience via television, the newspaper, or personal contact?" "To what extent will a media campaign be counteracted by messages from other people close to the audience member?" "What can be done to neutralize the impact of interpersonal communication?" These problems in manipulative uses of communication have built a body of knowledge called "administrative research."[3]

From the second, receiver-oriented perspective, the distinctions among channels, and even between channel and source, are much less salient. We do not ordinarily think of the channels through which we get our information about the world as in competition with one another, nor do we differentiate clearly between a person who generates a message ("source") and one who relays a message that was created elsewhere ("channel"). We would often find it demeaning to consider ourselves objects of "persuasion," or even of "influence"; these are source-oriented concepts. A great deal of research on people's reception of information has, nevertheless, been geared toward assessing the relative efficacy of various channels. The purpose of this paper is to analyze what goes on between people who are parties to communication transactions in a society with many mass media channels and where people upon occasion engage heavily in interpersonal discussion as well.

Basic Assumptions and Terms

Conclusions drawn from any single perspective are likely to be misleading in our attempts to comprehend the outlines of the overall process of social communication. A number of different viewpoints need to be examined, drawing on studies of different kinds of social behavior, if we are to piece together a coherent picture.

An empirical study tells us only *what has been* the case under a specific set of circumstances. We need to compare studies that find different results under different circumstances to get an idea of the range of possibilities. For example, studies on some topics of persuasion have concluded that the possible impact of communication is very limited because a campaign has not brought about much change. This empirical observation is mistaken for an estimate of theoretical potential. Social conditions vary from time to time and place to place, and we should expect that communication—often called the basic social process—should vary accordingly. Research on advertising in the midst of affluence, for example, is no sure guide to its potential in an underdeveloped country or at a time of severe recession. Studies of a presidential campaign may tell us little about getting a local referendum passed. Surveys showing that people rarely discuss foreign events are not likely to apply when a war has just erupted in the Middle East. Only when we find similar results across a wide variety of social conditions should we begin to consider generalizations.

Accessibility and Flow

The sources one consults for information, and thus the seeming "influences" on one's behavior, are determined mainly by (a) their accessibility; and (b) the likelihood that they will contain the information one might be seeking. Accessibility is the more pervasive factor, involving variation in both the source's and the receiver's behaviors: how frequently does a message's source contact the person via a given channel? And how easy is it, physically or psychologically, for the would-be receiver to consult an information source via a given channel? The second question comes up less often, because much of the information flowing through society simply comes to us whether we seek it or not. Indeed, in modern society it takes a fair amount of effort to avoid receiving messages from a number of channels.

Convergence and Complementarity

The relationship between mass media and interpersonal sources is not clearcut. While different channels may be competitive from a sender's viewpoint, they are more likely to be convergent or complementary when viewed from a receiver's perspective. Convergence occurs when different channels provide the same or overlapping messages. This is the usual case, and it serves to increase a person's confidence in such messages. In the rarer case of divergence—when different sources provide contradictory information—one's belief in the message is called into question. This is a question of "credulity" regarding the correctness of one's information, and often results in seeking convergent information on one side or the other from additional sources. Although there have been many studies devoted to the inherent "credibility" of various channels, we shall see that there is little evidence that people make such a judgment about a channel; few of these studies have been conducted under conditions of divergent information from supposedly competing channels. Instead, a hypothetical situation is posed, one that rarely if ever occurs; example: "If you got opposite news reports from newspapers and television, which would you believe?"

Complementary relationships between channels occur when information is carried in one but not another, or when a person who lacks access to one channel gets information from another. Ordinarily the choice of channels is not a matter of great moment to an individual; information is received, or sought, from the most accessible source. Motivation to seek information is aroused mainly in the rare instance when a person contemplates a change in behavior or a personal decision and sees a risk of adverse consequences if the choice is not a wise one.[4] In such a case, one might reasonably seek information from several accessible channels, seeking convergence, with little regard to whether the channel is a mediated or personal one "at the mouth."

Channel Competition: The Conventional Wisdom

It has become conventional in communication theory to assume that interpersonal channels are more persuasive than mass media. This is the wisdom passed on as a policy generalization to professional communicators responsible for conducting campaigns on behalf of candidates, products, causes, and the like. It seems to stem from attempts to interpret receiver-based data from field surveys in terms of the source-oriented effects model.

As will become evident, there are conditions under which communication via mass media is more effective—for the purposes of either source or receiver—and other conditions under which interpersonal channels are preferable. Because human communication is a continuous process over a series of different situations, statistics that sum across many events over time can be a poor guide for anticipating what will occur under specific circumstances. Nonetheless, it is important to know what statistical generalizations have been drawn, as a first step in breaking down the conventional wisdom based upon them. The following observations ought to be accounted for by any theory of social communication:

1. In the study of adoption of innovations, mass media tend to predominate in making people aware of the innovation, but by the time an individual decides to adopt it most of his communication about it is interpersonal.[5]
2. A person's social contacts tend to be with others who are similar to him in demographic characteristics, and also in terms of social values, political opinions, economic resources, etc. In homespun words, "Likes talk to likes"; in fancier terminology, conversations are mostly "homophilic," not "heterophilic." [6]
3. A message from a source that is untrustworthy or that lacks expertise on the topic is less likely to be accepted than is information from an expert source or one with no reason not to be truthful.[7] (Channel differences, and divergent messages, are not ordinarily examined in this research; comparisons are made of the degree of belief in a single message propagated through either media channels of varying expertise and trustworthiness or interpersonal sources that differ in these respects.)

The Homophily-Credibility Explanation

An interconnected set of social psychological processes has been inferred to tie the empirical observations to the conclusion that interpersonal channels are more effective than mass media. Perhaps the most central of these presumed relationships is the one between channel-receiver similarity or homophily, and the degree of credibility the receiver attributes to a channel.[8] Interpersonal contacts, the reasoning runs, are homophilic and therefore credible; consequently the messages they deliver should be accepted. Messages from the impersonal mass media are not readily believed, because channel-receiver heterophily (or non-homophily) implies lower credibility. A media message could be learned, but only tentatively accepted until corroborated via a homophilic personal channel. Decision or action, then, would be withheld pending interpersonal discussion.

Although this explanation would be consistent with the empirical findings noted above, and while it describes processes that do occur under certain limited conditions, there is considerable evidence to suggest that it does not account for the general case.

First, credibility is not a stable attribution that a person assigns consistently to a channel. Several studies have shown that credibility is highly situational, in that it can be modified significantly by sending the person a message that is different from the one expected.[9] Nor is credibility a singular dimension of judgment; in one analysis it was found to fragment into forty-one different factors.[10] The most important factors are expertise, which is an attribute of a source rather than a channel per se, and trustworthiness, which a receiver likewise attributes to the source rather than the channel as a rule. (The source-channel distinction is of course often blurred even in mass communication, as in the case of the widely trusted "anchor man" on a network newscast.)

When a message has been sent, as in a persuasion experiment, the source's expertise and trustworthiness may indeed govern its acceptance. But this does not particularly mean that these factors are important in a person's handling of channels of information, or day-to-day acceptance of information from them. It is likely that untrustworthy sources of competing intentions could, if they provided convergent information, be collectively at least as believable as would one, or even two, more trusted sources.[11] For example, if opposing candidates for office agree in their accounts of a recent event, this common interpretation is probably no less credible than if it had been transmitted by the AP and/or UPI without attribution to either source.

When information is sought, source expertise is probably an important criterion, although not so important as is channel accessibility. This distinction between accessibility as an interaction between receiver and channel, and expertise as an attribute of a source is critical with respect to mass media—channels in which inexpert reporters and editors gather and cross-check information from more expert sources. In interpersonal communication, the person might consult either an expert source, such as a "cosmopolite" or a technical specialist, or he might consult a close peer.[12] Almost by definition, a lay person's relationship to an expert will be heterophilic, and to a peer more homophilic. This leads to the interesting prediction that the expertise dimension of source credibility should be *negatively* related to interpersonal channel homophily when people consult experts directly. Put another way, there is more to learn from people who are different than from people who are a lot like oneself. In diffusion research, this paradox is called "the strength of weak ties," referring to the fact that contacts between dissimilar people are rare ("weak") but when they occur they are more likely than other contacts to result in information transfer ("strength").[13]

Several studies demonstrate that homophilic interpersonal networks often carry highly inaccurate information, much of it internally inconsistent.[14] People seem to sense this. For instance, when President John F. Kennedy was shot, the news was so rapidly disseminated that some 90 percent of U.S. citizens had heard about it before he died.[15] One study found that 44 percent of those who first heard about it via television completely believed it; but only 24 percent believed the news when they heard it first from even a good friend.[16] A 1978 Utah survey of dissemination of the revelation that black members of the Mormon church would henceforth be eligible for ordination produced similar findings.[17] This surprising but happy news traveled so rapidly that 94 percent heard about the day it was announced. Of those who first heard interpersonally, 63 percent doubted it enough to seek confirmation; of those who learned of it via television, only 39 percent checked it further before accepting it as accurate. Confirmation was sought predominantly from media, not interpersonally. A study of reactions to the Watergate scandals of early 1973, when the veracity of the charges against the Nixon administration was still very much in doubt, found that other people were believed less often than *any* mass media channel of Watergate news.[18]

Most studies that report positive correlations between channel use and source credibility involve topics on which there is very little interpersonal message flow.[19] Several surveys have reported null or even negative correlations between channel use and credibility; generally interpersonal communication has been more prevalent in these cases.[20]

The simple assumption that homophilic sources are more effective was directly contradicted in an advertising experiment in Hong Kong.[21] Five ads were prepared in two dialects: Cantonese, which was the regional dialect and therefore presumably homophilic, and Mandarin, a northern Chinese dialect traditionally associated with the elite class. Recall of content from the ads was greater among those who had read the Mandarin (heterophilic) versions, and among older subjects, at least, the products themselves were rated more favorably after the Mandarin ads than the Cantonese ads. This result could be easily explained on the basis of, say, status appeal, but it does not jibe at all with a homophily-breeds-credibility explanation of message reception and acceptance.

The Frequency Criterion

Two convergent bodies of research are often cited to support the general conclusion that interpersonal contacts are more persuasive than media channels. In keeping with the actuarial nature of communication research conducted from the sender's viewpoint, both rely on frequency as the criterion for inferring impact. By far the more thoroughly investigated of these two has been the diffusion of innovations, where the statistical conclusion can scarcely be in doubt. The second is the study of influence in election campaigns, where the evidence is much more limited and questionable.

Diffusion research is ordinarily conducted in rural, traditional societal settings, where a "modern" innovation is being presented for possible adoption. In such situations there are usually a few relatively more "modern" people, who more readily learn of and adopt the innovation; these people are also more cosmopolitan, in that they have both personal and media contacts outside the immediate locale.[22] Later adopters (called "laggards" by program sponsors impatient with delays in the adoption process) are more likely to rely on interpersonally transmitted information. Media channels are less accessible to them (for such reasons as illiteracy and poverty), and by the time they have heard much about the innovation there are plenty of other people in the area who know a lot about it so interpersonal sources are highly accessible. We should expect, then, that their channels will be primarily interpersonal by the time they hear about and adopt the innovation.[23]

These findings do not, however, lead inevitably to the conclusion that interpersonal channels are *preferred* by the poor and illiterate, nor that "modern" people are quick to adopt life-style changes on the basis of a media message alone. A variety of studies show that the more educated strata delay longer in making the decision to change their behavior.[24] For instance, a survey of 500 Taiwanese women found that those who were younger and more educated were better informed about family planning, discussed it more with their husbands, were more likely to consult specialists in clinics and hospitals, got more information from television and other media, and were more likely to adopt a family planning method.[25] Similarly, during a disease inoculation program in Honduras, a comparison was made of "instantaneous" vs. "protracted" deciders.[26] The first group consisted of those who had first heard of the inoculation on the day they came to get their shots. The "protracted" decision group, i.e., people who had heard about it before the day they came for shots, were both more literate and more likely to have discussed it with other people.

In general, then, the distinguishing features of more educated people include (1) a disinclination to adopt an innovation precipitately; and (2) a tendency to take control of their communication environment by seeking additional viewpoints via accessible channels to informed sources before making a personal decision. Whether the channels of contact with those sources are direct or mediated apparently makes no difference in terms of either the credence given the information or its influence on the decision made. The statistical tendency for less educated people to adopt innovations later is probably due to their becoming aware much later; they apparently spend less time between the points of awareness and adoption. Both these time-lag differences would be due to their lower levels of relevant communication and information handling.

The fallacy of using frequency of use as a criterion for evaluating either the effectiveness or the attractiveness of a channel can be demonstrated by a few raw data comparisons. In the diffusion of news, for instance, there are large differences from one news item to another in the percentage who learn of it interpersonally. Unexpected, dramatic, and important items are often heard from others who are relaying the news: the death of leaders like Franklin D. Roosevelt[27] and Chiang Kai-Shek,[28] the assassinations of the Kennedys,[29] the shooting of Gov. George Wallace,[30] and (in a Harvard student survey) the resignation of Vice President Spiro T. Agnew.[31] These and other studies consistently find that it is the younger, college-educated person who is most likely to *tell others* of news he has heard.[32] But there is also a lot of news that doesn't seem important enough to pass on. Examples include a major papal encyclical (heard of interpersonally by just 2 percent)[33] and the political assassinations of George Lincoln Rockwell, Medgar Evers, and Malcolm X (each 3 percent).[34] Timing of events also determines where one learns news. In 1964 President Lyndon B. Johnson announced that he would not run for re-election on an evening telecast to which almost all households were tuned in. So even though it aroused a lot of discussion only 5 percent first heard about it interpersonally.[35] Obviously these huge differences in frequency of interpersonal reception are no indicator of people's channel preferences. They are due to such structural and environmental factors as timing and newsworthiness as judged by potential interpersonal disseminators of the news.

Election campaign research has, since the classic 1940 Erie County study, been widely thought to demonstrate the superiority of interpersonal over mass communication as a social influence.[36] Examination of the original data, however, reveals that the media—even in that pretelevision era— were judged more powerful by most voters. A majority cited either radio or newspapers as the most important single source in making their voting decisions, and two-thirds found each of these media helpful.[37] About one-half of those who changed their voting intentions during the campaign cited something learned from either the newspaper or radio as the main reason.[38] On the other hand, less than half mentioned any personal contact as an influential source, and less than one-fourth considered an interpersonal source as the most important one.[39] Apparently the emphasis on interpersonal influence emanating from the Erie County study was due more to the contrast between these figures and the researchers' expectations for far more dramatic evidence of media impact. Figures from the 1948 Elmira study are not appreciably different, and yet the stress on interpersonal influence persisted in the interpretations drawn.[40] Subsequently the same research group undertook a concerted study of personal influence across a wider variety of topics.[41] As the authors reported, 58 percent of the reported opinion changes "were apparently made without involving any remembered personal contact, and were, very often, dependent upon the mass media."[42]

Since those are the studies repeatedly cited as basic evidence on the question of media vs. interpersonal influence, one might be tempted to take them at face value and conclude that mass media communication is more persuasive. But just as frequency of use is not a valid criterion for inferring higher credibility or preference for a channel, neither is recalled influence a valid criterion for concluding that one channel *is capable of* achieving stronger effects than another. Mass media, when they carry information relevant to a decision facing the person, seem to have some advantages. Media reports represent professional reporting, editing, and verification processes, and probably for that reason are on the average more believed. Far more important, the media are more amenable to control—by both the sender and the receiver—for various purposes. Sources can to a great extent determine what information they will release via the media. Receivers expect the media to provide them with certain kinds and amounts of information in a relatively coherent package. But wise users of information rarely rely on mass media alone; they do well to check with experts, compare notes with peers, and otherwise attempt to validate media content for themselves before acting upon it. This is what we find better-educated receivers doing, in all kinds of situations. The question of which channel reaches a person first, or where a person turns for information when he needs it, does not tell us much of importance about the people involved.

Getting and Giving Information

General statements about communication behavior can be addressed more directly in terms of what people do rather than their orientations toward channels. The static concept of "interpersonal channels" slightly masks the fact that people are actively doing several things with the information flowing from mass media. They are both asking and telling one another about it, often with a good deal of personal interpretation and opinion mixed in. Only as an outgrowth of these behaviors of asking and telling (sometimes after being asked) is there an interpersonal dissemination of information; this is the transaction that carries the possibility of personal influence as a communication process. A small research literature has, almost by inadvertence, built up on each of these specific interpersonal behaviors. We know a few things about the kinds of people involved, and their motivations, in each specific role in interpersonal dissemination: finding out, telling, asking, and being asked.

Motivations in Disseminating Information

Recommunication of messages to others appears to be at least as important as is intrapersonal use of information by the individual, as an explanation for mass media consumption. That is, many people seem to gather news and other media content largely for the purpose of passing it on to others. In studies of self-reported "gratifications" of media use, this interpersonal motive tends to be rated low; there may be some social undesirability associated with so commonplace a purpose. But it is a strong correlate of information seeking.[43] Becker found in two studies that interpersonal utility motives predicted attention to and knowledge of political news more strongly than did measures specifically related to knowledge-acquisition motivations.[44] Another survey found requests for partisan campaign materials higher among people who expected to be discussing the election.[45] The phenomenon is not limited to political topics. Adolescents' information-seeking regarding both symphony music and popular music, for example, is strongly related to the existence of others with whom this type of music is discussed.[46]

A number of explanations have been suggested to account for this tendency to use mass media in anticipation of interpersonal communication. It is a time-honored notion in sociology that people seek social approval and stature by appearing to be well informed.[47] One study concluded that it was "obvious how this use of the newspaper serves to increase the reader's prestige among his fellows."[48] Listening to popular music is a way in which adolescents who perform poorly in school can gain compensating peer approval.[49] Another motivation, more difficult to isolate empirically, is simply to have a basis for initiating a desired interaction—"small talk" or "breaking the ice."[50] There are also other-centered, altruistic motivations. It is possible that a person would seek, or at least pass on, information for the benefit of other people who might need it. This was one self-reported reason for interpersonal dissemination within a "distance running community" of the accidental death of a famous runner.[51] People also talk about the news simply for the opportunity to express their opinions about it.[52]

But the motivation that dominates the research literature, and probably the real world as well, is to have information that can be used in the service of interpersonal influence attempts. In election surveys especially, those who report that they try to persuade others to support their candidate are consistently found to be the heaviest consumers of news media.[53] This includes both discussions with friends and family, and writing letters to public officials—another, less personal, attempt at political influence.[54]

A modest study using a quite different method gives us some idea of the extent to which media content is employed in interpersonal influence. Students in a college class were assigned to keep records on conversations they overheard in public places.[55] Not only was information from news media frequently cited in support of overheard arguments, but this was more often the case when the target person expressed a change in opinion (i.e. when persuasion was apparently successful). Politics, which constitutes the bulk of news media content, is the dominant topic in this connection; 76 percent of conversations dealing with political topics included media references, compared with only 40 percent of other conversations.

Argumentative discussion does not necessarily reflect a strong motivation on the part of one person to influence another, of course. News events create new demands on a person for an ordered construction of the world; much of conversation may consist of people comparing their separate constructions of reality, and perhaps modifying them. The important fact is that the media "set the agenda" of much interpersonal communication.

Asking as a Transaction

Neither information nor influence attempts flow in one direction. A number of studies have found that the predominant interpersonal pattern is *exchange,* in that most people who try to persuade others are themselves likely to be targets of similar attempts.[56] And as has already been noted here, those who seek information are also inclined to pass it along to others. Researchers have not ordinarily looked at communication transactions from the viewpoint of each party separately. In an interpersonal transaction, if one person is *asking* for information, the other person is *being asked.*

Little specific attention has been given to the phenomenon of being asked for information, or even for opinion. We know from experimental studies of small, task-oriented groups that *opinions are given* more often than information, whereas *information is sought* more often than opinion.[57] Messages of both types are sent much more often than they are requested. A few studies give us at least a preliminary picture of the relationship between those who request information and those who respond to such requests. Where asking is concerned, we cannot distinguish clearly between information and opinion; more researchers have been interested in opinion flow, and that is the type of request they have typically examined. (From the viewpoint of the asker this is probably not terribly important, since much of information-seeking is evaluative and active seekers are usually comparing viewpoints from different perspectives. To ask for an opinion may well be the predominant and most enriching mode of eliciting information flow interpersonally.)

One survey specifically measured a person's likelihood of being asked for opinion—aside from his being motivated to influence someone else. Those who were asked their opinions ("opinion leaders") were more likely to be active members of organizations, to regularly read news magazines and newspapers, and to discuss public affairs.[58] Targets of personal information requests have the characteristics we should expect of informational channels: they are accessible for discussion and are likely to have information due to their heavy media use.

The profile of askees is more complicated then that, though. One analysis separated people who tried to influence someone else ("talkers") from those who made no such effort but who were nevertheless asked their opinions ("passive leaders").[59] The talkers were more informed than were the passive leaders, although both groups were much better informed than other people. In another study, giving advice about shopping was not significantly correlated with either attempted influence or media exposure.[60] (Influence attempts and media use were, as in other studies above, strongly intercorrelated.) A survey in Chile found no appreciable demographic difference between people who were asked their opinions on current problems and others; the nondistinguishing variables included income, class, education, occupation, and age.[61] The unique characteristic of the askees was that, when asked by the interviewer for an opinion (about local newspapers), they were four times as likely to express one as were other respondents.

It is the asker-askee relationship that, when separated from influence attempts, seems to be the homophilic one. Those of whom opinions are requested, and who otherwise do not volunteer their views or exercise persuasive designs on their listeners, are indeed demographically similar to their interaction partners. They are a bit more attentive to the media, a bit more informed, and do answer questions when the occasion arises. But these homophilic relationships are more involved in the flow of information than in any active influence process, and it is not clear that these are especially informative transactions. (Whether askers purposely seek homophilic informants, or simply seek informants locally and therefore find homophilic ones, cannot be determined from the data available.)

Seekers of information (and opinion), on the other hand, appear to be quite different from other people. An extensive review of studies of exposure to information[62] found that people tend to seek out viewpoints they have not yet heard—whether they agree with the opinions expressed or not—when those viewpoints would be useful to know about. Other strong predictors of voluntary exposure to information are education (and correlated social class), and a previous history of exposure to the same topic.[63] Taking these characteristics as a group produces a sensible generalization: potentially useful information is most likely to be sought by a person who knows enough (about the subject) to recognize deficiencies in his knowledge.

Subsequent research has borne this out in various ways. A survey of people who sought published information (about civil defense) found that these seekers had already been more informed about the subject than were other people.[64] Predictably too, they were more likely to ask others about it, and to be themselves asked for such information. A field experiment in which some people were mailed a brochure (on lawn care) had the effect of stimulating them to seek further information from expert sources.[65] A survey dealing with family planning found a positive correlation between socioeconomic status and interpersonal acquisition of *rare* information about birth control, but a negative association between SES and consultation of interpersonal sources regarding methods that were widely diffused.[66] People with a greater range of social skills are probably more able to exploit the resources in their local information environments. Mass communication about a subject seems to stimulate people's interest, which in turn leads to further communication of various kinds.

Opinion-seeking is a bit different from information-seeking, and the people who specifically seek (without giving) opinions appear to be more dependent than those who actively search for information and offer their own opinions. For example, people who say they are more likely than others to ask for voting advice during an election campaign tend to be young, and low in political interest, knowledge, and party identification.[67] They rely more on TV for news than do those who give or share opinions with others. Opinion-seeking, it should be remembered, is not a very common behavior, although when it occurs the opinion expressed may prove quite influential.

Overview

The underlying theme of this essay has been its focus on variabilities in the flow of communication due to both structural factors and micro-social relationships. The point of view has necessarily shifted back and forth between those of the separate parties to various types of communication transactions. People who assume the role of either a source (e.g., a communication campaign) or a channel communicator (e.g., a reporter or editor) can be more effective if they understand what goes on at the "other end of the line," rather than try to plan their efforts according to a mechanistic design based upon faulty generalizations. People who participate in social communication in other roles (e.g. expert, teacher, or persuader) likewise need to see the process from a more Olympian perspective, one that considers the total communication environments that other people construct and utilize.

Normally the mass media and the people in our daily settings serve complementary roles for most of us. We absorb a great deal of information from both kinds of channels. Only on a topic of unusual importance or concern are we likely to go out of our way either to seek information or to pass it on to others. The giving of information is often associated with attempts to influence others. When we seek information it is often for corroboration or comparison with prior constructions of reality, and we seek it through those channels that are most accessible to us and are likely to have something additional to say on the subject. Whether these are media or interpersonal channels depends largely on the topic, timing, and immediate accessibility. We can also count on others to bring us news of very important and unanticipated events, and often to give us their opinions whether we ask for them or not. While the professionalized mass media are on the average more reliable sources of information, they are not always accessible. Inaccessibility can be a psychological condition; many people, for example, are not accustomed to using libraries or other information archives.

There are also certain topics on which the mass media carry little or no information; other people may be our best sources on matters of taste or local fashion, or on very personal problems. When we turn to other people for information, we are most likely to seek it either from an expert source, or from an "interpersonal channel," which is to say a person who is well versed on the topic either through contact with an expert or from the mass media. Those who bring us information without our even asking for it tend to be well informed on the topic, but they are likely also to have persuasive intentions toward us.

In general, then, while daily social interaction is largely homophilic, instances of acquisition of information about the world beyond our immediate lives are not. When complementary channels present divergent or dubious information, the most likely result is that the person will seek further information from other channels. For most people, especially those who are poorly educated or otherwise unprepared to consult media and expert sources directly, there are more accessible interpersonal channels than formal channels to consult. Social communication consists of an ongoing series of transactions between people and the channels that bring them information, not a finite competition among these channels. The traditional concept of a directional "two-step" or "multi-step" flow fails to capture the cyclical and reciprocal nature of this process.

The most likely "effect" of communication, we might conclude, is further communication. The more one knows about a topic, the more one tries to find out and the more skilled one is in that effort. The more contact we have with people we would not normally interact with, the more we learn. The more people talk with one another about information from the mass media, the greater is the total impact of the media on social action.

Notes

1. Harold D. Lasswell, "The Structure and Function of Communication in Society." In Lyman Bryson (ed.), *The Communication of Ideas* (New York: Harper and Row, 1948), pp. 37–51.
2. Jay G. Blumler and Elihu Katz (eds.), *The Uses of Mass Communications* (Beverly Hills: Sage Pubns., 1974).
3. The term "administrative research" was coined by Paul F. Lazarsfeld, a pioneer in the field. This usage should not be confused with the pejorative application of the term to all empirical mass communication research by critical writers who are unversed in empirical scholarship.
4. Raymond A. Bauer, "The Obstinate Audience: The Influence Process from the Point of View of Social Communication." *American Psychologist* (1964) 19: 319–28.
5. Everett M. Rogers with F. Floyd Shoemaker, *Communication of Innovations* (New York: Free Press, 1971). See especially pp. 255–58.
6. *Ibid.* "Homophilic" literally means liking the same things, and "heterophilic" means liking different things; the terms have latterly been generalized to mean, roughly, "similar" and "different." Also see Steven H. Chaffee, "The Interpersonal Context of Mass Communication." In F. Gerald Kline and Phillip J. Tichenor (eds.), *Current Perspectives in Mass Communication Research* (Beverly Hills: Sage Pubns., 1972), pp. 95–120.
7. This finding is well established in experimental literature dating from Carl I. Hovland, Irving L. Janis, and Harold H. Kelley, *Communication and Persuasion* (New Haven: Yale University Press, 1953) Ch. 2.
8. The line of reasoning outlined here is oversimplified in comparison with the best theoretical literature. Rogers and Shoemaker (*op. cit.*, note 5) view homophily and credibility as parallel factors that both predict success by change agents (pp. 240–46). They note that commercial change agents, while they can encourage trial of an innovation, are not as persuasive as peers (or noncommercial change agents) because they lack credibility. Later, Rogers found that change agents were judged most credible by those with whom they worked most frequently (*Modernization Among Peasants*, New York: Holt, Rinehart & Winston, 1969, pp. 184–86), but also that media credibility had little relationship to media effects upon modernization. Katz suggests that peer interpersonal communication is mainly important for "legitimation" of information received from less credible sources. Elihu Katz, "The Social Itinerary of Technical Change." In Wilbur Schramm and Donald F. Roberts (eds.), *Process and Effects of Mass Communication, Rev. Ed.* (Urbana: University of Illinois Press, 1971), pp. 761–97. Many writers stress that a limitation on the effectiveness of mass media is their impersonality and distance from the individual

receiver, but this makes the media more useful for some audiences (*see* Chaffee, note 6).

9. Don D. Smith, "Some Effects of Radio Moscow's North American Broadcasts." *Public Opinion Quarterly* (1970–71) 34: 539–51. Harold B. Hayes, "International Persuasion Variables are Tested Across Three Cultures," *Journalism Quarterly* (1971) 48: 714–23. Vernon A. Stone and Thomas L. Beell, "To Kill a Messenger: A Case of Congruity." *Journalism Quarterly* (1975) 52: 111–14.

10. Michael W. Singletary, "Components of Credibility of a Favorable News Source." *Journalism Quarterly* (1976) 53: 316–19.

11. Florangel Z. Rosario, "The Leader in Family Planning and the Two-Step Flow Model." *Journalism Quarterly* (1971) 48: 288–97.

12. On the distinction between "cosmopolite" and "localite" channels (sources), see Rogers and Shoemaker, *op. cit.*, note 5, pp. 258–59.

13. Everett M. Rogers, "Network Analysis of the Diffusion of Innovations." In Daniel Lerner and Lyle Nelson (eds.), *Communication Research—A Half-Century Appraisal* (Honolulu: University Press of Hawaii, 1977). William T. Liu and Robert W. Duff, "The Strength in Weak Ties." *Public Opinion Quarterly* (1972) 36: 361–66.

14. Niels G. Roling, Joseph Ascroft, and Fred Wa Chege, "The Diffusion of Innovations and the Issue of Equity in Rural Development." *Communication Research* (1976) 3: 155–70. F. Jane Marceau, "Communication and Development: A Reconsideration." *Public Opinion Quarterly* (1972) 36: 235–45.

15. Bradley S. Greenberg, "Diffusion of News of the Kennedy Assassination." *Public Opinion Quarterly* (1964) 28: 225–232.

16. Thomas J. Banta, "The Kennedy Assassination: Early Thoughts and Emotions." *Public Opinion Quarterly* (1964) 28: 216–24.

17. Edwin O. Haroldsen and Kenneth Harvey, "The Diffusion of 'Shocking' Good News." *Journalism Quarterly* (1979) 56: 771–75.

18. Alex S. Edelstein and Diane P. Tefft, "Media Credibility and Respondent Credulity with Respect to Watergate." *Communication Research* (1974) 1: 426–39.

19. Richard F. Carter and Bradley S. Greenberg, "Newspapers or Television: Which Do You Believe?" *Journalism Quarterly* (1965) 42: 29–34. Bradley S. Greenberg, "Media Use and Believability: Some Multiple Correlates." *Journalism Quarterly* (1966) 43: 665–70. Lee B. Becker, Raymond A. Martino and Wayne M. Towers, "Media Advertising Credibility." *Journalism Quarterly* (1976) 53: 216–22. Eugene F. Shaw, "Media Credibility: Taking the Measure of a Measure." *Journalism Quarterly* (1973) 50: 306–11.

20. Hilde Himmelweit and Betty Swift, "Continuities and Discontinuities in Media Usage and Taste: A Longitudinal Study." *Journal of Social Issues* (1976) 32: 133–56. Jack M. McLeod, Ramona R. Rush, and Karl H. Friederich, "The Mass Media and Political Knowledge in Quito, Ecuador." *Public Opinion Quarterly* (1968–69) 32: 575–87. Chaffee, *op. cit.*, note 6.

21. Luk Wah-shing, "Measurement of the impact of dialect in print media advertising copy." M.B.A. thesis, Chinese University of Hong Kong, 1973. Ab-

stracted in Godwin Chu (ed.), *Research on Mass Communication in Taiwan and Hong Kong* (Honolulu: East-West Center Communication Institute, 1977) pp. 106–7.

22. Rogers and Shoemaker, *op. cit.*, note 5.

23. Steven H. Chaffee, "The Diffusion of Political Information." In Chaffee (ed.), *Political Communication* (Beverly Hills: Sage Pubns., 1975), Ch. 3.

24. This is presumably because they are gathering more information, not because they are slow to make up their minds. Time itself is an ambiguous variable in field studies.

25. Chia-shih Hsu, "The Response of Taipei Housewives to the Family Planning Campaign." *Mass Communication Research* (Taipei, Taiwan, 1974) 14: 1–73. Abstracted in Chu, *op. cit.*, note 21.

26. Nan Lin, "Information Flow, Influence Flow and the Decision-Making Process." *Journalism Quarterly* (1971) 48: 33–40.

27. Richard J. Hill and Charles M. Bonjean, "News Diffusion: A Test of the Regularity Hypothesis." *Journalism Quarterly* (1964) 41: 336–42.

28. Christopher Y. Chao, "Sources and Diffusion of an Important Event: A Study of Public Reactions to the News of President Chiang's Death." *Mass Communication Research* (Taipei, Taiwan, 1975) 15: 11–44. Abstracted in Chu, *op. cit.*, fn. 23.

29. Sheldon G. Levy, "How Population Subgroups Differed in Knowledge of Six Assassinations." *Journalism Quarterly* (1969) 46: 685–98.

30. David A. Schwartz, "How Fast Does News Travel?" *Public Opinion Quarterly* (1973–74) 37: 625–27.

31. Gary Alan Fine, "Recall of Information About Diffusion of a Major News Event." *Journalism Quarterly* (1975) 52: 751–55.

32. M. Timothy O'Keefe and Bernard C. Kissel, "Visual Impact: An Added Dimension in the Study of News Diffusion." *Journalism Quarterly* (1971) 48: 298–303. Asghar Fathi, "Diffusion of a 'Happy' News Event." *Journalism Quarterly* (1973) 50: 271–77.

33. John B. Adams, James J. Mullen, and Harold M. Wilson, "Diffusion of a 'Minor' Foreign Affairs News Event." *Journalism Quarterly* (1969) 46: 545–51.

34. Levy, *op. cit.*, note 29.

35. Irving L. Allen and J. David Colfax, "The Diffusion of News of LBJ's March 31 Decision." *Journalism Quarterly* (1968) 45: 321–24.

36. Paul F. Lazarsfeld, Bernard Berelson, and Hazel Gaudet, *The People's Choice* (New York: Columbia University Press, 1944).

37. *Ibid.*, Chart 35. The exact total was 51 percent, with 38 percent citing a radio message and another 23 percent something read in a newspaper.

38. *Ibid.*, Chart 39.

39. *Ibid.*, Note 1 to Chapter XV.

40. Bernard R. Berelson, Paul F. Lazarsfeld and William N. McPhee, *Voting* (Chicago: University of Chicago Press, 1954).

41. Elihu Katz and Paul F. Lazarsfeld, *Personal Influence* (Glencoe: Free Press, 1955).

42. *Ibid.*, p. 142.

43. Steven H. Chaffee and Fausto Izcaray, "Mass Communication Functions in a Media-Rich Developing Society." *Communication Research* (1975) 2: 367–95.

44. Lee B. Becker, "Two Tests of Media Gratifications: Watergate and the 1974 Election." *Journalism Quarterly* (1976) 53: 28–33, 87.

45. Steven H. Chaffee and Jack M. McLeod, "Individual vs. Social Predictors of Information-Seeking." *Journalism Quarterly* (1973) 50: 237–45.

46. Peter Clarke, "Teenagers' Coorientation and Information-Seeking About Pop Music." *American Behavioral Scientist* (1973) 16: 551–66; "Children's Responses to Entertainment." *American Behavioral Scientist* (1971) 14: 353–70.

47. Robert Merton, *Social Theory and Social Structure* (New York: Free Press, 1949), pp. 406–9. Charles Wright, "Functional Analysis and Mass Communication." *Public Opinion Quarterly* (1960) 24: 605–20.

48. Bernard Berelson, "What 'Missing the Newspaper' Means." In Paul F. Lazarsfeld and Frank Stanton (eds.), *Communications Research, 1948–1949* (New York: Harper, 1949), p. 119.

49. Roger L. Brown and Michael O'Leary, "Pop Music in an English Secondary School System." *American Behavioral Scientist* (1971) 14: 401–14.

50. Chaffee, *op. cit.*, note 6. Walter Gantz and Sarah Trenholm, "Why People Pass on News: Motivations for Diffusion." *Journalism Quarterly* (1979) 56: 365–70.

51. Walter Gantz, Sarah Trenholm, and Mark Pittman, "The Impact of Salience and Altruism on Diffusion of News." *Journalism Quarterly* (1976) 53: 727–32.

52. Gantz and Trenholm, *op. cit.*, note 50.

53. Jerome D. Becker and Ivan L. Preston, "Media Usage and Political Activity." *Journalism Quarterly* (1969) 46: 129–34.

54. *Ibid.*

55. Saadia R. Greenberg, "Conversations as Units of Analysis in the Study of Personal Influence." *Journalism Quarterly* (1975) 52: 128–31.

56. Verling C. Troldahl and Robert C. Van Dam, "Face-to-Face Communication About Major Topics in the News," *Public Opinion Quarterly* (1965–66) 29: 626–34. Lloyd R. Bostian, "The Two-Step Flow Theory: Cross-Cultural Implications," *Journalism Quarterly* (1965–66) 29: 626–34. Lloyd R. Bostian, "The Two-Step Flow Theory: Cross-Cultural Implications," *Journalism Quarterly* (1970) 47: 109–17. Garrett J. O'Keefe, "Interpersonal Communication in Political Campaigns," paper presented to Midwest Association for Public Opinion Research, Chicago, November 1979.

57. Robert F. Bales, "How People Interact in Conferences," in Alfred G. Smith (ed.), *Communication and Culture* (New York: Holt, Rinehart and Winston, 1966), pp. 94–102.

58. Verling C. Troldahl and Robert C. Van Dam, "A New Scale for Identifying Public-Affairs Opinion Leaders," *Journalism Quarterly* (1965) 42: 655–57.

59. John W. Kingdon, "Opinion Leaders in the Electorate," *Public Opinion Quarterly* (1970) 34: 256–61.

60. Herbert Hamilton, "Dimensions of Self-Designated Opinion Leadership and Their Correlates." *Public Opinion Quarterly* (1971) 35: 266–74.
61. Roy E. Carter Jr. and Orlando Sepulveda, "Some Patterns of Mass Media Use in Santiago de Chile," *Journalism Quarterly* (1964) 41: 216–24.
62. David O. Sears and Jonathan L. Freedman, "Selective Exposure to Information: A Critical Review," *Public Opinion Quarterly* (1967) 31: 194–213.
63. *Ibid.*
64. Verling C. Troldahl, Robert Van Dam, and George B. Robeck, "Public Affairs Information-Seeking from Expert Institutionalized Sources," *Journalism Quarterly* (1965) 42: 403–12.
65. Verling C. Troldahl, "A Field Test of a Modified 'Two-Step Flow of Communication' Model," *Public Opinion Quarterly* (1966–67) 30: 609–23.
66. Liu and Duff, *op. cit.*, note 13.
67. O'Keefe, *op. cit.*, note 56.

WILBUR SCHRAMM

Channels and Audiences

Professor Schramm, a leading authority on mass communication, describes the various channels of media used to carry messages in our society. He analyzes the ways audiences, from one-person to mass, are influenced by media channels. Marshall McLuhan's concept of the "medium is the message" is scrutinized, and although Schramm is not fully in agreement with McLuhan, he does believe that media channels have powerful effects on messages and audiences. What Schramm presents is, in effect, a communications model which makes the channel and medium equally as important as the source, message, and receiver.

Channel is a word borrowed from telecommunication and applied to a number of different aspects of the communication process. One may talk, for example, of *sensory* channels, of *interpersonal* channels, or of *mass media* channels. Here the word *channels* will be used broadly to refer to the ways the signs in a message are made available to a receiver.

Audience is a word borrowed from the performing arts and public speaking, and is used to describe receivers or potential receivers of messages. These receivers may be of any number, and they may be engaged in a variety of behaviors; they may be related in a variety of ways to the sender, and they may make a variety of uses of the message. Here *audience* will be used simply to mean receivers of messages; however, we shall devote much of our attention to the receivers who have been most studied—the audiences of the mass media.

The Nature of Channels

One of the reasons for treating channels and audiences together is that we have come increasingly to posit an active and selective, rather than a passive, audience. Consequently, the analogy derived from electronic or hydraulic channels has proved less and less adequate to describe the relationship between senders and receivers of human communication.

Different kinds of channels are involved in the communication process, and different kinds of signals pass through them—e.g., light and sound waves through the atmosphere, and electrical impulses over neural pathways. But no one signal passes from cortex to cortex. The image of human communication that seems to be emerging is one of a relationship between two or more active persons, entered into with the aid of shared signs. Whereas the relationship between a power source and the filament of a light bulb might be described adequately in terms of a connecting channel to a passive receiver, the relationship between sender and receiver has proved to be immensely more complex. To describe it, communication scholars have had to take into account the motivations and activity of two parties, and to specify a number of elements in the communication situation in addition to channels.

Deutschmann (1957) suggested a simple classification for communication situations, to which we have added examples of each type (see Table 1).

Other people have complicated this classification. The size of the assembled group obviously makes a difference: a two-person group, a group small enough for a living room, a group that requires a public hall or other meeting place. Clinical sociologists have argued that "context is content," which has a McLuhan-like ring but means essentially that the social setting and the shared or differing goals of the participants help to determine the nature of the communication relationship. In other words, it makes sense to assume that the different relationships of, say, two lovers under a moon, or a potential client to a salesman with his foot in the door, or a student to his teacher, or a father to his son, or a demagogue to an aroused audience will make some difference in the way communication occurs. The agreed-upon goals have some effect upon the relationship: for example, the goals of a discussion group versus those of a football team versus those of the

Table 1. Communication situations

Private		Public		
Face-to-face	*Interposed*	*Face-to-face*	*Interposed*	
			Assembled	Nonassembled
two people converse at dinner	two people converse on telephone	public meeting	movie theater audience	viewing television at home

crowd that gathered in Yankee Stadium to participate in the Papal Mass. As Blumer (1946) has pointed out, the situation for communication in a mob, or an acting crowd, is different from that in a work group or a play group.

It has also been said that the constrictions of the sign system itself are essential elements in the relationship. Thus Innis (1950, 1951) and McLuhan (1962; 1964) have concerned themselves with the determinism of printed signs. And critics have often pointed out, for example, that the relationship of a painter and someone viewing the painter's work is considerably different from the relationship of the maker of a road sign and the viewer of a road sign.

The simplifying insights are not yet at hand to explain this very complicated situation by which persons share a symbolic message and usually arrive at some degree of commonality of understanding. Theory in both the behavioral and the natural sciences typically moves ahead in an accordionlike pattern through alternating simplifications and complications. At the moment we can say that the idea of "channel" to describe the relationship of sender to receiver has proved too simple, and a principal trend of the last twenty years has been to complicate it by introducing new elements and new concepts.

"Naïve Psychology" of Channels

In the absence of more general theoretical insights, researchers have typically worked on parts of the relationship—selective attention or perception, sensory-channel capacity, or learning through audio-visual presentation as opposed to audio presentation or printed media, to take a few examples. We shall have more to say about some of their results.

Some of the most useful generalizations in the area were made twenty-five or more years ago, and were based not so much on new research as on the kind of approach that Heider and his contemporaries called "naïve psychology." This is not at all a pejorative term. It refers to insightful and stimulating observations that were only partly, if at all, supported by existing research but that contributed to useful understanding and to future research. We refer to books like *The Psychology of Radio* (Cantril & Allport, 1935), and *Radio and the Printed Page* (Lazarsfeld, 1940), and to the historic paper by Lazarsfeld and Merton (1948), "Mass Communication, Public Taste, and Organized Social Action," writings of a kind too infrequently seen in communication scholarship today.

Approaches of this kind have offered a kind of common sense basis for at least partially classifying delivery systems. For example:

1. *The senses affected.* Face-to-face communication makes it possible to stimulate all the senses, if necessary and desirable. When anything is interposed in communication, some restriction is put on the use of the senses. Thus television and sound movies reach the eye and the ear (although McLuhan says, without evidence, that television affects the tactile sense also). Radio and the telephone reach only the ear, and print only the eye (although we must not underestimate the tactile pleasure of handling a beautifully made book). This line of classification calls for study of the handling of information in different sensory apparatus.

2. *The opportunity for feedback.* In a face-to-face situation the opportunity for quick exchange of information is maximal. As the face-to-face group grows larger, attention is diffused and a smaller proportion of the available feedback is used by any given person. When anything is interposed, the feedback is attenuated. For example, a telephone restricts not the speed but the amount of feedback because it is limited to one kind of sensory input. A *photo*-telephone would supposedly provide more feedback. Interposing a mass medium restricts both the speed and the amount of feedback, and the impersonality of media organization discourages it. When feedback to mass media is regarded as very important—as, for example, in teaching by television—devices such as pretesting, studio audiences, and reports from the classroom are introduced to approximate as closely as possible the face-to-face situation. This line of classification calls for research on how feedback is used and how communication can best be conducted when feedback is less than efficient.

3. *The amount of receiver control.* In face-to-face communication, a person can ask questions, help steer the conversation, and exert some control over the pace of it. A person reading print can set his own pace, pause to think over a point, repeat a passage, or reread the whole book or article if he thinks it necessary or desirable to do so. A listener to radio, or a viewer of films or television has no such control. To be sure, he can turn off the receiver, leave the theater, or allow his attention to wander, but he cannot control the pace or cause the flow of information to repeat or pause while he thinks. This is one of the reasons why television advertising has drawn more complaint than newspaper advertising, and why printed texts have proved so effective for individual study.

Traditionally, people have believed that sender control makes far more effective persuasion, receiver control for more effective learning. During the last decades, technology has moved to satisfy both—to provide more efficient circulation of information from a central point (e.g., via satellites) and to provide more control to the receiver (e.g., by recording devices and computerized methods of individualizing instruction). The problem is how to combine these two advantages.

4. *The type of message-coding.* In face-to-face communication, a high proportion of all the available information is nonverbal. This is only slightly less true of television and sound movies, still less true of radio and silent movies, and least true of print. Therefore, the silent language of culture, the language of gesture and emphasis and body movement, is more readily codeable in some delivery systems than in others.

A high proportion of printed communication is coded in orthographic signs compared to a very low proportion of television and movies, while almost no painting, sculpture, music, or dance is coded orthographically. Thus, it is possible in printed media to abstract easily; in the audiovisual media, to concretize. This leads to a series of questions still not fully answered about the effects of different sign systems on individuals and societies, and the most effective combinations of sign types for given purposes.

5. *The multiplicative power.* Face-to-face communication can only be multiplied with great effort. Mass media, on the other hand, have an enormous ability to multiply a message and make it available in many places. They can overcome distance and time and, in developing regions, the audio-visual media can also overleap the barriers of illiteracy. Therefore, the advantages of this multiplicative power must be weighed against the advantages of the feedback provided by face-to-face communication.

A considerable amount of attention has been given in recent years to combinations of the two, in an effort to salvage some of the best of each: for example, the radio rural forum in which face-to-face groups meet together to hear and discuss broadcasts made especially for them, and the combination of television teaching with related, face-to-face activities in the classroom. Attention has also been given to the ways in which face-to-face communication is itself extended, either by very large meetings or by interpersonal networks. For example, when one hundred thousand people come together at a sports event or a political rally, the crowd effects are themselves an element of great importance in the communication. When a message is spread person-to-person, the networks may be spectacularly effective, as they were when the news that "Gandhi-ji is dead!" spread by word of mouth throughout India. Such messages may be distorted, however, as the students of rumor have discovered (see, for example, G. W. Allport & Postman, 1945; Festinger & Thibaut, 1951).

6. *The power of message preservation.* Face-to-face communication is evanescent. So, without recording machines, are the electronic media. It is difficult, therefore, for a person to relive a moving experience or enjoy a television program again, except in memory. The printed media have a great advantage in being able to preserve facts, ideas, pictures. Not until a way was found to record meaningful visual symbols was it possible to preserve human records, except on monuments or in the memories of old men and women. The importance of libraries, archives, and encyclopedias testifies to the significance of this function today. Now that the glut of information is so great, new retrieval systems are needed to supplement the storage of information; now that the audiovisual media are so important in our lives, new storage and retrieval mechanisms are needed for them also.

These are a few of the qualities of distributive systems that seem to be self-evident. But it must be admitted that the implications of these qualities are not always so clear as they might seem, nor is it always easy to test the implications by research.

Selective Attention and Perception

Regardless of how the signs are made available, no communication will take place except as a receiver selects from the signs available to him, processes the resulting stimuli, and translates them into something cognitive or behavioral. Much of the theorizing and research in this part of the communication process has been organized around two sets of behaviors usually called selective attention and selective perception.[1]

Any individual has available to him many more cues than he can possibly accept. It is necessary, therefore, for him to give his attention selectively. What he selects is not a random sample of what is available. The question is, What determines how he draws the sample?

Over fifteen years ago this author suggested a rule-of-thumb approach to this question which he called a "fraction of selection":

$$\frac{\text{expectation of reward}}{\text{effort required}}$$

This fraction of selection was designed to help determine the probability of any particular communication being selected. When one tries to translate this into specific terms, however, the situation looks far less simple than the fraction would make it seem.

Freedman and Sears (1965) have reviewed the literature on selective exposure, seeking to answer the question. What do we know about the motivation that leads an individual to expose himself to one set of communication stimuli rather than another? With this excellent summary of selective exposure readily available, it will not be necessary to go over the same ground here.

They conclude that there is good evidence, mainly from field studies, that exposure to communication really is selective, and that regularities within the pattern suggest a tendency for people to expose themselves to information with which they agree rather than to information with which they do not.

> Republican rallies are mainly attended by Republicans, Baptist services are attended mainly by Baptists, the readers of the *New Republic* are mostly liberals and those of the *National Review* mostly conservatives. AMA journals are read primarily by doctors, and APA journals primarily by psychologists. The audiences for most mass communications are disproportionately made up of those with initial sympathy for the viewpoints expressed (Freedman & Sears, 1965:61).

They point out, however, that none of this indicates a general psychological tendency to prefer supportive information. As a review of their examples indicates, there may be many other reasons—useful information, friendships, social roles and customs, for example—that help to explain such selective exposure.

Examining the laboratory studies bearing on the proposition that individuals seek information in agreement with their opinions, Freedman and Sears found five studies that seemed to support it, five that showed the opposite tendency, and seven that appeared inconclusive. They also tested against the literature the proposition that subjects under high dissonance will show a greater preference than those under low dissonance for supportive over nonsupportive information. This proposition was supported by only one study out of nine.

After some discussion of alternative reasons for exposure, they concluded as follows:

1. People are, in fact, exposed to disproportionate amounts of supportive information, although this is not an overwhelming nor completely ubiquitous phenomenon.
2. Laboratory evidence does not support the hypothesis that people prefer to be exposed to supportive as opposed to nonsupportive information.
3. The evidence does not support the hypothesis that the greater the magnitude of cognitive dissonance the greater will be the relative preference for exposure to supportive as opposed to nonsupportive information.
4. Although a variety of other factors such as confidence and familiarity may

limit the conditions under which selective exposure occurs, at the present time there is not sufficient evidence to support any hypothesis concerning the effect of these factors on selectivity.

5. It is suggested that research in this area turn away from questions dealing primarily with the selective exposure hypothesis, and focus more on the questions of what factors chiefly determine voluntary exposure to information and how people resist persuasive messages with which they have been confronted (Freedman & Sears, 1965:94–95).

These results suggest that selective exposure is due to a complex set of causes, some of which may be operative at one time, some at another, and any of which in any particular case may be more powerful than the tendency to try to reinforce one's own opinions. What might some of these causes be?

1. *The availability of the stimulus.* How easily at hand is it? Advertisers know that more people look at large ads than at small ones, and political candidates know that if they saturate a broadcasting station with spot announcements most listeners will attend to at least one of them. Similarly, it is easier to see an audiovisual program on one's television screen than in the movie theater, although there may be other compelling reasons for going to the movies; and one is more likely to read a magazine if it is beside one's easy chair than if one has to go out and buy it.

2. *The contrast with its background.* Does the stimulus stand out from the field around it? How big is it? How loud? How much in contrast to the colors or patterns around it? All of us have had our attention jerked to a sudden contrast or change in our environment: a swift movement in a calm forest, a baby's wail in the night, a few seconds of silence in the midst of a rock-and-roll party, a falling star against the sky, a spot of orange against the blue of the sea. We find our attention drawn to large headlines and, if we are parents, we know that we must raise our voices if we want our children to "pay attention" while they are playing.

3. *The set of the receiver.* A person comes to any communication supermarket by previous experiences to look for certain things. A fisherman is set to look for fish rather than wildflowers beside the stream. A student goes to class prepared to look for different cues than he seeks in the cafeteria.

4. *Estimated usefulness of the stimuli.* At any given time, a subject may be seeking information that he needs for a particular purpose—to pass a test, to decide whether to take along an umbrella, to find a quotation for a talk he has to give, or merely to be informed about a topic that he is likely

to have to talk about. Some sources will prove over time to have utility for certain kinds of information, some for others, and thus an individual tends to develop habits and patterns of information seeking. A student who has been in class long enough knows pretty well what he must pay attention to, and how much attention. When a physician looks at a patient he looks for certain signs of illness or of well-being. When a commuter settles down into his seat with a familiar newspaper, he is set to look at certain parts of that paper and probably in a certain order. Most of us, as Stephenson (1967) cogently points out, are likely to learn that the act of reading or viewing or listening is pleasant in itself—other things being equal—and to develop habits of satisfying this pleasure, such as reading the newspaper at breakfast or turning on the television, without much regard for the program, to relieve a boring evening.

5. *Education and social status of the receiver.* Finally, some qualities within the experience of any individual help to determine his communication behavior. Chief among these are education and social class. Freedman and Sears (1965: 80–81) review some of this evidence and note that there is perhaps no other correlation with information-seeking that is so strongly supported in the literature. For example, more education goes with more frequent choice of television news, information, and public affairs shows (for one national study supporting this, see Steiner, 1963: 168–170). Both social class and education relate to preference for print over television and to the use of educational television (see Schneider & Lysgaard, 1953; Schramm, Lyle, & Parker, 1961; Schramm, Lyle, & Pool, 1963). Education, especially, seems to be a function both of reading skill and of an appetite for information built up by acquiring a wider knowledge (see Wade & Schramm, 1969).

Obviously, there is a great deal more to be found out before the reasons for patterns of selective exposure are made completely clear.

The situation is much the same with selective perception and selective recall, except that data are somewhat harder to obtain. After a person has directed his attention to some set of stimuli, he organizes them according to his experience with coding data, his estimate of probable need for them, and the other information he has already stored. We really know surprisingly little about this coding process, but it is what we call selective perception—meaning that some elements in the available information are emphasized more than others, some are rejected entirely, and some or all are reinterpreted to fit into the frame of reference of the receiver. Over time the selective processes are further intensified as selectiveness in recall eliminates that which contradicts the receiver's predispositions (Hovland, Lumsdaine, & Sheffield, 1949) or his needs (Zimmerman & Bauer, 1956).

The need to organize information received is a deep human characteristic. If we see a pattern of dots on a television screen, we make figure and ground of it. If we look at an ink blot, we are likely to see in it a picture or story that tells more about us than about the ink blot. When we meet another person, we need to classify and code him in relation to the categories and classes of persons we have developed out of our experience. When we are confronted with an idea, we are likely to code it according to our established system rather than looking at it fresh. If our codes are few and rigid, both persons and ideas may be forced into rigid stereotypes—Communist, imperialist, leftist, rightist, hippie, or the like.

It is clear, then, that we are compelled to perceive any new information in terms of our frame of reference, meaning our funded and organized store of experience. If we hear the word *dog,* we can interpret it only in terms of the kinds of dog we have known. If we meet information for which we have no referable experience, it bothers us, and we seek closure, either by pretending it never happened, by reinterpreting it until it becomes comfortable, or by seeking new information to put it in its niche.

As we select against a background of our needs, we perceive personal characteristics, relevant group relationships, values, and beliefs. We interpret cues, once they are selected, to fit as comfortably and usefully as possible. This has been many times documented, and it is necessary here only to mention the Mr. Biggott study (Kendall & Wolf, 1949), in which prejudiced people completely missed the point of antiprejudice cartoons by interpreting them in such a way as to support prejudiced viewpoints; and the Asch (1958) studies, in which group influences led to the misperceptions of physical phenomena that were objectively verifiable.

Hsia (1968), Travers (1964), and others have emphasized the significance of the fact that the central nervous system can apparently handle only a small part of the information that the sense receptors and the peripheral nervous system are capable of receiving. The human capacity to process sensory information has been measured in various ways and with various results,[2] but it is clearly much less than the amount of information available to the channel. Jacobson (1950: 1951a; 1951b) estimates that the input channel can handle only one percent of the information that can be taken in by the ear. Therefore, some mechanism of selection has to exist beyond selective exposure. It is reasonable to think that when the combined input from the two senses exceeds the amount of information the central system can handle, the conditions of interference are set up; and unfortunately this means that interference between channels may occur at any rate of presentation except a very slow one.

Broadbent (1958) has interpreted some of the selective process and interference phenomena in terms of a one-channel model for human information processing, and Feigenbaum and Simon (1961) also have suggested a simulated model that includes a single channel as a limit on the ability to process information. Travers (1964), following closely on Broadbent's model, has suggested that many of the results of learning experiments on single versus multiple channels can be interpreted if it is posited that the human system for utilizing information "has the properties" of a single channel.

It is important to speak of "properties" in this case, because the neural channels from the sense receptors are clearly separate. Travers' modification of Broadbent's model provides for a series of "compressions" of information, first by the sense organs and the peripheral nervous system, then by recoding and categorizing the input.[3] Then he assumes a short-term memory (maximum of two or three seconds) which can store information from one channel while the other channel is discharging through some gatekeeping and organizing mechanism.

Individual differences enter into the relative ability to learn from different channels, as May (1965) points out. A Soviet psychologist, Nebylitsyn (1961), found very low correlation between individuals' rankings for auditory acuity and visual sensitivity. Asher (1961) found that students who were visually dominant learned Spanish vocabulary with fewer errors when the stimulus words were presented visually and the response words were spoken than when the stimuli were presented aurally and the response words were spoken; he found the opposite to be true of those students who were aurally dominant.

Thus the learning effectiveness of different channels and combinations of channels seems to depend even more on how the channels are used, and for whom, than on the channels themselves. There is no particular magic in multimedia presentation per se. Hartman gives some advice to movie and television producers about using audiovisual media. If the conditions for interference are present, he warns, multiple channels

> may actually produce inferior learning because attention is divided and optimal learning is not possible in any of the channels . . . Pictorial illustrations in many cases may distract rather than illustrate. Attention-getting devices are of value only if they neither distract from learning which is already taking

place nor continue in competition with the material to which they are supposed to direct attention. The tradition in the television message is to place the majority of the information in the verbal audio channel and to attract attention and illustrate it in the pictorial. Too often the picture is not properly related to the sound and a real barrier to effective communication is created by a tendency to focus attention on the picture when the message to be learned has been coded in the sound track (Hartman, 1961:41).

McLuhan and Social-Channel Effects

An argument impossible to disprove is that studies of learning from different media channels are necessarily incomplete measures of learning, and that in particular what is learned from pictorial material is much more than any of the tests measures (for one thing because the tests are made by print-oriented scholars). One writer who would so argue is Marshall McLuhan (1962; 1964). Like his mentor, Innis (1950; 1951), McLuhan interprets the history of the modern West as "the history of a bias of communication and a monopoly of knowledge founded on print." The quotation is from an extraordinary paper by Carey (1967); because of McLuhan's somewhat oracular style of writing, it is often more satisfactory to quote his interpreters than his own statements.

Innis and McLuhan are technological determinists, concentrating on the influence of communication, and especially the influence of the printed media. The growth of communication through print, Innis argues, has killed the oral tradition, replaced the temporal organization of Western society with a spatial organization, transformed religion, shifted the locus of authority from church to state, brought about a relativity of values, and encouraged rampant nationalism. McLuhan is in accord with this but, as Carey points out, his approach is psychological rather than institutional, and is not unlike the Sapir-Whorf hypothesis that the language a person uses influences his view of the world and the nature of his thought (cf. Whorf, 1956). McLuhan extends the idea of "language" to media. His central idea, as Carey (1967:18) says, is that

> Media of communication . . . are vast social metaphors that not only transmit information but determine what is knowledge; that not only orient us to the world but tell us what kind of world exists; that not only excite and delight our senses but, by altering the ratio of sensory equipment that we use, actually change our character.

McLuhan (1962, 1964) is not the first to claim that "the things on which words were written down count more than the words themselves," but his way of saying it is the one most often quoted: "The medium is the message."

McLuhan's chief contribution to the understanding of communication channels is his analysis of the supposed effect of print which, he contends, imposes a "particular logic on the organization of visual experience." It leads us to break down reality into discrete units, logically and causally related, perceived linearly, abstracted from the wholeness and disorder and multisensory quality of life. It "privatizes" man, encouraging withdrawal and individual study rather than communal activities. It "detribalizes" man, removes him, as Carey says, from the need to participate in a tightly knit oral culture. Finally, it encourages nationalism by standardizing the vernacular and making possible the growth of large political institutions.

For both McLuhan and Innis, the growth of print seems disastrous. McLuhan, however, looks beyond the age of print (which he considers dead) to a new age of television. Television, he believes, will restore the balance of the senses, "retribalize" man, lead him back to the communal experiences of an oral culture, encourage talking rather than reading, involvement and participation rather than withdrawal, action rather than mediation. It is this vision of the effect of television—conceived at a time when many other persons are deploring the effects of television's materialism and violence—that more than anything else has been responsible for McLuhan's recent vogue.

Research on Media as Social Channels

These propositions, exciting as they are, do not readily lend themselves to testing. Moreover, McLuhan holds that testing is illegitimate because, among other reasons, modern research has a bias toward print. But so far as social research on the media can be summed up (e.g., in Berelson, Lazarsfeld, & McPhee, 1954; Katz & Lazarsfeld, 1955; Klapper, 1960; DeFleur, 1966; and the like), the findings seem to suggest that effects are more likely to arise from variability within media than from variability between media.[4]

Here, for example, are some of the generalizations it seems justifiable to make with respect to the effectiveness of the media as social channels:

1. Media have the power to focus attention, and thus to direct much of the interpersonal discussion within society. One of the first scholars to develop this point was Lasswell (1948). All the media seem to have this

power. An exposé in print is as likely to focus attention as an event on radio or television.

2. Media have the power to confer status, as Lazarsfeld and Merton (1948) pointed out. Men like James Reston and Walter Lippmann have acquired special status from their writing in print, just as Edward R. Murrow and H. V. Kaltenborn acquired it from radio, and Walter Cronkite and David Brinkley from television.

3. The best evidence available indicates that face-to-face persuasion is more effective than persuasion on the audiovisual media, and that it is more effective than persuasion in print. But as Klapper (1960: 109) points out, "Some topics . . . may be susceptible of better presentation by visual rather than oral means, or by print rather than by film, while for other topics no such differences exist. The relative persuasive power of the several media is thus, in real-life situations, likely to vary from one topic to another."

4. A combination of face-to-face and media communication is likely to be more effective than either alone. But this seems to be true of all media, as can be shown from the effects of the radio rural forum in countries like India, the great-books discussion groups in the United States, the combination of television teaching with classroom teaching in use in many countries.

5. A great part of any social effect of any medium depends on the audience at any given time. Indeed, one of the most solid findings in this area was expressed by Waples in 1940: "What reading does to people is not nearly so important as what people do to reading" (cited by Berelson & Steiner, 1964:529), and reiterated by Schramm, Lyle, and Parker (1961: 2):

> What television is bringing to children . . . is not essentially different from what radio and movies brought them; but what children bring to television is infinitely varied . . . When we talk about the effect of television on children, we are really talking about how children use television.

Most of the variables . . . that have been shown by research to be related to the social effects of the mass media channels are content or audience variables: prestige or perceived trustworthiness of the source, nature of the appeals, repetition, practice, order of presentation, age, ability, attitudes, motivations of the audience, salience of group relationships, and so forth. This is not to say that there are no media effects apart from content and audience; indeed, there is good reason to think that there are such effects, whether or not they are as powerful as McLuhan suggests. But there is at least as good reason to think that there are powerful effects arising from the content, and especially from the interaction of content characteristics with audience characteristics. The message is more than the medium.

Notes

1. The scholarly literature on attention and perception is too large to treat in detail here. The Freedman and Sears (1965) article has no counterpart in the field of selective perception. A helpful nontechnical introduction can be found in Berelson and Steiner (1964:100ff., 529ff.), and in Berlo (1960). More technical treatments are in Osgood (1953), F. H. Allport (1955), and Broadbent (1958).
2. Jacobson (1951a) estimated the maximum input from reading at 50 bits/sec. Pierce and Karlin (1957) estimated 43 bits/sec. for reading, and 78 bits/sec. for receiving music. Travers and Bosco (1967) estimated the possible reading input at 79 bits/sec.
3. George A. Miller (1956) says that this process of recoding sensory information, in particular linguistic recoding, is "the very lifeblood of the thought process" and deserves much more explicit attention than it has received.
4. Research on the media as social institutions, and the effects of the media, are treated elsewhere in this volume.

WALTER J. ONG

Interfaces of the Word: Television as Open System

Walter Ong has written a number of important works: *The Presence of the Word; Rhetoric, Romance and Technology; Interfaces of the Word*. His theme is the evolution of human communication, in which the individual's sense of self and reality is altered by each technological advance. In this essay from *Interfaces of the Word* he defines and compares "open" and "closed" models of communication systems. Ong would have us think of communication as an ecological system with human consciousness at its center. In this respect his analysis is different from other system approaches. Read the essays by Brent D. Ruben and Lee Thayer in this section for interesting comparisons.

Television as Open System

The most spectacular and intrusive of the recent technological transformations of the word, television, manifests perhaps most clearly, and certainly most massively and deeply, the breaking up of the closed systems associated with the verbal art forms generated by writing and print. Television blurs the fictional with the real on a scale previously inconceivable. It does so not through deliberate choices made by executives, directors, writers, technicians, performers, or viewers, but rather of its very nature. The "tube of plenty" has generated an other-than-real world which is not quite life but more than fiction.[1]

Both visually and aurally (sound is of the essence of television), the instrument takes a real presence from the place where it is real and present and represents it in other localities where it is neither real nor truly present. This representation is not a report. The football game you view on television is going on, its outcome unrealized as yet, and thus unknown. Reports are essentially ex post facto. Not all television presentations are simultaneous with reality, but, in a way, all television presentations seem to be; the fact that the instrument is capable of such presentations defines its impact.

Before television no human psyche had experienced visually and aurally events actually going on in the real present but in an extraneous locale. Various signs (smoke, bonfires) could give crude reports. Radio could do better, providing detailed oral accounts of distant events. But an oral account is always in essence a report: however recent, the event described is over with. The speaker knew the *fait accompli* before the hearer did. Television is different. The voice on a live television sports broadcast lags behind the audience's perceptions. Jack Ruby was viewed by millions while he was actually murdering Lee Harvey Oswald in Dallas. But he was murdering him in Dallas, not in hundreds of thousands of homes into which the killing was artificially projected as it took place. This intrusion creates a new unreality of presence, grotesquely assertive in the case of such tragic violence. The event in Dallas and the synchronized nonevent in living rooms across the country corresponded in time, though not even remotely in human context. More routinely but no less really than the Ruby-Oswald killing, such conditions obtain in a live television presentation of scheduled events, such as football games. Living in the ambience of such nonpresent present events has reorganized human consciousness, which is to say, the individual's own sense of presence in and to himself and in and to the world around him.

The individual's sense of presence to himself and others is not always rendered grotesque by television, as it was in the case of the Ruby-Oswald killing. It can be a healing and strengthening sense, too. Television coverage of the funeral ceremonies and related matters made the entire United States into a community in a new and healing way as the country mourned collectively the assassination of President Kennedy in 1963. Something similar happened at the national mourning for the assassination of Dr. Martin Luther King. In both these cases the collective self-presence, the sense of community, came into being around live events. More recently, a similar collective healing and strengthening has been experienced through the television presentation of Alex Haley's *Roots*, where the events were not live. Although the story was basically historical (with many fictional elements) and in this sense real, it was played by actors and its historical (and fictional) events belonged to the past. But the participatory sense conveyed by television, plus the fact that the events were symbolically momentous in national history, again created a sense of community. It has become a commonplace to remark about *Roots* that nothing like the same effect would have been achieved had the story been put out as a movie, so that the experience of viewing it could not have been shared, as it was on television, by millions simultaneously, blacks and whites and others. As in the John F. Kennedy and Martin Luther King tragedies, the audience could sense its own vast unity.

The audience in television is, however, a puzzling actuality on the whole. The writer's audience, it has been said earlier in this book, is always a fiction. So is the television "audience" in its own way: it is never present, though performers and audience alike pretend that it is. And it is never a unitary group as the audience in a theater is. The problems are particularly evident when television is presenting not live events but some sort of "show," something "staged," such as drama, vaudeville, give-away programs, discussions, or interviews.

Taping or performing before a live audience does not eliminate the paradox but only enhances and complicates it. For instead of merely one audience, the performer is now dealing with two. The "live" audience in the studio is not the real audience at all. It serves as a substitute for the audience of those watching the TV screen who are by implication not "live" but somehow "real." But these watchers are not a real audience at all either in the sense that they are not present to the performers—which is why the studio audience is set up. Nevertheless, the nonpresent viewers are in effect more real as audience than the seemingly "real" studio audience, for the studio audience appears as part of the show on the television screen for the nonpresent audience, and thus disqualifies itself as an audience by becoming part of the show. To complicate interrelations further, laughs of this televised studio audience or even laughs from old tapes encourage and add substance to the real laughs of the nonpresent real audience. Open systems with a vengeance. A tangle of apertures. The effect is again reminiscent of the transactions between reader and fictional narrative in *Don Quixote,* but *Don Quixote* is much less open.

Introversions and extroversions and convolutions are limitless here. At the Encuentro Mundial de Communicación in Acapulco in October 1974, as a hall of some six hundred persons listened to and saw live panelists engaged in discussion on the dais before them, television cameras in the rear of the hall picked up the panelists and projected them onto a huge sixteen-by-twenty-foot screen (my own calculations on the spot) suspended above the panelists' heads. The audience was thus encouraged to view not the live panelists but the television projection of the live panelists, more assertive in its assault on the senses than the live panelists it was presenting.

At times the cameras would enlarge their field and pick up the entire hall, including, besides the panelists, members of the audience (the backs of heads and shoulders) as well as the huge screen itself, which was, with everything else, projected onto itself. At this point the audience found itself on the equivalent of a one-way electronic hall of mirrors. On the huge screen appeared images of the panelists, audience, and the screen itself as a part of the hall's equipment. On this smaller screen thus projected onto the larger screen appear the same elements as upon the larger screen: panelists, audience, and screen again, which once more was reproduced with panel, audience, and screen, still smaller, and so on, until too tiny to discern. To the question I put to the panel, "What is the purpose, conscious or unconscious, of this curious exercise in introversion or narcissism, and of the blending of image and actuality?" no direct answer in depth was available. This Encuentro Mundial de Communicación was a world-wide meeting of the media greats, got together by the major Mexican television chain Televisa. The impression one got was that you do these things because the medium makes it possible to do these things. This is what television essentially is: interplay between actuality and image. The more such interplay, the more the medium is true to itself.

The in-and-out relationship of television as an art form with its audience in the real world is maximized with videotape, whereby a taped past performance can be played back into the present and merged on another videotape with a live performance so that the composite can be presented on monitors to the live performers who, as part of their performance, can view themselves interacting simultaneously with what is real and what is fictitious. This kind of introversion—more complex than the Acapulco phenomenon because it is also diachronic and not merely synchronic—was adumbrated a good many years ago, though in simpler form, by Samuel Beckett in *Krapp's Last Tape,* in which the protagonist enters into a dialogue with his voice taped some years earlier. Such intro-introversion on television makes it clear that the new medium is not just a new way of purveying what other media purvey in their own ways, but is rather the implementation of a new state of awareness and of a new gaming relationship with both space and time, which of course affects our sense of real time.

A recent book by Paul Ryan, which comes out of extensive experimentation with videotape, treats relationships made possible with videotape by analogy with Klein bottles or "kleinforms" (more elaborate, more introverted Klein bottles).[2] A Klein bottle is a construct, well known in mathematics, made by passing the narrow end of a tapered tube back through the side of the tube and flaring out the narrow tube end to join the other end from the inside. The resulting form is something analogous to a Moebius strip devised in a world of solids. As a Moebius strip is a surface with no other side, a Klein bottle is a container with no bottom. In a Klein bottle or other kleinform, the container is also the contained, and vice versa. The television audience and the television show can likewise contain one another, as we have seen. In elaborated kleinforms, a tube containing part of itself can in turn be contained in another part of itself, or can emerge from itself again and re-enter. In kleinforms, closures are open. The analogy with television, if not total, is nevertheless apt.

The open relationship between television and nontelevised actuality puts a special premium on preserving spontaneity—which in fact for television products mostly means creating spontaneity. All art forms to some degree tend to pass themselves off as in one way or another unprogramed, spontaneously achieved actuality: *ars celare artem.* Art consists in concealing art. The ballet dancer or trapeze artist or figure skater makes his or her movements look completely effortless and natural: paradoxically (and all art is a paradox), you have to work harder to make essentially difficult actions appear easy. The easier you want them to appear, the harder you have to work. But in television the spontaneity cultivated by art is more essential than in other art forms and more complexly artificial.

Drama has always exploited planned spontaneity: since Greek antiquity the text composed in writing has been made by actors to sound, more or less, like spontaneous speech. Still, everyone knows that a play's a play (with the seeming exceptions for "living theater" noted earlier in this chapter). In the classic play-within-a-play, such as in Shakespeare's *A Midsummer Night's Dream,* the lines between fictionalized fiction (the play-within-a-play), mere fiction (the play), and actuality are still relatively easy to draw. Lines are also easy to draw in the play-outside-the-play, such as Francis Beaumont's *The Knight of the Burning Pestle,* where a grocer in the audience insists that his apprentice Ralph have his own idiosyncratic part in the play being staged by a troup of professional players, who then have desperately to keep their own play going in the midst of the melodrama being enacted by Ralph. There is no mistaking here that the grocer and his wife and Ralph are fictional, too, though at a different level than the other characters.

In television the line between the show and actuality is often much more difficult to assess. Besides the cases already noted, give-away shows are a case in point. They must presumably be honestly run, so that the recipients of the prizes cannot be known in advance and thus the receiving of the prizes cannot be rehearsed. The recipients are to be purely parts of the natural world, as against the world of art. However, not any old recipient will really do: the recipient must fit a certain mold, be assimilable to the show through his or her proper grooming. And thus the entire audience is somehow carefully screened, so that whoever from among those in the audience receives a prize is properly attired in effective television garb. The "natural" audience consists exclusively of potential performers. Since the studio audience of this sort is tacitly expected to be representative of all mankind, or at least in the United States, roughly representative of all the country's citizenry, the implication is that everybody in the world dresses in clothes suited to television, and the implication of this implication is that television dress is the natural way to dress.

The implication of such an implication in this art form has a real and immediate effect. Much art has been fed back into the directly lived world, but none more than that of television. Fashion design has often imitated Hollywood movie costumes. But television has projected a walking replay of itself on United States streets. The garish garb fashionable today appears largely as a spin-off from the color-television screen: real life adopts the psychedelic colors and costumes that work best, or are thought to work best, in television fantasia, such as that of Sonny and Cher or of rock musicians, or even in newscasts, where the drab objectivity of "facts" and generally quite "square" personalities come into the screen in glowing clothes or against contrasting contrived-color backgrounds. Color television does not merely present high-contrast colors: it replicates them in the real lives of its viewers.

The blurring of the edge between art and reality on television as in other art forms, however, is not an innocent achievement. It is not sinister either. But it is dangerous, and tragedy lurks at the interface between unrehearsed actuality and fiction on which this medium is forced to live. With cultivated nonplanning, as is well known, a documentary of a real family in the United States was televised a few years ago, and in the course of the documentary, the family broke up. It would appear that the break-up was earlier on its way, for it is hard to see how a normally cohesive family could have consented to this savage and inhuman invasion of its privacy, but television provided the ultimate format for real-life catastrophe. Still, the break-up comes through in the medium as essentially unpremeditated and unforeseen. It is the essence of television to give all it touches at least some gloss of spontaneity. To this day, the greatest television scandal in the United States has been that of the "Sixty-Four-Thousand-Dollar Question" of a few decades ago, when responses programed as unrehearsed and spontaneous turned out to have been planned in advance. They were programed as unrehearsed and were magically successful as unrehearsed because television favors the unrehearsed show.

Television in the United States is often noted as different from that of other countries because it is commercialized, or more commercialized than elsewhere. What is probably more distinctive of United States television, however, as conversations at international media meetings have suggested to the author, is that in the United States, where the medium is relatively free of the heavy hand of partisan governmental control, the interior dynamics of television have more fully asserted themselves than they have elsewhere. Although social pressures—commercial, religious, educational, ethnic, and other—distinctive of the United States of course shape the United States television phenomena, to know what television as such really is, you will probably do best to study it in the United States because there it registers a wider range of social pressures than elsewhere (though it never registers them quite equally or equitably, of course). Elsewhere, television tells you basically what government wants it to say, to a greater or lesser degree, to the obscuring of its own nature.

Whether television's more full-blown state of existence in the United States is due precisely to commercialization is an interesting question. It may be, and this may indeed indicate that television is in some very deep sense, and even essentially, a commercial medium. It was certainly brought into being by commercial cultures, not by others. It may even ultimately promote or reinforce commercial culture wherever it becomes prominent. But whatever its alignments with commerce, the open-system qualities of the medium, such as those just mentioned, appear more markedly in the United States than anywhere else.

If it is the essence of the present state of consciousness to cultivate open-system models and if television itself essentially promotes such models, being itself essentially open-system (whatever constraints may be put on it from the outside), the strong and widespread feeling that television is in some deep sense the modern medium of communication par excellence can be to a certain extent accounted for. But because of its curious, and by no means understood, ways of intertwining unreality with reality, the alignments and cultural implications of television remain a tangle of unsolved mysteries.

● ● ●

Earlier Open-System and Closed-System Models

The open-system paradigm which has asserted itself so forcefully in recent years had antecedents of course far back in time, many of them of major consequence in intellectual or cultural history. One can readily instance a few more or less relevant to the matters of the present book. In Western antiquity, Socratic dialogue and Platonic dialectic were consistently open-system. So in another way was the preaching of Jesus and his followers: the Kingdom is good news to be shared, thought of in the parables as a mustard plant growing from a tiny seed (Matthew 13:31–32) or as yeast spreading through dough (Matthew 13:33)—this latter model is caught in the term "catholic" (*katholikos,* a Greek word adopted also by the Latin Church), which means not "universal" (that is, "inclusive," "encompassing," and hence by implication to some degree bounding) but rather, in its Greek etymology, *kata + hōlos,* through-the-whole, outgoing, expansive. The rhetorical and dialectical methods of teaching which dominated intellectual activity in the West from classical antiquity through the eighteenth century perpetuated something of the Socratic and Platonic paradigms: thought was always open to attack. Countless other early examples of more or less open-system models abound. The point here is simply that significant ones were available and in use.

But early open-system models existed in a climate which within the past four or five centuries came to favor closure of thought in significant ways. The tendency to closure had to do with a state of mind encouraged by print and its way of suggesting that knowledge, and thus indirectly actuality itself, could somehow be packaged.[3] Though of course there were other factors at work besides print, it would appear that many if not most of the other factors can be related dynamically to print. In *System and Structure* Anthony Wilden has discussed some of the ways in which widely dominant Cartesian and Newtonian frames of reference relied on "closed-system energy models of all reality."[4]

Backtracking, one finds that there are many pre-Cartesian representatives of closed-system thinking, just as there are many representatives of open-system thinking who are contemporaries of Descartes (Wilden instances Pascal, who is also discussed along with related thinkers by Lucien Goldmann[5]) or who belong to the later Cartesian age (Wilden instances Rousseau). Perhaps the most tight-fisted[6] pre-Cartesian proponent of the closed system, one not mentioned by Wilden, was the French philosopher and educational reformer Pierre de la Ramée or Petrus Ramus. Ramus' close-field thinking is absolute and imperious, welling out of unconscious drives for completeness and security, (and thus in some ways regressive to the self-enclosed, infantile stage represented by the uroboros, the serpent with its tail in its mouth—the thumb-sucking infant).[7] It is unencumbered by any profound philosophical speculation, and yet it is supposed to apply to every field of knowledge.[8] Insofar as a strong stress on closed-system thinking marks the beginning of the modern era, Ramus, rather than Descartes, stands at the beginning.

The closed-system paradigm was encouraged by the new science of the sixteenth and seventeenth centuries in its reliance on seemingly closed-system mathematics: the physical universe was assimilated to a closed system, or, rather, a system of systems, each operating on purely mathematical laws. The term *systema* itself, with its implication of closure, became widely current, as it had not been before, and a whole armory of related closed-system terms for fields of knowledge achieved spectacularly wide, almost ubiquitous, currency, particularly in text books: *idea, typus* (imprint, outline), *fabrica* (fabric), *corpus* (body), *series* (array), *tabella* (table), *tabula* (chart) *synopsis,* and many more.[9] Frank E. Manuel's brilliant and incisive Fremantle Lectures, *The Religion of Isaac Newton,* show how Newton's fascination with closure began in the realm of physics and carried far beyond. In the latter half of his long life (1642–1727), the discoverer of the laws of gravitation devoted a major part of his energies to theological writing centered on the interpretation of prophecies, undertaking to construct a system of interpretation which exhausted all the possible meanings of the prophetic symbols in the Bible so that "there was nothing left over, no random words still unexplained, no images that were superfluous. The system was closed, complete, and flawless."[10] Newton really thought he could manage the meaning of Ezekiel and of the Book of Revelation this way. Newton's success in physics was for him a limited success, significant largely because it provided a miniature model for his total ambition, which was "to force everything in the heavens and on earth into a grandiose but tight form from which the most minuscule detail could not escape."[11] The German Ramist Ioannes Piscator (1546–1626) had been bitten earlier by a like ambition, as had many other Ramists.[12] Piscator undertook to do a "logical analysis" of each book of the Bible to state explicitly and totally in his analysis exactly what the book was really saying: the rest of the given book, that is, whatever his analysis did not contain, was understood to be pure ornament, to make the content attractive.[13] After Newton, closed-system theology was given another kind of try by Richard Jack in his *Mathematical Principles of Theology, or the Existence of God Geometrically Demonstrated* (London, 1747).

Closed-system paradigms were maximized by Kant. Noumena are untouched by phenomena; practical reason is disjunct from pure reason. Almost incredibly for a person of such intelligence, Kant believed . . . that logic was so much a closed system that nothing new in it had been discovered or could be discovered after Aristotle. The closed-system paradigms favored by Newtonian physics dominated many views of language, such as those of John Wilkins in *An Essay towards a Real Character and a Philosophical Language* (1668) or Johann Nicolaus Funck (Funckius) who in his six Latin volumes, *De origine Latinae linguae* (1720) and *De pueritia Latinae linguae* (1720) through *De inerti ac decrepita Latinae linguae senectute* (1750), treats the Latin language as a historically closed system which came into integral existence at a certain moment, went through an infancy, adolescence, and maturity and then grew old and prepared to die. The antecedent life of Latin in its preclassical forms and its evolution into the modern Romance languages, though these had been perfectly normal and ordinary linguistic developments, somehow did not fit Funckius' closed-system model.

The closed-system paradigms were peremptorily disqualified in the early twentieth century with the development of quantum theory and with relativity theory, which brought the observer into consideration. But throughout the Western intellectual world closed systems were under particularly vigorous attack, more or less overt, more or less subtle, from the time that the romantic movement gained enough strength to cast suspicion on the claims of extreme rationalism. In keeping with the romantic sensibility, through its dialectical approach to history Hegel's philosophy was more open than Kant's. Darwin's and Wallace's discoveries regarding natural selection and the selection and evolution of species dealt probably the heaviest blow to closed-system models. . . . Not only individual organisms, but the hitherto supposedly fixed species were open, as species, to change through natural selection, powered by individuals' interaction with environment. In the Darwinian world, ecosystems were far more crucial for life in every one of its specific forms than had ever before been proved.

In the currents feeding out of the romantic movement and related evolutionary thinking, countless other instances of open-system paradigms can be found. Among these would be those favored by phenomenology and by intersubjectivity as it has been developed in recent philosophy and psychology. Intersubjectivity is the open-system paradigm directly countering the closed-system paradigm of solipsistic activity which had characterized Cartesian epistemology and the implied epistemology of Ramist logic. In his *Studies in Ethnomethodology* and other works Harold Garfinkel has effected another opening, showing how the communication of abstract reasoning comes about not simply in a closed, abstract world, but only insofar as this reasoning is embedded in tacitly used or implied practical reasoning, which is to say in social behavioral settings.[14]

This sketchy overview or sampling of some of the fortunes of closed-system and open-system paradigms is meant only to be suggestive. It treats of these paradigms sometimes as consciously and articulatedly appropriated (in ecological planning or in "living" theater) and sometimes as simply present and operative without fully reflective, conscious appropriation. Paradigms of this latter source may be embedded in theories (Cartesian epistemology) or simply in ways of life (uncontrolled exploitation of natural resources). They represent what Thomas H. Kuhn means by "paradigms" in *The Structure of Scientific Revolution*.[15]

Interfaces of the Word and Evolution of Consciousness

The place at which independent systems meet and act on one another or communicate with one another is called an interface. The concept "interface," so defined, presents difficulties, for if the systems are independent, how can they be interacting? The difficulties are due not merely to the concept of "interface" itself but more directly to that of "system," and especially that of "independent system," for the independence of a system is in the last analysis always relative independence. In Paul A. Weiss's definition, . . . a system is a "rather circumscribed complex" of "relatively bounded phenomena" which retains a "relatively stationary pattern" despite a "high degree of variability, . . . among its constituent units." The "rather" and "relatively" are deliberate and crucial. In short, no system is ever totally closed, ever totally independent. They all interact with something other than themselves.

This is why, paradoxically, discussion of systems generates discussion not merely of containedness, of closure, but eventually and inexorably the discussion of exchange, of outwardness, and ultimately of communication. The forces at work in any in-depth consideration of systems are caught in the title of the book by Anthony Wilden noted above, *System and Structure: Essays in Communication and Exchange,* and in the anthropological and linguistic as well as biological and mathematical subject matter that the book treats. System and structure directly involve insidedness and imply outsidedness, otherness. And communication and exchange become issues both inside a system (between the elements within the system) and outside a system (communication between systems). In depth, the discussion of systems becomes another avatar of the metaphysical question of the one and the many.

The concept of communication refers basically to our experience of the living world, of interrelations between unitary organisms, particularly sentient organisms. Even to think of messenger RNA as "communicating" within a cell is to stretch the term a bit: RNA does not "communicate" in quite the sense in which two male mockingbirds communicate at the edges of their respective territories, warning each other off. By comparison, RNA simply "registers" and transports a given structure. This does not mean that it is illegitimate to say that RNA "communicates," but only that this sense of "communicate" is adjusted somewhat from the basic sense.

In the world of living, sentient organisms, communication exists at its peak among human beings. The reason is that communication requires closure, or unification and distinctiveness of a being, maximum interiority, organization from within, like that of a system, and openness, or access to whatever is outside the closure. Human beings are both closed and opened to the maximum.

The focus of closure and openness in human beings is human consciousness itself. What is meant by human consciousness here can be understood by treating it at its center, as caught up in the "I" that I utter. The "I" that I utter is open only to me and closed to all outside me. No one else knows what it feels like to be me. I do not know what any other human being experiences when he or she says "I." In a way it would seem to be "like" what I feel when I say "I," but I am aware that every bit of any other person's sense of "I" is totally different from mine. I simply do not know what it feels like to be the other person. Each of us is isolated, sealed off from every other in this way, even husband from wife and wife from husband, father and mother from daughter and son, brother from brother and sister from sister.

Yet it is only such isolated consciousnesses that can truly communicate, that can share, as no brute animal—that cannot say "I"—can share. What we mean by communication at its maximum intensity, its peak, is what goes on between human beings. Paradoxically, communication demands isolation. Unless a being is somehow closed in on itself, self-possessed from within, able to say "I" and to know in the saying that this "I" is completely and indestructibly unique, separate from all else, that there is simply no possibility that any more of the four billion other human beings alive today is also the same "I," there is no sharing to be done, no communication possible. I can share only what I have control of. If I do not lay hold of myself by reflection, do not know the "taste of self, more distinctive than ale or alum" (in Gerard Manley Hopkins' words), I cannot give myself to another or to others. I have nothing to give—for I have no self, no person, to give.

Communication does not have simply to do with oneself, but in fact can concern anything and everything. But it always involves the self, for communication, whatever it is concerned with, is a conscious activity, and the "I" which I speak and which I alone can speak lies at the center of my consciousness. It is the most insistently accessible of all things in my world, the ground and border of all my waking experience of everything, and even of my dream experience. I can do nothing outside its presence, more or less directly adverted to. In this "I," I am totally open and transparent to myself: by comparison, all else is dark and opaque, including even my own body, which is somehow included in the "I" but in some strange ways also feels a bit external to me. "The heavy bear who goes with me," Delmore Schwartz calls the body in his poem of that name.

Yet, though isolated and unique, in one way open only to itself, in another way the "I" is necessarily and essentially open to others, too. For me to have matured into the self-knowledge whereby I can say "I," there had to be other persons around me, each of them, even mother and father, unique and isolated but communicating with me from infancy, coaxing and coaching me into talking and thinking simultaneously, and into the unique interior awareness of myself that none of them, all strangers, had access to.

The strangers not only coaxed and coached me into an awareness of myself but also guided me into an awareness of the rest of actuality around me impinging on myself. They, isolated though they were, helped me, isolated though I was, and am, to open my consciousness to all being. For, as earlier noted in this chapter, the human person is open to other beings not only physically and physiologically but intellectually—and through his intellect, which is part of his consciousness, to anything and everything. There is no particular limit to how much actuality the human consciousness, directly or indirectly, can pull itself into.

Human consciousness is open closure.

The "I" interfaces with everything.

There can be little doubt that our central experience of unity, the foundation of what we mean by oneness, the datum of experience on which we build (with the help of other data, too, of course) our concept of the "one," of unity, is our conscious experience of self that we capture in the saying of "I." Nothing else in our experience is so irrefragable, so palpably indivisible. Whatever our interior multiplicities, somatic, sensory, psychological, noetic, or other—and we do have experiences of these multiplicities—our sense of "I" somehow transcends them. The "I" cannot be split into simpler units. What could it be severed into? This is a central paradox of existence. How can it be that with all my interior divisions and multiplicities—my welter of sensations, feelings, thoughts, my bodily parts outside parts—this "I" is so purely and indissolubly one? Here my sense of self is my immediate experience in my own life of the paradox of the one and the many which has an infinite number of versions, cosmological and metaphysical and other.

Since my concept of unity is so tied up with my sense of self expressed in "I," the "I" serves as a kind of paradigm for the notion of system, a paradigm, that is, in Thomas Kuhn's sense of a model or frame of reference that is not consciously adverted to as a model but that nevertheless determines the way one thinks about things. A system is a multiplicity, somehow one, separate, self-sustaining (up to a point) in a way that at least unconsciously suggests this center of consciousness, this paramount unity, the "I" that I can utter and that in the welter of other experiences impinging on me at any given time (synchronically) or over a period of time (diachronically) provides me with an experience and concept of oneness, and more specifically of oneness despite diversity.

Looked at carefully, a system does indeed resemble the "I" in being in one way closed but in another way not entirely closed at all. Thus the "I" itself can be thought of as a system, in a certain sense. The difference between systems and the unique "I" are, however, manifold. Basically, systems are neither so definitely closed as is the "I" nor so utterly open. A system is not so definitely closed as is the "I" in that it cannot pull itself together inside itself to the extent that it knows from inside itself that it is different from every other being simply because it experiences itself directly for who it is. For a system is not a "who" but a "what"—which is to say it is not open to itself from the inside, but only more or less open to other things outside.

As communication is a concept derived from the world of living things and then extended to nonliving activities, so a system is a concept derived from the mechanical world and then extended to living things. System and communication stand in complementary relationship to one another.

Because essentially it is modeled on nonlife, a system is not so utterly open as is the "I": it is not receptive to all of being. So likewise, human consciousness, centered in the "I," is not strictly a system, only something like a system, or, better, something that systems are like. Human consciousness is the open-and-closed unity that a system can only approach more and more closely without achieving. For the living world, and more specifically the human world, is ultimately the measure of the mechanical, and not vice versa.

The technological world is part of the human world. There is no technology not totally dependent on man (which is not to say that any technology is totally under conscious control). Technology enters into consciousness more intimately than has commonly been thought, for the technologies of writing and print and electronic devices radically transform the word and the mental processes which are the coefficients of speech and of which speech is the coefficient. These technological "systems" of writing and print and electronic devices interface with one another. . . . Writing grows out of oral speech, which can never be quite the same after writing is interiorized in the psyche. Writing leads verbalization out of the agora into a world of imagined audiences—a fascinating and demanding and exquisitely productive world. Print grows out of writing and transforms the modes and uses of writing and thus also of oral speech and of thought itself. Electronic devices grow out of writing and print, and also transform writing and print, so that books of an electronic age can be distinguished by their very organization of thought, from those of earlier ages.

And beneath it all, consciousness, insofar as it can be considered by analogy with a system, interfaces with everything. Human beings still say "I" and each "I" is always unique. Each "I" is also open, but the world on which consciousness opens today impinges on consciousness in ways different from the ways of earlier ages. More than ever before, the alert individual consciousness feels that it must do more interfacing, that it must be more "open."

There is no reason to believe that the present hospitality to open-system paradigms in the exercises of conscious activity presages a stage of millennial bliss for mankind either in the West or elsewhere in the world. Wrongdoing appears as rampart as ever before, and some of our most open-system mass media are willing to make real-life tragedy a part of entertainment and to be as venal otherwise as human beings have always tended to be. Still, the drive to openness on the whole does appear to be advantageous and to represent progress in a deep sense of this term. The tendency to openness appears to mark a new and more advanced stage in the evolution of consciousness. Closure can be protected and desirable at times, and it is particularly necessary at earlier stages of thought to rule out distractions and achieve control. But programmed closed-system thinking, whether in matters of science, history, philosophy, art, politics, or religious faith is ultimately defensive and, although defenses may be always to some degree necessary, to make defensiveness on principle one's dominant mood and program forever is to opt not for life but for death. The great forces in psychic life, the thirst for knowledge, love for others, religious faith, certainly the Christian faith, are not essentially forces favoring closure, but drives to openness. "The truth shall make you free."

Openness does not mean lack of organization, lack of principle, or lack of all resistance. For the human being, at least, it means quite the contrary: the strengthening of organization, principles, and resistance where needed, so that interaction with the outside can be strong and real. Indeed, paradoxically again, openness means strengthening closure itself.

Ultimately, openness calls for strengthening of closure because of the dialectical relationship of the two in consciousness. When one is heightened in a way, the other normally undergoes heightening in another way. The age of "togetherness," of open-system paradigms, of noetic "kleinforms" that open actuality and fiction into and out of one another in amazing ways, is also the age of the isolated individual. But how isolated can the individual be in an age more openly and explicitly concerned about the individual—in literature, psychology, sociology, philosophy, theology, social legislation, and otherwise—than any earlier age has been? Discussion of the "I" such as that just undertaken here would have been impossible a few centuries ago. Consciousness was not yet ready for it. Such discussion is a twentieth-century phenomenon. We can face the isolation or closure of the "I" with equanimity today because society's openness serves as a counterpoise to the individual's isolation and reminds us that such isolation is a foundation for openness. We can all tolerate being very much alone and acknowledging we are alone so long as we are all alone together.

The closure implemented by print was a prelude to the openness of the television age. And since television has not destroyed print but interfaced with it, the closure is in some ways with us still. There are problems and opportunities with both closure and openness, and we all are going to have to live with the problems and opportunities there are, and more.

Notes

1. For a good overview of the history of television, see Erik Barnouw, *Tube of Plenty: The Evolution of American Television* (New York: Oxford University Press, 1975).
2. Paul Ryan, *Cybernetics of the Sacred* (Garden City, N.Y.: Anchor Press, Doubleday, 1974); first published as *Birth and Death and Cybernation* (New York: Gordon & Breach, Science Publishers, 1973).
3. See Walter J. Ong, *Ramus, Method, and the Decay of Dialogue* (Cambridge, Mass.: Harvard University Press, 1958), pp. 151–152, 307–318.
4. Wilden, *System and Structure,* pp. 213–217, and *passim.*
5. *The Hidden God: A Study of Tragic Vision in the Pensées of Pascal and the Tragedies of Racine,* trans. Philip Thody (New York: Humanities Press, 1964).
6. Since at least the time of Zeno of Citium, logic has been compared to the closed fist, rhetoric to the open hand. See Wilbur Samuel Howell, *Logic and Rhetoric in England, 1500–1700* (Princeton, N.J.: Princeton University Press, 1956), pp. 14–15, 33, 51, 141, 208, 315, 365, 374, 377, 378. All of these places in Howell report on citations of Zeno's model by various ancient and Renaissance philosophers. The "closed fist of logic" was a widely current closed-system model for centuries, though it served also simultaneously as a model for other things, such as power.
7. See Erich, Neumann, *The Origins and History of Consciousness,* trans. R. F. C. Hull (New York: Pantheon Books, 1954), pp. 5–38.
8. Ong, *Ramus, Method, and the Decay of Dialogue,* pp. 36–49, 224–269, and *passim.*
9. Walter J. Ong, " 'Idea' Titles in John Milton's Milieu," *Studies in Honor of DeWitt T. Starnes,* ed. Thomas P. Harrington, *et al.* (Austin, Texas: University of Texas Press, 1967), pp. 227–239.
10. Oxford: The Clarendon Press, 1974, p. 98.
11. Page 103.
12. Ong, *Ramus, Method, and the Decay of Dialogue,* pp. 295–318.
13. Ong, "Ioannes Piscator: One Man or a Ramist Dichotomy?" *Harvard Library Bulletin,* 8 (1954), 151–162.
14. Harold Garfinkel, *Studies in Ethnomethodology* (Englewood Cliffs, N.J.: Prentice-Hall, 1967). See also Aaron V. Cicourel, *Cognitive Sociology* (Harmondsworth, England: Penguin Education, a Division of Penguin Books, 1973), pp. 99–140.
15. Second enlarged ed. (Chicago: University of Chicago Press, 1970).

BRENT D. RUBEN

Intrapersonal, Interpersonal, and Mass Communication Processes in Individual and Multi-Person Systems

This chapter from the book *General Systems Theory and Human Communication* links all communication, from intrapersonal to mass, as one continual process in which the individual comes "to know and be" in relationship to the world. Brent Ruben contends we cannot study and understand one form of human communication apart from all other kinds of human communication. Each form is part of a complex network of functionally interrelated communication acts in multi-individual systems. The basic function of this network is information processing. Ruben considers "information" to be all the inputs and outputs that flow through the human communication system producing the thoughts, feelings, and actions that we label as human. If you understand and accept Ruben's systems theory, you should be able to relate all the ideas presented in this collection of readings to a general system of human communication.

For communication study, one of the particularly significant contributions of C. West Churchman is his application of the concept of functionality. In *The Systems Approach,* Churchman differentiates between what might be termed *functional analysis,* which he contends is essential to the development of a systems orientation, and *descriptive analysis* which he believes is antithetical to system thinking. To make clear the difference, Churchman uses the automobile as an example. Where a descriptive analysis of an auto begins by listing the parts: wheels, axles, alternator, frame, and so on, analysis of function proceeds instead by considering how automobiles are used—what they are for.[1] The strength of this paradigm when applied to human communication study is that it draws one's attention to the predominantly descriptive traditions reflected in the majority of definitions of communication, while at the same time suggesting an alternative approach.

Descriptive Analysis in Human Communication Thought

That communication has been conceived of primarily in terms of "how-it-works" becomes apparent from even a most cursory consideration of the history of thought about the phenomenon. Since Aristotle set forth his concept of rhetoric, communication has primarily been examined in descriptive, component-oriented fashion:

> Since rhetoric exists to affect the giving of decisions . . . the orator must not only try to make the argument of his speech demonstrative and worthy of belief, he must also make his own character look right and put his bearers, who are to decide, into the right frame of mind.[2]

With his concern for a person who speaks, the speech to be given, and the person who will listen, Aristotle underscored in *Rhetoric* the same elements of communication as do most contemporary descriptions.

The descriptive mode of analysis was also evident in the classical portrayals of communication advanced by Lasswell,[3] Shannon and Weaver,[4] and Schramm,[5] whose models focus generally upon the same components as did Aristotle.[6] Lasswell,[7] of course, posited the well-known *"Who* said *what* in *which channel* to *whom* with *what effect,"* and Shannon and Weaver[8] listed source, transmitter, signal, receiver, and destination as primary ingredients in their analytic scheme which was intended to characterize communication in mathematical terms. Similarly, Schramm[9] referenced the elements of source, encoder, signal, decoder, destination.

The more elaborate "two-step flow" paradigm advanced by Katz and Lazarsfeld[10] evidenced a similar descriptive focus. In that definition, communication was conceived of in terms of messages flowing from impersonal sources to opinion leaders who in turn influenced nonleaders through interpersonal means. Riley and Riley[11] provided a scheme which integrated aspects of previous models yet maintained a primarily descriptive component orientation, though giving some attention to sociological processes, structures, and functions.

The models provided by Westley and MacLean,[12] and Berlo[13] were intended to focus more upon communication as a *process,*[14] and particularly the Westley-Maclean[15] model better accommodated the communicative implications of non-purposive behavior than had previous characterizations. Broadened in application and increased in sophistication, these two pervasive models further reflected, and no doubt contributed significantly to, the penchant for descriptive portrayal of communication.

Speech-communication schemes, while often considering more elements, have maintained a predominantly descriptive focus. Barker and Kibler[16] provide a useful compilation of the variety of dimensions in terms of which writers in speech communication have chosen to characterize and examine communication. Their list includes: verbal and nonverbal communication; interpersonal, intrapersonal, group, mass and cultural communication; oral and written communication; formal and informal communication; intentional and unintentional communication; and logical and emotional communication.[17]

Brooks,[18] in like manner, presents a taxonomy of communication which focuses upon verbal, interpersonal, nonverbal, dyadic, and small group communication, and utilizes the basic Lasswellian paradigm of an initiator, message, and recipient(s). Samovar and Mills[19] offer a model which also stresses the elements of encoder, message, channel, and receiver. Miller,[20] Becker,[21] and Hasling[22] similarly conceptualize communication descriptively in terms of a speaker, messages, and listener(s).

In mass communication, descriptive analysis and consequent emphasis upon specific components has perhaps been more pronounced than in the writings on speech-communication.[23] The "how-it-works" orientation has been manifest in the tendency to focus upon the technology of the mass media as if it were the same as the mass communication *phenomenon*. One finds, for example, the terms mass media and mass communication used more or less interchangeably in Barnouw,[24] Stephenson,[25] and DeFleur.[26] This same descriptive focus leads other popular authors to fail to differentiate conceptually between mass communications (messages), and mass communication. This is the case, for example, in Schramm;[27] Emery, Ault and Agee;[28] and Rivers, Peterson and Jensen.[29]

Typically stressing *channel*—and sometimes *message*—as opposed to *source* and *receiver,* such schemes for conceiving of communication (and mass communication) have both reflected and reinforced the descriptive orientation.

The writings of journalism, taken to a generic level of analysis, indicate a similar proclivity for descriptive analysis, although the focus is generally more upon the *message* than *source, channel,* or *receiver.* Hohenberg,[30] Brown,[31] and Charnley[32] are examples. The literature of persuasion, whether approached from speech, social psychology, or mass communication evidences this pattern also, as Miller and Burgoon[33] suggest by implication. The works of Rosnow and Robinson,[34] Bettinghaus,[35] and Rogers and Shoemaker[36] are illustrative.

Clearly, there has been a great deal of attention devoted to models explaining how *communication works*. Like the definition of the automobile in terms of its parts and how they work together, communication has been characterized largely by focusing upon *source, message, channel,* and *receiver* and operational interactions between them.

What is noticeably lacking are models of the phenomenon which utilize functional analyses of the sort Churchman suggests. Few researchers who conceive themselves (and are conceived by others) to be in the field of communication appear to be focusing their efforts in any direct fashion toward an exploration of the *functions* of communication—what it is for, and how it is used.

Functional Analysis in Human Communication Thought

There are no doubt various explanations for this imbalance. Some would argue that the attention given to descriptive analysis indicates the lack of appropriateness, validity, and/or utility of functional modes of characterization. Others would point out that findings of descriptive analysis seem to have a clearer relevance for communication practitioners (e.g., journalists, speakers, librarians, writers, announcers, managers, information system managers, counselors) and that directions of scholarship in the field have been impacted centrally by a desire for finding which will help the practitioner on an operational level. Others have suggested that the shape and direction of scholarship in communication has come about more by default—through socialization and homogenization of individuals entering the field—than by conscious choice.

For these and perhaps other reasons many—if not most—of those contributions which are most central to characterizing human communication in functional terms, have been provided by individuals whose work falls outside the boundaries of "the field" as it is generally defined in reviews of the literature in many major journals and volumes.

One such source of analysis of function in human communication is provided in the works of Berger,[37] Luckman,[38] Holzner,[39] and McHugh,[40] whose research focus upon the social origins of information and knowledge and functions of the informational relationships between the individual and social reality.

Other sociologists, including Goffman,[41] Duncan,[42] and Blumer,[43] have provided particularly useful analysis for understanding communication in terms of its social functions.

Another pertinent area is general semantics with its focus upon the functions of information for science and reality mapping. The work of Korzybski,[44] Johnson,[45] and Brown,[46] are especially relevant here.

Additionally, the general semanticists' interest in human information ecology has in many respects been complemented by work on the role of communication in human adjustment of Rogers;[47] Ruesch;[48] Bateson;[49] Watzlawick, Beavin, and Jackson;[50] Grinker,[51] Shands,[52] Speigel,[53] and Quill.[54]

Still another source of input for functional research on human communication and individual behavior comes from a group of scholars with a psychological background. The writings of Thayer;[55] Allport;[56] Church;[57] Kelley;[58] Maslow;[59] Schroder, Driver and Streuffert;[60] and Lindsay and Norman[61] are among these contributions.

Other works, by individuals often not centrally associated with communication, and yet especially useful for conceiving of communication in functional terms, have been provided by Delgado,[62] Young,[63] Laszlo,[64] and Smith,[65] relative to the neurophysiological, biological, epistemological, and cultural functions of information for man.

Given this wide-ranging diversity, it is apparent that a functional approach to human communication would have, of necessity, a multi-disciplinary heritage. And to the extent that one seeks to develop a system paradigm that meets the criteria suggested by von Bertalanffy, Boulding, and Rapoport, as well as by Churchman, the framework must be valid and useful in cross-disciplinary application.

As a foundation for such a conceptualization of communication and communication systems, J. G. Miller's[66] view of information processing as one of two basic processes of living systems is especially valuable. Building on this notion, communication can be meaningfully defined as *the process of information metabolism,* and understood to be of parallel importance to living organisms as the processes involved in the metabolism of matter-energy. In this light, communication can be regarded as essential to the birth, growth, development, change, evolution, and survival or death of all that is human.[67]

To further refine one's scheme for categorizing the processes of information metabolism, and hence communication, the concept of *symbol* is important.[68] There are, for man, but two sorts of possible exchanges with the environment: those involving bio-physical transactions and those involving symbolic transactions. And in a number of instances the two operate conjunctively. While man is clearly not the only living organism that processes information about his milieu, nor is he the only animal who can be said to utilize language, man alone has the capacity for inventing, accumulating, and attaching meanings and significance—through symbols—to the entirety of his biophysical and social environment and to himself.

Unlike other non symbol-using animals, man uniquely has the capacity and the necessity of accumulating information cast in the form of knowledge, behavior and culture for diffusion to and inculcation among his contemporaries and members of subsequent generations. Further, unlike other non symbol-transacting animals, man alone has the capacity and therefore the necessity of acquiring membership in the various social collectivities upon which he depends solely through the identification and internalization of the significant symbols of the social unit.

The study of communication systems is, therefore, logically understood as the study of the role of symbols, symbolization, and symbol internalization in the creation, maintenance, and change of all human individual and multi-individual organization.

In order to develop a communication system paradigm, it is therefore necessary to develop a scheme for categorizing information-metabolizing structures in terms of the symbolic processes involved. For present purposes, the first such classificatory unit will be labelled the *individual system* and the second, the *multi-individual system.*[69] In considering the former, the focus of this chapter will be upon what can be termed the *intrapersonal functions of human communication.* Examination of the multi-individual system will center on the *interpersonal and socio-cultural functions of human communication.* The processes at the first of these levels of analysis will be termed *personal communication,* and those at the second level, *social communication.*

Personal Communication

Personal communication can be thought of as sensing, making sense of, and acting toward the objects and people in one's milieu. It is the process by which the individual informationally fits himself in (adapts to and adapts) his environment.

As the individual organizes himself in and with his milieu, he develops ways of comprehending, seeing, hearing, understanding, and knowing his environment. Largely as a consequence of this process, no two individuals will view the objects or people in their environment in the same way.

What an individual becomes is therefore a function of having organized himself in particular ways with the objects and people in his milieu. Allport[70] describes this fundamental process of personality development as becoming. General semanticists refer to this process as abstracting and speak of it in terms of a mapping of the territory.[71] Thayer refers to this as in-formation.[72] In a neuro-physiological context one could think of personal communication as a process of intracerebral elaboration of extracerebral information.[73] Berger[74] characterizes the process as internalization.

From a variety of disciplinary viewpoints then, personal communication can be conceived of as that active process by which the individual comes to know and be in relationship in his world. Unlike lower animals who are genetically organized with their environments in relatively fixed and determinant ways, man must organize himself.[75] He can and must invent his rules for attaching significance and meaning to his milieu and the people in it. It is man's organize-ability which would seem to most clearly distinguish him from lower organisms, and which here serves to clarify the nature of *personal* communication.

The necessary condition for these complex adaptive functions may be termed *reality integration,* and understood to be a most basic and essential information metabolizing function of personal communication. It is simply that function which allows and compels the individual to organize himself with—to come to know, to map the territory—his milieu, and therefore to become what he is and will be.

Personal communication, and the *reality integration function* can be categorized based upon the particular adaptive functions subserved. Such a classification includes: (1) biological adaptation; (2) physical adaptation; (3) interpersonal adaptation; (4) sociocultural adaptation.

Biological Integration
Through personal communication an individual develops, maintains, and alters the knowledge and "maps" necessary for his biological functioning. He comes to understand procreation and with whom, where, when, and under what circumstances it is appropriate. With regard to the processes involved in the metabolism of matter-energy, he comes to know what, when, where, and how to eat and excrete wastes. Through personal communication the individual learns about those aspects of his physical and biological environment which may threaten his well-being as a living system. He also comes to understand what data he must gather, how the data are to be processed, and how decisions are to be made in order to avoid

collision with other structures; some of which are stationary, and others having patterns and rates of movement he must discern.[76] Personal communication functions also to enable the development and assertion of the individual's identity and territoriality as a human creature distinct from, and yet dependent upon, all others of the species. This occurs through the use of symbolic and geographical distancing utilizing a wide range of symbolic markers such as beach blankets, houses, autos, clothes, perfumes, hair stylings, and so on.

Physical Integration

Personal communication also functions to enable the individual to develop, maintain, and alter his explanations of the *nonhuman objects* in his environment. For present purposes, it is meaningful to distinguish between physical matter which is contrived and that which is noncontrived. Within the category of contrived objects are those nonliving things which man has created, like cars, tools, buildings, furniture, and processes like sawing, lawn-mowing, writing, and so on. Personal communication also enables the individual to develop and maintain understandings of physical properties and processes such as the atmosphere, metabolism, geological structures, evolution, rivers, communication, plants, animals, living/dying as well as other substances and processes generally assumed not to be human in origin.

Interpersonal Integration

One increasingly popular research area regards the functions of personal communication through which the individual comes to conceive of people—himself and others. It is this function of personal communication that enables the individual to know who he thinks he is, what he is like and who and what others in his milieu are about.

Sociocultural Integration

One of the least familiar, yet centrally important functions of personal communication relates to the symbolic reality systems of the various multiperson organizations in which all individuals operate. It is through personal communication that the individual comes to know what is informationally and behaviorally expected of him if he is to participate in such collectivities as friendships, passengers on an elevator, families, clubs, fraternities, religious sects, political parties, professional and vocational groups, societies, and so on.

Personal communication functions to enable the individual to internalize, symbolically, the accepted organizational truths, operating principles, habits, norms, rituals, protocol, conventions, explicit and implicit goals, required competencies, ethical standards, laws, rules, and so on. He learns what most people seem to say, what most people seem to do, how they dress, and where he fits.

Of particular importance also is the learning personal communication affords relative to the accepted modes of explanation. In an organization of social scientists, for example, "science" provides the explanatory framework which one must learn. In another organization, a "religious" mode of explanation may be more popular.

A related function of personal communication regards an individual's symbol internalization of prescribed and prohibited behaviors, which are both implicit and explicit in nature. The individual learns the nature and price of membership, "the coinage of the realm,"[77] the significant and sacred symbols, flags, words, behaviors and the consequences of failure to posture oneself in an organizationally consistent manner.

At the level of analysis of the individual system then, personal communication operates such that the individual is able to identify and internalize through symbolic information processing those biological, physical, interpersonal, and sociocultural realities necessary for him to adapt in his environment.

Social Communication

Social communication is the process underlying *intersubjectivization,* a phenomenon which occurs as a consequence of public symbolization and symbol utilization and diffusion. It is through this information metabolism process that the world we know is defined, labeled, and categorized, our knowledge of it shared and validated, and our behavior toward it and one another regularized and regulated. It is through this same process that multi-person organization, social order, control and predictability are achieved.[78] The most basic transaction of social communication is two or more individuals organizing with one another, knowingly or not, in an effort to adapt to or adapt their environment.[79]

Because of the nature of human communication—and personal communication—achieving this goal requires active participation in the invention, construction, and maintenance of a plethora of overlapping and non-overlapping organizations.[80] Organization through social communication varies from the relatively simple informational-behavioral interdependency patterns man creates and perpetuates with other passengers riding an elevator, to the extremely complex and varigated organization necessary to the emergence, continuity, and evolution of a society.

Clearly then, the specific consequences of social communication may vary greatly from one multi-person organization to the next in terms of complexity and function. The basic information metabolizing processes by which these organizations are initiated and maintained, however, do not. When people organize with one another, in an elevator, a friendship, or a society, they discover, create, and share informational and behavioral realities.[81] In so doing, the whole they define together becomes more than a simple sum of the parts. This discovery, creation, sharing, socialization process can be termed intersubjectivization. Were there no intersubjective reality structures, there could be no multi-person organization. Thus "values," "norms," "knowledge," and "culture" may all be viewed as instances of intersubjectivated realities, defined and diffused through social communication.

Considered in this light, reality definition, standardization, and diffusion can be viewed as both necessary and sufficient conditions for social organization and joint-adaptation, and may be understood to be the primary function of social communication. The process of social communication can be further delineated in terms of particular biological, physical, and socio-cultural functions.

Biological Definition
Through social communication, multi-individual organizations define, label, and standardize information-behavior patterns relative to a wide range of human biological functions. Intersubjectivizations, variously termed knowledge, norms, and rituals that relate to sexual and reproductive practices, food consumption and excretory functions, medical care and medication are exemplars. It is not the intention to detail specifics in each case here, and it is adequate simply to note the rather obvious point that within multi-person systems rather specific socially defined legal, medical, and normative guidelines are constructed and shared with regard to where, under what conditions and with whom sexual relations are appropriate. Similarly, conventions are created and maintained with regard to conventions of food procurement, preservation, and preparation as well as excretion. It is also clearly through social communication that both organic and psychological illness and health are defined, and labels created, agreed

upon and attached to what are conceived to be maladies.[82] It is this same process by which strategies for treatment are invented, tested, applied or discarded, and validated.

Additionally, it is through social communication that both explicit and implicit rules for locomotion—time-place movement—are developed, standardized, and diffused. Rules for passing oncoming pedestrians and cars on the right rather than left, as well as conventions governing right-of-way, pedestrian crosswalks, and red lights on street signs are examples.

It is also through social communication that the concepts of personal space and protection and differentiation from the environment are defined and institutionalized, and methods for marking and separating territories invented and regularized.[83] Architecture plays a central role with regard to the institutionalization of this social communication function. The nature and placement of construction, size, accessibility, and location of boundaries within physical structures exemplify the process and consequences of intersubjectivization.[84] Related also are multi-individual system conventions as to whom and under what conditions several persons can appropriately inhabit a single structural domain, and customs developed pertaining to the use of boundaries (e.g., walks, windows, doors) to isolate or protect individuals within one dwelling (or portion of a dwelling) from individuals in another portion of that dwelling or another structure.

Physical Definition

Intersubjectivization with regard to geophysical and biophysical substances in an important function of social communication. It is through social communication that informational-behavioral orientations relative to substances like granite, telephones, water, and books, as well as plants and animals are defined, standardized, classified, and those intersubjectivizations perpetuated and validated.

Social communication functions such that biophysical and geophysical substances and processes are classifiable in a systematic taxonomical framework in which each substance is defined in terms of constituent subclasses and is itself categorized as one component of the next larger encompassing classification.[85] It is through these same processes that biophysical and geophysical phenomena like evolution or metabolism are discovered, defined, and shared. It should be noted also that the instruments by which these and other biophysical and geophysical definitions are validated are themselves products of social communication and standardization, as with the rock-hardness scale or the Richter Scale.

A distinct function of social communication is the invention, production, marketing, utilization, and validation of technological devices, manufactured products, and consumer goods in general.[86] Thus, social communication is as critical to the production and definition of books, automobiles, or typewriters as it is to systems for the metaorganization of information about them.[87]

Sociocultural Definition

It is through social communication that sociocultural patterns essential to the functioning of all multi-person systems are defined, standardized, and diffused. While specific consequences in terms of complexity and goals will vary from one multi-person unit to the next—from an organization consisting of passengers on an elevator, to a friendship, family, club, business organization, professional group, or society—the fundamental information metabolizing processes and often the functions subserved remain constant. Informational-behavioral patterns related to roles, rules, language-use patterns, values, habits, norms, appropriate jargon, protocol, ethics, aesthetics and even requisite vocational competencies are created, shared, and perpetuated through social communication.

Social communication performs another critical socio-cultural function involving the establishment and maintenance of particular organizational truths, operating principles, or belief structures around which a multi-person system is formed. It is also through social communication that a characteristic mode of explanation for the events that beset members of the collectivity are created, implemented, and validated. Religion and science each exemplify the notion of mode of explanation in the sense suggested here.[88] For each multi-person system, social communication allows for the creation, utilization, and institutionalization of significant symbols such as flags, trademarks, political campaign posters and buttons, dress or any organization-specific insignias which function to identify and differentiate one multi-person system from another.

Another critically important sociocultural function of social communication relates to the enabling of transactions between members of a system. It is through social communication that social currency, and hence an economy, becomes possible. Without intersubjectivization and hence shared concepts of intrinsic value, comparative value, and symbolic value, neither a barter system nor a token-utilizing economic system is achievable. Further, these same economic functions may be said to be subserved in even the simplest multi-person systems such as friendships, where the coinage of the realm—the means of transaction—may be understood to be language and nonverbal symbols rather than more familiar monetary markers.

Mass Communication

The institutionalization, by multi-person systems, of the processes by which informational-behavioral patterns are diffused and perpetuated, may be termed *mass communication*. Such a definition, it should be noted, suggests that the mass communication process is neither media centered, nor purposive in the sense most definitions imply. Rather, mass communication is conceptualized in terms of function served rather than mode of transmission, size or nature of an audience, or goals of a communicator.

Thusly viewed, mass communication is an aspect of social communication; it serves the diffusion function necessary for intersubjectivization. By this definition, restaurants, schools, churches, supermarkets, highways, the clothing industry, and political campaigns are defined as mass communication institutions along with the mass media, theatre, museums, art galleries, and libraries in that all serve a reality diffusion and intersubjectivization function. A related function of mass communication pertains to the perpetuation function, which may be thought of in terms of time and space binding.[89] Through the institutionalization of diffusion processes, informational-behavioral realities are perpetuated across time, geographical distances, new members of multi-person systems, and new generations.

Transactions

Social communication, it has been said, is fundamental to the definition, categorization, and standardization of information-behavioral patterns; mass communication is essential to their diffusion; personal communication to the manner in which they are sensed, made sense of, and acted upon by the individual. Clearly, these three functions are not accomplished by independent activities, but rather operate in a continuous, interpenetrating, transactional fashion.

● ● ●

The information metabolizing functions of informational-behavioral *definition, standardization, diffusion,* and *integration* are as basic to the *individual–multi-individual suprasystem,* as sensing, making sense of, and acting toward are to the individual system and defining, standardizing, and diffusing are to the multi-person system. Implied is that what an individual becomes and can become is largely a consequence of how he or she organizes with the informational-behavioral patterns and demands of his or her milieu. Implied also is that the patterns with which the individual organized are consequences of the activities of multi-person system information metabolizing processes, which in turn, are a consequence of the social synthesis of the individual behaviors of its constituent members. Thus . . . society can be viewed as a multi-person communication system and understood to be defined and perpetuated by the behaviors of citizens. Information necessary for the individual citizens to adapt is provided by the multi-person system and digested and acted upon by the individual citizens, such as to continually redefine the society for themselves and one another. . . .

Conclusion

This, then, is the basic paradigm. In sum, the perspective developed provides a view of human enterprise as a complex network of functionally interrelated individuals in multi-individual systems, who, through the information metabolizing processes of intrapersonal, interpersonal and mass communication, enable and constrain, satisfy and frustrate, create and destroy, change and not, in all that is human.

The view of communication systems which emerges draws heavily on many fundamental open systems concepts, particularly multi-lateral causality, equi-finality, multi-finality, functionality, dynamic stabilization, organic growth and change, and interdependent, hierarchically ordered levels of organization. Basic notions of symbolic interaction, general semantics, transactional psychology, and sociology of knowledge are also heavily utilized.

While far from comprehensive in its present form, the paradigm would seem also to satisfy the systems criteria of cross-disciplinary validity and interdisciplinary applicability, and in this sense may serve as an outline for the subsequent development of more elaborate and detailed operational models.

Notes

1. C. West Churchman, *The Systems Approach,* New York: Delacorte, 1968.
2. This point is presented and discussed by Richard F. Hixson, "Mass Media: An Approach to Human Communication," *Approaches to Human Com-*

munication, Richard W. Budd and Brent D. Ruben, eds., Rochelle Park, N.J.: Hayden Book Co. (Spartan), 1972.

3. Harold D. Lasswell, "The Structure and Function of Communication in Society," *The Communication of Ideas,* Bryson Lyman, ed., Institute for Religion and Social Studies, 1948. Reprinted in *Mass Communications,* Wilbur Schramm, ed., Urbana, Ill.: University of Illinois Press, 1960, 1966, pp. 117–130.

4. Claude Shannon and Warren Weaver, *The Mathematical Theory of Communication,* Urbana, Ill.: University of Illinois Press, 1949.

5. Wilbur Schramm, "How Communication Works," *The Process and Effects of Mass Communication,* Wilbur Schramm, ed., Urbana, Ill.: University of Illinois Press, 1960, 1966, pp. 3–26.

6. This point is discussed by John Hasling, *The Message, The Speaker, The Audience,* New York: McGraw-Hill, 1971, pp. 2–3.

7. Harold D. Lasswell, "The Structure and Function of Communication in Society," p. 225.

8. Claude Shannon and Warren Weaver, *The Mathematical Theory of Communication,* Urbana, Ill: University of Illinois Press, 1949. *See also* Donald K. Darnell, "Information Theory: An Approach to Human Communication," *Approaches to Human Communication,* Rochelle Park, N.J.: Hayden Book Co. (Spartan), 1972.

9. Wilbur Schramm, "How Communication Works," *The Process and Effects of Mass Communication,* Wilbur Schramm, ed., Urbana: University of Illinois Press, 1960, 1966, pp. 3–26.

10. Elihu Katz and Paul F. Lazarsfeld, *Personal Influence,* New York: Free Press, 1960. *See also* earlier work of Paul Lazarsfeld, Bernard Berelson, and Hazel Gaudet, *The People's Choice,* New York: Columbia University Press, 1944, 1948. Discussion by Bernard Berelson, "Communication and Public Opinion," *The Process and Effects of Mass Communication,* Wilbur Schramm, ed., 1954, 1965, pp. 343–356, and Elihu Katz, "The Two-Step Flow of Communication," *Mass Communications,* Wilbur Schramm, ed., pp. 346–365.

11. John W. Riley, Jr. and Matilda White Riley, "A Sociological Approach to Mass Communication," *Sociology Today,* Robert K. Merton, Leonard Broom and Leonard S. Cottrell, Jr., eds., Basic Books, 1959. *See* "Sociology: An Approach to Human Communication," *Approaches to Human Communication,* Rochelle Park, N.J.: Hayden Book Co. 1972.

12. Bruce H. Westley and Malcolm S. MacLean, Jr., "A Conceptual Model for Communication Research," *Journalism Quarterly,* Vol. 34, 1957, pp. 31–38.

13. David K. Berlo, *The Process of Communication,* New York: Holt, Rinehart and Winston, 1960.

14. An excellent discussion of the status of "process" in conceptualizations of communication is provided in "Communication Research and the Idea of Process," by David H. Smith, *Speech Monographs,* August 1972. Smith argues that most models of communication which have purported to integrate the process concept have generally failed in their attempts.

15. The Westley-MacLean model is referenced in most contemporary com-

munication volumes. *See* for example, discussion in *Communication—The Study of Human Interaction,* C. David Mortensen, New York: McGraw-Hill, 1972. An excellent critical discussion of the Westley-MacLean, Berlo, and other popular models of communication provided by John Y. Kim in "Feedback and Human Communication: Toward a Reconceptualization," an unpublished doctoral dissertation, University of Iowa, 1971.

16. Larry L. Barker and Robert J. Kibler, *Speech Communication Behavior,* Englewood Cliffs, N.J.: Prentice-Hall, 1971.

17. Ibid. pp. 3–8.

18. William D. Brooks, *Speech Communication,* Dubuque, Iowa: W. C. Brown, 1972.

19. Larry A. Samovar and Jack Mills, *Oral Communication,* Dubuque, Iowa: W. C. Brown, 1968, 1972, pp. 3–5.

20. Gerald R. Miller, *An Introduction to Speech Communication,* Indianapolis, Ind.: Bobbs-Merrill, 1972, p. 58. *See also* Gerald Miller, "Speech: An Approach to Human Communication," *Approaches to Human Communication,* Rochelle Park, N.J.: Hayden Book Co., 1972.

21. Samuel L. Becker, "What Rhetoric (Communication Theory) Is Relevant for Contemporary Speech Communication?" presented at the University of Minnesota, 1968, Spring Symposium on Speech-Communication.

   A presentation of the model with discussion is also provided in C. David Mortensen, *Communication—The Study of Human Interaction,* New York: McGraw-Hill, 1972, pp. 46–48.

22. J. Hasling, *The Message, the Speaker, The Audience,* New York: McGraw-Hill, 1971, pp. 3–5.

23. It is interesting to note that although descriptive component-oriented analysis predominates in both speech and mass communication, there is remarkably little evidence of conceptual cross-fertilization between these disciplines despite some rather obvious philosophical and operational similarities.

24. Erik Barnouw, *Mass Communication,* New York: Holt, Rinehart and Winston, 1956. That mass communication is understood to be defined in terms of the mass media (channel component) is suggested by the subtitle of this volume: "Television, Radio, Film, Press." The point is underscored in Section 1 entitled "The History of Mass Communication," which consists of the following chapters: "The Paper Tide," "The Moving Image," "Signals in the Air," and "Of Words and Mousetraps."

25. William Stephenson, *The Play Theory of Mass Communication,* Chicago: University of Chicago Press, 1967. Stephenson begins Chapter 1, "Two New Theories of Mass Communication Research," as follows:

> From its beginnings, in 1924 or so, mass communication theory has concerned itself primarily with how the mass media influence the attitudes, beliefs, and actions of people. There was little evidence up to 1959, however, that the mass media had any significant effects on the deeper or more important beliefs of people . . .
>   . . . it is the thesis of this book that at its best mass communication

allows people to become absorbed in *subjective play.* People read newspapers, magazines, and paperbacks in vast numbers, and there are ever increasing audiences for movies, radio, records, and television.

26. Melvin L. DeFleur, *Theories of Mass Communication,* New York: McKay, 1966, 1970. While DeFleur argues initially that mass communication is a special case of communication, five of the eight chapters in the volume focus on the mass media.

27. Wilbur Schramm, *Mass Communication,* Urbana, Ill.: University of Illinois Press, 1960, 1966.

    On page 3, Schramm says:

> When did mass communication begin? The date usually given is that of the beginning of printing from movable metal type, in Western Europe in the fifteenth century, but the roots are much earlier and the flowering much later.
>
> The *mass media* are the resultant forces set in motion when groups of manlike animals first huddled together against the cold and danger of primitive times. . . . In Korea, where they had paper, ink and metal type first, conditions were not ripe for the growth of *mass communication;* in Western Europe, when Gutenberg began to print, society was more nearly ready to develop *the new device.* (italics added)

    The volume includes sections on "The Structure and Function of Mass Communications" which consists of articles by Lasswell, Lerner, Breed, and others about the structure and function of *mass communication* as a process.

    In other sections, such as "The Development of Mass Communications," Schramm seems clearly to be referring to the development of the *mass media.* In yet another section, "Responsibility for Mass Communication," references are to *messages.*

28. Edwin Emery, Philip H. Ault, and Warren K. Agee, *Introduction to Mass Communications,* New York: Dodd, Mead, 1960, 1965, 1970. Of the 18 chapters in the volume, 13 are devoted to the mass media.

29. William L. Rivers, Theodore Peterson, and Jay W. Jensen, *The Mass Media and Modern Society,* New York: Holt, Rinehart, and Winston, 1971. On page 16, the authors state:

> Today one can more correctly speak of "mass communications" than of "journalism" when referring to media other than newspapers and magazines. In a sense, of course, every *communication* uses some medium, is committed to some channel for transmission. The letterhead or sheet of notepaper in correspondence, the sound waves utilized in conversation—these are channels or media. But in *mass communication,* a whole institution becomes the message carrier—a newspaper, a magazine, a broadcasting station . . .
>
> The term *mass communication* has sometimes been defined in two ways: *communication by the media* and *communication for the masses.* *Mass communication,* however, does not mean communication for everyone. (italics added)

The term "mass media" is used in the book to refer to channel, source, message, and sometimes receiver(s), as well. Included in the volume, for example, are chapters entitled "The Media as Persuaders" and "The Media as Informers and Interpreters."

30. John Hohenberg, *The Professional Journalist,* New York: Holt, Rinehart, and Winston, 1960, 1969.

31. Lee Brown, "Journalism: An Approach to Human Communication," *Approaches to Human Communication,* Rochelle Park, N.J.: Hayden Book Co. (Spartan), 1972.

32. Mitchell V. Charnley, *Reporting,* New York: Holt, Rinehart, and Winston, 1959, 1966.

33. Gerald R. Miller and Michael Burgoon, *New Techniques in Persuasion,* New York: Harper and Row, 1973, pp. 1–3.

34. Ralph L. Rosnow and Edward J. Robinson, *Experiments in Persuasion,* New York: Academic Press, 1967.

35. Erwin P. Bettinghaus, *Persuasive Communication,* New York: Holt, Rinehart, and Winston, 1968.

36. Everett M. Rogers and E. Floyd Shoemaker, *Communication of Innovations,* New York: Free Press, 1971. A related discussion is provided by Everett Rogers in *Communication and Social Change,* Rochelle Park, N.J.: Hayden Book Co.

37. Peter L. Berger and Thomas Luckmann, *The Social Construction of Reality,* Garden City: Doubleday, 1966 and Peter L. Berger in *The Sacred Canopy,* Garden City: Doubleday, 1969.

38. Peter L. Berger and Thomas Luckmann, *The Social Construction of Reality,* Garden City: Doubleday, 1966.

39. Burkart Holzner, *Reality Construction in Society,* Cambridge, Mass.: Schenkman, 1966.

40. Peter McHugh, *Defining the Situation,* Indianapolis, Ind.: Bobbs-Merrill, 1968. The central concepts undergirding the frameworks of Berger Luckmann, Holzner, and McHugh are reflective of the contributions of Schutz, Sorokin, Scheler, Mannheim, and Durkheim to the study of epistemology and the "sociology of knowledge."

A discussion of their work and of the sociology of knowledge in general, is provided by Robert Merton in *Social Theory and Social Structure,* New York: Free Press, 1949, 1957, 1968, pp. 510–562. *See also* Werner Stark, *The Sociology of Knowledge,* London: Routledge and Kegan Paul, 1958, 1960, 1967, and W. J. H. Sprott, *Science and Social Action,* London: Watts, 1954, 1961.

41. Of the contributions of Erving Goffman, *Relations in Public,* New York: Basic Books, 1971; *Interaction Ritual,* Garden City: Doubleday, 1967; *The Presentation of Self in Everyday Life,* Garden City: Doubleday, 1959; and *Strategic Interaction,* Philadelphia: University of Pennsylvania, 1969, are most particularly relevant.

42. Hugh D. Ducan, *Symbols in Society,* London: Oxford University, 1968; *Communication and Social Order,* Oxford University, 1962; and *Symbols and Social Theory,* New York: Oxford University, 1969.

43. Herbert Blumer, *Symbolic Interactionism,* Englewood Cliffs: Prentice-Hall, 1969. Portions appear as "Symbolic Interaction: An Approach to Human Communication," *Approaches to Human Communication,* Rochelle Park, N.J.: Hayden Book Co., 1972.

44. Alfred Korzybski, *Science and Sanity,* Lakeville, Conn.: International Non-Aristotelian Library, 1933, 1948. *See also* discussion by Richard W. Budd, in "General Semantics: An Approach to Human Communication," *Approaches to Human Communication,* and *Communication: General Semantics Perspectives,* Lee Thayer ed., Rochelle Park, N.J.: Hayden Book Co., 1970.

45. Wendell Johnson, *People in Quandaries,* New York: Harper, 1946 and *Coping With Change* (Wendell Johnson and Dorothy Moeller), New York: Harper and Row, 1972.

46. Roger Brown, *Words and Things,* New York: Free Press, 1958, 1968.

47. Of Carl Rogers many contributions, *On Becoming a Person,* Boston: Houghton-Mifflin, 1961, and *Encounter Groups,* New York: Harper and Row, 1970, are particularly relevant as input for analysis of function in communication.

48. Major summary contributions of Jurgen Ruesch include *Communication: The Social Matrix of Society* (with Gregory Bateson), New York: Norton, 1951, 1968; *Nonverbal Communication* (with Veldon Kees), Stanford: University of California, 1956, 1972; *Therapeutic Communication,* New York: Norton, 1961; and *Disturbed Communication,* New York: Norton, 1957, 1972.

49. Major summary contributions of Gregory Bateson include *Communication: The Social Matrix of Society* (with Jurgen Ruesch), New York: Norton 1951, 1968; and *Steps to an Ecology of the Mind,* New York: Ballantine Books, 1972.

50. Paul Watzlawick, Janet Beavin, and Don D. Jackson, *Pragmatics of Human Communication,* New York:: Norton, 1967.

51. Roy R. Grinker, Sr., *Toward a Unified Theory of Human Behavior,* New York: Basic Books, 1956, 1967.

52. Harley C. Shands, *Thinking and Psychotherapy,* Cambridge, Mass.: Harvard University Press, 1960.

53. John Spiegel, *Transactions,* New York: Science House, 1971.

54. Quill, William G., *Subjective Psychology,* Rochelle Park, N.J.: Hayden Book Co., 1972.

55. Major summary contributions of Lee Thayer especially relevant for functional analysis of communication: *Communication and Communication Systems,* Homewood, Ill: Irwin, 1968; "Communication—*Sine Qua Non* of the Behavioral Sciences," *Vistas in Science,* D. L. Arm, ed., Albuquerque: University of New Mexico, 1968; *Communication: Concepts and Perspectives,* Rochelle Park, N.J.: Hayden Book Co., 1967; *Communication: Theory and Research,* Springfield, Ill.: Thomas, 1967; "Communication and the Human Condition," prepared for the VII Semana de Estudios Sociales "Mass Communication and Human Understanding" Instituto de Siencias Sociales, Barcelona, Spain, November, 1969; "Communication and Change," *Communication and Social Change,* Rochelle Park, N.J.: Hayden Book Co., "On Communication and Change: Some Provocations," *Systematics,* Vol. 6, No. 3, December, 1968;

"On Human Communication and Social Development," presented at the first World Conference on Social Communication for Development, Mexico City, March, 1970.

56. Gordon W. Allport, *Becoming*, New Haven: Yale University, 1955.
57. Joseph Church, *Language and the Discovery of Reality*, New York: Vintage Books, 1961.
58. George A. Kelly, *A Theory of Personality*, New York: Norton, 1955, 1963.
59. Abraham H. Maslow, *Toward a Psychology of Being*, New York: Van Nostrand, 1968, and *Motivation and Personality*, New York: Harper and Row, 1954, 1970.
60. Harold M. Schroder, Michael J. Driver, and Seigfried Streufert, *Human Information Processing*, New York: Holt, Rinehart, and Winston, 1967.
61. Peter H. Lindsay and Donald A. Norman, *Human Information Processing*, New York: Academic Press, 1972.
62. José M. R. Delgado, *Physical Control of the Mind*, New York: Harper and Row, 1969, portions of which appear as "Neurophysiology: An Approach to Human Communication," *Approaches to Human Communication*, Rochelle Park, N.J.: Hayden Book Co., 1972.
63. J. Z. Young, *Doubt and Certainty in Science*, Oxford University, 1970, and "Biology: An Approach to Human Communication," *Approaches to Human Communication*, Rochelle Park, N.J.: Hayden Book Co., 1972.
64. Particularly relevant contributions of Ervin Laszlo include *System, Structure and Experience*, New York: Gordon and Breach, 1969, *The World System*, New York: Braziller, 1972, and "Basic Concepts of Systems Philosophy" in this volume.
65. Of the numerous contributions of Alfred G. Smith, *Communication and Culture*, New York: Holt, Rinehart, and Winston, 1966, "Anthropology: An Approach to Human Communication," *Approaches to Human Communication*, Rochelle Park, N.J.: Hayden Book Co. and "Change, Channels and Trust," *Communication and Social Change*, Rochelle Park, N.J.: Hayden Book Co. (in preparation) are especially relevant.
66. James G. Miller, "Living Systems," *Behavioral Science*, Vol. 10, 1965, p. 338.
67. *Cf.* Lee Thayer, *Communication and Communication Systems*, Homewood, Ill.: Irwin, 1968, p. 17.
68. *Cf.* Kenneth Boulding, "General System Theory—Skeleton of Science," *Management Science*, Vol. 2, 1956, edited and included as Chapter 2 of this volume.
69. Additional discussion of the concepts of individual and multi-person systems is provided on pp. 137–140 "General System Theory: An Approach to Human Communication," *Approaches to Human Communication*, Rochelle Park, N.J.: Hayden Book Co., 1972.
70. Gordon W. Allport, *Becoming*, New Haven: Yale University, 1955.
71. Alfred Korzybski, *Science and Sanity*, Lakeville, Conn.: International Non-Aristotelian Library, 1933, 1948; Wendell Johnson, *People in Quandaries*, New York: Harper, 1946 and Richard W. Budd, "General Semantics: An Approach to Human Communication," *Approaches to Human Communication*, Rochelle Park, N.J.: Hayden Book Co., 1972.

72. Lee Thayer, "On Human Communication and Social Development," a paper presented at the first World Conference on Social Communication for Development, Mexico City, March, 1970.
73. Jose M. R. Delgado, *Physical Control of the Mind*, New York: Harper and Row, 1969 especially Ch. 5–7. See "Neurophysiology: An Approach to Human Communication," *Approaches to Human Communication*, Rochelle Park, N.J.: Hayden Book Co., 1972.
74. Peter Berger and Thomas Luckman, *The Social Construction of Reality*, Garden City: Doubleday, 1966; and Peter Berger, *The Sacred Canopy*, Garden City, Doubleday 1969, Ch. 1.
75. *Cf.* Anatol Rapoport, "Man—The Symbol-User," *Communication: Ethical and Moral Issues*, Lee Thayer, ed., New York: Gordon and Breach, 1973.
76. *Cf.* Erving Goffman, *Relations in Public*, New York: Basic Books, 1971. Ch. 1.
77. A phrase for which I am indebted to David Davidson.
78. *Cf.* Hugh D. Duncan, *Symbols in Society*, London: Oxford University, 1968. *Communication and Social Order*, Oxford University, 1962, and *Symbols and Social Theory*, New York: Oxford University, 1969.
79. *Cf.* Anatol Rapoport, "Man, The Symbol-User," *Communication: Ethical and Moral Issues*, New York: Gordon and Breach, 1973.
80. Lower-order animals function in some rather sophisticated multi-individual collectivities, but the nature of those organizations and the requisite individual roles are usually genetically predetermined and highly predictable. In contradistinction, human communication makes possible—in fact requires—active participation in these processes.
81. *Cf.* Herbert Blumer, *Symbolic Interactionism*, Englewood Cliffs: Prentice-Hall, 1969 and "Symbolic Interaction: An Approach to Human Communication," *Approaches to Human Communication*, Rochelle Park, N.J.: Hayden Book Co.
82. *Cf.* Paul Watzlawick et al., *Pragmatics of Human Communication*, New York: Norton, 1967; R. D. Laing, *The Politics of Experience*, London: Penguin, and Thomas Szasz, *The Manufacture of Madness*, New York: Harper and Row, 1970. An interesting example of the point was provided at an annual conference of the American Psychological Association, held in April 1974, where by a majority vote, it was determined that homosexuality is no longer an illness.
83. *Cf.* Erving Goffman, *Relations in Public*, New York: Basic Books, 1971, Ch. 2.
84. *Cf.* Christian Norberg-Schulz, *Existence, Space and Architecture*, New York: Praeger, 1971 and *Shelter: The Cave Re-examined*, Don Fabun, Beverly Hills: Glencoe Press, 1971.
85. *Cf.* Albert Upton, *Design for Thinking*, Stanford: Stanford University Press, 1961 and *Creative Analysis* (with Richard W. Samson), New York: E. P. Dutton, 1961.
86. *Cf.* Alfred G. Smith, in "Anthropology: An Approach to Human Communication," and Bent Stidsen, "Economics: An Approach to Human Communication," *Approaches to Human Communication*, Rochelle Park, N.J.: Hayden Book Co., 1972.

87. *Cf.* Magorah Maruyama, "Metaorganization of Information," *General Systems Yearbook,* Society for General Systems Research, Vol. XI, 1966.
88. *Cf.* Wendell Johnson and Dorothy Moeller, *Coping With Change,* New York: Harper and Row, 1972, pp. 3–55, a discussion of "scientific" versus "magic" explanation. For an exploration of religious explanations, see Peter Berger, *The Sacred Canopy,* Garden City: Doubleday, 1969.
89. *Cf.* Richard W. Budd, "General Semantics: An Approach to Human Communication," *Approaches to Human Communication,* Rochelle Park, N.J.: Hayden Book Co., 1972.

On the Mass Media and Mass Communication: Notes Toward a Theory

It is necessary to understand the meaning of terms such as "media," "mass communication," "mediated communication," and "interpersonal communication." Adequate definitions help clarify the processes and concepts central to the study of human communication. Lee Thayer provides some operational definitions that clarify the "basic dynamic" of mass communication, i.e., the uses to which each of us put the media and their fare. He describes five major ways we use the mass media and the resultant effects upon the media themselves. Perhaps you have always thought of the mass media as affecting people—most persons do. Try the opposite: what are your *uses* of media?

Some Preliminary Definitions

Definitions do not make a theory, of course. But some preliminary redefinitions of terms consistent with the preceding analysis may help to set the stage for an alternative conceptual framework.

Media

By the term *media,* we should be referring to *all* of the means—all of the devices, technologies, etc.—utilized for acquiring, storing, transporting, displaying "messages" (i.e., codified data). The human ear is thus a medium, as are human languages.[1] The microscope and the telescope are media. A piece of parchment, like the wall of an inhabited cave, when used to inscribed "messages," is also a medium. Most of the popular media are compounded: radio requires not only the devices which broadcast and which receive codified signals, but the natural "medium" of "air waves." Historically, the most ubiquitous and significant of all of the media have been people themselves: people may be utilized, or utilize themselves, as a *means* of storing, transporting, acquiring, or displaying "messages" presumed to have some potential relevance or meaningfulness for others.

There are many ways of categorizing media. Some we take ourselves to (e.g., museums and churches), others are more portable (e.g., radio, photographs). Some can be privately utilized (e.g., books); others are necessar-

From *Beyond Media: New Approaches to Mass Communication.* Edited by Richard Budd and Brent Rubin. (Rochelle Park, N.J.: Hayden Book Co., 1978.)

ily more public (e.g., circuses[2]). Some are simple (e.g., the human ear, the newspaper); others are compound (e.g., roads and highways, which are used to transport people, who store and transmit "messages," and television, which displays people talking to each other by telephone). But the essential point is that the media include *all* means of acquiring, storing, transporting, or displaying "messages."

Communication Messages and Mass Communication Messages

A communication message is one which is addressed to a specific person or to specific persons who are functionally related to the source in some way. A mass communication message is of the sort: to whom it may concern; the addressees are essentially anonymous; and a mass communication message neither implies nor requires a personal relationship, even though the conventional uses to which people put the media or media fare over time establishes a reciprocal relationship, a special form of "institutionalization" which will be discussed below. A piece of mail addressed to John Jones by a friend or a legitimate creditor is a communication message. A piece of mail in his mail box addressed to "Occupant" or to "John Jones" from someone unknown and unrelated is a mass communication message. By its nature, a television network cannot transport communication messages; it can transport only mass communication messages. The telephone and telegraph systems, like the postal system, can transport either kind of message. The ultimate distinction between the two is this: a communication message involves two or more people reciprocally, and in terms of their relationship; a mass communication message is of the sort: to whom it may concern; it is impersonal in the sense that either or both the source and the consumer are anonymous.

A weakness of existing formulations is the typical assumption that non-mediated (e.g., "face-to-face") communication is always personal, while mediated communication is generally impersonal. A letter or telephone call between friends is certainly mediated; but it can be extremely personal. On the other hand, the ritual pleasantries we exchange at cocktail parties, although "face-to-face," are typically impersonal, such "messages" as "The weather has certainly been unusual," or "Hello, how are you?" can be addressed to anyone who cares to listen; they are therefore essentially impersonal, in the manner of "to whom it may concern."

Communication Media and Mass Communication Media

Whether a given medium is a communication medium or a mass communication medium therefore depends entirely upon how it is used. By their nature, some are more "usable" one way than the other. For example, the print and electronic media may lend themselves more to the transport and display of mass communication messages. While the major use of the telephone is for the transport of communication messages, it can be used the other way too. Film may be used to transport a movie to be viewed by millions; or it can be used to capture a special moment having special meaning for only one or two people—as when an absent lover sends a picture of himself. Memos between two principals of the "Watergate affair" may have been a communication medium prior to the investigation; but, if read by others, they become a mass communication medium.

So the distinction between the two is neither a dichotomous nor a mutually exclusive one. Entertainment media typically become more specialized over time by the uses to which their audiences put them. Specialized media having specifiable audiences are somewhere in the middle of the continuum from the exclusively personal to the indiscriminately impersonal.

Any means of storing or transporting or displaying what people say is a communication medium. The distinction is not in the technologies used, but in the uses to which they are put. Using two-way television for personal conversations in lieu of using the telephone doesn't alter the devices used: it merely alters their use.

Communication Networks and Mass Communication Networks

A much more important distinction, theoretically, is that between a communication network and a mass communication network. A communication network emerges from people talking to each other about matters that make a difference to them. It connects or links people functionally "in series." A mass communication network is superimposed or overlaid on existing communication networks (*viz.*, social structure) to the extent made possible by the available technology. It networks or connects people nonfunctionally "in parallel." *What is* and *what matters*—indeed, all human reality, all human values—are products of communication networks. There is more to be aware of in our physical and social environments than we could possibly be aware of; there is more to be known than we can possibly know. One function of a communication network is to sort out what we need to be aware of from what we don't, and what we need to know from what we don't. The mass media and their fare are ultimately no more than a part of our social environment. What aspects of that fare we need to be aware of depends generally upon who we talk to; what we need to know of what is provided by a mass communication network depends generally upon the communication networks to which we belong. In a free society, the relationship between people and the mass communication media is the same as that between people and their communication media—adaptive, emergent, and evolving. Therefore, the more subcultures (communication networks) there are in a given society, and the more heterogeneous they are, the more "selectivity" there is or the more specialized the mass communication media become. The demise of *Life* was but one of a long list of examples in recent U.S. history of what happens when a "something-for-everyone" medium fails to adapt to changing social conditions. Would the disciples of the cause → effect approach want to argue in this case that the "effect" of *Life* was to kill its audience?

Mediators

A mediator is someone who, intentionally or not, mediates for others some world, some domain of existence, some knowledge, etc., which is presently or permanently inaccessible to those others. Parents are, of necessity, mediators of the adult world for their children. Teachers are, by choice, mediators of knowledge and value for their pupils; priests are the mediators of other worlds for their parishioners, as movie and television and stage stars are for their followers, as sports or music celebrities are for their publics, as reporters and broadcasters are for their audiences, and as scientists are for laymen.

The nature of the relationship between a mediator and his constituency is such that what he says or how he acts about those inaccessible worlds he is mediating cannot be directly verified by those who, by necessity or by choice, comprise that constituency. Whether what we take to be public beliefs about "the Establishment" or about "Hollywood" are well-grounded or not cannot be decided by direct inspection. They can be validated only in communication with other persons, and these are typically other members of the same constituency. Whether a given public's image of the President is truly "accurate" cannot in fact be determined; it is acceptable as "true" to me or to you to the extent that its relevance to others confirms that image. "Is it true? Is it true that President Kennedy was shot?" was the question that was asked of millions by millions. There were, of course, the radio and television and newspaper "reports." But did the event in fact occur? And, if so, what does it *mean?* When we cannot see for ourselves, and often even when we can, we can determine the truth and the relevance and the *human* meaning of something or some event only by talking to each other. What the child's mother or teacher tells him about sex may be interesting; but is it *true?* For this, most children must turn to their peers.

Mediators may create, in what they say or what they do, some possibilities. But the social significance and the social reality—whether of Vietnam or Santa Claus—has to be created by those for whom given social realities have reliable social utility. Thus the distinction between "reality" and myth is a blurred one. The beliefs and opinions of various publics about Vietnam, like the beliefs and opinions of various publics about the sex lives of movie stars, emerge not directly out of what our mediators of those worlds say and do, but out of the ways in which we talk to other people about those worlds. The assumption made—whether by reporters or researchers or parents or preachers—that what we say as mediators of an inaccessible world determines the image that people will have of it, or the opinions they will develop about it, is a grossly naive one. The opinions and images that various publics hold of mediated worlds are products not of what mediators say, but of the ways in which their constituents come to talk about what those mediators say.

It will occasionally be useful to distinguish two kinds of mediators. There are *instrumental* mediators—those who perform their function more or less anonymously. There are also *consummatory* mediators—those who mediate other worlds for us by embodying those other worlds. The local weather forecaster reports the weather news; Jane Fonda *is* news. An instrumental mediator is one *through* whom we are enabled to see or vicariously experience other worlds which are at least at that moment inaccessible to us. A consummatory mediator is one *in* whom we see and vicariously experience those other worlds. The consummatory mediator is a celebrity; the instrumental mediator is a functionary. The two are not mutually exclusive; many mediators, for example parents, function as a little of both. But, in the extreme, the distinction is useful. For example, the industries which arise around the revelation of the lives of celebrities may be economically far more important than what the celebrity actually does. For example, the President of the United States has a fixed salary. But the time and money invested in reporting on and reading and hearing and talking about the President undoubtedly runs to many times what the President makes.

Consummatory mediators are *institutionalized*—taken together with their constituencies and the beliefs and images that their constituencies have of them, the whole is as much a social institution as any other. Bob Hope is an American institution; can you imagine how difficult it would be for most people to take him seriously at the opening of his regular "specials"? Or how difficult it would be for us to accept Doris Day as a serious character actress? Or to accept the Pope as a practical joker? Or one's own parents as being lascivious?

The Basic Dynamic

The basic dynamic in the phenomena of mass communication, the pivotal mechanism out of which all else evolves, is not the technology, awesome as that has become. Nor is it the "message," or the implicit culture imparted in the "content" of the media. Nor is it the "effects" which the media are purported to have. The basic mechanism inheres in the *social and personal uses* to which people put the media and their fare.[3] It is this basic dynamic which any relevant theory of mass communication will have to be based upon.

The historically and theoretically significant phenomenon, and the measurable and explicable one, is not that of the "effects" of the media on people, but that of the effects *on* the media of the *uses* to which people put the media and their fare.[4] Books, as such, have had no measurable effect upon people, for example; but the uses to which books have been put by people have altered the structure of that industry over the years, and have had identifiable social and human consequences. So it has been with radio, and with movies and museums and the greeting card and recording industries. The change and evolution of mass communication systems in the context of particular societies, and the change and evolution of particular human societies networked by certain kinds of mass communication systems having certain kinds of characteristics: these are matters of central theoretical importance. And they can be validly approached only from this point of departure: that the basic dynamic is the uses to which people put the media and their fare. All the rest is incidental to this.

The producers and distributors of mass communication messages can and do use the media for the transportation and display of those messages. But in the same way that "I love you" has no relevance for the people involved apart from the ways in which it is taken into account by people. And our ways of taking mass communication messages into account hinge generally upon the personal and social uses to which they can be put.

Uses of the Mass Media and Their Fare

The uses to which people put the mass media and their fare, in approximately descending order of importance or magnitude, are these:

1. The primary use to which people put the media and their fare is that of providing something to talk about in ritual, non-vital encounters with other people. The more complex and the more mobile a society, the more frequent are such encounters, and hence the more functional the media and their fare. Betrand de Jouvenel wrote:

> The more society is mixed, the more a man needs to know what to expect of the unlike-seeming stranger. He needs security for and against the behavior of another.[5]

Using media fare as something to talk about provides just this kind of security. People who live in relatively non-complex, non-mobile societies have little occasion to use the media and their fare in this way, except perhaps for the purpose of talking to an occasional tourist or anthropologist from this culture! Thus having a radio or a television has a quite different meaning for such people than it does for us. A businessman drawn into a casual conversation with a tourist in a Hong Kong bar will need to know the current ball standings, the current "front page news," the names of the characters in the currently "in" TV programs (e.g., Archie Bunker), or something of that sort which would serve as a basis for the conversation. Wherever you go today, whether to your own village or shopping center, or to any of the world's cities, it will be possible to talk with almost anyone about current news events or media celebrities, in the same way that we use talk about the weather to ease through such ritual encounters. And the fact that people can talk to each other without threat using media fare as a basis has some very real consequences for what media producers can and cannot do, as we shall see below. So this primary use that people make of media fare—that it gives them something to talk about—is not trivial; it is, in fact, of major theoretical import.

2. The second use to which people put the mass media and their fare, in order of importance or magnitude, is as the central component of personal identity or reality *rituals*. There are two aspects of this use that deserve attention. First, more than is often recognized, the routinization of our lives around certain regular, predictable happenings on a day-to-day basis is crucial to the maintenance of a sense of personal identity. The marking of time by certain rituals is common to people in every culture.

Those who have the media available for such rituals can use them in this way: I know it's Saturday (or whenever) because "All in the Family" is on tonight. "You know I don't like to talk in the morning until after I've had a chance to look at the paper." There is "travelling music" and special traffic news during commuters' hours, silence in church, the indestructibility of Little Orphan Annie, the unchanging pulchritude of Daisy Mae, and the "profundity" of Peanuts. There is the "six o'clock news" which reliably comes on at six o'clock and structures that end of the day. There is knowing what to expect in the latest issue of your favorite magazine, with only the details to be filled in. And there is listening to (but not hearing) the "top forty" pop records over and over again for several days in a row. And so on. We need to know that we're in a structural and predictable world, and that the world is as we remembered or expected. The media and their fare can go far toward providing such props for our personal identity rituals.

There is another aspect to the ritual uses of the media and their fare. To the extent that we have our sense of being "in" the world through being like "others" and doing as "others" do, we will feel constrained to attend to the media and their fare according to our beliefs about how "others" are attending to the media and their fare. To the extent that we believe "everyone else" takes a daily newspaper, and to the extent that being like "everyone else" is vital to our own sense of being "in" the world, we will go through the ritual of "taking" a daily newspaper. If large numbers of people believed that "everyone else" attended a museum once a week, more people than now do so would go through the ritual of attending a museum. Suffering the nth repetition of a "top ten" tune being played that day, young people are no longer hearing it; they are performing a ritual— one which keeps each one tacitly in touch with all the "others."

Thus there comes to be a structuring of the media and their fare more or less consistent with the structure of the lives of those who use them in similar ritualistic ways. We speak of "curling up" with a good book. And most people comprehend the image of watching the late night television shows over one's bare feet. There are sermons on Sunday, but rarely any lectures. People go to see movies that other people are going to see, with likely little or no thought as to real personal preferences. Expressions like "Would you believe?" become public rituals.

In a complex society, these rituals are more and more frequently identification rituals for those who belong to the same "epistemic communities" or the same "interest groups" or the same "communication networks."

But there are still some which are more national in scope. What adults in the U.S. do not feel a stirring of emotion when witnessing a colorful street parade? In 1973, what American could afford not to know *something* about the Watergate "scandal," even though he may have had no vital interest in it one way or the other?

All such rituals in which we engage the media and their fare provide us a sense of reality, and of being "in" the world with others, which is the only way we *can* be "in" the world. What is real to people, and what is indispensable to their sense of being "in" the world is of fundamental theoretical importance. The fact that what is real to people and what is indispensable to their sense of being "in" the world more and more involves ritual uses of the media and their fare makes it no less important.

3. The third use to which people put the media and their fare is the *mythical*. There are three levels at which this use of the media and their fare can be observed.

First, because no "recipes" for living are given in man's genes—as they are totally or largely given for all of the other creatures of the earth—these "recipes" have to be created and perpetuated in some way. No one of us can for long go without a feeling that our way of living is reasonable, just, proper, and "right." Whether in matters of morality, esthetic sensitivity, value, ideology, or of just everyday comportment, we need to be able to find in our social and/or physical surroundings some regular confirmation for our own "recipes" for living. All cultural and subcultural "recipes" for living are like myths: they are created and sustained by tacit covenant[6] and behavior. They are not absolute. Nor is there any ultimate test of their "rightness" beyond self-affirmation. To the extent that such cultural or subcultural "recipes" for living are functional and operative, they must be pervasive in that culture or subculture. Those "recipes," or aspects of them, must pervade what the members of that culture or subculture do and do not do, the manner in which they do and do not behave, the way they invent and deploy their artifacts and technologies, the stories they tell and the generic beliefs they hold, and so on. Thus, to the extent there are operative cultural "recipes" for living, they will be, covertly or overtly, intentionally or inadvertently, built into the fare of the mass media.[7] And we will sense them there; we will find there confirmation of the "recipes" for living by which we are guided, and we will find there alternative recipes for living, some of which may be feasible, as well as others we can only fantasize about. We may be surprised to learn that the Russian people are not that much different from us. But most of us can only fantasize about the "recipes" by which native islanders of the South Seas or the "beautiful people" of the "jet set" live.

Second, there are many aspects of our human existences which can be explained *only* by metaphor or myth. Humans are by nature the only creatures on earth who must explain the inexplicable. How are we to explain just what we are, where we came from, where we are going? How are we to comprehend death? Or life? Or love? These are questions whose ultimate and absolute answers must seemingly be always just out of reach. What we don't or can't know, we make up; myths undergird the existences or people of every culture.[8] Watts defined myth as follows: "Myth is to be defined as a complex of stories—some no doubt fact, and some fantasy—which, for various reasons, human beings regard as demonstrations of the inner meaning of the universe and of human life."[9] Again, to the extent these myths are cultural, they will necessarily be pervasive, and largely covert or tacit. Those who create and produce the fare of the mass media will not be able to avoid imbuing what they do with cultural myth. And those who consume the media and their fare will not be able to avoid finding in that fare some confirmation—or disconfirmation—of the "recipes" upon which their ways of seeing and knowing and being are based.

Third, neither of these mythical uses of the mass media and their fare is limited to "content." To the contrary, it seems altogether likely that the "deeper" and hence the more influential myths are sensed not in the "content" of the myriad of "messages" and "stories" to which the average person in the U.S. subjects himself every day, but in their individual structure and their aggregate patterning.[10] For example, it has been suggested that advertising (always good news) represents heaven, juxtaposed with "the news" (almost always bad news) which represents hell. The "story" which embodies the cultural myth of the western hero is not to be found so much in the plot or even in the theme, but in the structure of the action. And there is presently some research into the structure of the total pattern of television programming as being the mythically important aspect of television.[11] Whatever the outcome of these more contemporary approaches to the study of myth, it is clear that the most fundamental cultural myths are codified in the *patterns* of the things we say and do, and that being socialized into one culture rather than another means that we are empowered to "read" the patterns of our own culture and thus nurture those guiding and orienting myths within ourselves. To the extent that these patterns or "structures" get codified in the media or their fare, people will be able to "read" them there, and to use them for the purposes to which all cultural myths are put.

4. People use the fare of the mass media also for the purpose of providing varied experiences. In their book, *The Functions of Varied Experience,* Fiske and Maddi conclude that there are three broad positive functions of variation in experience: (a) it contributes to the normal development and to the normal functioning of organisms; (b) it is sought out for its own sake; and (c) it is one factor contributing to the affective state of human beings.[12] Some of this seeking out or "tuning in" may derive from pure curiosity—from a sheer curiosity to know what's "there" or what's "going on." Such curiosity may or may not be socially-inspired, may or may not be expected to produce socially-useful experiences or knowledge. But, just as the laboratory rat which explores a maze out of curiosity, then learns how to "run it" in order to reach food at the other end, the varied experience that one has in exploring the fare of the mass media out of curiosity becomes a part of that person and therefore has potential utility for personal ritual or as social currency.

Perhaps the major impetus behind this particular use of the fare of the mass media, however, is that of *compensation.* Although we all work out individual patterns, our psychological and social equilibrium depends upon compensating for too much, *or too little,* uncertainty, chance, risk, variety, etc.[13] There are many activities which we can turn to for such compensation: drinking, wilderness vacations, hobbies, eating, travelling, etc. To achieve that pattern of stimulation which, intuitively at least, seems "right" to use individually, we turn to what is available. The more available the fare of the mass media, the more possibilities there are for more people to use the media and their fare to compensate for too much, or too little, uncertainty, chance, riskiness, variety, etc., in the balance of their lives. This use of the media and their fare is related to people's individual life patterns, and not to any particular set of demographic factors, such as age or income level. A highly paid executive might be as bored with his everyday life as a housewife might be with hers. Yet their compensatory uses of media fare, or of any other compensatory activities, are not a function of "boredom" as such, but of the total life patterns of the two particular individuals. The fact that it is presumed to be "manly" in the U.S. to be interested in certain sports should not, therefore, be viewed as "mass" compensation or as a sufficient explanation of why more men than women watch professional football on television; different viewers may be putting this "same" fare to different uses. Or, to take another, perhaps too obvious example, the subscribers and readers of *Playboy* magazine do not constitute a homogeneous audience, except perhaps in a very naive microeconomic sense. Different subscribers and readers put *Playboy* to different uses. Some may use it as a status prop; others for purpose of phantasy; still others as a basis for confirming "nonconventional" values; and so on. It makes considerable theoretical difference whether we differentiate audiences by use rather than, for example, age or geographic location or social position, as is customarily done.

All audiences and all consumer aggregates of media fare are thus self-selecting. If a medium or one of its products were to be said to have an "effect" on people, it would have to have that "effect" on a *random* sampling of people. If the "effect" is discernible only in the case of a self-selected audience or consumer aggregates, the direction of the "effect" is the other way around. It is the *uses* to which people put the media and their fare that differentiates audiences and consumer aggregates, not demographic "variables" and not the "content" of that fare or the static "personality characteristics" of the people involved.

5. People make other uses of the media and their fare, certainly. A television set may be used as a status symbol; a head-set radio to isolate oneself from the rest of the world aurally; a library as a place to sleep or meet; a particular stereo amplifier or a trip to a particular art gallery for prestige; a highway as a challenge; a book to press leaves or a newspaper to wrap garbage; a particular magazine dropped on a suburban coffee table for snob appeal; a greeting card to hide indifference or inarticulateness; and so on and on. The "hardware" can be put to many diverse uses, in the same way that the "software" can be put to many diverse uses by people in the context of their personal and social existences.

People do use the media as a source of information for purchases they are going to make, have just made, or might make. There is the housewife whose primary use of the newspaper is that of clipping supermarket or other sale ads. There is the fellow who carefully reads advertisements for a certain Chevrolet automobile or a certain tour because he has just bought one. And there are those who use certain media as a source of information about next fall's or next spring's fashions—whether in clothing, party-giving, travel, reading, or office decor.

People use the media as a source of information about work- or hobby- or leisure-time-related interests. There is the executive who scans particular newspapers for news and ideas pertinent to his company. There are those who have a low attention threshold for ideas about golfing or wood-working or skydiving or mink-breeding or baby-raising or car repair, whatever the medium. And there are those who gain access to diffused subcultures like recreational vehicle owners by paying attention to media fare on that subject.

Some people may use media fare for educational purposes. This is not related to enterprises like "educational television," which serves mainly the purposes of those who make their living in it, or in related industries (e.g., "educational technology," which is a euphemism for all kinds of products and services that are sold primarily to schools and to "educators" and not to students). Rather, this refers to the *systematic* use of the media as a means of carrying out one's own educational plans and goals. Someone who could not afford books, for example, might set out to become an Elizabethan scholar by using the public libraries. Or, one might invest his time in media fare on the basis of his intent to become an expert on public affairs. It has been said that only about 15 percent of the people in the U.S. *can* learn from books. Whether it is the same 15 percent who *could* learn from television or from museums, or some other 15 percent of the people, remains to be determined. In any case, this use of the media is relatively minor.

And people do, of course, sometimes use media fare for purposes of pure entertainment. But in the overall view, this is also a relatively minor use of media fare, contrary to much popular belief. For a media experience to be used as sheer entertainment, it would have to remain personal. The experience would have to be the end in itself. When one talks to others about media fare, he is using it not only as "entertainment," but for social purposes or ends as well; and the latter may be the more important. We may "enjoy" a movie; but most people sooner or later talk to others about the movie's relevance, its "truth," its artistry, its "meaning," or its quality relative to other movies made by the same director or producer. Americans give considerable lip service to the value of communication "work" over communication "play." Regardless, almost, of how we may individually use television fare, we find it easy to agree that there should be "better" television programs. When you ask people how "good" television is in their part of the country or their part of the world, they will most likely describe to you the public affairs programs, the documentaries, the differ-ent ethnic programs, and the like. But if you ask them what they in fact "watch," you hear a different description. Given the alternative, a majority of Britons seem to prefer cops-and-robbers shows to ballet, domestic comedy to news analysis. Even so, there is no basis for assuming that "Gun-smoke" is entertainment and that a documentary is not. People can use either one in many ways. And it is these uses which define mass communication systems, mass communication audiences, and future alternatives, not arbitrary form or "content" classifications.

The several uses of the media and their fare described here do not exhaust the possibilities, of course. Nor are such uses mutually exclusive. One may put media fare to several uses simultaneously. And consumer uses of media fare are not always obvious or specific. We may not even be aware of the uses to which we put the media and their fare. And certainly the importance of one use relative to another may change over time. Nevertheless, for all such reservations and qualifications, the key to any empirically-sound theories or generalizations about mass communication lies not in the "effects" which the media have on people, but in the uses to which people put the media and media fare.

Institutionalization of Media and Media Fare

The uses to which people put the media and media fare have consequences for the future possibilities of those media and their fare. This is a condition of social life, it is a condition of social order. From a casual friendship to the largest, most complex human society, there must be order, structure. And this order or structure comes from the reliable expectations people have about how other people are going to behave. It comes from being able to depend upon what one expects, whether of other people, of one-self, or of things. Out of necessity for their own continuity, people base their lives on the dependability of their conceptions of the world. How we conceive of tables and cabbages may be as important socially as how we conceive of ideas and kings. The only difference is that, as far as we know, it doesn't make any difference to the table how we conceive of it. But it does make a difference to other people how we conceive of them. If other people don't behave according to our expectations, we have no way of relating to them. And this is as true for every other person as it is for us.

For example, someone in a community who has come to be known as the "town gossip" over a period of time will be expected by people who "know" this to continue providing "the gossip." If for some reason the "gossip's" resources dry up, or if he or she wishes to change from that expected role in the community, it will be at the considerable peril of losing the security of a known role and a reliable set of expectations; and this would threaten the psychological continuity of those people who had these expectations as much as it would the psychological continuity of the one "known" as the "gossip." Our expectations of others over time serve to *institutionalize* our relationships with them. It happens with husbands and wives. They come to expect certain behaviors of one another, and these expectations function as real constraints on the other. Husbands and wives *institutionalize* their relationships with each other. Or, consider the case of Joe Namath: it is conceivable that he could revert to a withdrawing, family-man type of role if he wanted to; but who could accept that image immediately beyond those who didn't already "know" who he is? We who "know" him have *institutionalized* him. We get impatient quickly with an automobile we have come to expect to start easily; we have more patience with one which we are less familiar with, in the same way that we have less patience with the unexpected behavior of others we "know" well than we would have with the unexpected behavior of strangers. We want the world to fit our expectations of it, and most of us are ready most of the time to exert whatever influence we can to *make* the world fit our expectations of it, for good or ill, right or wrong.

It is so for all humans in all human societies, and it is so in our relationships with the media and their fare. The crux of the matter is this: The conventional uses to which the media and media fare are put by people *over time* constitute an *institutionalization* of those media and of that fare. That is, when the uses to which people put particular media and particular fare become an integral part of their everyday lives, or an integral part of the basis on which people relate to each other over time, then those media and that fare have become institutionalized. When we can take our expectations for granted, we are relying upon a social institution. Joe Namath is a social institution, in much the same way that "the news" is a social institution; what we get is what we expect, and what we expect is what we get.

Consider ball game scores or stock market reports. If it becomes conventional for people to use this information as a basis for starting or sustaining a conversation (in a bar, a subway or train, or barber shop, etc.), then such "knowledge" has social utility. And this social utility can be exploited by an enterprising mediator. A Picasso exhibit may draw some who are just curious; but what makes such an exhibit economically feasible or practical are those for whom "knowing about" and talking about Picasso and his paintings has social utility—i.e., those who can be expected to *use* the occasion as a basis for talking to each other, or in some other way having social currency. The daily or hourly repetition of the top ten popular tunes provides listeners with something they can use: it confirms their expectations and hence serves as a kind of identity ritual. Then there is "the news." For the most part, "the news" has to be what people expect; it has to provide assurance that what they are talking about is what they should be talking about, because it is what "people" are talking about. Anything truly novel or "new" and unexpected has unknown social currency; perhaps none. Thus broadcasting or printing much that is really "new" or unexpected or unassessable in terms of its social currency would be an extremely high-risk venture, both for the broadcaster or editor, and for the consumer. Neither the economics nor the politics of the mass media can stand very much real "news." You can bet that the ABC, CBS, and NBC evening "news" will cover the same "news" in essentially the same order. This is due to no conscious conspiracy. The more people who get the same "news," even on different channels, the more assurance we can have as individuals that we really got "the news"—and that what we now "know" about what is going on is what we *need* to "know."

Examples are legion. The central theoretical issue, however, is this: The conventional ways in which people over time come to use places and people and ideas and things—including media and media fare—constitute a mutual constraint on both producer and consumer, both source and audience.[14] The producer is constrained to deploy the media and to produce that fare which people have a use for, when and where and how they have come to use the media and their fare. And users are reciprocally constrained by the ways in which particular personal and social "usefulnesses" are built into and out of the particular media and media fare available. This reciprocally-constraining system is never perfect, of course. The producer may misinterpret user interest or expectation. Or, the producer may be moved, for whatever reason, to produce something which he thinks people *ought* to have available. The producers of media fare do not live by bread alone, any more than do the consumers. Sometimes they simply experiment. These and other "imperfections" on the producer's side keep the system from being perfect. So, too, do users upset the inertia in the system. People are sometimes "obstinate."[15] They don't always react to media fare in the way even seasoned producers of that fare expect them to react. People may not always pay attention to what would be in their own best interest. Sometimes people will listen to what they "ought" to know about; and sometimes they won't. And, as consumers of the media and their fare, people are sometimes apparently just "fickle." Just when they seem to have taken a program or a feature or a new celebrity or some "current event" to their hearts, the affair may be over as quickly and as inexplicably as it started, and they begin to warm up to some new celebrity or some new cause [16] or Social Issue or some new feature. Even "Peanuts" no longer has the same appeal to the same people it once had, and "Star Trek" and the original "Laugh In" are now history. The "ecological crisis" has apparently given way to the "energy crisis" and this to the "Watergate crisis." Just as there are fashions in the way bathrooms are used, there are fashions in the usefulness of media fare. There are those people who don't know what they want in the fare of the media, simply because they are uncertain about the social currency it might have for them. Sometimes users don't go at all for the obvious. On other occasions they go overboard for the inobvious in what they buy or use. Who would have predicted the "hoola hoop" craze? Thus there are a great many imperfections in this reciprocally-constraining system, and this contributes to its continuous evolution and change. The mutual constraints which tend to "close" the system and to bring it into the perpetual equilibrium of perfect redundancy also provide for the dialectics of change. People want the security of the familiar and the routine and the predictable. But they also want the stimulation of the unfamiliar, the nonroutine, and the unpredictable. We want sameness; but we want some variety and change too—in our media fare as in other aspects of our lives.

The reaction of people to something truly novel cannot, of course, be predicted. And what is at work in the emergence or the decline of a current public fashion—whether in topical interests or clothes or media fare—is a set of variables so complex, so self-determining, that the particulars cannot be predicted. In the same way that the most accurate prediction we can make of tomorrow's weather is that it will be the same as today's, the most reliable prediction anyone can make about public tastes in media fare tomorrow is that they will be the same as today. This is why there is so much imitation and redundancy in programming, advertising, book publishing, songwriting, and so on. It is not that the producers conspire to present more of the same or similar media fare. It is that nothing succeeds like success. Except within very minor variations on already institutionalized themes, programs, formats, etc., the producers of media fare cannot predict what will appeal to consumers, and sometimes not even then. So when something seems to be "going," people get on the bandwagon, producer and consumer alike. An art exhibitor has some basis for calculating the appeal of a Renoir exhibit. He has no basis for predicting the public appeal of a totally unknown painter (unless, of course, there is already an audience institutionalized around the value of going only to exhibits of unknown painters, which happens). This is not "crassness" on the part of the exhibitor. He is constrained as much by the system as are those to whom he exhibits. People go to a Renoir exhibit because other people go. They don't go to the exhibits of painters to which no one else goes. This is as true in those nations where the media and the arts are mainly tax-supported as it is in the U.S., where they are not. The exhibitor might be a philanthropist, however; he might undertake to exhibit the work of un-known painters simply because he believed it would be "good" for people to look at something different for a change. But if no one came, then no one else would come; and our altruistic exhibitor would thereby be jeop-ardizing the future possibilities of the very work he wanted to make known.

These are not trivial matters. All of this is in the nature of the conditions of everyday social life. These conditions are not different elsewhere simply because of a different political or economic suasion. The constraints of social institutionalization are real, and they are significant. *Any* sensed threat to an institutional relationship—any threat to the conventional uses (or non-uses) to which people put other people and the artifacts of their en-vironment—is a threat not just to that relationship. It is a threat to the very existences of the people involved, sometimes minor, sometimes major. Every human existence hinges upon the conventional, institutionalized re-lationships that obtain between and among individuals in their environ-ments over time. Without these, we could not have human existence as we know it. So when we speak of the institutionalization of, for example, a television star, we are not talking about whimsy. We are talking about the fundamental stuff of social life. And that is not trivial. In the same way that social order depends upon the reliable continuity of most of the peo-ple of that society, the reliable continuity of every individual depends upon social order. And the ways in which we institutionalize media fare as a part of that predictable social order is just as important to our existences as the conventional uses to which we put other people and the other arti-facts of our environment.

What could be more traumatizing than to discover one day that every-thing one "knew" about what-is-going-on had no social currency at all, that what one "knew" seemed totally irrelevant to what everyone else was talking about, and that what everyone else was talking about seemed strange and without any personal relevance? The fact that this does not occur gives ample evidence of the underlying social processes at work. What has personal or social utility for us establishes real constraints on what it is feasible or possible for the producers of media fare to provide us. And what is provided places limits on what can be found in media fare having personal or social utility.

We create these mutually-constraining systems through our conventional uses of the media and media fare over time. The uses to which people put the media and media fare in their everyday personal and social activities serve to institutionalize particular media and particular media fare in particular ways. The time and the place and the manner of institutionalization of media and media fare can no more be predicted than can the time and place and manner of genetic mutation. The specifics of social evolution are as indeterminable as are the specifics of biological evolution. In a totally controlled society, which could exist only hypothetically, the "controllers" might well concern themselves with the achievement of wanted "effects" and with the elimination of unwanted "effects" of the media and media fare. But in a free or "open" society, these are matters which emerge from the social behavior of people in the course of their everyday lives. They are not matters to be decided for them and imposed upon them.

Thus it is that in a free or "open" society the theoretical point of entry is that of the institutionalization of the uses to which people put the media and media fare.

• • •

The Proliferation of Publics

The greater the variety of alternative media or media fare, the more audiences there will emerge. And, the more audiences or publics there are, the more alternative possibilities there are for the media and for media fare. But this differentiation is essentially from within. It is not unlike the literacy problem. Producing and distributing more different kinds of books will not necessarily increase the literacy of a society-at-large. But it will go hand in hand with a further differentiation of the existing book-reading public into several specialized audiences, with some attributing more "significance" or value or usefulness to biographies, others to fiction, others to documentaries, and so on. Or, to take another example: the more conflicting political points of view made available to a public, the more fragmented that public will likely become. Not all of the alternatives offered will "catch on," but those that do will be given the legitimacy of an audience, and that audience the security of having its differentiated beliefs confirmed and legitimized. What is measurable is that where the media and their fare are more heterogeneous, publics proliferate—and conversely. This raises some intriguing questions about the relationship between the rate of proliferation of publics and social order.

Media Alternatives and Social Order

The more real alternatives there are for people in a given society, the more internally differentiated that society will be. And the more differentiated publics there are in a society, the more possibilities there are for additional variety in ideas, things, tastes, fashions, etc. Where there may have been but one guiding ideology or world-view in earlier societies, one could be either for it or against it. Because he was not *for* the dominant world-view of his time, Galileo was presumed to be *against* it. Where there are alternative world-views espoused by different publics within the same society, one has some choice of which publics to subscribe to. When there was but one type of sword, one either liked it or did not. When a different kind of sword was introduced, there could be factions; there were undoubtedly fights and skirmishes between those who were convinced that the one was better than the other. When there was but one kind of music, or when there was but one music celebrity at a time, it was difficult to get into an argument about which was best; today one can overhear such arguments everywhere. In the early days of television, there was little talk about how "bad" it was; people even sat around watching the test pattern. We may suffer now in the U.S. the consequences of too many alternatives. There could not be differences of opinion if there were not real alternatives for people.

Perhaps what distresses some of the more "intellectual" critics of our present situation is the range of the alternatives, the scope of the choices becoming available to more and more people. Of course television could be "better." It could be "better" in France, too, and in Japan and England. But the question is, better *for whom?* We "intellectuals" *know* that a revered ballet is "better" television fare than a quiz show. We "intellectuals" *know* that a higher ratio of social documentaries to "escape" fare on television would raise social consciousness and improve the lot of people in the process. But we have no evidence of this. Is our dogma less irrational than any one else's? Contrary to current folklore—and this is generally how we deal with the popular media these days, from the current folklore about it—there is some evidence that there is more public affairs broadcasting on television in the U.S. than in England.[17] The B.B.C. may not be the end-all for everyone.

People seek the security of the familiar; but people also seek the stimulation of the novel. The normal individual needs the comfort of the expected; but he also needs the perturbation of the unexpected. We all need certainty. Couple this with the institutionalization of the things we use and the people we see and the talk we engage in every day, and we have that certainty. But we also need variety. Couple this with the technological inventiveness and the affluence of a society such as that of the U.S., and we have that variety, whether in can openers, home music amplifiers, automobiles, spectacles, or television fare.

The more real alternatives there are for people in mass media fare, the more the society becomes differentiated. Yet the more differentiated the society becomes, the more utility there is in the fare of the mass media as a basis for social integration on another level. Another paradox. It is not unlike the process of socialization itself, through that process, we mold new members into cogs that fit the existing social machinery. But through that same process we also necessarily foster and nurture their individuality. The apparent need that people have to differentiate themselves into smaller communities having interests, values, tastes, beliefs, etc., different from other such communities has led in the past to a specialization of the media. *Life*, in attempting to be *something* to *everyone*, failed, as had many other such magazines in the years since World War II. While most of the general "mass" circulation magazines have declined and disappeared, a great many new specialized periodicals have emerged. As such specialization increases, there is a parallel increase in the need for something which would contribute to communication *between* the increasingly specialized or differentiated audiences. Certain media fare—such as "the news," as already suggested—can be used in this way.

In his recent book, *World Communication: Threat or Promise?*, Colin Cherry raises the issue in this way: threat *or* promise?[18] In free societies, if unimpeded by well-intentioned but misguided policy-making, the continuing increase in alternative media and media fare is *both*, both threat *and* promise. It has been both since the first troubadour wandered into a remote village.

And this raises some intriguing questions about the ultimate compatibility of *mass* media and democracy. In his essay *On Liberty*, John Stuart Mill wrote that "The individual must be protected . . . against the tyranny of the prevailing opinion and feelings. . . ." To the extent there are many specialized worlds, not one general one, the individual would thus be protected. But if government policy requires that all television programming, for example, as well as all stations, be "balanced," how are we to maintain our separate worlds? [19]

An approach such as this raises a great many such questions. They cannot all be answered here, if at all. The challenge is that we must learn to think both more substantively and creatively about these issues. Hopefully the approach outlined here makes some small contribution to the possibilities for doing so.

Notes

1. On Languages as media, see Marshall McLuhan, "Myth and Mass Media," in H. A. Murray (ed.), *Myth and Mythmaking* (Boston: Beacon Press, 1968). On the "languages" of the media, see E. Carpenter, "The New Languages," in E. Carpenter and M. McLuhan (eds.), *Explorations in Communication* (Boston: Beacon Press, 1960).
2. See Paul Bouissac, "Poetics in the Lion's Den: The Circus Act as a Text," *Modern Language Notes*, 86:6 (December) 1971.
3. This was the gist of Katz's paper on mass communication research in 1959, and others have argued in this direction, with apparently little or no "effect". In response to the question of what makes a book sell, Charles Darwin replied to Samuel Butler, "Getting talked about is what makes a book sell."
4. This is of course true of all human inventions and artifacts. The wheel as such had no social effects; it was and is the uses to which wheels are put that have had social and human consequences.
5. In *The Art of Conjecture* (New York: Basic Books, 1967).
6. On the relevance of the concept of covenant for this kind of inquiry, see J. F. A. Taylor, *The Masks of Society: An Inquiry into the Covenants of Civilization* (New York: Appleton-Century-Crofts, 1966).
7. For a view of the role of one kind of fare—literature—in this regard, see ch. 5, "Literature and Society," of Leo Lowenthal, *Literature, Popular Culture, and Society* (Englewood Cliffs, N.J.: Prentice-Hall, 1961).
8. See, e.g., J. Campbell, *Myths to Live By* (New York: Viking, 1972); J. G. Frazer, *The Golden Bough* (New York: Macmillan, 1922); O. E. Klapp, *Heroes, Villains, and Fools* (Englewood Cliffs, N.J.: Prentice-Hall, 1962). For a contemporary analysis of the "mythic" function of mass entertainment, *c.f.* E. Morin, *The Stars* (New York: Grove Press, 1960).
9. Alan W. Watts, *Myth and Ritual in Christianity* (London: Macmillan, 1954).
10. *Cf.* Claude Lévi-Strauss, "The Structural Study of Myth," in T. A. Sebeok (ed.), *Myth: A Symposium* (Indiana University Press, 1955); and Roland Barthes, *Mythologies*, Trans. Annette Lavers (New York: Hill & Wang, 1972). For a general overview of the "Structuralist" approach, see Richard T. DeGeorge, *Structuralists: From Marx to Lévi-Strauss* (New York: Anchor Books, 1972). *Cf.* Mircea Eliade, *Myth and Reality* (New York: Harper, 1963).

11. E.g., R. C. Schmidt, "The Mythic Structure of Television Programming," Meeting of the International Communication Association, Montreal, April 1973.

12. Donald W. Fiske and Salvatore R. Maddi, *Functions of Varied Experience* (Homewood, Ill.: Dorsey, 1961), p. 13. If it seems paradoxical that people need both sameness and variety in some dialectical mixture, then it may be.

13. One might compare this with the concepts of *communication-pleasure* and *communication-pain* suggested by the psychiatrist T. A. Szasz in *Pain and Pleasure* (New York: Basic Books, 1957), and extrapolated by William Stephenson in *The Play Theory of Mass Communication* (University of Chicago Press, 1967); but I believe there is more than just "pain" and "pleasure" involved.

14. In "The Communicator and the Audience," *Journal of Conflict Resolution*, 2:1 (1958), pp. 67–77, Raymond Bauer proposes, on the basis of experimental evidence, that (a) images of the audience affect the communicator, and (b) users commit sources to a position.

15. *Cf.* R. A. Bauer, "The Obstinate Audience," *loc. cit.*

16. On the phenomenon of Social Issues in general, with the issue of our ecology as the exemplar, see L. Thayer "Man's Ecology, Ecology's Man," *Main Currents in Modern Thought*, 27:3 (January-February 1971), pp. 71–78.

17. E.g., Karen Possner, "A Comparison of a Week of Television Programming in New York and London," University of Iowa, School of Journalism, (unpublished ms., 1972).

18. (London: Wiley-Interscience, 1971).

19. On the necessity of isolating populations to optimize evolutionary health and vigor, see Garrett Hardin, *Nature and Man's Fate* (New York: Rineheart, 1959). A "global village" as a criterion for the species reflects the hubris and the myopia of technologism.

S. J. BALL-ROKEACH and MELVIN DEFLEUR

A Dependency Model of Mass Media Effects

Do the mass media effect us individually? To the degree that each of us is
dependent on the mass media, to that degree are we shaped as individuals.
Professors Ball-Rokeach and DeFleur claim that modern industrialized, urbanized society has made us all dependent on the media for information, for
news, for social correlation, and for value clarification because we no longer
depend on close communal interpersonal relationships to meet these needs.
What kinds of information can you obtain that is not mediated? Do the mass
media supply you with things to talk about to your friends? Figuring out how
dependent you are on the mass media might enable you to determine how
much they affect your values and your priorities. Read the essays in Section
4, "Media Values and Interpersonal Roles," for another perspective on media
dependency.

Do mass communications have widespread effects on individuals and society or do they have relatively little influence? It seems almost incredible
that after many decades of theorizing and empirical study, media researchers are still typically unable to give a straightforward answer to this
question. While the "hypodermic needle" theory was abandoned long ago
by communications researchers, the public continues to feel that the media
have direct, usually menacing, effects on their audiences. The scientific
community, on the other hand, almost reluctantly leaves the issue of direct
or "magic bullet" effects open because hundreds of studies have failed to
support such a conceptualization.

Research on communication is guided mainly by adaptations or elabora-
tions of learning theories that have emerged from psychological laboratories and animal studies. To a limited extent, sociological theories stressing such concepts as "diffusion" and "primary groups" have also played a
role in the development of communications theory. But the search for
the effects of the media has been guided primarily by conceptualizations
that focus on the stimulus-response probabilities of individuals acting
in a situational field. One generalization that can be drawn from detailed
reviews of such literature (Weiss, 1969) is that audiences frequently en-

From *Communication Research*, vol. 3, #1 (January 1976). © 1976 Sage Publications, Inc.
Reprinted by permission.

counter media messages about which they have preestablished beliefs and norms that are anchored in their group associations and that filter or recreate media messages to conform to the established social realities of the audience. While such generalizations are helpful in understanding the psychological and social processes which act as constraints on media influence, the conceptualizations on which they are based may not be the best guides for studying a complex social process such as mass communication.

It can be suggested that one of the reasons that there is such a lack of clarity as to whether or not the media have effects is that researchers have proceeded from the wrong theoretical conceptualizations to study the wrong questions. A more appropriate theoretical framework for the analysis of media effects originates in the classical sociological literature ranging from Durkheim (1933) to Marx (1961) to Mead (1934). Such literature, while not directly focused on the issue of media effects, encourages treatment of both the media and its audiences as integral parts of a larger social system. Peoples' social realities are regarded as not only a product of their social histories and current systems of symbolic interaction, but also as being fundamentally connected to the structural conditions of the society in which they live. As the social structure becomes more complex, people have less and less contact with the social system as a whole. In other words, they begin to be less aware of what is going on in their society beyond their own position in the structure. The mass media enter as not only economic systems engaged in deliberate attempts to persuade and entertain, but also as information systems vitally involved in maintenance, change, and conflict processes at the societal as well as the group and individual levels of social action.[1]

Thus, if one hopes to account for changes in the cognitive, affective, or behavioral aspects of people's social realities brought about by mass communicated information, one must take into account the interrelationships between audiences, media, and society. It is not sufficient to attempt to account for media alteration effects solely in terms of the audiences's psychological characteristics, prior socialization, on-going groups associations, or their social characteristics.

Mass communication, in other words, involves complex relationships between large sets of interacting variables that are only crudely designated by the terms "media," "audiences," and "society." It is through taking these sets of variables into account individually, interactively, and systematically that a more adequate understanding of mass communications effects can be gained. By taking this theoretical orientation, the present paper presents a theoretical approach toward the issue of media influences that identifies a number of observable effects of mass communications on individuals, groups, and society. The conceptualization stresses as a central issue the *dependency* of audiences on media information resources—a dependency that leads to modifications in both personal and social processes.

A Dependency Model of Mass Media Effects

We propose that it is the nature of the tripartite audience-media-society relationship which most directly determines many of the effects that the media have on people and society. While there are a number of aspects of audience-media-society relationships that could be discussed, the one we focus upon first is the high level of dependence of audiences on mass media information resources in urban-industrial societies. The primary reason for this focus is that the degree of audience dependence on media information is a key variable in understanding when and why media messages alter audience beliefs, feelings, or behavior.

Dependency is defined as a relationship in which the satisfaction of needs or the attainment of goals by one party is contingent upon the resources of another party. So defined, dependency on media information resources is an ubiquitous condition in modern society. One finds this condition in many settings, ranging from the need to find the best buys at the supermarket to more general or pervasive needs such as obtaining the kinds of information that will help to maintain a sense of connectedness and familiarity with the social world outside one's neighborhood. There are numerous ways in which people are dependent on media to satisfy information needs. For example, one form of dependency is based on the need to understand one's social world; another type of dependency arises from the need to act meaningfully and effectively in that world; still a third type of dependency is based on the need for fantasy-escape from daily problems and tensions. The greater the need and consequently the stronger the dependency in such matters, the greater the likelihood that the information supplied will alter various forms of audience cognitions, feelings, and behavior.

It can be assumed that as societies grow more complex, and as the quality of media technology improves, the media continuously take on more and more *unique information functions*.[2] These include information gathering, processing, and delivery. In the American society, for example, the media are presumed to have several unique functions. They operate as a

Fourth Estate, gathering and delivering information about the actions of government; they serve as the primary signalling system in case of emergencies; they constitute the principle source of the ordinary citizen's conceptions of national and world events; they provide enormous amounts of entertainment information for fantasy-escape.

Some media information functions are more socially central than others. In other words, some are more essential than others for societal and individual well-being. Centrality may vary over time, situation, and unit of analysis. For example, providing national sports coverage to politically active groups is probably a less central function than providing them with information about national economic or political decisions that strongly affect their lives, while the reverse may hold for politically apathetic groups. It can be hypothesized that the greater the number and centrality of the specific information-delivery functions served by a medium, the greater the audience and societal dependency on that medium.

The second condition in which dependency is heightened occurs when a relatively high degree of change *and* conflict is present in a society. Forces operating to maintain the structural stability of a society coexist with forces toward conflict and change. The relative distribution of forces for stability or for change varies over time and place. Societies undergoing modernization, for example, usually experience high levels of conflict until societal adaptations are made that promote new forms of structural stability. Social conflict and social change usually involve challenges to established institutions, beliefs, or practices. When such challenges are effective, established social arrangements become, to one degree or another, inadequate as frameworks with which members of a society can cope with their life situations. People's dependence on media information resources is intensified during such periods. This is a joint consequence of the reduced adequacy of their established social arrangements and the media's capacity to acquire and transmit information that facilitates reconstruction of arrangements. We can hypothesize, therefore, that in societies with developed media systems, audience dependency on media information increases as the level of structural conflict and change increases.

These basic propositions of dependency theory can be brought together and summarized as follows: The potential for mass media messages to achieve a broad range of cognitive, affective, and behavioral effects will be increased when media systems serve many unique and central information functions. That potential will be further increased when there is a high degree of structural instability in the society due to conflict and change.

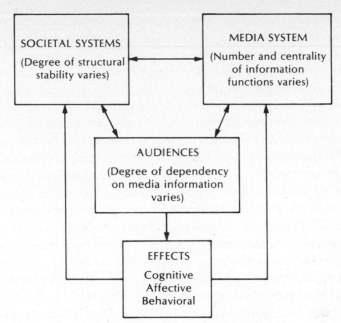

Figure 1. Society, Media, and Audience: Reciprocal Relationships

We need to add, however, the idea that altering audience cognitive, affective and behavioral conditions can feed back in turn to alter both society and the media. This is what was meant by a tripartite relationship between media, audience and society. Herein lies a key theoretical difference between the present dependency approach and the "uses and gratifications" approach of Blumler and Katz (1974). Proponents of the uses and gratification approach examine how audiences use the media to gratify similar information needs but do so by taking the audience as the focal point of analysis, not the interrelationships between audience, media, and society.

We can now illustrate how dependency theory predicts certain types of effects. The general relationships are presented in diagrammatic form in Figure 1. We now turn to identify specific kinds of cognitive, affective, and behavioral changes in people that are regularly brought about by the mass media because of individual and societal dependence on their information resources.

Cognitive Effects
The *creation and resolution of ambiguity* serves as the first example of a cognitive alteration effect which is particularly likely to receive the atten-

tion of investigators working from a dependency model. Ambiguity is a problem of either insufficient or conflicting information (Ball-Rokeach, 1973). Ambiguity can occur either because people lack enough information to understand the meaning of an event, or because they lack adequate information to determine which of several possible interpretations of an event is the correct one. Research evidence shows that when unexpected events occur, such as natural disasters or the assassination of a political leader, many people first become aware of such events through mass media information channels (e.g., Sheatsley and Feldman, 1969). When the initial information gathered and delivered by the media is incomplete, feelings of ambiguity are created whereby audience members know that an event has occurred, but do not know what it means or how to interpret it. More information will probably be sought in attempts to resolve such ambiguity. In many instances, the ambiguity resulting from incomplete or conflicting media reports is resolved by more complete information subsequently delivered by media to their audiences. In such cases, the media's role in ambiguity creation and resolution is relatively easy to see.

What is perhaps harder to see, but what may have greater sociopolitical significance, is the extent to which people are dependent on the media for continuous or ongoing ambiguity resolution. People living in times of rapid social change, who are in settings marked by relative instability or social conflict, or who are confronted with specific situations in which something unexpected has occurred, will often experience ambiguity. Such ambiguity is usually stressful. Ambiguity can be resolved in a matter of seconds, or it can persist for days, months, or even years in the absence of adequate information.

When people become heavily dependent upon the mass media for the information they need to resolve ambiguity, the defining or structuring effect of mass-mediated information is considerable. The media do not have the power to determine uniformly the exact content of the interpretations or "definitions of the situation" that every person constructs. But, by controlling what information is and is not delivered and how that information is presented, the media can play a large role in limiting the range of interpretations that audiences are able to make.

Examination of the essential roles played by the media in periods of modernization suggests that the media clearly have such a role in the construction of social reality (Lerner, 1959, 1969). Persons living in societies undergoing change from traditional to industrial forms experience pervasive ambiguity. This ambiguity is particularly acute during the period between their psychological unhitching from traditional customs, values, and world views and their adoption of more modern versions. The utility of having relatively standardized information packaged and transmitted via media by those agencies seeking to promote and control the modernization process has long been recognized. Control over such media information delivery is essential precisely because of the need to control how people resolve ambiguity.

A second cognitive effect that can be particularly common when audiences rely heavily upon media information resources to keep up with their changing world is *attitude formation*. During any year or decade in recent history, numerous instances of media-initiated attitude formation can be found. Publics have formed new attitudes about such events as lower speed limits, environmental problems, energy crises, specific wars, and political corruption. New attitudes are continually being formed as various persons gain the public eye. In modern society there is a constant parade of new political figures, religious leaders, sports personalities, scientists and artists. There is also a seemingly endless variety of social movements toward which orientations must be worked out. Even physical objects become the focus of attitude formation. These can include new household gadgets, clothing, birth control devices, car safety mechanisms, and innovations in communication technology. The media push a never-ending flow of such events, issues, objects and persons into public attention. People formulate their feelings toward them as they confront this flow.

We do not suggest that the media are monolithic in their influence on such attitudes. The selectivity processes emphasized in earlier perspectives undoubtedly play a role in the attitude formation process. Likewise, local community opinion leaders selectively channel people's attention to events and influence the content or intensity of the attitude formed. However, these psychological and social processes probably play more of a role in determining the specific content and intensity of the attitudes formed than they do in determining which events, people, or objects are likely to become candidates for attitude formation.

A third cognitive effect centers around the media's role in *agenda-setting*. Neither individuals themselves nor their opinion leaders control the selection activities of the media that sort among potential topics for presentation or among available sets of information about those topics. Moreover, even though the media deliver information on a broad range of topics, people have neither the time nor the energy to form attitudes and beliefs about everything. They must select some more limited set of topics and issues about which to concern themselves. It is out of this set of necessities that the effect of agenda-setting takes place.[3] We need to understand two major features of this process. First, why is there a considerable similarity in the agenda of concern regarding certain types of topics among members of the media audience? Second, in spite of such instances of similarity, why do members of the public who attend to the media show numerous differences in their personal agendas of concern regarding media-presented topics?

This seeming dilemma between tendencies toward both uniformity and differences in personal agendas can be resolved quite simply. To be certain, specific individuals will set their personal agendas in relation to their unique backgrounds of prior socialization, experience and personality structure. However, the society produces broad strata of people with sufficient uniformity of social circumstances that they share many problems and concerns in greater or lesser degree in spite of individual differences. In a society such as ours, for example, many people are wage-earners that have limited monetary resources to obtain their mass-produced necessities. In this sense they are alike regardless of their personality differences; they share a concern over such matters as rising prices, taxes, unemployment, and other economic matters that can quickly alter their standard of living. These override their individual differences. Thus, when the media present information of importance on economic matters, these topics can be expected to be placed high on their agendas of concern.

Where individual differences play an important role in agenda-setting is with respect to topics that are less tied to such social locations. Animal lovers of any social category because of their individual attitudes will be likely to attend to and respond strongly to media-delivered stories of mistreatment. People of all walks of life who enjoy fishing are likely to include in their agendas new policies of the fish and game department.

Agenda setting, in other words, is brought about by an interactional process. Topics are filtered through media information-gathering and processing systems and then selectively disseminated. The public then sorts out their interest and concern with this information as a function of both their individual differences in personal make-up and their location in societal strata and categories. Out of this sytem of variables and factors emerges a list of topics to which varying numbers of people give differential assignments of importance. That list constitutes the agenda of the media audience as a whole.

Still another cognitive effect that occurs in a media-dependent society is the *expansion of people's systems of beliefs.* Charles H. Cooley (1909) long ago used the term "enlargement" to refer to the idea that people's knowledge and belief systems expand because they learn about other people, places, and things from the mass media. This idea can be more specifically explained by examining what Altman and Taylor (1973) call the "breadth" dimension of belief structure. Beliefs are organized into categories. These categories, such as those pertaining to religion, family, politics, and the like reflect the major areas of a person's social activity. The categories. dimension refers to the number of categories in a belief system and how many beliefs are found in each category. Belief systems can be broadened (enlarged) by increasing either the number of categories or the number of beliefs in a given category. For example, the vast amount of new information about ecological matters disseminated by the media in recent years has surely fostered the enlargement of people's beliefs about everything from automobiles to "baggies," from babies to compacters. These can be incorporated into existing opinions, attitudes and values concerning free enterprise, recreation, work, religion, and the family. By their constant surveillance and presentation of aspects of the changing social and physical world we live in, the media have the effect of broadening their audiences' belief categories and enlarging their belief systems.

The final cognitive effect that needs consideration is the media's impact on *values.* Values may be defined as very basic beliefs that people hold about either "desirable end states of existence" (e.g., salvation, equality, freedom) or "preferred modes of conduct" (e.g., honest, forgiving, capable). Only under rare conditions would we expect mass media information to be able single-handedly to alter such basic beliefs.[4] Mass mediated information can, however, play an important part in creating the conditions for *value clarification.* One way that the media facilitate value clarification is by presenting information that precipitates *value conflict* within audience members and between social groups. For example, the recent civil rights and ecology movements not only received broad media coverage, but also involved fundamental value conflicts. Civil rights movements posed a conflict between individual freedom (e.g., property rights) and equality (e.g., human rights). Ecology movements bring economic value into conflict with aesthetic and survival values. Most people did not, however, have the interest, inclination, or information necessary to see these issues as value conflicts. Mass mediated information, in the form of reports of statements made by movement leaders, or in the form of interpretations of the movement's motives and actions, usually includes identification of the underlying value conflicts. Once the value conflicts inherent in such movements are posed and clarified by the media, audience members are moved to articulate the own value positions. Such articulation can be painful because it can force a choice between mutually incompatible goals and the means for obtaining them. However, for action to take place choices must be made. In the process of trying to decide which is more important in a particular case, general value priorities become clarified. Thus, the media indirectly have had a cognitive impact on members of their audiences.

Affective Effects

The impact of media messages on an audience's feelings and emotional responses is one of the least explored kinds of effects. However, a limited body of writing on the matter makes some suggestions. It has been hypothesized that prolonged exposure to violent media content has a "numbing" or de-sensitization effect (e.g., Wertham, 1954). Some observers suggest that such effects may promote insensitivity or the lack of a desire to help others when violent encounters are witnessed in real life (e.g., Rosenthal, 1964). Along a similar line, Hyman (1973) has pointed out that social scientists have not paid attention to the effects of violent media content on audience sentiments. There is some evidence to suggest that the level of physiological arousal caused by exposure to audio-visual portrayals of violence does decline over time. But such evidence is no substitute for the kind of direct research on emotional responses that Hyman is calling for.

Fear, anxiety, and trigger-happiness are illustrations of affective effects that could be researched. For example, prolonged exposure to news messages or even TV dramas that portray cities as violence-ridden jungles may increase people's fear or anxiety about living in or even travelling to the city. In a state of anticipation of the worst, city residents or visitors may be emotionally triggered to respond violently to others' actions. These kinds of effects may be particularly likely for residents of nonmetropolitan areas who depend largely on the media for information about what's going on in the cities, and who have little firsthand experience with city life.

Actually, almost all media effects could be examined in terms of their affective dimension. It is difficult to imagine the cognitive effect of attitude formation without accompanying affective effects. Sometimes the affective element of attitude formation can have serious social consequences. In periods of intense social conflict the police may form a number of attitudes from media characterizations about groups with which they have to deal.

If media-derived attitudes contain affective elements, such as anger, hostility, and frustration, it may retard the ability of the police to keep their cool when the encounter actually comes. Exactly this pattern developed in 1968 in Chicago during the disruptions of the Democratic National Convention.

Morale and *alienation* serve as the final examples of the kinds of alterations in audience affect that can result from media messages. Klapp (1972) has proposed that in societies in which the mass media play central communications roles, the nature of media information has substantial effects on people's morale and level of alienation. The reason why can be found in the pioneering writings of Emile Durkheim (1951). The sense of collective well-being and "we feeling" that promotes morale and that combats alienation is a fragile product of successful social relations that cannot be developed or maintained without effective communication systems. A key element in that effective communication is the presence of regular and positive information about the groups and categories to which people belong, such as their society, community, profession, or ethnic group. People who rely on mass media systems as a primary source of information about their groups and categories can, thus, experience changes in morale and level of alienation when there are notable changes in the quantity or quality of the information delivered by the media about those collectives. According to this line of reasoning, any number of groups including women, blacks, native Americans, or even Americans generally, would be expected to undergo increased or decreased morale and changes in level of alienation as the nature of media messages about them underwent change.

Behavioral Effects

Overt action is, of course, the kind of effect that most people are interested in. Changes in attitude, belief and affective states are interesting, but it is the degree to which they influence overt action that makes them important. Of the numerous effects of media messages on behavior that could be considered, we have chosen to discuss *activation* and *deactivation*.[5]

Activation refers to instances in which audience members do something that they would not otherwise have done as a consequence of receiving media messages. As we have already suggested, activation may be the end product of elaborate cognitive or affective effects. For example, people may engage in *issue formation* or *issue resolution* as a consequence of attitudes they have formed and feelings they have developed. Take as an illustration people whose primary contact with the contemporary women's movement is via the media. They may initially react to movement leaders' allegations of "sexism" with ambiguity, perhaps not even knowing what the term means. The problem of resolving ambiguity and the stress that accompanies it gain a high place on their cognitive agenda. Resolution of ambiguity leads to the formation of new attitudes and feelings about sexual equality and the women's movement. The culmination of this chain of effects is a felt need to act. Once established, the need to act is transformed into overt action by public expression of these new attitudes and feelings, thereby participating in issue formation. Subsequent media information, such as an announcement of a protest in support of a proposal made by a women's group, may further activate people to join the protest, while others may be activated to organize a counter protest. These overt actions become part of the issue resolution process.

Seymour-Ure (1974) notes the difference between primary effects on message receivers and secondary effects that occur because certain media messages are or are not transmitted. The *strategies of action* formulated by groups who are dependent upon media coverage to communicate their protest or point of view to the public and policy makers provide one example of what might be called a secondary activation effect. The Yippies of the 1960s, for example, seemingly took cognizance of what kinds of protest activities were and were not covered by the media. They created an almost classical strategy of action to gain media coverage which included explicit appeals to such media news criteria as drama, simple symbols and slogans, motion, and potential conflict or violence.

So much attention has been given to the undesirable behavioral consequences of television content that it might be well to mention briefly one socially desirable behavioral effect. Stein and Friedrich's (1971) recent research suggests that TV viewers may be activated to engage in both prosocial and antisocial behavior. Subjects in their research who viewed a popular children's show (Mr. Rogers) increased their level of cooperative activity over several weeks of exposure. Those subjects exposed to violent content, on the other hand, increased their level of aggressive activity. Thus, the research showed that both cooperation and aggression may be activated, depending on the nature of the television message received.

Research conducted in the 1940s suggests that media messages may activate *altruistic* economic behavior. Merton (1946) examined how a radio marathon featuring a well-known singer of that era (Kate Smith) activated large numbers of people to buy war bonds.

In many instances, such as voting and consumption, deactivation—or what people would have otherwise done, but which they *don't* do as a consequence of media messages—can be as important as what they are activated to do. Yet deactivation effects have not received as much research attention. Not voting and not consuming provide two examples of the kinds of deactivation effects which could be examined. Most people are heavily dependent on the media for information about state and national political contests and about the state of the economy. Political campaigns have not only become longer and longer, but have also depended more and more on the media to communicate to voters. Such campaigns may not change many established attitudes toward the contestants. They might, however, elicit affective responses, such as overwhelming boredom, disgust, or cognitive assessments such as that it makes no difference who wins. These inner states can culminate in voting or deactivation of people's intention to vote.

Likewise, when media messages help to create an affective state of fear about one's own and the nation's economic future or the belief that a depression is unavoidable, people may not buy stocks, new cars, certain foods, or a multitude of other products that they would have otherwise bought. This would actually have the effect of deepening a recession by too much deactivation of a consumption behavior.

Discussion

Persons as members of media audiences encounter media messages with both constructed social realities and considerable dependency on media information resources. The social realities people hold are the product of the processes by which the societal system enculturates and socializes persons and structures their social action. The dependencies people have on media information are a product of the nature of the sociocultural system, category membership, individual needs, and the number and centrality of the unique information functions that the media system serves for individuals and for society.

When media messages are not linked to audience dependencies and when people's social realities are entirely adequate before and during message reception, media messages may have little or no alteration effects. They may reinforce existing beliefs or behavior forms. In contrast, when people do not have social realities that provide adequate frameworks for understanding, acting, and escaping, and when audiences are dependent in these ways on media information received, such messages may have a number of alteration effects. Media messages, in this instance, may be expected to alter audience behavior in terms of cognitive, affective, and/or overt activity. Thus, both the relative adequacy of the audience's social realities and the relative degree of audience dependency on media information resources must be taken into account to explain and predict the effects of media messages.

Finally, the effects of media messages flow back to influence people's needs or psychological and social characteristics. And, in some cases, they flow back to alter the nature of the societal system itself. Behavioral alteration effects, for example, in some instances may take the form of massive protest which not only gets people involved in producing a new series of events to be covered by the media, but may also increase the level of societal conflict, alter societal norms, or create new social groups. This series of events, in turn, can force changes in the nature of the relationships between the sociocultural system and the media system, such as the passing of new laws designed to change the media's operating policies.

The dependency model avoids a seemingly untenable all-or-none position of saying either that the media have no significant impact on people and society, or that the media have an unbounded capacity to manipulate people and society. It allows us to specify in a limited way when and why mass-communicated information should or should not have significant effects upon how audiences think, feel, and behave.

Notes

1. These propositions can be accepted without reversion to a simplistic assumption of a mass society lacking meaningful group ties.
2. See C. Wright (1959; 1974) for a functional analysis of media information roles.
3. For a discussion of the various ways in which the term "agenda-setting" has been used, see J. McLeod et al. (1974).
4. For a thorough discussion of the values concept and the conditions under which values can be changed, see M. Rokeach (1973).
5. For an earlier discussion of activation effects, see O. Larsen (1964).

2
Media
and Interpersonal Intimacy

In "The Veldt," a short story by Ray Bradbury, the Nursery is a room in the future in which dreams and fantasies become reality. In this room the children are transported to any place in any time. Of late the children have been spending more and more time on the African veldt with its herds of wild beasts. The parents are anxious because the children are spending all their time in the Nursery. The father is discussing the effects of the Nursery on his children with a friend. The friend advises him,

> where before they had a Santa Claus [for a father] now they have a Scrooge. Children prefer Santa. You've let this room and this house replace you and your wife in your children's affections. This room is their mother and father, far more important in their lives than their real parents. And now you come along and want to shut it off. No wonder there's hatred here. You can feel it coming out of the sky. Like too many others, you've built it around creature comforts. Why, you'd starve tomorrow if something went wrong in your kitchen. You wouldn't know how to tap an egg. Nevertheless, turn everything off. Start new. It'll take time. But we'll make good children out of bad in a year, wait and see.[1]

This story of the future is interesting for what it reveals about media and interpersonal relationships. We find "The Veldt" intriguing because it implicitly relates the sophisticated media environment of the future with our private fears and dreams. The Nursery can turn our deepest fantasy into reality—a reality that leaves nothing to the imagination. "The Veldt" is interesting also because of what it implies about travel, space and privacy. Toward the end of the story the friend, Mr. Mclean, sees the two children seated in the Nursery having a picnic. He asks for their parents. The children answer, "They'll be here directly." "Good, we must get along," replied Mr. Mclean. In the distance he sees the lions fighting and clawing and then quieting down to feed in silence under shady trees. The story ends a paragraph or so later and we are left thinking about our own nurseries and the shocking possibilities.

Media Transcend Time and Space

One of the implications of Bradbury's short story is that media are doing terrible things to us. This is a misconception, but one that is quite common among media critics. It is the thing to be said: the media are doing bad things, good things, things, but certainly things are being done to us. It is an error to blame the media for everything we dislike, but it is not wrong to recognize our own confusion about the media, because media themselves create ambivalent and often contradictory relationships.

To exist in a media world requires an understanding of a number of contradictions which confound our concepts of time and space. For example, how can you be in two places at the same time? A simple answer is, give your friends a photograph of yourself. "Media and Interpersonal Intimacy," the title of this section, represents a paradox. In the process by

which media connect and transcend time and space our sense of personal space is altered and our spacial relationships are modified. In this section we explore the consequences of the changes in our concept of geographical and personal space resulting from the use of media to connect us with almost anyone, any place on the globe, and even on the moon.

We began this section with a fictional encounter of the future. Let us contrast that with a realistic encounter which occurred several years ago, but which then seemed like science fiction. On May 31, 1965, one of the editors of this book participated in the first intercontinental TV classroom exchange.[2] It took place between the United States and France. A French class at the West Bend High School, Wisconsin, assembled with its teacher at the unusual hour of 7:00 A.M. on the Memorial Day holiday. It is probable that only an international "incident" would entice students into school during a holiday.

On that particular morning, the class was to be combined for one hour with its counterpart at the Lycée Henri IV of Paris. The interconnection was accomplished by means of the Early Bird Satellite, with the TV unit of the University of Wisconsin handling the video and audio pick-up in the West Bend classroom. The signals from cameras and microphones were sent across the country by microwave to Andover, Maine (the North America ground station of the Communications Satellite Corporation).

At Andover, the picture and sound signals were transmitted 22,300 miles out into space to the Early Bird Communications Satellite which is a synchronous (stationary) orbiting instrument located above the Equator between Africa and South America. The signals were received by Early Bird and retransmitted 22,300 miles back to earth to be received at a European ground station located at Plemeur-Bodou, France. It was here that the American television picture consisting of 525 scan lines was translated to a French television picture consisting of 819 scan lines. The picture was then transmitted to the classroom of the Lycée Henri IV.

The French Broadcasting System had their cameras and microphones located in the classroom. The sound pictures originating there followed in reverse the same 47,000 mile route just described. Remember that this is almost twice the distance around the earth. When the hour-long class began it was 7:30 A.M. in West Bend and 1:30 P.M. in Paris. The American students spoke in French, the French students in English.

While such TV classrooms have not become commonplace, we have become accustomed to daily satellite communication. Print, radio, telephone, television and photography are transmitted via satellite without concern for geographic boundaries. The students in West Bend, Wisconsin and Paris, France spoke to each other only vaguely aware that they were separated by 3000 miles. The matter of 47,000 miles was never a consideration. The miles dissolved into mediated interpersonal relationships and the students' lives were changed by their participation in an event which altered their view of world geography. Think of that American student at home after this Trans-Atlantic experience, "I spoke to Jean in Paris today. He was wearing a Beatles button." "But you weren't in Paris, you never left Wisconsin." The argument is soon resolved, but the implications for interpersonal relationships are startling.

The Paradox of Communication

We became space travelers with Samuel Morse's invention of the telegraph. It allowed the sender/receiver to transcend space technically and symbolically. All subsequent inventions of media facilitated instantaneous transmission over time and space. (The word "television" is a derivation of the Greek word "tele," meaning at a distance, and the Latin verb "video," meaning "I see.")

Whether we are talking about sounds conveyed over a great distance or seeing and hearing over great distances, the model is always two individuals attempting to communicate with each other. There is no medium that cannot be used for interpersonal communication. There is no medium that cannot be used for mass communication. The telephone can be used to broadcast to many people. The television can unite two people in a dyadic relationship. It all depends on the intent of the sender and the choice of the receiver. In either case the function is to eliminate space and alter time.

Media affects how we relate to others and the circumstances in which those relationships exist. Is it necessary to visit a relative when a telephone call will do just as well? Why go to the trouble of going to a concert, or a drama or sports event? Space can be transcended by media and we can participate in relative comfort. Richard Sennett in *The Fall of Public Man* points out that electronic communication is one means by which the very idea of the "public" man has been put to an end. It is wrong though to believe that media alone are responsible for our loss of contact and intimacy. Sennett states the case clearly:

> the impulses to withdraw from public life began long before the advent of these machines; they are not infernal devices, according to the usual scenario of technological monster; they are tools invented by men to fulfill human needs. The needs which the electronic media are fulfilling are those cultural impulses that formed over the whole of the last century and a half to withdraw from social interaction in order to know and feel more as a person. These machines are part of the arsenal between social interaction and personal experience.[3]

We can see the formation of a strange paradox suggested by Sennett and intrinsic to media—the paradox of isolation and visibility. Our potential for relationships has been extended beyond the barriers of space and time. An environment in which we talk to each other and see each other while we are actually in the presence of the other is no longer necessary to interpersonal communication. This has produced a confusing paradox. Interpersonal intimacy has traditionally entailed physical and psychological closeness. We could be intimate only with those that we could be close to, physically and emotionally. As Edward T. Hall has pointed out in his works on nonverbal communication,[4] we actually divide personal space into intimate and social distance depending on how close we allow others to come.

The media, however, have made it necessary to rethink what we mean by space and environment. Space, defined as distance, is not relevant to a telephone call (until we receive the bill from the telephone company). There was a time not so long ago when a long distance call was accompanied by a lot of transmission noise. But every now and then the call would come through with such clarity that one would say, "It sounds like you're in the next room." It is now commonplace to extend our psychological, intimate selves as the physical space between ourselves and others has become irrelevant. If you live in an urban community, the chances are that you know very little about your neighbors, but are "intimate" with persons who live far from your neighborhood. It is likely that you have not visited a relative who lives in the same city in the recent past, but that you have seen Johnny Carson, Merv Griffin, and Dick Cavett, among others, on a regular basis. This is not meant to chastise, but to point out the paradoxical effects that media have on all our close relationships. Now, we are all space travelers.

It is difficult to resist the temptation to pass judgment on the effects of media on our relationships. It takes a bit of a struggle to stay away from the "technology as monster" type of analysis. We must recognize that there is a mixture of positive and negative elements influencing our interpersonal communication when it is mediated communication; that is, dependent upon media for completion.

Think of a very intimate relationship: the one with your doctor.

> In the near future automated histories may be taken with the patient being present before a computer. A patient can press the appropriate pushbutton on a Touch-Tone telephone in response to questions generated orally from a central computer console. The verbal questions emanating from the machine are prerecorded, and they, like the visual displays on the cathode ray tube, branch, depending upon the patient's answers. In the more distant future computers will be able to participate in a verbal dialogue with the patient.[5]

Which is more important to you: an intimate give-and-take relationship between yourself and the family doctor, or an efficient, accurate encounter with a talking computer? Be careful with your answer. A doctor can make a mistake or be influenced by his emotions, but the computer does not make errors. What will you risk?

The Expansion of Space and Nonphysical Intimacy

Each of us has a common set of expectations regarding interpersonal relationships. That is, we share a model of behavior in which participants expect to process the actions and reactions of other persons using the full complement of senses. It is also obvious that face-to-face interaction occurs only where the participants physically inhabit contiguous space.

The media relationships made possible by the interposition of typographical, iconic, and electronic media are distinctly different from the face-to-face relationship in several ways: by the elimination of the need for contiguity, by the shifting emphasis of sensory modes, and by the development of unique relationships that are media based—that is, without the medium the relationship would not exist. Thus, the telephone represents a relationship based solely upon the use of the auditory sense with the other senses—touch, sight, smell, and taste temporarily placed in reserve.

Obviously it is possible for relationships to be established with individuals who have never shared a contiguous place. We accept, sometimes even prefer, intimate relationships facilitated by media in which physical presence is not only absent, but is a prerequisite. It is probably true that at one time the motivation for all mediated communication was the transcendence of time and space to accommodate the limitations of place. The evolution of media technology has brought about the extraordinary separation of place from communication. Whereas formerly communication could occur only within the context of a place, place has become irrelevant as space has been bridged by the media. Each of us participates in media relationships in which we do not know where the other person is, nor does it matter. The telephone company provides the 800 number in order to facilitate transactions that do not require a place for completion. At one time we thought of radio and television in terms of the places from which the signals emanated. Satellite communication and cable connection have antiquated that notion. Now there is no space on earth far enough away to be insulated from the media of communication. The unusual has become the normal. The irony is that what counts is connection, not the places connected. We have made possible nonphysical intimacy, an intimacy that requires no face-to-face contact.

When you become aware of your place in a media-dependent world, the confusion between negative and positive effects of media appears. It is marvelous that contact and intimacy are not limited by distance. But does intimacy over distance suggest any negative features? That is not easy to answer. Let's look at a letter from the poet Dylan Thomas to his mother and father:

> Dear Mother and Dad,
> How are you both? It's a long, long time since a letter came from you; or is it that time moves so slowly here and one looks forward so much to the postman? Or, postwoman, rather, a little woman too, who walks about twenty miles a day, up & down these steep Florentine hills, in the baking sun. Whatever it is, we do want to hear from you soon. Letters from England seem to take, on the average, five days to get here.[6]

Is a Dylan Thomas letter different, aside from style and orality, from a telephone call, a home movie of the family, or a video cassette made from light portable equipment? Dylan Thomas writes his mother and father using a form of communication which is less than ideal. The ideal is for Thomas to be together with his parents, but because this is not possible he uses the postal letter. We have come to respect the letter form of interpersonal communication, but we are not as sure of ourselves when intimate communication involves the newer technological forms of communication. Doubts can arise when we see persons using the more sophisticated forms of communication to avoid the risk of direct interaction. "I'll talk to him/her on the phone because I can hang up when I want to." "I'd rather watch TV in my room than try to talk with my mother or father." "I just love Barry Manilow. He really understands me!" What does it mean when we are more "intimate" with media personalities than we are with people who are physically close to us?

Every medium of communication changes us. Every technological innovation has positive as well as negative potential. Holography will arrive in the not so distant future. Imagine a medium which will allow us to see and talk to each other over great distances and to "walk around" each other in an illusory third dimension. We will be able to approximate the ideal interpersonal communication with one major exception; we will not be able to touch or feel the warmth of each other. Will this increased "closeness" without touch be positive or negative? Some possible answers can be found in the following readings.

Notes

1. Ray Bradbury, "The Veldt," *The Illustrated Man.* (New York: Bantam Books, 1951).
2. Dreyfus, Lee S. and Gary Gumpert, "Students Visit Via Satellite," *The NAEB Journal*, Vol. 25, (May–June 1966), pp. 6–7.
3. Sennett, Richard, *The Fall of Public Man*, (New York: Alfred A. Knopf, 1977), pp. 282–83.
4. Hall, Edward T., *The Hidden Dimension*, (New York: Doubleday, 1969), and *The Silent Language*, (New York: Doubleday, 1959).
5. Maxmen, Jerrold S., *The Post-Physician Era: Medicine in the Twenty-First Century*, (New York: John Wiley & Sons, 1976), p. 18.
6. *Selected Letters from Dylan Thomas*, edited with commentary by Constantine Fizgibbon, (New York: New Directions Books, 1966), p. 310.

MARK R. LEVY

Watching TV News as Para-Social Interaction

Each evening almost 60 million Americans watch one of the network news-casts. While hearing the news they are also watching—interacting with—the newscasters. To many people the personality of the newscasters is as important as the news itself, if not more so. What is this fascination that we have with newscasters such as Walter Cronkite, John Chancellor, and Barbara Walters? What is their relationship to the viewer? Mark Levy has made a study of this relationship and he reports his finding in this essay. For a different view of relationships with media personalities, read Daniel J. Boorstin's essay "From Hero to Celebrity."

Introduction

In a well known article, Horton and Wohl suggest that the mass media have created a new form of social interaction, a relationship of "intimacy at a distance" in which audiences experience the illusion of face-to-face primary relations with actually remote mass media communicators.[1] Horton and Wohl call this form of interaction "para-social," and contend that in a para-social relationship, audience members react to mass media performers or the characters they portray *as if* the communicators or characters were part of the audience's peer group.

According to the concept of para-social interaction, the audience learns to recognize and more importantly to interact with the highly stylized "images" presented by the mass media communicators, especially those entertainers, talk show hosts, "personalities," and journalists who appear frequently on television. The communicators, or as Horton and Wohl call them, the personae, encourage this para-social relationship by speaking in conversational tones directly into the television camera, by engaging in clever monologues which appear to require audience reciprocity, and by interacting in a casual way with other media communicators ("side-kicks," confidants, antagonists, and the like). Since the televised appearances of the personae are often regularly scheduled and since at each appearance the personae perform in accordance with their basic "image," the personae take on the attributes of the "perfect" role partner: their behavior is highly predictable.

This article originally appeared in the *Journal of Broadcasting,* Winter 1979, 23: 1. Copyright © 1979 by the Broadcast Education Association. Reprinted by permission of the publisher.

Although the audience can not communicate directly with the mass media performers, viewers are still said to interact with the personae. Audiences are thought to "benefit from the persona's wisdom, reflect on his advice, sympathize with him in his difficulties, [and] forgive his mistakes." For most members of the audience, para-social interaction is considered complementary to social communication. However, for people with few or weak social ties, para-social interaction may offer a functional alternative for inadequate interaction opportunities.

Despite the plausibility of the para-social interaction concept, little systematic research has been directed toward understanding its place in the communication process and few studies have specifically examined the nature of the interaction between television newscasters and the news audience.[2] While numerous investigations have noted the ability of viewers to evaluate the characteristics or "appeal" of newscasters,[3] viewer evaluations or preferences do not necessarily demonstrate that audience members engage in para-social relations with the broadcasters. To rate a newscaster's skill or appearance, for example, implies only that audience members are aware of the news persona as a social object and that viewers can or do attribute meanings to the behavior and appearance of the journalists. To demonstrate that news audiences interact on a para-social level with news personae, it is necessary to show not only that viewers interpret and evaluate the behavior or "gestures" of the newscasters, but that audiences also act or react based on those attributed meanings.[4]

The first part of this article will offer data concerning the existence, quality, and extent of the para-social relationship between the television news audience and the personae who appear on the newscasts. These data seek to describe the nature of the para-social interaction process. In the second part of this report, two hypotheses will be tested:

> H1: The more opportunities an individual has for social interaction, the less likely it is that he or she will engage in a para-social relationship with news personae;
>
> H2: The stronger an individual's para-social interaction with television news personae, the more television news he or she will watch. This hypothesis assumes that audience members value their para-social interaction and that after an initial period during which the para-social tie is formed, viewers will attempt to maintain, if not maximize, that valued interaction by continuing to watch the news at a relatively high rate.

Methods

Focused group discussions were held with two dozen adults living in the greater Albany County, New York region. Focused group participants were selected from a wide variety of social backgrounds and all watched television news regularly. Transcripts of each hour-long discussion were analyzed for viewer attitudes toward television news programs and a propositional inventory of 42 uses and gratifications items was prepared from this analysis.[5] Based on the discussion of para-social interaction above, seven propositions were selected as possible indicators of para-social interaction.

During October and November, 1975, the inventory and other measures were administered by personal interview to a sample of 240 adults in the Albany County Urbanized Area. Respondents were chosen from 40 randomly selected housing clusters, with quota controls for respondent's sex, age, and work-force participation. Each respondent said he or she watched a minimum of one newscast a week. Respondents were asked to indicate their support for each para-social interaction proposition on a five-point scale, ranging from "strongly agree" to "strongly disagree."

Respondents' potential for social interaction was measured by two items. The first is an Index of Gregariousness[6] which ranks respondents as either "high," "medium," or "low" in grepariousness depending on both their total number of friendships and memberships in voluntary associations. The second measure of social interaction potential is based on responses to the question: "When you watch the TV news, do you usually watch alone or with someone else?" Since watching television and television news has been shown to be a highly social activity,[7] it was assumed that only persons living alone or temporarily without face-to-face interaction partners would watch the news in isolation.

Respondent exposure to television news was gauged by an index which takes into account the frequency with which a given respondent watches local and network newscasts in comparison to all other respondents in the sample.[8] Overall rates of exposure for each respondent were classified either "high," "medium," or "low."

Results

On the average, more than half (53%) of respondents agreed with the para-social interaction propositions, with support for the measures ranging

Table 1. Respondent support for various para-social interaction propositions

Proposition	Strongly Agree %	Agree %	Not Sure %	Disagree %	Strongly Disagree %
1. The newscasters are almost like friends you see every day.	6	46	12	31	5
2. I like hearing the voices of the newscasters in my house.	6	41	24	20	8
3. When the newscaster shows how he feels about the news, it helps me make up my mind about that news item.	4	27	16	45	9
4. I like to compare my own ideas with what the commentators say.	28	52	8	8	3
5. When the newscasters joke around with each other, it makes the news easier to take.	27	39	10	16	8
6. I feel sorry for the newscasters when they make mistakes.	14	37	12	23	14
7. Television shows you what people in the news are really like.	8	38	20	30	5

N = 240

from a low of 31% (Proposition 3 on Table 1) to a high of 80% (Proposition 4 on Table 1). This overall finding strongly suggests that para-social interaction with news personae is a common feature of the audience experience with television news.

The most general indicator of the para-social relationship is Proposition 1. More than half (52%) of respondents agreed that newscasters are *almost* like friends one sees every day. From the focused group transcripts it is clear that few, if any, viewers confuse the newscasters with their actual friends, but many do relate to the broadcasters as something "special."

As one focused group participant explained:

> I grew up watching Walter Cronkite. I guess I expect him to be there when I turn on the news. We've been through a lot together. Men on the moon and things like that.

This response suggests that the para-social relationship develops over time and is based in part on a history of "shared" experiences. It also implies that the daily "visit" of the newscaster is valued by the viewer, perhaps because the news persona, like a friend, brings "gossip" in the form of news, or perhaps because the nightly appearance of the broad-caster provides a temporal benchmark for the day's activities.[9]

While on its face, this proposition indicates only that some members of the television news audience attach the meaning of "friend" to the personae, evidence from the focused group discussions shows that this meaning often results in interaction. Some focused group participants said, for example, they had actually met the newscasters and looked forward to seeing them again, either in person *or* on television. Other focused group members said they occasionally responded to the newscaster's opening greeting (e.g. "Good evening from NBC News in New York") with a friendly salutation of their own (e.g. "Good evening, John."); and others recalled reacting to the anchorman's sign-off (e.g. "Thanks very much for watching" or "We'll have a complete update of the news at 11") with a reciprocating remark such as "You're welcome" or "See you later." Moreover, 68% of network news viewers said they noticed when the anchorman was off on vacation and 25% said the anchorman's absence "upset" them.

This sense of companionship with news personae is also found in Proposition 2. Nearly half (48%) of the respondents said they liked hearing the newscasters' voices in their homes. Focused group participants who lived alone or who frequently found themselves without face-to-face contacts particularly appreciated the audio "presence" of the newscasters. For these viewers, interacting with the news personae was an antidote for loneliness and even fear.

Some people who watch television news engage in a cognitively oriented interaction with the personae. More than three in ten (31%) use the newscaster as a cognitive guide with whom they "explore" the world (Proposition 3). By non-verbal cues such as "editorial eyebrows," headshakes, or smiles, or by a change in inflection, the newscaster provides some para-socially attentive viewers with a context for understanding the news. Many focused group participants commented on this type of interaction, with many saying they responded to the newscaster's behavior with similar gestures or remarks reflecting agreement, outrage, or amusement.

Television news commentators, particularly network commentators,[10] were likely to provide interaction on the cognitive level. More than three-quarters (80%) of all respondents said they compared their own ideas to those expressed by the commentators (Proposition 4). This finding has an interesting implication for the concept of opinion leadership.[11] While opinion leaders often derive their information and opinions from the mass media, opinion leaders are not generally thought of as mass media actors but rather as attentive members of the audience. However, if as this proposition suggests, some viewers interact with the news commentators as though they were physically present, then it is possible that under certain circumstances mass media actors might take on some of the functions normally reserved to the interpersonal communicator.

By contrast to this cognitive interaction, other aspects of the para-social relationship have an affective quality. Some 67% of respondents believed, for example, that the banter, jokes, asides, and "happy talk" between newscasters, especially local broadcasters, made the news "easier to take" (Proposition 5). What these audience members are saying is this: If the "knowledgeable" and "sophisticated" journalists have not lost their sense of humor, if these "busy" news professionals still find time to treat each other as friends, then perhaps things are not so bad after all.

Not all viewers enjoy this easy-going style of news presentation. Some focused group participants said they did not understand the "running gags" between the newscasters and felt "left out"; while better educated focused group participants often complained that the newscasters' behavior demeaned the importance of the news and was a waste of time. It should be noted, however, that both of these negative reactions imply that even critical viewers engage in some sort of affective interaction with the newscasters.

Additional evidence for the affective equality of the para-social relationship comes from Proposition 6. Half (51%) of all respondents felt sorry for the newscasters' mistakes. This response implies that some viewers are relatively attentive to the newscaster's performance and suggests a sense of viewer empathy with the difficulties of familiar, if actually remote, others. When the newscaster misreads his script or when a piece of news film breaks, the newscaster faces a momentary embarrassment and instead of being annoyed or indifferent some viewers share in the persona's discomfort.

Finally, the data show that para-social interactions are not limited to the newscasters. Almost half (46%) of respondents agreed with Proposition 7 that television shows them what "newsmakers" are "really like." Some focused group participants said, for example, that seeing public figures on the news gave them the opportunity to judge how those public actors might act "under pressure"; while some viewers, often the same ones, reported "talking back" to the newmakers, interacting with them in unreciprocated dialogues of praise, challenge, or disbelief.

Correlates of Para-social Interaction

In order to test the two hypotheses regarding the social and behavioral correlates of para-social interaction, an index of para-social behavior was created by summing each respondent's score on Propositions 1, 2, 3, and 7. These four items were selected because they were equally applicable to the audience experience with local and network news, and because it was felt that they represented the broad range of para-social behaviors. As measured by coefficient alpha,[12] the index has a reliability of .68.

With regard to H1, the data give some support to the hypothesized inverse relationship between social interaction opportunities and para-social interaction. An examination of the zero-order correlations shows that the degree of para-social interaction increases with respondent age ($r = .280$, $p < .01$) and that the strength of the para-social relationship varies inversely with viewer education ($r = -.52$, $p < .01$). However, respondent gregariousness is only weakly correlated with scores on the para-social interaction index ($r = -.12$, $p < .05$) and not correlated with whether the respondent watches the news alone or with others ($r = .02$, $p = .36$).

Since respondent education is so strongly associated with parasocial interaction scores, first-order partial correlations were calculated, controlling for education. This computation reduces the association between respondent age and scores on the index of parasocial interaction (first order $r = .19$, $p < .01$), and further reduces the correlations between para-social interaction and each of the direct measures of respondent social interaction potential.

Still, these results do not falsify the hypothesis, and indeed the correlations of respondents' education and age with para-social interaction can be interpreted as supporting the hypothesis. First with regard to respondent education, it should be noted that education is positively correlated with gregariousness. Both Table 2 and numerous other studies[13] show that as an individual's level of education increases, his or her social network increases as does the individual's potential for social interaction. Since parasocial interaction with news personae was assumed to be a functional complement or alternative for impaired or deficient social interactions, the better educated viewer may have less need for the para-social relationship and this is reflected in the strong negative correlation between education and para-social interaction.

Of course, it is possible that better educated respondents are simply more reluctant to disclose their para-social interactions. However, well-educated focused group participants generally talked quite freely about their para-

Table 2. Selected zero-order correlates of para-social interaction

		Variables			
Variables	2	3	4	5	6
1. Index of Para-Social					
Interaction	.28 **	−.52 **	.02	−.12 *	.22 **
2. Respondent Age		−.24 **	.00	.10	.25 **
3. Respondent Education			−.03	.15 *	−.08
4. Watch Alone				.01	−.03
5. Index of Gregariousness					.08
6. Total TV News Exposure					

$** p < .01$
$* p < .05$

Table 3. Selected first-order partial correlations with para-social interaction controlling for respondent education

		Variables		
Variables	2	3	4	5
1. Index of Para-Social				
Interaction	.19 **	.02	−.05	.21 **
2. Respondent Age		.00	.14 *	.24 **
3. Watch Alone			.01	−.03
4. Index of Gregariousness				.10
5. Total TV News Exposure				

$** p < .01$
$* p < .05$

social relations with those news personae whom the respondents believed to be especially talented, witty, or whose political or social attitudes the viewer inferred to be like their own.

Although the correlation between respondent age and scores on the para-social index is weak, it is statistically significant and in combination with previous studies[14] does lend some additional support to the hypothesis. Older viewers, in particular the housebound infirm, are often faced with decreasing opportunities for social interaction. For these viewers, the news personae may offer both a chance for surrogate friendship and the possibility to retain some vicarious ties with a world in which the viewer has a declining role.

As to the hypothesized relationship between para-social interaction and television news exposure, the data gave clear support to the hypothesis. Scores on the index of para-social interaction are significantly correlated in the predicted direction with levels of television newswatching ($r = .22$, $p < 0.1$). Since respondent education has been shown to be a major predictor of television news exposure[15] and since education is negatively associated with para-social interaction, first-order partial correlations between exposure and para-social interaction were computed, controlling for respondent's education. The first-order partial correlation was .21 ($p < .01$) and does not differ markedly from the zero-order correlation.

The causal direction of this association seems clear. People who watch television news engage in varying degrees of para-social interaction with the news personae. Those viewers who find the parasocial relationship particularly attractive or gratifying increase their exposure in order to increase their "contact" with the news personae. While it is possible that there is a threshold of exposure beyond which individuals will not increase their viewing in order to increase their para-social interactions, it is also likely that establishing and maintaining para-social interaction with the news personae is an important determinant of how much television news some people will watch.

Discussion

The para-social interaction between audiences and news personae shares attributes of both primary and secondary social relations.[16] First and foremost, the para-social relationship is based on an affective tie which many members of the audience create with the communicators. Even though this affective tie is completely the subjective invention of the audience, parasocially interactive viewers believe it is genuine and they interpret the behavior of the news personae as reciprocating this "real" bond. Further, like other primary relationships, the para-social interaction of audience and news personae often serves to meet the tension-release and integrative needs of the viewer. People who engage in para-social interaction are often reassured by a familiar, friendly "image" of their intimates-at-a-distance; and para-socially active viewers experience a sense of order, belonging, and context from their relationship with the news personae.

The para-social interaction of audience and news personae also has aspects of a secondary relationship. Except for a presumably complementary desire to inform and to be informed, there is little identity of goals between the audience and the personae. In fact, the para-social relationship might better be thought of as instrumentally oriented with audience members and personae seeking to use the relationship for different ends. Newscasters, for example, want to attract large audiences and may deliberately manipulate their self-presentation in order to evoke a para-social response. Newsmakers may also attempt to manipulate the public through their self-presentation. Clearly, these are not the goals of the audience, particularly those viewers for whom the para-social relationship is one of friendship or trust.

Notes

1. Donald Horton and R. Richard Wohl, "Mass Communication and Para-Social Interaction," *Psychiatry,* 19:215–229 (1956). An earlier version of this article was presented at the 1978 meeting of the American Sociological Association.

2. See, for example, P. Gregg, *Television Viewing As Parasocial Interaction for Persons 60 Years or Older,* master's thesis, University of Oregon, 1971; Karl Rosengren and Sven Windahl, "Mass Media Consumption as a Functional Alternative," in Denis McQuail, ed., *Sociology of Mass Communication* (Harmondsworth: Penguin, 1972), pp. 269–286; and Denis McQuail, Jay Blumler and J. R. Brown, "The Television Audience: A Revised Perspective," in McQuail, *op. cit.,* pp. 135–165; Jan-Erik Nordlund, "Media Interaction," *Communication Research,* 5:150–75 (April, 1978).

3. See, for example, William Cathcart, "Viewer Needs and Desires in Television Newscasters," *Journal of Broadcasting,* 14:55–62 (Winter 1969–1970); James McCroskey and Thomas Jenson, "Image of Mass Media News Sources," *Journal of Broadcasting,* 19:169–180 (Spring, 1975); and H. Shostek, "Factors Influencing Appeal of TV News Personalities," *Journal of Broadcasting,* 18:63–72 (Winter 1973–1974).

4. This distinction is based on Herbert Blumer, *Symbolic Interaction: Perspective and Method* (Englewood Cliffs, N.J.: Prentice-Hall, 1969).

5. For the complete propositional inventory, see Mark R. Levy, *The Uses and Gratifications of Television News,* doctoral dissertation, Columbia University, 1977.

6. Elihu Katz and Paul Lazarsfeld, *Personal Influence* (New York: Free Press, 1955).

7. Gary Steiner, *The People Look at Television* (New York: Knopf, 1963); Robert Bower, *Television and the Public* (New York: Holt, Rinehart and Winston, 1973).

8. For the rationale for this procedure, see J. Lyle, "Television in Daily Life: Patterns of Use Overview," in E. Rubinstein, G. Comstock, and J. Murray, eds., *Television and Social Behavior* (Washington, D.C.: Government Printing Office, 1972), Vol. 4, pp. 1–32; and for index construction, see Levy, *op. cit.*

9. See, for example, Mark R. Levy, "Experiencing Television News," *Journal of Communication,* 27:112–117 (Autumn, 1977).

10. At the time of this study, each of the three networks had a regularly scheduled commentary by either David Brinkley, Howard K. Smith, or Eric Severeid;

while the three Albany stations aired only occasional editorials within their newscasts.

11. Paul Lazarsfeld, Bernard Berelson and Hazel Gaudet, *The People's Choice* (New York: Columbia University Press, 1948).

12. L. Cronbach, "Coefficient Alpha and the Internal Structure of Tests," *Psychometrika,* 16:297–334 (1951). It should also be noted that the complete set of seven para-social interaction propositions have a mean inter-item correlation of .311 and an alpha coefficient of .73.

13. See, for example, Charles Wright and Herbert Hyman, "Voluntary Association Membership of American Adults: Evidence from National Sample Surveys," in B. Zisk, ed., *American Political Interest Groups: Readings in Theory and Research* (Belmont, Califronia: Wadsworth, 1969) and Sidney Verba and Norman Nie, *Participation in Democracy* (New York: Harper and Row, 1972).

14. R. H. Davis, "Television and the Older Adult," *Journal of Broadcasting,* 15:153–159 (Winter 1971).

15. Steiner, *op. cit.;* Bower, *op. cit.*

16. For an extended treatment of primary and secondary relations, see Kingsley Davis, *Human Society* (New York: Macmillan, 1948).

DONALD HORTON and R. RICHARD WOHL

Mass Communication and Para-Social Interaction: Observation on Intimacy at a Distance

This article first appeared in 1956 in the *Journal of Psychiatry*. It was one of the early explorations of the way media and media performers create the illusion of an interpersonal relationship. The authors call this a "para-social relationship" because it is based upon an implicit agreement between the performer and viewer that they will pretend the relationship is not mediated— that it will be carried on as though it were a face-to face-encounter. An example of this para-social relationship can be found among the viewers of the Johnny Carson show. Carson performs as though he were speaking directly to the viewer. They become a "team," where the viewer is privy to Carson's thoughts and feelings and Carson acts in a reciprocal manner. All other persons on the show are merely props used to enhance this "intimate" relationship between Carson and the viewer. As a consequence many viewers report that they "know" Johnny better than they do their next-door neighbor.

Notice how many television and radio shows utilize the "para-social" technique; *Eye Witness News*, for example, where the reporter-analyst-commentator is speaking directly to you, letting you in on feelings, jokes, and personal references. Does the radio DJ carry on a conversation with you as you drive along in your car? Think about how many of these surrogate interpersonal relationships you have with media performers.

One of the striking characteristics of the new mass media—radio, television, and the movies—is that they give the illusion of face-to-face relationship with the performer. The conditions of response to the performer are analogous to those in a primary group. The most remote and illustrious men are met as if they were in the circle of one's peers; the same is true of a character in a story who comes to life in these media in an especially vivid and arresting way. We propose to call this seeming face-to-face relationship between spectator and performer a *para-social relationship*.

In television, especially, the image which is presented makes available nuances of appearance and gesture to which ordinary social perception is

From *Psychiatry,* vol. 19, #3 (August 1956). Copyright © 1956 by The William Alanson White Psychiatric Foundation. Reprinted by special permission of the William Alanson White Psychiatric Foundation, Inc.

attentive and to which interaction is cued. Sometimes the "actor"— whether he is playing himself or performing in a fictional role—is seen engaged with others; but often he faces the spectator, uses the mode of direct address, talks as if he were conversing personally and privately. The audience, for its part, responds with something more than mere running observation; it is, as it were, subtly insinuated into the program's action and internal social relationships and, by dint of this kind of staging, is ambiguously transformed into a group which observes and participates in the show by turns. The more the performer seems to adjust his performance to the supposed response of the audience, the more the audience tends to make the response anticipated. This simulacrum of conversational give and take may be called *para-social interaction*.

Para-social relations may be governed by little or no sense of obligation, effort, or responsibility on the part of the spectator. He is free to withdraw at any moment. If he remains involved, these para-social relations provide a framework within which much may be added by fantasy. But these are differences of degree, not of kind, from what may be termed the ortho-social. The crucial difference in experience obviously lies in the lack of effective reciprocity, and this the audience cannot normally conceal from itself. To be sure, the audience is free to choose among the relationships offered, but it cannot create new ones. The interaction, characteristically, is one-sided, nondialectical, controlled by the performer, and not susceptible of mutual development. There are, of course, ways in which the spectators can make their feelings known to the performers and the technicians who design the programs, but these lie outside the para-social interaction itself. Whoever finds the experience unsatisfying has only the option to withdraw.

What we have said so far forcibly recalls the theatre as an ambiguous meeting ground on which real people play out the roles of fictional characters. For a brief interval, the fictional takes precedence over the actual, as the actor becomes identified with the fictional role in the magic of the theatre. This glamorous confusion of identities is temporary: the worlds of fact and fiction meet only for the moment. And the actor, when he takes his bows at the end of the performance, crosses back over the threshold into the matter-of-fact world.

Radio and television, however—and in what follows we shall speak primarily of television—are hospitable to both these worlds in continuous interplay. They are alternately public platforms and theatres, extending the para-social relationship now to leading people of the world of affairs, now to fictional characters, sometimes even to puppets anthropomorphically transformed into "personalities," and, finally, to theatrical stars who appear in their capacities as real celebrities. But of particular interest is the creation by these media of a new type of performer: quiz-masters, announcers, "interviewers" in a new "show-business" world—in brief, a special category of "personalities" whose existence is a function of the media themselves. These "personalities" usually, are not prominent in any of the social spheres beyond the media.[1] They exist for their audiences only in the para-social relation. Lacking an appropriate name for these performers, we shall call them *personae*.

The Role of the Persona

The persona is the typical and indigenous figure of the social scene presented by radio and television. To say that he is familiar and intimate is to use pale and feeble language for the pervasiveness and closeness with which multitudes feel his presence. The spectacular fact about such personae is that they can claim and achieve an intimacy with what are literally crowds of strangers, and this intimacy, even if it is an imitation and a shadow of what is ordinarily meant by that word, is extremely influential with, and satisfying for, the great numbers who willingly receive it and share in it. They "know" such a persona in somewhat the same way they know their chosen friends: through direct observation and interpretation of his appearance, his gestures and voice, his conversation and conduct in a variety of situations. Indeed, those who make up his audience are invited, by designed informality, to make precisely these evaluations—to consider that they are involved in a face-to-face exchange rather than in passive observation. When the television camera pans down on a performer, the illusion is strong that he is enhancing the presumed intimacy by literally coming closer. But the persona's image, while partial, contrived, and penetrated by illusion, is no fantasy or dream; his performance is an objectively perceptible action in which the viewer is implicated imaginatively, but which he does not imagine.

The persona offers, above all, a continuing relationship. His appearance is a regular and dependable event, to be counted on, planned for, and integrated into the routines of daily life. His devotees live with him and share the small episodes of his public life—and to some extent even of his private life away from the show. Indeed, their continued association with him acquires a history, and the accumulation of shared past experiences gives additional meaning to the present performance. This bond is symbolized by allusions that lack meaning for the casual observer and appear occult to the outsider. In time, the devotee—the "fan"—comes to believe that he "knows" the persona more intimately and profoundly than others do; that he "understands" his character and appreciates his values and motives.[2] Such an accumulation of knowledge and intensification of loyalty, however, appears to be a kind of growth without development, for the one-sided nature of the connection precludes a progressive and mutual reformulation of its value and aims.[3]

The persona may be considered by his audience as a friend, counselor, comforter, and model; but, unlike real associates, he has the peculiar virtue of being standardized according to the "formula" for his character and performance which he and his managers have worked out and embodied in an appropriate "production format." Thus his character and pattern of action remain basically unchanged in a world of otherwise disturbing change. The persona is ordinarily predictable, and gives his adherents no unpleasant surprises. In their association with him there are no problems of understanding or empathy too great to be solved. Typically, there are no challenges to a spectator's self—to his ability to take the reciprocal part in the performance that is assigned to him—that cannot be met comfortably. This reliable sameness is only approximated, and then only in the short run, by the figures of fiction. On television, Groucho is always sharp; Godfrey is always warm-hearted.

The Bond of Intimacy

It is an unvarying characteristic of these "personality" programs that the greatest pains are taken by the persona to create an illusion of intimacy. We call it an illusion because the relationship between the persona and any member of his audience is inevitably one-sided, and reciprocity between the two can only be suggested. There are several principal strategies for achieving this illusion of intimacy.

Most characteristic is the attempt of the persona to duplicate the gestures, conversational style, and milieu of an informal face-to-face gathering. This accounts, in great measure, for the casualness with which even the formalities of program scheduling are treated. The spectator is encouraged to gain the impression that what is taking place on the program gains a momentum of its own in the very process of being enacted. Thus Steve Allen is always pointing out to his audience that "we never know what is going to happen on this show." In addition, the persona tries to maintain a flow of small talk which gives the impression that he is responding to and sustaining the contributions of an invisible interlocutor. Dave Garroway, who has mastered this style to perfection, has described how he stumbled on the device in his early days in radio.

> Most talk on the radio in those days was formal and usually a little stiff. But I just rambled along, saying whatever came into my mind. I was introspective. I tried to pretend that I was chatting with a friend over a highball late in the evening. . . . Then—and later—I consciously tried to talk to the listener as an individual, to make each listener feel that he knew me and I knew him. It seemed to work pretty well then and later. I know that strangers often stop me on the street today, call me Dave and seem to feel that we are old friends who know all about each other.[4]

In addition to creating an appropriate tone and patter, the persona tries as far as possible to eradicate, or at least to blur, the line which divides him and his show, as a formal performance, from the audience both in the studio and at home. The most usual way of achieving this ambiguity is for the persona to treat his supporting cast as a group of close intimates. Thus all the members of the cast will be addressed by their first names, or by special nicknames, to emphasize intimacy. They very quickly develop, or have imputed to them, stylized character traits which, as members of the supporting cast, they will indulge in and exploit regularly in program after program. The member of the audience, therefore, not only accumulates an historical picture of "the kinds of people they really are," but tends to believe that this fellowship includes him by extension. As a matter of fact, all members of the program who are visible to the audience will be drawn into this by-play to suggest this ramification of intimacy.

Furthermore, the persona may try to step out of the particular format of his show and literally blend with the audience. Most usually, the persona leaves the stage and mingles with the studio audience in a question-and-answer exchange. In some few cases, and particularly on the Steve Allen show, this device has been carried a step further. Thus Allen has managed to blend even with the home audience by the maneuver of training a television camera on the street outside the studio and, in effect, suspending his own show and converting all the world outside into a stage. Allen, his supporting cast, and the audience, both at home and in the studio, watch together what transpires on the street—the persona and his spectators symbolically united as one big audience. In this way, Allen erases for the moment the line which separates persona and spectator.

In addition to the management of relationships between the persona and performers, and between him and his audience, the technical devices of the media themselves are exploited to create illusions of intimacy.

> For example [Dave Garroway explains in this connection], we developed the "subjective-camera" idea, which was simply making the camera be the eyes of the audience. In one scene the camera—that's you, the viewer—approached the door of a dentist's office, saw a sign that the dentist was out to lunch, sat down nervously in the waiting room. The dentist returned and beckoned to the camera, which went in and sat in the big chair. "Open wide," the dentist said, poking a huge, wicked-looking drill at the camera. There was a roar as the drill was turned on, sparks flew and the camera vibrated and the viewers got a magnified version of sitting in the dentist's chair—except that it didn't hurt.[5]

All these devices are indulged in not only to lure the attention of the audience, and to create the easy impression that there is a kind of participation open to them in the program itself, but also to highlight the chief values stressed in such "personality" shows. These are sociability, easy affability, friendship, and close contact—briefly, all the values associated with free access to and easy participation in pleasant social interaction in primary groups. Because the relationship between persona and audience is one-sided and cannot be developed mutually, very nearly the whole burden of creating a plausible imitation of intimacy is thrown on the persona and on the show of which he is the pivot. If he is successful in initiating an intimacy which his audience can believe in, then the audience may help him maintain it by fan mail and by the various other kinds of support which can be provided indirectly to buttress his actions.

The Role of the Audience

At one extreme, the "personality" program is like a drama in having a cast of characters, which includes the persona, his professional supporting cast, nonprofessional contestants and interviewees, and the studio audience. At the other extreme, the persona addresses his entire performance to the home audience with undisturbed intimacy. In the dramatic type of program, the participation of the spectator involves, we presume, the same taking of successive roles and deeper empathic involvements in the leading roles which occurs in any observed social interaction.[6] It is possible that the spectator's "collaborative expectancy"[7] may assume the more profound form of identification with one or more of the performers. But such identification can hardly be more than intermittent. The "personality" program, unlike the theatrical drama, does not demand or even permit the esthetic illusion—that loss of situational reference and self-consciousness in which the audience not only accepts the symbol as reality, but fully assimilates the symbolic role. The persona and his staff maintain the parasocial relationship, continually referring to and addressing the home audience as a third party to the program; and such references remind the spectator of his own independent identity. The only illusion maintained is that of directness and immediacy of participation.

When the persona appears alone, in apparent face-to-face interaction with the home viewer, the latter is still more likely to maintain his own identity without interruption, for he is called upon to make appropriate responses which are complementary to those of the persona. This 'answering' role is, to a degree, voluntary and independent. In it, the spectator retains control over the content of his participation rather than surrendering control through identification with others, as he does when absorbed in watching a drama or movie.

This independence is relative, however, in a twofold sense: First, it is relative in the profound sense that the very act of entering into any interaction with another involves *some* adaptation to the other's perspectives, if communication is to be achieved at all. And, second, in the present case, it is relative because the role of the persona is enacted in such a way, or is of such a character, that an *appropriate* answering role is specified by implication and suggestion. The persona's performance, therefore, is open-ended, calling for a rather specific answering role to give it closure.[8]

The general outlines of the appropriate audience role are perceived intuitively from familiarity with the common cultural patterns on which the role of the persona is constructed. These roles are chiefly derived from the primary relations of friendship and the family, characterized by intimacy, sympathy, and sociability. The audience is expected to accept the situation defined by the program format as credible, and to concede as "natural" the rules and conventions governing the actions performed and the values realized. It should play the role of the loved one to the persona's lover; the admiring dependent to his father-surrogate; the earnest citizen to his fearless opponent of political evils. It is expected to benefit by his wisdom, reflect on his advice, sympathize with him in his difficulties, forgive his mistakes, buy the products that he recommends, and keep his sponsor informed of the esteem in which he is held.

Other attitudes than compliance in the assigned role are, of course, possible. One may reject, take an analytical stance, perhaps even find a cynical amusement in refusing the offered gambit and playing some other role not implied in the script, or view the proceedings with detached curiosity or hostility. But such attitudes as these are, usually, for the one-time viewer. The faithful audience is one that can accept the gambit offered; and the functions of the program for this audience are served not by the mere perception of it, but by the role-enactment that completes it.

The Coaching of Audience Attitudes

Just how the situation should be defined by the audience, what to expect of the persona, what attitudes to take toward him, what to "do" as a participant in the program, is not left entirely to the common experience and intuitions of the audience. Numerous devices are used in a deliberate "coaching of attitudes," to use Kenneth Burke's phrase.[9] The typical program format calls for a studio audience to provide a situation of face-to-face interaction for the persona, and exemplifies to the home audience an enthusiastic and "correct" response. The more interaction occurs, the more clearly is demonstrated the kind of man the persona is, the values to be shared in association with him, and the kind of support to give him. A similar model of appropriate response may be supplied by the professional assistants who, though technically performers, act in a subordinate and deferential reciprocal relation toward the persona. The audience is schooled in correct responses to the persona by a variety of other means as well. Other personae may be invited as guests, for example, who play up to the host in exemplary fashion; or persons drawn from the audience may be maneuvered into fulfilling this function. And, in a more direct and literal fashion, reading excerpts from fan mail may serve the purpose.

Beyond the coaching of specific attitudes toward personae, a general propaganda on their behalf flows from the performers themselves, their press agents, and the mass communication industry. Its major theme is that the performer should be loved and admired. Every attempt possible is made to strengthen the illusion of reciprocity and rapport in order to offset the inherent impersonality of the media themselves. The jargon of show business teems with special terms for the mysterious ingredients of such rapport: ideally, a performer should have "heart," should be "sincere";[10] his performance should be "real" and "warm."[11] The publicity campaigns built around successful performers continually emphasize the sympathetic image which, it is hoped, the audience is perceiving and developing.[12]

The audience, in its turn, is expected to contribute to the illusion by be-lieving in it, and by rewarding the persona's "sincerity" with "loyalty." The audience is entreated to assume a sense of personal obligation to the performer, to help him in his struggle for "success" if he is "on the way up," or to maintain his success if he has already won it. "Success" in show business is itself a theme which is prominently exploited in this kind of propaganda. It forms the basis of many movies; it appears often in the patter of the leading comedians and in the exhortations of MC's; it domi-nates the so-called amateur hours and talent shows; and it is subject to frequent comment in interviews with "show people." [13]

Conditions of Acceptance of the Para-Social Role by the Audience

The acceptance by the audience of the role offered by the program involves acceptance of the explicit and implicit terms which define the situation and the action to be carried out in the program. Unless the spectator under-stands these terms, the role performances of the participants are mean-ingless to him; and unless he accepts them, he cannot "enter into" the per-formance himself. But beyond this, the spectator must be able to play the part demanded of him; and this raises the question of the compatibility be-tween his normal self—as a system of role-patterns and self-conceptions with their implicated norms and values—and the kind of self postulated by the program schema and the actions of the persona. In short, one may conjecture that the probability of rejection of the proffered role will be greater the less closely the spectator "fits" the role prescription.

To accept the gambit without the necessary personality qualifications is to invite increasing dissatisfaction and alienation—which the student of the media can overcome only by a deliberate, imaginative effort to take the postulated role. The persona himself takes the role of his projected audi-ence in the interpretation of his own actions, often with the aid of cues provided by a studio audience. He builds his performance on a cumulative structure of assumptions about their response, and so postulates—more or less consciously—the complex of attitudes to which his own actions are adapted. A spectator who fails to make the anticipated responses will find himself further and further removed from the base-line of common under-standing. [14] One would expect the "error" to be cumulative, and eventually to be carried, perhaps, to the point at which the spectator is forced to re-sign in confusion, disgust, anger, or boredom. If a significant portion of the audience fails in this way, the persona's "error in role-taking" [15] has to be corrected with the aid of audience research, "program doctors," and other aids. But, obviously, the intended adjustment is to some average or typical spectator, and cannot take too much account of deviants.

The simplest example of such a failure to fulfill the role prescription would be the case of an intellectual discussion in which the audience is presumed to have certain basic knowledge and the ability to follow the development of the argument. Those who cannot meet these requirements find the discussion progressively less comprehensible. A similar progressive alienation probably occurs when children attempt to follow an adult program or movie. One observes them absorbed in the opening scenes, but gradually losing interest as the developing action leaves them behind. Another such situation might be found in the growing confusion and restiveness of some audiences watching foreign movies or "high-brow" drama. Such resistance is also manifested when some members of an audience are asked to take the opposite-sex role—the woman's perspective is rejected more commonly by men than vice versa—or when audiences refuse to accept empathically the roles of outcasts or those of racial or cultural minorities whom they consider inferior. [16]

It should be observed that merely witnessing a program is not evidence that a spectator has played the required part. Having made the initial commitment, he may "string along" with it at a low level of empathy but reject it retrospectively. The experience does not end with the program itself. On the contrary, it may be only after it has ended that it is submitted to intellectual analysis and integrated into, or rejected by, the self; this occurs especially in those discussions which the spectator may undertake with other people in which favorable or unfavorable consensual interpretations and judgments are arrived at. It is important to enter a qualification at this point. The suspension of immediate judgment is probably more complete in the viewing of the dramatic program, where there is an esthetic illusion to be accepted, than in the more self-conscious viewing of "personality" programs.

Values of the Para-Social Role
for the Audience

What para-social roles are acceptable to the spectator and what benefits their enactment has for him would seem to be related to the systems of patterned roles and social situations in which he is involved in his everyday life. The values of a para-social role may be related, for example, to the demands being made upon the spectator for achievement in certain statuses. Such demands, to pursue this instance further, may be manifested in the expectations of others, or they may be self-demands, with the concomitant emergence of more or less satisfactory self-conceptions. The enactment of a para-social role may therefore constitute an exploration and development of new role possibilities, as in the experimental phases of actual, or aspired to, social mobility.[17] It may offer a recapitulation of roles no longer played—roles which, perhaps, are no longer possible. The audience is diversified in terms of life-stages, as well as by other social and cultural characteristics; thus, what for youth may be the anticipatory enactment of roles to be assumed in the future may be, for older persons, a reliving and reevaluation of the actual or imagined past.

The enacted role may be an idealized version of an everyday performance—a successful para-social approximation of an ideal pattern, not often, perhaps never, achieved in real life. Here the contribution of the persona may be to hold up a magic mirror to his followers, playing his reciprocal part more skillfully and ideally than do the partners of the real world. So Liberace, for example, outdoes the ordinary husband in gentle understanding, or Nancy Berg outdoes the ordinary wife in amorous complaisance. Thus, the spectator may be enabled to play his part suavely and completely in imagination as he is unable to do in actuality.

If we have emphasized the opportunities offered for playing a vicarious or actual role, it is because we regard this as the key operation in the spectator's activity, and the chief avenue of the program's meaning for him. This is not to overlook the fact that every social role is reciprocal to the social roles of others, and that it is as important to learn to understand, to decipher, and to anticipate their conduct as it is to manage one's own. The function of the mass media, and of the programs we have been discussing, is also the exemplification of the patterns of conduct one needs to understand and cope with in others as well as of those patterns which one must apply to one's self. Thus the spectator is instructed variously in the behaviors of the opposite sex, of people of higher and lower status, of people in particular occupations and professions. In a quantitative sense, by reason of the sheer volume of such instruction, this may be the most important aspect of the para-social experience, if only because each person's roles are relatively few, while those of the others in his social worlds are very numerous. In this culture, it is evident that to be prepared to meet all the exigencies of a changing social situation, no matter how limited it may be, could—and often does—require a great stream of plays and stories, advice columns and social how-to-do-it books. What, after all, is soap opera but an interminable exploration of the contingencies to be met with in "home life?" [18]

In addition to the possibilities we have already mentioned, the media present opportunities for the playing of roles to which the spectator has—or feels he has—a legitimate claim, but for which he finds no opportunity in his social environment. This function of the para-social then can properly be called compensatory, inasmuch as it provides the socially and psychologically isolated with a chance to enjoy the elixir of sociability. The "personality" program—in contrast to the drama—is especially designed to provide occasion for good-natured joking and teasing, praising and admiring, gossiping and telling anecdotes, in which the values of friendship and intimacy are stressed.

It is typical of the "personality" programs that ordinary people are shown being treated, for the moment, as persons of consequence. In the interviews of nonprofessional contestants, the subject may be praised for having children—whether few or many does not matter; he may be flattered on his youthful appearance; and he is likely to be honored the more—with applause from the studio audience—the longer he has been "successfully" married. There is even applause, and a consequent heightening of ceremony and importance for the person being interviewed, at mention of the town he lives in. In all this, the values realized for the subject are those of a harmonious, successful participation in one's appointed place in the social order. The subject is represented as someone secure in the affections and respect of others, and he probably senses the experience as a gratifying reassurance of social solidarity and self-confidence. For the audience, in the studio and at home, it is a model of appropriate role performance—as husband, wife, mother, as "attractive" middle age, "remarkably youthful" old age, and the like. It is, furthermore, a demonstration of the fundamental generosity and good will of all concerned, including, of course, the commercial sponsor.[19] But unlike a similar exemplification of happy sociability in a play or a novel, the television or radio program is real; that is to say, it is enveloped in the continuing reassurances and gratifications of objective responses. For instance there may be telephone calls to "outside" contestants, the receipt and acknowledgement of requests from the home audience, and so on. Almost every member of the home audience is left with the comfortable feeling that he too, if he wished, could appropriately take part in this healing ceremony.

Extreme Para-Sociability

For the great majority of the audience, the para-social is complementary to normal social life. It provides a social milieu in which the everyday assumptions and understandings of primary group interaction and sociability are demonstrated and reaffirmed. The "personality" program, however, is peculiarly favorable to the formation of compensatory attachments by the socially isolated, the socially inept, the aged and invalid, the timid and rejected. The persona himself is readily available as an object of love—especially when he succeeds in cultivating the recommended quality of "heart." Nothing could be more reasonable or natural than that people who are isolated and lonely should seek sociability and love wherever they think they can find it. It is only when the para-social relationship becomes a substitute for autonomous social participation, when it proceeds in absolute defiance of objective reality, that it can be regarded as pathological.[20]

The existence of a marginal segment of the lonely in American society has been recognized by the mass media themselves, and from time to time specially designed offerings have been addressed to this minority.[21] In these programs, the maximum illusion of a personal, intimate relationship has been attempted. They represent the extreme development of the para-social, appealing to the most isolated, and illustrate, in an exaggerated way, the principles we believe to apply through the whole range of "personality" programs. The programs which fall in this extreme category promise not only escape from an unsatisfactory and drab reality, but try to prop up the sagging self-esteem of their unhappy audience by the most blatant reassurances. Evidently on the presumption that the maximum of loneliness is the lack of a sexual partner, these programs tend to be addressed to one sex or the other, and to endow the persona with an erotic suggestiveness.[22]

Such seems to have been the purpose and import of *The Lonesome Gal,* a short radio program which achieved such popularity in 1951 that it was broadcast in ninety different cities. Within a relatively short time, the program spread from Hollywood, where it had originated, across the country to New York, where it was heard each evening at 11:15.[23]

The outline of the program was simplicity itself. After a preliminary flourish of music, and an identifying announcement, the main and only character was ushered into the presence of the audience. She was exactly as represented, apparently a lonesome girl, but without a name or a history. Her entire performance consisted of an unbroken monologue unembarrassed by plot, climax, or denouement. On the continuum of para-social action, this is the very opposite of self-contained drama; it is, in fact, nothing but the reciprocal of the spectator's own para-social role. The Lonesome Gal simply spoke in a throaty, unctuous voice whose suggestive sexiness belied the seeming modesty of her words.[24]

From the first, the Lonesome Gal took a strongly intimate line, almost as if she were addressing a lover in the utter privacy of some hidden rendez-vous:

> Darling, you look so tired, and a little put out about something this evening. . . . You are worried, I feel it. Lover, you need rest . . . rest and someone who understands you. Come, lie down on the couch, relax, I want to stroke your hair gently . . . I am with you now, always with you. You are never alone, you must never forget that you mean everything to me, that I live only for you, your Lonesome Gal.

At some time in the course of each program, the Lonesome Gal specifically assured her listeners that these endearments were not being addressed to the hale and handsome, the clever and the well-poised, but to the shy, the withdrawn—the lonely men who had always dreamed, in their inmost reveries, of finding a lonesome girl to comfort them.

The world is literally full of such lonesome girls, she urged; like herself, they were all seeking love and companionship. Fate was unkind, however, and they were disappointed and left in unrequited loneliness, with no one to console them. On the radio, the voice was everybody's Lonesome Gal:

> Don't you see, darling, that I am only one of millions of lonely girls. I belong to him who spends his Sundays in museums, who strolls in Central Park look-ing sadly at the lovers there. But I am more fortunate than any of these lovers, because I have you. Do you know that I am always thinking about you? . . . You need someone to worry about you, who will look after your health, you need me. I share your hopes and your disappointments. I, your Lonesome Gal, your girl, to whom you so often feel drawn in the big city where so many are lonely. . . .

The Lonesome Gal was inundated with thousands of letters tendering pro-posals of marriage, the writers respectfully assuring her that she was in-deed the woman for whom they had been vainly searching all their lives.

As a character in a radio program, the Lonesome Gal had certain advan-tages in the cultivation of para-social attachments over television offerings of a similar tenor. She was literally an unseen presence, and each of her listeners could, in his mind's eye, picture her as his fancy dictated. She could, by an act of the imagination, be almost any age or any size, have any background.

Not so Miss Nancy Berg, who began to appear last year in a five-minute television spot called *Count Sheep*.[25] She is seen at 1 A.M. each weekday. After an announcement card has flashed to warn the audience that she is about to appear, and a commercial has been read, the stage is entirely given over to Miss Berg. She emerges in a lavishly decorated bedroom clad in a peignoir, or negligee, minces around the room stretches, yawns, jumps into bed, and then wriggles out again for a final romp with her French poodle. Then she crawls under the covers, cuddles up for the night, and composes herself for sleep. The camera pans down for an enormous close-up, and the microphones catch Miss Berg whispering a sleepy "Good-night." From out of the distance soft music fades in, and the last thing the viewers see is a cartoon of sheep jumping over a fence. The program is over.

There is a little more to the program than this. Each early morning, Miss Berg is provided with a special bit of dialogue or business which, brief though it is, delights her audience afresh:

> Once, she put her finger through a pizza pie, put the pie on a record player and what came out was Dean Martin singing "That's Amore." She has read, with expression, from "Romeo and Juliet," "Of Time and the River," and her fan mail. She has eaten grapes off a toy ferris-wheel and held an imaginary telephone conversation with someone who, she revealed when it was all over, had the wrong number.[26]

Sometimes she regales her viewers with a personal detail. For instance, she has explained that the dog which appears on the show is her own. Its name is "Phaedeaux," she disclosed coyly, pronounced "Fido."

It takes between twenty and twenty-six people, aside from Miss Berg herself, to put this show on the air; and all of them seem to be rather bemused by the success she is enjoying. Her manager, who professes himself happily baffled by the whole thing, tried to discover some of the reasons for this success in a recent interview when he was questioned about the purpose of the show:

> Purpose? The purpose was, Number 1, to get a sponsor; Number 2, to give people a chance to look at a beautiful girl at 1 o'clock in the morning; Number 3, to do some off-beat stuff. I think this girl's going to be a big star, and this was a way to get attention for her. We sure got it. She's a showman, being slightly on the screwball side, but there's a hell of a brain there. She just doesn't touch things—she caresses things. Sometimes, she doesn't say anything out loud, maybe she's thinking what you're thinking.[27]

The central fact in this explanation seems to be the one which touches on Miss Berg's ability to suggest to her audience that she is privy to, and might share, their inmost thoughts. This is precisely the impression that the Lonesome Gal attempted to create, more directly and more conversationally, in her monologue. Both programs were geared to fostering and maintaining the illusion of intimacy which we mentioned earlier in our discussion. The sexiness of both these programs must, we think, be read in this light. They are seductive in more than the ordinary sense. Sexual suggestiveness is used probably because it is one of the most obvious cues to a supposed intimacy—a catalytic for prompt sociability.

Such roles as Miss Berg and the Lonesome Gal portray require a strict adherence to a standardized portrayal of their "personalities." Their actual personalities, and the details of their backgrounds, are not allowed to become sharply focused and differentiated, for each specification of particular detail might alienate some part of the audience, or might interfere with rapport. Thus, Miss Berg, despite the apparent intimacy of her show—the audience is invited into her bedroom—refuses to disclose her "dimensions," although this is a piece of standard information freely available about movie beauties.

The Lonesome Gal was even more strict regarding personal details. Only once did she appear in a public performance away from her radio show. On that occasion she wore a black mask over her face, and was introduced to her "live" audience on the same mysteriously anonymous terms as she met her radio audience. Rumor, however, was not idle, and one may safely presume that these rumors ran current to provide her with a diffuse glamour of a kind which her audience would think appropriate. It was said that she lived in Hollywood, but that she originally came from Texas, a state which, in popular folklore, enjoys a lively reputation for improbabilities and extravagances. Whispers also had it that French and Indian blood coursed in her veins, a combination all too likely to suggest wildness and passion to the stereotypes of her listeners. For the rest, nothing was known of her, and no further details were apparently ever permitted.

The Image as Artifact

The encouragement of, not to say demand for, a sense of intimacy with the persona and an appreciation of him as a "real" person is in contradiction to the fact that the image he presents is to some extent a construct—a facade—which bears little resemblance to his private character. The puritanical conventions of the contemporary media make this facade a decidedly namby-pamby one. With few exceptions, the popular figures of radio and television are, or give the appearance of being, paragons of middle-class virtue with decently modest intellectual capacities. Since some of them are really very intelligent and all of them are, like the rest of us, strong and weak, good and bad, the facade is maintained only by concealing discrepancies between the public image and the private life.

The standard technique is not to make the private life an absolute secret—for the interest of the audience cannot be ignored—but to create an acceptable facade of private life as well, a more or less contrived private image of the life behind the contrived public image. This is the work of the press agent, the publicity man, and the fan magazine. How successfully they have done their work is perhaps indicated by the current vogue of magazines devoted to the "dirt" behind the facade.[28]

Public preoccupation with the private lives of stars and personae is not self-explanatory. Sheer appreciation and understanding of their performances as actors, singers, or entertainers does not depend upon information about them as persons. And undoubtedly many members of the audience do enjoy them without knowing or caring to know about their homes, children, sports cars, or favorite foods, or keeping track of the ins and outs of their marriages and divorces. It has often been said that the Hollywood stars—and their slightly less glamorous colleagues of radio and television—are modern "heroes" in whom are embodied popular cultural values, and that the interest in them is a form of hero-worship and vicarious experience through identification. Both of these interpretations may be true; we would emphasize, however, a third motive—the confirmation and enrichment of the para-social relation with them. It may be precisely because this is basically an illusion that such an effort is required to confirm it. It seems likely that those to whom para-social relationships are important must constantly strive to overcome the inherent limitations of these relationships, either by elaborating the image of the other, or by attempting to transcend the illusion by making some kind of actual contact with him.

Given the prolonged intimacy of para-social relations with the persona, accompanied by the assurance that beyond the illusion there is a real person, it is not surprising that many members of the audience become dissatisfied and attempt to establish actual contact with him. Under exactly what conditions people are motivated to write to the performer, or to go further and attempt to meet him—to draw from him a personal response—we do not know. The fan phenomenon has been studied to some extent,[29] but fan clubs and fan demonstrations are likely to be group affairs, motivated as much by the values of collective participation with others as by devotion to the persona himself. There are obvious social rewards for the trophies of contact with the famous or notorious—from autographs to handker-chiefs dipped in the dead bandit's blood—which invite toward their pos-sessor some shadow of the attitudes of awe or admiration originally directed to their source. One would suppose that contact with, and recog-niton by, the persona transfers some of his prestige and influence to the ac-tive fan. And most often such attempts to reach closer to the persona are limited to letters and to visits. But in the extreme case, the social rewards of mingling with the mighty are foregone for the satisfaction of some deeply private purpose. The follower is actually "in love" with the per-sona, and demands real reciprocity which the para-social relation cannot provide.

A case in point is provided in the "advice" column of a newspaper.[30] The writer, Miss A, has "fallen in love" with a television star, and has begun to rearrange and reorder her life to conform to her devotion to this man whom she has never actually met. It is significant, incidentally, that the man is a local performer—the probability of actually meeting him must seem greater than would be the case if he were a New York or Hollywood figure. The border between Miss A's fantasies and reality is being steadily encroached upon by the important affective investment she has made in this relationship. Her letter speaks for itself:

> It has taken me two weeks to get the nerve to write this letter. I have fallen head over heels in love with a local television star. We've never met and I've seen him only on the TV screen and in a play. This is not a 16-year-old infatu-ation, for I am 23, a college graduate and I know the score. For the last two months I have stopped dating because all men seem childish by comparison. Nothing interests me. I can't sleep and my modeling job bores me. Please give me some advice.

The writer of this letter would seem to be not one of the lonely ones, but rather a victim of the "magic mirror" in which she sees a man who plays the role reciprocal to hers so ideally that all the men she actually knows "seem childish by comparison." Yet this is not the image of a fictional hero; it is a "real" man. It is interesting that the newspaper columnist, in replying, chooses to attack on this point—not ridiculing the possibility of a meeting with the star, but denying the reality of the image:

> I don't know what you learned in college, but you are flunking the course of common sense. You have fallen for a piece of celluloid as unreal as a picture

on the wall. The personality you are goofy about on the TV screen is a hoked-up character, and any similarity between him and the real man is purely miraculous.

This case is revealing, however, not only because it attests to the vigor with which a para-social relationship may become endowed, but also because it demonstrates how narrow the line often is between the more ordinary forms of social interaction and those which characterize relations with the persona. In an extreme case, such as that of Miss A, her attachment to the persona has greatly invaded her everyday life—so much so that, without control, it will warp or destroy her relations with the opposite sex. But the extreme character of this response should not obscure the fact that ordinarily para-social relations do "play back," as it were, into the daily lives of many. The man who reports to his friend the wise thing that Godfrey said, who carefully plans not to make another engagement at the time his favorite is on, is responding similarly, albeit to a different and milder degree. Para-social interaction, as we have said, is analogous to and in many ways resembles social interaction in ordinary primary groups.

The new mass media are obviously distinguished by their ability to confront a member of the audience with an apparently intimate, face-to-face association with a performer. Nowhere does this feature of their technological resources seem more forcefully or more directly displayed than in the "personality" program. In these programs a new kind of performer, the persona, is featured whose main attribute seems to be his ability to cultivate and maintain this suggested intimacy. As he appears before his audience, in program after program, he carries on recurrent social transactions with his adherents; he sustains what we have called para-social interaction. These adherents, as members of his audience, play a psychologically active role which, under some conditions, but by no means invariably, passes over into the more formal, overt, and expressive activities of fan behavior.

As an implicit response to the performance of the persona, this para-social interaction is guided and to some extent controlled by him. The chief basis of this guidance and control, however, lies in the imputation to the spectator of a kind of role complementary to that of the persona himself. This imputed complementary role is social in character, and is some variant of the role or roles normally played in the spectator's primary social groups. It is defined, demonstrated, and inculcated by numerous devices of radio and television showmanship. When it has been learned, the persona is assured that the entire transaction between himself and the audience—of which his performance is only one phase—is being properly completed by the unseen audience.

Seen from this standpoint, it seems to follow that there is no such discontinuity between everyday and para-social experience as is suggested by the common practice, among observers of these media, of using the analogy of fantasy or dream in the interpretation of programs which are essentially dramatic in character. The relationship of the devotee to the persona is, we suggest, experienced as of the same order as, and related to, the network of actual social relations. This, we believe, is even more the case when the persona becomes a common object to the members of the primary groups in which the spectator carries on his everyday life. As a matter of fact, it seems profitable to consider the interaction with the persona as a phase of the role-enactments of the spectator's daily life.

Our observations in this paper, however, are intended to be no more than suggestions for further work. It seems to us that it would be a most rewarding approach to such phenomena if one could, from the viewpoint of an interactional social psychology, learn in detail how these para-social interactions are integrated into the matrix of usual social activity.

In this connection, it is relevant to remark that there is a tradition—now of relatively long standing—that spectators, whether at sports events or television programs, are relatively passive. This assertion enjoys the status of an accredited hypothesis, but it is, after all, no more than a hypothesis. If it is taken literally and uncritically, it may divert the student's attention from what is actually transpiring in the audience. We believe that some such mode of analysis as we suggest here attunes the student of the mass media to hints *within the program itself* of cues to, and demands being made on, the audience for particular responses. From such an analytical vantage point the field of observation, so to speak, is widened and the observer is able to see more that is relevant to the exchange between performer and audience.

In essence, therefore, we would like to expand and capitalize on the truism that the persona and the "personality" programs are part of the lives of millions of people, by asking how both are assimilated, and by trying to discover what effects these responses have on the attitudes and actions of the audiences who are so devoted to and absorbed in this side of American culture.

Notes

1. They may move out into positions of leadership in the world at large as they become famous and influential. Frank Sinatra, for example, has become known as a "youth leader." Conversely, figures from the political world, to choose another example, may become media "personalities" when they appear regularly. Fiorello LaGuardia, the late Mayor of New York, is one such case.
2. Merton's discussion of the attitude toward Kate Smith of her adherents exemplifies, with much circumstantial detail, what we have said above. See Robert K. Merton, Marjorie Fiske, and Alberta Curtis, *Mass Persuasion: The Social Psychology of a War Bond Drive;* New York, Harper, 1946; especially Chapter 6.
3. There does remain the possibility that over the course of his professional life the persona, responding to influences from his audience, may develop new conceptions of himself and his role.
4. Dave Garroway as told to Joe Alex Morris, "I Lead a Goofy Life," *The Saturday Evening Post,* February 11, 1956; p. 62.
5. Garroway, *Saturday Evening Post,* p. 64.
6. See, for instance: George H. Mead, *Mind, Self and Society;* Chicago, Univ. of Chicago Press, 1934. Walter Coutu, *Emergent Human Nature;* New York, Knopf, 1949. Rosalind Dymond, "Personality and Empathy," *J. Consulting Psychol.* (1950) 14:343–350.
7. Burke uses this expression to describe an attitude evoked by formal rhetorical devices, but it seems equally appropriate here. See Kenneth Burke, *A Rhetoric of Motives;* New York, Prentice-Hall, 1950; p. 58.
8. This is in contrast to the closed system of the drama, in which all the roles are predetermined in their mutual relations.
9. Kenneth Burke, *Attitudes Toward History, Vol. 1;* New York, New Republic Publishing Co., 1937; see, for instance, p. 104.
10. See Merton's acute analysis of the audience's demand for "sincerity" as a reassurance against manipulation. *Mass Persuasion,* pp. 142–146.
11. These attributes have been strikingly discussed by Mervyn LeRoy, a Hollywood director, in a recent book. Although he refers specifically to the motion-picture star, similar notions are common in other branches of show business. "What draws you to certain people?" he asks. "I have said before that you can't be a really fine actress or actor without heart. You also have to possess the ability to project that heart, that feeling and emotion. The sympathy in your eyes will show. The audience has to feel sorry for the person on the screen. If there aren't moments when, rightly or wrongly, he moves the audience to sympathy, there's an actor who will never be big box-office." Mervyn LeRoy and Alyce Canfield, *It Takes More Than Talent;* New York, Knopf, 1953; p. 114.
12. Once an actor has succeeded in establishing a good relationship with his audience in a particular kind of dramatic role, he may be "typed" in that role. Stereotyping in the motion-picture industry is often rooted in the belief that sustained rapport with the audience can be achieved by repeating past success.

(This principle is usually criticized as detrimental to the talent of the actor, but it is a *sine qua non* for the persona whose professional success depends upon creating and sustaining a plausible and unchanging identity.) Sometimes, indeed, the Hollywood performer will actually take his name from a successful role; this is one of the principles on which Warner Brothers Studios selects the names of some of its actors. For instance, Donna Lee Hickey was renamed Mae Wynn after a character she portrayed, with great distinction, in *The Caine Mutiny*. See "Names of Hollywood Actors," *Names* (1955) 3:116.

13. The "loyalty" which is demanded of the audience is not necessarily passive or confined only to patronizing the persona's performance. Its active demonstration is called for in charity appeals, "marathons," and "telethons"; and, of course, it is expected to be freely transferable to the products advertised by the performer. Its most active form is represented by the organization of fan clubs with programs of activities and membership obligations, which give a continuing testimony of loyalty.

14. Comedians on radio and television frequently chide their audience if they do not laugh at the appropriate places, or if their response is held to be inadequate. The comedian tells the audience that if they don't respond promptly, he won't wait, whereupon the audience usually provides the demanded laugh. Sometimes the chiding is more oblique, as when the comedian interrupts his performance to announce that he will fire the writer of the unsuccessful joke. Again, the admonition to respond correctly is itself treated as a joke and is followed by a laugh.

15. Coutu, *Emergent Human Nature*, p. 294.

16. See, for example, W. Lloyd Warner and William E. Henry, "The Radio Day Time Serial: A Symbolic Analysis," *Genetic Psychol. Monographs* (1948) 37:3–71, the study of a daytime radio serial program in which it is shown that upper-middle-class women tend to reject identification with lower-middle-class women represented in the drama. Yet some people are willing to take unfamiliar roles. This appears to be especially characteristic of the intellectual whose distinction is not so much that he has cosmopolitan tastes and knowledge, but that he has the capacity to transcend the limits of his own culture in his identifications. Remarkably little is known about how this ability is developed.

17. Most students of the mass media occupy a cultural level somewhat above that of the most popular programs and personalities of the media, and necessarily look down upon them. But it should not be forgotten that for many millions indulgence in these media is a matter of looking up. Is it not also possible that some of the media permit a welcome regression, for some, from the higher cultural standards of their present status? This may be one explanation of the vogue of detective stories and science fiction among intellectuals, and might also explain the escape downward from middle-class standards in the literature of "low life" generally.

18. It is frequently charged that the media's description of this side of life is partial, shallow, and often false. It would be easier and more profitable to evaluate these criticisms if they were formulated in terms of role-theory. From the

viewpoint of any given role it would be interesting to know how well the media take account of the values and expectations of the role-reciprocators. What range of legitimate variations in role performance is acknowledged? How much attention is given to the problems arising from changing roles, and how creatively are these problems handled? These are only a few of the many similar questions which at once come to mind.

19. There is a close analogy here with one type of newspaper human-interest story which records extreme instances of role-achievement and their rewards. Such stories detail cases of extreme longevity, marriages of especially long duration, large numbers of children; deeds of heroism—role performance under "impossible" conditions; extraordinary luck, prizes, and so on.

20. Dave Garroway, after making the point that he has many "devout" admirers, goes on to say that "some of them . . . were a bit too devout." He tells the story of one lady "from a Western state" who "arrived in Chicago [where he was then broadcasting], registered at a big hotel as Mrs. Dave Garroway, opened several charge accounts in my name and established a joint bank account in which she deposited a large sum of money. Some months later she took a taxi to my hotel and informed the desk clerk she was moving in. He called a detective agency that we had engaged to check up on her, and they persuaded her to return home. Since then there have been others, but none so persistent." *Saturday Evening Post*, p. 62.

21. This group presumably includes those for whom "Lonely Hearts" and "Pen Pal" clubs operate.

22. While the examples which follow are of female personae addressing themselves to male audiences, it should be noted that for a time there was also a program on television featuring *The Continental*, who acted the part of a debonair foreigner and whose performance consisted of murmuring endearing remarks to an invisible female audience. He wore evening clothes and cut a figure in full conformity with the American stereotype of a suave European lover.

23. This program apparently evoked no very great amount of comment or criticism in the American press, and we are indebted to an article in a German illustrated weekly for details about the show, and for the verbatim quotations from the Lonesome Gal's monologue which we have retranslated into English. See "Ich bin bei dir, Liebling . . . ," *Weltbild* (Munich), March 1, 1952; p. 12.

24. This is in piquant contrast to the popular singers, the modesty of whose voice and mien is often belied by the sexiness of the words in the songs they sing.

25. The details relating to this show are based on Gilbert Millstein, "Tired of it All?" *The New York Times Magazine,* September 18, 1955; p. 44. See also "Beddy-Bye," *Time,* August 15, 1955; p. 45.

26. *The New York Times Magazine,* p. 44.

27. *The New York Times Magazine,* p. 44.

28. Such magazines as *Uncensored* and *Confidential* (which bears the subtitle, "Tells the Facts and Names the Names") enjoy enormous circulations, and

may be thought of as the very opposite of the fan magazine. They claim to "expose" the person behind the persona.

29. M. F. Thorp, *America at the Movies;* New Haven, Yale Univ. Press, 1939. S. Stansfeld Sargent, *Social Psychology;* New York, Ronald Press, 1950. K. P. Berliant, "The Nature and Emergence of Fan Behavior" (unpublished M.A. Thesis, Univ. of Chicago).

30. Ann Landers, "Your Problems," *Chicago Sun-Times,* October 25, 1955, p. 36.

KARL ERIK ROSENGREN and SWEN WINDAHL

Mass Media Consumption as a Functional Alternative

Professors Rosengren and Windahl have been studying groups in Sweden to determine under what circumstances people prefer media interaction over face-to-face interaction and what form this preference takes. They describe alternate ways available for gratifying our need for social interaction, i.e., parasocial interaction and character identification. What results is a typology of media consumption based on social needs.

Read the essay by Horton and Wohl for a more elaborate description of how and why we form para-social relationships with radio and television personalities.

. . . Our aim in this paper is to investigate a special family of media functions for the individual. We are trying to relate a certain type of gratification to a certain type of audience characteristic. Underlying this attempt is the conviction that sooner or later mass media research must cease using raw demographic variables for its independent variables, and simple amount of consumption for its dependent variable. Instead, various sociological and social psychological variables should be introduced as independent or intervening variables, while the dependent variable, the mass media consumption, should be qualitatively differentiated into various types of consumption. Before presenting our version of this programme, we must first discuss some relations between the individual, his needs and his possibilities to satisfy these needs in various ways.

We all have the most various types of needs. Suppose that we are interested in the study of one special, fairly well defined need.[1] Suppose there is more than one way of satisfying this need, ways numbering 1, 2, 3, . . . *n*. These are functional alternatives, one of which may, but not necessarily must, stand out as the natural one—for biological, psychological or cultural reasons.[2] Let us call this alternative "way 1." The possibilities to use way 1 of need satisfaction are supposed to vary on the individual and environmental levels. (Environment is here taken to include all extra-individual variables: social-psychological, social and societal.) When his individual and/or environmental possibilities to use this way of need satis-

From *Sociology of Mass Communications,* edited by Denis McQuail (Penguin Education, 1972), pp. 166–194. This selection copyright © Denis McQuail, 1972. Reprinted by permission of the publisher, Penguin Books Ltd.

faction are small or even non-existent, the individual tends to satisfy the same need by means of one or more of the functional alternatives offered by society and its culture, ways 2, 3, . . . n.

Given these assumptions, a typology of possibilities for need satisfaction may be established. Individual and environmental possibilities for need satisfaction in way 1 may each be divided into satisfactory and non-satisfactory, which gives us a typology of four cases.

Once the possibilities are organized in this way the four cells of the typology may be seen as the values of a new variable, *degree of dependence on the functional alternatives*. When an individual has satisfactory individual and environmental possibilities to satisfy the need in way 1, he is only to a small degree dependent on the functional alternatives. When he has non-satisfactory possibilities to satisfy the need in this way, he is very dependent on the alternatives. Cells 2 and 3 may be seen as intermediary cases, possibly resulting in the same intermediary degree of dependence on functional alternatives for need satisfaction.

As an example, let us take the need for social interaction, which we trust to be fairly general, demanding some capacities of the individual (e.g. a certain degree of extroversion, empathy and socialization) and of his environment (e.g. someone to interact with). Also, there is a "natural" way of satisfying the need: face-to-face interaction with real, living human beings; and there are functional alternatives for the satisfaction of the same need, for instance, writing letters, reading books, attending to such mass media as radio, television, newspapers, magazines.[3]

A well socialized person, high on extroversion and empathy, has satisfactory individual possibilities to satisfy his need for social interaction in the natural way, way 1, i.e. by means of interaction with real human beings. If he also has partners and other prerequisites (time, for instance), his environmental possibilities may also be said to be satisfactory, and, by definition, his dependence on such functional alternatives as reading books or listening in will be low (cell 1).

The highly introverted person, on the other hand, low on empathy, whose socialization leaves much to be desired, may be said to have non-satisfactory possibilities on the individual level to satisfy his need for social interaction in way 1. If his environment is equally lacking in this respect, he will be very dependent on such functional alternatives as may be offered, for instance, by the mass media (cell 4). And now let us continue our theoretical argument.

When we considered the suggested typology from the point of view of

	Environmental possibilities to find satisfaction in a given way:	
	Satisfactory	Non-satisfactory
Satisfactory	1	2
Non-satisfactory	3	4

Individual possibilities to find satisfaction in a given way:

Figure 1. Typology of possibilities to satisfy a given need in a given way

the individual and his relations to the functional alternatives, we arrived at the variable "degree of dependence." But one might equally well look at the typology from the angle of the functional alternatives and their relations to way 1. These relations may be seen as defined by the possibilities to satisfy the given need in way 1. That is, for each of the four cells of the typology of possibilities presented in Figure 1, we will get a special relationship of the functional alternatives to way 1. In this way some of the terms used in the debate may be given a somewhat more precise meaning.[4] This is done in Figure 2.

Figure 2, then, implies a suggestion for a more precise terminology. The terms themselves, of course, are mere labels, and could be changed without much ado. Nevertheless, it seems to us that when there are satisfactory individual and environmental possibilities to use way 1, a functional alternative is precisely a supplement. (See Webster's *Dictionary of Synonyms:* "*Supplemental* implies an addition to something relatively complete.") When neither of these possibilities is satisfactory or even existent, the functional alternative may with some justification be called a substitute for way 1. (See Webster's *Dictionary of Synonyms:* "*Substitute:* . . . surrogate, makeshift, stopgap.") A complement is what functional alternative is when

1 Supplement	2 Complement
3 Complement	4 Substitute

Figure 2. Relations of functional alternatives to way 1, as defined by possibilities of satisfying the given need in way 1 (see Figure 1)

there are individual but not environmental (or environmental but not individual) possibilities of satisfying the need in way 1. (See Webster's *Dictionary of Synonyms:* "Complement . . . implies a completing.") It should be pointed out that the labels are by no means intended to be evaluative, although, because of the paucity of the language, we have had to choose labels some of which sound nicer than others. This is in spite of the fact that all functional alternatives may serve in each of the four cells; that is, one man's substitute may very well be another man's supplement. Thus, the same functional alternative to actual social interaction—say, a TV play—may be either a supplement, a complement, or a substitute, depending on the circumstances.

The functional alternative may be sought by the individual for various reasons or motives. We believe that these motives should also preferably be defined in terms of the individual's possibilities to use way 1 for need satisfaction. So again we use the four cells of the typology of Figure 1, this time to distinguish between four types of motives (that is, here we find it meaningful to differentiate between the two intermediary cases). This is done in Figure 3.

1 Change	2 Compensation
3 Escape	4 Vicarious experience

Figure 3. Motives for seeking functional alternatives, as defined by possibilities of satisfying the given need in way 1 (see Figure 1)

Like Figure 2, Figure 3 implies a suggestion for a more precise terminology. Again the terms are but labels and could be changed without much consequence to our argument. But all the same we find them meaningful, at least to a degree. It is meaningful, we think, to assume that the man who has large individual and environmental possibilities to satisfy a given need in a given way is motivated by a wish for change when seeking functional alternatives to the first way of satisfaction. A man, on the other hand, who as an individual perfectly well could avail himself of the given way of finding satisfaction but whose environment offers no possibility to do so, such a man may with some justification be said to seek compensation in a functional alternative for what society denies him. The less talented or gifted, without individual possibilities for need satisfaction in the given way, but living—as far as our way 1 of satisfaction is concerned— in a world of plenty, may be seen as seeking escape from his frustrating situation. And the individual, finally, who has no possibilities of his own and is offered none from his environment either, his experience in this respect obviously will be vicarious. (To stick to our interaction example: this is the poorly socialized youngster without friends, who turns to the mass media, seeking a substitute—vicarious experience—for what his individual and environmental situation denies him.)

Starting from a typology of possibilities for need satisfaction (large and small individual and environmental possibilities for satisfaction in a given way), continuing by way of a new variable with three or four values (degree of dependence on functional alternatives) and a typology of functional alternatives (supplement, complement, substitute), we ended up with a typology of motives for seeking functional alternatives (change, compensation, escape, vicarious experience). How do we use all these concepts, the reader may rightly ask.

In principle they could be used whenever a social scientist is investigating individuals with needs that may be satisfied in a way that demands individual and social or societal resources of some kind, at the same time as there are other ways of finding satisfaction—the functional alternatives. In this paper we will apply the argument to the need for social interaction, which we have already used a couple of times for illustrative purposes.

This is hardly the first paper that has been devoted to the problem of mass media and the need for interaction. What one experiences, approaching the subject, is rather a feeling of *embarras de richesses,* and the embarrassment is caused not least by the richness of the terminological florilegium of the subject. There is hardly a dearth of terms like escape, substitute, compensation, fantasy, vicarious experience, etc. Before trying to express some of the thoughts hidden behind the terms, let us, however, introduce still another typology, pertaining to the special need on which we have now focused our attention: the need for interaction.

Interaction is a special type of relation between individuals. Another one is identification. If the first may be roughly determined as mutual stimulation and response, the other may be equalled for our purposes with the act of imagining oneself to be in the place of another person.[5] Stretching these somewhat elastic definitions, both relations may be said to exist also between a real human being and an individual—an "actor"—of the mass media world: the hero or anti-hero of the TV play or the magazine story, the well-known columnist of the newspaper, the disc-jockey of the radio programme. At least this is what has been contended in more than one investigation about uses and gratifications of the mass media. Identification, of course, in these cases may be highly temporary and shallow, existing, perhaps, only during the fleeting moments of a mass media scene of heightened tension of relief. Interaction must be imaginary (the audience partaking only imaginarily in the action), one-sided or mutual only in a very special way (for instance, an entertainer tells a joke and then pauses, to let the far-off audience laugh).

The two kinds of relations—identification and interaction—may be used to construct a typology of relations between a real individual and one or more "actors" of the mass media (Figure 4).

		Interaction	
		No	Yes
Identification	No	1 Detachment	2 Para-social interaction
	Yes	3 Solitary identification	4 Capture

Figure 4. Typology of relations between audience and actors of mass media

This fourfold table gives us four types of relation. We label them from the point of view of the public and call the relation contained within cell 1 *detachment*. (From the point of view of the "actor" we might have called it "lack of rapport," for instance.) This is the case when the individual neither identifies nor interacts with any actor of the mass media content he is consuming.[6]

The relation of cell 2 we call *para-social interaction*, borrowing the term from an imaginative and insightful paper by Horton and Wohl (1956). . . . In short it denotes the interaction with somebody of the mass media world more or less as if he were present in person, without losing even momentarily one's identity. The mutuality of this type of interaction is of a very special sort.

The relation of cell 3 we believe is very rare or virtually nonexistent in reality. We feel it is rather difficult to identify with somebody of the mass media content consumed, without at the seme time interacting with the rest of the cast. But especially in the case of a one-man show, or when one person or role is very dominating, identification without interaction may, of course, occur. We have named this type of relationship *solitary identification*.

The relation of cell 4 we call *capture*. This is the opposite of the relation of cell 1: the individual both identifies with one or more of the "actors" and also interacts with one or more other actors of the mass medium he is attending to. The interaction, of course, is imaginary.

The four types of relationship may be seen as forming the values of a new variable, which we prefer to call *degree of involvement*. The variable may be seen as having three values, that is, we prefer to collapse as before the two intermediate cases into one. We suggest the possibility of a positive correlation between degree of dependence as defined above and degree of involvement. The more dependent one is on one or more of the mass media as purveyors of functional alternatives to real interaction, the higher one's degree of involvement would tend to be (see Turner, 1958). We also hypothesize a positive correlation between degree of involvement and amount of consumption: the higher the degree of involvement, the larger the mass media consumption. In both cases the relationship probably is mutual or interdependent (see Zetterberg, 1965, pp. 72 ff.).

We believe that irrespective of degree of dependence on the mass media, irrespective of motives and degree of involvement, the need for interaction (and, indeed, all needs that may be satisfied, in one way or another, by the mass media) may be satisfied by almost any type of media content. But this does not mean that we must expect no correlation at all between preference for, and consumption of, certain types of media content on the one hand, and degree of dependence, motives for seeking the functional alternative of the news media, or degree of involvement, on the other. Therefore, our argument should be connected with a typology of content.

Again, we resort to a fourfold typology, obtained this time by cross-

		Content supplies explicit and concrete information	
		Yes	No
Content is fictional	No	1 News, current affairs, educational content, etc.	2 Entertainment, music, etc.
	Yes	3 Instructional plays, certain features, etc.	4 Drama, plays, novels, short stories, etc.

Figure 5. Typology of media content

tabulating the two concepts of fictitiousness and informativeness (Figure 5). We take it for granted that it is possible to distinguish between fictional and non-fictional media content, although we are of course aware of the fact that there must be borderline cases. Informative media content to us means such media content that by the communicator (yet another tricky concept!) is intended to convey explicit and concrete information of some sort.

The figure shows what types of content items we feel should be placed in the various cells, and we do not have to enlarge upon that any more, although we freely admit that the typology is primitive indeed and needs elaboration. We think that a better version of a media content typology of this kind (i.e. content seen from the point of view of the medium or the communicator) should ultimately be correlated with a typology of the kind suggested by Emmett (content seen from the point of view of the consumer) (1968). However, in this paper we will have to let suffice with the typology just offered.

In analogy with our previous strategy we may now see our four types of media content as values of a new variable, *degree of reality proximity of media content*. Content in cell 1, being nonfictional and supplying explicit and concrete information, is closer to reality, we feel, than content in cell 4, being fictional and non-informative, the contents of cells 3 and 4 coming in between these two extremes.

Let us remark here, parenthetically, that we are not unaware of the fact that we have not defined "reality" at all. Starting from another set of explicit or implicit evaluations than those that form the implicit platform of this paper, it is very easy to arrive at a different conception of reality and consequently at a different ordering of the cells on the variable "degree of reality proximity." Thus we would not quarrel if anybody suggested that at least some dramas and novels are very close to reality indeed— "reality" in a certain sense of the word, and "close" in a certain sense of the word, that is.

Accepting our definition of the variable "degree of reality proximity" we could correlate it with the variable "degree of dependence" and "degree of involvement" as earlier defined, and our hypothesis would be that high degree of dependence and involvement would tend to go together with preference for and consumption of media content with a low degree of reality proximity, both identification and interaction being easier to establish with this type of content. As before, we believe that the hypothesized correlations probably represent a mutual or interdependent relationship.

Finally, a word or two should be said about the effects of mass media consumption. As a rule, effect studies and functional studies are seen as belonging to two different approaches. The catchword "what do the media do to people, and what do people do with the media" is sometimes used to characterize the two different approaches. But according to Merton, functions are a certain type of effect (1963, p. 51), and even if in this case one takes functions to mean uses, types of gratification, etc., it is quite possible to ask what effect a given use made of the mass media, or a given gratification obtained from them, may have. Thus we are convinced that sooner or later the two traditions must merge.

Waiting for such a merger it is urgent that effect arguments be as sophisticated as possible. However, it seems that it is not possible to be very sophisticated at the present stage of mass communication research. A minimum requirement would be to distinguish between long-term and short-term effects, and between effects on the individual and on society or parts of society. It is to be expected that effects of mass media consumption should vary not only with amount of consumption, but also with degree of dependence, motives for seeking the functional alternatives offered by the mass media, degree of involvement and degree of reality proximity of the content consumed. Consequently, one should try to heed variables such as these. Also, evaluations should be kept out of the argument as much and for as long as possible, so that they may be made with greater precision, and perhaps, greater weight, when at last they really are made. . . .

Notes

1. We loosely equate need with drive. In many or most cases we are probably thinking of acquired drive: "a motive, need, or source of motivation (rarely defined) that is a product of learning" (Brown, 1968, p. 280).
2. Merton (1963, p. 34 *passim*). The arguments of the rest of this paper hold true even if the functional alternatives are equivalent, so there is no more or less self-evident 'way 1' among them.
3. "There is good reason to consider this *basic drive for contact* the most important factor in keeping all communication in operation" (Nordenstreng, 1969, p. 254).
4. An excellent overview of the literature on mass media as substitute, supplement, escape, etc., may be found in Lundberg and Hultén, 1968, ch. 9. Lundberg and Hultén refer to well-known works by, for instance, Bailyn, Berelson, Hemmelweit, Riley and Riley, Schramm, Steiner, and also to some less-known pieces of research.
5. See Theodorson and Theodorson (1970) and also, among others, Emery (1959), Kelman (1961) and the literature cited by these authors.
6. Note the related concept of "adult discount," introduced in Dysinger and Rucknick (1933) and Blumler, Brown and McQuail (1970, p. 31).

JOSHUA MEYROWITZ

Television and Interpersonal Behavior:
Codes of Perception and Response

This essay is a unique analysis of the relationship of space as portrayed through the television camera, and space experienced interpersonally. Very few studies have analyzed the photographic "grammar" of the televised image. Combining Horton and Wohl's concept of the "para-social relationship," in which the television performance is experienced like a live interaction, with the interpersonal theories of Edward Hall (*The Silent Language*) and Erving Goffman (*The Presentation of Self in Everyday Life*), Meyrowitz develops the concept of "para-proxemics." His point is that television shots (close-up, medium, and wide shots) and camera locations (behind the head, over the shoulder) are related to the way in which we perceive and react to interpersonal distance.

After reading this essay you will better understand how the television medium itself, quite apart from the content of the program, works to involve you with the image and to make you feel as though it were an interpersonal encounter. Read the essay by Horton and Wohl on para-social relationships to better understand Meyrowitz. Also, if you are not already familiar with the works of Hall and Goffman, two noted social anthropologists, you may want to acquaint yourself with their ideas about how we use space to communicate and how we develop personal relationships.

In 1956, Donald Horton and R. Richard Wohl wrote of the television viewer's "illusion of face-to-face relationship with the performer."[1] They called this phenomenon a *para-social relationship*. Horton and Wohl claimed that the "conditions of response to the performer are analogous to those in a primary group,"[2] and they described the ways in which the mediated relationship psychologically resembled real-life encounters.

Horton and Wohl's description of "para-social" interaction might logically have led other theorists to use the structure and characteristics of

This piece was written expressly for the first edition of *Inter/Media*. Copyright © 1978 by Joshua Meyrowitz.

The author wishes to acknowledge the helpful criticism and suggestions of Professor Joseph R. Dominick, University of Georgia, in the early stages of this research.

face-to-face interaction to explore response to television. But what are the "characteristics" of face-to-face interaction? When Horton and Wohl wrote their article, there were few, if any, theories of interpersonal behavior which could be "borrowed" and used to study the structure of television. As a result, researchers have generally looked elsewhere for sources of theories and methodologies. And yet over the same period of time in which television research has grown and multiplied, an increasing amount of important work has been done in describing the structure of interpersonal behavior and in identifying interpersonal behavior "codes." It may now be possible, therefore, to test, or at least further explore, Horton and Wohl's contention that television is experienced in a manner resembling live interaction.

Two significant researchers of interpersonal behavior are anthropologist Edward T. Hall and sociologist Erving Goffman. Hall has studied, among other things, the ways in which people use space and adjust interaction distances to suit different types of relationships. He has analyzed the "meaning" of different interpersonal distances. A significant part of Goffman's work deals with the ways in which people—both alone and in "teams"—constantly structure their appearance and behavior to convey socially meaningful messages and impressions.

Hall and Goffman present the kind of ethnographic data normally found in the work of anthropologists studying strange or primitive societies. Their observations, however, illuminate our own culture and behavior. Hall and Goffman try to make us aware of perceptions and actions which are normally intuitive and unconscious. Their work, therefore, does not tell us about behavior patterns which are foreign to us, but about patterns we know but do not usually know we know.

The work of Hall and Goffman suggests that there is an observable structure to interpersonal behavior—a structure that encompasses "elements" or "variables" which are commonly manipulated by people to create specific meanings and effects. It is possible that variables inherent in interpersonal behavior correlate in some way to variables used in television production. The "meaning" of a close-up or a long shot, for example, may have something to do with the meaning of different interpersonal distances. And the ways in which scenes and people are revealed to the viewer in television's para-social relationship may have something to do with the ways in which live impressions are given and received. This essay will explore the relevance to television of two interpersonal behavior codes: *proxemics* and *impression management*.

Proxemics

In the 1950s Edward T. Hall served as director of the State Department's Point Four Training Program for foreign-bound administrators and technicians. In the training process, Hall found that language was a surprisingly small problem. The disappearance or muting of the language barrier did not, in itself, open up communication between Americans and foreigners. Americans abroad still ran into tremendous difficulties accomplishing their goals. In fact, language gave them only a few clues to the general organization of behavior and lifestyle in other cultures. Many intercultural encounters ended badly, often with lingering mutual disrespect, and sometimes, more distressingly, with violence.

Hall contends that many such intercultural difficulties stem from Americans' ignorance of the structure of their own behavior and their belief that American behavior patterns are "natural" and "correct" while all other patterns are crazy or stupid. Often, claims Hall, we tend to see all foreigners as "underdeveloped Americans." [3]

Hall argues that nonverbal behavior varies as often and as consistently as linguistic behavior. He also believes that there are many unspoken, but very real patterns of behavior—what he calls *silent languages*—which serve to organize action and thought in any given culture. In the past, "culture" has often been dealt with as a single mass of undifferentiated behavior which must be understood through "empathy." Hall feels, however, that if there is any hope of establishing real channels of intercultural communication, *elements* of culture must be identified. If elements or "isolates" of culture can be found, then comparison and "translation" of some sort would be possible. With this in mind, Hall set out to identify and describe patterns of behavior which vary culturally.

Hall is best known for his work in *proxemics,* a term he coined to describe man's spatial behavior patterns. Man's perception and use of space are apparently biologically based, but they are modified by culture. Thus while people everywhere respond to spatial cues, each culture tends to organize space in its own specific way.

One aspect of proxemics which has been explored by Hall is the amount of distance established between two people when they interact. Hall has described the existence of four discrete and measurable *spatial zones: intimate, personal, social* and *public* (each with a near and far phase). Each zone represents a range of interpersonal distance and each tends to be used for a different type of interaction. People tend to select a given zone on the basis of their relationship and the given topic of conversation. A man and his wife, for example, tend to stand at a different distance from each other than a man and his secretary. (Indeed, a wife may become angry with her husband for simply exhibiting "inappropriate" spatial behavior with other women.) Gestures, voice volume, even choice of language, vary with distance.

Hall claims that the existence and use of these spatial zones is universal, but that the range of distance associated with each zone varies with culture. For similar types of interactions, for example, Latin Americans will likely choose an interpersonal distance different from that chosen by North Americans. Such variations in spatial behavior may cause misunderstandings in intercultural encounters. Members of other cultures, for example, may be perceived as "aggressive" or "cold" simply because they seem to stand "too close" or "too far away."

Hall's theory of proxemics has received support from many sources. Research has shown that a decrease in interpersonal distance causes an increase in galvanic skin response (GSR), a measure of stress and emotion.[4] Distance also affects the selective perception of available information; verbal messages, for example, are more easily attended to at a greater distance.[5] Further, the selection of a proxemic zone is apparently so consistent that distance has been suggested as one way of operationally defining interpersonal relationships.[6]

Hall's theory can also be "tested" informally. You may want to start paying attention to the amount of distance which you establish between yourself and others when you speak. Does it vary with relationships? Try to consciously change the distance during a conversation. Move closer, move farther away. What does the other person do? Do you feel uncomfortable moving during an interaction? If so, why? Perhaps you are changing the "meaning" of the interaction. See how close you can come to a stranger in an open space without feeling uncomfortable or obligated to speak to him. (You will probably find that this distance varies depending upon whether you approach face-to-face, back-to-back, and so forth.) Try to talk to a close friend about intimate personal matters while standing fifteen, or more, feet apart. Try to speak to someone about grand schemes and great expectations while standing nose-to-nose. While in an airport, or train station, or a large party, see how your involvement and response to conversations among other people varies with your distance from them. If you interact with a member of another culture or subculture, try to become aware of differences in the use of space. If you try any of these proxemic tests, you will probably become very much aware of the fact that "space speaks."

Para-Proxemics

What relevance might our perception and use of space have to the structure and "meaning" of televised sequences? An obvious point of departure is the "framing variable": the choice of close-ups, medium shots, or long shots to frame the portrayed scene. The very language of television and film shots suggests that distance is a factor in choosing them—*close*-up and *long* shot, for example. Oddly enough, however, shot selection is only rarely discussed in terms of distance. More often shots are analyzed in terms of image size or abstract concepts of "adjustment." Film scholar Lewis Jacobs, for example, notes that:

> The size of an object affects our feelings as well as our recognition and understanding of it. "Big" and "little" particularize and generalize. The close-up focuses attention on what is important through magnification of relevant details and exclusion of unwanted portions of a subject. The full shot encompasses all of a subject and facilitates recognition.[7]

And film theorist André Bazin explained the prevalence of the medium shot by suggesting that

> the director returns as often as he can to a shot of the characters from the knees up, which is said to be best suited to catch the spontaneous attention of the viewer—the natural point of balance of his mental adjustment.[8]

Hall's theory of proxemics, however, suggests a possible relationship between perception of interpersonal distance and the "framing variable." Hall indicates that at any given interpersonal distance one sees a specific amount of the other person clearly. Such descriptions may be relevant to television shots. While a television lens distorts visual cues to some extent (no binocular vision, no peripheral vision, a specific depth of field over which the individual has no control, etc.), any given shot of a person frames the individual in a certain way. It may show only his head, or only his head and shoulders, or it may picture his whole body with varying amounts of space around it. In a particular shot, therefore, the way in which a person is framed may suggest an interpersonal distance between that person and the viewer.

Are there any other indications that a "framed picture" is perceived in terms of distance? Artist Maurice Grosser's analysis of the portrait suggests that distance is a significant factor in shaping viewer response. Grosser notes that the portrait is distinguished from other painting formats in that the closeness of artist and model yields "the peculiar sort of communication, almost a conversation, that the person who looks at the picture is able to hold with the person painted there."[9] Indeed, Hall points out that Grosser's description of distance and communication in portraits coincides very closely with Hall's own description of spatial zones.

Implicit in Grosser's discussion of portraits is the fact that the absolute size of the figure is not the key variable determining response to a picture. What is important is the distance that is suggested by the *relative* size of the figure within the frame. Similarly, on television a close-up on a nine-inch screen may suggest the same interpersonal distance as a close-up on a twenty-one-inch screen.

The idea that *relative* size is more important than *absolute* size may seem unusual, but this is actually one of the ways in which we judge distance in everyday life. Psychologists have discussed the "constancy of size" phenomenon, whereby people and familiar objects are perceived as remaining the same size, even though the size of the image that they cast on the retina changes markedly.[10] When our friends walk away from us there is a decrease in the size of the retinal image of them. And yet, we do not think of our friends as getting smaller; we think of them as going further away. Similarly, regardless of the size of the image of a person within the television frame, we might react to the picture in terms of distance, not size. In television, perhaps, the screen becomes a kind of "extended retina" for the viewer. The relative size of people or objects within the screen, therefore, would serve as a cue to the distance of people and objects from the viewer. Following Horton and Wohl's lead, I call this a *para-proxemic* relationship.

Para-Proxemic Model

Several perceptual phenomena in television viewing might be described in terms of proxemics. One is the visual "relationship" between the viewer and the image. This relationship exists at every moment that a person watches television. In any one shot the viewer is shown a specific amount of a scene, person, or object. The subject may be shot in close-up, medium shot, or long shot. This *framing variable* creates a *mediated distance* between the viewer and the content of the image. Shots of a football game, for example, can "place" the viewer directly outside of the huddle or in the last row of the stands. The distance is "mediated" and not "real" because the image is flat, conveys a limited amount of sensory information, and thus abstracts for the viewer only a fraction of the contingencies of actual physical presence. Response may be further affected by such *situational variables* as the nature of the televised event (documentary versus fiction, for example), viewer distance from the screen, screen size, viewing angle, and other aspects of the immediate environment (lighting, noise, architecture, number of other people present). Nevertheless, the television shot suggests an approximate distance from the televised subject. At any point, the image can be compared to something seen live at distance X.

A second type of distance—*portrayed distance*—is an extension of the viewer/image distance. Not only does the viewer experience the image at a *mediated distance,* but he also sees spatial relationships within the image. For example, in addition to seeing the huddle at a certain "distance," the television football spectator also sees distances among the players in the huddle. *Portrayed distances* apply to relationships among people and objects within the medium. At any point during televised sequences the apparent distance between characters and objects might be estimated.

Portrayed distances can be divided into two categories—*portrayed objective distance* and *portrayed subjective distance;* that is, a division may be made on the basis of two types of shots—"objective" and "subjective." An "objective" shot is one that "maintains the role of a detached observer" of the action, where the camera assumes "whatever angle will best portray that action." [11] The point of view presented by the objective shot is not that of any particular person within the scene. Instead it selects an observation point for the viewer. One way to represent an interaction between two people, for example, is to show them both at the same time by using an objective shot. It is then possible to describe the physical distance at which they appear to be standing from each other.

On the other hand, an interaction between two characters can also be portrayed through "subjective" shots. A subjective shot "assumes the point of view of one of the characters"; [12] it shows the viewer what one person within the action sees. A subjective shot of a two-character interaction would show only one person, and the shot would be taken from the angle and viewpoint of the second person. Subjective shots are commonly used in television and film. In a conversation between person A and person B, for example, first a subjective shot of person A might be shown, then a subjective shot of person B, and then back to a subjective shot of person A. Although only one person is shown in any one such subjective shot, the manner in which the image is framed within the screen may suggest a physical distance between the two characters.

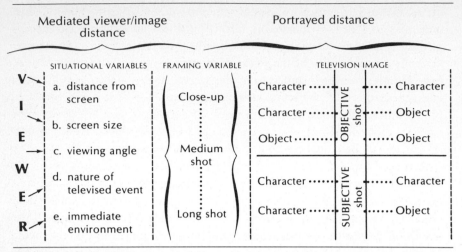

Figure 1.

There are thus at least three potential television "distances": (1) *mediated viewer/image distance,* (2) *portrayed objective distance,* and (3) *portrayed subjective distance* (Fig. 1).

A para-proxemic analysis of television shots has many significant implications for television theory. Proxemic conventions suggest both "appropriate" and "special effects" uses of media variables in relation to: (1) viewer orientation to a scene, (2) viewer perception and response to characters, and (3) viewer perception of relationships among characters.[13]

Viewer Orientation to a Scene. Live encounters do not begin suddenly. We approach buildings and rooms, see people first at a distance, and then come closer to begin interactions. At the end of interactions the process is generally reversed. On television as well, those scenes which seem to start and end "naturally" begin with long shots, progressively move in, and then end once again with long shots or a "fade-out." The fade-in and fade-out serve as a kind of shortcut "movement" into and out of scenes. Rarely do programs begin with a sudden cut from black, or a sudden cut to black.

The interpersonal experience of physical and perceptual transition can, however, be violated for special effects. Horror movies, for example, exploit sudden cuts into scenes and reorientations of the viewer without warning or transition. And a sudden cut to black can leave the viewer "hanging," still engrossed in the now unseen scene.

Once "brought into" a scene, the viewer must be gently moved around it, so as not to lose his bearing. Different shots may show him different parts of the scene—just as he would tend to look around a room—but if the shots alter the angle of viewing too drastically then the viewer may get lost. Shots, therefore, suggest visual behavior in live encounters. Indeed, although the "cutting" of shots is often thought of as a distortion of perception because we do not see the space in between (as we would in a "pan" shot), the cut actually closely resembles an individual's own scanning of a live scene. If I am watching two people talking in a live encounter, I will often look at one and then the other. I rarely attend to the space between them. In effect, I see in "cuts," not pans.

The interpersonal experience of orientation and vision can also be distorted for special effects. A director can purposely disorient the viewer by "moving" him around too violently. He can use "unnaturally" quick cutting or swift, long pans that give the viewer a swirling, spinning feeling. Such special effects give the viewer the sense of having "lost his ground." Both normal and special effects, therefore, can be related to live physical position and perception.

Viewer Perception of and Response to Characters. An understanding of proxemics is most helpful in analyzing our perception of and response to characters on television. Through para-proxemic variation, an actor in a television commercial, for example, may be presented to us either as an individual who makes a personal or intimate appeal (close-up) or as an authority whose approach is based on social role (medium or long shot).

Our response to what a character does or to what is done to him can also be interpreted in terms of proxemics. Actions in long shots, for example, tend to be viewed in terms of abstract "events," while close-ups focus attention on personal characteristics and response. If we see a policeman gunned-down in long shots, therefore, we tend to respond to the action: "shooting of a policeman." If, however, we come close enough to see tears running down the face of the wounded man, we have a very different response. Such variation in response is related to live experience.

The potential effect of para-proxemics on the perception of and identification with characters becomes clearer in a sequence involving more than one character. In a courtroom drama, for example, the director can juggle response to the judge and the defendant by simply varying the structure of the shots. If the judge is shown in long shots, the viewer's concern tends to be mainly with the judge's performance as a judge, while in close-ups the concern is with the judge's own feelings or his own response to his role. Alternating the types of shots presents a more complex response. The same manipulation is possible for the defendant. With shots that convey different distances, the director might be able to broadly recast the scenario: (1) judge vs. defendant (both seen in terms of "roles," in medium or long shot), (2) judge (medium shot) vs. man (close-up), (3) man vs. man (both close-ups), and so on. The notion that distance affects our response to characters can be further illustrated in a courtroom scene by the fact that many characters tend to serve only as "background." The court clerk, the stenographer, members of the jury, and others are not attended to very carefully *unless we see them close-up.*

It is important to note that many such changes in para-proxemic response are possible without any changes in dialogue or in much of what is often considered "content." Content variables, to be sure, interact with structural variables to mold the *exact* nature of our response, but the *intensity* of response is related to the distances established by shot structure. The content, therefore, may determine whether we feel sorry for a defendant or pray that he hangs; the content may determine whether we greatly admire the judge or are infuriated with his seeming bias. But the degree of response is related to para-proxemics. Similar content/structure interactions affect response in live encounters; distance determines intensity of relationships rather than specific behavior. Intimate space, for example, is the distance of both lovemaking *and* murder!

The ways in which we are para-proxemically oriented to characters in a scene may, at times, be a "distortion" of reality in that there could be no direct interpersonal analogue. We may, for example, see too much of too many people, too quickly from too many different perspectives to bear any direct relationship to actual physical presence. And yet the impact of such "distortion" may still be related to the types of feelings and response we experience in live encounters.

Viewer Perception of Relationships Among Characters. The framing variable in subjective shots also affects viewer understanding of the relationship among characters. Through subjective shots, the perceptions discussed in "response to characters" above are experienced through the eyes of a character within the drama. Para-proxemic variables in subjective shots indicate to the viewer the nature of a character's physical and psychological orientation to a scene. In a two-person interaction, for example, the framing variable will suggest distances between characters even though only one person is pictured in the shot. And the distances (as Hall suggests) indicate the intensity of the relationship among characters. Similarly, subjective shots portray general character orientation to actions and events.

Shots that portray the vision of a character can also distort "real" perception for special effects. If, for example, two people are shown in objective shots to be at opposite sides of a room, and yet in subjective shots they are shown to "see" each other in close-up, then psychological intimacy and emotional intensity is suggested. Conversely, if two people are shown in objective shots at "social" distance, and yet each views the other subjectively in long shots ("public" distance), then psychological isolation is suggested. Further, unmatched subjective shots may suggest nonreciprocal perception and response. A young man's sense of isolation from his parents, for example, might be portrayed through subjective shots. He may be "perceived" by his parents in medium shots, yet he "sees" them in long shots.

Hall's theory of proxemics, therefore, can be adapted to an analysis of television. The *framing variable* "places" the viewer within scenes or reveals spatial orientations of characters. Shots portray distances and therefore have a "meaning" which corresponds to the functioning of spatial cues in interpersonal interaction. My analysis of para-proxemics, however, suggests only a broad framework of viewer perception and response. Thus far, I have suggested how shots "position" the viewer, but I have not yet analyzed what the viewer sees from his position, how he makes any (social) sense of what he sees, and how and why he might choose to identify with some characters rather than others. Erving Goffman's theory of *impression management* suggests some preliminary answers to these questions.

Impression Management

In *The Presentation of Self in Everyday Life*,[14] Erving Goffman suggests that when a person enters a social situation he wants and needs to know something about the other participants and the given context. He may, for example, want to know the age, marital status, wealth, education, or intelligence of the other people. He may want to know the particular roles being played by others in the situation. He will need to know whether the situation is formal or informal, who is in charge, whom he must speak to first, and whether he is welcome or unwelcome. Conversely, people in the given setting will want to know something about the person who enters.

Goffman notes that much of this information is not "naturally" available. It may take years to fully know a person or understand how a group of people function in a given social establishment or institution. And yet, most social interaction requires instant judgments, alignments, and behavior. As a result, Goffman suggests, people are constantly mobilizing their energies to create socially meaningful "impressions."

Goffman argues that *impression management* has the character of "drama"; that is, all social roles are, in a sense, a performance where the individual actor highlights certain characteristics and conceals others. And just like any other drama, the stage must be properly set, the individual must often learn and rehearse his role, and he must coordinate his activities with fellow performers.

In most social encounters, Goffman argues, the individual tends to have a *front:* "that part of the individual's performance which regularly functions in a general and fixed fashion to define the situation for those who observe the performance." [15] Goffman discusses two aspects of *front:* the *setting,* and *personal front.*

The *setting* involves relatively fixed elements such as furniture, carpeting, statues, windows, and professional equipment. The setting itself establishes an expectation of roles and appropriate behavior. One of the differences between eating in Sardi's and eating in McDonald's is the distinctly different setting.

Variations in the *setting* influence the behavior of all involved. A scientist sitting in his laboratory both *feels* and *appears* more authoritative about his work than he does while playing golf. And a rock group leader may not feel he can give his "rap" to the audience unless he stands in front of his group with amplifiers and instruments at the ready. Similarly, the way in which a teenager arranges and decorates his room will suggest his attitude toward himself and his expectations in regard to formality and type of interaction with friends.

The *personal front* differs from the setting in that it is located within or on the performer himself. Personal front includes such features as age, height, sex, race, hair length, posture, style and quality of clothing, facial expression, and gesture.

Some aspects of personal front are fixed and do not change from situation to situation (unless one resorts to surgery or other drastic means). A good part of the personal front, however, can easily be changed or modified to suit the context and the role to be played in it.

In terms of a given interaction, Goffman divides personal front into *ap-*

pearance and *manner*. *Appearance* is that part of the personal front which includes such features as clothing, uniforms, and insignia, and which tells others the nature of the performer's social status in the given context. The same man will *appear* very different in a bathing suit than in a four-star general's uniform.

Manner is related to appearance, but it adds the dimension of the specific (and more variable) behavior which the individual exhibits in a given situation. Manner and appearance can be at odds. A person who appears to be of very high status, for example, may nevertheless behave toward others in a humble or egalitarian manner. A general, for example, may speak "man to man" to a private. Usually, however, we expect and experience some consistency between manner and appearance. We expect a man dressed in judge's robes (appearance) to behave sternly and judiciously (manner). And we expect a busboy (i.e., someone dressed as a busboy) to be humble and inconspicuous.

While we often believe that it is dishonest to "put on" a character or "play" a role, Goffman suggests that this is a foolish belief. Some people, it is true, may purposely give misleading impressions (con men, spies, undercover agents), but *all* individuals must give *some* impression. Thus, while a dishonest judge may pretend to be an honest judge, an honest judge must also play the role of "honest judge." He may, for example, have to avoid being seen in questionable places with questionable characters even if there is nothing "actually" inappropriate about his behavior. And even an honest judge must dress up properly, wearing black, not pink, robes. Impression management, therefore, serves as a kind of social "shorthand" through which people identify themselves and provide expectations about their behavior.

One of Goffman's most interesting observations about the management of impression is that any individual's behavior in a given setting can generally be broken down into two broad categories: what Goffman calls *back region* or backstage behavior, and *front region* or onstage behavior. In front regions, the individual is in the presence of his "audience" and he plays out a relatively ideal conception of the social role. A waiter is in a front region when he serves people in a restaurant. He is polite and respectful. He does not enter into the dinner conversations of his patrons. He does not comment on their eating habits or table manners. He rarely, if ever, eats while in their sight. In the dining hall, setting, appearance, and manner are carefully controlled. When the waiter steps from the dining room into the kitchen, however, he suddenly crosses the line between onstage and backstage. He enters an area which is hidden from the audience and which he shares with others who perform the same or similar roles. Here, then, the waiter may make remarks about the "strange" people at table number seven, he may imitate patrons, he may give advice to a "rookie" waiter on methods of getting big tips, he may get out of role by sitting or standing in a sloppy manner. He may even get out of costume.

Goffman suggests that all people—from porters to presidents—share this distinction in behavior. All social roles depend upon selected behaviors. A doctor, for example, tends to hide his doubts, times of depression, sexual feelings, and personal likes and dislikes of patients. Similarly, virtually all role performers tend to have back regions where they and their "teammates" (those who share the same role or work to foster the same performance) relax, rehearse, make jokes about behavior in front regions, and sometimes work out strategies for future performances. When not in a courtroom, even a judge may joke about the physical appearance of a witness, he may ask a court clerk to speak more slowly when announcing the judge's entrance (a "stage direction") or he may telephone another judge to explore a legal technicality about which he is uncertain. All roles depend upon the performer having a back region. At the same time, all front region roles rely upon keeping the audience out of back regions. The social performer, like the stage actor, must have a private place to learn and rehearse his role. If he does not, he cannot build up to or maintain a performance which impresses his audience.

Teammates always have a different perception of the situation than do audience members. For the benefit of the audience, errors tend to be corrected before they can be seen, only end products are shown, and the dirty aspects of work are concealed. Many features of the performance, including the individual's perspective on his role, are saved for teammates. Even when an audience is present, teammates may furtively exchange glances, grimaces, or knowing winks.

Televised Impressions and Teams

The characteristics of live interaction which Goffman outlines may be related to perception of television drama in terms of (1) identifying situations and characters, (2) aligning (or teaming) the viewer with selected characters, and (3) revealing relationships among characters.

Identifying Situations and Characters. As Goffman describes it, *front* plays a very significant, though often unnoticed role in the perception of television scenes. Opening shots of sequences generally reveal the *setting* and then the *appearance* of characters. Indeed, when a single shot of a setting or of a character is not sufficient for identification, there may be a slow scan of the scene or of the individual. To set the scene for "the eccentric millionaire," for example, there may be an opening shot of a mansion followed by a pan of a collection of strange and extravagant art works. The "highly decorated general" may himself be slowly scanned to reveal his medals and stern demeanor. In virtually all television drama such "establishing" shots begin sequences and set expectations for the type of interaction that is to come.

Further, shots throughout a sequence allow the viewer to monitor variations in the *manner* of characters. They reveal the character's changing orientation to ongoing events. Such shots combined with information about the setting help to flesh-out the fine points of character and behavior.

Television shots, therefore, especially "establishing shots," reveal to us what we would normally look for upon entering a live encounter. If impression management is a kind of social shorthand, then television shots are a shorthand of a shorthand. Shots quickly display those aspects of setting and personal front which "performers" in live interactions purposely highlight and express.

Aligning (or Teaming) the Viewer with Selected Characters. In many social situations we find ourselves in one of two positions in relation to each other person: we are either an audience to their front region role, or we are a teammate concerned to some extent with their "carrying off" their performance before others. Our perception and orientation to situations varies tremendously depending upon those in the situation whom we see as teammates. There is, for example, a great difference between visiting a classroom, where one of our friends is a student, and visiting a classroom where one of our friends is the teacher. We tend to view the "action" from the perspective of our "team." We are generally concerned that our teammates perform their roles well and make good impressions. And as teammates, we are usually given access to back region rehearsals, relaxations, comments about the "audience," and teammates' perceptions of their own roles.

In television drama as well, the structure and arrangement of shots can establish a "character" for the viewer; that is, the camera can make the viewer a teammate of selected characters.

Sometimes the camera makes the viewer a teammate by simply "placing" him in a back region or giving him the back region view of the front region performance. If we see a judge from *behind* his bench, and we see him scratch his legs or twiddle his thumbs, we have a significantly different relationship with him than if we view him from the front and at a low angle. Such variables combine with para-proxemic effects to align the viewer with characters. And again, dialogue and abstract descriptions of actions will tell us only a small fraction of the "meaning" of televised sequences.

A key to the structure of many detective dramas rests in the timing and extent of the revelation to the viewer of the criminals' back region behavior. Do we have the same information as the detective? Less or more? Are we teamed with the detective or with the criminals? The order in which we get to "know" characters (as is often the case in real-life) can also affect our alignment. If we get to know the detective first, we may become aligned with him. Even if we later see the criminals in their back regions, we may view ourselves as spies, not teammates. On the other hand, if we get to know the criminals very well and see law enforcement personnel in their front region roles only, we may align with the criminals. Such variables can account, in part, for the markedly different viewer attitude toward the criminals in *The Untouchables* and *The Godfather*.

Alignments and teaming are used most unabashedly in war and cowboy dramas. Here, the perspective established by chosen shots clearly distinguishes "them" from "us." The enemy is generally seen in front region roles only. But "our boys" are seen in both back and front regions. Further, we tend to be shown situations from the position of "our side." Indeed, we literally see scenes primarily from one *side*. Often we are "placed" right behind our men, as if we stand with them. When the enemy fires, he fires on us. When one of our boys is wounded, we are upset; but a hundred Indians, outlaws, or Germans can be blown to bits, and we cheer. That such response has more to do with structure than ideology is demonstrated by some antiwar films which show both sides alternately and equally (giving us the perspective of God?). Here the futility and stupidity of war seems apparent.

Even "objective" shots, therefore, are rarely objective in the larger sense. When a character enters a room, for example, the side of the door from which the viewer watches the action is significant. The shot may not portray the vision of any specific character in the action, but the perspective established by it selects a position, and therefore a general response, for the viewer. At any given point in a television scene we may ask: Whose perspective do I have? What do I know about these characters? Who are my "teammates"? Who do I see only in their front region roles? Who do I like and why?

Revealing Relationships Among Characters. Through subjective shots the viewer sees those aspects of setting and personal front which a character observes. A common technique in detective dramas, for example, is to show the viewer features of the setting or personal front which the detective finds odd or suspicious. Subjective shots can also reveal to the viewer the nature of alignments among characters. Subjective shots may reveal collusive looks between characters suggesting a teammate relationship. In a murder drama, for example, a gun may be found behind a bush, and the viewer may see a collusive look between the widow of the murdered man and the next-door neighbor. Through subjective shots, therefore, the viewer learns whether characters view themselves as teammates or as audience members for each other's roles.

In summary, Goffman's theory of impression management is of relevance here because it suggests a number of similarities between interpersonal interaction and the structure of television sequences. Both are dramatic in nature, highly structured, rehearsed, and planned. Both involve highlighting socially significant cues. Both involve the perception of action and character in terms of social context and personal alignments.[16]

Conclusion

Proxemics and impression management are only two of many interpersonal behavior codes which have been outlined by researchers in recent years. They alone, however, provide a rich source of insight into the nature of viewer response to television.

Content/Structure Interaction. Television research has generally focused on content *or* on structure. The analysis presented here, however, suggests that televised sequences are understood through a structure/content interaction. The key to the "meaning" of such an interaction lies in the content/structure interface of live perception and response. A shout in real experience has one meaning at 25 feet and quite another at 25 inches; a "member of the opposite sex" has one meaning at 5 feet and another at 5 inches. Moreover, a person's response to a given person or event depends upon his perception of the social context and his knowledge of, and identification with others in the situation.

In the same way, a piece of television content—such as an act of violence—has no meaning in and of itself. The intensity of response is affected by the "distance" from the action. And the nature of the response will vary with the viewer's relative relationship with characters. A violent attack, for example, may be committed (1) on a teammate by a stranger, (2) on a stranger by a teammate, (3) by one teammate on another teammate, or (4) by one stranger on another stranger. In each case the viewer's response would be different.

Furthermore, just as a unit of television content has no meaning apart from the way in which it is presented, so does a production variable have no inherent meaning apart from the portrayed content and relevant social context. A low angle shot, for example, might be understood in one way when picturing a judge or a politician (people who are "looked up to" in real life) and another way when picturing a young boy or a waiter. A low angle shot may in one case enhance credibility and in another cause uneasiness, mistrust, or fear. Again, the real-life matrix of meaning provides the framework for perception and response.[17]

Implications for Directors. Many of the television "grammar" studies are designed to systematically investigate the validity of production guidelines that have developed through intuition and trial-and-error. The analysis presented here suggests a source of the director's intuition: the unconscious behavior codes of interpersonal behavior. Production guidelines, therefore, may need less experimental investigation than is often assumed. In television, as in interpersonal behavior, if it "feels" right, it probably is right.

A major exception to the "feeling right" rule, however, is intercultural communication. If television cues are "equivalent" to interpersonal cues, then perception of a given television sequence will vary culturally. All cultures, for example, may be able to "understand" paraproxemics (just as all cultures "understand" proxemics). Yet, response to a given shot may be quite different in different cultures. A Latin American, for example, may perceive people on North American television as being cold and unfriendly, even to each other; North Americans may find people on Latin American television pushy and aggressive.[18] While intercultural communication through distribution of film is often thought of as a means of

enhancing understanding and good-will, visual media may actually reinforce stereotypes and prejudices. Some cross-cultural translation of visual
material may be necessary.

Impact of Media on Interpersonal Behavior. Interpersonal behavior preceded television. To describe a structural similarity between television and
live encounters, therefore, is to demonstrate the ways in which interpersonal behavior affects media. And yet, if there is a strong common denominator between television "relationships" and face-to-face interaction, then
the widespread use of television may also have an impact on interpersonal
behavior. Television may, for example, teach or reinforce proxemic behavior patterns for children. Television may sensitize individuals to significant
aspects of *setting* and *personal front* in given contexts. Indeed, worldwide
distribution of television programs may create a trend toward homogenization of previously variant proxemic patterns and characteristics of impression management.

Furthermore, if Goffman is correct in assuming that interpersonal behavior is a kind of drama where the "scripts" depend upon controlling
performances carefully and *restricting* access to performers, then electronic
media may be restaging the social drama as a whole. Electronic media may
change the arenas in which many people play their roles and alter the identity and size of their audiences. As a result, electronic media may change
the type and amount of access that people have to each other and thereby
affect the nature of the roles that can be successfully played. I have explored some of these possibilities elsewhere.[19]

A Symbolic Link. Even when the content of television programs is nonfictional, there is a limit to the extent to which the analogue between live and
para-social interaction can be taken. After all, television images are only
images. They convey a limited amount of sensory data, they give the
viewer little choice over field of view and focus, and they therefore present
only a small range of the perceptual and psychological phenomena associated with physical presence. There can, for example, be no real threat
or seduction in television—even when a shot is para-proxemically "equivalent" to intimate distance. And rarely could a viewer be expected to actually foster the performance of a televised "teammate." We are, therefore,
left with the question: What is the nature of the connection between interpersonal codes and our understanding of televised sequences of action?

I suggest that the link is a symbolic one. Television images are symbolic of live experience. That is, we do not respond to the televised situation as we would to a real situation, but we respond to the *concept* of the real situation.[20]

This symbolic link is similar to "suspension of disbelief" in drama. When we watch someone being attacked on the stage we do not yell "Police!" but we do feel pity; that is, we respond to the *idea* of attack. Similarly, the meaning of many television cues may rest in unconscious interpersonal codes such as proxemics and impression management. When we see a performer in a close-up, therefore, we do not get directly sexually aroused or frightened, but we respond to the idea of intimacy or aggression. Similarly, when we are set up as the teammate of an outlaw we respond to the concept of being a criminal.

This symbolic link explains why distortion in the image or in the combination of images does not negate the relationship between television and interpersonal reality. Distortion must be distortion of something. The basis of comparison remains the nature of perception and response in real-life social encounters.

Notes

1. "Mass Communication and Para-Social Interaction," *Psychiatry,* 19 (1956), p. 215.
2. Ibid., p. 215.
3. The discussion of Hall's work is based on two of his books: *The Silent Language* (Greenwich, Conn.: Fawcett, 1959) and *The Hidden Dimension* (Garden City, N.Y., Anchor, 1966).
4. G. McBride, M. G. King, and J. W. James, "Social Proximity Effects on Galvanic Skin Responses in Adult Humans," *Journal of Psychology,* 61 (1965), 153–157.
5. Bernard Steinzor, "The Spatial Factor in Face to Face Discussion Groups," *Journal of Abnormal and Social Psychology,* 45 (1950), 552–555.
6. Frank N. Willis, Jr., "Initial Speaking Distance as a Function of the Speakers' Relationship," *Psychonomic Science,* 5 (1966), 221–222.
7. Lewis Jacobs, "The Meaningful Image," in *The Movies as Medium,* ed., Lewis Jacobs (New York: Farrar, Straus and Giroux, 1970), p. 25.
8. André Bazin, "The Evolution of the Language of Cinema," in *What is Cinema?* by André Bazin, ed. and trans. Hugh Gray (Berkeley: University of California Press, 1967), p. 32.
9. *The Painter's Eye* (New York: Rinehart, 1951), p. 9.
10. See, for example, William H. Ittelson, *Visual Space Perception,* (New York: Springfield, 1960), pp. 169–188.
11. Herbert A. Lightman, "The Subjective Camera," in *The Movies as Medium,* ed. Lewis Jacobs (New York: Farrar, Straus and Giroux, 1970), p. 61.

12. Lightman, p. 62.
13. While the focus in this discussion is on television drama, much of the analysis is relevant to nonfiction television programs (documentaries, televised trials, videotaped court testimony, Congressional hearings and debates, etc.) and even to perception of other visual media such as cinema and still photography.
14. (New York: Anchor, 1959).
15. Goffman, p. 22.
16. Some social critics have argued that America is losing a grip on "reality" as an outcome of high media use. In *The Image* (Atheneum, 1961), for example, Daniel Boorstin describes the great outbreak of "pseudo-events." Yet Goffman's model of face-to-face encounters suggests that *all* social interaction is staged. Indeed the significance of our new forms of communication may be that the planning and staging of media events cannot be hidden as simply as can the planning of simpler face-to-face encounters. A President, for example, cannot hide his media advisors as easily as the average businessman can hide the suggestions of his wife and his tailor. Media, therefore, do not present events which are inherently "false"; they do, however, present events that are *seemingly* less "real." Media do not *create* pseudo-events, but they do make the falseness of events visible.
17. The social context variable explains some of the seemingly contradictory findings of television "grammar" studies. The difference in results in camera angle investigations can be explained in terms of a shot/context interaction.
18. Other interpersonal codes which vary with culture and which may affect perception of television include: rules of eye behavior, pace of interactions, and value orientations. See, for example, Edward T. Hall, *The Silent Language* and Edward C. Stewart, *American Cultural Patterns: A Cross Cultural Perspective* (Pittsburgh: Regional Council for International Education, 1972).
19. For a general theory on the impact of television on the performance of social roles, see Joshua Meyrowitz, *No Sense of Place: A Theory on the Impact of Electronic Media on Social Structure and Behavior,* Doctoral Dissertation, New York University, 1978. For a specific application of the theory to political communication, see Meyrowitz, "The Rise of 'Middle Region' Politics," *Et cetera,* 34 (1977), 133–144.
20. The ability to maintain distance from an event and yet respond to it *as if* it were real was described in 1912 by Edward Bullough in " 'Psychical Distance' as a Factor in Art and an Esthetic Principle," reprinted in *A Modern Book of Esthetics,* ed. Melvin Rader (New York: Henry Holt and Co., 1952). The application of "psychical distance" to television has been suggested by Gary Gumpert in "Psychical Distance and Television Theatre," unpublished paper, University of Wisconsin, 1963.

From Hero to Celebrity:
The Human Pseudo-Event

Daniel Boorstin is the Chief Librarian of the Library of Congress and has written a number of books exploring contemporary American life. In this selection from *The Image: A Guide to Pseudo-Events in America,* Boorstin describes the role of the celebrity in our media world. The celebrity is a
phenomenon of the media age created to gratify the public need for heroes
and the advertiser's need for recognizable figures to sell their products. According to Boorstin, the celebrity is a human pseudo-event, or a heroic
image, rather than a heroic individual. The probing eye of the camera brings
us "close" to the celebrity, but what do we see? What is our relationship to
the celebrity? The secret of the celebrity's successes is to appear intimate
while never allowing the public to penetrate the barrier that would destroy
the media magic surrounding him or her.

Our age has produced a new kind of eminence. This is as characteristic of
our culture and our century as was the divinity of Greek gods in the sixth
century B.C. or the chivalry of knights and courtly lovers in the middle
ages. It has not yet driven heroism, sainthood, or martyrdom completely
out of our consciousness. But with every decade it overshadows them
more. All older forms of greatness now survive only in the shadow of this
new form. This new kind of eminence is "celebrity."

The word "celebrity" (from the Latin *celebritas* for "multitude" or
"fame" and *celeber* meaning "frequented," "populous," or "famous")
originally meant not a person but a condition—as the Oxford English Dictionary says, "the condition of being much talked about; famousness, notoriety." In this sense its use dates from at least the early seventeenth century. Even then it had a weaker meaning than "fame" or "renown."
Matthew Arnold, for example, remarked in the nineteenth-century that
while the philosopher Spinoza's followers had "celebrity," Spinoza himself
had "fame."

For us, however, "celebrity" means primarily a person—" a person of
celebrity." This usage of the word significantly dates from the early years

of the Graphic Revolution, the first example being about 1850. Emerson spoke of "the celebrities of wealth and fashion" (1848). Now American dictionaries define a celebrity as "a famous or well-publicized person."

The celebrity in the distinctive modern sense could not have existed in any earlier age, or in America before the Graphic Revolution. *The celebrity is a person who is known for his well-knownness.*

His qualities—or rather his lack of qualities—illustrate our peculiar problems. He is neither good nor bad, great nor petty. He is the human pseudo-event. He has been fabricated on purpose to satisfy our exaggerated expectations of human greatness. He is morally neutral. The product of no conspiracy, of no group promoting vice or emptiness, he is made by honest, industrious men of high professional ethics doing their job, "informing" and educating us. He is made by all of us who willingly read about him, who like to see him on television, who buy recordings of his voice, and talk about him to our friends. His relation to morality and even to reality is highly ambiguous. He is like the woman in an Elinor Glyn novel who describes another by saying, "She is like a figure in an Elinor Glyn novel."

The massive *Celebrity Register* (1959), compiled by Earl Blackwell and Cleveland Amory, now gives us a well-documented definition of the world, illustrated by over 2,200 biographies. "We think we have a better yardstick than the *Social Register,* or *Who's Who,* or any such book," they explain. "Our point is that it is impossible to be accurate in listing a man's social standing—even if anyone cared; and it's impossible to list accurately the success or value of men; but you *can* judge a man as a celebrity—all you have to do is weigh his press clippings." The *Celebrity Register*'s alphabetical order shows Mortimer Adler followed by Polly Adler, the Dalai Lama listed beside TV comedienne Dagmar, Dwight Eisenhower preceding Anita Ekberg, ex-President Herbert Hoover following ex-torch singer Libby Holman, Pope John XXIII coming after Mr. John the hat designer, and Bertrand Russell followed by Jane Russell. They are all celebrities. The well-knownness which they have in common overshadows everything else.

The advertising world has proved the market appeal of celebrities. In trade jargon celebrities are "big names." Endorsement advertising not only uses celebrities; it helps make them. Anything that makes a well-known name still better known automatically raises its status as a celebrity. The old practice, well established before the nineteenth century, of declaring the prestige of a product by the phrase "By Appointment to His Majesty" was, of course, a kind of use of the testimonial endorsement. But the King was in fact a great person, one of illustrious lineage and with impressive actual and symbolic powers. The King was not a venal endorser, and he was likely to use only superior products. He was not a mere celebrity. For the test of celebrity is nothing more than well-knownness.

Studies of biographies in popular magazines suggest that editors, and supposedly also readers, of such magazines not long ago shifted their attention away from the old-fashioned hero. From the person known for some serious achievement, they have turned their biographical interests to the new-fashioned celebrity. Of the subjects of biographical articles appearing in the *Saturday Evening Post* and the now-defunct *Collier's* in five sample years between 1901 and 1914, 74 percent came from politics, business, and the professions. But after about 1922 well over half of them came from the world of entertainment. Even among the entertainers an ever decreasing proportion has come from the serious arts—literature, fine arts, music, dance, and theater. An ever increasing proportion (in recent years nearly all) comes from the fields of light entertainment, sports, and the night club circuit. In the earlier period, say before World War I, the larger group included figures like the President of the United States, a Senator, a State Governor, the Secretary of the Treasury, the banker J. P. Morgan, the railroad magnate James J. Hill, a pioneer in aviation, the inventor of the torpedo, a Negro educator, an immigrant scientist, an opera singer, a famous poet, and a popular fiction writer. By the 1940s the larger group included figures like the boxer Jack Johnson, Clark Gable, Bobby Jones, the movie actresses Brenda Joyce and Brenda Marshall, William Powell, the woman matador Conchita Cintron, the night club entertainer Adelaide Moffett, and the gorilla Toto. Some analysts say the shift is primarily the sign of a new focus of popular attention away from production and toward consumption. But this is oversubtle.

A simpler explanation is that the machinery of information has brought into being a new substitute for the hero, who is the celebrity, and whose main characteristic is his well-knownness. In the democracy of pseudo-events, anyone can become a celebrity, if only he can get into the news and stay there. Figures from the world of entertainment and sports are most apt to be well known. If they are successful enough, they actually overshadow the real figures they portray. George Arliss overshadowed Disraeli, Vivian Leigh overshadowed Scarlett O'Hara, Fess Parker overshadowed Davy Crockett. Since their stock in trade is their well-knownness, they are most apt to have energetic press agents keeping them in the public eye.

It is hardly surprising then that magazine and newspaper readers no longer find the lives of their heroes instructive. Popular biographies can offer very little in the way of solid information. For the subjects are themselves mere figments of the media. If their lives are empty of drama or achievement, it is only as we might have expected, for they are not known for drama or achievement. They are celebrities. Their chief claim to fame is their fame itself. They are notorious for their notoriety. If this is puzzling or fantastic, if it is mere tautology, it is no more puzzling or fantastic or tautologous than much of the rest of our experience. Our experience tends more and more to become tautology—needless repetition of the same in different words and images. Perhaps what ails us is not so much a vice as a "nothingness." The vacuum of our experience is actually made emptier by our anxious straining with mechanical devices to fill it artificially. What is remarkable is not only that we manage to fill experience with so much emptiness, but that we manage to give the emptiness such appealing variety.

We can hear ourselves straining. "He's the greatest!" Our descriptions of celebrities overflow with superlatives. In popular magazine biographies we learn that a Dr. Brinkley is the "best-advertised doctor in the United States"; an actor is the "luckiest man in the movies today"; a Ringling is "not only the greatest, but the first real showman in the Ringling family"; a general is "one of the best mathematicians this side of Einstein"; a columnist has "one of the strangest of courtships; a statesman has "the world's most exciting job"; a sportsman is "the loudest and by all odds the most abusive"; a newsman is "one of the most consistently resentful men in the country"; a certain ex-King's mistress is "one of the unhappiest women that ever lived." But, despite the "supercolossal" on the label, the contents are very ordinary. The lives of celebrities which we like to read, as Leo Lowenthal remarks, are a mere catalogue of "hardships" and "breaks." These men and women are "the proved specimens of the average."

No longer external sources which fill us with purpose, these new-model "heroes" are receptacles into which we pour our own purposelessness. They are nothing but ourselves seen in a magnifying mirror. Therefore the lives of entertainer-celebrities cannot extend our horizon. Celebrities populate our horizon with men and women we already know. Or, as an advertisement for the *Celebrity Register* cogently puts it, celebrities are "the 'names' who, once made by news, now make news by themselves." Celebrity is made by simple familiarity, induced and re-enforced by public means. The celebrity therefore is the perfect embodiment of tautology: the most familiar is the most familiar.

The hero was distinguished by his achievement; the celebrity by his image or trademark. The hero created himself; the celebrity is created by the media. The hero was a big man; the celebrity is a big name.

Formerly, a public man needed a *private* secretary for a barrier between himself and the public. Nowadays he has a *press* secretary, to keep him properly in the public eye. Before the Graphic Revolution (and still in countries which have not undergone that revolution) it was a mark of solid distinction in a man or a family to keep out of the news. A lady of aristocratic pretensions was supposed to get her name in the papers only three times: when she was born, when she married, and when she died. Now the families who are Society are by definition those always appearing in the papers. The man of truly heroic stature was once supposed to be marked by scorn for publicity. He quietly relied on the power of his character or his achievement.

In the South, where the media developed more slowly than elsewhere in the country, where cities appeared later, and where life was dominated by rural ways, the celebrity grew more slowly. The old-fashioned hero was romanticized. In this as in many other ways, the Confederate General Robert E. Lee was one of the last surviving American models of the older type. Among his many admirable qualities, Southern compatriots admired none more than his retirement from public view. He had the reputation for never having given a newspaper interview. He steadfastly refused to write his memoirs. "I should be trading on the blood of my men," he said. General George C. Marshall (1880–1959) is a more recent and more anachronistic example. He, too, shunned publicity and refused to write his memoirs, even while other generals were serializing theirs in the newspapers. But by his time, few people any longer considered this reticence a virtue. His old-fashioned unwillingness to enter the publicity arena finally left him a victim of the slanders of Senator Joseph McCarthy and others.

The hero was born of time: his gestation required at least a generation. As the saying went, he had "stood the test of time." A maker of tradition, he was himself made by tradition. He grew over the generations as people found new virtues in him and attributed to him new exploits. Receding into the misty past he became more, and not less, heroic. It was not necessary that his face or figure have a sharp, well-delineated outline, nor that his life be footnoted. Of course there could not have been any photographs of him, and often there was not even a likeness. Men of the last century were more heroic than those of today; men of antiquity were still more heroic; and those of pre-history became demigods. The hero was always somehow ranked among the ancients.

The celebrity, on the contrary, is always a contemporary. The hero is made by folklore, sacred texts, and history books, but the celebrity is the creature of gossip, of public opinion, of magazines, newspapers, and the ephemeral images of movie and television screen. The passage of time, which creates and establishes the hero, destroys the celebrity. Onc is made, the other unmade, by repctition. The celebrity is born in the daily papers and never loses the mark of his fleeting origin.

The very agency which first makes the celebrity in the long run inevitably destroys him. He will be destroyed, as he was made, by publicity. The newspapers make him, and they unmake him—not by murder but by suffocation or starvation. No one is more forgotten than the last generation's celebrity. This fact explains the newspaper feature "Whatever Became Of . . . ?" which amuses us by accounts of the present obscurity of former celebrities. One can always get a laugh by referring knowingly to the once-household names which have lost their celebrity in the last few decades: Mae Bush, William S. Hart, Clara Bow. A woman reveals her age by the celebrities she knows.

There is not even any tragedy in the celebrity's fall, for he is a man returned to his proper anonymous station. The tragic hero, in Aristotle's familiar definition, was a man fallen from great estate, a great man with a tragic flaw. He had somehow become the victim of his own greatness. Yesterday's celebrity, however, is a commonplace man who has been fitted back into his proper commonplaceness not by any fault of his own, but by time itself.

The dead hero becomes immortal. He becomes more vital with the passage of time. The celebrity even in his lifetime becomes passé: he passes out of the picture. The white glare of publicity, which first gave him his specious brilliance, soon melts him away. This was so even when the only vehicles of publicity were the magazine and the newspaper. Still more now with our vivid round-the-clock media, with radio and television. Now when it is possible, by bringing their voices and images daily into our living rooms, to make celebrities more quickly than ever before, they die more quickly than ever. This has been widely recognized by entertainment celebrities and politicians. President Franklin Delano Roosevelt was careful to space out his fireside chats so the citizenry would not tire of him. Some comedians (for example, Jackie Gleason in the mid1950s) have found that when they have weekly programs they reap quick and remunerative notoriety, but that they soon wear out their images. To extend their celebrity-lives, they offer their images more sparingly—once a month or once every two months instead of once a week.

There is a subtler difference between the personality of the hero and that of the celebrity. The figures in each of the two classes become assimilated to one another, but in two rather different ways. Heroes standing for greatness in the traditional mold tend to become colorless and cliché. The greatest heroes have the least distinctiveness of face or figure. We may show our reverence for them, as we do for God, by giving them beards. Yet we find it hard to imagine that Moses or Jesus could have had other special facial characteristics. The hero while being thus idealized and generalized loses his individuality. The fact that George Washington is not a vivid personality actually helps him serve as the heroic Father of Our Country. Perhaps Emerson meant just this when he said that finally every great hero becomes a great bore. To be a great hero is actually to become lifeless; to become a face on a coin or a postage stamp. It is to become a Gilbert Stuart's Washington. Contemporaries, however, and the celebrities made of them, suffer from idiosyncrasy. They are too vivid, too individual to be polished into a symmetrical Greek statue. The Graphic Revolution, with its klieg lights on face and figure, makes the images of different men more distinctive. This itself disqualifies them from becoming heroes or demigods.

While heroes are assimilated to one another by the great simple virtues of their character, celebrities are differentiated mainly by trivia of personality. To be known for your personality actually proves you a celebrity. Thus a synonym for "a celebrity" is "a personality." Entertainers, then, are best qualified to become celebrities because they are skilled in the marginal differentiation of their personalities. They succeed by skillfully distinguishing themselves from others essentially like them. They do this by minutiae of grimace, gesture, language, and voice. We identify Jimmy ("Schnozzola") Durante by his nose, Bob Hope by his fixed smile, Jack Benny by his stinginess, Jack Paar by his rudeness, Jackie Gleason by his waddle, Imogene Coca by her bangs.

With the mushroom-fertility of all pseudo-events, celebrities tend to breed more celebrities. They help make and celebrate and publicize one another. Being known primarily for their well-knownness, celebrities intensify their celebrity images simply by becoming widely known for relations among themselves. By a kind of symbiosis, celebrities live off one another. One becomes better known by being the habitual butt of another's jokes, by being another's paramour or ex-wife, by being the subject of another's gossip, or even by being ignored by another celebrity. Elizabeth Taylor's celebrity appeal has consisted less perhaps in her own talents as an actress than in her connections with other celebrities—Nick Hilton, Mike Todd, and Eddie Fisher. Arthur Miller, the playwright, became a "real" celebrity by his marriage to Marilyn Monroe. When we talk or read or write about celebrities, our emphasis on their marital relations and sexual habits, on their tastes in smoking, drinking, dress, sports cars, and interior decoration is our desperate effort to distinguish among the indistinguishable. How can those commonplace people like us (who, by the grace of the media, happened to become celebrities) be made to seem more interesting or bolder than we are?

JAMES W. CHESEBRO and JOHN D. GLENN

The Soap Opera as a Communication System

Are you a soap opera addict? Do you arrange your weekday schedule so as not to miss an episode of "General Hospital?" Or do you dismiss soaps as mindless entertainment to fill the afternoons of tired housewives? Whatever your view, it is apparent that soaps are not only here to stay, they are capturing an ever larger following and are proliferating in TV's prime time programming. They are an important part of our culture and are worthy of examination in terms of their interpersonal implications. Chesebro and Glenn argue that soaps are a unique type of communication that help form the symbolic reality of a major portion of the American public. You may or may not agree with their conclusion, depending on your own involvement with the soaps.

Soap operas are derided by some, ignored by others, but watched by tens of millions. It is unlikely that the aesthetic issues created by the soap opera can be resolved. However, it is both possible and appropriate to identify the role, characteristics, uniqueness, and functions of the soap opera as a communication system. Toward these ends, this essay posits four interrelated arguments. First, we argue that these soap operas are a major part of the popular culture and therefore worthy of consideration if—for no other reason—we are to acknowledge and understand the nature of the "symbolic reality" of a major portion of the American public. Second, we argue that the soap opera, both in content and form, is particularly susceptible to a communication analysis, for the content and form of the soap opera is "talk" rather than action. Having established this context, we affirm a third argument that the soap opera is a unique genre or type of communication. As we move toward our fourth and final argument, we adopt an evaluative stance. Our investigation leaves us with but one conclusion, namely that an entertainment format of millions is a form of pathological communication. However, before developing such a critical stance, it is initially appropriate to identify the place of the soap opera among contemporary popular media.

The Role of the Soap Opera in the Contemporary American Media

Soap operas occupy a prominent place in the national mass media, particularly as a major feature of contemporary television. Sixteen soap operas are nationally broadcast: thirteen appear on daytime television from Monday through Friday; two appear weekly during prime time and are touted as "adult serial dramas"; and one, *Soap,* is a soap opera but also a comic parody of the genre of soap operas.[1]

These soap operas receive some of the highest popularity ratings. *As the World Turns,* for example, has captured as much as 33 percent of the viewing audience and thus has had one of the highest Nielsen ratings. On the average day, some eight million watch the *World.* Similarly, *Search for Tomorrow* has, on the average, six million daily viewers. Overall, on the average, some 30 million people watch daytime soap operas at least one hour every day.

The prime-time soap operas are equally successful. *Dallas,* one of the weekly evening adult series, was ranked third in Nielsen's top twenty prime-time television shows for the broadcast year 1979–1980. *Dallas* has created its own spin-off as well as encouraging the other networks to add series with this format to their fall 1980 programming lineup.

Additionally, soap operas have established some of the most remarkable endurance records on television. Multiple generations of viewers have literally watched multiple generations of soap opera characters grow up, grow older, and pass from the series. *As the World Turns* and *Search for Tomorrow,* for example, have each been on the air for more than twenty years.

Beyond the extensive airing of soap operas on television, the soap opera is becoming a multimedia experience. Publications about soap operas are becoming a significant mass communication phenomenon. *Soap Opera Digest,* the largest of the national soap opera publications, has a circulation of 750,000 right now, with a projected circulation of one million for 1980–1981.[2] Additionally, there are five other national soap opera publications with a circulation of between one quarter to one half million each.

Thus, regardless of any popular assessment of the soap opera, we must admit that the soap opera occupies a prominent place in the popular mass media. Given the significance of the soap opera, an investigation of the messages and strategies of the format is appropriate. Accordingly, we ask: "What are the formal and substantive features of the soap opera as a communication system?"

The Soap Opera as a Communicative Activity

In content and form, the soap opera is a profoundly symbolic activity. The soap opera is a product of a communication medium, television. Accordingly, few would argue that the format of the soap opera is noncommunicative in nature. However, the content of the soap opera is equally communicative. Granted, soap operas have now matured and deal with contemporary social issues such as abortion, infidelity, premarital relationships, and venereal diseases. However, these do not appear directly on the screen. Soap opera characters talk. They *talk* about their lives, *talk* about their relationships, *talk* about their neighbors, and *talk* about their possible futures. The physical actions related to these conversations seldom appear on the screen itself. In sharp contrast, the actual shooting or robbery that generates the plot for prime-time evening television series is actually seen on the screen. The soap opera character only talks about the events that have occurred or will occur off-screen. The soap opera is a world of words, not deeds. On *General Hospital,* for example, Rick and Monica *talk* about their respective upcoming divorces and *talk* about their faint hope of spending the rest of their lives together. Likewise, Luke *talks* about his unrequited love for Laura and *talks* about the possibility of death and violence befalling him or his loved ones. In content, then, the soap opera is a profoundly communicative activity. It is a series of "talking heads" or close-ups of the head and shoulders of the actors and actresses talking. In essence, the soap opera is decisively a communicative activity in both form and content.

As a mode of public communication, the soap opera also has an identifiable "target audience." The daytime soap opera is directed toward and watched by the housewife and homemaker. Eighty-four percent of the viewers are women, most of whom do not work outside of the home.[3] In this vein, prime-time evening soap operas have traditionally been unsuccessful. *Return to Peyton Place,* when offered as a commodity to a television audience of greater demographic diversity, performed poorly in the network rating competition. Insofar as prime-time evening soap operas such as *Dallas* and *Knott's Landing* are successful, the content of these soap operas is changed for evening viewing. The evening soap opera shifts from an oral communication emphasis to physical action. We actually see, for example, the shooting of J. R. For most daytime soap operas—our central focus of concern here—women, in the relatively isolated environment of the home, are the predominant viewers. At the same time, we should note that the daytime soap opera viewers may be diversifying. The second largest body of viewers is college students. However, the college student responds in a more participatory fashion to the soap opera, for most of the fan mail from college students typically takes the form of petitions in which requests are made to have a plot developed in one fashion rather than another. Nonetheless, women still constitute the single largest group of viewers.

In our view, then, we are not remiss in treating the soap opera as a communicative activity. Both in content and form, communication dominates the soap opera. Moreover, an identifiable target audience can be specified—the housewife and homemaker—which allows us to identify the meaning of the soap opera to its viewers. As a preliminary analysis of the day-time soap opera as a mode of communication, we would argue that the day-time soap opera is a unique mode of television communication. The daytime soap opera is, in other words, unlike other modes of television communication such as network news programs, prime-time dramas, or documentaries. To demonstrate our point, we compare the daytime soap opera with its closest ally, the prime-time evening episode such as *Charlie's Angels* or *Laverne and Shirley*. Such a comparison has led us to conclude that the day-time soap opera is a unique type, class, or genre of television communication.

The Generic Features of the Soap Opera

Soap operas constitute a genre of television communication unique among network broadcasting. At the broadest level of abstraction, soap operas are part of the "art" of television drama rather than television comedy, television documentaries, or television news programs. In this sense, the daytime soap opera is closely affiliated with the prime-time evening drama. However, we would make a distinction between the daytime soap opera and the prime-time evening drama. The former we identify as *series* while we view the latter as *episodes*. These two forms of drama, we would maintain, are generically distinct. At least four factors distinguish these two forms of drama. Table I summarizes these differences.

First, episodes and series differ temporally or in their use of time. The episodic drama has an identifiable action which occurs within a fixed time period, typically thirty, sixty, or ninety minutes. Each of the prime-time evening episodes possesses its own sense of closure; the drama ends. In contrast, the daytime serial drama employs an open-ended time period.

The dramatic action of the daytime serial drama may, and does, go on for months or years with no indication of when, how, or even if, the drama will complete itself. In *General Hospital*, for example, Jeff wants to marry Anne. However, Jeff's wife is in a mental hospital. Jeff must wait five years before he can divorce and marry Anne. With the input of other characters, the plot is open to innumerable changes, twists, and contortions, with no one being able to predict the outcome. On the other hand, the prime-time evening episodic drama has an identifiable inciting incident be that incident a murder, rape, or whatever, with a specified "hero" or "heroine" whom the viewers "know" will solve the problem within half an hour to ninety minutes. The murderer or rapist is apprehended as the episode closes and the drama is completed. The soap opera offers no such closure within any predictable time period. In fact, the soap opera celebrates in the unending, increasing complex, nature of human dilemmas. Accordingly, one of the messages of the daytime serial soap opera is that "Human beings may never resolve their dilemmas and every effort toward resolution may, in fact, compound the resolution of the drama."

Second, the central characters function differently in the episodic and serial dramas. The episodic drama employs actors and actresses who are known "stars" with identifiable and unique personalities. The unique personality of the actor or actresses is an indication of the way in which the drama will be resolved. Correspondingly, because the personality of the actor or actress is unique and becomes part of the definition of the central character of the episodic drama, the actor or actress is extremely difficult to replace. It is, for example, extremely difficult to think of substituting another actor for Carroll O'Connor in *Archie's Place* or to imagine another actor replacing Peter Falk as Columbo. The unique personality and appearance of particular actors and actresses are associated with central characters in the prime-time evening episodic dramas. In contrast, the serial dramas employ highly stereotyped roles in the creation of the daytime soap opera. The central characters of the soap opera are so unidimensional that

Table 1. Factors distinguishing the serial and episodic dramatic genres

Distinguishing Factor	Series	Episode
1. Time	Open-ended	Fixed
2. Central character	Role	Star
3. Content	Words	Behavior
4. Form	Multiple subplots	Single plot

virtually any actor or actress can, and frequently have been, employed as substitutes for a single character. The role of the character is all-important and can exist independent of the actor or actress' personality. Rachel on *Another World* has, for example, been played by over five different actresses without apparently disturbing the viewers. In fact, one of these Rachels, Robyn Strauser, has since gone on to play Dorian Lord on *One Life to Live*. Viewers are not upset by such changes, for the role of the character is far more important on the soap opera than is the actor's or actress's unique personality. Accordingly, a second message of the daytime serial soap opera is that, "Human beings are role-players or stereotypical."

Third, episodic and serial dramas differ with respect to content. As we have already suggested, the content of the episodic drama is action-centered. A sequence of behavioral actions and reactions physically dominate the plot of the episodic drama. In the detective show, for example, a murder occurs on screen, a shrewd detective is called in on the case, and the viewers actually see the physical actions that the detective must go through to ultimately apprehend the murderer. A specific behavioral action starts the drama of the episode, and specific behavioral actions follow that ultimately provide the foundation for resolution and closure of the drama. In contrast, the content of the serial drama, as we have already argued, is verbal. The characters *talk* about life's perils. Typically, in fact, their words are extremely selective and reflect middle-class values, life-styles, and settings. But more important than this class bias, their words are about words; rarely do they actually act and do. From a communication perspective, the soap opera's verbal emphasis is particularly problematic, for it seems to suggest that verbal communication is more important than nonverbal communication. From a larger societal perspective, such an emphasis conveys a third message, namely, that "The realm of human action is predominantly limited to verbal description and interpretations rather than social change."

Fourth and finally, the episodic and serial dramas differ in form. Episodic dramas have one single major plot line with few subplots. The plot develops and concludes in what might be called a "vertical arrangement with few branches." Serial dramas, on the other hand, employ multiple subplots rather than a single or major plot line. The plot develops from several independent branches, and it is more appropriate to observe that soap operas have plots rather than a single plot as we anticipate in most dramas. These plots can develop independently for years if the soap operas' writers prefer. The plots can, in fact, be so independent that a single character can be introduced into a different subplot of the same soap opera after a profoundly traumatizing experience in another subplot without any noticeable effects. Rick, for example, died in one subplot[4] of *General Hospital* in 1976 and yet he is now alive and well, still living in Port Charles, and talking about divorce and remarriage in a different *General Hospital* subplot. By shifting Rick from one subplot to another, it was "discovered" that Rick was not really dead after all. More generally, as one watches an hour-long soap opera on any given day, one notices that the program is typically divided into three to four major subplots; each subplot is independently developed as the days pass. The viewer must watch the soap opera every day if the coherence of each subplot is to be understood. Ultimately, then, multiple subplots define the structure of the daytime serial soap opera. Accordingly, a fourth message is conveyed by the soap opera: "Human beings function in relatively discrete social units, seldom affecting one another, and ultimately diminishing the significance of societal identifications and interactions, societal identities, and collective action."

These four generic features of the daytime serial soap opera provide a foundation for an overview of the messages ultimately conveyed to soap opera viewers. An extremely selective perspective of the human being is constructed by the soap opera. The human being is cast as pathetic, helpless, and isolated. Particularly, human beings are—we are told in the contemporary American soap opera—caught in a series of unending dilemmas with few creative options for change through individual, physical, or social action. Essentially, the soap opera portrays the human being as frustrated, immobile, and isolated. Such a view of the human being requires a critical response.

The Soap Opera: An Interpretation and an Evaluation

Having specified the descriptive characteristics of the soap opera, it is appropriate to turn our attention to an interpretation and finally an evaluation of soap operas as communication. As a communicative drama, we may profitably recall the classical distinction between comedy and tragedy as our foundation for interpreting the social meaning of the soap opera.

For classical critics, comedy highlights *how* something is done; the form, way, or method in which an act is executed receives attention in a comedy. Consequently, we identify Laurel and Hardy films as comedies because they highlight the mode of operation rather than the societal issues and meanings at hand. Tragedy, on the other hand, focuses upon the issues and the substance of the drama: *what* is occurring is the concern. In our view, soap operas are appropriately interpreted as tragedies. Characters on these soap operas seldom perceive themselves as humorous nor do they view their actions as satirical. More important, the viewer is asked to concentrate upon *what* is said. The viewers' attention is not to be focused on how someone is doing something but rather on what he or she is doing. Thus, soap operas function as tragic drama. Having offered such a broad interpretation, we need to extract the social meaning therefrom. To identify the social meaning of the soap opera, we have found it convenient to employ a modified form of Kenneth Burke's conception of the tragic drama.[5]

From a Burkeian view, all human dramas pass through four discrete stages: *pollution, guilt, purification,* and *redemption.* Each stage raises a critical question relevant to the sequential development of the drama. These four critical terms and their concomitant questions are: (1) *Pollution*— "What norms are violated?" (2) *Guilt*—"Who or what is held responsible for the pollution?" (3) *Purification*—"What acts are initiated to eliminate the pollution and guilt?" and (4) *Redemption*—"What order is created by passing through the process of pollution, guilt, and purification?" These four stages provide a convenient critical framework for the examination of soap operas as a type of tragic drama.

Soap operas seldom pass through all four of these critical stages. In our view, soap operas are incomplete dramas, for the actions of the soap opera deal only with pollution, guilt, and purification, but never with redemption. Continuing and overwhelming pain is the focus of the soap opera. Pollution is rampant: murder, rape, blackmail, adultery, and incest can define the human situation. Guilt for these acts is likewise a frequent topic of conversation, and in the course of these discussions, the soap opera characters identify the erring party. Purification, necessary for the elimination of the pollution and guilt, is attempted over and over again. Characters are continually offering solutions and following advice. But, the steps to purification do not succeed. In fact, each attempt at purification only compounds the initial problem and sense of guilt, ultimately creating only additional pollution and guilt for the new errors. Accordingly, the errors of the characters continue to grow and multiply. A new order, a new social system, or redemption is never established. The characters are trapped by their own values, and their values preclude the resolution of their problems. They are fated not only to relive all of their past mistakes perpetually, but to compound them. In this sense, soap operas are unredeemed dramas.

Besdies this interpretation of soap operas as unredeemed dramas, we would also observe that the soap opera employs modes of mystification and deception. Mystification, according to R. D. Laing,[6] is to "befuddle, cloud, obscure, or mask whatever is going on, whether this be experience, action, or process, or whatever is the issue. It induces confusion . . . and a failiure to distinguish or discriminate the actual issues."[7] Laing goes on to identify the two primary functions of mystification: (1) "to maintain the status quo," and (2) "to maintain stereotyped roles."[8] One employs a mystifying strategy if one says to another, "I know you are upset. We should go out tonight and have a good time so that you can get your mind off your troubles." Such statements are mystifying for they tell one how to feel about a particular problem but not how to redeem the drama. In our view, then, the soap opera is not only an unredeemed drama, but a communication system that precludes the resolution of the unredeemed drama by virtue of the communicative strategies built into the soap opera.

Besides functioning as an unredeemed and mystifying symbolic form, the soap opera can also be appropriately interpreted as a form of deception. Deception is used here in the common-sense meaning of the word: intentionally to omit information or to provide misleading or incorrect information. Deception (or lying) thus becomes a strategic form of communication among soap opera characters primarily functioning as a self-protection device among these characters. Characters deceive in order to prevent others from discovering the "truth." And, while the characters may voice regrets over their deceptions in subsequent conversations, they are trapped by a pattern, for each vow to start a new life is tarnished and constrained by the previous deception.

In interpreting the soap opera, then, we are left with the conclusion that the soap opera is an unredeemed drama that perpetuates a mode of communication that makes it impossible to define the nature of the unredeemed drama either because of mystification or because of deception. The soap opera thus functions as a closed-communication system; it is impossible to redeem the human dilemma because the purification process includes the seeds of its own destruction, namely, mystification and deception.

From an evaluative stance, we are finally left with the view that the soap opera is a pathological mode of communication, particularly for the viewers of these series. We envision the following scenario: some 30 million housewives are home alone, watching hours of soap operas in which human beings are cast as isolated, helpless, and incapable of action. Life becomes, in this view, incapable of reaching fulfillment primarily because human beings are incapable of defining the problems before them or honestly responding to the problem even if the problem has been accurately diagnosed. In the isolation of the home, this is the view of human existence that is portrayed.

The question emerges: "How does the housewife respond to such a view of human existence?" Unfortunately, few efforts have been made at carefully surveying the responses of housewives to soap operas. In fact, we know of no attempt to identify the consequences of prolonged soap-opera viewing in social isolation. Accordingly, we can only offer only theoretical and speculative indications of the consequences of soap opera viewing. However, such a set of explorations can be formally structured and guided by the research of others who have examined the social consequences of other types of television programming upon viewers. Typically, these research efforts are classified under the heading of "uses and gratification research." The effort of the uses/gratification researchers is simply to determine what uses viewers make of television and/or what needs are gratified by viewing television.[9] Given the nature of these research programs, it would seem that the American housewife might make but four uses of the soap opera.

First, the American housewife might employ the soap opera as a medium for "exploring reality." Employed for such a purpose, soap operas would be utilized as an indication of what people actually do and how they do it. If used for such an end, we anticipate that housewives are likely to believe that any effort at change would be meaningless, for the soap opera casts life as an unredeemable drama.

Second, the American housewife might employ the soap opera as a form of "escapsim." Escapist entertainment provides a way of avoiding involvement in ongoing life-experiences and substituting vicarious thrills for the immediate environment. But if the soap opera is more rewarding than housewive's own environments, the very existence of the soap opera is an indictment of the lifestyle of some 30 million people. Can so many people actually prefer the suffering of others (soap opera characters) to their own ongoing life-experiences?

Third, the American housewife might employ the soap opera for "character reference." In this view, the soap opera characters are employed as models for human interaction. If used for such an end, we anticipate that American housewives can only compound their problems, for mystification and deception are the common communicative norms of soap opera characters.

Fourth and finally, the American housewife might employ the soap opera for "personal reference." We can anticipate that some housewives will find particular and unique guidelines for living that others might ignore or dismiss. Again, we would suggest that if used for such an end, we anticipate that elements of mystification and deception are likely to be a dimension of the cues adopted for personal use.

If the soap opera serves any one of these four purposes, we believe that a pathological mode of communication dominates the viewing time of some 30 million Americans. If our speculations are correct, we are frankly amazed that the American housewife has survived as a healthy human being. Unfortunately, we also suspect that the kind of communication norms fostered by soap operas are reinforced by other modes of communication and that these counterproductive forces might be linked to the decline of the nuclear family, the dissatisfaction which many women have experienced in marriage environments, and the increasing anomie that characterizes the American culture. We frankly hope that our speculations are wrong, but we fear that we may be correct.

Notes

1. We have avoided detailed footnoting regarding the number, frequency, ratings, and endurance of soap operas because these data are so regularly available in publications such as *Soap Opera Digest* on virtually all newsstands on a tri-weekly basis or monthly basis. We would suggest that the reader consult these publications for current and specific statistics.
2. Personal telephone conversation with Wendy Schreiber, Assistant Editor, *Soap Opera Digest*.
3. Fergus M. Bordewich, "Why Are College Kids in a Lather Over TV Soap Operas?" *New York Times*, October 20, 1974, section 2, p. 31.
4. See *Soap Opera Digest*, June 1976, p. 74.
5. For greater details regarding this modification, see James W. Chesebro, "Communication, Values, and Popular Television Series—A Four Year Assessment," in *Inter/Media*, ed. by Gary Gumpert and Robert Cathcart (New York: Oxford University Press, 1979).

6. R. D. Laing, "Mystification, Confusion, and Conflict," in *Intensive Family Therapy*, ed. by Ivan Boszormenyi-Nagy and James Frama.
7. Laing, pp. 343–363.
8. Laing, pp. 343–363.
9. F. Gerald Kline and Phillip J. Tichenor, Editors, *Current Perspectives in Mass Communication Research*, Sage Publications, Beverly Hills, London, 1974.

DAVID L. ALTHEIDE and ROBERT P. SNOW

The Grammar of Radio

Radio has been with us much longer than television, but it has never evoked the intense study and interest in its effects that TV has. Still, it is an extremely important medium, one that has changed dramatically in its form and function during the past several decades and that touches on the lives of all of us. David L. Altheide and Robert P. Snow describe the ways in which radio interacts with our daily existence, how it structures time, sets the tempo for our day, connects us with the community, caters to our moods, and provides us with dee-jay role models.

Is radio your first media contact of the day? Would you ever drive an automobile without the radio on? Could this medium be one of your closest and most important companions? Read "Mass Media and Face-to-Face Communication: Bridging the Gap," by Robert Avery and Thomas McCain in Section 1 for an analysis of people's use of "talk" radio.

Radio's appeal is that it serves both utilitarian or practical tasks and playful moods without immobilizing the listener. In describing the functions of radio, Harold Mendelsohn argued that, in addition to simply transmitting news, time, and temperature, radio brings the outside world into the home or car; provides an organization for the routines of the day; and serves as a social lubricant. As an organizer of daily routine, radio wakes us in the morning, gets us to work, and provides a variety of moods for evening and late-night activity. As a social lubricant, radio provides content to talk about with others, we may interact vicariously with the radio personality, or we may play and sing along with the program. To understand the media culture of radio, we will examine radio format in terms of the grammar of radio; factors that influence radio content; the radio personality; and, finally, speculate on some hypothetical consequences of radio format.

The grammar of radio consists of ways in which the use of time, the organization of content, and conversation make this a very personalized medium. In brief: time follows the listener's pace through daily routine; content is organized into segments that meet music subculture requirements as well as daily routine activities; and radio talk augments the time and organizational factors of grammar. In making sense of radio grammar it also must be remembered that entertainment is the basic underlying form for this grammar.

Uses of Time

Unlike television, radio presents time according to "normal" everyday routine. Whereas television alters time in drama, news, and comedy programs, radio follows an exact linear progression of time, keeping pace with the listener's sense of real time throughout the day. This enables the listener to use the radio as a clock and a metronome; during the hurried pace of the morning and afternoon rush-hour periods, radio constantly reports the time to the listener, and maintains a tempo that keeps pace with the listener's use of time. For example, the morning drive-time is a hurried pace of getting dressed, fed, and off to work. The midday period is a relaxed moderate pace, with things picking up again during the afternoon rush-hour period. Early evening is usually a time to wind down, and the late-night hours can range from slow romance to the funky beat of nighthawks. The type of tempo variation not only caters to listener routines, it helps establish these routines.

The most important element of time and tempo is the music presented by radio stations. Since each musical piece has a particular tempo, a record can sustain an intended pace and flow of time. Rock stations are almost frantic, while "beautiful music" stations maintain a slow, soothing tempo. In addition, a particular rhythm is established by alternating slow, moderate, and up-tempo records. This rhythmic variation provides a sense of balance within the general tempo of a time segment. Developing this rhythmic balance has become such a sophisticated operation that many stations now employ computer technology to insure appropriate music scheduling.

To augment and support music tempo, disc jockeys establish an appropriate conversational tone and pace. During drive-time periods, they project calm sympathy for the rush-hour-bound commuter. At midday periods, their tone and pace is relaxed and comforting. With changes occurring throughout the day, the conversational tone and pace of the "deejay" corresponds to the music tempo and, consequently, the routines of the listener. For example, rock stations use a ten-to-twenty second interval between records with a voice-over the end of one record, a short quip, and a voice-over the beginning of the next record. In this fashion, conversation is integrated into the music tempo without mood interuption. Easy-listening stations string three or four records together without interruption and then identify the artists. In this case, talk is a momentary pause that prevents the tempo from becoming too monotonous. Jazz station deejays often use their knowledge of music to "back" one record over another with no change in the beat. Following this feat of skill, the jazz jock may give a lengthy reporting of the individual artists, tell when the recording was made, and make some comment about its quality. Here, the conversation is used partially to legitimize the particular musical selection.

To summarize, radio time corresponds to how listeners carry out their daily routines. In this sense, radio time is subordinate to listener time, with radio facilitating and helping to establish the sense of time a listener wants to achieve. For many listeners, using radio to establish and sustain their uses of time has become a routine in itself.

Organization and Scheduling

The organization of content in radio programs has become a sophisticated procedure in the past twenty years. During the mass-audience period of the 1930s and early '40s, radio used block programming much as television uses today. In radio, block programs were homogeneous segments of quarter-, half-, or hour-long periods in which the music of a band or artist was supported by one or two advertisers. As the record industry expanded (with nonbreakable 45s and LPs) the hit parade was born, and radio scheduled music according to its popularity. With the baby boom and the advent of youth-oriented rock 'n' roll, the record industry boomed and began pressuring radio stations to create and play hits. Radio was now in a position to exercise greater control over music entertainment through new formats.

The most successful new format, sometimes called the Drake Format after its originator, developed in rock music and gradually spread to middle-of-the-road popular music stations. In this format the radio hour is broken into three or four separate segments, with each segment further organized into specific categories of record popularity, such as a hit, an "up-and-comer," a "golden oldie," and so on. With this format a station could use as few as 30 records for an entire broadcast day. One consequence of this format was a high degree of standardization for a particular station and similar stations throughout a music subculture. Program directors now had absolute control over what records were played and when they were scheduled.

Given the apparent success of what is now called "formated" radio, it is difficult to find a so-called "free form" station—one in which the disc jockey selects the records and determines when they are played. Today, music is scripted according to a grammar that in part programs the listening audience.

Special Features of Vocal Communication

Radio achieves an intimate interpersonal character referred to earlier by serving specialized audiences and subcultures. To reach these specialized audiences, the station must speak the appropriate subculture language; bubblegum rock, jazz, country, soul, and the rest are uniquely different in jargon, rhythm, pitch, and other speech characteristics. On bubblegum stations the deejay speaks fast, using teenage slang. In contrast, jazz audiences require a slow, cool style. On news, talk radio, and background music stations, the communicators follow a "middle-of-the-road" policy that some listeners describe as middle-class anonymity. Given the unique language character of a subculture, radio stations follow the language of their audience, rather than forcing listeners to accept something that is dissonant.

Radio communication is also clear, crisp, pleasing to the ear, and devoid of long (dead air) pauses. The talk of radio professionals appears articulate and polished, although on occasion we hear glaring bloopers and inane comments. But in major radio markets mistakes are rare, and so, for the average listener, the radio personality represents an ideal model of communication within a specialized subculture. In some cases, such as large urban MOR stations, the talk may even be described as "slick." To be slick is to flaunt a skill or talent beyond what is necessary for the situation—extraordinary behavior that is a vital element of entertainment.

Finally, radio grammar has a low degree of ambiguity. A radio may be switched on at any time and a listener will immediately understand what is happening. Several factors contribute to low ambiguity. Each music type is very distinctive, and after hearing only a few bars, almost anyone can identify the type of content that will follow. Voice rhythm is also an indication of content—compare religious radio to news, rock, or classics and the rhythm is readily apparent. Voice types are also standardized according to a station's content so that, even if you tune in during a break in the music, the station is identifiable. Content is instantly intelligible in radio and other "live" electronic media—there is no opportunity for an instant replay.

Definition of Content

In addition to the content of radio discussed in the preceding section, there are nongrammatical factors that influence radio format. One of these factors is the limitations of Federal Communications Commission regulations and the self-imposed broadcasting code. Since the airwaves are defined as public domain, radio stations are required to be licensed by the federal government. Regulated by the FCC, these licenses stipulate the frequency band and broadcasting power limitations of a station. In addition, the FCC requires a specific amount of broadcast time be devoted to public service announcements. Beyond these technical restrictions, the FCC supports the self-imposed code of ethics developed by the National Association of Broadcasters. In addition to such guidelines as the amount of advertising that is suggested in a given period of time, the code serves as a framework for upholding community values and norms to the extent that a lack of proper public spirit and decorum could actually result in the loss of a station's license. But on an informal level, media tend to regard themselves as guardians of community well-being. This ethical gatekeeping responsibility function is a well-established tradition and, as such, it is part of the overall media logic. Of course, what constitutes the media's sense of guardianship and what actually happens through media action may be quite different. At any rate, radio defines its content in terms of ideals and ethics designed to serve the station's definition of community well-being.

In addition to the formal and informal aspects of broadcasting codes, radio stations establish program content according to specific audience requests. These requests may range from the familiar music request line to demands by irate listeners offended by apparent attacks on what they hold sacred. With respect to music requests, large urban stations seldom play specific requests, although they do use this audience contact as an indicator of music and program popularity. Regarding irate listeners, stations distinguish between the common "crank call" and those influentials who represent potential bad public relations for the station. Radio is thus highly sensitive to audience response as advertising rates rise and fall according to audience size.

The final, and perhaps most important, factor in defining radio content is the entertainment perspective. As entertainment, radio meets all the criteria of entertainment previously discussed. Music is extraordinary in the talent and skill of the performer, in the moods and enjoyment that emerge while listening, and in the star character that musical groups provide to the members of various music subcultures. Talent and skill are judged differently by different listeners, but every music aficionado can recognize the presence or absence of those qualities. Radio stations occasionally try to "hype" a performer of dubious talent, but this is rarely successful. Even established stars who sluff-off or "lose it" are quickly dropped by a listening audience. Music stars who maintain their status represent what is extraordinary about the entertainment part of a subculture. The group "Kiss" is outrageous, Dolly Parton is country innocence with pizzazz, Herbie Hancock is a jazz genius, and Elvis is immortal.

Music is also a critical part of the vicarious character of entertainment. Music makes the mood that is important in achieving vicarious involvement as well as overt commitments. To this end, radio supplies the music that listeners need to facilitate various behaviors, both entertaining and nonentertaining. Since a radio can be carried anywhere, the variety of music available on radio makes it possible to dial in and out of various moods at will. A listener may tune in MOR for getting to and from work, listen to mellow mood music for lounging or romance, get hard rock or disco for Friday night, dial in country for long night drives, and listen to classics on Sunday morning. Every mood is formated by specialized ratio. Above all else, radio is enjoyable as a background or foreground activity.

The Radio Personality

The "personality" has been a fixture in radio for some time. Arthur Godfrey was king in this category, establishing the criteria by which radio communicators are still judged today. Although the format has changed considerably over the past two decades, the "personality" is still the factor that makes entertainment radio work. Throughout the broadcast day, the "air" personality develops a personal relationship with listeners. At one time or another we have had our favorites: Imus in New York, Bill Haywood in Phoenix, Steve Cannon in Minneapolis, and the likes of Cousin Brucie, the Real Don Steele, Jazzbo Collins, Daddy O'Dailey—the list seems endless. These personalities seem to accomplish two things: first, they talk to us personally and we feel part of an exclusive club, and second, they entertain, using every feature of the entertainment format.

The radio personality usually employs comedy; with well-planned "ad lib," a successful deejay enlivens the mundane and eases the listener's tensions. For most listeners, the drive-time hour of the day are difficult periods. Getting out of bed to face another routine day, fighting traffic to and from work, going home to perhaps more routine, the listener may be in a fairly anxious and negative mood. During these periods, the radio comedians usually have a funny story, a few wry quips, or perhaps a comedy routine. Even the practical information that listeners need, such as time, temperature, and road information, is spiced with comedy—a joke about the weather, a satirical comment on city hall, a jibe at traffic engineers or auto mechanics, and the inevitable reference to sex are all part of the comedy routine. Life during this drive-time period is serious business, but it is a relief to "take it on the lighter side."

When radio personalities develop the skills and talent to attract large audiences, they may become role models in specific music subcultures and for middle-of-the-road audiences. The role model of a music subculture involves both verbal behavior and a physical appearance image. The rock-jock is a young, hip, zany male with lots of hair and the clothes of a well-heeled teenager. Talk on the air must be spiced with plenty of teenage jargon. Never mind that some rock-jocks are bald and over forty—it's the image that counts. Jazz-jocks must demonstrate knowledge about the music and artists, be "up" on the latest sounds, and preferably have a very "cool" style. Middle-of-the-road personalities may run a wide range of verbal behavior and appearance, but they must be respectable. While these descriptions are overgeneralizations, the point is that part of the media culture of radio is an on-the-air personality who typifies the music.

Radio stations realized the power of the disc jockey in the early 1960s when they initiated disco concerts at which the deejay would play records at the local armory or high school gym. Soon the stations were doing weekend remotes and finally promoting big name concerts—SEE THE BEATLES with Murray the K (often called the Fifth Beatle). The same phenomena occurred for country music, middle-of-the-road, jazz, and, of course, soul. Listeners reasoned that if the radio personality was at the concert, then the music must be good. Soon deejays were selling products on television, appearing at charity affairs, and even conducting workshops at local schools on everything from the problems of communicating in today's world to drugs and dating. Radio personalities have become influential. As a part of media culture, the radio personality is a focal point and semi-leader of the music subcultures. How the radio personality behaves represents that music subculture both to those in the subculture and to outside observers. The radio personality is part of the music itself—as much a star as the recording artists.

In the 1960s, rock deejays became so powerful that a few developed cult followings. Record companies treated these personalities royally—the money was big and the prestige high. While it is doubtful these radio stars could "break" a musical group, they could be very helpful in promoting a newcomer or assisting a rise on the sales charts. A good word from Wolfman Jack and who knows what heights could be reached. But radio personality influence is not limited to rock music. Late night talk show hosts are currently the giants of the industry. Appearing knowledgeable on every subject, they are highly influential with their listeners.

The radio personality's influence is vast: we may emulate the role modeling behavior of the radio personalities; we may buy products they personally endorse. When they talk about a subject, it may legitimize that subject for us—we may even pay more attention to them than to the experts. Radio personalities form an inextricable part of the culture in which they participate. They don't simply transmit culture, they *are* media culture.

Hypothetical Consequences

One of our primary concerns in this book is to identify the extent to which people tend to adopt the logic of media, which in turn affects their definitions of reality. With radio, this is a difficult task. People use radio for purposes that are extraneous to the medium. With television, the captive viewer becomes immersed in whatever is being presented on the screen and often, for the moment, accepts what the medium offers. In contrast, people use radio to facilitate other activities, such as getting to work, eating, reading, making love, and so on. Even when radio is being listened to attentively, the listener is often engaged in some other activity. Consequently, listeners employ radio to stay in touch with realities that are formed in other contexts. This is not to say that radio is without influence, for it serves as a guideline, reference point, and legitimizer for those realities established in other contexts.

Listeners basically trust their radio stations to play quality music that is current. In this sense, radio serves as guiding framework and reference point for maintaining contact with a particular music subculture. The listener can be informed and at the same time feel in touch with like-minded people. However, this is a vicarious involvement, and over a long period of time the listener may feel estranged and require face-to-face contact with others in this subculture. To meet this need, radio promotes live concerts. Therefore, radio can mediate contact among members of a subculture and also stimulate or perpetuate a particular type of music.

Radio is also a legitimizing agent. As mentioned previously, radio personalities discussing a subject or playing a song demonstrate the legitimacy of that content. Given trust in a station by its listeners, the content of that station represents knowledge and evidence in a practical sense. Just as the content of a news program is accepted as "news," so too are the music and talk of a favorite radio station accepted as truth. The danger here is that "hype" can become a powerful media tool—listeners may be unaware they are being "hyped" to buy a particular record or attend a particular concert but influenced just the same. Radio may create a feeling that if you do not follow the subculture's lead, you will be "out of it."

Radio format also has a major influence on the recording industry. While the record companies are constantly looking for that new sensation, they must make hits to stay in business. For a record to get air play it must fit a station's format. It is one thing to make albums that sell, but quite another to make a record fit the time requirements and the tempo of the radio format. Given these requirements, record companies often make single copies that are shorter in length than the same piece on an album. They may also arrange music for each instrument and have artists record each arrangement separate from the others. The final product is then mixed according to the formula dictated by the record company. Thus, radio format has a definite influence on what is recorded and how it is recorded.

Another consequence of radio is the rapid consumption of talent. With our capability of instant dissemination of information and the apparent desire for instant knowledge, a situation exists in which a musical hit is established everywhere at the same time. Consequently, hits rise and fall at a rapid pace. If a song writer and musician wish to stay atop the charts, they must constantly create new material and maintain contact with the public. The schedule and pressure is so intense that few artists last more than several years at the hit level. This talent consumption is part of the larger issue David Riesman et al. discussed in *The Lonely Crowd*—we live in a consumption society. Radio and other media simply increase the pace of consumption, especially for musical entertainment.

There are other problem areas that deserve elaboration, but brief mention must suffice. One is the socializing impact of radio. Such stars as David Cassidy, Shaun Cassidy, Donny Osmond, and Andy Gibb are recent examples of the "boy next door" who provides a wholesome come-on or vicarious education and seduction prior to real dating. Later on, hard rock, country, and MOR tell the listener about the real problems of love, family, work, and so on. As with the case of preadolescent girls, radio also serves as a facilitator for adjusting to various turning points in one's life. Radio may be a companion for those with the "blues," such as the recently separated or divorced, or those who have lost a job or a loved one. As a facilitator, radio also helps recapture the "good old days," as evidenced by the current rash of nostalgia radio programs.

In summary, the consequences of an entertainment perspective worked through radio format are varied. Through radio, music entertainment is changed, talent is consumed, radio personalities may become influential role models, and listeners may become dependent on radio for seeking what they feel is legitimate information. While radio is a culture of its own, it also serves as the unique character of various subcultures. To this extent, radio, as a specialized medium, may serve as a model for what television could become.

SIDNEY H. ARONSON

The Sociology of the Telephone

Telephoning has been described as "interposed" private communication. While it is not strictly speaking a mass medium, it is a type of mediated communication that exists on a massive scale: a potent instrument of social change, as sociologist Sidney Aronson points out. Like other media of communication, it has significant effects on our interpersonal lives. Aronson describes the effects of the telephone on social institutions.

Can you conceive of carrying on your interpersonal relationships without the aid of the telephone? Do you feel cut off from your friends when you can't be reached by phone? Does the telephone ever permit more intimacy than face-to-face communication?

Amid the welter of recent writing on the phenomena of "modernization" and social change, scant attention has been granted to technological innovations themselves as direct sources of new human needs and behavior patterns. Yet it seems apparent that the kind of modernization experienced by the Western world, and more specifically the United States, over the past century is intimately tied, both as cause and effect, to the availability of the telephone as an easy, efficient and relatively inexpensive means of communication. This may seem only to restate the obvious, yet how rarely is the telephone so much as mentioned in contemporary discussions of social change or modernization?[1] This is the more remarkable as the process of communication, generically considered, has come to be recognized as *the* "fundamental social process" without which society and the individual self could not exist. Communication-in-general (if such a thing can be imagined) has been much studied, but the meaning and the consequence for individuals of being able to pick up something called a telephone and rapidly transmit or receive messages have been all but ignored. As with so many other aspects of social life, that which we take most for granted usually needs to be most closely examined.

This inattention to the social consequences of the telephone is the more surprising still in light of the importance usually attached to the presence or absence of mass media of written communication in explaining dif-

From the *International Journal of Comparative Sociology,* vol. 12, #3 (September 1971). Reprinted by permission of the publisher.

ferences among societies. It has become usual to distinguish between pre-industrial and industrial societies, each type manifesting distinctive characteristics partly attributable to the widespread dissemination and accessibility (by way of general literacy) of the printed word. It is surely conceivable that the presence or absence of a system of two-way oral-aural communication may account for equally important differences between types of societies, that the distinction between a society with and one without a developed telephone system may be as great as that between one with and one without a developed system of printed media or even as great as that between a literate and a nonliterate society. A necessarily brief examination of the history of the telephone in the United States will support these assertions.

Whether a matter of social structure or of "national character," American society not only fosters technological innovation but typically embraces it with alacrity once it occurs. The introduction and almost immediate acceptance of the telephone in the United States after 1876 is characteristic. That Americans at that particular moment in history wanted to or "needed" to communicate in new and faster ways facilitated the transformation of their behavior and the structure and character of their society.[2] The remainder of this article will present a brief survey of some of the areas of American life where the "modernizing" impact of the telephone has been most pervasive and obvious. If the discussion that follows may seem, by implication at least, to give to the telephone an unwarranted primacy as an agent of modernization, such an overstatement of the case can be justified as an understandable reaction to ninety-odd years of scholarly neglect, not to say disdain. The telephone, like modernization itself, has insinuated itself into even the most remote crevices of American life; the ubiquity of its ringing as an accompaniment to our daily lives can perhaps best be compared to the ever present tolling of church bells in a Medieval village or *bourg*. The railroad, the electric light, the automobile, even the bathroom—not to speak of the more dramatic radio and television—have all been granted their moment on the scholarly stage, to be examined more or less intensively, more or less dispassionately. The time seems overripe for a comprehensive examination of the slighted telephone. Nor is the story by any means all told. The recent development of a "picturephone," which adds the visual capability of television to the traditional telephone, promises to make a new chapter in the history of Bell's creation as well as a new dimension to human communication.

The Telephone and the Economy

What can be said regarding the most pervasive effects of the telephone on the organization and conduct of American economic life, aside from the obvious rise of the American Telephone and Telegraph Company itself as an economic monolith?

Perhaps the most conspicuous of these effects has been the dramatic contraction in the time needed to establish communication, transmit orders and consummate business transactions, what for the sake of brevity, may be called "transaction time." By bringing two or more persons, often separated by long distances, into direct and immediate communication, the telephone eliminated much of the time which otherwise would have been spent in writing letters or traveling to meetings. Telephoning did not, of course, replace written communication and face-to-face meetings; it rather supplemented them and altered somewhat their character. The telephone greatly speeded the pace and the responsiveness of business at the same time that it tended to change the relations among businessmen from those between whole personalities to those between differentiated, functionally specific "roles," a fact which may help to explain the almost compulsive informality and conviviality that obtains when businessmen finally do come together face-to-face. This suggests that the increased efficiency of doing business may have been paid for, in part, by a decrease in the personal and emotional satisfactions of business activity. We are, for example, all aware that the insistent ringing of the telephone usually takes priority even over an ongoing face-to-face business conversation. The significance of this ordering of priorities needs to be examined as does the actual extent to which various kinds of businesses are dependent for their conduct on telephonic conversation.[3]

● ● ●

The Telephone, the Community and Social Relationships

The transformation of many aspects of urban life can be traced to the influence of the telephone either directly or in combination with other aspects of modernization. For the sake of convenience one can divide these effects into three classes: effects on the physical appearance of the community; effects on social interaction, and effects on patterns and models of communication among people.

The influence of the telephone on the design of urban and suburban areas has probably been minor compared to that of innovations in the realm of transportation (including the elevator) and the effects of building and zoning codes. But the telephone probably facilitated the separation of workplace from residence so characteristic of the American economy.

Far more important have been the effects of the telephone on the patterns and the quality of social relationships in urban areas. Those sociologists and social cirtics who studied the urban environment during the first thirty years of this century almost universally lamented the waning role in society played by primary groups and the declining solidarity of the neighborhood itself. They contrasted the impersonal, fragmented quality of contemporary urban life with an image of warm personal relationships believed to have characterized small towns and urban neighborhoods of an earlier age. (The degree to which this image corresponded to reality is not significant in this connection.) Earlier communities were thought of essentially as interacting groups of kinsmen and neighbors (who were also one's friends). In such communities all but the very wealthy were likely to confine their social contacts to members of their extended families and those living in close physical proximity; it was difficult and costly (of time if not always of money) to get to know others and it was not considered necessary. People's horizons were limited, in large part by the difficulties of other than purely local transportation and communication. The invention of the telephone, among other developments, helped to extend those horizons.

The breakdown of the earlier style of community life is regarded by most sociologists as the consequence chiefly of large scale industrialization and urbanization, of all that is connoted by the development of a "mass society." The extended family, the most important primary group, often disintegrated and dispersed as its consistuent units, responding to expanding economic opportunities, scattered over an ever widening geographical area. Although later studies have shown that the conjugal family is less isolated than once thought and although sociologists have discovered new types of primary groups in American life they have tended to see the latter as shifting friendship groups and cliques grounded either in the formal work situation or in informal associational activities rather than as stable groups on the model of the family. Completely overlooked has been the changing nature of the "neighborhood," made possible by the almost universal availability of the telephone.

With the spread of the telephone, a person's network of social relationships was no longer confined to his physical area of residence (his neighborhood, in its original meaning); one could develop intimate social networks based on personal attraction and shared interests that transcended the boundaries of residence areas. It is customary to speak of "dispersed" social networks to denote that many urban dwellers form primary groups with others who live physically scattered throughout a metropolitan area, groups which interact as much via the telephone as in face-to-face meetings.[4] Such primary groups constitute a person's "psychological neighborhood." Modern transportation, of course, makes it possible for such groups to forgather in person, but it is highly doubtful that they could long sustain their existence without the cohesion made possible by the telephone.

The nature, the structure and the functions of such psychological neighborhoods and telephone networks, whether or not they are considered to be "primary" groups, are very obscure. The author has discovered one such network consisting of a group of elderly widows living alone who maintain scheduled daily telephone contacts as a means of insuring the safety, health, and emotional security of the group's members. The questions yet to be answered are, in brief, who talks to whom, for how long, for what reasons and with what results?

By this circuitous route we return to the question raised earlier, that of what functions the use of the telephone serves for individuals rather than for the structure of the society as a whole or its constituent institutions. This question requires detailed investigation but it may be suggested that among the most likely functions are the reduction of loneliness and anxiety, an increased feeling of psychological and even physical security and the already mentioned ability to maintain the cohesion of family and friendship groups in the face of residential and even geographic dispersion. Recent sociological inquiries have illuminated somewhat the role of the telephone in maintaining the cohesion of families in the face of pressures of industrialization, but little is known about the variables (e.g., distance, degree of kinship, stage of the family cycle) associated with variations in these patterns.

Finally, it may not be amiss to suggest that, at least in the early years of its existence, the possession of a telephone may have served both to define and to enhance the social status of individuals, a function which, for a time, probably every consumer-oriented technological innovation has served.

While the various questions and hypotheses we have examined above have been raised in relation to urban life, they are no less valid when applied, *mutatis mutandis,* to the conditions of rural life. The rural, relatively isolated "folk" society (gemeinschaft) has frequently been idealized by nostalgic critics of contemporary "mass society" (gesellschaft) because such writers deplore the loss of those warm, primary-group relations and that sense of belonging to an organic, solidary community which they believe—or imagine—to have characterized earlier rural and small town life. The type case of such a social order—as the origin of the idea in late nineteenth century German sociological romanticism immediately suggests—was rather the European peasant village or castle town of the High Middle Ages than the American farming community of the 1880s or 1890s. The typical American rural family of that period lived on its own farm, separated from any neighbors by distances ranging from a quarter mile to five miles or more. In consequence, the local town, which had to be within a few hours ride by horse and wagon, served chiefly as a trading center rather than as the scene of a richly textured organic community life. This is not to deny, however, that such towns served important socializing functions, especially on those occasions—weekends and holidays—when all the families from the hinterland gathered there to renew acquaintanceships, buy provisions, compare experiences and entertain themselves and each other. The persistent theme of loneliness in accounts of nineteenth century American farm life suggests, however, that the "official" model of rural American society is closer to ideological fiction than to historical fact.[5] For these reasons it may be suggested that the increasing modernization of rural America, far from eroding primary group ties, actually strengthened them by expanding the area from which primary (and secondary) group members could be selected while simultaneously freeing people from social and psychological dependence on what may at times have been uncongenial neighbors. The telephone broke through the isolation of the rural family.

Moreover, the very construction of telephone lines in rural areas often gave impetus to social solidarity, as farmers frequently organized informal groups to string wires.[6] That these early farmers' mutual societies were organized so that all the farms in a given locality were on the same telephone line probably contributed further to the sense of shared communal identity. The whole area served by a telephone cooperative could intercommunicate simultaneously and, apparently, it was not unusual for all the families served by a single line to get on the phone at the same time to hear the latest news and discuss common problems. Since farmers' wives were especially susceptible to feelings of loneliness and isolation, the telephone here too helped to allay personal anxiety.[7]

The following statistic may illuminate both the importance of the telephone on the farm and its rapid acceptance by the rural population (which is typically thought to be more tradition bound than urban dwellers): according to the special telephone census of 1907, 160,000 (73 percent) of Iowa's approximately 220,000 farms were already supplied with telephone service.[8] The major share in this development was the work of farmers' cooperatives. Assuredly, other factors such as the need for mutual aid and the economic advantages of being able to obtain up-to-date information on market conditions in the cities and towns played their part in the rapid spread of rural telephone service, but the importance of more strictly sociological and psychological factors must not be underestimated.[9]

If the suggestions thus far advanced are ultimately confirmed by additional research it may turn out that the extent to which rural life in America actually does or ever did exhibit the characteristics of a solidary, organic community so often imputed to it is primarily the result of modernization and specifically of the introduction and spread of the telephone. This would also help to explain the greater uniformity of values and attitudes among the rural population; for people who share common problems and interact frequently with one another tend to develop similar values and attitudes and to inhibit the expression of deviant sentiments. That rural areas have typically been served by party rather than individual lines has tended to make rural telephone conversations relatively public, thus facilitating both the reinforcement of dominant attitudes and the suppression of deviant ones.[10] This situation stands in sharp contrast to that prevailing in the heterogeneous urban residential neighborhood with its mixing of people from many "psychological neighborhoods," within which no single set of attitudes or behaviors could easily be imposed. In urban areas telephone messages tended to be transmitted on one- or two-party lines and even if one's physical neighbors took exception to one's expressed values or behavior a person could usually find support for his "deviance" within his psychological neighborhood. Urban "deviance" is thus but the Janus face of privacy.

A discussion of the social effects of the telephone would, however, be incomplete were reference to its relationship to other modes of communication omitted. In the absence of research one can only suggest these relationships through a series of questions. Does telephone communication lessen or increase total face-to-face communication? Does it supplement or replace the letter? How does telephone communication change the character of face-to-face and of written communications? What effects has use of the telephone had on the rate of use of the telegraph and on the letter writing habits of Americans? Has there occurred specialization within the media of communication wherein certain kinds of messages are considered appropriate for transmission by telephone while other kinds are transmitted by telegraph (e.g., the congratulatory message) or by letters? And if so, why? What is the effect—in political campaigns and direct selling—of a telephone message directed to a particular person as against a newspaper, radio, or telephone message addressed to a mass, anonymous audience? [11]

Although these questions have not as yet been subjected to systematic research, some of them have been the subject of discussion and study.

Among the first generation of Americans to use the telephone were those who were concerned about the ways in which people behaved while talking on the phone and the rules evolving to govern that behavior. Some objected to Bell's invention precisely because it seemed to generate new codes of conduct which were at variance with those governing face-to-face relationships. One can easily imagine the responses of men and women of social standing at discovering a social climber at the other end of the line. Other critics were shocked by the apparent absence of inhibitions when people spoke on the phone. One wrote of impulsive women who "say things to men and to each other over the telephone that they would never say face to face." Others complained about people who made calls at inappropriate times, or who phoned last minute invitations, or about the obligation to return a call if one was missed.[12]

An early, more scientific approach to the question of how people behave on the telephone consisted of a study of the words spoken. The study, conducted in New York City in 1931, analyzed 1000 telephone conversations. Eighty-thousand words were spoken in that sample of calls. Only 2240 (3 percent) different words were employed and 819 of these were used only once. Thus 1421 of the total number were words used over and over again. The study demonstrated not only the diminutive character of the vocabulary of the average American telephoner but suggested, at least, the general contents of the conversations: the most frequently used words were "I" and "me."[13]

In recent years, it has been observed that for some time the telephone has come to be used as an instrument of aggression and hostility. Such uses for the phone can probably be traced back to its earliest days, but the additional anonymity provided by automatic dialing no doubt greatly encouraged the use of the telephone for such purposes. The behavior ranges from the standard April Fool joke (i.e., calling the zoo and asking for Mr. Wolf) to the sex deviants who call women unknown to them personally and whose conversational style varies from the use of seductive language to enormous obscenity. There is also a kind of "persecution" apt to occur between acquaintances and friends which consists of calling at intervals, letting the phone ring until it is answered and then hanging up. "Crank-calls" probably are akin to poison pen letters.

The opportunity to talk on the phone may also function to limit and to deflect the expression of hostility. Loud haranguing on the wire can mitigate situations that might otherwise lead to blows if the antagonists were face-to-face. The practice of screaming at the operator may serve as a safety-valve. Whether she is employed by the telephone company or handles the switchboard for a large firm, the operator can be a built-in victim or target for the caller.

Over the past century the telephone has been diffused throughout America. As it has done so, it has helped to transfor life in cities and on farms and to change the conduct of American business, both legitimate and illegitimate; it imparted an impetus toward the development of "mass culture" and "mass society" at the same time it affected particular institutional patterns in education and medicine, in law and warfare, in manners and morals, in crime and police work, in the handling of crises and the ordinary routines of life. It markedly affected the gathering and reporting reporting news and patterns of leisure activity; it changed the context and even the meaning of the neighborhood and of friendship; it gave the traditional family an important means to adapt itself to the demands of modernization and it paved the way both technologically and psychologically, for the thematically twentieth century media of communication: radio and television.[14]

The Comparative Perspective

While this discussion has concentrated on the cumulative impact of the telephone on American society over the past century, there are obvious advantages to examining its effects both in other industralized societies of differing cultural traditions and in newly industrializing areas. The consequences of the telephone in other industrial societies have not necessarily been identical to those in American society and may, in fact, have been quite different, for any number of reasons. Only a comparative historical approach can distinguish recurrent structural and psychological effects of the telephone (or any other technological innovation) from idiosyncratic ones, can delineate the range of varying cultural contacts in channeling the effects of technological innovation. Studying the consequences of the telephone as it is being introduced in developing nations is, on the other hand, analogous to observing an experiment, with history as the laboratory.

Furthermore, there are theoretical issues at stake which perhaps can only be resolved through comparative study. What degree of modernization in the American or Western sense is, for example, possible in the absence of a well-articulated telephone system? A reflection on Daniel Lerner's *The Passing of Traditional Society* (New York, 1958) may be pertinent here. Either there were no developed telephone systems in the Middle East in the mid-1950s (almost certainly not true in the case of Turkey) or the author overlooked their significance for, despite an incisive analysis of the role of mass communications in the modernization of such societies, he nowhere mentions the telephone in that connection. It may be that essential social communication in such societies emanates from a few strategic elite groups and is disseminated among the largely illiterate masses primarily by way of radio and television. Is an elaborate widely-dispersed telephone system necessary to successful modernization given the existence of the latter? The role of the transistor radio in the modernization of underdeveloped nations certainly cries out for analysis. These are more than idle questions for postprandial senior common room debate: governments for developing societies require a rational basis for assigning priorities and allocating resources for the development of communications systems.

Notes

1. The number of telephones present in a country is frequently used as an indicator of "modernization" by sociologists, but the process by which telephone communications contributed to the changes implied by that term are not considered.
2. This statement should not be taken as advancing a monocausal theory of social change predicated on the idea of direct technological determinism. Far from it. Mutual independence has always characterized technicological and social change.
3. On the extent to which American businessmen hastened to take advantage of the telephone, see American Telephone and Telegraph Company, *National*

Telephone Directory (New York, October, 1894), (New York, October, 1897); Department of Commerce and Labor, United States Bureau of the Census, *Special Reports Telephones: 1907* (Washington, 1910), 74–75; Herbert N. Casson, *The History of the Telephone* (Chicago, 1910), 204–211.

4. On the notion of "social networks" see Elizabeth Bott, *Family and Social Network* (London, 1957).

5. Pound, *The Telephone Idea*, 32; *Special Reports: Telephones 1907*, 75.

6. United States Department of Agriculture, Farmers' Bulletin No. 1245, *Farmers' Telephone Companies* (Washington, 1930), 5–6; Frank Gordon, "To Teach Farmers Telephone Repairing," *World Repairing," Word*, XXII (January, 1915), 722.

7. H. P. Spofford, "Rural Telephone: Story," *Harper's Monthly Magazine*, Vol. 118 (May, 1909), 830–837; H. R. Mosnot, "Telephone's New Uses in Farm Life," *World's Work*, IX (April, 1905), 6103–4; "Spread of the Rural Telephone Movement," *Scientific American*, Vol. 104 (February 18, 1911), 162; Frederick Rice, Jr., "Urbanized Rural New England," XXXIII (January, 1906), 528–548.

8. *Special Reports: Telephones 1907*, 18, 23.

9. *Ibid.*, 74–75. Access to the Telephone was regarded as being so essential to life on the farm that the United States Department of Agriculture issued a bulletin in 1922 designed to assist farmers in establishing and improving telephone service. See *Farmers' Telephone Companies.*

10. Spofford, "Rural Telephone: Story," 830–837; Mosnot, "Telephone's New Uses in Farm Life," 6103–4.

11. For a discussion of some of these questions see G. S. Street, "While I Wait," *Living Age*, Vol. 276 (March 15, 1913), 696–7; Antrim, "Outrages of the Telephone," 125; Andrew Lang, "Telephone + Letter-Writing," *The Critic* XLVIII (May, 1906), 507–508; "Telephone and Telegraph Prospects," *The Journal of Political Economy*, XXII (April, 1914), 392–394.

12. Antrim, "Outrages of the Telephone," *Lippincotts' Monthly Magazine*, Vol. 84 (July 1890), 125–126.

13. "The Frequency of Words Used Over the Telephone," *Science*, Vol. 74 (August 14, 1931) supplement, 11–13. Everyday conversations have more recently been studied by a number of ethnomethodologists. See Emanuel A. Schegloff, "Sequencing in Conversational Openings," *American Anthropologist*, Vol. 70 (December, 1968), 1075–1095; *The First Five Seconds: The Order of Conversational Openings*, Unpublished Ph.D. dissertation, Department of Sociology, University of California, Berkeley, 1967; Emanuel A. Schegloff and Harvey Sacks, "Opening Up Closings" unpublished manuscript; Donald W. Ball, "Toward a Sociology of Telephones and Telephoners," in Marcello Truzzi, ed., *Sociology and Everyday Life* (Englewood Cliffs, N.J., 1968), 59–74.

14. Virtually each topic deserves at least a chapter of its own. The following references are intended as a guide to subjects not discussed elsewhere in this paper. "Improvements in the Telephone," *Literary Digest*, Vol. 92, (January 1, 1927), 42–49; "Few Telephones Mean High Death Rate," *Ibid.*, Vol. 105

(May 24, 1930), 105; H. T. Wade, "Telephones Throughout the Fleet," *World's Work*, XV (March, 1908), 9991–2; "Battles by Telephone," *Literary Digest*, Vol. 50 (June 19, 1915), 1464; "Directing An Attack," *Scientific American*, Vol. 83 (March 17, 1917), Supplement, 166; M. B. Mullett, "How We Behave When We Telephone," *American Magazine*, Vol. 86 (November, 1918), 44–45; Dr. Alfred Gradenwitz, "A German Police Telephone: Scientific Aids for Patrol Service," *Scientific American*, Vol. 75 (January 25, 1913), Supplement, 61; "A Pocket Telephone," *Literary Digest*, Vol. 44 (March 30 1912), 639; "Private Telephone System in School," *Journal of Education*, (March 31, 1910), 355; William F. McDermott, "Emergency Calls," *Today's Health*, XXIX (November, 1951), 38; "Mine Rescue Telephone Equipment," *Scientific American*, Vol. 109 (November 1, 1913), 340; "Telephone in the Mississippi Flood," *Literary Digest*, Vol. 99 (August 20, 1927), 21; Alfred M. Lee, *The Daily Newspaper in America* (New York, 1937); A. H. Griswold, "The Radio Telephone Situation," *Bell Telephone Quarterly*, I (April, 1922), 2–12; S. C. Gilfillan, "The Future Home Theatre," *The Independent*, LXXIII (October 10, 1912), 886–891; W. Rupert Maclaurin, *Invention and Innovation in the Radio Industry* (New York, 1949).

EDWARD M. DICKSON

Human Response to Video Telephones

It may sound futuristic, but the technical means are already available and tested for the transmission of the human image over a telephone circuit. Edward Dickson, a researcher in telecommunications, provides us with a fascinating look at the potential uses of this new medium of communication. In this chapter from *The Video Telephone: Impact of a New Era in Telecommunications,* Dickson considers the impact on our social norms and interpersonal behavior as videophones become widespread.

Will videophoning make interpersonal conversation less or more formal than does the telephone? What changes in your telephone manner will you make when you can see and be seen? Will there be times you will want to turn off the video segment of the phone?

Introduction

This should be the most important chapter of this [Dickson's] book. It should set out the motivation for the development of a video telephone in terms of human needs. This should also be the chapter that reports experimental measurements demonstrating the superior effectiveness of video telecommunications, thereby justifying the development of the video telephones. Unfortunately, this chapter will not be able to do either of these things because, as Alex Reid laments:

> Although the study of human interactions occupies a central place in a number of disciplines, the human aspects of person-person telecommunications have been curiously ignored. The well-organized platoons of the established disciplines have marched around, rather than across, this area of research. . . . It is necessary to make the negative point that in all this huge body of experimental social psychology research, the question of communication by any media other than face-to-face has been virtually ignored.
> . . . Despite their obvious relevance to each other, the fields of social psychology and telecommunications engineering have made little contact.[1]

Most new technological devices are not made in response to well researched studies of human needs and the comparative effectiveness of new technologies for satisfying these needs. Rather, most new products represent sophisticated consideration of technological and concomitant economic feasibility with only intuitive and often superficial assessment of human needs and comparative effectiveness. The video telephone appears to be no exception. The Picturephone ®, for example, was technologically ready for the marketplace before the question of the effectiveness of video telecommunications was taken seriously. Although most large telecommunications administrations have social psychologists researching questions of human communications, these activities tend to follow technological feasibility rather than to guide the search for it, and most frequently involve issues that are more properly termed human engineering (matching the human-machine interface to the human senses and skills). This shows signs of change.

This chapter will draw upon the few investigations directly relevant to video telephones to present speculations about human-oriented questions that will be raised by video telephone communication. Hopefully, in the future, more social scientists will conduct research in this vitally important but highly neglected area of human interactions. The Communications Studies Group, Joint Unit for Planning Research (University College London and London School of Economics) formerly headed by Alex Reid, has begun serious interdisciplinary research into these basic questions. However, in Britain there is less technological pressure for a video telephone, partly because the per capital number of audio telephones lags so far behind the number in the USA. Consequently, with the work of the Communications Studies Group, Britain is beginning with consideration of the need and effectiveness of video telephones before developing plans for deployment.

This chapter will be concerned with person-person usage of video telephones and will not confront the questions of human responses to video telephones used for person-computer or person-machine interactions. Privacy, self-consciousness, eye contact, status, prestige, and etiquette are the kinds of topics now to be discussed.

Privacy

Privacy is an important issue today with strong civil libertarian overtones. Although the word privacy correctly includes concern with surveillance, secret files, computerized activity records, and wire-tapping, it also includes more fundamental considerations such as absence of intrusion, quiet, composure and shyness. A sense of privacy can be as adversely affected by a poorly placed window as by a hidden microphone. In many ways, the video telephone may be regarded as a new window offering a view into the lives of users.

In absolute terms the audio telephone has probably decreased human privacy in the last 100 years. It has also changed human behavior. Before the telephone, people could communicate at a distance only by letter, carefully moderating the image they intended to project. Alternatively, people could arrange to meet in order to communicate face-to-face, with countenance, body motion, posture, skin coloration, and other non-verbal cues enriching the transfer of information.[2] With the advent of the telephone, a state seemingly intermediate between face-to-face conversation and letter writing was established in which real-time response was possible, but was devoid of all nonverbal cues with the exception of sighs, coughs, finger-tapping, and other audible secondary communications behavior. Upon closer examination, however, the telephone appears to have special properties that makes it more than a simple intermediate between a letter and a personal encounter.

In particular, the telephone lacks manners. It rings when one is talking to others, when one is eating dinner, when one is deep in thought, when one is lost in affection, and when one is bathing. Since it is part of an enormous random access system, it is impossible to know who is at the other end of the ringing telephone and this drives all but the superbly disciplined to answer the telephone no matter what other activity is being interrupted. The persistence of the telephone's ring further guarantees that a telephone call is not ignored. Faced with standing in a line to make inquiries, some people have learned to go across the room to a public telephone. A call to the person serving the line interrupts the normal transactions and effectively moves the caller to the head of the line.

Thus the person placing a call can intrude, divert attention and accomplish *his* task at the expense of the activities of the recipient of the call. It is no accident, therefore, that in order to insure stretches of time unbroken by telephone intrusions, many people have secretaries to answer the telephone, filter the calls for those which the person truly cares about, suggest times to call back that would be more convenient, extend promises (sometimes false) that the call will be returned, and simply lie about the presence of the person.

Virtually everyone who is inconvenienced by the telephone is at another time himself an agent of inconvenience. Telephone users have learned to employ the invisibility of the telephone conversation to advantage, indulging in activities while communicating by telephone that might be considered forward or rude in actual face-to-face contact, such as intruding where not wanted, doodling, gesturing to people in the room, simultaneously reading and writing on an unrelated topic, and expressing non-complimentary reactions such as grimacing disapproval, rolling one's eyes, and picking one's nose.

The blindness of the telephone conversation also renders ineffective the trappings people array to complement their personality, to establish their status, and perhaps even to awe others.[3] Without these reminders of status, the caller is sometimes emboldened to intrude upon people he would not feel secure in approaching face-to-face. Replacing the audio telephone with a video telephone would strip away this visual anonymity behind which the caller can shield his emotions.[4]

Studies have shown that individuals are very concerned with the way that they are perceived by others, and this often results in rather elaborate maneuvers to avoid embarrassment and to save face when things do not proceed as hoped.[5] On the audio telephone this preoccupation is lessened by the severely truncated "self" that is actually revealed. Most people have learned to control their aural image to some extent, but few people are similarly adept at controlling their visual image.[6]

Certainly if the contemporary American telephone ethic were applied to video telephony, the person receiving a video call might well feel that his privacy had been more compromised because his appearance and emotional state would be immediately on view. Conversely, since the person making the call would also be visible, perhaps he would be more reticent and more sensitive to the mood of the respondent.

To date, relatively few people have routinely used video telephones, and these few are secure in the knowledge that only a very limited number of other people possess a telecommunications instrument to contact them visually. In addition, most of the people who have routine experience in face-to-face video telephone usage have either been in a pro-video telephone environment (e.g., Bell Laboratories), or are executives whose privacy is protected by secretaries. How people in general will respond to the video telephone's ability to strip away visual privacy is essentially an unexplored question.

It needs to be emphasized, however, that the "normal" behavioral response that people have developed to cope with the audio telephone is itself only about one hundred years old. Reid speculates that it may take a generation for a new communications technology to become fully assimilated and notes that old people or people unfamiliar with audio telephones approach the device with reservation compared to the casual, matter-of-fact approach by people long accustomed to it. Consequently, while seeking to understand the beneficial and detrimental impacts of a technological change, it is well to keep in mind that value-laden evaluations made by one generation may be viewed quite differently by succeeding generations.

With this caveat in mind, we now offer a partial list of unanswered questions related to individual privacy which will be raised by use of video telephones.[7] Since economic cost will insure that video telephones will become common in work situations before in residences, certain privacy issues are more immediate than others:

1. Will people feel more self-conscious or vulnerable on video telephones? Under what circumstances will the camera be disabled? How will people regard correspondents who disable their cameras? Will movement "out of view" be considered rude? What etiquette will develop to regulate the circumstances for disabling the camera?

2. Will people learn to be less revealing in their nonverbal expression? when will people view themselves rather than their respondent? Will people become more concerned about their appearance and about their background? When video telephones begin to appear in homes, what rooms will be favored for installation?

3. Will obscene video telephone calls become a significant intrusion of privacy? Will a new class of voyeur arise, one who is intrigued by a glimpse into the place of a "wrong number"?

4. Against what norms should the questions be judged—those common in face-to-face interactions, audio telephone interactions, or some other standard?

Distortions of Face-to-Face

Besides the obvious facts of a limited field of view, lower resolution, and at present, lack of color, there are several less obvious ways in which video telephones fail to be electronic equivalents of face-to-face encounters.

For example, two deviations of Picturephone ® from exact replication of face-to-face encounters can be rather inhibiting. The present Picturephone camera has excellent sensitivity in the infrared part of the spectrum. Human skin is partially transparent to infrared. The camera is able to see whiskers still beneath the skin of men with heavy beards, even when they are cleanly shaven, especially when background lighting is dim.[8] Reputedly the nature of the Picturephone camera's spectral sensitivity also enables toupees and wigs to be identified more easily. Whether these effects and others like them will lead to mass avoidance of face-to-face encounters on video telephones for cosmetic reasons remains to be seen. In the future, camera technology will probably be changed to account for this effect.

Second, it has been observed that in all cultures there are distances of personal approach appropriate for different situations.[9] Hall has categorized five distances:[10] "Intimate," from contact to eighteen inches; "personal," from eighteen inches to four feet; "social," close phase, from four feet to seven feet; "social," far phase, from seven to twelve feet; and "public," above twelve feet. In the Picturephone, as in most video telephones, the optimum viewing distance is about three feet and thus falls within Hall's "personal" category, no matter whether the conversation is with a friend or with a famous and distinguished person normally viewed only at "public" distance. Thus video telephone conversations force everyone into the same distance category while also diminishing the awareness of many of the props normally arrayed to enhance status distinctions. This artificial leveling process has the potential to lead to discomfort on both the part of the person reduced in apparent status and to the interloper made to feel uncommonly close to a person otherwise unapproachable.

To countervail this "distance" effect, etiquette may develop that would essentially forbid video calls between people of different social stations. Technological aids such as subtitles giving the person's title might be employed to re-establish status relationships. Attention might also be turned to establishing a rich, studiolike backdrop for video telephone use in an effort to restore some of the visual clues that might suggest behavior appropriate to the encounter. In the long run, video telephones may somewhat level status distinctions.

A potentially disturbing aspect of video telephones arises from eye contact. Unless an etiquette develops that permits users to gaze anywhere in the room rather than rivet their attention on the video display, eye contact patterns will be encountered that are seldom established in actual face-to-face conversations. During conversations in person, eye contact is repeatedly made and broken.[11] The person talking seldom looks his correspondent in the eye, but instead gazes off in all directions. Meanwhile, the person listening tends to look at the person talking, often at his eyes. The person talking only occasionally looks at the listener to get feedback, to check for cues, to relinquish the floor, and sometimes to exert dominance. When the role of speaker and listener exchanges, so, generally, does the pattern of eye behavior. When conversing on a video telephone and looking at the video display screen, both correspondents will tend to think that they are being looked in the eye for abnormally long periods of time. This abnormal eye contact probably increases tension during the conversation.[12]

Most people are completely unaware of this elaborate eye contact ritual during conversations. Without prior coaching, shyness coupled with an abnormal eye contact is likely to give many people an unpleasant sensation on their first interactions by video telephones, somewhat souring their attitudes towards them. Very likely this is a short-lived feeling that is overcome with continued use. The principal author has observed personnel at Bell Laboratories who have used Picturephone for several years interact by Picturephone without inhibition. The men were observed when video calls interrupted conversations with the author; they became preoccupied with the call and had no idea that the author was relishing this opportunity to note the behavior of experienced users of Picturephone. The man who had used Picturephone for the shortest amount of time had two conversations with his superior. Both times, he looked intently at the screen, while the supervisor was very blasé and only infrequently glanced at his display (or, therefore, into his camera). Instead the supervisor left the device aimed vaguely in his direction, and usually only his profile was seen by his subordinate. Another man, who had used Picturephone since about 1968, often initiated or received his calls standing up and frequently did not bother to sit down to move his face into view of the camera. Occasionally he looked obliquely at the display of his correspondent's face, who in turn saw only this man's torso. Perhaps these more experienced users are unconsciously avoiding the unpleasant sensation of excessive eye contact. When use of video telephones for face-to-face interactions becomes this casual, it is difficult to see how it can be argued that they enhance communication by allowing reception of the full range of nonverbal cues.

Interesting and potentially useful experiments relating to behavioral consequences of video telephones might compare patterns of eye movements during audio telephone conversations and eye contacts during video telephone conversations with actual face-to-face encounters. Whether excessive eye contact is avoided on video telephones could then be correlated with studies of the effectiveness of video telecommunications. It would also be useful to learn how this behavior changes with increased experience with the medium.

Effectiveness

All of the foregoing considerations that affect the attitude of the user towards the video telephone surely have some consequences for the ultimate effectiveness of video telephones as a tool for human communications. These subtleties have been scarcely investigated; indeed, studies of the net effectiveness of various communications media are just beginning. Preliminary experiments by Reid and his colleagues in the Communications Studies Group indicate, tantalizingly, that for many kinds of communications tasks there may be no clearcut advantage of video telecommunication over audio telecommunication.[13] There are hints, in fact, that for bargaining and negotiating, the *absence* of a video channel may be a positive advantage, enabling users to better manage their presentation by hiding certain counterproductive nonverbal communications.[14]

Meier has thought beyond the relative effectiveness of telecommunications channels and has speculated that even today, without video telephones, some segments of American society are suffering from "communications stress." A sheer overload of information beyond the human ability to respond and cope is the hypothesized cause of communications stress.[15] According to Meier, persons involved in professional activities that require a great deal of communication often retreat to places where "the telephone can't ring," such as the wilderness or the ocean, in order to escape from communications stress. Because little experimentation has been done to determine the relative effectiveness of various communications media or the actual pathology of communications stress, it is not known whether video telephones would actually result in a *net* increase or decrease in the ability of humans to receive, digest, and act upon information. The trend, however, seems to be that improved technology for information processing serves to increase the information "throughput" of an individual rather than to simply lessen the total time spent on a constant volume of information, thus potentially contributing to communications stress.

The audio telephone is currently used as a secondary form of communication between people who already know each other, providing a means to continue and enrich their relationship. It is also used as an exploratory form of communication to identify and locate new contacts and to gather new information. It is fairly clear that video telephones would likely enhance communications between good friends, close associates, or loved ones. However, it is not clear that either party would relish the use of video telephones in exploratory communications, for suddenly and continually confronting new people face-to-face is something many people avoid. The audio telephone has significantly extended our ability to explore for information without the commitment of seeing a stranger face-to-face each time a call is placed.

In the work environment, repeated telephone contacts can lead to telephone "friendships" (somewhat analogous to "pen pals" by mail) that are never reinforced with personal meetings. The correspondents have only a mental image of the other person's physical appearance. Actually meeting such a telephone "friend" can be extremely disappointing, since the mental image must invariably be discarded in favor of reality. Video telephone usage in work activity may ultimately lead to closer, more substantial telephone friendships than are possible on audio telephones; this, in turn, may result in an increase of on-the-job time spent in non-business cordialities. An increase in these "affective" communications at the expense of "task-oriented" communications[16] might enhance the emotional satisfaction of the user while actually decreasing the effectiveness of the video telephone (measured in terms of the volume of communication handled per person per day).

Diffusion of Technology

With the spread of new techniques or technologies there is a progression of adoption from the first users to the last that is governed by more than chance. Studies employing "sociograms" (simply diagrams showing who influences whom) have examined the diffusion among physicians of the prescription of new drugs.[17] Within fairly well defined circles of physicians there are leaders, followers, holdouts, and mavericks. Studies of the social determinants of the diffusion of innovation will find interesting application in a full technology assessment of video telephones.

The major thrust for adoption of video telephones could come from executives and managers at the top of the organizational hierarchies where the device could be treated as a luxury and status symbol. Alternatively, the major thrust of adoptions could come from the staff whose major task is information processing and who recognize the potential for the device to make transmission and manipulation of information more efficient. Depending upon the character of the bulk of the initial adoptions and the connotations that arise, the subsequent pattern of adoption could be rather different.

If executives adopt the video telephone first, it will probably arise from the face-to-face communication potential, be seen as a substitute for some (but not nearly all) inconvenient travel, and as a means to exert charisma at a distance. It would probably join carpeting, fine furniture, and art to become one of the tangible trappings employed to emphasize the organizational hierarchy. As an emphasis of the chain of command, an etiquette could develop in which video telephone calls were initiated only by superiors calling laterally or downward in the organizational pyramid. To call upward in the pyramid of power, a person might initiate only an audio call, awaiting an invitation to establish full video contact. If, like carpeting, the possession of a video telephone begins with an executive, luxury connotation, it need not be justifiable in a strictly economic sense. Only executives would carry home with them the desire, based upon actual personal experience, to install a video telephone at home. As a result of interactions between executives of different organizations, it is easy to imagine demand for video telephones being stimulated by competition in the acquisition of status symbols.

If adoption begins with usage by members of the information processing staff as a means to expedite or alter the nature of their work, the device will need to pass a more strict test for economic justification. Versatility, resolution, and ancillary services such as hard copy and computer graphics format, will become the dominant considerations. Status will be less involved and the device will be considered as a work tool more like a desk calculator than as an item of prestige. Since there are more people employed in information processing than in high level management, if diffusion begins at the information processing level the spread is likely to be more rapid.

Rogers has suggested that early adopters of technological innovations possess certain common characteristics.[18] They are generally young, high-risk takers, financially well off, respected, and social leaders with interactions beyond their immediate environment. Although executives often fit part of this description, they are seldom young and tend to be conservative. Since the visage of the user of the video telephone is thrust within the "personal distance" of his respondent, and the full aura of the executive suite cannot be conveyed by video telephone, there is some risk that executive authority will be compromised by video telephones if they are used in the face-to-face mode. Consequently, executives may not be eager to adopt video telephones. However, if used as an information processing tool, these limitations will be far less important than technical limitations upon transmission quality. There is little concrete evidence to categorize the characteristics of the first substantial wave of innovators, but based upon the listings in the Chicago Picturephone directory, there is a suggestion that they will be the information processors.

Discrimination

There are many ways in which people discriminate against other people. The USA is struggling to overcome overt discrimination against blacks, Chicanos, Puerto Ricans, and Indians. There is lingering ethnic discrimination against people of Italian and Polish descent and people of Jewish heritage. The audio telephone is actually a slightly positive instrument of antidiscrimination because, on the basis of voice alone, it is usually not possible to establish a person's color, religion or ethnic background without an additional clue of a name, an accent or a dialect. However, on a video telephone some of these distinguishing characteristics are visible.

Although a video telephone will reveal some nonverbal communications cues, it will probably prove easier to say "no" over a video telephone than in person. Consequently, there lurks the danger that subtle, difficult to establish discrimination could be fostered by video telephones if they were used for initial employment screening, in real estate transactions, and in similar activities where discrimination has been a problem. Fortunately, perhaps, video telephones will not be in general residential use for many years, so that the nearest term threat lurks mainly in the work environment where video telephones will appear first. The elimination of sexist stereotypes for women could easily suffer a setback since receptionists who use video telephones may not only have to sound nice but have to look nice as well.

Conclusion

Fundamental knowledge of the relative effectiveness and human responses to various telecommunications channels and systems is essentially unknown. There remains a great deal of useful and interesting work in this field for social scientists. Telecommunications planners and engineers (and ultimately the public) could profit from an interdisciplinary dialogue with social scientists. The following list of research priorities put forth by Reid[19] seems sensible:

1. A program to develop, and test, effective methods of surveying all forms of interpersonal communication, including face-to-face, tele-

phone, and mail, so that a reliable and comprehensive picture of existing communication patterns may be established.
2. A program to evaluate, by means of controlled laboratory experiments,
the comparative effectiveness of a wide range of interpersonal communication media, when used for a variety of purposes.
3. A program to evaluate, by means of field trials, the comparative effectiveness of a range of telecommunications systems.
4. A program to maintain continuous observation of the commercial introduction of novel person-person telecommunications systems, so that
users' reactions may be studied under real conditions.
5. A program to develop mathematical models of the interaction between
telecommunications technology and other aspects of the environment,
such as location of employment and traffic patterns, so that the wider
impacts of telecommunications innovation may be predicted.
6. A program to investigate the extent to which handicaps such as isolation, immobility, loneliness, or old age, may be mitigated by the effective application of telecommunications technology.

Notes

1. Alex Reid, "New Directions in Telecommunications Research," a report prepared for the Sloan Commission on Cable Communications, June 1971.
2. E. T. Hall, *Silent Language,* (Doubleday) 1959; and T. Burns, "Non-Verbal
Communication," *Discovery,* Oct. 1964.
3. Erving Goffman, *Presentation of Self in Everyday Life,* (Doubleday) 1959.
4. Patrick Ryan, "And the Last Word . . . on Picturephones," *New Scientist,*
Aug. 19, 1971, p. 401; and Andre Modigliani, "Embarrassment and Embar-
rassability," *Sociometry 31,* 1968, pp. 313–26.
5. Erving Goffman, "On Facework," *Psychiatry 18,* 1955, pp. 213–31, Fritz
Heider, *The Psychology of Interpersonal Relations,* (Wiley) 1958; and Brown
and Garland, "The Effects of Incompetency, Audience Acquaintanceship, and
Anticipated Evaluative Feedback on Face Saving Behavior," *J. Experimental
Social Psychology 7,* 1971, pp. 490–502.
6. Omar Khayyam Moore, quoted by George R. Wratney in "Expanded Educational Horizons," *News Bulletin,* Bell of Pennsylvania and Diamond State
Telephone, May 28, 1971.
7. Speculations about the impact of the "vuphone" upon a household are amus-
ingly set forth in a short story by Jack Wodhams. Jack Wodhams, "Stormy
Bellweather," *Analog/Science Fiction Science Fact,* Jan. 1972, pp. 140–57.
8. The principal author observed this effect when testing the "Vu-Self" mode of
Picturephone. This significantly increased his self-consciousness in subsequent
tests of Picturephone.
9. R. Somers, *Personal Space* (Prentice Hall) 1969.

10. E. T. Hall, *The Hidden Dimension* (Anchor, Doubleday & Co.) 1966.
11. Kenneth Strongman, "Communicating with the Eyes," *Science Journal* (British) Mar. 1970, pp. 47–52, Michael Argyle, *The Psychology of Interpersonal Behavior* (Penguin Books) 1967; and A. Kendon, "Some Functions of Gaze Direction in Social Interaction," *Acta Psychologica 26*, 1967, pp. 1–47.
12. In a personal encounter this increased tension is easily verified. While speaking, intentionally look the *listener* in the eye. The conversation often quickly goes awry, with the listener acting as if he were very uncomfortable.
13. "Interim Report," Communications Studies Group, Joint Unit for Planning Research (University College London) July 1971.
14. W. Sinaiko, "Teleconferencing: Summary of Preliminary Research Project," Institute of Defense Analysis, 1963; and W. Richard Kite and Paul C. Vitz, "Teleconferencing: Effects of Communication Medium, Network and Distribution of Resources," Institute of Defense Analysis, Mar. 1966.
15. Richard L. Meier, "Urban Ecostructures in a Cybernetic Age: Response to Communications Stress," *Communications Technology and Social Policy: Understanding the New Cultural Revolution,* George Gerbner, et al. eds. (Wiley-Interscience) in press.
16. Bales in *Social Interaction,* Michael Argyle, Ed. (Aldine) 1969.
17. Herbert Menzel and Elihu Katz, "Social Relations and Innovation in the Medical Profession: The Epidemiology of a New Drug," *The Public Opinion Quarterly,* Winter 1955–56, pp. 337–52, and Coleman et al, "Social Processes in Physicians' Adoption of a New Drug," *J. Chronic Diseases 9,* 1959.
18. E. M. Rogers, *Diffusion of Innovation* (Free Press) 1962.
19. Alex Reid, op. cit.

HOLLIS VAIL

The Home Computer Terminal: Transforming the Household of Tomorrow

Using your home computer you may soon be able to do your homework, conduct business, shop for dinner, and have your ailments diagnosed without leaving the house. With the full development of an interactive potential you will be able to vote, select the ending of plays, and immediately tell advertisers if you approve of their shows. Hollis Vail describes the present state of computer development and suggests that before long we might live in a society where work life and home life merge and where our most important home service will be the information utility.

"John, when are you going to finish with the terminal? I need to send some messages."

"Just a bit, Mom. I have to have this paper for school tomorrow and the speller's been acting up."

"No wonder! If you learned to spell some of the words yourself, the computer wouldn't have so much trouble. Spelling "physical" f-i-s-i-k-a-l! No wonder you have trouble!"

"Well, they ought to spell it fisikal. That's how it sounds."

Susan Young wondered if they should buy John his own terminal. He had his own phone and television. So why not? Then a terminal would be available when she wanted it. Except, of course, when her husband Bill was playing games on it. That *really* tied it up.

The terminal Susan is thinking about looks like a television with a typewriter keyboard in front. It also has a place for the phone so that the terminal can be connected to a computer some distance away.

When connected, the terminal is used like a typewriter except that the typed words appear on the screen. Also, the computer writes on the screen as it responds to Susan or whoever is using the terminal. John was doing this when he commanded the computer to check his spelling. The computer checked each word against its word dictionary and then played out the possibles until John selected one. In the case of "fisikal," the computer

From *The Futurist* (December 1980), published by the World Future Society, 4916 St. Elmo Avenue, Washington, D.C. 20014.

had the same problem we have when we do not know the first two or three letters of a word and its sound misleads us.

Many Services Available Today

The home of Bill and Susan Young is located a few years in the future, but only a very few years. Already thousands of American families have discovered the possibilities of a terminal in the home for phone and cable TV services. They also are pioneering, for the "information utilities" are in their infancy. Many of the potential services are available today. But today's users must also live with the growing pains of the industry.

Let us go forward again to Bill, Susan, and son John. Susan wanted to send some messages. This can be done today. It is one of the better developed services of these utilities. The main difference between what Susan could do and today is the number of people she could reach. When terminals become as common as phones or televisions, then almost anyone will be on a system and thus able to receive and send messages. Today, of course, the number of possible "addresses" is much smaller.

Sending a message via a terminal is simple. Susan first tells the computer she wants the SEND MAIL service by typing SEND MAIL. The computer connects her to its program for sending and receiving messages and writes "To:" on the screen and waits for Susan to enter the "address" (similar to a phone number) of each person she wants the message to go to. Then the computer asks for a subject line. Next, it asks for the text. When she finishes the message, Susan types a SEND command and the message is sent to the people on the "To:" line.

The message is not actually sent, as one would send a letter. Instead, the computer assigns a unique electronic mailbox to each person using the service. Susan's message is stored in each person's mailbox, where it waits until they come on line and ask for their mail.

Today such messages can be sent to and from over 300 cities in the United States and Canada and between many cities elsewhere in the world as well, just by dialing a local phone number. This number connects the user to a long-distance network that specializes in carrying messages between terminals and computers. Thus, Susan can send a message from her home in Richmond, Virginia, to a friend in Seattle, Washington, as easily (and as inexpensively) as to a friend across town. Also, the computer involved may be in some other city such as Silver Spring, Maryland.

At the end of the day, Bill "signs on" (establishes electronic contact with the computer). Bill has a portfolio of stocks that he follows, so he tells the computer to search for the stocks in his portfolio. Susan and Bill have invested in a printer that is coupled to their terminal, so Bill has the quotes printed out in "hard" copy.

Bill then asks for information on a number of companies that he thinks might be promising investments. The computer shifts to another data bank and prints out financial and other information on these companies. Bill then leaves a message for his broker.

Next, Bill posts the checks he wrote that day. In posting, he notes whether they are tax deductible and assigns them to various family accounts. He also directs the computer to generate "checks" for bills that came in that day and "posts" these checks. The computer then comes back saying:

"You have a balance of $302.37 in your savings/checking account."

At this point, Susan calls out, "Don't sign off, Bill. I have something I want to do."

"How long will you be? A group of us were going to get on tonight to play poker in about 20 minutes."

"I'll be done by then. I just want to plan the dinner we are having Friday."

Planning a Dinner Menu

Soon Susan sits down and types in MENU. The computer delves into its memory bank and locates a program called MENU. This program then tells the computer to look up Susan's cooking profile, which contains information about Susan's cooking preferences and information on her common guests. In this case, the profile tells the computer that Susan has a microwave oven, a slow cooker, a food processor, and the other usual kitchen appliances. It includes a listing of the dishes she has chosen for menus during the past year and indicates that she likes to experiment with new dishes, but only when entertaining old friends.

"Who are your guests?" the computer asks.

Susan types in the names of her guests. The computer matches the names with prior guest lists and, where they match, notes the preferences and diet restrictions that Susan had previously entered for each guest. Since new guests are on Susan's list, the computer asks Susan to provide what she knows about the new guests' preferences.

The computer is now ready to help Susan work out a dinner menu. In its memory are the recipes for over 5,000 dishes. It also holds information on how to cook exotic foods. A built-in clock/calendar enables the computer to keep track of changing seasons, so it knows what is likely to be available in Susan's market. It can even estimate the amount of a dish needed to feed heavy, moderate, or light eaters—and project the approximate cost of each dish. So the dialogue begins:

> COMPUTER: Quick, slow cooking, or prepared?
> SUSAN: Quick, slow cooking.
> C: Fish, chicken, beef, or meatless?
> S: Chicken, meatless.
> C: American or other?
> S: General.
> C: Familiar?
> S: Yes.
> C: Expense?
> S: Moderate.
> C: Your files show you have cooked the following dishes two or more times during the last year: Chicken Tarragon, Chicken Kiev, Quick spaghetti with soup and bacon, Quiche Lorraine.
> S: Can Chicken Kiev be cooked in the microwave?
> C: Yes.

At nine o'clock, Bill and his friends—Alan in Cleveland, Robert in Atlanta, Lester in Denver, and Henry in Seattle—settle down for an evening of poker. Bill is particularly anxious to play this evening, for he has added a probability subroutine that he thinks might help him make his bets.[1]

The Information Utility: An Infant Industry

This scenario of a day in the life of the Youngs could include many other uses of the information utility. John could use it to study subjects such as math, history, and geography. Bill could use it to enhance his management skills through the use of simulation games. The family could store many documents and records in the computer's magnetic memory file. The possibilities exceed today's imagination, for the information utility is definitely in its early infancy. And, as with any infant industry, its future can take many courses. Some of today's pioneers may go broke while others prosper. The information utility concept is certainly not without its risks and problems.

Ironically, the requirement that users have a terminal is one of the lesser problems. Not many homes have terminals today, but in a country of 80 million homes it is quite reasonable to get 100,000 homes to buy termi-

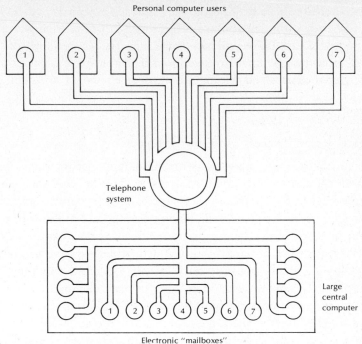

Personal computer users

Telephone system

Large central computer

Electronic "mailboxes"

The term "information utility" is used to describe a system that supplies information as routinely as the traditional utilities supply water, gas, and electricity. Today's information utility generally works by connecting many small personal computers to a large central computer over ordinary telephone lines. This central computer is able to receive and store typed messages in specially labeled electronic "mailboxes" where they can be located and read by the individual system users to whom they are addressed. The central computer also contains data bases from which information of many kinds can be drawn. Personal computer users on the system can order up news reports, statistics, games, etc., for display on their own viewscreens or printing terminals. In the future, information utilities may use satellite or radio facilities to link central computers with users all over the world.

nals, and an information utility probably could remain solvent with 100,000 subscribers. The more serious problems involve developing a base of steady users and working out the difficulties posed by competition between information utility vendors.

The needs of industry in recent years have called into being and are paying for the specialized telecommunications networks that now permit companies to link their far-flung units to a central or integrated computer system. These systems now transmit tremendous volumes of information over virtually the entire globe. Perhaps the most visible examples of this activity are the computerized reservations systems used by airlines and motels.

So far, the information utilities have been piggybacking on existing computer centers and telecommunications networks to gain the national and international user base they need. They also have priced their services to encourage their subscribers to use the cheaper, off-peak time periods (evenings and weekends). The day may come, though, when these utilities will be so big that they will have to use more than the spare capacity of existing computer centers and telecommunications networks and will develop new ones of their own.

Computer Responsiveness and Other Problems

The technical capability now exists for building a telecommunications system large enough to serve millions of users. The "ports" through which subscribers reach the computers can be expanded in number and the storage capacity needed to store millions of messages and millions of personal files can be assembled. These capacities, however, may not be added fast enough to meet the demand, so users will probably have to endure the trials of getting on to an overly busy system. Once on, they may find the system painfully slow to respond at times of peak demand.

This matter of computer responsiveness is an important one. Computers can serve many users at the same time because the computer is so fast. A computer needs only a tiny fraction of a second to search Susan's cooking portfolio and decide what next to ask her. If she were the only user, the computer would then have to wait "ages" (to it) until she replied. The computer does not wait, though. It goes to the next user and does its bit there, then goes to the next user and does its bit there, then goes to the next user, and so forth. Eventually Susan answers, which puts her back in the queue the computer is serving. If this queue is not too large, the computer will appear to each queue member to be responding immediately. Too many users, however, can make Susan wait. When this wait is more than a few seconds, we say the computer is unresponsive.

The limited computer capacity available means that today's users, the information utility pioneers, will often experience annoying delays and interruptions until the necessary telecommunication and computer capabilities are installed. These are not, however, the only problems facing the user or the information utility industry.

Today the industry has not standardized many of its procedures. As a result, users must learn different commands and routines to obtain essentially the same information or service from different utilities. Those who subscribe to more than one service have to remember different procedures for each service. On one service you may "login" and on another you "logon."

In this case, the difference of a single letter in the opening command will bar you from entering the system. The same holds true for signing off. Some use "logout," others "logoff," and some just "off." Command terms differ completely among different services, so "list," "file," "change," and other terms may mean entirely different things on different systems. A "file" in one system is a "record" in another and a "segment" in a third.

More frustrating still is the diversity of procedures for working with the different services. Each text-editing service, for example, has its own procedure and its own terminology for the steps in that procedure. To store information, you say "save" in one system, "write" in another system, and "store" in a third. Some text-editing routines use constantly numbered lines while in others the line numbers change.

Access to data banks is one of the key services offered by information utilities. As these services expand, the number, size, and variety of data banks they offer will sharply increase. Encyclopedic services such as the New York Times Information Bank and topical services such as the UPI news stories will coexist with reservation banks (make your airline reservations at home), cookbooks, entertainment calendars, catalogs (shopping by computer), and personal data banks. Today, however, there is little consistency in the procedures for using and searching such data banks.

An almost untouched area is that of interactive services. The education field has done some good work in developing interactive program instructions. Such instructions go beyond simply posing problems or questions and making different responses according to the student's answers. Interactive programs can develop a profile for each student that "judges" his or her individual strengths and weaknesses and offers instructions keyed to each unique profile. Also, such programs enable students to ask for and get special information or extra practice. A great part of the computer's future lies in the development of interactive programs. Just as Susan used the computer to help her deal with the many variables of planning a dinner party, many other programs are needed that can respond appropriately to the unique requirements of each individual using the system.

Planning a Vacation

One instance might be planning a vacation. There are thousands of vacation options, most of which we never think of. Have you, for instance, considered a flight in a glider over the Arizona mountains?

In interacting with Bill and Susan, the computer might start by asking for information that will set firm limits within which the vacation must occur. How much money can they spend? How many days do they have available? Do they prefer an active or leisurely pace? Scenery or night life? Will they drive their own car? Will they stay in motels or campgrounds? Etc.

Once the parameters are set, the computer can stimulate Bill's and Susan's imaginations. Gliding? White-water rafting? Seeing glass being made and cut? Finding and polishing rocks? Exploring the "buried" cities in Central America? Participating in a scientific expedition?

As Bill and Susan narrow their vacation options, the computer helps them keep track of comparative figures on cost and time. And, once they make their decision, the computer can arrange for a reservation and obtain travel material. It could also remind them to stop the newspaper delivery and arrange for having the lawn mowed while they are gone.

As the information utilities address and resolve the problems facing them and the number of their subscribers increases, other changes will probably take place, changes in society itself.

Work Life, Home Life May Merge

For example, work life and home life may merge. Susan is active in an association that supports the expansion of pocket parks throughout the United States and Canada. These parks are small plots of ground in urban areas that provide opportunities for open air meals and relaxation, play space for children, scenic locales for artists, and self-cycling ecological environments. Susan's professional responsibilities include preparing and editing a newsletter and maintaining a data bank on the many types of ecological environments created in these parks.

Park association members from all over the United States and Canada send Susan messages on pocket park activities in their locales. Susan reads through these messages and selects those worthy of mentioning in the newsletter or adding to the data bank. She also uses the information utility for conducting "written" interviews and to gather background on the items for the newsletter and data bank.

Finally, using the utility's text editor, Susan composes her newsletter and sets up the data bank items. She then transmits the newsletter to the association headquarters in Washington, D.C. They, in turn, edit the newsletter in final form and transmit it to a printer located in Phoenix, Arizona.

The association that Susan belongs to has had to radically alter its structure as its members began to subscribe to the information utility. At one time, Susan's involvement would have been limited to a local chapter. Now the activities of the association are dispersed across the membership regardless of where the individual members live. Soon, the newsletter will not actually be printed. Members will receive it through their computer terminals.

Bill and Susan have also become the customers of businesses that saw opportunities in the growing number of information utility subscribers. A major news service recognized that people who moved around wanted to maintain contact with hometown events. Which high schools won last night's games? Did the city council decide to buy the old Henry estate? So the news service contracted with city newspapers for access to the files they maintain on local news. The Youngs had recently moved from Denver to Richmond and John wanted to keep tabs on his old high school. Susan, incidentally, continued her newsletter activity when the family moved, since it did not matter where she lived as far as this activity was concerned.

The entertainment world, too, was interested in the information utility since it provided an inexpensive way for theaters, restaurants, and other entertainment spots throughout the country to advertise their special features and events to potential visitors from distant places. Thus, subscribers planning a trip could learn in advance about plays, concerts, shows, or local celebrations and could often make advance reservations.

Banks, too, quickly got into the act—offering people like Bill and Susan direct access from their homes and offices to their personal checking and savings accounts. Now, Bill and Susan could know at any moment which checks had cleared and which were still outstanding. They could pay bills through the bank, and the bank would even answer financial questions and provide income tax service.

Soon, mail-order houses across the country were taking orders via the information utility and accepting payment directly through the same utility.

Hotels and motels also began to provide terminals, first in special "information centers," later in every room, so Bill and Susan never needed to be far away from their records, their data bases, their mail, or contact with their bank. Nor could John get far away from school, for he could always sit down wherever he was and study his lessons.

This scenario hardly begins to suggest the potential uses of information utilities. Strong evidence suggests that terminals will someday contain their own computer capabilities and memory storage. Some will come stocked with prepackaged programs for those who do not want to learn how to program computers. Others will be programmable so that those who use them can develop programs "hand tailored" to their special needs. Competition among information utility companies is just starting. Who knows where this will lead the industry? It certainly will lead to diversity as competing utilities explore and nurture more and more potential service opportunities. It also could mean some very different subscribing patterns. For example, the giant telecommunications companies might absorb these new small information utility firms and emerge as a unified information and computer supplier that connects people to many specialized services.

Whatever the future direction of information utilities, the likelihood is high that the 1980s will see computer terminals added to the list of essential household items. Today's school-aged children will grow up using these computer-based services as routinely and as easily as their parents now use libraries, checking accounts, credit cards, and other "modern" devices.

Note

1. Interstate betting on poker raises complex legal questions, and an information utility might not offer poker or other betting games. But it is practical today for people to play games in which a computer supplies variables and monitors the "legality" of their moves, even when the participants are located in different cities.

JEFFREY IAN COLE

Interactive Media: New Relationships

In what ways will your life styles and relationships be altered by the new technologies: computers, satellites, two-way cablevision, and information bubbles? Do you have any fears that the "machine" will take over and that you will lose your privacy as well as the ability to make your own decisions? Or do you take the position that a technologically dominated world is merely science fiction and that we will continue to deal with our problems and relationships in pretty much the same ways that we always have? The reactions to the new communication technologies vary from antipathy to enthusiasm.

Jeffrey Ian Cole assures us that the communication revolution is already here. He addresses himself to the six common fears that people have about the effects of communication technology upon their future lives.

A Day in 1982
Before I do anything else, I have to fill the car with fuel. Then, after hunting for a parking place I wait in a long line at the bank to deposit my checks and get some money. Next stop is the post office where I wait in another line to buy stamps. Next it's off to the supermarket, department store, and the local ticket agency to buy Dodger tickets. All errands require parking and then waiting. Finally I head to the library to check a fact and then end the day in another line at the polling booth. I spend the better part of a day and tank of gasoline on these essential errands.

A Day in 2012
I sit at my television-computer-printer console and press the "Begin Transaction" key. With the entry of a few numbers, I pay all my bills, send electronic mail, order groceries and my mother's birthday gift, select movie tickets to Superman XIII and cast a vote in a national election. Of course my bank account is tied into the computer, which immediately verifies my ability to pay (thus ending "bad" checks). Total time for all these transactions: five to ten minutes. Gasoline used: none. Frustration and emotional energy expended: very little. The only thing left to do is decide how to spend the rest of the day.

Science fiction or fantasy? Neither. Everything predicted for 2012 is easily possible today. The communications revolution (one of the few times the term revolution is justified) is not coming, it is here. All the time-saving things we dream about are completely feasible. The only factors inhibiting the widescale use of these new technologies are less than complete penetration into the nation's households and the public's long-standing apprehension toward a technology it does not fully understand.

The real revolution in communications has been the television's transition from an entertainment to an information center. Until recently television brought us ten or eleven channels and only three real choices. The spark responsible for the transition of television and the beginning of the communications revolution was cable television. Originally cable television served the simple but important function of bringing the ten or eleven broadcast channels to homes where the signal was blocked by mountains standing. Cable television, unlike the over-the-air radio spectrum, has always had the potential to deliver more than blocked broadcast signals. One small coaxial cable, traveling throughout our cities along with telephone and electrical wires, has the capability of bringing dozens, even hundreds, of channels into our homes. Fiber optics will multiply this channel capacity into the thousands.

Home Box Office's (HBO) 1975 move to distribute uncut motion pictures by means of a geosynchronous satellite immediately created an economical and efficient national system of filling many of these available channels. With the launching of one RCA Satcom satellite the cable subscriber's choices included twenty-four-hour news (Cable News Network), sports (ESPN), religion (TBN, CBN, and PTL), music (Music TV), children's programming (Nickelodeon and Calliope) and the House of Representatives (C-SPAN). The era of narrowcasting had begun.

Even more channels still went unfilled while cable's greatest resource, the ability to become interactive, went untapped. By pressing a button on a computer-like keyboard, the subscriber can send a message to the cable operator. For the first time in the history of mass mediated communication, the passive receiver can become an active source. He or she can tell the country what he or she is thinking. Interactive, or two-way cable, is being used for home security, public opinion polling, audience participation in game shows, and television ratings. With the integration of the television and the computer, still a terrifying thought to many Americans in 1982, the world can be reached from the security and privacy of the home. Banking, shopping, voting, corresponding around the world, monitoring our bodies during sleep—all are easily accomplished with interactive technology.

The potential of this technology has generated many fears, such as "will we ever leave the home?" Our comparison shows that what took several hours and much frustration in 1982 can be achieved in a few minutes at a television console in 2012. But at what price? Our personal communication patterns are about to undergo a significant change. What happens to us as social creatures if indeed we do not leave the home? How much is our life affected by the performance of those simple everyday errands we all have to do? Does society benefit when we have to leave the home physically and enter the outside world? If we relate to others through machines, will we lose our interpersonal skills and retreat into human shells? Some sociologists' greatest fear is that our communities will shrink from several hundred or thousand to four small walls. Will there even be such a thing as sociology in 2012 if we all stay in our homes?

In *The Naked Sun,* a 1957 science fiction classic, Isaac Asimov tells of a planet, Solaria, that is so sparsely populated that its inhabitants can only communicate with each other through tridimensional viewing. This viewing is so realistic that the need to actually see another person firsthand disappears. Solarians communicate through mediation and most have not "seen" anyone besides their spouses for years. There simply is no need to be in the physical presence of others. All the necessary information can be communicated through viewing. Being present, because of the threat of contagious disease, becomes quite unpleasant and distasteful. The lowest-status occupation on Solaria is a physician, because he or she may occasionally have to see or even touch another person. The sign of status is to never see anyone. Asimov writes:

> A Solarian takes pride in not meeting his neighbor. At the same time, his estate is so well run by robots and so self-sufficient that there is no reason for him to have to meet his neighbor. The desire not to do so led to the development of ever more perfect viewing equipment, and as the viewing equipment grew better there was less and less need ever to see one's neighbor. It was a rein-forcing cycle, a kind of feedback.[1]

In the absence of actual experience with the most advanced of the new technologies, it is easy to believe that Earth might become like Asimov's Solaria. When viewed as a completely new and unique phenomenon, the communications technologies pose a frightening scenario for the future of human relationships. When examined in the context of past adaptations to technology, however, what is happening in America in the 1980s is neither unique nor frightening. We have adjusted to technology before without losing the essence of what it means to be a human being.

One hundred years ago when we used the telephone we heard the familiar voice of the local switching operator who placed our calls. This was a very personal and community-oriented method of communication. It also was not very efficient. Automatic dialing has made communication less community oriented. When the last dialing operator was replaced on Catalina, a small and quiet island off the coast of Los Angeles, several local residents mounted a protest. They felt they were losing an important and personal link with their community. What could be more personal than the local operator who knows your voice (and most of your private affairs)? We lost something indefinable and important when the last local operator was lost. At the same time we gained the ability to make quick, efficient, and private phone calls. The same transition is currently taking place as many overseas operators are being replaced by automatic international dialing. Each new technology involves a trade-off of some personal contact for efficiency. The question is whether the technology of 2012 involves too much of a trade-off.

Today's mail carrier coming to our homes once a day, six days a week is as antiquated as yesterday's community operator. We will lose something nostalgic (there is a folklore involving mailmen: "his appointed rounds," mailmen and biting dogs) when the last carrier delivers his mail, but we will get mail twenty four hours a day, seven days a week. In the next few years we will lose many bank tellers, sales clerks, and office personnel to interactive processes. Once again we have to make a trade. In an era of rising crime, scarce fuel, and increasing congestion and pollution, does it make sense to put people on the streets and freeways of our cities when they can perform the same tasks in their homes?

The new interactive technologies have been wired into only a few homes across the nation. Most of the current services are to protect the home against fire and theft. Each portal of the home and every smoke detector can be connected to the local cable operator. When a signal is sent from the home, the operator immediately notifies the police or fire departments, who dispatch someone to the scene. In 1982 the more sophisticated interactive systems are just beginning to be introduced into homes. Throughout America experiments are currently taking place testing home shopping, banking and information retrieval systems. We can be reasonably certain of the technical integrity of these new systems. They work, are easy to operate, and eventually will be no more expensive than the average color television receiver. But until these new services reach a significant home penetration level of perhaps 50 percent, we can only speculate about the effect on human beings and their interpersonal relationships. Some of the common fears about the technology of 2012 can be spelled out and examined based on our best speculative powers.

Fear No. 1: We will never need to see other people. No matter how realistic our future mediated communications, even if we develop systems like Asimov's Solarians, we will still want to be around other people. With very few exceptions, we all possess an interpersonal imperative compelling us in a basic and perhaps animalistic way to be *with* other people. Much of our face-to-face communication can be transmitted much more efficiently over the telephone with no loss of information. Few of our messages need such a face-to-face channel; it is our choice to *see* the other person. Many of us will go to great effort and inconvenience to see another person even when the message could be communicated by telephone or letter. There is a need and a pleasure in being with people.

If the telephone were being invented today, we would hear fearful predictions about its detrimental effects on face-to-face communication. Why see a fellow human being when you can send the message from the home? Yet the telephone has been with us for over 100 years with no significant impact on the quantity or quality of our face-to-face communication. We still see one another. Despite its convenience many people use the telephone only for trivial exchanges of information and to arrange future personal meetings. The telephone, rather than inhibiting interpersonal communication, has extended its range from the community to the world.

Conversation is not the only activity that can be accomplished just as easily through mediation. Another example is teaching. It has been possible for years to videotape lectures and then play them back to students at some assigned time. This is a cheaper and easier way of distributing information. The best teachers can distribute their messages far beyond their own local colleges. But even if the same information can be exchanged through videotape, something important and intangible is lost: the personal touch and the synergy that come from being with other people and reacting to their feedback. So even though we can dispense with this face-to-face channel, we continue to meet in person because it is our collective decision that this is the best way to learn. The new technologies may decrease our need to have to be with each other, but never our desire.

Fear No. 2: We will develop fewer interpersonal relationships. At each place we visit—the bank, market, library and polling booth—there exists the potential of initiating a conversation that will develop into a relationship. In principle, the most intimate relationships can come from a five-minute wait in a supermarket line. The typical day in 2012 will not be filled with as many possibilities for these chance encounters. Does this mean we will develop fewer relationships? It would be unrealistic to overestimate the importance of these irregular and unpredictable encounters. Out of these very casual and temporary meetings usually come very casual and temporary relationships. The friendship arising from a short line at a market seldom outlasts the even shorter walk to the car. Without the frequent trips to the bank or market, we may make fewer casual acquaintances and recognize fewer familiar faces, but we are unlikely to experience much change in our serious life relationships.

Fear No. 3: The frustrations of life will reach new and higher levels. It's a familiar story: A nasty letter arrives warning us of the third notice of a long overdue bill. If we do not pay immediately, a collection agency will investigate and our credit rating may suffer. One problem: we never bought the merchandise we are being billed for. We send letter after letter trying to rectify the mistake, but the computer generating the threats never seems to listen. Few things in life are as frustrating as trying to correct a computer error. What will happen when all our transactions are conducted by computer? How will we react upon receiving a $13.6 million phone bill? Frustrations will soar to new levels and all we will be able to do is kick the television-computer screen. The only beneficiaries of this scenario will be television repairmen. If only .000001 percent of all transactions contain an error, then based on the billions of possible transactions, many people will be affected. We will become frustrated and alienated consumers.

One of the new occupations to evolve in the twenty-first century to solve this problem will be the consumer-computer ombudsman. Somewhere in all this technology there must be a human voice and face. The ombudsman will listen to the consumer's complaint and will launch an investigation. The consumer's complaint will authorize the ombudsman to inspect all relevant records. After the investigation is completed, the ombudsman will file a report and make necessary adjustments and changes. Frustrations can be diffused when the consumer knows somewhere beneath all the wires there is a human being who can be reasoned with. The well-trained ombudsman will symbolize a personal step in an otherwise impersonal process.

Fear No. 4: The workplace will be transformed, if not destroyed. Our approach to work is about to undergo an enormous transformation. It will be far less necessary to work in a factory or office and much more advantageous to work inside the home. Alvin Toffler understands this when he writes in his recent book, *The Third Wave:*

> Today it takes an act of courage to suggest that our biggest factories and office towers may, within our lifetimes, stand half empty, reduced to use as ghostly warehouses or converted into living space. Yet this is precisely what the new

mode of production makes possible: a return to cottage industry on a new, higher, electronic basis, and with it a new emphasis on the home as the center of society.[2]

The thought that much of 2012's work can be conducted in the home sends fears through many important groups in American society. The decentralization of the workplace causes us to rethink our need for labor unions, workman's compensation, and two-week vacations. Society at large benefits, however, when much of the working force can be concentrated in the home. Working at home becomes a significant factor in the conservation of fuel and the lessening of congestion and pollution in the cities. Homes that are occupied for more hours of the day become a deterrent to burglary. Less commuting means less need to enter the city and it becomes easier to live in distant suburbs. This is one way to make housing affordable. Many of the disadvantages in living further out where housing is less expensive tend to diminish.

The nuclear family also benefits from working at home. One or both parents are likely to be present and provide supervision for children. Those who find it difficult to commute—the handicapped, elderly, part-time employees, working parents, and pregnant women—all benefit from the opportunity to work at home. Even those with contagious diseases can continue to work.

Fear No. 5: People cannot be taught to use the new technology. Some human beings have a strong resistance to technological innovation. The Bell System found many of its customers terrified of touch-tone telephones. The fourteen buttons on a simple calculator panic some Americans. What will happen when our technology-shy parents are introduced to computers? The great challenge of the next thirty years will be easing the transition to the new technology. A full-scale, non-threatening effort must be mounted to educate consumers on how to use all this new and strange-looking equipment. In *2081: A Hopeful View of the Human Future,* Professor Gerald O'Neill of Princeton encourages us to:

> acquire a firm basic knowledge in communication and in technology. Learn to use your native language well and precisely, because ours is and will become even more a communicating society. Equally important, learn the basis of the technological world. If you don't understand the laws of Newton, or don't know the difference between volts and amperes, you'll have little hope of understanding this next century. Trace the functions on a pocket calculator to make such concepts as exponential growth and sinewave oscillation less of a mystery.[3]

This effort in education is already happening: many elementary-school children find computers as easy to operate as the telephone. The systems of the future are designed for simplicity. They require little technical knowledge. Still, it will take an effort to help people overcome the initial panic of sitting at a sophisticated console.

Fear No. 6: We will never leave the home. It is naive to think we will never leave the home. We'll leave when we want to see a movie on a large screen or to be with other people. No matter how realistic our mediated communication is, we will always want to sit at the ocean or walk through a forest. Watching faraway places on a big screen has never lessened our desire to travel in person to those places. We will leave the home when we want to. We will not have to leave the home when we are tired or sick. We will be spared the frustration of looking for parking places and waiting in lines.

All is not completely rosy, however, in our picture of the future. There are still enormous problems of privacy to be worked out. Anyone able to tap the wires coming into our homes can put a complete dossier together on our lives. Strong security measures will have to be built into the systems and legislation will have to be passed. Despite these temporary problems, there is nothing frightening about the future. We have adapted to technology before with an increase in productivity and improvement in the quality of our lives. What the communications revolution is really about is more choices. Each of our homes becomes the center of the universe. Beneath all the jargon, we become more the masters of our own lives. We will have more options and more free time. We can use that time to think, explore, and be with each other.

Notes

1. Isacc Asimov, *The Naked Sun*. (New York: Fawcett Crest Books, 1979) p. 117.
2. Alvin Toffler, *The Third Wave* (New York: William Morrow and Co., 1980), p. 194.
3. Gerald O'Neill, *2081: A Hopeful View of the Human Future* (New York: Simon and Schuster, 1981), p. 266.

3

Reality and Media Perception

Flip the switch and the world is yours. There is no need to pretend. Space is irrelevant—it dissolves with electronics. Time is altered. The past can be preserved. The present frozen. You can be assured that the future will be stored and saved, in case you missed it. What was it like to hear music only when musicians were present? What was it like to depend on travelers for news about relatives who lived a hundred miles away? There was a time when our contact with the world was pretty much limited to what we could see, hear, touch, feel and smell. There was no doubt when we said "I know it! I can see it, touch it, feel it!" That was direct sensory experience. But what does it mean today when we say "I can see it" or "I can hear it!"? It has become increasingly difficult to distinguish between that which is real—directly sensed first hand, and that which is "real"—indirectly sensed through media.

Time and Space Binding

In our interaction with the environment we are, by definition, selective. Through our selective perception we transform disorder into order. To that task we bring our past experiences, our past relationships, and our unique personalities. Each of us perceives the environment through idiosyncratic filters. We each create a reality from the world "out there."

The process of selecting and abstracting is, at times, quite direct. We feel the heat, we smell the aroma. But an existence limited to direct sensory experience would be so primitive it would prevent human development. Ultimately, we require some form of media to extend our abstracting capabilities. Psychologist James J. Gibson, in his study of human perception, made the following pertinent observation:

> In speaking, painting, sculpting, and writing, the human animal learns to *make* sources of stimulation for his fellows, and to stimulate himself in doing so. These sources, admittedly, are of a special sort, unlike the sources in the "natural" environment. They are "artificial" sources. They generate a new kind of perception in man, which might be called knowledge, or perception at

DAY FIELD NEWSPAPER SYNDICATE

11-9 © 1980 JULES FEIFFER

second hand. The so-called accumulation of knowledge in a society of men, however, depends wholly on communication, on ways of getting stimuli to the sense organs of individuals.[1]

Essential to communication is the dissemination of knowledge over time and space. Essential to the dissemination of knowledge over time and space are media. Media has time and space binding capability.

Media are the means for the present to understand the past. Media function throughout time to generate and preserve knowledge. Cave drawings, gravestones, footprints in cement, graffiti on public walls, and even libraries are ways of the past to communicate with the future. It is this process of time and space binding, more than anything else, that shapes our perception of reality.

Reality Confirmation

The essence of living is "now" and experientially our concern is with the moment. Once the moment occurs, however, it is gone. The present melts into memory. Media, however, intercede between the moment and the memory. They capture and freeze the moment, preserving it in its "real" form. The memory as well as the moment are altered by the presence of media artifacts. The fleeting moment of "now" is de-emphasized. It need not be experienced firsthand. It is replaced by the artifact of "now"—the media-constructed reality.

Is the essence of experience the moment or the photograph of the moment? The still photograph illustrates how a medium can alter the relationship between the individual and the dimension of time that surrounds events. It is interesting to see how the photograph has more and more become a form of reality confirmation rather than merely a record of the past or an individual artistic expression. Have you "experienced" the Spanish Steps in Rome, the Eiffel Tower in Paris, or Westminster Abbey in London unless you have a record of the visit—a photograph? Without the photographic record what would be the proof that you had been there—proof to others and proof to yourself?

If you want instant proof you can use a Polaroid camera. (The Polaroid Corporation announced the development of the instant motion picture system on April 14, 1977.) The advantage is obvious. The long time delay in processing is eliminated. If you "missed" the first time, there is always a second chance. Proof of one's presence at a site or event is provided while still on the spot. Confirmation of reality need not wait.

Audio tape-recordings are another example of media altering the moment and memory. Everything is placed on tape: baby's first words, the wedding ceremony, the funeral ceremony, telephone conversations, interviews. Increasing numbers of students attend classes armed with tape recorders. While most see this as an aid to note taking, the presence of the tape recorder alters the event. A classroom lecture is a participatory activity involving both the teacher and the student at the moment of delivery. The tape recording, though faithfully preserving the professor's comments, alters the event. The professor becomes performer while the student becomes spectator.

An intriguing use of audio tape-recording is revealed in the Watergate Hearings. President Nixon recorded conferences and meetings involving himself and aides—without the participants' awareness. Why? One possible answer is that a recorded conversation is more "official" than a nonrecorded one. "On the record" is a frequently used phrase in Washington to identify official statements. Consider the implications of that phrase. Conversations actually occur which do not officially exist. These are "off the record." So the President of the United States is involved in "off the record" conversations which he secretly knows are "on the record." It is assumed that the presence of the tape recorder did alter the President's conversations and actions. The President was seemingly more concerned with future judgment than with present interaction. Conversations become objects or artifacts when preserved on tape. In this case, the Presidential tapes were the "real" objects that determined Nixon's future.

The addition of the "instant replay" to the technical repertory of television is another example of reality confirmation and reality selection. Not only can any play in a game be shown immediately after the event occurred, but it can be frozen, played backwards, and several versions from various cameras can be shown, sometimes simultaneously. To what extent are we developing a dependency on instant replay to confirm reality? The answer is evident when we see the latest use of instant replay. Now videotape playback is shown not only to the home viewer, but shown also on a giant screen to the audience at the arena or stadium. Both the home viewer and the stadium spectator can concentrate less on the execution of an intricate play because, if it is important, the replay will be available. Instant replay tells us what is important and confirms the reality of what is before our eyes.

The Media Jet

The issues examined here reveal that subtle shifts in our perception of reality have occurred and are occurring. Yet, we often are unaware of these changes and the role of media in bringing them about. For example, we all know how important it is to be in the proper location for seeing an event as it happens. We usually report exactly where we were standing when we witnessed an accident, or how far away we are from an object being described. But where are we when we watch a televised event? This is difficult to answer. The obvious response is that we are sitting in the living room, or family room, or bathroom—wherever the ubiquitous television set is located. But beyond our physical presence in front of the set, where are we? Where are our senses in relationship to the event being televised?

The phrase "I'm looking at the television set" is not an adequate description of perceiving events on the screen. Individuals neither watch a TV set nor look at the screen. The viewer may be physically outside the screen, but is psychologically beyond the screen. An explanation of this can be found by examining the television process itself. Let's look at a hypothetical but common television presentation. A visiting dignitary comes to visit the United States and is greeted, not only by the necessary officials, but also by a host of TV cameras and personnel. The plane taxis down the runway, the dignitary comes down the steps, proceeds along the red carpet with the hosts and is introduced to the American people. The visitor delivers a short speech, gets into a car and leaves the airport in a motorcade. You can imagine the television coverage. A number of cameras have been placed strategically to achieve adequate vantage points. The television director switches from one camera to another, from a view of the celebrity to the sight of visitors standing in the background. As the coverage unfolds, the director chooses the wide shot being transmitted from the left of the dignitary and then switches to a close-up from the right side. And so it goes from camera to camera, from shot to shot. Do you assume that each camera represents a different personality viewing the event? No! You view the event through a single proxy—the television eye. The person at home, while sitting in a stationary position, is not static psychologically. The viewers accept psychological multiplicity. Multiple cameras do not suggest or represent various personalities, rather they constitute one personality capable of radical shifts in time and space. If the individual viewer were outside the screen psychologically, he or she could never accept this extraordinary manipulation of presence through time and space. That is, one would have to articulate that each camera represented a view of separate individuals and not that of oneself. That is not what happens when we participate in a television event.

Just as we do not assume several personalities while watching a televised event, we are not "at home" while watching the event. That is, we are not seeing the event from our home. The "media jet" teleports us, at least psychologically, to the event. To what degree do we distinguish between "the" event and a mediated event? How dependent are we on being at media events? To what extent have media events become substitutions for our participation in "real" events?

If the "media jet" did *not* teleport us, at least psychologically, through time and space, we could readily distinguish between experiencing firsthand events and secondhand events. But as urban society continues to extinguish agrarian existence, human beings become increasingly sedentary and more dependent upon mediated contact with the environment. The paradox for twentieth-century urban citizens is that while we have gained a tremendous number of mediated contacts with a world far beyond, we have lost some of the relationship with immediate community and present environment: a relationship achievable primarily through primary sensory contact. The importance of immediate local environment has been negated or de-emphasized in the creation of a global community not based upon the usual limitations of time and space.

Media Semantics

Some clarification may be needed at this point to escape a potential semantic morass. Central to this discussion of reality and perception is a distinction between the nature of mediated and nonmediated experience. Obviously, it would be foolish to claim that media relationships with reality are nonexperiences, just as it would not be helpful to place a value judgment on media experience in relation to nonmedia experience. Ideally we want to heighten experiential awareness and develop experiential differentiation, not do away with any sensory experiences.

To watch a play on television and to see a play in the theater are two distinct experiences, even though the same play and cast are involved. A wildlife TV program about the prairie dog is not the same as an actual encounter with a prairie dog. At some point the omnipresence of media does begin to negate sensory differentiation. "I talked to her yesterday," is quite different from "I talked to her on the telephone yesterday." "I saw the game" and "I saw the game on television" are phrases referring to totally different experiences. And, as the videophone becomes commonplace, what does "I talked to her yesterday" really signify? One does not have to be an alarmist to see an increasing degree of experiential ambiguity resulting from the increasing amount of technologically mediated communication. The woman who phones her grocer and has the order sent out says, "I did my shopping." At what point do people who watch the telecast of the arriving dignitary say, "I was there"? Who can deny that, to a certain extent, the statement is true?

The probability seems high that in an urban society the vicarious media experience might push the firsthand encounter into the background. And why not? The nature of urban contact can be unpleasant, uncertain, and often confusing. The safety of a mediated environment in which the human being is enclosed and protected, but not isolated, is very appealing. To go to the ballgame means a chance encounter with inclement weather, discomfort with crowds of strangers, and contact with smells that might be offensive. It's easier to watch a show on the Florida Everglades than to venture into an area which can be dangerous and where insect life would certainly make its presence known. Some might argue that the tremendous growth of tourism has placed an increased importance on firsthand experience with the world. But is that really the case? Upon examination, we find that tourism is as mediated as that magic seat in front of the TV set. The shift from the living room environment to the encapsulated world of the jumbo jet, to the uniform boxes of hotels and motels, is not a radical change in sensory experience but merely an amplification of the media jet. It is virtually impossible to exist in contemporary society without developing a dependency on or addiction to media.

Media Distinctions

The intersection of reality and media perception occurs in three major ways. (1) All mediated representations are circumscribed by the defining properties of a specific medium. That means that each medium's treatment of the same event would differ in terms of what would be transmitted and received. Therefore, the televised political convention is not the political gathering that would have been observed within the confines of the arena and is distinct from a newspaper account of the proceedings. (2) We process media information by learning and internalizing a receptive mode for each medium, i.e., we learn and accept the conventions for watching a film, which contrast with the convention and techniques required for reading a newspaper or a book (even in the latter case there are differences; one cannot read a newspaper with the mind set required for a book). The creation of a narrative by an author assumes certain abilities on the part of the consumer, particularly the ability to read. The reconstruction of a film involves a decoding ability which necessitates the transformation of two dimensional images into three dimensional imagined images. (3) The internalization of processing requirements for each medium is absorbed into the cognitive options we have in communication processing. The prevalence of different media with their own depictions require multiple perspectives of reality. Each one of us is capable of looking at a non-mediated situation with a media filter. We are able to experience directly sensed situations as if a medium had been interposed between the event and our perceptions of that event. For example, many of us look at the world as if we were a camera. One indication that this phenomenon actually occurs is the prevalence in our language of media metaphors. A "close-up" experience, a "frame" of reality, "focusing" in on a problem—all suggesting media perspectives that accompany our daily encounters. What is being examined in this section is our media interaction and its influence upon our perceptions of reality.

Note

1. Gibson, James J., *The Senses Considered as Perceptual Systems* Boston: Houghton Mifflin Co., 1966, pp. 26–27.

ROSS SNYDER

Architects of Contemporary Man's Consciousness

Unlike the other authors in this section who view with alarm what the electronic media are doing to our perception of reality, theologian Ross Synder takes a dispassionate view of the new electronic media. Snyder neither condemns nor praises the new media, rather he probes into the relationships among mind, world, and media processing. He looks into the ways that electronic media attach the human brain to the world creating a new media habitat. The new architects are those who create the habitat of the "lived moment." The media architects alter our concepts of time and space just as did the architects of the past.

We suggest that you read the essays of Edmund Carpenter and Marshall McLuhan along with this one to gain a more comprehensive view of a world; not where messages about the real world are carried to us by the media, but where the media and their messages *are* the real world.

I choose to think of the people who program television, movies, and radio, as architects. I believe that APBE [Broadcast Education Association] members ought to see themselves as *teachers of architects*. Architects of the meaningful space in which contemporary man will live and move and have his being.

Broadcasters are designers and builders of habitat for modern man. They also sell him a mode-of-being-*in*-the-world. Habitat is geography transformed into personal world. An opening in time and social space that is his to colonize and make livable, marked with some trails through what is otherwise wilderness, containing the aroma of his kin. A home territory which this person has helped organize, and is filled with his intentions and the intensities of his labors and celebrations. Every person must find and help create his habitat—else he is anxiously alone and defective. A new consciousness and a new habitat for man is being formed by electronic communications—man's brain is being connected with the world in a new way. This is not just a matter of giving Oldtime Man new information and entertainment. New modes of communication reshape the human mind. New qualities and powers of consciousness emerge with electronic communication. Via electronic communications the human brain is now being

From the *Journal of Broadcasting*, vol. 10, #4 (Fall 1966). Reprinted by permission.

attached to the world in a new way. Some people are saying that this new way is "programmed sensations"; that this phrase is the clue to what television, movies, recordings are to be. I am going to say instead that the inherent clue is "new power in sensing and realizing."

The human brain is molded by the flood of incoming stimuli to resemble the world it has been privileged (and often damnably sentenced) to perceive. The quality, taste, design of the communicated world structures the quality, taste, patterns of his consciousness. So the world to which our brains are attached is now different: partly because we are no longer living in an agricultural society but a commercial and city society, but more importantly because of electronic communications, man's mind and emotions are no longer basically attached to the world of nature, but to the "soft ground" of people—their inner world and their history making.

My mind and personality early knew the world of nature—the sun, the good earth and what it yielded if we but rightly treated it, the organic rhythms of sowing and harvest, wintry dying and spring rising again, lightning and thunder; within this structure, I also lived with people. But the universe was the ground design which provided a setting for life.

The television generation in a metropolitan civilization is not primarily rooted in such a world. A member of "masscom" hardly experiences this world of nature, let alone is formed by it. His brain is now immersed in the unpredictable history-making of people in a time of world-creating thrust. His mind is formed by their equally fantastic inner world of sensations, actings out, surrealist dreamings. This "people world" he willingly invites into himself via electronic communications. Which means that the invited people are not the inhabitants of a village where he touches, encounters first hand, has two-way communication with, tests out in action the citizens' fidelity to him. The people and events of electronic communication are *presented*. They come at him through the television screen.

So, in between the viewer-listener and the presented people and events he sees and hears is always the intervening variable which he does not see—the men who determine what will be presented to him and why. Out of all that is going on—both in contemporary history-making and in the present bubbling consciousness of the peoples of the earth—some group of men has to select what is to be presented, how it is to be presented, what is background and what is of fringe importance, what is to be highlighted. Thereby they determine the meaning of those events.

That this has to be done is inevitable. The question is—can it be done in a professionally adequate way by men of principled originality? Men who are devoted to human civilization? I conclude that broadcasters, teachers of communications, must become consciously a profession—constantly searching out what is their basic truth, what is their rightful and inescapable role in dealing with mankind's present problems and new possibilities. They must constantly be establishing live hypotheses, testing methods, and collecting the data of their profession.

It is toward this effort that I offer what I hope are some fruitful hypotheses. First of all, electronic communications fit, in a quite special way, a world in which from now on there is only world history and mankind learning to live simultaneously with history making. They are rather naturally a part of the making of the new relevant consciousness. At last we are all so interrelated that historians such as McNeill see our era as the closure of a world of household of man.[1] No nation can any longer have just its own history, but is inescapably a part of world history.

Television is a forming agent of our era, and an expression of it. So much so that we can say that television's potential is not being realized unless it is so functioning. As in other eras, a new style, new power, and new horizons of communication will form a human consciousness, culture, and method of making history that will be different from anything we now have. In ancient days, Joshua blew the trumpets and the walls came tumbling down. Once more the walls are already down because of a new trumpet: electronic communications. Events all over the world are now its content. Space and walls are constantly being annihilated in this new era. Broadcasting is a reaching out to the multitude, to all citizens of the inhabited household. A reaching out, not just to "our kind," but to all human beings. By its very nature mass communications is toward a world ecumene. Hopefully it might become of the world household.

Millions of people all over the world can be present at the funeral procession of a President of the United States, have their own heart-beat blocked by the heartless roll of the drums in that procession, feel as never before the threat against all men of Arrogant Death. A social worker told me recently, "Any dance invented by a group of kids any place in the world is being danced the next evening by the young people who come to our Youth Center." All over the world, thanks to transistor radios and television, even the most distant have access to immediate events. Explosions of white man's brutality in America are experienced by the new African, the sheik of the lonely Middle East oasis, the laborer of Japan. Even the poorest and most ignorant cannot be shut out of what is happening. All men have access to original sources and inside dopesters.

History is no longer a something we read about in textbooks, but what we are living *in*. It isn't just that we *know* that something is happening. Because of the peculiar immediacy of the sound-seeing image coming through the television screen, we are *present* in it. And always *news*, rather than *views*, finally and immediately determine public opinion. Now we have the instrument par excellence of communicating the news event in its full actuality and the same day and instant it is happening. Radio and television influence public opinion the instant it is being formed. For always within the presentation itself is an interpretation of the meaning of that event. But not only to present the news, but to enable the citizen to make sense of that news, is the big possibility of broadcasting.

McLuhan maintains that one way to understand the story of man is to see that communication is so basic in the making of man that the prevailing mode of communication creates the mind man lives with. In this conviction he is supported by the social psychology of George Herbert Mead whose basic tenet is that mind, self, and society is constituted by significant symbol. But the exciting, brilliant hypothesis McLuhan has brought off is to succeed in dividing the long experiment of man into three epochs, according to the dominant mode of communication. He illuminates with startling clarity what is happening now—which is that electronic communication is doing us over. As with all other areas of life, today's man is a synthesis of all three eras of communication style, not as a piling on top of each other, but as a leap up into a new existence, which both uses and re-shapes the past. So communicators need to understand thoroughly all three communication modes. But especially the emerging dominant one.

Primitive man lived face to face. He encountered first-hand those with whom he talked, the situations he talked about. He lived in small clusters and in a habitat that was hollowed-out space in a wilderness. He had a language which only his people understood. His ethic, his sense of belonging stopped with the perimeters of his village—with his kind of people with whom he was in communication. In a wilderness world, sound and movement are the basic clues. They are the primal indicators of how the other realities are tuning into you. Without them, the world is empty; meaningless. Even face-to-face communication is not all verbal. Primarily it is by means of the feeling arts of the face and voice and body. By gesture. By communal dance where the crisis experiences and tensions of common life are worked out in symbol, and the traditions of "this people" are enacted and organically possessed. Face-to-face communication is also *living speech*, addressed to each other in the midst of enterprises, communal conflict, decision, celebration. This primitive mode of communication is the elemental communication which has made and sustained human beings from the time of earliest men. Every human society must be constantly renewed by face-to-face communication in the immediacy of life's world-for-me.

With the inventing of printing, a new power and mode of communication brought new power and extension to man's consciousness. The invention of movable type made man's mind print-conscious. The immediate perceptual stimulus to the brain now was marks on a piece of paper; hieroglyphs rather than the living personal reality or the immediacy of total event. There was no sound, no movement. The grammar of sentence structure structured man's mind, rather than the global immediacy of the perceptual encounter. The mind plodded along step by step, piece by piece, from left to right along the trail of words in approved sequence. Which was fine for logic—but what happens to man's consciousness?

Print communication made possible the man of principle. Man need no longer be victimized by total immersion in immediate event or by his provincial village's customs. He could stand outside immediacy, reflect, make sense of his world, transcend it. He had available for his thinking the best that man had thought any time, any place. He no longer had to hear by word of mouth or consult the power structures who controlled the few manuscripts available. The ploughboy of England might understand the New Testament better than the King of England—provided that he could read. And he could read whenever he wanted to. He could read his book when he was by himself and in his own habitat. But certain disasters—which show up starkly in some of today's brilliant college students—also characterize print consciousness. Print consciousness becomes *alienated* man. For he is communicated to, not in the very midst of encounter and presence of other people, but by absent, de-fleshed man. Print consciousness is not an experience of being *immersed,* with warm humanity all around him. The reader's perceptual field is non-human marks in a book. The reality with which he has to come to terms is a printed page. The great goal of education comes to be "know the book," rather than to know life. He is impoverished by the loss of sound and motion; by the loss of perceptual experiencing. For the printed page, at best, depends upon calling up experiences and sensations the reader already has, instead of presenting to him new sensation and new experiencing. Print consciousness becomes emotionally impoverished.

And now in the third epoch of communication, contemporary man the world over is emerging as a new consciousness and a new mode of being-in-the-world. McLuhan says, "With the omnipresent ear and moving eye, we have abolished writing, the specialized acoustic-visual metaphor that established the dynamics of Western civilization. . . . The age of writing is past." [2] Today, with electronic communications, man lives in one global village, with throbbing drums, beating tom-toms, dozens of loudspeakers blaring all at once, both sacred and profane liturgies pulsing and recoiling upon one another. He is living in a total communication, with news and stimuli stabbing all his senses like a cloud of arrows from all directions. The noise, pace, sense of unknown risk, is terrific. He is living the *beat, beat, beat of time* rather than in confined geographical space. He "lives simultaneous." He lives with "dramatic truths," rather than with conceptual truths. The meaning must be in the happening itself; electronic mind is against interpretation. What something is, is what the mind perceives and experiences as of this moment. Reflection and analysis would destroy the lived moment, and to take time to develop a logical chain of thought would be to miss the next programmed sensation.

The omnipresent ear and the moving eye report to him a kaleidoscope of fragments of reality. In each fragment are forces in tension with each other, only *in process* of taking on form. In each fragment are the complex ambiguities, mixtures of promise and threat, life and death that life on earth is. No longer does his stream of consciousness flow out of the threaded-together story of a small community, but is jerked along by "happenings"—here, there, everywhere. Consciousness is brief flutters, broken mosaic, peerings into sudden openings and then on to the next. As "blippy" as the points appearing on the screen. Contemporary electronic consciousness is like the sea otter, who because of man's inhumanity has forsaken the established beaches and now swims ceaselessly in a large circuit of islands, never landing, but each night wrapping himself up in the tendrils of offshore kelp, undulating with the waves. And then on to the next.

We can now at least understand McLuhan's forceful point that the electronic medium itself is the message—the forming mind factor. And that the new media are not bridges between man and nature. They *are* nature. This is a tricky and complex point. First of all, McLuhan is referring to the nature of the electronic mode of communication just in and of itself—what electronic communication does to the human mind regardless of content. The thesis is that our consciousness takes on the structures of the media of communication. And back of that thesis, the mind is a working replica of the world fed into it; of the rhythms, pace, tune, quality which its receptors pick up persistently in the world.

But the content of the program is also important. To be sure, the nature of the medium determines what kinds of content can be communicated. For example, thought is very difficult to picture or put into flowing sounds! So the medium is the fundamental factor—whose influence is compounded when the television viewer accepts the world presented to him via television as the real world, rather than the flesh and blood world actually about him. A recent striking illustration of this location of "the world" comes from a time of flood near Hamburg. People kept sitting in front of their television sets totally engrossed, in spite of frantic warnings that the flood was coming their way and they must get out. Their real world was in the television program!

A much more common confirmation would seem to be that the youthful television viewer often is sure that the "real" world is not that of his own parents, or his teachers, but rather, the world that youth culture has programmed for him electronically. And he shapes his family relationships and community activities and youth culture of his own community to resonate with this real world. Indeed, television—by nature and program—is adolescent culture.

There are the three epochs of mankind according to the rise of new modes of communication. We now live with all of them available to us, and our job is to combine them all towards a new actualization of man. But the mode of communication which structures and tinctures the emerging new consciousness of mankind is the electronic. Strangely, we are back—in a new way—to primitive man. Back to a face-to-face that now comes *through a television screen* to us. Back to a primarily perceptual grasp of the world—but a world selected out, programmed, present in the television set. Back to living in community-that-has-experiences. But now to a diffuse, conflictful, anonymous, earth-circling opinion just being formed. Back to the horizonless dark of primordial feeling: "We have evoked a super-civilized, sub-primitive man. . . . We begin again to structure the primordial feelings and emotions from which 3000 years of literacy divorced us."[3]

So how do we begin? We begin by taking seriously perceptual learning, the lived moment, image, and presence, as chief means of communication in this new era. All four of these are of one piece, but let's begin with television's particular genius: the presentation of the lived moment, in all its immediacy and fullness.

Those teaching and creating communications need a thorough grounding in the contemporary thrust of phenomenology in psychology and philosophy. I endeavor to train my students in what we call "existential-phenomenological-developmental style." Practically, this means acquiring the power to catch and symbolize what is going on inside a person in a given situation, and to be the kind of person he will want to know these things about him. Part of our training is a clinical course where students must learn to perceive the "organizer" of a lived moment of a child, and the instant it is happening be able to put it into words which the child accepts as true report of his experiencing, his existence condition, the world as it presents itself to him in this immediacy.

What is involved in the lived moment approach was called "the poetry of the present" by D. H. Lawrence. This image and conception should permeate every cell of a television communicator's mind:

> The strands are all flying, quivering, intermingling into the web, . . . The living plasm vibrates unspeakably, it inhales the future, it exhales the past, it is the quick of both, and yet it is neither . . .
>
> The whole tide of all life and time suddenly heaves, and appears before us as an apparition, a revelation. We look at the very white quick of nascent creation. A water-lily heaves herself from the flood, looks around, gleams, and is gone. . . . We have seen, we have touched, we have partaken of the very substance of creative mutation.
>
> Give me the still, white seething, the incandescence and the coldness of the incarnate moment: the moment, the immediate present, the Now. . . . Here in this very instant moment, up bubbles the stream of time, out of the wells of futurity, flowing on to the oceans of the past."[4]

The lived moment, adequately presented, enables sensing and realizing. People are not just being imprinted with programmed sensations. There is some chance for the discriminating and intellectualizing operations of the mind. The hearer is treated as a consciousness, as a personality that goes beyond raw sensation into wanting to know "What is this before me? How do I see into it?" Part of what is meant here is McLuhan's distinction between "hot" communication and "cool." The first type attempts to overpower and thoroughly immerse the hearer, the other invites construction and "putting the mosaic together" by the viewer.

We come next to the primacy of perception. Man is a constituting consciousness that goes on from there. We expose people to the actual, instead of telling them about it. In effect we say "Look! See and feel for yourself.

Meet the live energies of your times. Live contemporary with them. We bring the world to you for you to *perceive*—to sense, to realize."

Probably the most alive common memory we have of effective perceptual learning via television is the Nixon-Kennedy debates in the campaign of 1960. On these programs Nixon appeared to be a dour, irascible man trying to assert that he was superior; he appeared so concentrated on this contentiousness rather than on thinking about the nation's problems that he seemed to have a very sluggish mind. And so the voters left him in droves. What formed their decision was the image left in their minds as to what kind of a person he was. They had learned perceptually.

Every perception has built into it an implicit judgment and feeling attitude toward what we are encountering. Feeling and judgment of what something intends toward us are not added on to, but are a quality of each perception. Our fleeting seeings coalesce into a sensing of the *kind* of person that is before us, combined with liking or not-liking him. So it is not heresy to propose that the image of the central person in a television show is more important than the content of the program. Or more accurately, the major content of any television show is images produced in the listener of the possibilities of human life.

Today's generation of minds produced by television does not have logical definitions and clear concepts of what might be meant for instance by "freedom"—they *feel* what freedom is with the aid of the image of Sammy Davis in free-swinging-ballet (full of grace and truth) surrounded by four adolescent girls. For one whole generation of youth, the movies *West Side Story* and *David and Lisa* are still interpretive myths by which they understand life. And how we all now miss the image of Khrushchev! He was a crucial aliveness in our moment of history. We knew what the world was like so long as he dependably appeared. He was a familiar figure to all Americans; more vivid and constant in their minds than the people in the apartment next door. With his disappearance, something significant in us has died. So I conclude that no one is fit to teach communication who has not delved and dug into "just what is an image?" For the carrier of communication is no longer the printed page or the spoken word, but the image.

An image is not just a photographic picture, or a bit of poetry such as "wet leaves against dark branches." An image is what happens in the consciousness of the person perceiving; it must be an eruption of *his* memories, feelings, struggle for realization. A destiny-for-me must be coming through what is "out there" toward him. Let me offer three images of what an image is. You are trying to work your way through a jungle; you are surrounded on all sides by jungle. Suddenly the tip of a lion's nose and the glitter of his eyes begin to come out at you from the jungle. The body is yet to appear, but you know that it will. An image is a broad V of golden geese swimming on a blue lake in sunset autumn. Suddenly the dispersed V is startled and cleaves the sky, wing to wing. An image is the awesome mystery when a man opens a long-closed barn door. He has not been there for fifty years, and he tries to re-assemble once-vivid acts and objects from the dim interior. And the whole barn is filled and heavy with the fatefulness of his life.

To be more prosaic and precise about it—an image cannot be static, but is on its way *becoming* something. An image is filled, suffused with feeling (and to quote William James, "Our judgments concerning the worth of things, big or little, depend on the *feelings* the thing arouses in us"). An image stirs up other experiences, becomes filled with their residues, pulls them all together into pattern and new intensity. We begin to see the energies below the surfaces of life, at the *documentary* level. And finally an image is instinct with potential. More truth and light is yet to break forth. It is a vision of possibility coming out of the actual.

Finally, television brings a strange new kind of face-to-face communication. A new kind of presence. "Presence" is what the person has turned on the television set to find. He turns on the set not primarily for information or even entertainment. Rather he wants a cure for his loneliness and a sensing that the world is still in touch with him. He wants a vivid human being right there before him. Not just their surface, but the struggling, enjoying part of them. That's what presence is.

The heart of television is presence. Women who have followed a soap opera for a considerable time have experienced more self-revelation from the chief character of the program than they have from their neighbors or husband all their life. Small wonder that the hero and heroine are a presence to them in a way that most people are not. Yet on the television screen there is merely an electronic representation of a person! How can this give strong sense of presence? Surely there is a difference in everybody's mind between these electronic blips and *living with* a person. The intense hunger of Beatle fans to touch them would seem some evidence in this direction. How are we to understand this strange new kind of face-to-face communication . . . one way communication mediated by electronic patterns.

Notes

1. McNeill, William Hardy. *The Rise of the West*. Chicago: University of Chicago Press, 1963.
2. McLuhan, Marshall and E. S. Carpenter (eds.). *Explorations in Communication*. Boston: Beacon Press, 1960. p. 208.
3. *Ibid.*, p. 308.
4. Lawrence, D. H. *Complete Poems*. New York: Viking Press, 1964. pp. 182–183.

MICHAEL NOVAK

Television Shapes the Soul

This article makes two points: (1) that television affects our perception of reality and (2) that television effects spring from a "class bias." Michael Novak points out a fascinating but often overlooked point about the television industry: that the writers, producers, network executives and others in positions of authority represent the ten percent of our population who have had four or more years of college. They are the intellectual elite. He believes that this educated, affluent and, for the most part, liberal elite is imposing its perceptions and values on the rest of society. Even though you might not agree with Novak, depending on the motives you attribute to those who produce television, you will have to admit that it is not the uneducated who have control of the electronic media. Read the Chesebro article on values and popular TV series in Section IV to see how values are manipulated through television.

For twenty-five years we have been immersed in a medium never before experienced on this earth. We can be forgiven if we do not yet understand all the ways in which this medium has altered us, particularly our inner selves, the perceiving, mythic, symbolic—and the judging, critical—parts of ourselves.

Media, like instruments, work "from the outside in." If you practice the craft of writing sedulously, you begin to think and perceive differently. If you run for twenty minutes a day, your psyche is subtly transformed. If you work in an executive office, you begin to think like an executive. And if you watch six hours of television, on the average, every day . . . ?

Innocent of psychological testing and sociological survey, I would like to present a humanist's analysis of what television seems to be doing to me, to my students, to my children, and, in general, to those I see around me (including those I see on television, in movies, in magazines). My method is beloved of philosophers, theologians, cultural critics: try to *perceive,* make *distinctions, coax into the light* elusive movements of consciousness. It goes without saying that others will have to verify the following observations; they are necessarily in the hypothetical mode, even if some of the hypotheses have a cogency that almost bites.

From Leonard L. Sellars and Wilbur C. Rivers, eds., *Mass Media Issues* (New York: Prentice-Hall, 1977). Reprinted by permission of Michael Novak and Aspen Institute for Humanistic Studies.

Two clusters of points may be made. The first, rather metaphysical, concerns the way television affects our way of perceiving and approaching reality. The second cluster concerns the way television inflicts a class bias on the world of our perceptions—the bias of a relatively small and special social class.

Television and Reality

Television is a molder of the soul's geography. It builds up incrementally a psychic structure of expectations. It does so in much the same way that school lessons slowly, over the years, tutor the unformed mind and teach it "how to think." Television *might* tutor the mind, soul, and heart in other ways than the ways it does at present. But, to be concrete, we ought to keep in view the average night of programming on the major networks over the last decade or so—not so much the news or documentaries, not so much the discussions on public television or on Sundays, not so much the talk shows late at night, but rather the variety shows, comedies, and adventure shows that are the staples of prime-time viewing. From time to time we may allow our remarks to wander farther afield. But it is important to concentrate on the universe of prime-time major network programming; that is where the primary impact of television falls.

It is possible to isolate five or six ways in which television seems to affect those who watch it. Television series represent genres of artistic perfomance. They structure a viewer's way of perceiving, of making connections, and of following a story line. Try, for example, to bring to consciousness the difference between the experience of watching television and the experience of learning through reading, argument, the advice of elders, lectures in school, or other forms of structuring perception. The conventions of the various sorts of television series re-create different sorts of "worlds." These "worlds" raise questions—and, to some extent, illuminate certain features of experience that we notice in ourselves and around us as we watch.

Suppose that you were a writer for a television show—an action-adventure, a situation comedy, even a variety show. You would want to be very careful to avoid "dead" spots, "wooden" lines, "excess" verbiage. Every line has a function, even a double or triple function. Characters move on camera briskly, every line counts, the scene shifts rapidly. In comedy, every other line should be a laugh-getter. Brevity is the soul of hits.

Television is a teacher of expectations; it speeds up the rhythm of attention. Any act in competition with television must approach the same pace; otherwise it will seem "slow." Even at an intellectual conference or seminar we now demand a swift rhythm of progressive movement; a leisurely, circular pace of rumination is perceived as less than a "good show."

But not only the pace is fast. Change of scene and change of perspective are also fast. In a recent episode of *Kojak,* action in three or four parts of the city was kept moving along in alternating sequences of a minute or less. A "principle of association" was followed; some image in the last frames of one scene suggested a link to the first frames of the new scene. But one scene cut away from another very quickly.

The progression of a television show depends upon multiple logics—two or three different threads are followed simultaneously. The viewer must figure out the connections between people, between chains of action, and between scenes. Many clues are *shown,* not *said.* The viewer must detect them.

The logic of such shows is not sequential in a single chain. One subject is raised, then cut, and another subject is picked up, then cut. Verbal links—"Meanwhile, on the other side of the city . . ."—are not supplied.

In teaching and in writing I notice that for students one may swiftly change the subject, shift the scene, drop a line of argument in order to pick it up later—and not lose the logic of development. Students understand such a performance readily. They have been prepared for it. The systems of teaching which I learned in my student days—careful and exact exegesis proceeding serially from point to point, the careful definition and elucidation of terms in an argument and the careful scrutiny of chains of inference, and the like—now meet a new form of resistance. There has always been resistance to mental discipline; one has only to read the notebooks of students from medieval universities to recognize this well-established tradition of resistance. But today the minds and affections of the brighter students are teeming with images, vicarious experiences, and indeed of actual travel and accomplishments. Their minds race ahead and around the flanks of lines of argument. "Dialectics" rather than "logic" or "exegesis" is the habit of mind they are most ready for. I say this neither in praise nor in blame; pedagogy must deal with this new datum, if it is new. What are its limits and its possibilities? What correctives are needed among students—and among teachers?

The periodization of attention is also influenced by the format of television. For reasons of synchronized programming the ordinary television show is neatly divided into segments of approximately equal length, and each of these segments normally has its own dramatic rhythm so as to build to dramatic climax or sub-climax, with the appropriate degree of suspense or resolution. Just as over a period of time a professor develops an instinct for how much can be accomplished in a fifty-minute lecture, or a minister of religion develops a temporal pattern for his sermons, so also the timing of television shows tutors their audience to expect a certain rhythm of development. The competitive pressures of television, moreover, encourage producers to "pack" as much action, intensity, or (to speak generally) entertainment into each segment as possible. Hence, for example, the short, snappy gags of *Laugh-In* and the rapid-fire developments of police shows or westerns.

Character is as important to successful shows as action; audiences need to "identify" with the heroes of the show, whether dramatic or comic. Thus in some ways the leisure necessary to develop character may provide a counter-tendency to the need for melodramatic rapidity. Still, "fast-paced" and "laugh-packed" and other such descriptions express the sensibility that television both serves and reinforces.

Television tutors the sensibilities of its audience in another way: it can handle only a limited range of human emotions, perplexities, motivations, and situations. The structure of competitive television seems to require this limitation; it springs from a practiced estimation of the capacity of the audience. Critics sometimes argue that American novelists have a long tradition of inadequacy with respect to the creation of strong, complicated women and, correspondingly, much too simple and superficial a grasp of the depths and complexities of human love. It is, it is said, the more direct "masculine" emotions, as well as the relations of comradeship between men, that American artists celebrate best. If such critical judgments may be true of our greatest artists working in their chosen media, then, a fortiori, it is not putting down television to note that the range of human relations treated by artists on television is less than complete. The constraints under which television artists work are acute:the time available to them, the segmentation of this time, and the competitive pressures they face for intense dramatic activity. To develop a fully complicated set of motivations, internal conflicts, and inner contradictions requires time and sensitivity to nuance. The present structure of television makes these requirements very difficult to meet.

This point acquires fuller significance if we note the extent to which Americans depend upon television for their public sense of how other human beings behave in diverse situations. The extent of this dependence should be investigated. In particular, we ought to examine the effects of the growing segregation of Americans by age. It does not happen frequently nowadays that children grow up in a household shared by three generations, in a neighborhood where activities involve members of all generations, or in a social framework where generation-mixing activities are fairly common. I have many times been told by students (from suburban environments, in particular) that they have hardly ever, or never, had a serious conversation with adults. The social world of their parents did not include children. They spent little time with relatives, and that time was largely formal and distant. The high schools were large, "consolidated," and relatively impersonal. Their significant human exchanges were mostly with their peers. Their images of what adults do and how adults think and act were mainly supplied by various media, notably television and the cinema. The issue such comments raise is significant. Where *could* most Americans go to find dramatic models of adult behavior? In the eyes of young people does the public weight of what is seen on television count for more than what they see in their private world as a model for "how things are done"? Indeed, do adults themselves gain a sense of what counts as acceptable adult behavior from the public media?

If it turns out to be true that television (along with other media like magazines and the cinema) now constitutes a major source of guidance for behavior, to be placed in balance with what one learns from one's parents, from the churches, from one's local communities, and the like, then the range of dramatic materials on television has very serious consequences for the American psyche. While human behavior is to a remarkable extent diverse and variable, it tends to be "formed" and given shape by the attraction or the power of available imaginative materials: stories, models, symbols, images-in-action. The storehouse of imaginative materials available to each person provides a sort of repertoire. The impact of new models can be a powerful one, leading to "conversions," "liberations," or "new directions." The reservoir of acquired models exerts a stong influence both upon perception and upon response to unfamiliar models. If family and community ties weaken and if psychic development becomes somewhat more nuclearized or even atomized, the influence of television and other distant sources may well become increasingly powerful, moving, as it were, into something like a vacuum. Between the individual and the national source of image-making there will be little or no local resistance. The middle ground of the psyche, until recently thick and rich and resistant, will have become attenuated.

The point is not that television has reached the limit of its capacities, nor is it to compare the possibilities of television unfavorably with those of other media. It is, rather, to draw attention to television as it has been used in recent years and to the structures of attention that, by its presentations, it helps to shape.

The competitive pressures of programming may have brought about these limits. But it is possible that the nature of the medium itself precludes entering certain sorts of depths. Television may be excellent in some dimensions and merely whet the appetite in others.

Television also seems to conceive of itself as a national medium. It does not favor the varieties of accent, speech patterns, and other differences of the culture of the United States. It favors a language which might be called "televisionese"—a neutral accent, pronunciation, and diction perhaps most closely approximated in California.

Since television arises in the field of "news" and daily entertainment, television values highly a kind of topicality, instant reflection of trends, and an effort to be "with it" and even "swinging." It values the "front edge" of attention, and it dreads being outrun by events. Accordingly, its product is perishable. It functions, in a way, as a guide to the latest gadgets and to the wonders of new technologies, or, as a direct contrary, to a kind of nostalgia for simpler ways in simpler times. Fashions of dress, automobiles, and explicitness "date" a series of shows. (Even the techniques used in taping shows may date them.)

Thus television functions as an instrument of the national, mobile culture. It does not reinforce the concrete ways of life of individual neighborhoods, towns, or subcultures. It shows the way things are done (or fantasized as being done) in "the big world." It is an organ of Hollywood and New York, not of Macon, Peoria, Salinas, or Buffalo.

I once watched television in a large hut in Tuy Hoa, South Vietnam. A room full of Vietnamese, including children, watched Armed Forces Television, watched Batman, Matt Dillon, and other shows from a distant continent. Here was their glimpse of the world from which the Americans around them had come. I wanted to tell them that what they were watching on television represented *no place,* represented no neighborhoods from which the young Americans around them came. And I began to wonder, knowing that not even the makers of such shows lived in such worlds, whose real world does television represent?

There are traces of local authenticity and local variety on national television. *All in the Family* takes the cameras into a neighborhood in Queens. The accents, gestures, methods and perceptions of the leading actors in *Kojak* reflect in an interesting and accurate way the ethnic sensibilities of

several neighborhoods in New York. The clipped speech of Jack Webb in
Dragnet years ago was an earlier break from "televisionese." But, in general, television is an organ of nationalization, of homogenization—and, indeed, of a certain systematic inaccuracy about the actual, concrete texture
of life in the United States.

This nationalizing effect also spills over into the news and the documentaries. The cultural factors which deeply affect the values and perceptions
of various American communities are neglected; hence the treatment of
problems affecting such communities is frequently oversimplified. This is
especially true when matters of group conflict are involved. The tendency
of newsmen is subtly to take sides and to regard some claims or behavior
as due to "prejudice," others as rather more moral and commendable.

The mythic forms and story lines of the news and documentaries are not
inconsonant with the mythic forms represented in the adventure stories
and Westerns. "Good" and "evil" are rather clearly placed in conflict.
"Hard-hitting" investigative reporting is mythically linked to classic American forms of moral heroism: the crimebuster, the incorruptible sheriff.
The forces of law and progress ceaselessly cut into the jungle of corruption. There is continuity between the prime-time news and prime-time
programming—much more continuity than is detected by the many cultivated Cyclopses who disdain "the wasteland" and praise the documentaries. The mythic structure of both is harmonious.

It should prove possible to mark out the habits of perception and mind
encouraged by national television. If these categories are not decisive, better ones can surely be discerned. We might then design ways of instructing
ourselves and our children in countervailing habits. It does not seem likely
that the mind and heart tutored by many years of watching television (in
doses of five or six hours a day) is in the same circumstance as the mind
and heart never exposed to television. Education and criticism must, it
seems, take this difference into account.

The Class Bias of Television

Television has had two striking effects. On the one hand, as Norman
Podhoretz has remarked, it has not seemed to prevent people from reading; more books are being published and mass marketed than ever before
in American history. It is possible that television stimulates many to go
beyond what television itself can offer.

Secondly, television works, or appears to work, as a homogenizing world to a national audience. In many respects, it could be shown, the overall ideological tendency of television productions—from the news, through the talk shows, to the comedy hours, variety shows, and adventure, crime, and family shows—is that of a vague and misty liberalism: belief in the efficacy of an ultimate optimism, "talking through one's problems," a questioning of institutional authorities, a triumph of good over evil. Even a show like *All in the Family,* beneath its bluster and its violation of verbal taboos, illustrates the unfailing victory of liberal points of view: Archie Bunker always loses. A truly mean and aggressive reactionary point of view is virtually non-existent. There is no equivalent on national television to *Human Events* and other right-wing publications, or to the network of right-wing radio shows around the nation. While many critics of right and left find prime-time television to be a "wasteland," few have accused it of being fascist, malicious, evil, or destructive of virtue, progress, and hope. Television's liberalism is calculated to please neither the new radicals nor the classic liberals of the left, nor the upbeat, salesmanlike exponents of the right. In harmony with the images of progress built into both liberalism and capitalism, television seems, however gently, to undercut traditional institutions and to promote a restless, questioning attitude. The main product—and attitude—it has to sell is the new.

This attachment to the new insures that television will be a vaguely leftist medium, no matter who its personnel might be. Insofar as it debunks traditions and institutions—and even the act of *representing* these in selective symbolic form is a kind of veiled threat to them—television serves the purposes of that large movement within which left and right (in America, at least) are rather like the two legs of locomotion: the movement of modernization. It serves, in general, the two mammoth institutions of modern life: the state and the great corporations. It serves these institutions even when it exalts the individual at the expense of family, neighborhood, religious organizations, and cultural groups. These are the only intermediate institutions that stand between the isolated individual and the massive institutions.

Thus the homogenizing tendencies of television are ambivalent. Television can electrify and unite the whole nation, creating an instantaneous network in which millions are simultaneous recipients of the same powerful images. But to what purpose, for whose use, and to what effect? Is it an unqualified good that the national grid should become so pre-eminent, superior to any and all local checks and balances? The relative national power and influence of state governors seems to have been weakened, for example; a state's two senators, by comparison, occupy a national stage and can more easily become national figures.

But in at least five other ways national television projects a sense of reality that is not identical to the sense of reality actual individuals in their concrete environments share. Taken together, these five ways construct a national social reality that is not free of a certain class and even ethnic bias. The television set becomes a new instrument of reality—of "what's happening" in the larger, national world, of "where it's at." In some sense what isn't on television isn't quite real, is not part of the nationally shared world, will be nonexistent for millions of citizens. Three examples may suggest the power of this new sense of reality.

Experiments suggest (so I am told) that audiences confronted with simultaneous projection on a large movie screen and on a television set regularly and overwhelmingly end up preferring the image on the smaller set. The attraction of reality is somehow there.

On the political campaign, or at a sports event, individuals seem to seek to be on camera with celebrities, as if seeking to share in a precious and significant verification of their existence. A young boy in Pittsburgh exults, "I'm real!" as he interposes himself between the grinding cameras and a presidential candidate in the crowd. Not to be on television is to lack weight in national consciousness. Audience "participation" (the ancient platonic word for being) fills a great psychic hunger: to be human in the world that really counts.

Finally, anyone who has participated in a large-scale event comes to recognize vividly how strait and narrow is the gate between what has actually happened and what gets on television. For the millions who see the television story, of course, the story is the reality. For those who lived through a strenuous sixteen-hour day on the campaign trail, for example, it is always something of a surprise to see what "made" the television screen—or, more accurately, what the television screen made real. That artificial reality turns out to have far more substance for the world at large than the lived sixteen hours. According to the ancient *maya*, the world of flesh and blood is an illusion. And so it is.

Television is a new technology and depends upon sophisticated crafts. It is a world of high profit. Its inside world is populated by persons in a high income bracket. Moreover, television is a world that requires a great deal of travel, expense-account living, a virtual shuttle between Los Angeles and New York, a taste for excellent service and high prestige. These economic factors seriously color television's image of the world.

The glitter of show business quickly spread to television. In the blossomy days when thinkers dreamed of an affluent society and praised the throwaway society, the shifting and glittering sets of television make-believe seemed like a metaphor for modern society. Actually, a visit to a television studio is extraordinarily disappointing, far more so, even, than a visit to an empty circus tent after the crowd has gone. Cheaply painted pastel panels, fingerprints sometimes visible upon them, are wheeled away and stacked. The cozy intimacy one shares from one's set at home is rendered false by the cavernous lofts of the studio, the tangle of wires, the old clothing and cynical buzzing of the bored technicians, crews, and hangers-on. Dust and empty plastic coffee cups are visible in corners where chairs compete for space. There is a tawdriness behind the scenes.

In a word, the world of television is a radically duplicitous world. Its illusions pervade every aspect of the industry. The salaries paid to those who greet the public remove them from the public. The settings in which they work are those of show business. Slick illusion is the constant temptation and establishes the rules of the game.

Moreover, the selling of products requires images of upward mobility. The sets, designs, and fluid metaphors of the shows themselves must suggest a certain richness, smoothness, and adequacy. It is not only that writers and producers understand that what audiences desire is escape. (One can imagine a poor society in which television would focus on limited aspiration and the dramas of reality.) It is also the case, apparently, that an inner imperative drives writers, producers, and sponsors to project their *own* fantasies. Not all Americans, by far, pursue upward mobility as a way of life. A great many teach their children to have modest expectations and turn down opportunities for advancement and mobility that would take them away from their familiar worlds.

The myths of the upwardly mobile and the tastes of the very affluent govern the visual symbols, the flow, and the chatter of television.

The class bias of television reality proceeds not only from the relative economic affluence of the industry and its personnel. It springs as well from the educational level. "Televisionese" sends a clear and distinct message to the people, a message of exclusion and superiority. (George Wallace sends the message *back;* he is not its originator, only its echo.) It is common for a great many of the personnel connected with television to imagine themselves as anti-establishment and also perhaps as iconoclastic. Surely they must know that to men who work in breweries or sheet metal plants, to women who clean tables in cafeterias or splice wires in electronic assembly plants, they must seem to be at the very height of the Establishment. Their criticisms of American society—reflected in *Laugh-In,* in the nightclub entertainers, and even in the dialogue of virtually every crime or adventure show—are perceived to be something like the complaints of spoiled children. There seems to be a self-hatred in the medium, a certain shame about American society, of which Lawrence Welk's old-fashioned, honeyed complacency and the militant righteousness of Bob Hope, John Wayne, and *Up With America!* are the confirming opposites. To confuse the hucksterism of television with the real America is, of course, a grievous error.

Television is a parade of experts instructing the unenlightened about the weather, aspirins, toothpastes, the latest books or proposals for social reform, and the correct attitudes to have with respect to race, poverty, social conflict, and new moralities. Television is preeminently a world of intellectuals. Academic persons may be astonished to learn of it and serious writers and artists may hear the theme with withering scorn, but for most people in the United States television is the medium through which they meet an almost solid phalanx of college-educated persons, professionals, experts, thinkers, authorities, and "with it," "swinging" celebrities: i.e., people unlike themselves who are drawn from the top ten percent of the nation in terms of educational attainment.

It is fashionable for intellectuals to disdain the world of television (although some, when asked, are known to agree to appear on it without hesitation). Yet when they appear on television they do not seem to be notably superior to the announcers, interviewers, and performers who precede them on camera or share the camera with them. (Incidentally, although many sports journalists write or speak condescendingly of "the jocks," when athletes appear as television announcers—Joe Garagiola, Sandy Koufax, Frank Gifford, Alex Karras, and others—the athletes seem not one whit inferior in intelligence or in sensitivity to the journalists.) Television is the greatest instrument the educated class has ever had to parade its wares before the people. On television that class has no rival. Fewer than ten percent of the American population has completed four years of college. That ten percent totally dominates television.

It is important to understand that the disdain for "popular culture" often heard in intellectual circles is seriously misplaced. Television, at least, more nearly represents the world of the educated ten percent than it reflects the world of the other ninety percent. At most, one might say in defense, the world of television represents the educated class's fantasies about the fantasies of the population. To say that *kitsch* has always required technicians to create it is not a sufficient route of escape. Do really serious intellectuals (i.e., not those "mere" technicians) have better understandings of where the people truly are? What, then, are those better understandings?

The interviews recorded by Robert Coles, for example, tend to show that persons of the social class represented by Archie Bunker are at least as complicated, many-sided, aware of moral ambiguities, troubled and sensitive, as the intellectuals who appear on television, in novels, or in the cinema. Artists who might use the materials of ordinary life for their creations are systematically separated from ordinary people by the economic conditions of creativity in the United States.

The writers, producers, actors, and journalists of television are separated from most of the American population not only by economic standing, and not only by education, but also by the culture in which their actual lives are lived out. By "culture" I mean those implicit, lived criteria that suggest to each of us what is real, relevant, significant, meaningful in the buzzing confusion of our experience: how we select out and give shape to our world. The culture of prime-time television is, it appears, a serious dissolvant of the cultures of other Americans. The culture of television celebrates to an extraordinary degree two mythic strains in the American character: the lawless and the irreverent. On the first count, stories of cowboys, gangsters, and spies still preoccupy the American imagination. On the second, the myth of "enlightenment" from local standards and prejudices still dominates our images of self-liberation and sophistication. No doubt the stronghold of a kind of priggish righteousness in several layers of American history leads those who rebel to find their rebellion all too easy. It is as though the educated admonish one another that they "can't go home again" and that the culture against which they rebel is solid and unyielding.

But what if it isn't? What if the perception of culture on the part of millions is, rather, that chaos and the jungle are constantly encroaching and that the rule of good order is threatened in a dozen transactions every day—by products that don't work, by experts and officials who take advantage of lay ignorance, by muggings and robberies, by jobs and pensions that disappear, by schools that do not work in concert with the moral vision of the home?

Television keeps pressing on the barriers of cultural resistance to obscenities, to some forms of sexual behavior, and to various social understandings concerning work and neighborhood and family relationships. A reporter from the *New York Times* reports with scarcely veiled satisfaction that *Deep Throat* is being shown in a former church in a Pennsylvania mining town, as though this were a measure of spreading enlightenment. It might be. But what if our understanding of how cultural, social, and moral strands are actually interwoven in the consciousness of peoples is inadequate? What if the collapse of moral inhibition in one area, for a significant number of persons, encourages a collapse at other places? What if moral values cannot be too quickly changed without great destructiveness? The celebration of "new moralities" may not lead to the kind of "humanization" cultural optimists anticipate.

Television, and the mass media generally, have vested interests in new moralities. The excitement of transgressing inhibitions is gripping entertainment. There are, however, few vested interests wishing to strengthen the inhibitions which make such transgressions good entertainment. Television is only twenty-five years old. We have very little experience or understanding proportionate to the enormous moral stakes involved. It is folly to believe that *laissez-faire* works better in moral matters than in economic matters or that enormous decisions in these matters are not already being made in the absence of democratic consent. When one kind of show goes on the air others are excluded during that time. The present system is effectively a form of social control.

I do not advocate any particular solution to this far-ranging moral dilemma; I do not know what to recommend. But the issue is a novel one for a free society, and we do not even have a well-thought-out body of options from which to choose. In that vacuum a rather-too-narrow social class is making the decisions. The pressures of the free market (so they say) now guide them. Is that so? Should it be so?

Because of the structure and history of the social class that produces prime-time television, group conflict in the United States is also portrayed in a simplistic and biased way. The real diversity of American cultures and regions is shrouded in public ignorance. Occasional disruptions, like the rebellion of West Virginia miners against certain textbooks and the rebellion of parents in South Boston against what they perceived as downward mobility for their children and themselves, are as quickly as possible brushed from consciousness. America is pictured as though it were divided between one vast homogeneous "middle America," to be enlightened, and the enlighteners. In fact, there are several "middle Americas."

There is more than one important Protestant culture in our midst. The

Puritan inheritance is commonly exaggerated and the evangelical, fundamentalist inheritance is vastly underestimated (and under-studied). Hubert Humphrey is from a cultural stream different from that of George Wallace or of John Lindsay. There are also several quite significant cultural streams among Catholics; the Irish of the Middle West (Eugene McCarthy, Michael Harrington) often have a quite different cultural tradition from the Irish of Philadelphia, Boston, or New York. Construction workers on Long Island are not offended by "pornography" in the same way as druggists in small midwestern towns; look inside their cabs and helmets, listen to their conversations, if you seek evidence. There is also more than one cultural stream among American Jews; the influence of the Jews of New York has probably misled us in our understanding of the Jewish experience in America.

It seems, moreover, that the social class guiding the destiny of television idealizes certain ethnic groups—the legitimate minorities—even while this class offers in its practices no greater evidence of genuine egalitarianism than other social classes. At the same time this class seems extremely slow to comprehend the experiences of other American cultures. One of the great traumas of human history was the massive migration to America during the last 100 years. It ought to be one of the great themes of high culture, and popular culture as well. Our dramatists neglect it.

Group conflict has, moreover, been the rule in every aspect of American life, from labor to corporate offices to neighborhoods to inter-ethnic marriages. Here, too, the drama is perhaps too real and vivid to be touched: *these* are inhibitions the liberal culture of television truly respects. Three years ago one could write that white ethnics, like some others, virtually never saw themselves on television; suddenly we have had *Banacek, Colombo, Petrocelli, Kojak, Kolchack, Rhoda, Sanford,* and *Chico.* Artists are still exploring the edges of how much reality can be given voice and how to voice it. These are difficult, even explosive matters. Integrity and care are required.

It must seem odd to writers and producers to be accused of having a "liberal" bias when they are so aware of the limitations they daily face and the grueling battles they daily undergo. But why do they have these battles except that they have a point of view and a moral passion? We are lucky that the social class responsible for the creative side of television is not a reactionary and frankly illiberal class. Still, that it is a special class is itself a problem for all of us, including those involved in it.

GARY GUMPERT

The Ambiguity of Perception

"It's a poor sort of memory that only works backwards."

LEWIS CARROLL
Through The Looking Glass

This article was written for an issue of *Et cetera* devoted to "Media and Culture." In it, Gumpert examines a new, and as yet relatively unexamined, aspect of the electronic media—the widespread use of videotaping. He describes the situation where the majority of everything we see on TV is videotaped. (The same is true for radio shows where audiotaping is widespread and where all "live talk" shows are delayed seven seconds before being transmitted.) This time-freezing process makes it possible to alter, edit, reshoot, etc., while allowing the source to present the material as though it were "live."

Gumpert asks us to consider the psychological ramifications of a situation where we can no longer depend on our senses to perceive what is "live" and what has been "recorded." Consider how we decide when something presented on the electronic media is "live" and what difference that makes in our judgment. What distinguishes listening to a rock group on a recording that has been contrived by putting together dozens of tracks from various taping sessions, and seeing and hearing a "real live" performance? Which do you prefer, "electronic perfection," or face-to-face interaction with all its possible slip-ups and errors?

We depend upon concepts of time and space in order to function in and interpret reality. Here and there, now and then, what was and what will be—all are percepts which guide us through the world. Without these operational frames life would be absolutely chaotic. Fantasy could not be distinguished from reality, tomorrow would be today, and history would never have occurred. We assume that all "normal" individuals operate in a universe essentially agreeing on basic definitions of time and space; for all, there is a yesterday and a tomorrow. But the world is changing and today is repeatable, yesterday can be preserved, and we can be here and there simultaneously. The development of modern media technology is altering

From *Et cetera*, vol. 34, #2 (June 1977). Reprinted by permission of the International Society for General Semantics.

the perceptual frames through which individuals operate in their daily lives.

In most circumstances the frame of reality is quite evident. We believe we are aware of where and when we are. The writer is aware of words being typed. Fingers are in contact with typewriter keys in an attempt to convey thoughts through individual signs and symbols. Through auditory, tactile, and visual senses the writer knows and is aware of what is happening "now." "Now" is momentary, fleeting, a transition between past and future, defined by what has happened and what will occur. We are bound to the present because of a belief that it is controllable, that the manipulable "now" determines the undetermined future. The author's "now" is transformed into the reader's "now" as these past thoughts are read.

An awareness of time and space is taken for granted in the process of communication. We know where we are when we communicate. The conventions are not generally articulated. On a simplistic level, if in the course of this essay the author addresses you in the present tense, you play a game with him: you pretend that the author is uttering the words as you are reading them, although you know that this is certainly not the case. This process involves both a physical and psychological dimension, but the awareness of process and convention is central to the manipulation of time and space in communication. As the technology of communications media grows more complex, as we absorb that technology into our lives, we become less aware of process and this signals the potential alteration or perhaps obliteration of time and space conventions. This in turn determines our perception of reality. Two facets of our changing perceptions of reality will be examined in this essay: What is "now," and what is "perfection"?

The Perception of Now

The increasing use of videotape recording provides an intriguing example of technological effect upon psychological process. The President of the United States addresses the American people through the means of a live, televised broadcast. Time has not been altered, while space is bridged by the medium of television. Distance is dissolved through electronic connection. The viewer can be several hundred or several thousand miles away from the White House. The event is concurrent with its perception. The President is speaking at the very moment that individuals are watching and listening to him. The speech exists in time. Ideas through words, tone, and gesture have been developed, are developing, and will develop. Theoretically, no linguistic or environmental possibilities are locked out from potential occurrence. The viewer does not know what will happen as the President speaks to the nation. Indeed, the President himself, while having developed a plan or strategy, can never be totally sure of what will happen during the next few minutes. He might make a mistake, a stranger conceivably might wander in front of the cameras thereby distracting him. An illness might suddenly surface. Perhaps a new idea may suddenly occur which the President might insert into his prepared text. The possibilities are infinite. The tension of unpredictability always hovers over the moment.

This dramatic aspect of viewer-speaker confrontation is quite different when a newsclip portion of the speech is included in the late evening television news coverage. The viewer knows (is conditioned to a convention) that the news includes the coverage of past events.

Because of the existence of videotape recording, the President, for a number of reasons, may decide to prerecord his speech. He can achieve a greater degree of perfection by using tape. The danger of mistakes in an important address can be totally avoided. A nervous mannerism or some faltering in delivery can be eliminated. Whatever the reason, the videotaped speech is substituted for the live broadcast. Is there a difference between watching an unedited recording of the address and a live broadcast of the same event? Most people are not able to distinguish a difference. (The author has not conducted formal research on this question. It is certainly an area that should be carefully examined.) If both events are hypothetically identical, do psychological differences exist between those two situations because one is recorded and one is live?

Let us assume that the viewer at home cannot detect a difference between the live and the taped speech, and that the latter is being transmitted, but *is not identified as a videotaped event*. No problem exists if the viewer does not know of the possibility of videotape recording. Obviously he must assume that the broadcast is live. But if the viewer has an awareness of the possible use of the technology of videotape, psychological differences can become rather important.

An immediate sense of ambiguity is introduced, since an either/or situation exists. Is the speech live or taped? Is it happening now? If it is taped, it is not happening now. If it is taped, where is the President of the United States while he is appearing on television? When was the speech recorded? If the speech is (was) taped, even though the content has not yet been revealed, what will happen has already occurred. The content of the video-tape is predetermined. Therefore the relationship between subject and speech is altered by an awareness of technological means. The viewer is no longer a participant in an actual event, since participation is never prede-termined. The viewer of the videotaped speech does not participate, but reacts to an orchestrated event.

Participant versus viewer is a contrast of activity versus relative pas-sivity. In that regard, the nature of the medium is relevant. In the case of film projected in a theater, in those days when news was an integral part of the movie theater experience, there was never a confusion in regard to the "nowness" of the depicted event. People knew that they were watching something that had been filmed at a prior time. Film has to be developed, shipped to a location, projected upon a screen via a mechanical device. People are aware of this process. Film is not confused with the reality of liveness. When President Roosevelt appeared on film in the motion picture theater, it was not assumed that he was sitting in the White House at the same time that the viewer was observing him in the theater. The genre of drama is being excluded from this discussion since it involves a special set of conventions based upon an act of self-deception which allows the fic-tional to assume the cloak of reality. Nevertheless, general technical obser-vations can be made comparing television and film which transcend genre, and the effect of which is intuited on a perceptual level.

> In film, the time continuum is broken down into a series of separate, dis-crete, frozen nows. Each frame represents an arrested now, *a state of being*. We have an accurate record of this now—as it was. In reality, the film is a selection of *past* moments. *The film is a record of the past.*[1]
>
> In live television, the time continuum is represented by an integrated contin-uously moving image. The now cannot be pinpointed; it is in a *state of becom-ing*. While each film frame is a record of the past, the *television frame is a reflection of the living present.*[2]

The nondramatic cinematic event is not confused with the object. The screen is not the event. The screen reflects the event. In television the event exists through the screen. While film involves a separation in time and space (by mere definition of process), television potentially dismisses time and emphasizes space.

In television the live event invites participation because the lack of pre-destination places a degree of potency in the hands of the individual. If the future is not determined ahead of time, perhaps the individual can hope, wish, charm, or even cast a spell which will affect that which has not yet happened. It is the case of the sports fan *involved* in a tense moment during the baseball game. He yells, perhaps pounds the table, or strokes his lucky charm, in an effort to will circumstances in the favor of his team. He believes that his will can determine the future. Of course, this fantasy represents an impossibility. The cold hand of logic is clear. An individual separated by miles from the contest cannot affect the outcome of the contest, but nevertheless, the rituals are enacted. There is an implicit belief that the participant can determine the future. *We all play the game.* The same belief applies to the situation of the broadcast of a presidential address. To some degree the individual viewer believes in his potential power over the event. The viewer seeks the aura of uncertainty in which he can cast his evil spell, dispense a blessing, or merely hope.

A further example of the effect of videotape upon the nature of viewer experience, related to the example of the presidential address, can be demonstrated through the analysis of the telecasting of a sports event. The spectator at a football game is caught up in the atmosphere surrounding him and probably identifies with one of the teams. It has been the author's experience that even if he is unfamiliar with the teams, he nevertheless quickly identifies with one of them. To some extent, the athletic event is the modern version of a morality play, inviting identification with the "good guys" who hopefully will win over the "forces of evil." On a second level, we have the situation in which the same event is seen live on television. Certainly the force of atmosphere disappears, but the tension of unpredictability remains, along with the "morality" aspect of the contest. Probably the spectator now has a "better seat" through the magnification and editing process of live television. On a third level, we have the same event, but the entire game has been videotaped. If the viewer is unaware of the technology of videotape or actually believes that what he is seeing is live, there is no change in his relationship to the game. The degree of tension has not been defused. On a fourth level, the individual watches a videotaped game, knows that it has been videotaped, but does not know the outcome. Now a subtle change occurs, because of the awareness that the outcome is predetermined, since all the forces in action were resolved and completed at a prior time. The edge of excitement has been blunted. The viewer in this situation is forced to assume the dramatic convention of the "willing suspension of disbelief" in order to recapture the keen excitement of the game: "I'll pretend that it hasn't happened yet." (This author has even gone to the trouble of hiding the newspaper and avoiding any newscasts so that he would be unaware of the outcome in order to preserve the suspense of "not knowing.") On the last level, the viewer is involved with a videotape of a game which has already occurred, and he is aware of the outcome. At this point, the total relationship of the individual to the game changes radically. The excitement of conflict, of the unpredictable morality play, vanishes and gives way to an analytical mode of viewing. It is not who won or lost the game that matters so much; *how* the game was won or lost is of primary importance. The morality play has given way to a display of skill. Clearly, it is the presence of videotape that has affected the psychological relationship between viewer and event.

In the case of the President addressing the nation, the frame of reality, or the degree of "nowness," is clear when the videotape process is identified. When it is unidentified and a realization of process (an awareness of the technology) is present, a state of dissonance is introduced. Note that a non-videotaped program must also be identified, since the potential presence of videotape suggests that *all* programs may be videotaped. In short, if viewers are aware of the existence of videotape technology and its uses in television, but are *not* clearly informed about which broadcasts are taped and which are not, they must always experience some ambiguity about the time frame in which the events they are seeing actually occur.

Because a state of ambiguity is generated by the introduction into television of the videotaping process, an atmosphere of cynicism and doubt surrounds viewer responses to televised events. Perhaps the President does not really exist. The videotape could have been produced several months or several years ago. The giant conspiracy syndrome can make sense, if time and process are not labeled accurately. If videotapes are not identified or authenticated for date, the conclusion can be reached that *all* programs are completed and taped before transmission. Since the seeds of scepticism have been planted . . . When *did* the President actually make the speech? Hours, days, or weeks ago? If he isn't talking to us now, where is he? Could he be ill? Perhaps the country is run by a group of powerful individuals who control a file of prepared videotaped Presidential addresses. How many people have seen the President, without benefit of television, within the past year? How many persons have ever seen him at all? Perhaps . . .

But back to reality and a very real example of the problem. It is assumed that television newscasts are live broadcasts with filmed and videotaped news inserts. Authenticity is a basic value inherent in the transmission of the newscast. The concept of the newscast suggests that the format is flexible enough to allow for the inclusion of late developments which occur during the course of the broadcast. The latest news will be presented to the public. Indeed, the "on the spot reporter" capability distinguishes the electronic news services from newspapers and periodicals, which can cover events in greater depth and perspective. Several years ago the formats and presentational style of television newscasts were altered in order to present to the public an atmosphere of a *real* working newsroom. The trend has been away from a formalized, artificial, presentational style. Often, in the background, one can see busy editors in their shirtsleeves while the news is being presented. It is therefore surprising to discover that the CBS television newscast is taped at 6:30 p.m. (Eastern Standard Time) and, while it is broadcast live to a limited number of stations on the East coast, most of the East coast receives the broadcast at 7:00 p.m. via tape. The rest of the nation receives a taped version later, depending upon the time zone involved. If late items do develop, the video tape is interrupted with a live insert. It is possible, of course, to broadcast live if necessitated by a major late-breaking news event. To some extent, the aura of "immediacy" which pervades the newscast is a facade which is manufactured for authenticity.

The relationship of the videotaping process to our perception of reality has been discussed so far in rather absolute terms, but there are additional factors which complicate the issue. Let us examine a relatively simple interview between two people which has been videotaped. A number of assumptions are made by the viewer about such a situation: the tape which is broadcast is a faithful copy of the original event; that event was an ongoing interaction between two people which began at one point in time and ended at a later point in time. These assumptions are quite tenuous, since videotape editing can alter and rearrange events. The question is not whether programs should be recorded, but rather, to what extent should tape be *edited* when a program is recorded? At the root of the problem is the audience's perception of the event before editing and the degree of manipulation involved as editing is introduced. Any edited event has an idealized basis existing in the world of real time and space. Even the simple concept of a close-up assumes an understanding that the head has not been severed from the body and in "real" time and space a totally connected individual exists safe and sound.

The purist's position would be to object to any editing of videotape. That is not the position being taken here. Editing can be a useful and creative tool. When is it objectionable? To answer that question, let us return to that hypothetical interview. Scene one takes place in the garden. The interviewee is wearing a yellow dress. The interviewer says, "Let's go into the house now." Scene two is juxtaposed to the previous one, and the interviewee is now wearing a brown dress. The edit is obvious. There was no time (on the tape) for the pair to walk into the house. It is taken for granted that cameras and recorders stopped to allow for a change in location and dress. The viewer does not object, because the convention is understood and the viewer was not deceived. Now the circumstances are altered slightly. Instead of recording the interview for the purpose of broadcast, the producer has recorded it for the purpose of editing for broadcast. Instead of recording the amount required for the broadcast, he has recorded double that amount, with the understanding that the material will be reduced by half through editing. A sentence or two is eliminated. Several large sections are rather dull and are dropped. Comments made late in the interview are shifted to the beginning. Eventually the interview will be broadcast, but it has assumed the character of a pseudo-event (fabricated, manufactured, rearranged for presentation), although it is presented as if the interaction now being witnessed has actually once existed in real time. The audience is not supposed to know about the procedures utilized to create the event. For lack of a more descriptive phrase, this type of manipulation of the perception of reality can be called "hidden tampering." The product is objectionable, because it has no relationship to what it pretends to be—a real interview. It is a created situation delivered as an authentic event.

It seems puzzling that most people are not concerned with the matter of accurate labeling in the case of television recording. Perhaps the reasoning runs this way: "What does it matter? So what if the videotape is substituted for the live broadcast? The content has not changed! The speaker intended to communicate a specific series of points to the public and has used the latest technology in order to assure himself that the message is conveyed as he intended." Or, "What does it matter if sections were shifted around or perhaps eliminated? I'm only going to judge what I see on the tube." How does one reply to such hypothetical reactions? The matter goes beyond that of content; it involves authenticity of experience with content. We discern a difference between a roaring fire and a photograph of a roaring fire. If these differences were not apparent, potential calamity would await the individual so confused. But even minor or insignificant confusion of authenticity should be important. There is a need to be able to tell the difference between real and artificial, between a creation of nature and an artifact of man, between fantasy and reality, between what was, what is, and what will be. Just as we are impelled to classify and label objects in our environment in order to achieve structure and order, we should be driven to authenticate mediated events in time and space. The lack of apparent concern with this specific question suggests the degree to which our sensory awareness or acuity has been narcotized, the degree to which we have abdicated sensory responsibility. Sensory responsibility requires a degree of accuracy in recognizing the nature and magnitude of sensory impression.

There is also an ethical dimension to the problem. Does the producer of a nondramatic, unedited videotape substituted for a live broadcast have a responsibility for identifying that act? Should deceptive types of editing be identified? The answer to both questions is, Yes! Anything short of that action is manipulation. Duplicity is discernable, manipulation is not. Individuals have the ability to discern truth and falsehood. However, there is no way to distinguish an unedited videotape from a live broadcast—if minimal technical standards are maintained. If the individual cannot discern "then" from "now" or the "real" from the "specious," manipulation is a distinct possibility. It seems quite clear that the individual has the right not to be deceived, that he or she should have the tool to avoid manipulation—the proper labeling of a videotaped production.

The Perception of Perfection

Human beings have always had the desire to record and to preserve events. It is a long way from prehistoric cave paintings to electronic and filmic recording, although the motivation for such acts is probably quite similar. In the previous section of this essay we explored the confusion which can result when time and space distinctions are altered through the nonlabeling of recordings. The issue to be examined now is how the presence of recordings has altered, or can alter, our perception of a live event.

One source of the appeal of a live event is its fallibility. Something can go wrong. A mistake or error always lurks in the wings of the performance. Indeed, the extraordinary performance rests on a precarious tightrope where a slight error in judgment results in failure. The abysmal performer does not take a chance; neither does the dull, prosaic display of talent ever approach the daring of the extraordinary. One index of a great performance is the degree to which the ordinary, the mundane, is transcended. Greatness is the transcendence of failure.

Why are we so fascinated by the tightrope act, the lion tamer, or the flying trapeze artists? Is it the beauty and grace of movement? Perhaps, but it seems that, in addition, the danger involved in each of these acts is a pre-dominating attraction for the spectator. A strange contradiction in emotion is inherent in the appreciation of an act surrounded by risk or danger. We require that the potential for calamity be present, to a frightening, imaginary degree, although the fruition of that calamity is not desired—or is it? The threat cannot merely remain a threat. The frightful moment must occur to someone in order to underscore the fact that "the daring young man on the flying trapeze" is truly "daring." The potentiality for tragedy, for disaster, for failure, underscores and defines success. This observation is not limited to spectacular performances which involve physical danger. The principle applies to all arts. The rendering of one composition is exceptional, the other merely adequate. Why? The audience sits quietly bored at one performance and is electrified at the next. "There's magic in the air!" An actor knows when a fellow thespian goes beyond the normal enactment of a role and wanders into the shadowy domain where greatness and failure are almost fraternal.

But the technology of recording has altered the relationship between spectator and event. The audience has been so indoctrinated in the cult of perfectability that the concept of the "perfect" has become almost meaningless. The nature of the altered relationship between spectator and event can be demonstrated by examining any number of areas in the performing arts. In this case, the focus will be on music.

Certainly, the technology of recording has affected both the audience and artists of music. The late piano virtuoso Artur Schnabel articulated his concern in regard to recordings:

> In 1929 I was asked once again whether I would not agree to make records. Until then I had consistently refused to do so. One of the chief reasons for my refusal was that I did not like the idea of having no control over the behavior of the people who listen to music which I performed—not knowing how they would be dressed, what else they would be doing at the same time, how much they would listen. Also I felt that recordings are against the very nature of performance, for the nature of performance is to happen but once, to be absolutely ephemeral and unrepeatable. I do not think there could ever have been two performances of the same piece by the same person which were absolutely alike. That is inconceivable.[3]

It is fortunate that Schnabel agreed to record, because a record of his artistry has been preserved for today's listeners. At the same time, his hesitancy can be respected and his premise that the same artist could not duplicate two identical performances is significant because replication is the major motive for purchasing a record. The record performance never changes until the disc is worn out, at which point it is repurchased. Today the medium of music is the recording. "Where music was once propagated locally by the individual, it is now propagated generally by the phonograph record, the radio and the motion picture sound track. . . ."[4] Today, the greatest proportion of musical contact is not with the performer, but with sound.

The art of audio technology has progressed to a point where a performance is no longer merely recorded. A recording can be produced with the aid of twelve or sixteen separate tracks and a host of electronic effects. The results are often highly inventive and brilliant. But in what way has this development altered our perception of musical perfection? Before its impact can be appreciated, some distinction should be made between types of recordings in relation to performance.

1. A *"live"* recording is the record of a performance. It is essentially unedited and can be considered a faithful facsimile of a prior event.

2. The *"live augmented"* recording uses studio facilities to enhance a basically live performance. The artist or producer seeks the best possible recording, in terms of quality of performance and audio fidelity. This is achieved through the use of multiple tracks, countless takes, and electronic enhancement, but the purpose is to refine the original rendering of the artist. This type of recording can, through the aid of electronic technology, provide the perfectability which is the goal of any artist. It should be pointed out that it is possible, and it is a frequent occurrence, to achieve a perfect recording of an artistically inferior performance, and generally critics will evaluate recording and performance separately.

3. The *"studio"* recording is not restricted by what might or might not happen in a live performance, but uses audio technology as an additional musical instrument. The result is a performance *not possible* under normal live conditions. The technology is integral to the ultimate recording. This category of recording does not pretend to be anything other than what it is—a studio-produced work of art. The source of the problem is in the confusion which arises between the "live" recording and the "live augmented" recording.

Formerly, the live concert was the stimulus for record sales. "That was great. Has it been recorded? Let's buy it." The live concert was the criterion upon which a recording was judged. "It's almost as if I were there. I can remember the moment." Today, the live concert is judged by the standard of the recording, which may provide the motivation to attend the concert. "The record was fantastic. Let's go see him in person." This is a reversal in motivation, and the problem arises when the audience is disappointed by the performance. The audience is unhappy because the performer has not lived up to the virtuosity displayed on the recording. In all probability the recording has been artificially enhanced, and the audience, unaware of the fact (confusion of recording categories one and two), evaluates the live performance (nonrecorded) against standards that truly reside only in the realm of the ideal. Note that there is probably little confusion between the "studio" recording the "live" recording.

If a performer is talented, and on a given day plays with talent, and is inspired by the gods, he or she might almost reach the level of performance which is achieved every day in the recording studio—a level of performance which need not tolerate mistakes. There is no room for a mistake in a world when perfection can be manufactured—why should there be? If that note slightly off pitch can be fixed, why allow it into the home, where it reflects upon both artist and producer? The struggle of an artist to enter the realm of perfectability is awesome compared to the ease with which the studio technician can change, substitute, alter, or manufacture notes, passages, and sections. Yet the two processes compete for critical and commercial acceptance. Obviously, a recording studio can take a performance and perfect it, as long as the artist provides a basic level of competence in the rendering of the composition. But a great live performance cannot be manufactured; furthermore, it requires a milieu in which the nonperfect and potential failure exist side by side. An audience accustomed to the perfect has no patience for the fallible performer who walks an artistic tightrope—not when the perfect is so easily obtained by turning on the stereo. The perfect is accessible and repeatable. The struggle for perfection and its relationship to the human spirit is submerged and lost.

There is another dimension to the cult of perfectability, and that is centered in the nature of the experience and its environment. Greater and greater stress has been placed on the quality of musical sound. The automobile, that home away from home, is equipped with stereophonic tape decks. Sound in the home itself has progressed from high fidelity to stereophonic and to quadrophonic sound. The room has "living presence." The wired room is not a substitute for attending the concert; rather, electronics have transformed the living room into the concert hall—even though the room is comparatively miniscule when compared to the hall. The dimensions of the environment become even less important with the addition of earphones which allow for unadulterated, ear-to-ear sound. Now the concert hall is in your head. If the concert is literally shifted into the living room, is the aesthetic ambience of the concert hall also moved into the environment of the home? The two experiences are quite dissimilar, although the lines which distinguish between them have become increasingly blurred. Paradoxically, as multichannel sound streams into modern, boxlike living rooms, the live concert hall experience becomes increasingly more alien. The stress is placed on perfecting the auditory sense, to the degree that the total sensory involvement found in the live situation is absent. Lost is the dynamic involvement of individual and performer in which the auditory, visual, and tactile senses all play an important role. Parenthetically, living room habits have invaded many public events such as concerts and films, as extraneous conversations increasingly compete for attention.

Undoubtedly audio technology has altered our standards of excellence because of the ambiguity involved in the perception of medicated events. Concert hall is confused with living room. Mechanical and electronic perfection are jumbled with artistic quality. Part of the problem could be solved by identifying recordings which are "electronically enhanced." The solution of greater import is the education of the public to distinguish between modes of performance and the performance itself. In addition, it is necessary to articulate criteria in judging each form.

The perception of reality is increasingly dependent upon media technology, but our vision of the world, while increased in scope, is also distorted by the very media which serve us. The perception of now indicates that mediation can deemphasize authenticity while stressing availability of experience. The perception of perfection reveals how the struggle for purity of expression has been placed in the background as multiplicity of the unflawed is accentuated. The impact of media might be self-evident, but the effects upon our perception of reality are hidden behind the seductive rewards of media technology. Are the issues discussed in this essay important ones which require discussion and resolution, or is the ambiguity of perception merely an exercise in philosophical inquiry? The very fact that this question is asked in proxy for the reader suggests the degree to which the problems discussed have been lost in the exhilaration of technological progress.

> "Portions of this program
> were pre-recorded."
> Which portions?

Notes

1. Herbert Zettl, *Sight, Sound, Motion: Applied Media Aesthetics* (Belmont, California: Wadsworth Publishing Company, 1973), p. 254.
2. *Ibid.*, p. 255.
3. Artur Schnabel, *My Life and Music* (New York: St. Martin's Press, 1961), p. 96.
4. Henry Pleasants, *Serious Music—And All That Jazz!* (New York: Simon and Schuster, 1969), p. 91.

The Electric Revolution

Are you aware of the development of "schizophonia?" Do you partake of "audio analgesia?" These are terms coined by R. Murray Schafer. He refers to our sonic environment and implies the psychological changes resulting from the acoustical revolution. Schafer claims that the telephone, phonograph, and radio have produced portable acoustic space; this in turn has changed our definition of what is signal and what is noise. Human beings have always been surrounded by sound, but now we can and do create our own sonic environments and take them with us wherever we go.

The Electric Revolution extended many of the themes of the Industrial Revolution and added some new effects of its own. Owing to the increased transmission speed of electricity, the flat-line effect was extended to give the pitched tone, thus harmonizing the world on center frequencies of 25 and 40, then 50 and 60 cycles per second. Other extensions of trends already noted were the multiplication of sound producers and their imperialistic outsweep by means of amplification.

Two new techniques were introduced: the discovery of packaging and storing techniques for sound and the splitting of sounds from their original contexts—which I call schizophonia. The benefits of the electroacoustic transmission and reproduction of sound are well enough celebrated, but they should not obscure the fact that precisely at the time hi-fi was being engineered, the world soundscape was slipping into an all-time lo-fi condition.

A good many of the fundamental discoveries of the Electric Revolution had already been made by 1850: the electric cell, the storage cell, the dynamo, the electric arc light. The detailed application of these inventions occupied the remainder of the nineteenth century. It was during this period that the electric power station, the telephone, the radio telegraph, the phonograph and the moving picture came into existence. At first their commercial applications were limited. It was not until the improvement of the

From *The Tuning of the World: Toward a Theory of Soundscape Design,* by R. Murray Schafer. Copyright © 1977 by R. Murray Schafer. Reprinted by permission of Alfred A. Knopf, Inc.

dynamo by Werner Siemens (1856) and the alternator by Nikola Tesla (1887) that electrical power could become the generating force for the practical development of the discoveries.

One of the first products of the Electric Revolution, Morse's telegraph (1838), unintentionally dramatized the contradiction between discrete and contoured sound which, as I have said, separates slow from fast-paced societies. Morse used the long line of the telegraph wire to transmit messages broken in binary code, which still relied on digital adroitness, thus maintaining in the telegrapher's trained finger a skill that related him to the pianist and the scribe. Because the finger cannot be wiggled fast enough to produce the fused contour of sound, the telegraph ticks and stutters in the same way as its two contemporary inventions, Thurber's typewriter and Gatling's machine gun. As increased mobility and speed in communication continued to be desired, it was inevitable that, together with the act of letter-scratching, the telegraph should give way to the telephone.

The three most revolutionary sound mechanisms of the Electric Revolution were the telephone, the phonograph and the radio. With the telephone and the radio, sound was no longer tied to its original point in space; with the phonograph it was released from its original point in time. The dazzling removal of these restrictions has given modern man an exciting new power which modern technology has continually sought to render more effective.

The soundscape researcher is concerned with changes in perception and behavior. Let us, for instance, point up a couple of observable changes effected by the telephone, the first of the new instruments to be extensively marketed.

The telephone extended intimate listening across wide distances. As it is basically unnatural to be intimate at a distance, it has taken some time for humans to accustom themselves to the idea. Today North Americans raise their voices only on transcontinental or transoceanic calls; Europeans, however, still raise their voices to talk to the next town, and Asians shout at the telephone when talking to someone in the next street.

The capacity of the telephone to interrupt thought is more important, for it has undoubtedly contributed a good share to the abbreviation of written prose and the choppy speech of modern times. For instance, when Schopenhauer writes at the beginning of *The World as Will and Idea* that he wishes us to consider his entire book as one thought, we realize that he is about to make severe demands on himself and his readers. The real depreciation of concentration began after the advent of the telephone. Had

Schopenhauer written his book in my office, he would have completed the first sentence and the telephone would have rung. Two thoughts.

The telephone had already been dreamed of when Moses and Zoroaster conversed with God, and the radio as an instrument for the transmission of divine messages was well imagined before that. The phonograph, too, has a long history in the imagination of man, for to catch and preserve the tissue of living sound was an ancient ambition. In Babylonian mythology there are hints of a specially constructed room in one of the ziggurats where whispers stayed forever. There is a similar room (still in existence) in the Ali Qapu in Isfahan, though in its present derelict state it is difficult to know how it was supposed to have worked. Presumably its highly polished walls and floor gave sounds an abnormal reverberation time. In an ancient Chinese legend a king has a secret black box into which he speaks his orders, then sends them around his kingdom for his subjects to carry out, which I gloss to mean that there is *authority* in the magic of captured sound. With the invention of the telephone by Bell in 1876 and the phonograph by Charles Cros and Thomas Edison in 1877 the era of schizophonia was introduced.

Schizophonia

The Greek prefix *schizo* means split, separated; and *phone* is Greek for voice. *Schizophonia* refers to the split between an original sound and its electroacoustical transmission or reproduction. It is another twentieth-century development.

Originally all sounds were originals. They occurred at one time in one place only. Sounds were then indissolubly tied to the mechanisms that produced them. The human voice traveled only as far as one could shout. Every sound was uncounterfeitable, unique. Sounds bore resemblances to one another, such as the phonemes which go to make up the repetition of a word, but they were not identical. Tests have shown that it is physically impossible for nature's most rational and calculating being to reproduce a single phoneme in his own name twice in exactly the same manner.

Since the invention of electroacoustical equipment for the transmission and storage of sound, any sound, no matter how tiny, can be blown up and shot around the world, or packaged on tape or record for the generations of the future. We have split the sound from the maker of the sound. Sounds have been torn from their natural sockets and given an amplified and independent existence. Vocal sound, for instance, is no longer tied to a hole in the head but is free to issue from anywhere in the landscape. In the same instant it may issue from millions of holes in millions of public and private places around the world, or it may be stored to be reproduced at a later date, perhaps eventually hundreds of years after it was originally uttered. A record or tape collection may contain items from widely diverse cultures and historical periods in what would seem, to a person from any century but our own, a meaningless and surrealistic juxtaposition.

The desire to dislocate sounds in time and space had been evident for some time in the history of Western music, so that the recent technological developments were merely the consequences of aspirations that had already been effectively imagined. The secret *quomodo omnis generis instrumentorum Musica in remotissima spacia propagari possit* (whereby all forms of instrumental music could be transmitted to remote places) was a special preoccupation of the musician-inventor Athanasius Kircher, who discussed the matter in detail in his *Phonurgia Nova* of 1673. In the practical sphere, the introduction of dynamics, echo effects, the splitting of resources, the separation of soloist from the ensemble and the incorporation of instruments with specific referential qualities (horn, anvil, bells, etc.) were all attempts to create virtual spaces which were larger or different from natural room acoustics; just as the search for exotic folk music and the breaking forward and backward to find new or renew old musical resources represents a desire to transcend the present tense.

When, following the Second World War, the tape recorder made incisions into recorded material possible, any sound object could be cut out and inserted into any new context desired. Most recently, the quadraphonic sound system has made possible a 360-degree soundscape of moving and stationary sound events which allows any sound environment to be simulated in time and space. This provides for the complete portability of acoustic space. Any sonic environment can now become any other sonic environment.

We know that the territorial expansion of post-industrial sounds complemented the imperialistic ambitions of the Western nations. The loudspeaker was also invented by an imperialist, for it responded to the desire to dominate others with one's own sound. As the cry broadcasts distress, the loudspeaker communicates anxiety. "We should not have conquered Germany without . . . the loudspeaker," wrote Hitler in 1938.

I coined the term schizophonia in *The New Soundscape* intending it to be a nervous word. Related to schizophrenia, I wanted it to convey the same sense of aberration and drama. Indeed, the overkill of hi-fi gadgetry not only contributes generously to the lo-fi problem, but it creates a synthetic soundscape in which natural sounds are becoming increasingly unnatural while machine-made substitutes are providing the operative signals directing modern life.

Radio: Extended Acoustic Space

A character in one of Jorge Luis Borges's stories dreads mirrors because they multiply men. The same might be said of radios. By 1969, Americans were listening to 268,000,000 radios, that is, about one per citizen. Modern life has been ventriloquized. The domination of modern life by the radio did not take place unnoticed; but whereas opposition to the Industrial Revolution had come from the working classes, who feared the loss of their jobs, the principal opponents of the radio and the phonograph were the intellectuals. Emily Carr, who wrote and painted in the British Columbia wilderness, hated the radio when she first heard it in 1936.

> When I go to houses where they are turned on full blast I feel as if I'd go mad. Inexplicable torment all over. I thought I ought to get used to them and one was put in my house on trial this morning. I feel as if bees had swarmed in my nervous system. Nerves all jangling. Such a feeling of angry resentment at that horrid metallic voice. After a second I have to clap it off. Can't stand it. Maybe it's my imperfect hearing? It's one of the wonders of the age, simply marvelous. I know that but I *hate* it.

Hermann Hesse, in *Der Steppenwolf* (1927), was disturbed by the poor fidelity of the new electroacoustical devices for the reproduction of music.

> At once, to my indescribable astonishment and horror, the devilish metal funnel spat out, without more ado, its mixture of bronchial slime and chewed rubber; that noise that possessors of gramophones and radio sets are prevailed upon to call music. And behind the slime and the croaking there was, sure enough, like an old master beneath a layer of dirt, the noble outline of that divine music. I could distinguish the majestic structure and the deep wide breath and the full broad bowing of the strings.

But more than this, Hesse was revolted by the schizophonic incongruities of broadcasting.

> It takes hold of some music played where you please, without distinction or discretion, lamentably distorted, to boot, and chucks it into space to land where it has no business to be. . . . When you listen to radio you are a witness of the everlasting war between idea and appearance, between time and eternity, between the human and the divine . . . radio . . . projects the most

lovely music without regard into the most impossible places, into snug draw-
ing-rooms and attics and into the midst of chattering, guzzling, yawning and
sleeping listeners, and exactly as it strips this music of its sensuous beauty,
spoils and scratches and beslimes it and yet cannot altogether destroy its spirit.

Radio extended the outreach of sound to produce greatly expanded profiles, which were remarkable also because they formed interrupted acoustic
spaces. Never before had sound disappeared across space to reappear again
at a distance. The community, which had previously been defined by its
bell or temple gong, was now defined by its local transmitter.

The Nazis were the first to use radio in the interests of totalitarianism,
but they have not been the last; and little by little, in both East and West,
radio has been employed more ruthlessly in culture-molding. Readers of
Solzhenitsyn's novel *Cancer Ward* will recall the "constant yawping" of
the radio which greeted Vadim when he went to the hospital and the way
he detested it. I recall, twenty years ago, hearing the same loudspeakers
blaring out their cacophonies of patriotism and spleen on station platforms
and in public squares throughout Eastern Europe. But broadcasting has
now gone public in the West as well. It may be hard for younger readers
to appreciate what has happened but, up until about a decade ago, one of
the most salient differences between cities like London or Paris and Bucha-
rest or Mexico City was that in the former there were no radios or music
in public places, restaurants or shops. In those days, particularly during
the summer months, BBC announcers would regularly request listeners to
keep their radios at a low volume in order not to disturb the neighborhood. In a dramatic reversal of style, British Railways recently began
beaming the BBC regional service throughout railway stations (I have heard
it over loudspeakers in Brighton Railway Station, 1975). But they still have
a long way to go to catch Australian Railways, which plays the ABC light
program on trains from 7 a.m. to 11 p.m. during the three-day run from
Sydney to Perth. In my compartment in 1973 it was impossible to shut it
off.

In the early days one listened to the radio selectively by studying the
program schedule, but today programs are overlooked and are merely overheard. This change of habit prepared modern society to tolerate the walls
of sound with which human engineering now orchestrates the modern environment.

The radio was the first sound wall, enclosing the individual with the
familiar and excluding the enemy. In this sense it is related to the castle
garden of the Middle Ages which, with its birds and fountains, contra-

dicted the hostile environment of forest and wilderness. The radio has actually become the bird-song of modern life, the "natural" soundscape, excluding the inimical forces from outside. To serve this function sound need not be elaborately presented, any more than wallpaper has to be painted by Michelangelo to render the drawing room attractive. Thus, the development of greater fidelity in sound reproduction, which occupied the first half of the present century—and in a way may be thought of as analogous to the development of oil paints, which also rendered possible greater veracity in art—is now canceled by a tendency to return to simpler forms of expression. For instance, while the transition from mechanical to electrical recording (Harrison and Maxfield) extended the available band width from three to seven octaves, the transistor radio reduced it again to something like its former state. The habit of listening to transistor radios outdoors in the presence of additional ambient noise, often in circumstances which reduce the signal-to-noise ratio to approximately one to one, has in turn suggested the inclusion of additional noise which, in some popular music, is now engineered right onto the disc, often in the form of electroacoustical feedback. This, in turn, leads to new evaluations of what is signal and what is noise in the whole constantly changing field of aural perception.

The Shapes of Broadcasting

Radio programing needs to be analyzed in as much detail as an epic poem or musical composition, for in its themes and rhythms will be found the pulse of life. But detailed studies of this kind appear never to have been undertaken. . . . [I]t will not be out of place here to make a few general comments.

At first radio broadcasts were isolated presentations, surrounded by extended (silent) station breaks. This occasional approach to broadcasting, now absent from domestic radio, can still to some extent be experienced with shortwave broadcasts, where station breaks are often several minutes long and are accompanied by short musical phrases or signature tunes. (This attractive practice is only slightly spoiled by the unlikely choice of instruments used on some stations: thus, the calls of Jordan and Kuwait are played on the clarinet, those of Jamaica and Iran on the vibraphone—that is, they are played on instruments so distinctly non-indigenous that one might suppose they were originally recorded in New York.)

During the 1930s and 1940s schedules were filled out until the whole day was looped together in unsettled connectivity. The modern radio

schedule, a confection of material from various sources, joined in thoughtful, funny, ironic, absurd or provocative juxtapositions, has introduced
many contradictions into modern life and has perhaps contributed more
than anything else to the breakup of unified culture systems and values. It
is for this reason that the study of joins in broadcasting is of great importance. The montage was first employed in film because it was the first art
form to be cut and spliced; but since the invention of magnetic tape and
the compression of the schedule, the shapes of broadcasting have followed
the editor's scissors also.

The function of the montage is to make one plus one equal three. The
film producer Eisenstein—one of the first to experiment with montage—
defines the effect as consisting "in the fact that two film pieces of any kind,
placed together, inevitably combine into a new concept, a new quality,
arising out of that juxtaposition." The *non sequiturs* of the montage may
be incomprehensible to the innocent though they are easily accommodated
by the initiated. I recall one night in Chicago, at the height of the Vietnam
War, listening to an on-the-spot report of the grisly affair, sponsored by
Wrigley's Chewing Gum, whose jingle at the time was "Chew your little
cares away!" I mentioned the experience to a class of students at Northwestern University the next day. They were interested in my opposition to
the war, but failed to see my point about the gum. For them the elements
had been montaged as part of a way of life.

Since the advent of the singing commercial on North American radio,
popular music and advertising have formed the main material of the radio
montage, so that today, by means of quick cross-fades, direct cuts or "music under" techniques, songs and commercials follow one another in quick
and smooth succession, producing a commercial life style that is entertaining ("buy baubles for your bippy") and musical entertainment that is profitable ("five million sold").

Radio introduced the surrealistic soundscape, but other electroacoustical
devices have had an influence in rendering it acceptable. The record collection, which one may observe in almost every house of the civilized world,
is often equally eclectic and bizarre, containing stray items from different
periods or countries, all of which may nevertheless be stacked on the same
phonograph for successive replay.

I am trying to illustrate the irrationality of electroacoustic juxtposition-
ing in order that it might cease to be taken for granted. One last story. A
friend was once on an aircraft that supplies a selection of recorded programs of different types for earphone listening. Choosing the program of

classical music he settled back in his seat to listen to Wagner's *Meistersinger*. As the overture soared to a climax, the disturbed voice of the stewardess suddenly interrupted the music to announce: "Ladies and gentlemen, the toilets are plugged up and must be flushed with a glass of water."

As the format of radio tightened, its tempo increased, substituting superficiality for prolonged acts of concentration. Heavyweight fare like the famous BBC Third Programme was dismissed to be replaced by material with more twist and appeal. Each station and each country has its own tempo of broadcasting, but in general it has been speeded up over the years, and its tone is moving from the sedate toward the slaphappy. (I am speaking here only of Western-style broadcasting; I am not sufficiently familiar with the monolithic cultures of Russia or China.) In the West, material is being increasingly pushed together, overlapped. In a World Soundscape Project in 1973 we counted the number of separate items on four Vancouver radio stations over a typical eighteen-hour day. Each item (announcement, commercial, weather report, etc.) represented a change of focus. The results ran as follows:

Station	Total Number of Items	Hourly Average
CBU	635	35.5
CHQM	745	41.0
CJOR	996	55.5
CKLG	1097	61.0

Stations broadcasting popular music are the fastest-paced. The duration of individual items of any kind rarely exceeds three minutes on North American pop stations. Here the recording industry discloses a secret. On the old ten-inch shellac disc, the recording duration was limited to slightly over three minutes. As this was the first vehicle for popular music, all pop songs were abbreviated to meet this technical limitation. But curiously, when the long-play disc was introduced in 1948, the length of the average pop song did not increase in proportion. This suggests that some mysterious law concerning average attention span may have been inadvertently discovered by the older technology.

One acoustic effect is rarely heard on North American radios: silence. Only occasionally, during broadcasts of theater or classical music, do quiet and silence achieve their full potentiality. A graphic level recording of a popular station will show how the program material is made to ride at the maximum permissible level, a technique known as compression because the available dynamic range is compressed into very narrow limits. Such broadcasting shows no dynamic shadings or phrasing. It does not rest. It does not breathe. It has become a sound wall.

Sound Walls

Walls used to exist to delimit physical and acoustic space, to isolate private areas visually and to screen out acoustic interferences. Often this second function is unstressed, particularly in modern buildings. Confronted with this situation modern man has discovered what might be called *audioanalgesia*, that is, the use of sound as a painkiller, a distraction to dispel distractions. The use of audioanalgesia extends in modern life from its original use in the dental chair to wired background music in hotels, offices, restaurants and many other public and private places. Air-conditioners, which produce a continuous band of pink noise, are also instruments of audioanalgesia. It is important in this respect to realize that such masking sounds are not intended to be listened to consciously. Thus, the Moozak industry deliberately chooses music that is nobody's favorite and subjects it to unvenomed and innocuous orchestrations in order to produce a wraparound of "pretty," designed to mask unpleasant distractions in a manner that corresponds to the attractive packages of modern merchandising to disguise frequently cheesy contents.

Walls used to exist to isolate sounds. Today sound walls exist to isolate. In the same way the intense amplification of popular music does not stimulate sociability so much as it expresses the desire to experience individuation . . . aloneness . . . disengagement. For modern man, the sound wall has become as much a fact as the wall in space. The teenager lives in the continual presence of his radio, the housewife in the presence of her television set, the worker in the presence of engineered music systems designed to increase production. From Nova Scotia comes word of the continuous use of background music in school classrooms. The principal is pleased with the results and pronounces the experiment a success. From Sacramento, California, comes news of another unusual development: a library wired for rock music in which patrons are encouraged to talk. On the walls are signs stating NO SILENCE. The result: circulation, especially among the young, is up.

> They never sup without music; and there is always fruit served up after the meat; while they are at table, some burn perfumes and sprinkle about fragrant

ointments and sweet waters: in short, they want nothing that may cheer their spirits.

Sir Thomas Moore, *Utopia*

Moozak

If the Christmas card angels offer any proof, utopian creatures are forever smiling. Thus Moozak, the sound wall of paradise, never weeps. It is the honeyed antidote to hell on earth. Moozak starts out with the high motive of orchestrating paradise (it is often present in writings about utopias) but it always ends up as the embalming fluid of earthly boredom. It is natural then that the testing-ground for the Moozak industry should have been the U.S.A., with its highly idealistic Constitution and the cruddy realities of its modern life styles. The service pages of the telephone directories beam out its advertisements to clients in every North American city.

MUZAK IS MORE THAN MUSIC—PSYCHOLOGICALLY PLANNED—FOR THE TIME AND PLACE—JUST FLIP THE SWITCH—NO MACHINES TO ATTEND / FRESH PROGRAMS EACH DAY—NO REPETITION—ADVISED BY BOARD OF SCIENTIFIC advisors—OVER 30 YEARS OF RESEARCH—PAGING AND SOUND SERVICE—FAST ROUND-THE-CLOCK SERVICE—MUZAK BRAND EQUIPMENT—OFFICES—INDUSTRIAL PLANTS—BANKS—HOSPITALS—RETAIL STORES—HOTELS AND MOTELS—RESTAURANTS—PROFESSIONAL OFFICES—*SPECIALISTS IN THE PSYCHOLOGICAL AND PHYSIOLOGICAL APPLICATIONS OF MUSIC.*

Facts on Moozak program design are elementary. The programs are selected and put together in several American cities for mass distribution. ". . . program specialists . . . assign values to the elements in a musical recording; i.e., tempo (number of beats per minute); rhythm (waltz, fox trot, march); instrumentation (brass, woodwinds, strings), and orchestra size (5 piece combo, 30 piece symphony, etc.)." There are few solo vocalists or instrumentalists to distract the listener. The same programs are played to both people and cows, but despite the happy claim that production has in both cases been increased, neither animal seems yet to have been elevated into the Elysian Fields. While the programs are constructed to give what the advertising calls "a progression of time"—that is, the illusion that time is dynamically and significantly passing—the implicit malaise behind the claim is that for most people time continues to hang heavily. "Each 15-minute segment of MUZAK contains a rising stimulus which provides a logical sense of forward movement. This affects boredom or monotony and fatigue."

Although no precise growth statistics have ever been published, there can be no doubt that these bovine sound slicks are spreading. This does not perhaps so much indicate a lack of public interest in silence as it demonstrates that there is more profit to be made out of sound, for another claim of the Mooze industry is that it provides a "relaxed background to profit." When we interviewed 108 consumers and 25 employees in a Vancouver shopping mall, we discovered that while only 25 percent of the shoppers thought they spent more as a result of the background music, 60 percent of the employees thought they did.

Against the slop and spawn of Moozak and broadcast music in public places a wave of protest is now clearly discernible. Most notable is a resolution unanimously passed by the General Assembly of the International Music Council of UNESCO in Paris in October, 1969.

> We denounce unanimously the intolerable infringement of individual freedom and of the right of everyone to silence, because of the abusive use, in private and public places, of recorded or broadcast music. We ask the Executive Committee of the International Music Council to initiate a study from all angles—medical, scientific and juridical—without overlooking its artistic and educational aspects, and with a view to proposing to UNESCO, and to the proper authorities everywhere, measures calculated to put an end to this abuse.

There is a parallel to this resolution: when, in 1864, Michael Bass proposed his Bill to prohibit the sounds of street singing in the city of London, he drew substantial support from the musical profession itself. With the 1969 UNESCO resolution sonic overkill was apprehended by the musicians of the world as a serious problem. For the first time in history an international organization involved primarily with the *production* of sounds suddenly turned its attention to their *reduction*. In *The New Soundscape* I had already warned music educators that they would now have to be as concerned about the prevention of sounds as about their creation, and I suggested that they should join noise abatement societies to familiarize themselves with this new theme for the music room.

In any historical study of the soundscape, the researcher will repeatedly be struck by shifts in the perceptual habits of a society, instances where the figure and the ground exchange roles. The case of Moozak is one such instance. Throughout history music has existed as figure—a desirable collection of sounds to which the listener gives special attention. Moozak reduces music to ground. It is a deliberate concession to lo-fi-ism. It multiplies sounds. It reduces a sacred art to a slobber. Moozak is music that is not to be listened to.

By creating a fuss about sounds we snap them back into focus as figures. The way to defeat Moozak is, therefore, quite simple: listen to it.

Moozak resulted from the abuse of the radio. The abuse of Moozak has suggested another type of sound wall which is now rapidly becoming a fixture in all modern buildings: the screen of white noise, or as its proponents prefer to call it "acoustic perfume." The hiss of the air-conditioner and the roar of the furnace have been exploited by the acoustical engineering profession to mask distracting sound, and where they are in themselves not sufficiently loud, they have been augmented by the installation of white noise generators. A desideratum from America's most prominent firm of acoustical engineers to the head of a music department shows us that if music can be used to mask noise, noise can also be used to mask music. It ran: "Music Library: There should be enough mechanical noise to mask page turning and foot movement sounds." The mask hides the face. Sound walls hide characteristic soundscapes under fictions.

Prime Unity or Tonal Center

In the Indian *anāhata* and in the Western Music of the Spheres man has constantly sought some prime unity, some central sound against which all other vibrations may be measured. In diatonic or modal music it is the fundamental or tonic of the mode of scale that binds all other sounds into relationship. In China an artificial center of gravity was created in 239 B.C. when the Bureau of Weights and Measures established the Yellow Bell or Huang Chung as the tone from which all others were measured.

It is, however, only in the electronic age that international tonal centers have been achieved; in countries operating on an alternating current of 60 cycles, it is this sound which now provides the resonant frequency for it will be heard (together with its harmonics) in the operation of all electrical devices from lights and amplifiers to generators. Where C is tuned to 256 cycles, this resonant frequency is B natural. In ear training exercises I have discovered that students find B natural much the easiest pitch to retain and to recall spontaneously. Also during meditation exercises, after the whole body has been relaxed and students are asked to sing the tone of "prime unity"—the tone which seems to arise naturally from the center of their being—B natural is more frequent than any other. I have also experimented with this in Europe where the resonant electrical frequency of 50 cycles is approximately G sharp. At the Stuttgart Music High School I led a group of students in a series of relaxation exercises and then asked them to hum the tone of "prime unity." They centered on G sharp.

Electrical equipment will often produce resonant harmonics and in a quiet city at night a whole series of steady pitches may be heard from street lighting, signs or generators. When we were studying the soundscape of the Swedish village of Skruv in 1975, we encountered a large number of these and plotted their profiles and pitches on a map. We were surprised to find that together they produced a G-sharp major triad, which the F-sharp whistles of passing trains turned into a dominant seventh chord. As we moved about the streets on quiet evenings, the town played melodies.

The Electric Revolution has thus given us new tonal centers of prime unity against which all other sounds are now balanced. Like mobiles, whose movements may be measured from the string on which they are suspended, the sound mobiles of the modern world are now interpretable by means of the thin line fixture of the operating electrical current.

The Imprisoning of Reality

Does the camera "see" things better than you do? Are photos more "real" than what you saw or can remember? These and other related questions are explored by Susan Sontag in this excerpt from her provocative book, *On Photography*.

Although most of us do not think of photography as a mass medium in the usual sense, Sontag describes how it is a mediated experience which is carried out on a massive scale; one which has become institutionalized in our society. What is more important, she explains, is that reality is defined by photography.

Reality has always been interpreted through the reports given by images; and philosophers since Plato have tried to loosen our dependence on images by evoking the standard of an image-free way of apprehending the real. But when, in the mid-nineteenth century, the standard finally seemed attainable, the retreat of old religious and political illusions before the advance of humanistic and scientific thinking did not—as anticipated—create mass defections to the real. On the contrary, the new age of unbelief strengthened the allegiance to images. The credence that could no longer be given to realities understood *in the form of* images was now being given to realities understood *to be* images, illusions. In the preface to the second edition (1843) of *The Essence of Christianity*, Feuerbach observes about "our era" that it "prefers the image to the thing, the copy to the original, the representation to the reality, appearance to being"—while being aware of doing just that. And his premonitory complaint has been transformed in the twentieth century into a widely agreed-on diagnosis: that a society becomes "modern" when one of its chief activities is producing and consuming images, when images that have extraordinary powers to determine our demands upon reality and are themselves coveted substitutes for firsthand experience become indispensable to the health of the economy, the stability of the polity, and the pursuit of private happiness.

Feuerbach's words—he is writing a few years after the invention of the camera—seem, more specifically, a presentiment of the impact of photography. For the images that have virtually unlimited authority in a modern society are mainly photographic images; and the scope of that authority stems from the properties peculiar to images taken by cameras.

Such images are indeed able to usurp reality because first of all a photograph is not only an image (as a painting is an image), an interpretation of the real; it is also a trace, something directly stenciled off the real, like a footprint or a death mask. While a painting, even one that meets photographic standards of resemblance, is never more than the stating of an interpretation, a photograph is never less than the registering of an emanation (light waves reflected by objects)—a material vestige of its subject in a way that no painting can be. Between two fantasy alternatives, that Holbein the Younger had lived long enough to have painted Shakespeare or that a prototype of the camera had been invented early enough to have photographed him, most Bardolators would choose the photograph. This is not just because it would presumably show what Shakespeare really looked like, for even if the hypothetical photograph were faded, barely legible, a brownish shadow, we would probably still prefer it to another glorious Holbein. Having a photograph of Shakespeare would be like having a nail from the True Cross.

Most contemporary expressions of concern that an image-world is replacing the real one continue to echo, as Feuerbach did, the Platonic depreciation of the image: true insofar as it resembles something real, sham because it is no more than a resemblance. But this venerable naïve realism is somewhat beside the point in the era of photographic images, for its blunt contrast between the image ("copy") and the thing depicted (the "original")—which Plato repeatedly illustrates with the example of a painting—does not fit a photograph in so simple a way. Neither does the contrast help in understanding image-making at its origins, when it was a practical, magical activity, a means of appropriating or gaining power over something. The further back we go in history, as E. H. Gombrich has observed, the less sharp is the distinction between images and real things; in primitive societies, the thing and its image were simply two different, that is, physically distinct, manifestations of the same energy or spirit. Hence, the supposed efficacy of images in propitiating and gaining control over powerful presences. Those powers, those presences were present in *them*.

For defenders of the real from Plato to Feuerbach to equate image with mere appearance—that is, to presume that the image is absolutely distinct from the object depicted—is part of that process of desacralization which separates us irrevocably from the world of sacred times and places in which an image was taken to participate in the reality of the object depicted. What defines the originality of photography is that, at the very moment in the long, increasingly secular history of painting when secularism is entirely triumphant, it revives—in wholly secular terms—something like the primitive status of images. Our irrepressible feeling that the photographic process is something magical has a genuine basis. No one takes an easel painting to be in any sense co-substantial with its subject; it only represents or refers. But a photograph is not only like its subject, a homage to the subject. It is part of, an extension of that subject; and a potent means of acquiring it, of gaining control over it.

Photography is acquisition in several forms. In its simplest form, we have in a photograph surrogate possession of a cherished person or thing, a possession which gives photographs some of the character of unique objects. Through photographs, we also have a consumer's relation to events, both to events which are part of our experience and to those which are not—a distinction between types of experience that such habit-forming consumership blurs. A third form of acquisition is that, through image-making and image-duplicating machines, we can acquire something as information (rather than experience). Indeed, the importance of photographic images as the medium through which more and more events enter our experience is, finally, only a byproduct of their effectiveness in furnishing knowledge dissociated from and independent of experience.

This is the most inclusive form of photographic acquisition. Through being photographed, something becomes part of a system of information, fitted into schemes of classification and storage which range from the crudely chronological order of snapshot sequences pasted in family albums to the dogged accumulations and meticulous filing needed for photography's uses in weather forecasting, astronomy, microbiology, geology, police work, medical training and diagnosis, military reconnaissance, and art history. Photographs do more than redefine the stuff of ordinary experience (people, things, events, whatever we see—albeit differently, often inattentively—with natural vision) and add vast amounts of material that we never see at all. Reality as such is redefined—as an item for exhibition, as a record for scrutiny, as a target for surveillance. The photographic exploration and duplication of the world fragments continuities and feeds the pieces into an interminable dossier, thereby providing possibilities of control that could not even be dreamed of under the earlier system of recording information:writing.

That photographic recording is always, potentially, a means of control was already recognized when such powers were in their infancy. In 1850, Delacroix noted in his *Journal* the success of some "experiments in photography" being made at Cambridge, where astronomers were photographing the sun and the moon and had managed to obtain a pinhead-size impression of the star Vega. He added the following "curious" observation:

> Since the light of the star which was daguerreotyped took twenty years to traverse the space separating it from the earth, the ray which was fixed on the plate had consequently left the celestial sphere a long time before Daguerre had discovered the process by means of which we have just gained control of this light.

Leaving behind such puny notions of control as Delacroix's, photography's progress has made ever more literal the senses in which a photograph gives control over the thing photographed. The technology that has already minimized the extent to which the distance separating photographer from subject affects the precision and magnitude of the image; provided ways to photograph things which are unimaginably small as well as those, like stars, which are unimaginably far; rendered picture-taking independent of light itself (infrared photography) and freed the picture-object from its confinement to two dimensions (holography); shrunk the interval between sighting the picture and holding it in one's hands (from the first Kodak, when it took weeks for a developed roll of film to be returned to the amateur photographer, to the Polaroid, which ejects the image in a few seconds); not only got images to move (cinema) but achieved their simultaneous recording and transmission (video)—this technology has made photography an incomparable tool for deciphering behavior, predicting it, and interfering with it.

Photography has powers that no other image-system has ever enjoyed because, unlike the earlier ones, it is *not* dependent on an image maker. However, carefully the photographer intervenes in setting up and guiding the image-making process, the process itself remains an optical-chemical (or electronic) one, the workings of which are automatic, the machinery for which will inevitably be modified to provide still more detailed and, therefore, more useful maps of the real. The mechanical genesis of these images, and the literalness of the powers they confer, amounts to a new relationship between image and reality. And if photography could also be said to restore the most primitive relationship—the partial identity of image and object—the potency of the image is now experienced in a very different way. The primitive notion of the efficacy of images presumes that images possess the qualities of real things, but our inclination is to attribute to real things the qualities of an image.

As everyone knows, primitive people fear that the camera will rob them of some part of their being. In the memoir he published in 1900, at the end of a very long life, Nadar reports that Balzac had a similar "vague dread" of being photographed. His explanation, according to Nadar, was that

> every body in its natural state was made up of a series of ghostly images superimposed in layers to infinity, wrapped in infinitesimal films. . . . Man never having been able to create, that is to make something material from an apparition, from something impalpable, or to make from nothing, an object—each Daguerreian operation was therefore going to lay hold of, detach, and use up one of the layers of the body on which it focused.

It seems fitting for Balzac to have had this particular brand of trepidation—"Was Balzac's fear of the Daguerreotype real or feigned?" Nadar asks. "It was real . . ."—since the procedure of photography is a materializing, so to speak, of what is most original in his procedure as a novelist. The Balzacian operation was to magnify tiny details, as in a photographic enlargement, to juxtapose incongruous traits or items, as in a photographic layout: made expressive in this way, any one thing can be connected with everything else. For Balzac, the spirit of an entire milieu could be disclosed by a single material detail, however paltry or arbitrary-seeming. The whole of a life may be summed up in a momentary appearance.[1] And a change in appearances is a change in the person, for he refused to posit any "real" person ensconced behind these appearances. Balzac's fanciful theory, expressed to Nadar, that a body is composed of an infinite series of "ghostly images," eerily parallels the supposedly realistic theory expressed in his novels, that a person is an aggregate of appearances, appearances which can be made to yield, by proper focusing, infinite layers of significance. To view reality as an endless set of situations which mirror each other, to extract analogies from the most dissimilar things, is to anticipate the characteristic form of perception stimulated by photographic images. Reality itself has started to be understood as a kind of writing, which has to be decoded—even as photographed images were themselves first compared to writing. (Niepce's name for the process whereby the image appears on the plate was heliography, sun-writing; Fox Talbot called the camera "the pencil of nature.")

The problem with Feuerbach's contrast of "original" with "copy" is its static definitions of reality and image. It assumes that what is real persists, unchanged and intact, while only images have changed: shored up by the most tenuous claims to credibility, they have somehow become more seductive. But the notions of image and reality are complementary. When the notion of reality changes, so does that of the image, and vice versa. "Our era" does not prefer images to real things out of perversity but partly in response to the ways in which the notion of what is real has been progressively complicated and weakened, one of the early ways being the criticism of reality as façade which arose among the enlightened middle classes in the last century. (This was of course the very opposite of the effect intended.) To reduce large parts of what has hitherto been regarded as real to mere fantasy, as Feuerbach did when he called religion "the dream of the human mind" and dismissed theological ideas as psychological projections; or to inflate the random and trivial details of everyday life into ciphers of hidden historical and psychological forces, as Balzac did in his encyclopedia of social reality in novel form—these are themselves ways of experiencing reality as a set of appearances, an image.

Few people in this society share the primitive dread of cameras that comes from thinking of the photograph as a material part of themselves. But some trace of the magic remains: for example, in our reluctance to tear up or throw away the photograph of a loved one, especially of someone dead or far away. To do so is a ruthless gesture of rejection. In *Jude the Obscure* it is Jude's discovery that Arabella has sold the maple frame with the photograph of himself in it which he gave her on their wedding day that signifies to Jude "the utter death of every sentiment in his wife" and is "the conclusive little stroke to demolish all sentiment in him." But the true modern primitivism is not to regard the image as a real thing; photographic images are hardly that real. Instead, reality has come to seem more and more like what we are shown by cameras. It is common now for people to insist about their experience of a violent event in which they were caught up—a plane crash, a shoot-out, a terrorist bombing—that "it seemed like a movie." This is said, other descriptions seeming insufficient, in order to explain how real it was. While many people in non-industrialized countries still feel apprehensive when being photographed, divining it to be some kind of trespass, an act of disrespect, a sublimated looting of the personality or the culture, people in industrialized countries seek to have their photographs taken—feel that they are images, and are made real by photographs.

A steadily more complex sense of the real creates its own compensatory fervors and simplifications, the most addictive of which is picture-taking. It is as if photographers, responding to an increasingly depleted sense of reality, were looking for a transfusion—traveling to new experiences, refreshing the old ones. Their ubiquitous activities amount to the most radical, and the safest, version of mobility. The urge to have new experiences is translated into the urge to take photographs: experience seeking a crisis-proof form.

As the taking of photographs seems almost obligatory to those who travel about, the passionate collecting of them has special appeal for those confined—either by choice, incapacity, or coercion—to indoor space. Photograph collections can be used to make a substitute world, keyed to exalting or consoling or tantalizing images. A photograph can be the starting point of a romance (Hardy's Jude had already fallen in love with Sue Bridehead's photograph before he met her), but it is more common for the erotic relation to be not only created by but understood as limited to the photographs. In Cocteau's *Les Enfants Terribles*, the narcissistic brother and sister share their bedroom, their "secret room," with images of boxers, movie stars, and murderers. Isolating themselves in their lair to live out their private legend, the two adolescents put up these photographs, a private pantheon. On one wall of cell No. 426 in Fresnes Prison in the early 1940s Jean Genet pasted the photographs of twenty criminals he had clipped from newspapers, twenty faces in which he discerned "the sacred sign of the monster," and in their honor wrote *Our Lady of the Flowers;* they served as his muses, his models, his erotic talismans. They watch over my little routines," writes Genet—conflating reverie, masturbation, and writing—and "are all the family I have and my only friends." For stay-at-homes, prisoners, and the self-imprisoned, to live among the photographs of glamorous strangers is a sentimental response to isolation and an insolent challenge to it.

J. G. Ballard's novel *Crash* (1973) describes a more specialized collecting of photographs in the service of sexual obsession: photographs of car accidents which the narrator's friend Vaughan collects while preparing to stage his own death in a car crash. The acting out of his erotic vision of car death is anticipated and the fantasy itself further eroticized by the repeated perusal of these photographs. At one end of the spectrum, photographs are objective data; at the other end, they are items of psychological science fiction. And as in even the most dreadful, or neutral-seeming, reality a sexual imperative can be found, so even the most banal photograph-document can mutate into an emblem of desire. The mug shot is a clue to a detective, an erotic fetish to a fellow thief. To Hofrat Behrens, in *The Magic Mountain*, the pulmonary x rays of his patients are diagnostic tools. To Hans Castorp, serving an indefinite sentence in Behrens's TB sanatorium, and made lovesick by the enigmatic, unattainable Clavdia Chauchat, "Clavdia's X-ray portrait, showing not her face, but the delicate bony structure of the upper half of her body, and the organs of the thoracic cavity, surrounded by the pale, ghostlike envelope of flesh," is the most precious of trophies. The "transparent portrait" is a far more intimate vestige of his beloved than the Hofrat's painting of Clavdia, that "exterior portrait," which Hans had once gazed at with such longing.

Photographs are a way of imprisoning reality, understood as recalcitrant, inaccessible; of making it stand still. Or they enlarge a reality that is felt to be shrunk, hollowed out, perishable, remote. One can't possess reality, one can possess (and be possessed by) images—as, according to Proust, most ambitious of voluntary prisoners, one can't possess the present but one can possess the past. Nothing could be more unlike the self-sacrificial travail of an artist like Proust than the effortlessness of picture-taking, which must be the sole activity resulting in accredited works of art in which a single movement, a touch of the finger, produces a complete work. While the Proustian labors presuppose that reality is distant, photography implies instant access to the real. But the results of this practice of instant access are another way of creating distance. To possess the world in the form of images is, precisely, to reexperience the unreality and remoteness of the real.

The strategy of Proust's realism presumes distance from what is normally experienced as real, the present, in order to reanimate' what is usually available only in a remote and shadowy form, the past—which is where the present becomes in his sense real, that is, something that can be possessed. In this effort photographs were of no help. Whenever Proust mentions photographs, he does so disparagingly: as a synonym for a shallow, too exclusively visual, merely voluntary relation to the past, whose yield is insignificant compared with the deep discoveries to be made by responding to cues given by all the senses—the technique he called "involuntary memory." One can't imagine the Overture to *Swann's Way* ending with the narrator's coming across a snapshot of the parish church at Combray and the savoring of *that* visual crumb, instead of the taste of the humble madeleine dipped in tea, making an entire part of his past spring into view. But this is not because a photograph cannot evoke memories (it can, depending on the quality of the viewer rather than of the photograph) but because of what Proust makes clear about his own demands upon imaginative recall, that it be not just extensive and accurate but give the texture and essence of things. And by considering photographs only so far as he could use them, as an instrument of memory, Proust somewhat misconstrues what photographs are: not so much an instrument of memory as an invention of it or a replacement.

It is not reality that photographs make immediately accessible, but images. For example, now all adults can know exactly how they and their parents and grandparents looked as children—a knowledge not available to anyone before the invention of cameras, not even to that tiny minority among whom it was customary to commission paintings of their children. Most of these portraits were less informative than any snapshot. And even the very wealthy usually owned just one portrait of themselves or any of their forebears as children, that is, an image of one moment of childhood, whereas it is common to have many photographs of oneself, the camera offering the possibility of possessing a complete record, at all ages. The point of the standard portraits in the bourgeois household of the eighteenth and nineteenth centuries was to confirm an ideal of the sitter (proclaiming social standing, embellishing personal appearance); given this purpose, it is clear why their owners did not feel the need to have more than one. What the photograph-record confirms is, more modestly, simply that the subject exists; therefore, one can never have too many.

The fear that a subject's uniqueness was leveled by being photographed was never so frequently expressed as in the 1850s, the years when portrait photography gave the first example of how cameras could create instant fashions and durable industries. In Melville's *Pierre*, published at the start of the decade, the hero, another fevered champion of voluntary isolation,

> considered with what infinite readiness now, the most faithful portrait of any one could be taken by the Daguerreotype, whereas in former times a faithful portrait was only within the power of the moneyed, or mental aristocrats of the earth. How natural then the inference, that instead of; as in old times, immortalizing a genius, a portrait now only *dayalized* a dunce. Besides, when every body has his portrait published, true distinction lies in not having yours published at all.

But if photographs demean, paintings distort in the opposite way: they make grandiose. Melville's intuition is that all forms of portraiture in the business civilization are compromised; at least, so it appears to Pierre, a paragon of alienated sensibility. Just as a photograph is too little in a mass society, a painting is too much. The nature of a painting, Pierre observes, makes it

> better entitled to reverence than the man; inasmuch as nothing belittling can be imagined concerning the portrait, whereas many unavoidably belittling things can be fancied as touching the man.

Even if such ironies can be considered to have been dissolved by the completeness of photography's triumph, the main difference between a painting and a photograph in the matter of portraiture still holds. Paintings invariably sum up; photographs usually do not. Photographic images are pieces of evidence in an ongoing biography or history. And one photograph, unlike one painting, implies that there will be others.

"Ever—the Human Document to keep the present and the future in touch with the past," said Lewis Hine. But what photography supplies is not only a record of the past but a new way of dealing with the present, as the effects of the countless billions of contemporary photograph-documents attest. While old photographs fill out our mental image of the past, the photographs being taken now transform what is present into a mental image, like the past. Cameras establish an inferential relation to the present (reality is known by its traces), provide an instantly retroactive view of experience. Photographs give mock forms of possession: of the past, the present, even the future. In Nabokov's *Invitation to a Beheading* (1938), the prisoner Cincinnatus is shown the "photohoroscope" of a child cast by the sinister M'sieur Pierre: an album of photographs of little Emmie as an infant, then a small child, then pre-pubescent, as she is now, then—by retouching and using photographs of her mother—of Emmie the adolescent, the bride, the thirty-year old, concluding with a photograph at age forty, Emmie on her deathbed. A "parody of the work of time" is what Nabokov calls this exemplary artifact; it is also a parody of the work of photography.

Photography, which has so many narcissistic uses, is also a powerful instrument for depersonalizing our relation to the world; and the two uses are complementary. Like a pair of binoculars with no right or wrong end, the camera makes exotic things near, intimate; and familiar things small, abstract, strange, much farther away. It offers, in one easy, habit-forming activity, both participation and alienation in our own lives and those of others—allowing us to participate, while confirming alienation.

Note

1. I am drawing on the account of Balzac's realism in Erich Auerbach's *Mimesis*. The passage that Auerbach describes from the beginning of *Le Père Goriot* (1834)—Balzac is describing the dining room of the Vauquer pension at seven in the morning and the entry of Madame Vauquer—could hardly be more explicit (or proto-Proustian). "Her whole person," Balzac writes, "explains the pension, as the pension implies her person. . . . The short-statured woman's blowsy *embonpoint* is the product of the life here, as typhoid is the consequence of the exhalations of a hospital. Her knitted wool petticoat, which is longer than her outer skirt (made of an old dress), and whose wadding is escaping by the gaps in the splitting material, sums up the drawing-room, the dining room, the little garden, announces the cooking and gives an inkling of the boarders. When she is there, the spectacle is complete."

GEORGE LELLIS

Perception in the Cinema: A Fourfold Confusion

This article presents a unique view of cinema form and function. It describes the four fundamental perceptual contradictions which define the film experience. It is this confounding of perception, according to Lellis, that makes motion pictures interesting and exciting. We all know that movies are not "real," yet filmic technique presents actions and locations so realistically that we are transported to another time and place where objects and events have their own reality. If, as the author contends, films produce their own reality, do other media also have a unique reality?

Movies mix perception with deception. Film is a medium which helps us to see the world as we might not otherwise. Our perception of the world through film is based on four fundamental areas of perceptual confusion:

1. the technical area, whereby most movies seek to hide the methods by which they produce their illusions
2. the boundary between theatrical presentation and what we customarily call "real life"
3. the contradictory nature of cinema as both public entertainment and a replication of subjective, individual, and often dreamlike experience
4. our tendency to experience a film as spontaneous, uninterpreted reality, even while the very nature of the medium tends to invest a movie's imagery with symbolic force and significance.

The pleasure of watching a film comes from the constant interplay and dialectic between these contradictory tendencies.

The Confusion of Continuity

Film historians often trace the birth of the storytelling film to Georges Méliès, who performed trick photography to dazzle his audiences with fantastic, unreal images. Méliès had originally been a magician, a conjurer, and he found in the film medium an extension of a whole tradition of magical illusion making.

387

All movies are a kind of magical conjuring of images. Moving pictures are not really pictures that move, but rather a succession of still images projected so quickly that they appear to move. Cinema is, in the words of theorist Pascal Bonitzer, "interested in what it cannot be." That is, it is built on two other fundamental illusions: the illusion of off-screen space and the illusion of continuity between shots.[1]

The traditional movie seeks always to imply a world larger than what is in a particular frame at the moment. (In reality what is usually beyond the frame are a cameraman, a director, lighting and sound equipment, visitors to the set, and a host of other people and objects which would destroy the illusion the film is creating.) We are encouraged to think of what is in the frame as part of a larger whole.

Filmmakers use editing to create a sense of both spatial continuity (by showing what is implied beyond the edges of the frame of a previous shot) and temporal continuity. Although movies are usually photographed out of sequence and in bits and pieces, these pieces are assembled in such a way as to minimize audience consciousness of that process. Filmmakers attempt to create the illusion of a smooth, uninterrupted continuity between shots in a given scene while they hide the process whereby they create this convincing illusion.[2] The standard Hollywood rules of filmmaking are that the best creative decisions in terms of framing, cutting, camera angles and movement are those that do not call attention to themselves but allow the viewer to become involved in the plot, characters and action. They are a form of magic and deception that we take for granted.

Film magic differs from the kind that can be achieved in a live performance. Theorists of the medium such as Hugo Münsterberg and Jean Mitry have observed how every technique of all but the most primitive filmmaking is an analogue to some type of physiological human perception.[3] The close-up simulates actual physical intimacy by narrowing the field of what one can see. Camera movement approximates the sensations of human movement through space (to a point where some viewers may get nauseous when a camera is placed on a moving roller coaster). Mitry considers the use of the zoom displeasing precisely because there is no physiological analogue to it in human perception.

Thus the film medium becomes a form of participatory magic. In the traditional theater, one can never be more than just an extremely involved observer to the action. In film, however, a subjective camera shot can show the viewer exactly what a character sees; a tracking shot allows him to move exactly as the character is moving; a pan allows him to "turn his head." In the theater, the willing suspension of disbelief on which drama is based is primarily an intellectual exercise. At the movies, one submits to an experiential contradiction whereby one has physiological sensations of what one knows to be false.

Film is a medium in which inanimate, discreet, two-dimensional pictures are made to simulate subjective human experience. Our pleasure at watching a film is based on the essential contradiction between what is real and what is illusory, between what we believe and what we pretend to believe.

In this respect, the kind of recording of an actor's performance that goes on in a film is very different from that of a musical performer on a phonograph record. Although there are some noteworthy exceptions, in most cases even the best stereophonic, high fidelity phonograph equipment is still viewed as a substitute for a live performance. The attraction of seeing, let us say, Liza Minnelli or Richard Burton on the screen is very different from the satisfaction we get from a live stage performance. With the latter, one can only observe from a distance. On screen, one can approach them without fear, get closer to them by means of the close-up than would otherwise be socially acceptable, invade what anthropologists would call their "personal space."[4] Movie stars are literally larger than life when projected on the screen and part of the magic of film is to give us the feeling of relating intimately to them.

Most of the so-called techniques of the narrative film are deceptions. They create a sense of spatial and temporal continuity where none may previously have existed. They create the false sense of a complete world within the film.

The Confusion of Reality

In any film we are aware of two levels of reality. One is the movie's natural reality; the second its theatrical reality. On the natural level, a film documents the reality that is put in front of it. We see what certain locations look like and the physical qualities of certain actors. In some instances we may see real people doing activities which they would still be doing even if the camera were not there. On the theatrical level, we realize that some things may have been staged for the camera. Actors may be reciting lines that were written for them. There may be artificial sets or lighting effects. And if nothing has been staged or arranged for the camera, certain things may still be dramatized or emphasized through effects of composition, camera movement and editing.

Few films can escape combining these levels. Scientific documents recording natural phenomena probably seek to avoid the theatrical level. A totally animated film may have no natural level. But theatrical or fiction films combine these two to an extent. A film may emphasize one level or another, but even some films we label "documentary" have a highly developed theatrical side.

The result of this mixture is that filmmakers and audiences alike often confuse the two levels of reality. Sometimes the confusion is intentional, sometimes it is not. Films tend either to dramatize the natural reality they record, or naturalize the dramatic substance of what they present. In the first case, the film medium changes our perception of the real world. In the second, the filmmaker uses the real world to make a fictional story more credible. Let us consider each case.

Films May Dramatize the Natural

The very act of making a film often encourages a filmmaker to bring out what is inherently theatrical in his subject. The simple need to edit material forces him to pick out what may be most unusual or dramatic. The very insertion of a close-up privileges one object or face over another, and suggests the reshaping of materials from reality into some sort of familiar structure.

It is standard practice to praise a documentary filmmaker for his sense of dramatic structure. That is, documentary material becomes most effective, most watchable, most appreciated by an audience when it is manipulated to give shots a sense of progression and point. Critics consider Robert Flaherty to be the father of the documentary film, yet what Flaherty did in *Nanook of the North* and other works was not simply to show exotic and far away places; countless newsreels had done that from almost the very beginning of the medium. Rather, Flaherty's contribution was in his use of dramatic structure and filmmaking technique. Flaherty was, not surprisingly, also accused of falsifying Eskimo life. The world's first great documentary filmmaker achieved his status precisely by injecting elements of theatricality into his work.

All of those elements that give a documentary a look of professionalism, such as smooth continuity, music or the use of commentary, are elements that impose something of an artificial structure on the materials being shaped. The more control a filmmaker exercises over his materials, the more risk there is of falsifying them. Yet attempts to avoid the falsification that comes with slickness do not necessarily avoid the confusion of reality with fiction. Filmmakers in the *cinéma vérité* movement, where camera-men with lightweight equipment follow people around at their everyday business with relative spontaneity, have observed that the process of pho-tographing people brings out a certain latent exhibitionism. Critics often accuse the subjects of these films of overprojecting their feelings, of drama-tizing themselves—in short, of acting. Even if filmmakers are simply more inclined to turn their cameras on people with a flair for self-disclosure, the subject is rendered theatrical in either case.

One approach of the modern cinema has been to use a natural setting as the starting point for a film and to let a story seem to grow out of that set-ting.[5] The Italian cinema from Rossellini through Antonioni has produced numerous films which emphasize a natural, untheatrical sense of place (through location shooting) and people (often through nonprofessional ac-tors) onto which is grafted a story which is purposely episodic and under-stated. Often the acting in such films is improvised, which further blurs the line between theatricality and reality.

Critics often praise such works for their truthfulness, minimizing the es-sential contradictions of them as staged works about reality. For these critics the process of finding drama in real life is more honest than its op-posite, adding the impression of real life to the dramatic.

Films May Naturalize the Dramatic

The introduction of elements of natural reality or documentary into a fic-tional film increases its credibility. One can more easily suspend one's dis-belief when the place where the action is occurring looks real and when the actors do not look like actors. The lesson which Hollywood learned from Italian neo-realism was not so much to look to the common people for stories from everyday life, but that even the most ridiculous story ap-pears a little more reasonable if shot on a real street instead of in a studio.

The shooting of a fiction film in the style of a documentary is a common technique of the modern cinema. A film like Gillo Pontecorvo's *The Battle of Algiers* is a textbook example of the fiction film that aspires to a docu-mentary style. It uses grainy, newsreel style photography to restage events from the Algerian war, and has been widely praised for its honest sense of reality. This use of high speed, grainy film is a direct example of exploiting an audience's associations to create an impression of reality. That is, the film's graininess does not show us more of the natural setting or of the physical qualities of its North African nonprofessional actors. Rather, Pon-tecorvo uses it because the audience is accustomed to graininess in newsreels. It becomes easier to believe that the director's restaging is authentic because of it, even though he has carefully constructed it for dramatic impact.

We find also in cinema a tendency toward what some critics call a dedramatization of theatrical situations, particularly with regard to acting. Writers have long commented on how subtle (restrained) acting is far more effective in a medium which traditionally relies heavily on the close-up to communicate the feelings of dramatic characters. Critics commonly cite such acting as realistic, and certainly it is compared to the stylization prevalent in the theater in the early part of the century. But writer Jean Cayrol has suggested that film encourages conventionalized acting and gestures precisely because if we were to see extremes of real emotion expressed under the scrutiny of the camera's lens, in close-up, the result would be too disturbing, unsettling or even unbelievable.[6] We prefer the comfortable alternative of understatement and supposed subtlety.

We see here a kind of compensatory mechanism. The close-up makes the scene more intense, so the actor underplays it to bring it down to an acceptable level. Indeed, the objection made earlier to the way in which *cinéma vérité* causes people in real life to dramatize themselves may in this light be an oversimplification. What may cause the objection is the refusal by the audience to accept what real expression of emotion looks like. Psychologists note the relative taboo in our culture against looking at people at those times when they express intense, intimate emotion. Yet that is exactly what film invites us to do.

While film can give the ordinary places, objects and events of everyday life a dramatic dimension, it can also make the dramatic or theatrical seem ordinary and everyday. Several years ago I visited the city of Lyon a few months after having seen the film *The Clockmaker,* which takes place in that city. Much of the action of the film—clearly shot on real locations— takes place in and around the clockmaker's store. In walking through the old quarter of the city, I ran across the very shop used in the film, but was amazed to find that it was hardly a typical shop, but rather one of the most picturesque storefronts in the whole city. A Frenchman might have recognized the poetic license involved, but my assumption in watching the film—supposedly about an ordinary clockmaker—was that the location was also typical and unexceptional.

In every case, this naturalization of the dramatic comes in part from the way we put the film we are watching into a context built up by other movies we have seen. We judge the realism of photography from other films which emphasize natural lighting and spontaneous shooting, the realism of a performance from other performances as much as from watching behavior in life, the realism of a location from both its context in the film and the way locations are usually used in films.

The Confusion of the Collective Dream

Critics and psychologists have long commented on the superficial similarities between moviegoing and the dreaming state.[7] One attends a film in a darkened room, in a state of physical immobility (usually at night), frequently to see fantasylike stories acted out. Even more striking is the way movies resemble dreams by creating a sense of experiencing events physically as well as mentally (as opposed simply to watching them, as one would do with a stage production). People go to the movies for many of the same reasons that they dream—to fantasize their desires, to put certain disturbing elements of the world around them into a context whereby they make poetic (if not always logical) sense, to escape from the pressure of the real world and regain a certain psychological equilibrium with regard to it.

Yet moviegoing is also dreaming made social. Most people prefer not to go to the movies alone, and many films, particularly comedies, play much better to a full auditorium than to an empty one. Roland Barthes has commented on the almost orgylike quality of the usual moviegoing experience: one has an intimate, often erotic and dreamlike experience with a crowd of strangers. This is quite the opposite, Barthes points out, of television viewing, the physical circumstances of which are both familiar and familial.[8]

This leads to a third confusion inherent in film. We are alone with the film (since it reproduces subjective experience), yet we are not alone (there is the audience around us). This presence of the audience adds to our simultaneous sense of belief and disbelief. Hardly anyone thinks twice about watching a film on television alone. The small screen, the lights on in the room, the commercial interruptions all establish a contact with the real world that renders the experience nonthreatening and often rather shallow. It is much harder to imagine sitting alone in a large theater to watch a Cinerama or widescreen 70 mm production without the comfort of a surrounding audience. Moviegoing involves making oneself physically immobile and submitting to a passive experience very much akin to a dream during sleep. The larger the screen, the more complete one's immersion in the image. And the more one needs the assurance that there are other spectators. Only the real movie buffs sit in the front row.

This blend in moviegoing between a communal experience and one that is physiologically and subjectively involving has been the film medium's most vital response to the challenge of television. The *Ben Hur* style spectacle films of the 1950s, the "head films" of the 1960s, the *Star Wars* and *Close Encounters* of the 1970s all offer this alternative. In watching them, the audience wants to stretch itself in both directions—toward surrender to magical illusion or trance on the one hand, without sacrificing the security of the group on the other.

Ideal movie going conditions involve a delicate balance. We are annoyed when the person behind us talks or the person in front of us is wearing a wide brimmed hat, yet we like to be able to turn to a companion during a particularly frightening episode. We like to reserve the right to believe or disbelieve what we see on the screen.

The Confusion of the Symbolic[9]

The nature of moviegoing as a social, public activity has yet another purpose. We use our companions in the audience to *make sense* of what we have seen. The discussion that may follow a film becomes one reason for going: there is a common experience to talk about to a date, a spouse or a visiting uncle. This collective making sense of a film becomes an equivalent to the secondary elaboration process described by Freud with regard to dreams. When awake, the dreamer adds information to his dreams to give them sense and coherence.

For the moviegoer, simple value judgments of "good" or "bad" may sometimes suffice, whereas this process of making sense may become more complicated if the film is confusing, disturbing or challenging. The conclusions drawn need not coincide with those intended by the filmmaker, as evidenced by the rednecks who cheered *Easy Rider* when the hippies were massacred. Each person makes sense according to his own experience.

To the extent that a film exploits what I have called our theatrical awareness, we feel a need to make sense of it as a film. When we sense the filmmaker as a manipulator or a magician, we try to determine what he is saying. If we believe a documentary completely, as a totally honest representation of the world, we don't attempt to make sense of the documentary, but of the world itself. Let us put it differently: to the extent that a film makes us aware of a theatrical level, it creates for itself a symbolic level. A character is no longer a specific individual, but representative of a kind of person. The milieu in which a film takes place is no longer just a place, but representative of a country, a region or a culture.

Here the analogy to dreaming becomes particularly interesting. The dreamer takes pieces of his experience and re-experiences them while dreaming in a form that gives them symbolic meaning. The filmmaker does something very similar. He takes pieces of the real world he records, reshapes them through editing and other means, and gives them meaning. For the viewer, the material is experienced first as an imitation of immediate, direct, subjective consciousness. On reflection (which may be almost immediate), he gives this meaning. The illusion of physiological involvement that the film medium provides makes it very much a form of *human consciousness made symbolic*. This confusion between the film experience as a form of raw, uninterpreted, immediate experience and reflective, symbolic experience is the fourth area of confusion in the medium.

Film theories that see motion pictures simply as recorders of reality ignore the way in which the context of putting something into a film always makes the image mean more than what it simply is. (We dream in images of specific people, but that does not prevent these mental images from frequently having the most general and unspecific meanings.) In rare instances film material may be virtually nonsymbolic. A doctor may use a movie camera with x-ray equipment to record a patient's breathing or swallowing patterns. For that doctor, it would be simply a way of seeing that patient's abnormality—like a mirror. When that footage is put into a medical training film, however, it becomes symbolic or a whole pattern of medical aberration. Theatricalized even further in a fiction film, this image could gain further meanings, depending on its context.

Film is not merely a transmitter of images from the real world. Rather, it is a medium which comes to invest those images with meanings derived from the contexts under which they are sent and received.

The Pleasure of the Confusion

The attraction of the film medium lies in the enjoyment we get from these varied confusions. Critics have long been aware of the ambiguities between natural and theatrical levels of reality. As George Amberg has written:

> The elaborate strategy of realism, developed and perfected in the film studios over the years, is more than a bagful of technical tricks: it is a cunning device *to make facts sell fiction*. The encounter with the unfamiliar, the illicit, the daring, the impossible, or the improbable within a verifiable frame of reference allows the audience to enjoy the experience as though it were authentic. This compromise between the quest for truth and the quest for wonder, a compromise that is uniquely cinematic, provides a neat solution for the average spec-

tator's ambivalent attitude toward vicarious gratification. For, on the one hand, he craves to be carried away into experiences transcending his own limitations; on the other, he is haunted by the fear of becoming the victim of a fraud.[10]

What Amberg ignores is that the reverse is also true: that films also use many structures of fiction to sell facts. The favorite structure of the effective propaganda film is to organize facts and events from the real world into effective drama. By dramatizing reality, the medium is often used for educational and persuasive purposes. We admire an effective piece of socially conscious filmmaking for its ability to sell ideas without making its manipulations falsify the truth.

The classic cinema seeks to minimize or ignore any explicit contradiction between the magical and material, the natural and theatrical, the specific and symbolic levels of a film. The modern cinema—the works of Godard, Fassbinder, the *cinéma vérité* movement or John Cassavetes—often underlines and emphasizes the ways in which one level may influence another. Modern films may use editing which calls attention to itself, emphasize improvised acting whereby the spontaneous emotions or thoughts of the actor mix with the character he is portraying, or even show the process whereby the film is being photographed. Even when the contradictions are made explicit, they are still a source of fascination.

If we look at the confusions inherent in the medium we can understand why the portrayal of certain subjects, such as sex and violence, are among the most popular and controversial uses to which film is put. Our reaction to the realistic portrayal of violent actions is all the stronger because of the medium's ability to make us feel like participants rather than spectators. We react in part physiologically. Our instincts of self-preservation cause us to. This physiological reaction may range from fainting at the sight of blood on the screen to a slight shudder at the same stimulus. In either case our physical reaction (be it mild fear or intense revulsion) is a step ahead of our mental processes (which tell us it isn't real). When it *is* real, as in newsreel footage of war, violence on the screen can be justly disturbing. When it is faked, it is one of the strongest magic tricks the medium can effect. Unlike on the stage, where we have the security of seeing actors take curtain calls, we may even be uncertain whether to believe or not.

Some people thus react to violence on the screen on the aesthetic grounds that it makes them respond physically to images they do not wish to respond to. Yet it is presumably the charge of this physiological response that also makes violence so popular. It is such an intense illusion. Others object to graphic violence on the screen on the grounds that it naturalizes the dramatic. With repetition, the extraordinary, dramatic depiction of violence becomes ordinary because the other contexts of the film are ordinary and believable. A murder becomes like the clockmaker's storefront—extraordinary to experience in real life, taken for granted on the screen.

A similar process holds true for the portrayal of sex. Watching real or simulated sexual activity on the screen seems to produce actual physiological arousal even more strongly than similar portrayals in print or still photography. This physiological arousal is one of the most extreme forms of confusion between the dramatic and the natural. Pornographic films are used as a direct substitute for voyeurism and often make little use of the technical developments of the medium. The precious distinction between hard and soft core is a distinction between direct recording of reality and theatrical fakery.

As with the violent film, the objections to pornography come from people who wish to maintain a rational control over their bodies. And again the pornographic genre is accused of trivializing something which should not be treated casually. Pornography particularly begs the issue of whether film is a private or public experience. Because of the taboos in our culture against the public experience of sexuality, people who are comfortable banishing eroticism to the ghetto of the skin flick house, where it is the private experience of solitary, middle-aged males, may be uncomfortable with a change in mores that makes it acceptable as public entertainment for mixed company.

Even those who object strongly to portrayals of violence or sex in film still seek physiological involvement in what they see. Those who avoid erotic or violent cinema often seem to prefer comedies, which provide for a physical surrender to laughter. It takes a real puritan (be he a Pentacostal or a post-Brechtian theorist) to object to all theatrical situations in which the mind does not completely dominate one's physiological reactions.

The pleasure that we get from technological innovation in the cinema comes from the way in which new techniques create their own confusions and unique perceptual situations. Color, for example, at once makes images more lifelike and prettier, so that it intensifies both sides of the natural/theatrical confusion. Sound completes a film's illusion of reality, but also provides for commentative effects. The failure of 3-D movies to take significant hold may be attributed to the way in which they stylize the film image in an unrealistic way.[11] Each technology provides for a new kind of magical illusion.

Conclusion

Because it involves a dialectic among four essential confusions of perception, the film medium has grown to become a potent, entertaining and controversial form of expression. As a type of magic, it presents fragments of film as a continuity existing in space and time. Through its relatively accurate recording of the surface qualities of reality, it blurs the audience's awareness of what is real and what is theatricalized. Through the similarities between standard film exhibition and the dreaming state, we experience a film both individually and as an audience. Finally, most films achieve a balance between simulating unstructured, immediate experience and allowing for reflection and conceptualization about that experience.

Notes

1. Pascal Bonitzer, "Hors-champ (un espace en défaut)" *Cahiers du Cinéma*, No. 234–35 (December 1971–January 1972), pp. 16–18.
2. We refer here to the rule (the Hollywood cinema) rather than the exceptions (filmmakers like Eisenstein, Godard or Duras).
3. Hugo Munsterberg, *Film: A Psychological Study* (New York: Dover Publications, 1969); Jean Mitry, *Esthétique et psychologie du cinéma*, two volumes (Paris: Editions universitaires, 1963).
4. Edward T. Hall, *The Hidden Dimension* (Garden City, N.Y.: Doubleday & Company, Inc., 1966).
5. In his *Theory of Film*, Siegfried Kracauer discusses a similar idea which he calls the "found story" (New York: Oxford University Press, 1960), pp. 245–51.
6. Jean Cayrol and Claude Durand, *Le droit de regard* (Paris: Editions du Seuil, 1963), pp. 61–65.
7. See especially Christian Metz, "Le film de fiction et son spectateur (Etude metapsychologique)," *Communications*, No. 23 (1975), pp. 108–35, and Susanne K. Langer, *Feeling and Form: A Theory of Art* (New York: Charles Scribner's Sons, 1953), pp. 411–15.
8. Roland Barthes, "En sortant du cinéma," *Communications*, No. 23 (1975), pp. 104–107.
9. We use the term "symbolic" in the broad sense, to refer to all forms of communication which establish meaning by convention.
10. George Amberg, "The Ambivalence of Realism: Fragment of an Essay," in *The Art of Cinema: Selected Essays*, edited by George Amberg (New York: The Arno Press and The New York Times, 1972), pp. 151–52.

11. "One mistake of early 3-D movies was the advertising. It was claimed 3-D made movies more realistic when in fact 3-D is about as realistic as Orphan Annie. It was the heightened, surreal, distorted sensation that made it fun." (Tom Shales, "If You Can't Take It, Remove Your Glasses," *The Washington Post*, September 2, 1977, p. B–3).

LANCE STRATE

Media and the Sense of Smell

Even though we are aware of the odors around us, we seldom think of our sense of smell as important to communication. Even more rarely do we associate our olfactory sense with modern technology. This is not surprising inasmuch as telephone, TV, radio, and film do not utilize an olfactory channel. Aside from a few unusual excursions into "smellovision" and "odorama," smell has not been used in a technological medium of communication. This unusual essay by Lance Strate explores the nuances of olfactory communication, revealing it as a dynamic phenomenon interacting with our social, cultural, and technological environment. He points out that the function of and our reliance on the olfactory sense are being changed by our dependence on the new technology of communication. Will the sense of smell be incorporated into future media and be used to persuade and entertain us?

During one episode of *Monty Python*[1] we were given a rare glimpse of an outsider's view of America. As a scene shifts to the Pentagon, the music swells, and there, sitting behind an immense desk, is a five-star general. Acting as if he were unaware of the camera, he sniffs each of his armpits. Apparently, our British cousins find our concern over body odor odd and amusing. They seem to be saying that we are overly anxious about the scent of our armpits. The question behind *Monty Python*'s observation is why is it that when we say that something smells, we mean that it smells *bad?*

To answer this question, the olfactory component of the act of communication need be examined. That is one of the purposes of this article; to explain the nature and function of olfactory communication. The other purpose is to explore the relationship among olfactory media, mass media, and interpersonal intimacy. The act of communication is a multisensory, multichannel transaction. Olfaction is a significant, albeit often overlooked, factor in communication, and thus an analysis of olfactory communication and media should further our understanding of the act of communication.

The Characteristics of Olfactory Communication

We can begin by listing several basic characteristics of olfactory communication. The first is that olfactory communication, like any other communication, is a transaction; the individual is both perceiver and producer of odor (and anyone who has ridden a rush-hour subway during the summer months can attest to this fact). Furthermore, the effects of olfactory communication are difficult to gauge, and are relative to individual and cultural characteristics. Finally, olfactory communication aids in the individual's boundary maintenance; it is a factor in the individual's perception of personal distance and personal space. Thus, olfactory communication is modified by the individual's perception of olfactory space.

If our understanding of olfactory communication is based on a transactional process, then the individual can be examined as a producer of odors as well as a perceiver of odors. Individual body odors vary according to age, sex, complexion, and diet. One aspect of human odor production presently being studied is the likelihood of human pheromones. Pheromones are a group of biologically active substances, similar to hormones. There are two types of pheromones: primer pheromones, which trigger permanent physiological changes in the receiver, and releaser pheromones, which evoke immediate and reversible change in behavior. Among mammals, pheromones are involved in the formation of social hierarchies, territorial behavior, individual imprinting, and primary reproductive effects. Alex Comfort cites several factors that support the hypothesis that pheromones exist in humans. The first factor is that pheromone interaction is present in social mammals, including primates. Moreover, human beings have organs whose equivalents among lower animals serve a pheromone-producing function. There is also some evidence of cross-specific reactions (i.e., humans react to musk; bulls, goats, and monkeys react to the odor of women). Finally, Comfort notes the following:

> Humans have a complete set of organs which are traditionally described as non-functional, but which, if seen in any other mammal, would be recognized as part of a pheromone system. These include apocrine glands associated with conspicuous hair tufts, some of which do not produce sweat and most presumably produce some other functioning secretion; a developed prepuce and labia, and the production of smegma (the sebaceous secretion that collects beneath the prepuce or around the clitoris). This system in adults seems over-elaborate for the relatively small releaser role of odor in most cultures. The amputatory assault on these recognizable pheromone-mediating structures in many human societies implies an intuitive awareness that their sexual function

goes beyond the decorative. A conspicuous and apparently unused antenna array presupposes an unsuspected communications system.[2]

Carl Sagan makes a similar observation:

> Other methods of finding a mate have been developed in reptiles, birds, and mammals. But the connection of sex with smell is still apparent neuroanatomically in higher animals as well as anecdotally in human experience. I sometimes wonder if deodorants, particularly "feminine" deodorants, are an attempt to disguise sexual stimuli and keep our minds on something else.[3]

According to Comfort, the production of odors by humans probably has subliminal effect on other humans. However, the effects are confounded by other stimuli transmitted over other channels. Thus, the effects are difficult to measure. Part of the problem is that humans are the least distinguished of all the animal species as olfactory perceivers. The evolutionary process that brought humans to their present erect, upright position also brought their nose away from the ground, thus reducing the effectiveness and importance of olfactory perception (while simultaneously increasing the effectiveness and importance of visual and auditory perception). Also, it is difficult to gauge the effects of olfactory sensations on the human psyche. Havelock Ellis discusses this point:

> The sense of smell still remains close to touch in the vagueness of its messages though its associations are often highly emotional. It is the existence of these characteristics—at once so vague and so specific, so useless and so intimate—which has led various writers to describe the sense of smell as, above all others, the sense of imagination. No sense has so strong a power of suggestion, the power of calling up ancient memories with a wide and deep emotional reverberation, while at the same time no sense furnishes impressions which so easily change emotional color and tone, in harmony with the recipient's general attitude. Odors are thus specially apt both to control the emotional life and to become its slaves. Under the conditions of civilization the primitive emotional associations of odor tend to be dispersed, but, on the other hand, the imaginative side of the olfactory sense becomes accentuated, and personal idiosyncrasies tend to manifest themselves in this sphere.[4]

Odors, in a general, nonspecific manner, affect our emotions, trigger memories, and affect our interpersonal communication (especially in regard to courtship and sexual relations). Specific effects of olfactory substances are difficult to measure; scientists have so far been unable to generate a system of primary units of olfactory information. R. H. Wright states that the *minimum* channel capacity of the nose is twenty-eight bits per second.[5] R. W. Moncrieff[6] could isolate olfactory effects only in terms of a hedonic (pleasure-giving) classification system. He found that age, sex, and, to a lesser degree, temperament (extrovert/introvert) all are determinants in the perception of relative pleasantness or unpleasantness of odors. He also found that there was greater consensus among his subjects in the perception of relative unpleasantness of odors than in relative pleasantness. Among the substances perceived as unpleasant were products with a "fecal note in their odor." Moncrieff also noted that children were more tolerant toward this type of substance. Circumstantial evidence can be found to support the association of fecal odor with unpleasantness as either inherent biologically or as derived through socialization. Obviously, there is a need for cross-cultural studies of odor preferences. Edward T. Hall has noted cultural differences in olfactory communicative behavior:

> Arabs apparently recognize a relationship between disposition and smell. The intermediaries who arrange an Arab marriage usually take great precautions to insure a good match. They may even on occasion ask to smell the girl and will reject her if she "Does not smell nice," not so much on esthetic grounds but possibly because of a residual smell of anger or discontent. Bathing the other person in one's breath is a common practice in Arab countries. The American is taught not to breathe on people. He experiences difficulty when he is within olfactory range of another person with whom he is not on close terms, particularly in public settings. He finds the intensity and sensuality overwhelming and has trouble paying attention to what is being said and at the same time coping with his feelings. In brief he has been placed in a double bind and is pushed in two directions at once. The lack of congruence between U.S. and Arab olfactory systems affects both parties and has repercussions which extend beyond mere discomfort or annoyance.[7]

Hall states that olfaction plays a role in the individual's boundary maintenance and his concept of personal distance and personal space. Olfactory space is thus a component of personal space. As previously noted, Comfort states that among mammals pheromones are involved in the formation of social hierarchies and territorial behavior. Therefore, the phenomenon of olfactory space has a biological basis. However, both Comfort and Sagan try to explain the use of deodorants through the likelihood of human pheromones; in this endeavor they commit the error of ethnocentricity. Hall and *Monty Python* demonstrate that Americans have a relatively exaggerated sense of olfactory space. Moreover, deodorants are as much a technology as a cultural artifact.

The Functions of Olfactory Media

Throughout history, the human race has attempted to modify and control its environment. Olfactory space and olfactory communication are modified and controlled by olfactory technology, that is, olfactory media. Our contemporary olfactory media include perfumes, incense, cologne, dental preparations such as toothpaste and mouthwash, shaving preparations such as shaving cream and aftershave, deodorants, tobacco, and the list goes on. The use of incense, which is often associated with religion, mysticism, and meditation, is probably related to the ability of olfactory sensations to affect emotional states and invoke memory. Perfume has been used for hierarchical purposes. In Exodus 30:1–38 we find the first recorded recipe for perfume, along with instructions for its use. The holy perfume was only to be used by the priests. The anointing of the kings of the Israel was a symbolic act, allowing the fledgling royalty into the olfactory environment of the priests. However, the most celebrated function of perfume is that of increasing interpersonal attractiveness. Ellis speculates on the origin of this function:

> Since there are chemical resemblances and identities even of odors from widely remote sources, perfumes may have the same sexual effects as are more primitively possessed by the body odors. It seems probable that . . . perfumes were primitively used by women, not as is sometimes in civilization, with the idea of disguising any possible natural odor, but with the object of heightening and fortifying the natural odor. If the primitive man was inclined to disparage a woman whose odor was slight or imperceptible—turning away from her with contempt as the Polynesian turned away from the ladies of Sydney: "They have no smell!"—women would inevitably seek to supplement any natural defects in the same way as, even in civilization, they have sought to accentuate the sexual prominences of their bodies.[8]

According to Ellis, perfume was first used as an olfactory form of falsies. Similarly, Marshall McLuhan defines media as extensions of human faculties. In this sense, perfume is an extension of the individual's ability to produce odors. Respect for and fear of this extension is revealed in an act of the English Parliament in 1770:

> That all women, of whatever age, rank, profession, or degree, whether virgins, maids, or widows, that shall, from and after such Act, impose upon, seduce, and betray into matrimony, any of his Majesty's subjects, by the scents, paints, cosmetic washes, artificial teeth, false hair, Spanish wool, iron stays, hoops, high-heeled shoes, bolstered hips, shall incur the penalty of the law in

force against witchcraft and like misdemeanours and that the marriage, upon conviction, shall stand null and void.[9]

It is not until the twentieth century that we encounter a whole new array of olfactory media whose primary function is not to enhance body odors, but to mask them (i.e., deodorants, feminine hygiene spray, mouthwash, air freshener, etc.). The cultural attitude that has developed along with the new olfactory media is best exemplified by the following passage from *The Mala Rubinstein Book of Beauty*, under the heading of "The All-Importants":

> There's a part of your body that is invisible—but can make or break the impression you create; can make you nice to be near—or decidedly *not*. That, of course, is body odor. Regardless of how often you bathe, use of a deodorant daily is a "must." The type you use depends upon individual need and preference. Best for most women is an anti-perspirant deodorant, which serves the dual purpose of eliminating unpleasant odor and keeping the underarms dry.
>
> Fastidious care must, of course, extend to the vaginal area. The frequency and type of douche you use depends on you and your doctor's recommendation. A reliable vaginal deodorant used after the bath or morning shower should be part of your daily routine. It surprises me that Americans, who often make a cult of cleanliness, have never adopted the European bidet. For freshness throughout the day—where the bidet doesn't exist—there are pre-moistened paper towelettes that also deodorize.[10]

Not only does our friend Mala provide us with a strong and zealous view of our present cultural attitudes toward odor, but she also gives us a clue to its development. Odorlessness is associated with cleanliness. Odor and dirt are associated with disease. The association between odor and disease is not recent, however. The ancient Babylonians and Assyrians used fumigations and incense as medical treatment; perfume was an ingredient in the embalming oil of the ancient Egyptians. Incense and perfumes remained popular as remedies for diseases during the Middle Ages. When the scientific paradigm about the causes of disease changed, public belief did not. Beginning in 1860, Louis Pasteur, Joseph Lister, and Robert Koch contributed to the development of the antiseptic. Inherent in the idea of the antiseptic is that invisible disease can be eliminated. If disease is still associated with odor in the public mind, doesn't the antiseptic suggest the elimination of invisible odor through a deodorant? Theodor Rosebury[11] criticizes the common misconception in our culture that the cleaner we and our environment are, the healthier we are. While this may have been true once, we have carried the concept to such extremes as to make it dysfunctional. The use of deodorants, feminine hygiene sprays, etc., have no health value and can even create health problems. Our cult of cleanliness includes the worship of the mystical properties of soap, a situation Roland Barthes is highly critical of:

> L'important, c'est d'avoir su masquer la fonction abrasive du détergent sous l'image délicieuse d'une substance à la fois profonde et aérienne qui peut régir l'ordre moléculaire du tissu sans l'attaquer.[12]

Ivan Illich[13] criticizes our attitudes toward pharmaceuticals, toward the ability of medicine, of the pill, to cure disease. Given our association of odor and disease, our mystification and overuse of soap and deodorants is consubstantial with our attitudes toward pharmaceuticals. We deify the cure-all product, and it is not coincidental that this attitude fits in nicely with our consumerism-based economy. Mass production techniques also had a significant influence. The 1870s saw the rise of mass production in the soap industry as well as the introduction of perfumed soap. Also, synthetic perfumes were accidentally discovered by organic chemists in the late nineteenth century. This discovery led to increased production of perfumery materials at a much lower cost, and consequently, increased consumption of these materials, promulgated by the mass media. The use of "scare techniques" became popular in the twentieth century, leading to advertising copy such as "My first date with *HIM* tonight! So I'm bathing with fragrant cashmere bouquet soap . . . it's the *lovelier way* to avoid offending!" and "Are you as dainty at night as you are by day? Charming wives *never* risk offending. . . ."[14] The purpose of olfactory media is no longer to increase relative pleasantness in the individual, but to avoid unpleasantness. While the mass media are often accused of the creation of needs where there are none, it seems that in this instance the mass media were merely playing upon pre-existing cultural values toward odor, cleanliness, and disease. To avoid offending, one must be clean in the antiseptic sense, free of odor and disease. The invasion of olfactory space becomes a signal of contagion.

Mass Media and Olfactory Space

The exaggerated sense of olfactory space was probably further influenced by what Richard Sennett refers to as "the fall of public man."[15] Sennett's thesis is that over the past three centuries people in Western societies have shifted from playing socially accepted public roles to viewing social rela-

tions as self-disclosure. The nineteenth century was particularly characterized by a profound fear of involuntary personal disclosure. This was the
Victorian era. The fear of involuntary self-disclosure also extended to the
olfactory realm. Sennett cites a physician on the faculty of the University
of Marburg, Carl Ludwig. Ludwig felt that the origin of the "green sick-
ness," a euphemism for chronic constipation in women, lay in "the fear
women have had of accidentally farting after eating, leading to a constant
tensing of the buttocks." [16] Sennett states that our present era is a product
of a flip-flop from fear of involuntary disclosure to emphasis on self-
disclosure and the desire to indiscriminately place all social relations on
an intimate basis. However, our sense of olfactory space has not made the
transition. We have remained Victorian in our management of our olfactory space. Perhaps our attitudes toward odor, cleanliness, and disease have
prevented the changeover.

It is interesting to note that, in contemporary society, perfume advertisements are usually markedly different from deodorant advertising. While
the latter is often based on the aforementioned scare techniques, the former does not seem to be. Perfume advertising seems to appeal to a sense
of identity, to the type of person who would wear the particular perfume.
Perfume ads also usually contain abstract visual imagery, perhaps in an
attempt to visualize the emotional and memory-inducing effects of scent.
When perfume advertisements are related to social interaction, it is generally from a positive perspective. Instead of the subtle threat of social un-
acceptability, perfume ads tend to emphasize increased success in social
interactions. What is consistently deemphasized in advertisements is perfume's characteristic of being an odorous substance. A study comparing
perfume and deodorant advertising would be very enlightening.

The mass media also affect our attitudes toward odor in a less blatant
manner. Marshall McLuhan [17] has noted that the transition from print media to electronic media has ended the monopoly of the visual, and reinte-
grated our senses. Foremost among the electronic media is television, which
appeals to us on a visual, auditory, and (according to McLuhan) tactile
level. Notably absent from these elements of the sensorium is the olfactory
component. Susan Sontag [18] states implicitly, and Gary Gumpert [19] explicitly, that our mass media have altered our standards of perfection. Through
photographic and recording media we are presented with a standard of
perfection unrealizable in the non-mediated world. Photographic techniques such as retouching allow women of almost mythic quality to grace
the centerfold of *Playboy* and, amazingly enough, this perfect beauty is
also free of any offending odors.

The media also affect our sense of olfactory space through personal distance cues. Hall states that a culture's personal distance cues are implicit within a culture's art forms. The artist works from the existing personal distance cues of the culture that produced him. The relationship of the viewer to the work of art is determined by the personal distance cues transmitted by the work of art. The intimate personal distance cues given by television and other electronic media parallel the emphasis on intimacy and self-disclosure associated, in the twentieth century, with the fall of the public man. However, the intimate personal space is odorless; the news anchorman never has perspiration odor, the disc jockey never has bad breath. We are given an exaggerated perception of our own olfactory space, or at least reinforced in our desire to keep our olfactory space free of invasion (or infection) of outside odors. Edward Bullough recognized the dual-edged sword of cultural art forms:

> The working of distance is, accordingly, not simple, but highly complex. It has a *negative,* inhibitory aspect—the cutting-out of the practical sides of things and of our practical attitude to them—and a *positive* side—the elaboration of the experience on the new basis created by the inhibitory action of Distance.[20]

Our mass media present us with an odor-free world, which reinforces our over-exaggerated sense of olfactory space. With this in mind, is it any wonder that so many people can accept (and even prefer) the display of plastic flowers and plastic fruit? Another technological innovation that has reinforced this situation is the development and widespread use of ventilation systems and air conditioning during the 1940's. William N. McCord and William N. Witheridge[21] state that the foremost function of these inventions is to rid the air of offensive odors, thus protecting and expanding the individual's olfactory space. Recent attempts at antismoking regulation are an assertion of the olfactory space of the nonsmoker. It is significant that this issue manifests itself after widespread acceptance of the idea that smoking is injurious to health, in light of our association of odor and disease.

Our deodorizing imperative seems to indicate that olfactory stimulation is perceived as noise. When competing stimuli create noise, channel inhibition constitutes noise reduction. While we have traditionally studied the media of communication, it seems that we also must study the media of inhibition—blindfolds, sunglasses, earplugs, and sound-proofing.

The function of olfactory media has not been limited to the inhibition of odors. T-shirts and women's underwear with fragrances are now available (good for up to fifteen washings) in such scents as orange, fish odor, diesel fuel, marijuana, whiskey, and pizza. Ruth Winter states that scented ink with a bacon aroma was once used in a newspaper ad, but problems arose when neighborhood dogs began taking the papers from the porches where they were delivered and chewing them up.[22] Future technological developments may provide us with the ability to implant odor on a long term basis, and perhaps we will be able to obtain an olfactory version of a tatoo.

The Future of Olfactory Media

The subtler effects of odors are also being exploited. In the 1970s, twenty percent of all fragrance manufactured was used in perfume and toiletries. The rest was used to scent a variety of products including detergents, furniture polish, tobacco, tea, medicine, window cleaners, stationery, paints, pens, nail polish, greeting cards, stockings, used cars, and glue factories. The addition of a lemon scent to Joy detergent in 1966 proved successful, and since that time marketing experts have been using fragrance not just to cover bad odors, but to increase the attractiveness of the product. Future technologies may bring us an olfactory form of muzak (aimed at behavior modification).

It is likely that most developments in olfactory technologies will be used in conjunction with other technologies in a multi-channel presentation. Microfragrances, commonly known as scratch-and-sniff, are particularly suited for print media. By scratching, the receiver breaks millions of miniscule plastic bubbles, releasing fragrances. While mostly used for advertising, microfragrances have also been used in educational material, especially for the blind. The use of scratch-and-sniff cards as an integral part of the movie *Polyester* failed precisely because microfragrances are print-biased. The one-at-a-time scratching of microfragrance areas is not suited to the continuous flow of the motion picture; the connections between the visual image and the fragrance become strained and caricature-like. Aldous Huxley conceived of a much more elegant multichannel presentation almost fifty years ago. The following passage is a description of the olfactory medium used in Huxley's "feelies":

> The scent organ was playing a delightfully refreshing Herbal Capriccio— rippling arpeggios of thyme and lavender, of rosemary, basil, myrtle, tarragon; a series of daring modulations through the spice keys into ambergris; and a slow return through sandalwood, camphor, cedar, and newmown hay (with occasional subtle touches of discord—a whiff of kidney pudding, the faintest

suspicion of pig's dung) back to the simple aromatics with which the piece began. The final blast of thyme died away; there was a round of applause; the lights went up.[23]

Technological innovation, such as Huxley describes, can modify our olfactory communication and our sense of olfactory space. Still, change in our sense of olfactory space will probably be predicated on change in our attitudes towards cleanliness and disease. In the future, we may be able to tolerate an olfactory environment with more than just a faint trace of ozone. We may no longer feel compelled to sniff our armpits or to think that everything that smells, smells bad. But then again, who nose?

Notes

1. Monty Python is a comic / satiric television series produced by the BBC and often aired in the USA on PBS stations.
2. Alex Comfort, "The Likelihoood of Human Pheromones," in Martin C. Birch, *Pheromones* (New York: North-Holland Pub., 1974), p. 388.
3. Carl Sagan, *The Dragons of Eden* (New York: Random House, 1974), p. 69.
4. Havelock Ellis, *Psychology of Sex* (New York: Mento Books, 1963), p. 46.
5. R. H. Wright, *The Science of Smell* (New York: Basic Books, 1964), p. 82.
6. As described in *Odour Preferences* (New York: John Wiley, 1966).
7. Edward T. Hall, *The Hidden Dimension* (Garden City: Doubleday & Co., 1969), p. 49.
8. Ellis, *op. cit.,* pp. 49–50.
9. William A. Poucher, *Perfumes, Cosmetics, and Soaps, Vol. II* (New York: D. Van Nostrand Co. Inc., 1936), pp. 16–17.
10. Mala Rubinstein, *The Mala Rubinstein Book of Beauty* (Garden City: Doubleday & Co., 1973), pp. 159–160.
11. Theodore Rosebury, *Life on Man* (New York: Viking Press, 1969).
12. Roland Barthes, *Mythologies* (Paris: Éditions du Seuil, 1957), p. 40.
13. Ivan Illich, *Medical Nemesis, the Expropriation of Health* (New York: Pantheon Books, 1976).
14. Ann Bramson, *Soap, Making It, Enjoying It* (New York: Workman Publishing, 1975), pp. 78; 80.
15. Richard Sennett, *The Fall of Public Man* (New York: Vintage Books, 1978).
16. *Ibid,* p. 182.
17. Marshall McLuhan, *Understanding Media, The Extensions of Man* (New York: New American Library, 1964).
18. Susan Sontag, *On Photography* (New York: Farrar, Straus, Giroux, 1978).
19. Gary Gumpert, "The Ambiguity of Perception," *Et Cetera* Vol. 34, no. 2 (June 1977).
20. Edward Bullough, " 'Psychical Distance' As A Factor in Art and An Esthetic Principle," in Melvin Rader, ed., *A Modern Book of Esthetics* (New York: Holt, Rinehart and Winston, 1960), p. 396.

21. William N. McCord and William N. Witheridge, *Odors, Physiology and Control* (New York: McGraw-Hill Books, 1949).

22. Ruth Winter, *The Smell Book* (New York: J. B. Lippincott & Co., 1976), p. 123.

23. Aldous Huxley, *Brave New World* (New York: Harper & Row, 1946), pp. 198–201.

SHERRY TURKLE

Computer as Rorschach

The computer is being introduced rapidly into our office and homes as another component in a huge media system. A new relationship is being formed, one in which we will no longer be passive receivers of electronic fare, but will interact directly with media sources and channels.

According to Sherry Turkle of the Massachusetts Institute of Technology, some of us suffer from "computerphobia," others from "computer addiction." Almost all of us are in awe of this powerful new "machine" but perhaps only a few of us realize how many computer-human interactions are being imposed upon us without choice. Turkle examines our subjective reactions to a medium that is altering our concepts of self.

There is an extraordinary range of textures, tones, and emotional intensity in the way people relate to computers—from seeming computer addiction to confessed computerphobia. I have recently been conducting an ethnographic investigation of the relationships that people form with computers and with each other in the social worlds that grow up around the machines. In my interviews with people in very different computing environments, I have been impressed by the fact that when people talk about computers they are often using them to talk about other things as well. In the general public, a discourse about computers can carry feelings about public life—anxieties about not feeling safe in a society that is perceived as too complex, a sense of alienation from politics and public institutions. Ideas about computers can also express feelings about more private matters, even reflecting concerns about which the individual does not seem fully aware. When we turn from the general public to the computer experts, we find similar phenomena in more developed forms. There, too, ideas about computers carry feelings about political and personal issues. But in addition, the expert enters into relationships with computers which can give concreteness and coherence to political and private concerns far removed from the world of computation. In particular, the act of programming can be an expressive activity for working through personal issues relating to control and mastery.

Published by permission of Transaction, Inc. from *Society*, Vol. 17, No. 2, Copyright © 1980 by Transaction, Inc.

Of course, among technologies, the computer is not alone in its ability to evoke strong feelings, carry personal meaning, and create a rich expressive environment for the individual. People develop intense and complex relationships with cars, motorbikes, pinball machines, stereos, and ham radios. If computers are an exception to the general rule that there is a subjective side to people's relationships with technology, it is insofar as they raise this commonly known phenomenon to a higher power, and give it new form as well as new degree.

Other technologies, knives for example, can serve as projective screens: do we associate them with butter or with blood? But we can come close to having people agree that before it is a part of eating or killing, a knife is a physical object with a sharp edge. We shall see that the elusiveness of computational process and of simple descriptions of the computer's essential nature undermine such consensus and make the computer an exemplary "constructed object," a cultural object which different people and groups of people can apprehend with very different descriptions and invest with very different attributes. Ideas about computers become easily charged with multiple meanings. In sum people often have stronger feelings about computers than they know.

The Subjective Computer

A ticket agent who uses computers to make airline reservations begins a conversation about the computer by presenting it as a totally neutral object—programmed, passive, completely under the control of its operators and their input, threatening only in its impersonality—and then moves on in the same conversation to descriptions of the machine as a presence in which the line between person and thing seems nearly to dissolve. When confronted in a conversation by the possibility of computers which might serve as psychotherapists, judges, or physicians—that is, whose functions would be ones which are now seen as quintessentially "human"—many people react with a force of feeling by which they themselves are surprised. Some people try to neutralize feelings of discomfort by denying that such things as intelligent computers could exist outside of science fiction, but then try to buttress their arguments by adding in unabashed self-contradiction that while such things may be possible, they "ought not be allowed to happen." In talking about computers, people often make implicit reference to two scenarios that have long been explicit in science fiction plots: computers might change something about the way people think, and computers might develop minds of their own. In the complexity of our responses to the idea of machine intelligence, we see an expression of our stake in maintaining a clear line between the human and the artificial, between what has consciousness and autonomy and what does not, between a notion of "mechanical" calculation and of "human" judgment and emotion. The fact that the computer touches on a sphere—intelligence—that man has long thought to be uniquely his, means that even popular discourse about computers can raise tense questions about what is man and what is machine.

Questions like this are posed, if only implicitly, by our everyday use of language; that is, by our use of computational metaphors. In our culture, the fact that there is talk about such things as repression, the unconscious, and the superego, influences the way in which people think about their problems, their pasts, and their possibilities, even for people who do not "believe in" psychoanalysis. In the case of psychoanalysis, technical ideas were taken up as powerful metaphors by a nontechnical public and used as building blocks in a discourse about politics, education, and the self; that is, as building blocks in the development of a psychoanalytic culture. These ideas took many shapes and turned up in many different places as they became integrated into advice to the lovelorn as well as into theories of psychology. Computers, too, introduce a world of new language to those who work with and around them. And since this language is about cognitive processes that often seem at least superficially analogous to those which go on in people, this language is brought into everyday vocabulary.

Students speak of "dumping core" when they are asked to spill back course contents during an exam. Engineers complain of being "stuck in a loop" when problem solving is difficult and all paths lead to dead ends. A travel brochure for a condominium village in Hawaii assures the reader that a stay in Wailea means a sure addition to his "fond memory bank." Today's language for thinking about thinking is growing richer in computational metaphors. When we say that we have an idea that needs to be "debugged," we are referring to a computational model of dealing with global complexity through local intervention. When a computer scientist refuses to be interrupted during an excited after-dinner conversation and explains that he needs to "clear his buffer," he is using an image of his mental terrain in which access to interactive processing capacity can be blocked by a buffer zone that must be empty before it can be crossed.

We do not yet know whether these metaphors, commonly dismissed as "manners of speaking," are having an effect on the way we think about ourselves, perhaps by effecting an unconscious transfer between our ideas about machines and our ideas about people. In academic psychology, however, such transfer has become explicit: in the mid-1950s, the presence of the computer, a complex material embodiment of cognitive functions, gave American psychologists a new model for thinking about cognition, one which stressed the need to posit complex internal processes in order to understand even simple behavior (something that traditional behaviorism, in its attempts to avoid theorizing about internal states and processes, had declared outside the realm of good science). For example, behaviorists had spoken of the behavior of "remembering," but computational models reintroduced the notion of "a memory" into general psychology. Today, computational and information-processing models seem on their way to becoming the new dominant paradigm in psychology and have made serious inroads in other behavioral and social sciences. It is a plausible conjecture that, as in the case of psychoanalysis, today's technical computational language will filter into tomorrow's popular language.

Some might imagine that such subjective aspects of the computer presence and the use of computation for model building are either a private matter, of concern to the individual involved, or of interest to the theoretical psychologist, but without any bearing on issues of public concern except insofar as *misinformation* about computers can obscure discussion of public problems. In fact, the situation is more complex. We can observe the "subjective computer" in the language and the projections of individuals, but it does impact on the collectivity. There are several ways in which it can influence our approach to issues concerning computers in public life. First, when the computer acts as a projective screen for other social and political concerns, it can act as a smokescreen as well, drawing attention away from the underlying issues and onto debate "for or against computers." Second, feelings about computers (often largely projective in origin) can become formalized into "ideologies" of computer use, that is, into beliefs about what the computer can, will, and should do. These powerful computer ideologies can decrease our sensitivity to the technology's limitations and dangers as well as blind us to some of its positive social possibilities. And finally, along with the "constructed computer" comes the social construction of computer expertise.

When a school wishes to purchase a computer system, whom shall they consult? There are at least a hundred thousand Americans who have bought small, personal computers for their homes. Many are parents—it is natural that the school and the PTA should look to them as experts. And from a purely technical point of view, many of them are. But we shall see that the relationship of many computer hobbyists to the computer carries a vision of what is important in computation that systematically leaves some things out. Other "expert" groups introduce different biases.

The general public tends to think of a computer expert as defined by purely technical criteria but, in fact, computer experts are often distinguished from each other by subjective stances (such as an emotional feeling about what is important about computation) as well as by their technical capabilities. Even people who are extremely sensitive to the way in which personal preoccupations and political preferences can masquerade as "neutral" expertise in other technical fields often think that in computer science, things are different. One popular image is that computer expertise is a neutral quantity that can be acquired like a piece of hardware and be relied upon to perform in a steady and reliable way. It is as though people tend to see computer experts (often referred to as "computer people") as being "like computers." But different relationships with computers, different aesthetics of how to use them and what they are good for, structure computational value systems whose implications extend far beyond the technical. Even preferences among styles of programming can have a politics. One programming aesthetic puts a premium on having all elements of the program "on the table" and available to the programmer as "primitives." With so many little pieces, each one has to be made as small as possible to get them to all fit into the workspace, and so the criteria of elegance for this "flat" style of work are associated with highly condensed programming at the bottom level. Before the recent plummeting in the cost of memory, this ground floor condensation allowed economies of memory space that made its elegance highly cost effective. But because the structural building blocks are small, condensed, and numerous, modifications are virtually impossible without changing the whole system. An alternative aesthetic (top down, structured programming) builds up hierarchical programs using large, internally unmodifiable modular blocks. This often uses more memory but allows easy modifications with less reliance on a master programmer. The system is socially desirable, but some programmers find it constraining, unaesthetic, "good for organization, but bad for the artist." We shall return to the question of computational values and politics. Here I want only to suggest that understanding different subjective relationships with computation may be necessary to understanding and evaluating the views of computer experts on issues of public policy such as what kind of computer system needs to be built in a given situation. Indeed, such understanding may be a necessary step towards a kind of computer literacy that prepares the citizen to make responsible political judgments.

Computer as Smokescreen

Computational metaphors are only one element in the construction of a new, highly charged, and often highly self-contradictory popular discourse about computers. There is the everyday reality: the average American meets computer power when he makes a telephone call, uses a credit card, books a motel room, goes to the bank, borrows a library book, or passes through the checkout counter of the local supermarket. There is the science-fiction surrealism: the computer of the future is presented as threatening (HAL in *2001*), all-knowing (the "Star Trek" computers), and all-powerful (in the movie *Demon Seed*, a computer succeeds in impregnating a woman, resulting in a computer-human baby). And there is media image making, as television, popular journalism, advertisements, even games and toys, bombard us with an extraordinary range of images about what the computer really is and what it might be. The computer is portrayed as supercalculator, superenemy, superfriend, supertoy, supersecretary, and in the case of the bionic people who populate television serials and children's imaginations, computer as a path into a future of supermen and women.

Computers are portrayed as good and bad, as agents of change and of stagnation. Talking about computers and money, computers and education, computers and the home, evokes tension, irritation, anticipation, excitement. Some of the intensity reflects the schizophrenic splittings in the images of computers in our culture. But some of it comes from the use of the computer as a projective screen for other concerns. And although we do not yet know if computational metaphors and ideas about computers are changing the way we think, it is already clear that our popular and highly projective discourse about computers can discourage us from thinking things through.

Consider, for example, the problem of how computers make it easier to violate the privacy of the individual through the automatic accumulation of data about him. Traditional notions of the right to privacy are challenged when most social transactions leave an electronic trace. The computer presence has made the problem of privacy more urgent and visible. More attention is being devoted to it because decisions about its protection can no longer be postponed when there is the prospect of their being "hard-wired" into national information systems. But all too often, discussions of computers and privacy focus on the computer. This draws attention off the fact that organizations violated citizen privacy long before there were computers to help them do the job. And attention is drawn off the fact that the root of this serious problem lies not in our computer systems but in our social organization and political commitments and that its solution must be searched for in the realm of political choice, not of fancier technology. On the issue of privacy, the computer presence could serve to underscore an underlying problem; instead, talk about the computer serves as its smokescreen.

A similar smokescreen effect is present in the following images of the computer, all of them comments made by computer science professionals at a recent symposium on computers and society.

The Computer that Constrains:

You get on an elevator and you're wearing a badge in a particular office building and you try to go to the fifth floor. The computer in the elevator says, "No, that's not your floor."

The Computer that Encourages Violence:

A group of students were standing around a console playing Space War and I heard one student say to the other: "Don't you think we should get more points for killing than for merely surviving?" It was a perfectly reasonable statement in that context, and I'm afraid it may turn out unhappily to become a slogan for the era of the home computer.

The Computer that Atrophies the Mind:

Now that we're using calculators and no longer multiply in our heads, we may find an almost epidemic rise in things like dyslexia, learning disabilities, inability to work, a propensity to industrial accidents and auto accidents.

Let us consider the third image: the computer that atrophies the mind. Later discussion made it clear that the speaker who prophesied that the calculator age meant an increase in learning disabilities was deeply concerned about the contemporary crisis in education, where functional illiteracy after a high-school career has become commonplace. But our understanding of that crisis is not advanced if concern about a falling educational standard is expressed as complaints about calculators that may disenable multiplication neurons. The other images carry similar dangers. The fact that computer games are violent, like the fact that television programs are violent, makes a statement not about technology but about our society. The most disturbing thing about the student's comment about the game of Space War has nothing to do with computers. Its language is not very different than that which was used while our government was fighting and justifying the war in Vietnam, to take only one example. That we now see it reflected back to us on television and CRT screens is a comment not on the computer presence but on the internalized violence of our society.

Sophisticated information systems do facilitate increased surveillance of individuals, and shoot 'em down video games on personal computers can multiply the images of violence that enter our livingrooms. This tendency of computers to increase the urgency of many problems could in principle give rise to sharper social criticism. But in practice this seldom happens. Complaints about *computers* invading privacy and about *computer* games being violent are daily used to short-circuit discussion of political responsibility and the banalization of violence. Behind our conversations about the computer that constrains us (the computer that "won't let you off on the fifth floor," or, as in another common example, "won't let you change your airline reservation") is often our sense of having limited access to what we want to see and understand. There are people and large organizations behind the "computer" that constrains. When people's sense of political limitation is translated into statements about technology, about computers "hiding things from us," political discussion has been neutralized and the possibility for appropriate action has been subverted.

It is easy to catalogue the interests (industrial, governmental) that tend to be served when political choices are represented as technical problems. These interests exert forces from without. But other forces, harder to catalogue, also encourage this same kind of obfuscation. In a certain sense, these come from within. If a memory or a dream disturbs our sense of who we are as individuals, we "forget" it—we make it unconscious. As a society, we also find ways to "forget" the collectively unacceptable. Comfortable and habitual inactions are threatened by serious talk about such matters as how the decisions of large corporations affect our political and biological environment or about the consequences of gross inequalities of resources and power. We develop a paradoxical language for talking about such matters that allows us to forget the real issues. And one of the most powerful of these languages is technical. The strategy is not new, and insofar as the computer has a role here, it is to provide new means towards already familiar ends. But the new means make a difference.

People are particularly willing to embrace the computer as a technical explanation for things that might otherwise raise disturbing questions. Consider the situation of the airline clerk we met earlier. She frequently finds herself confronted by the anger of clients whose reservations cannot be honored. Her standard excuse is "Our computer fouled up." Like workers in a thousand other bureaucracies all over the world, the airline clerk need never call the organizational policies of her company into question. She need never call her employer into question because the computer is there to blame. It is felt by her to be an autonomous entity (it can act with agency) and so it is *blamable,* yet it is not a fellow worker to whom she would feel bonds of loyalty. This permits her a conscience-calming collusion with the client without jeopardizing her security as a "company person." What is it about the computer that makes it such an effective actor in situations like this? In order to answer this question we need to step back and try to understand people's tendency to anthropomorphize computers. Most particularly, we need to appreciate that it is deeply rooted in the nature of the computer itself. It does not necessarily reflect a lack of information or naive beliefs in the "intelligence of machines," either present or future. Many who find the anthropomorphization of computers offensive would like to make it go away by educating the public to understand "what computers really are." But they miss an epistemological issue: computation is irreducible. We can know more and more about it, but we never come to a point where we can completely define it in terms of more familiar things.

The computer theorist, like other scientists, sets up a conceptual frame of reference within which he works, and defines the computable within this framework. But even then, what he has isolated as the computable, the "essential computer," presents no easy analogies with other objects in the world (as the airplane does the bird)—except, of course, and this is a point to which we shall return, for its analogies with people. To explore this further requires that we proceed by a kind of paradox. We try to understand the epistemological isolation of the computer by looking at some of the many ways in which people try to projectively relate it to other things, each valid within a particular horizon, although many are inconsistent with each other.

Computer as Rorschach

The computer's capacity as a projective device resembles that of the Rorschach, perhaps the best known and most powerful of psychology's projective measures. In the Rorschach, the individual is presented with an ambiguous stimulus, a set of inkblots. How he responds to them is a window onto his deeper concerns. And so it is with the computer. First, as in the case of the Rorschach, whose blots suggest many shapes but commit themselves to none, we have noted that the computer is difficult to capture by simple description. We can say that it is made of electrical circuits, but it does not have to be. A computer can be made (and several—for fun— have been) of tinkertoys, and quite serious computers have been made using fluidic rather than electrical circuits. Although airplanes can come in all shapes and can be described in all sorts of ways, there is no conceptual problem in stating their essential function: they fly. There is no equally elegant, compelling, or satisfying way of defining the computer. Of course, one could say that it computes, that it executes programs. But the execution of a program can be described on many levels: in terms of electronic events, machine language instructions, high-level language instructions, or through a structured diagram which represents the functioning of the program as a flow through a complex information system. There are no necessary one-to-one relationships between the elements on these levels of description, a feature of computation which has led philosophers of mind to see the computer's hardware-software interplay as highly evocative of the irreducible relationship between brain and mind. The irreducibility of the computer to other things encourages, indeed it even seems to coerce, its anthropomorphization. This is further reinforced by the computer's interactive properties (you type to it and it types back to you) and by the unpredictability of programs (although the programmer inputs all instructions, their interaction soon becomes sufficiently complex that one can seldom foresee the results of their operation).

Computers are certainly not the only machines that evoke anthropomorphization. We often talk about machines as though they were people: we complain that a car "wants to veer left." We even talk to machines as though they were people: we park a car on a slope and warn it to stay put. But usually, when we "talk to technology," we have a clear path in mind for transforming any voluntary actions we may have ascribed to a machine into unambiguously mechanical events. We know that friction on the wheels caused by the emergency brake will prevent gravity from pulling the car down the hill. But when we play chess with a computer and say that the computer "decided" to move the queen, it is much harder to translate this decision into physical terms. Of course, an engineer might well reply that "all the computer really does is add numbers." And indeed, in a certain sense, he is right. But thinking of the computer as adding does not get us very far towards understanding why the computer moved the queen. Saying that the computer decided to move the queen by adding is a little like saying Picasso created *Guernica* by painting. And there is more than a touch of irony in the engineer's trying to undermine the anthropomorphization of the computer by using what is ultimately an anthropomorphic imagine of adding.

The reaction to ELIZA, a conversational natural language program that simulated the responses of a Rogerian psychotherapist, threw people's tendency to attribute human characteristics to computers into sharp relief. By picking up on key words and phrases it had been programmed to recognize, the program was able to ask questions and make responses ("I AM SORRY TO HEAR YOU ARE DEPRESSED," "WHAT ELSE COMES TO MIND WHEN YOU THINK OF YOUR FATHER?") that made "sense" in its conversational context (a therapy session).

Most of those who originally had access to ELIZA knew and understood the limitations on the program's ability to know and understand. The program could recognize character strings, but it could not attribute meaning to its communications or those it received. And yet, according to its creator, Joseph Weizenbaum, and much to his consternation, the program seemed to draw some of them into closer relationships with it. People confided in the program, wanted to be alone with it, seemed to attribute empathy and understanding to it. In my conversations with students about their experiences with ELIZA, the personalization of the involvement with the program often seemed tied to the issue of predictability. Many referred to the feeling of being "let down" when the program became predictable. When they had cracked the code, when they knew which inputs would provoke which responses, when they knew which inputs would cause the program to become "confused," then "computer confidences" became boring.

People tend not to experience themselves or other people as completely predictable. When asked what it means to be a person and not a machine, most people use plain talk to describe what the more philosophically minded might call the "ineffable." Machines are most people's everyday metaphor for invoking predictability and, insofar as the computer is able to simulate the kind of unpredictability we associate with people, it threatens our concept of machine. Here is a machine that is not "mechanistic." Locally, it has mechanistic components, but seen globally, these disappear and you are dealing with a system that surprises.

Something else that makes analogies between the computer and mechanical antecedents (like adding machines) unsatisfactory is that computers can be programmed into autonomy from their human users. On the simplest level, after a few sessions of an introductory computer science course, the novice programmer knows how to write programs that would, in principle, go on forever, let us say, because step three is an instruction that says return to step one. Such programs will never stop; that is, until somebody "kills" them by pulling out the plug, turning off the machine, or pressing a special control key on the computer terminal which is designed for just such moments. I interviewed a group of college students as they went through an introductory programming course and most could remember strong feelings about what one referred to as his first "forever program."

"Forever" is overwhelming because we can't know it or our place in it. Perhaps a "forever program" gives a glimpse, however ephemeral, of what it might mean. Such glimpses are rare, sometimes occasioned by looking at a mountain, or at a sunset, and are almost always accompanied by strong emotions. In the case of the iterative program, the image of "forever" is created by the programmer himself, perhaps intensifying its evocative power, its fascination.

The computer demonstration called the GAME OF LIFE has this evocative quality. The game begins with a checkerboard of dark and light cells in a given state; cells turn from dark to light and light to dark depending on the state (dark or light) of their immediate neighbors. Such local instructions produce a changing, evolving global pattern. Like a biological system, this computer program can generate global complexity out of local simplicity. The game fascinates, touching on our fascination with self-perpetuating systems, with generativity, and "forever." It also brings into focus a compelling tension between local simplicity and global complexity in the working of the computer. Locally, each step can be predicted from the step before. But the evolution of the global pattern is not graspable. This play between simplicity and complexity is among those things that makes computation a powerful medium for the expression of issues related to control. And perhaps it is in the range of programming relationships that this projective potential is maximally realized.

Programming as Projective

Depending on how the programmer brings the computer's local simplicity and global complexity into focus, he will have a particular experience of the machine as controlled or controlling. Both levels are there; people display different patterns of selective attention to each of them and end up with different relationships to control and power in their programming work. Out of this range of relationships we will look at two very different ones. We see a first style in X, an ex-programmer, now a university professor who describes himself as "having been a computer hacker." X experiences his computer power as a kind of wizardry. Wizards use spells, a powerful local magic. X's magic was local too. He described his "hacker's" approach to any problem as a search for the "quick and dirty fix" and described his longterm fantasy that he could walk up to any program, however complex, and "fix it, bend it to my will." As he described his intervention, he imitated the kind of hand gestures that a stage magician makes towards the hat before he pulls out the rabbit.

X's involvement was in a struggle with the program's complexity—what was most gripping for him was being on the edge between winning and losing. He described his hacking as walking a narrow line: make a local fix, stay aware of its potential to provoke unpredicted change or crash the system, test each system's flexibility to the limit. For X, the narrow line has "holding power." Stories of weekends at the terminal with little to eat and little or no rest were common, as were reflections on not being able to leave the terminal when debugging a program clearly required getting some sleep and looking at the whole in the morning instead of trying to "fix it" by looking at it line by line all night. For X it was his style of programming that led him to identify with what was for him a computer "subculture," that of the hacker. His process of identification seemed analogous to that of a creative independent virtuoso who recognizes his peers not by the "job" they have nor by their academic credentials, but because they share his sense of the personal importance, the urgency of creating in the medium in which they work.

Many hackers have dropped out of academic programs in computer science in order to devote themselves exclusively to computers. Based neither on a formal job nor on a research agenda, the coherency of the hacker subculture follows from a relationship with the "subjective computer": that is, with a set of values, a computational aesthetic, and from a relationship with programming that may be characterized as devotion to it as a thing in itself. In university settings all over the country, where hackers are often "the master programmers" of large computer operating systems, academic computer scientists complain that the hackers are always "improving the system," making it more elegant according to their aesthetic, but also more difficult to use.

Some have characterized the hacker's relationship with computation as "compulsive," but its urgency can be otherwise described. The hacker grapples with a computational essence—the issue of how to exert control over global complexity by mastery of local simplicity. The mechanism embodied in the lines of code under his immediate scrutiny is always simple, determined, certain—but the whole constantly strains to escape the limit of his ability to "think of it all at once," to see the implications of his actions on the larger system. And this is precisely what he finds so exciting.

A second programmer, Y, is also a computer professional, a microprocessor engineer who works all day on the development of hardware for a large industrial data system. He has recently built a small computer system for his home and devotes much of his leisure time to programming it. Whereas for hacker X, the excitement of programming is that of a high-risk venture, Y likes it as a chance to be in complete control. Although Y works all days with computers, his building and programming them at home is not "more of the same." He experiences his relationship to the computer as completely different in the two settings. At work he describes himself as part of a whole that he cannot see and over which he feels no mastery or ownership: "At work what I do is part of a big system; like they say, I'm a cog." At home he works on well-defined projects of his own choosing, projects whose beginning, middle, and end are all under his control. To him, the home projects seem a kind of compensation for the alienation of his job. He observes that he works most intensively on his home system when his tasks at work seem mostly a project of "somebody else having parceled things out . . ." and furthest away from any understanding of "how the whole thing fits together."

X and Y have very different senses about what is most satisfying about programming. These translate into different choices of projects, into different computational values, and ultimately into what we might call different computational aesthetics. X likes to work on large, "almost out of control" projects; Y likes to work on very precisely defined ones. X finds documentation a burdensome and unwelcome constraint. Y enjoys documentation; he likes to have a clear, unambiguous record of what he has mastered. Much of his sense of power over the program derives from its precise specifications and from his attempts to continually enlarge the sphere of the program's local simplicity. There is certainly no agreement between X and Y about what constitutes a "good" program or a "good" computer application.

X, like many other people I have spoken to who identify with the hacker subculture, sees business systems and IBM and its products (FORTRAN,

COBOL, IBM timesharing, and IBM computers themselves) as particularly "ugly." A company like IBM is interested in system reliability, and this means trade-offs in the system's "plasticity." A hacker may complain that such systems hold back both the computer and the programmer. He is often more sympathetic to computer applications which touch on the area of Artificial Intelligence, the enterprise of programming computers to do things (like having vision, speech, and chess-playing ability) that are usually considered intelligent when done by people. His sympathy is not surprising. In Artificial Intelligence projects, the hacker can see an embodiment of his sense of what is most exciting about the computer—the way unpredictable and surprising complexity can emerge from clever local ideas. At the other extreme, programmer Y's commitment to computers is to what is most precise, predictable, and controllable. For Y, what is powerful about the computer is definitionally in a different realm than the human mind with its vagueness and unpredictability. He may rule Artificial Intelligence out of court because there is as yet no agreed upon specification of what it is to be "intelligent." ("How can you build something which has not been reduced to 'specs'?") For the hacker, this usually poses no problem. In fact, his sense of computational power is incompatible with "specs."

People bring computers into their homes for many different reasons, but questionnaire data on over a hundred computer "hobbyists" (here defined as people who have had a computer in their home for several years—that is, before the advent of mass marketed "turnkey" systems) and nearly 150 hours of follow-up interviews with 30 of them suggested that Y's style of dealing with the computer, his computational values and aesthetics, are widely shared in this group. Like Y, other hobbyists have built their computers from kits, and many continue to work as close to the machine as possible, preferring assembly language to higher level languages, and preferring to write their own assemblers even when commercial ones are easily available. The hobbyist's relationship with the computer he has worked on, often built "from scratch," and nearly always carefully documented, can be heavily invested with a desire for a kind of personal control that can be passed on to his children.

Although advertisements for personal computers have stressed that they are an investment in your child's education—that computers have programs that can teach algebra, physics, the conjugation of French verbs— hobbyists don't speak about the importance of giving their children a competitive advantage in French, but of a competitive advantage in "the computer." Most hobbyists feel that the stakes are high. They believe that computers will change politics, economics, and everyday life in the twenty-first century. Owning a piece of it, and having complete technical mastery over a piece of it, is owning a little bit of control over the future.

For many hobbyists with whom I spoke, the relationship with their home computer carries longings for a better and simpler life in a more transparent society. *CoEvolution Quarterly, Mother Earth News, Runner's World,* and *Byte* magazine lie together on hobbyists' coffee tables. Small computers become the focus of hopes of building cottage industries that will allow the hobbyist to work out of his home, have more personal autonomy, not have to punch a time card, and be able to spend more time with his family and out-of-doors.

Some see personal computers as a next step in the ecology movement: decentralized technology will mean less waste. Some see personal computers as a way for individuals to assert greater control over their children's educations, believing that computerized curricula will soon offer children better educations at home than can be offered in today's schools. Some see personal computers as a path to a new populism: personal computer networks will allow citizens to band together to run decentralized schools, information resources, and local governments.

Many of the computer hobbyists I have interviewed talk about the computers in their livingrooms as windows onto a future where relationships with technology will be more direct, where people will understand how things work, and where dependence on big government, big corporations, and big machines will end. They represent the politics of this computer-rich future by generalizing from their special relationship to the technology, a relationship characterized by simplicity and a sense of control. In this tendency to generalization, they are not alone. People often take a particular way of relating to the computer; that is, they take their personal sense of what is important, interesting, and valuable about computers, and generalize it into beliefs about "computers in general." This process of generalization and ideology formation can be rapid. I saw it begin with a group of 25 college students, computer "newcomers," whom I followed through their first computer science course. I spoke to them several times during the course about their reactions to learning about computers and programming: how did they see the computer, how did they feel about what they were learning.

Many of the students began the course with an image of the computer as a complex and powerful entity. But for some, with an elementary knowledge of the machine and of programming came a way of thinking about the computer that began to approach the view we have characterized as common to many hobbyists, a view of the computer as simple and controllable. ("The machine is dumb; just a giant calculator.") And for about half of the students, an image of a primitive computer whose power was based on the ability to perform arithmetic functions became their image for all of computation. In the process, their attention turned away from questions relating to the complexity of computation. They showed little interest in highly speculative issues about the future of Artificial Intelligence or in such down-to-earth problems of sloppily written complex systems that have gotten out of hand. Such systems (written, rewritten, and locally revised by different programmers, indeed by different teams of programmers through the years) can become a patchwork of local fixes, each with an inevitable, but often unknown, impact on the working of the whole. If you need to change such programs, the change can only take the form of yet another local fix, and the results of doing so are unpredictable. When we refer to such systems as incomprehensible, this does not mean that we cannot understand their local workings. It means that we cannot act on the program as though we understood it as a whole. We cannot know the consequences of our actions. The programs become autonomous in the sense that making changes to them becomes too "dangerous" to try. But because the students saw the programs they were writing in their course as easily modifiable, they could not really see how such problems could arise. Several dismissed the very possibility with the phrase "Garbage in—Garbage Out" (GIGO).

One might think that the problem here is in the nature of "introductory" material. In the teaching of chemistry, for example, we usually find that it makes most sense to begin with the simplest stuff, with the material that will give students the most confidence that they can make the subject "their own." And then when they move on from their high-school to their college chemistry classes, they are shown how to cast aside their high-school models of atoms as "wrong." Images of electron shells and precise orbits are replaced by models of orbitals, suborbitals, and probability densities. But in the case of the computer, things are different. The kind of programming that typically goes on in an introductory course encourages an emphasis on the "local simplicity" view of the computer. But at every level of expertise you can have a choice of focusing on simplicity or on complexity. There is no "truth" in the Rorschach inkblots that you finally see if you examine them long enough, and a particular set towards computation can be maintained at very different levels of expertise.

By the end of their one semester course, most students in my study had averaged seventy-five hours at the computer terminal. Many of the hobbyists I interviewed who had logged many thousands of hours and had completed some very complex projects were as solidly committed as the students to a view of the computer that focused on its local simplicity. And like the students, they, too, used their experience with the computer as a basis for dismissing issues that might emerge from computational complexity. It may well be that for some of them, their use of the computer as enblematic of the personally and politically controllable gave them strong reasons to want to hold on to this view. But that they were *able* to do so reflects something about the nature of computation. The view of computation as locally simple can be shared by programmers at very different levels of expertise because it is not technically wrong: all programs can be described locally, and *at least in principle* all programming goals can be achieved while retaining complete control over the system. *In practice,* many hobbyists are led by their passion for documentation to become masters of the art of local (most often line-by-line) description of programs and are led by the individualism of their computer culture into habits of work and choices of programming projects that reinforce a style of highly controlled programming. Thus a tradition, an aesthetic, and relationships both with people and machines maintain a sense of computation similar to that which tends to be encouraged by working with the small, tightly controlled programming projects typical of first courses.

The "blind spots" of those who invoked formulas like GIGO to dismiss the problem of incomprehensible programs went beyond the inability to see the consequences of computational complexity. The remark reflects a vision of programming as a technical act and as an individual act: if a program is incomprehensible, it is because someone wrote bad code. For an individual working alone that might be true, but it is a mistake to think about computation in other settings as an extension of the computation that one does in one's home or for a problem set.

Computation is a social act, the sum total of everything it takes to make a particular computational event occur: the hardware, the teams of people creating the necessary software, the organizations of people, bureaucracies, and industries in which it happens. The incomprehensibility of the large programs used by such organizations as the Internal Revenue Service can have a great deal to do with such social factors as the uncommitted relationship between the programmers and the organization, the structure and the instability of the programming teams, the way in which authority is delegated. Even the programming environment in which the work is done (what languages are used, what debugging systems are available, etc.) can depend on political choices within the organization. None of these factors is intrinsic to computation. None of these factors is made apparent by extrapolating from most experiences of recreational or classroom computation.

Our discussion of "blind spots" and of programming experience helps us to bridge our earlier distinction between social problems that follow from what computers do and those that follow from how people think about computers. The social problems that arise from the presence of cumbersome, effectively unmodifiable programs in large organizations are in the class of problems raised by "what computers do." These problems may be compounded by difficulties in understanding their nature that are rooted in more subjective perceptions. The way in which we, as a society, deal with problems posed by what computers do is influenced by our ways of thinking about computers. The subjective side of computation is not without its objective consequences. The blind spots that I noticed among my sample of beginning students and hobbyists are only one example. We spoke about the computer "as Rorschach." But of course there is a difference. Unlike Rorschach blots, computers are also powerful social actors, and what people project onto them—these "socially constructed computers"—can themselves become social presences that influence policy makers, educators, engineers and the general public. In the last analysis, how people think about computers *is* "something that computers do."

Computer Literacy

The observation that the way people think about computers can exacerbate problems caused by what computers do leads easily to a standard response: educate them. There is an active movement of advocates and activists of "computer literacy," the minimum that everyone needs to know about computers in order to function effectively as a citizen. Schools and federal agencies, magazines and clubs, the computer industry, even the manufacturers of children's games are all entering the business of educating the public. There is no doubt that people are learning more about computers. But our glimpse of the subjective side of computation alerts us to some potential problems about what they may be learning. In most cases, and certainly in computer literacy courses that use curricula designed for grade school and adult education classes, people are learning simple programming skills and a set of "facts" about the computer. But we have seen that "facts" about the computer do not come in neutral information packets. Computer literacy is usually defined as knowledge about the computer. If we accept the idea of computation as a social act, it would be more appropriate to define it as knowledge about computers and people. In this essay, we have raised several issues that need to be taken into account by this kind of humanistic computer literacy movement.

We have seen that what seems like the obvious first step in computer education, learning to write small programs, can lead to a paradox. The computer educator hopes to give the student a more objective understanding, but the result can be to bias the student's perception of computation against recognizing phenomena associated with complexity. Several possible strategies have been suggested for dealing with this paradox. The student's model of computation might develop differently if his first computer experience was to modify a large pre-existing program rather than to create his own tiny ones. Explicit discussion of issues related to system complexity could be introduced into elementary computer education.

A second issue relates to selection. There clearly are different styles of relating to computers. The styles are so distinct that those who practice one are prone to see those who practice another as wrong, fuzzy headed, even bizarre. When speaking about programmers and their styles, we used the metaphor of subcultures. A standard computer literacy curriculum easily could become the vehicle which defines the "normal" and the "deviant" among these cultures. Any educationally "official" computer culture will encourage only some people to think of working with computation as being a good "fit" with who they are. When we think about computer education in the next decade, we are no longer talking about the education of a small group of people who will become computer specialists, computer experts. We are talking about computer literacy for the masses of people who will need to feel comfortable with computers in order to feel comfortable and unintimidated by daily life. The goal should be to give as many of them as possible the sense of belonging in a computer-rich society.

A third issue has to do with an unknown: how different styles of relating to computers may transfer to other things. We have noted that choosing a programming language and a programming style implies a cluster of cultural characteristics, values, ways of thinking, X's and Y's programming styles suggest strategies for dealing with problems that have nothing to do with the computer. There may be a transfer of some of these ways of thinking from computation to other things. If we acknowledge that a computer literacy program may be training in habits of thought, then it must be evaluated in these larger terms.

There is the fourth issue of anthropomorphization. The phenomenon makes many people uneasy. Some hope that objective knowledge about how computers "really" work will make it go away. But anthropomorphic imagery, supported by the computer's projective capacities, seems deeply embedded in the nature of computation. A responsible approach to computer education must take it more seriously, must understand its genesis and multiple functions, whether in the end it decides to oppose, exploit, or ignore it.

A fifth and final issue touches on the way in which the computer—as it becomes implicated in ways of thinking about politics, religion, psychology, and education—can raise challenging, even disturbing, questions for individuals. For example, in an introductory programming course, a college sophomore saw how seemingly intelligent and seemingly autonomous systems can run on programs. This led him to his first brush with the idea (which others have first encountered via philosophy or psycholoanalytic thought) that there might be something illusory in people's subjective sense of autonomy and conscious self-determination. Having seen this idea, he rejected it, with arguments about the irreducibility of man's conscious sense of himself that paralleled those of Freud's more hostile contemporaries both in their substance and in the emotion behind them. In doing so, he made explicit a commitment to a concept of man to which he had never before felt the need to pay conscious attention.

The reference to psychoanalysis brings us full circle to an analogy I made at the beginning of this article. There, I noted that twentieth-century popular culture has appropriated psychoanalytic ideas that were first developed in a technical context, and I conjectured that computational models for thinking about the mind might undergo a similar fate. Here I consider a very different aspect of the analogous relationship between computation and psycholanalysis—not how they can be similarly *accepted* but how they both carry messages which are likely to be resisted and *rejected*. Psychoanalytic notions of the unconscious, of infantile sexuality, and of Oedipal relationships provoked strong resistance before being accepted into either academic or popular cultures. Psychoanalysis is a framework for thinking—we might call it a "subversive science"—that challenges humanistic and "common sense" models of man as an autonomous agent. In doing so, it calls into question some of our taken-for-granted ways of thinking about ourselves. Computational frameworks share some of this "subversive" quality. They, too, provoke strong feeling. Opinions are divided: some people welcome computational analogies with people as the basis for a new kind of scientific humanism, while others warn that such models deny us that which is specifically human in our nature. Some embrace the prospect of Artificial Intelligence as an adventure for the human spirit, while others see much about the enterprise as obscene.

Although the phenomena around the "subjective computer" we have dealt with in this essay are highly visible in our culture, the groups that are most involved in computer education and the computer literacy movements tend to ignore them. Each has a different reason for doing so. The computer industry is committed to presenting computers as neutral technical objects that can enter daily life in a non-disruptive way. The personal computer magazines and hobbyist movement have a different motive for "normalization." Their effort is to assimilate everything to activities within the technical reach and the intellectual style of the owner of a very small system. Schools are intent on avoiding the controversial. They have had enough trouble with sharp debates over sex education and such experiments as the Man as a Course of Study program. They are willing to "take on" computation as a cost-effective adjunct to their standard curricula. It is not in their immediate interest to "see" other aspects of the computers they have taken on.

The leadership of industrial, recreational, and educational computing share a language for talking about computer education and computer literacy that is technical and instrumental and selectively ignores the more highly charged aspects of the computer presence. When these do come up, they tend to be denied as nonexistent, viewed as transitional phenomena that people need to be educated out of so that computers may more appropriately be seen as "just a tool." Of course the computer is a tool, but man has always been shaped by his artifacts. Man makes them but they in turn make him. In the case of the computer, we may confront a tool that can catalyze a change in how we think about ourselves; for example, by making us aware on a daily basis of being only one among many other possible forms of "rule driven" intelligence.

We spoke of the emergence in the mid-twentieth century of a psychoanalytic culture, a culture that had an influence on how people thought about

their lives, about raising their children, and about the stability and instability of political systems. It is too soon to tell whether we are entering a
computer culture that will have anything near this level of impact on us. But
in our discussion of the subjective computer we began to see traces of such
a culture in formation. There is the rapid spread of computional ideas into
everyday language, there is the appropriation of information-processing
models in psychology as well as in other behavioral and social sciences. If
psychoanalytic ideas became culturally embedded through their embodiment in therapeutic practice, computational ideas are growing their own
roots in education. There are cultures growing up around the computer
that use the machines as metaphors for thinking about people and social
organization. We wear a dangerous set of blinders if we do not appreciate
and further explore how computers can become the carriers of culture and
of a challenge to our way of thinking about ourselves. If nothing else, a
fuller appreciation of this subjective side of the technology should lead us
to a critical reexamination of what each of us takes for granted about "the
computer" and to an attitude of healthy skepticism towards any who propose simple scenarios about the "impact of the computer on society."

EDMUND CARPENTER

The New Languages

Brain of the New World,
What a task is thine,
To formulate the modern
. . . to recast poems, churches, art
WHITMAN

Anthropologist Edmund Carpenter takes issue with those who hold that one medium, such as the printed word, is more accurate or factual than another. It is his position that each medium has its own language and bias; therefore ideas or events are best communicated through the medium which has the most appropriate "language" or "bias" for that idea or event. The important concept is that "each medium, if its bias is properly exploited, reveals and communicates a unique aspect of reality, of truth."

When reading in Carpenter you may have to withhold your usual notions about language—that is, if you think of language mainly as the words, sentences and grammatical rules that you were taught in connection with learning to read and write. Think of language as the camera lens, the close-up, the montage, the split screen, the quick cut, the voice-over, sounds unconnected with objects. How does the medium put things together? What about the spaces and time units that are part of its grammar? if you begin to think of language in this way you will understand what Carpenter means by the "new" languages.

English is a mass medium. All languages are mass media. The new mass media—film, radio, TV—are new languages, their grammars as yet unknown. Each codifies reality differently; each conceals a unique metaphysics. Linguists tell us it's possible to say anything in any language if you use enough words or images, but there's rarely time; the natural course is for a culture to exploit its media biases.

Writing, for example, didn't record oral language; it was a new language, which the spoken word came to imitate. Writing encouraged an analytical mode of thinking with emphasis upon lineality. Oral languages tended to be polysynthetic, composed of great, tight conglomerates, like twisted knots, within which images were juxtaposed, inseparably fused; written communications consisted of little words chronologically ordered. Subject became distinct from verb, adjective from noun, thus separating actor from action, essence from form. Where preliterate man imposed form diffidently, temporarily—for such transitory forms lived but temporarily on the tip of his tongue, in the living situation—the printed word was inflexible, permanent in touch with eternity: it embalmed truth for posterity.

This embalming process froze language, eliminated the art of ambiguity, made puns "the lowest form of wit," destroyed word linkages. The word became a static symbol, applicable to and separate from that which it symbolized. It now belonged to the objective world; it could be seen. Now came the distinction between being and meaning, the dispute as to whether the Eucharist *was* or only *signified* the body of the Sacrifice. The word became a neutral symbol, no longer an inextricable part of a creative process.

Gutenberg completed the process. The manuscript page with pictures, colors, correlation between symbol and space, gave way to uniform type, the black and white page, read silently, alone. The format of the book favored lineal expression, for the argument ran like a thread from cover to cover, subject to verb to object, sentence to sentence, paragraph to paragraph, chapter to chapter, carefully structured from beginning to end, with value embedded in the climax. This was not true of great poetry and drama, which retained multi-perspective, but it was true of most books, particularly texts, histories, autobiographies, novels. Events were arranged chronologically and hence, it was assumed, causally; relationship, not being, was valued. The author became an *authority;* his data were serious, that is, *serially* organized. Such data, if sequentially ordered and printed, conveyed value and truth; arranged any other way, they were suspect.

The newspaper format brought an end to book culture. It offers short, discrete articles that give important facts first and than taper off to incidental details, which may be, and often are, eliminated by the make-up man. The fact that reporters cannot control the length of their articles means that, in writing them, emphasis can't be placed on structure, at least in the traditional linear sense, with climax or conclusion at the end. Everything has to be captured in the headline; from there it goes down the pyramid to incidentals. In fact there is often more in the headline than in the article; occasionally, no article at all accompanies the banner headline.

The position and size of articles on the front page are determined by interest and importance, not content. Unrelated reports from Moscow, Sarawak, London, and Ittipik are juxtaposed; time and space, as separate concepts, are destroyed and the *here* and *now* presented as a single Gestalt. Subway readers consume everything on the front page, then turn to page 2 to read, in incidental order, continuations. A Toronto banner headline ran: TOWNSEND TO MARRY PRINCESS; directly beneath this was a second headline: *Fabian Says This May Not Be Sex Crime.* This went unnoticed by eyes and minds conditioned to consider each newspaper item in isolation.

Such a format lends itself to simultaneity, not chronology or lineality. Items abstracted from a total situation aren't arranged in casual sequence, but presented holistically, as raw experience. The front page is a cosmic *Finnegans Wake.*

The disorder of the newspaper throws the reader into a producer role. The reader has to process the news himself; he has to co-create, to cooperate in the creation of the work. The newspaper format calls for the direct participation of the consumer.

In magazines, where a writer more frequently controls the length of his article, he can, if he wishes, organize it in traditional style, but the majority don't. An increasingly popular presentation is the printed symposium, which is little more than collected opinions, pro and con. The magazine format as a whole opposes lineality; its pictures lack tenses. In *Life,* extremes are juxtaposed: space ships and prehistoric monsters, Flemish monasteries and dope addicts. It creates a sense of urgency and uncertainty: the next page is unpredictable. One encounters rapidly a riot in Teheran, a Hollywood marriage, the wonders of the Eisenhower administration, a two-headed calf, a party on Jones beach, all sandwiched between ads. The eye takes in the page as a whole (readers may pretend this isn't so, but the success of advertising suggests it is), and the page—indeed, the whole magazine—becomes a single Gestalt where association, though not causal, is often lifelike.

The same is true of the other new languages. Both radio and TV offer short, unrelated programs, interrupted between and within by commercials. I say "interrupted," being myself an anachronism of book culture, but my children don't regard them as interruptions, as breaking continuity. Rather, they regard them as part of a whole, and their reaction is neither one of annoyance nor one of indifference. The ideal news broadcast has half a dozen speakers from as many parts of the world on as many subjects. The London correspondent doesn't comment on what the Washington correspondent has just said; he hasn't even heard him.

The child is right in not regarding commercials as interruptions. For the only time anyone smiles on TV is in commercials. The rest of life, in news broadcasts and soap operas, is presented as so horrible that the only way to get through life is to buy this product: then you'll smile. Aesop never wrote a clearer fable. It's heaven and hell brought up to date: Hell in the headline, Heaven in the ad. Without the other, neither has meaning.

There's pattern in these new media—not line, but knot; not lineality or causality or chronology, nothing that leads to a desired climax; but a Gordian knot without antecedents or results, containing within itself carefully selected elements, juxtaposed, inseparably fused; a knot that can't be untied to give the long, thin cord of lineality.

This is especially true of ads that never present an ordered, sequential, rational argument but simply present the product associated with desirable things or attitudes. Thus Coca-Cola is shown held by a beautiful blonde, who sits in a Cadillac, surrounded by bronze, muscular admirers, with the sun shining overhead. By repetition these elements become associated, in our minds, into a pattern of sufficient cohesion so that one element can magically evoke the others. If we think of ads as designed solely to sell products, we miss their main effect: to increase pleasure in the consumption of the product. Coca-Cola is far more than a cooling drink; the consumer participates, vicariously, in a much larger experience. In Africa, in Melanesia, to drink a Coke is to participate in the American way of life.

Of the new languages, TV comes closest to drama and ritual. It combines music and art, language and gesture, rhetoric and color. It favors simultaneity of visual and auditory images. Cameras focus not on speakers but on persons spoken to or about; the audience *hears* the accuser but *watches* the accused. In a single impression it hears the prosecutor, watches the trembling hands of the big-town crook, and sees the look of moral indignation on Senator Tobey's face. This is real drama, in process, with the outcome uncertain. Print can't do this; it has a different bias.

Books and movies only pretend uncertainty, but live TV retains this vital aspect of life. Seen on TV, the fire in the 1952 Democratic Convention threatened briefly to become a conflagration; seen on newsreel, it was history, without potentiality.

The absence of uncertainty is no handicap to other media, if they are properly used, for their biases are different. Thus it's clear from the beginning that Hamlet is a doomed man, but, far from detracting in interest, this heightens the sense of tragedy.

Now, one of the results of the time-space duality that developed in

Western culture, principally from the Renaissance on, was a separation within the arts. Music, which created symbols in time, and graphic art, which created symbols in space, became separate pursuits, and men gifted in one rarely pursued the other. Dance and ritual, which inherently combined them, fell in popularity. Only in drama did they remain united.

It is significant that of the four new media, the three most recent are dramatic media, particularly TV, which combines language, music, art, dance. They don't, however, exercise the same freedom with time that the stage dares practice. An intricate plot, employing flash backs, multiple time perspectives and overlays, intelligible on the stage, would mystify on the screen. The audience has no time to think back, to establish relations between early hints and subsequent discoveries. The picture passes before the eyes too quickly; there are no intervals in which to take stock of what has happened and make conjectures of what is going to happen. The observer is in a more passive state, less interested in subtleties. Both TV and film are nearer to narrative and depend much more upon the episodic. An intricate time construction can be done in film, but in fact rarely is. The soliloquies of *Richard III* belong on the stage; the film audience was unprepared for them. On stage Ophelia's death was described by three separate groups: one hears the announcement and watches the reactions simultaneously. On film the camera flatly shows her drowned where "a willow lies aslant a brook."

Media differences such as these mean that it's not simply a question of communicating a single idea in different ways but that a given idea or insight belongs primarily, though not exclusively, to one medium, and can be gained or communicated best through that medium.

Thus the book was ideally suited for discussing evolution and progress. Both belonged, almost exclusively, to book culture. Like a book, the idea of progress was an abstracting, organizing principle for the interpretation and comprehension of the incredibly complicated record of human experience. The sequence of events was believed to have a direction, to follow a given course along an axis of time; it was held that civilization, like the reader's eye (in J. B. Bury's words), "has moved, is moving, and will move in a desirable direction. Knowledge will advance, and with that advance, reason and decency must increasingly prevail among men." Here we see the three main elements of book lineality: the line, the point moving along that line, and its movement toward a desirable goal.

The Western conception of a definite moment in the present, of the present as a definite moment or a definite point, so important in book-dominated languages, is absent, to my knowledge, in oral languages. Absent as well, in oral societies, are such animating and controlling ideas as Western individualism and three-dimensional perspective, both related to this conception of the definite moment, and both nourished, probably bred, by book culture.

Each medium selects its ideas. TV is a tiny box into which people are crowded and must live; film gives us the wide world. With its huge screen, film is perfectly suited for social drama, Civil War panoramas, the sea, land erosion, Cecil B. DeMille spectaculars. In contrast, the TV screen has room for two, at the most three, faces, comfortably. TV is closer to stage, yet different. Paddy Chayefsky writes:

> The theatre audience is far away from the actual action of the drama. They cannot see the silent reactions of the players. They must be told in a loud voice what is going on. The plot movement from one scene to another must be marked, rather than gently shaded as is required in television. In television, however, you can dig into the most humble, ordinary relationships; the relationship of bourgeois children to their mother, of middle-class husband to his wife, of white-collar father to his secretary—in short, the relationships of the people. We relate to each other in an incredibly complicated manner. There is far more exciting drama in the reasons why a man gets married than in why he murders someone. The man who is unhappy in his job, the wife who thinks of a lover, the girl who wants to get into television, your father, your mother, sister, brothers, cousins, friends—all these are better subjects for drama than Iago. What makes a man ambitious? Why does a girl always try to steal her kid sister's boy friends? Why does your uncle attend his annual class reunion faithfully every year? Why do you always find it depressing to visit your father? These are the substances of good television drama; and the deeper you probe into and examine the twisted, semi-formed complexes of emotional entanglements, the more exciting your writing becomes.[1]

This is the primary reason, I believe, why Greek drama is more readily adapted to TV than to film. The boxed-in quality of live TV lends itself to static literary tragedy with greater ease than does the elastic, energetic, expandable movie. Guthrie's recent movie of *Oedipus* favored the panoramic shot rather than the selective eye. It consisted of a succession of tableaux, a series of elaborate, unnatural poses. The effect was of congested groups of people moving in tight formation as though they had trained for it by living for days together in a self-service elevator. With the lines, "I grieve for the City, and for myself and you . . . and walk through endless ways of thought," the inexorable tragedy moved to its horrible "come to realize" climax as though everyone were stepping on everyone else's feet.

The tight, necessary conventions of live TV were more sympathetic to

Sophocles in the Aluminium Hour's *Antigone*. Restrictions of space are imposed on TV as on the Greek stage by the size and inflexibility of the studio. Squeezed by physical limitations, the producer was forced to expand the viewer's imagination with ingenious devices.

When T. S. Eliot adapted *Murder in the Cathedral* for film, he noted a difference in realism between cinema and stage:

> Cinema, even where fantasy is introduced, is much more realistic than the stage. Especially in an historical picture, the setting, the costume, and the way of life represented have to be accurate. Even a minor anachronism is intolerable. On the stage much more can be overlooked or forgiven; and indeed, an excessive care for accuracy of historical detail can become burdensome and distracting. In watching a stage performance, the member of the audience is in direct contact with the actor playing a part. In looking at a film, we are much more passive; as audience, we contribute less. We are seized with the illusion that we are observing an actual event, or at least a series of photographs of the actual event; and nothing must be allowed to break this illusion. Hence the precise attention to detail.[2]

If two men are on a stage in a theater, the dramatist is obliged to motivate their presence; he has to account for their existing on the stage at all. Whereas if a camera is following a figure down a street or is turned to any object whatever, there is no need for a reason to be provided. Its grammar contains that power of statement of motivation, no matter what it looks at.

In the theater, the spectator sees the enacted scene as a whole in space, always seeing the whole of the space. The stage may present only one corner of a large hall, but that corner is always totally visible all through the scene. And the spectator always sees that scene from a fixed, unchanging distance and from an angle of vision that doesn't change. Perspective may change from scene to scene, but within it remains constant. Distance never varies.

But in film and TV, distance and angle constantly shift. The same scene is shown in multiple perspective and focus. The viewer sees it from here, there, then over here; finally he is drawn inexorably into it, becomes part of it. He ceases to be a spectator. Balázs writes:

> Although we sit in our seats, we do not see Romeo and Juliet from there. We look up into Juliet's balcony with Romeo's eyes and look down on Romeo with Juliet's. Our eye and with it our consciousness is identified with the characters in the film, we look at the world out of their eyes and have no angle of vision of our own. We walk amid crowds, ride, fly or fall with the hero and if one character looks into the other's eyes, he looks into our eyes from the

screen, for, our eyes are in the camera and become identical with the gaze of the characters. They see with our eyes. Herein lies the psychological act of identification. Nothing like this "identification" has ever occurred as the effect of any other system of art and it is here that the film manifests its absolute artistic novelty.

. . . Not only can we see, in the isolated "shots" of a scene, the very atoms of life and their innermost secrets revealed at close quarters, but we can do so without any of the intimate secrecy being lost, as always happens in the exposure of a stage performance or of a painting. The new theme which the new means of expression of film art revealed was not a hurricane at sea or the eruption of a volcano: it was perhaps a solitary tear slowly welling up in the corner of a human eye.

. . . Not to speak does not mean that one has nothing to say. Those who do not speak may be brimming over with emotions which can be expressed only in forms and pictures, in gesture and play of feature. The man of visual culture uses these not as substitutes for words, as a deaf-mute uses his fingers.[3]

The gestures of visual man are not intended to convey concepts that can be expressed in words, but inner experiences, nonrational emotions, which would still remain unexpressed when everything that can be told has been told. Such emotions lie in the deepest levels. They cannot be approached by words that are mere reflections of concepts, any more than musical experiences can be expressed in rational concepts. Facial expression is a human experience rendered immediately visible without the intermediary of word. It is Turgenev's "living truth of the human face."

Printing rendered illegible the faces of men. So much could be read from paper that the method of conveying meaning by facial expression fell into desuetude. The press grew to be the main bridge over which the more remote interhuman spiritual exhanges took place; the immediate, the personal, the inner, died. There was no longer need for the subtler means of expression provided by the body. The face became immobile; the inner life, still. Wells that dry up are wells from which no water is dipped.

Just as radio helped bring back inflection in speech, so film and TV are aiding us in the recovery of gesture and facial awareness—a rich, colorful language, conveying moods and emotions, happenings and characters, even thoughts, none of which could be properly packaged in words. If film had remained silent for another decade, how much faster this change might have been!

Feeding the product of one medium through another medium creates a new product. When Hollywood buys a novel, it buys a title and the publicity associated with it: nothing more. Nor should it.

Each of the four versions of the *Caine Mutiny*—book, play, movie,

TV—had a different hero: Willie Keith, the lawyer Greenwald, the United States Navy, and Captain Queeg, respectively. Media and audience biases were clear. Thus the book told, in lengthy detail, of the growth and making of Ensign William Keith, American man, while the movie camera with its colorful shots of ships and sea, unconsciously favored the Navy as hero, a bias supported by the fact the Navy cooperated with the movie makers. Because of stage limitations, the play was confined, except for the last scene, to the courtroom, and favored the defense counsel as hero. The TV show, aimed at a mass audience, emphasized patriotism, authority, allegiance. More important, the cast was reduced to the principals and the plot to its principles; the real moral problem—the refusal of subordinates to assist an incompetent, unpopular superior—was clear, whereas in the book it was lost under detail, in the film under scenery. Finally, the New York play, with its audience slanted toward Expense Account patronage— Mr. Sampson, Western Sales Manager for the Cavity Drill Company— became a morality play with Willie Keith, innocent American youth, torn between two influences: Keefer, clever author but moral cripple, and Greenwald, equally brilliant but reliable, a businessman's intellectual. Greenwald saves Willie's soul.

The film *Moby Dick* was in many ways an improvement on the book, primarily because of its explicitness. For *Moby Dick* is one of those admittedly great classics, like *Robinson Crusoe* or Kafka's *Trial*, whose plot and situation, as distilled apart from the book by time and familiarity, are actually much more imposing than the written book itself. It's the drama of Ahab's defiance rather than Melville's uncharted leviathan meanderings that is the greatness of *Moby Dick*. On film, instead of laborious tacks through leagues of discursive interruptions, the most vivid descriptions of whales and whaling become part of the action. On film, the viewer was constantly aboard ship: each scene an instantaneous shot of whaling life, an effect achieved in the book only by illusion, by constant, detailed reference. From start to finish, all the action of the film served to develop what was most central to the theme—a man's magnificent and blasphemous pride in attempting to destroy the brutal, unreasoning force that maims him and turns man-made order into chaos. Unlike the book, the film gave a spare, hard, compelling dramatization, free of self-conscious symbolism.

Current confusion over the respective roles of the new media comes largely from a misconception of their function. They are art forms, not substitutes for human contact. Insofar as they attempt to usurp speech and personal, living relations, they harm. This, of course, has long been one of the problems of book culture, at least during the time of its monopoly of Western middle-class thought. But this was never a legitimate function of books, nor of any other medium. Whenever a medium goes claim jumping, trying to work areas where it is ill-suited, conflicts occur with other media, or, more accurately, between the vested interests controlling each. But, when media simply exploit their own formats, they become complementary and cross-fertile.

Some people who have no one around talk to cats, and you can hear their voices in the next room, and they sound silly, because the cat won't answer, but that suffices to maintain the illusion that their world is made up of living people, while it is not. Mechanized mass media reverse this: now mechanical cats talk to humans. There is no genuine feedback.

This charge is often leveled by academicians at the new media, but it holds equally for print. The open-mouthed, glaze-eyed TV spectator is merely the successor of the passive, silent, lonely reader whose head moved back and forth like a shuttlecock.

When we read, another person thinks for us: we merely repeat his mental process. The greater part of the work of thought is done for us. This is why it relieves us to take up a book after being occupied by our own thoughts. In reading, the mind is only the playground for another's ideas. People who spend most of their lives in reading often lose the capacity for thinking, just as those who always ride forget how to walk. Some people read themselves stupid. Chaplin did a wonderful take-off of this in *City Lights,* when he stood up on a chair to eat the endless confetti that he mistook for spaghetti.

Eliot remarks: "It is often those writers whom we are lucky enough to know whose books we can ignore; and the better we know them personally, the less need we may feel to read what they write."

Frank O'Connor highlights a basic distinction between oral and written traditions: " 'By the hokies, there was a man in this place one time by name of Ned Sullivan, and he had a queer thing happen to him late one night and he coming up the Valley Road from Durlas.' This is how a folk story begins, or should begin. . . . Yet that is how no printed short story should begin, because such a story seems tame when you remove it from its warm nest by the cottage fire, from the sense of an audience with its interjections, and the feeling of terror at what may lurk in the darkness outside."

Face-to-face discourse is not as selective, abstract, nor explicit as any mechanical medium; it probably comes closer to communicating an unabridged situation than any of them, and, insofar as it exploits the give-take of dynamic relationship, it's clearly the most indispensably human one.

Of course, there can be personal involvement in the other media. When Richardson's *Pamela* was serialized in 1741, it aroused such interest that in one English town, upon receipt of the last installment, the church bell announced that virtue had been rewarded. Radio stations have reported receiving quantities of baby clothes and bassinets when, in a soap opera, a heroine had a baby. One of the commonest phrases used by devoted listeners to daytime serials is that they "visited with" Aunt Jenny or Big Sister. BBC and *News Chronicle* report cases of women viewers who kneel before TV sets to kiss male announcers good night.

Each medium, if its bias is properly exploited, reveals and communicates a unique aspect of reality, of truth. Each offers a different perspective, a way of seeing an otherwise hidden dimension of reality. It's not a question of one reality being true, the others distortions. One allows us to see from here, another from there, a third from still another perspective; taken together they give us a more complete whole, a greater truth. New essentials are brought to the fore, including those made invisible by the "blinders" of old languages.

This is why the preservation of book culture is as important as the development of TV. This is why new languages, instead of destroying old ones, serve as a stimulant to them. Only monopoly is destroyed. When actor-collector Edward G. Robinson was battling actor-collector Vincent Price on art on TV's *$64,000 Challenge*, he was asked how the quiz had affected his life; he answered petulantly, "Instead of looking at the pictures in my art books, I now have to read them." Print, along with all old languages, including speech, has profited enormously from the development of the new media. "The more the arts develop," writes E. M. Foster, "the more they depend on each other for definition. We will borrow from painting first and call it pattern. Later we will borrow from music and call it rhythm."

The appearance of a new medium often frees older media for creative effort. They no longer have to serve the interests of power and profit. Elia Kazan, discussing the American theater, says:

> Take 1900–1920. The theatre flourished all over the country. It had no competition. The box office boomed. The top original fare it had to offer was *The Girl of the Golden West*. Its bow to culture was fusty productions of Shakespeare. . . . Came the moving pictures. The theatre had to be better or go under. It got better. It got so spectacularly better so fast that in 1920–1930

you wouldn't have recognized it. Perhaps it was an accident that Eugene O'Neill appeared at that moment—but it was no accident that in that moment of strange competition, the theatre had room for him. Because it was disrupted and hard pressed, it made room for his experiments, his unheard-of subjects, his passion, his power. There was room for him to grow to his full stature. And there was freedom for the talents that came after his.[4]

Yet a new language is rarely welcomed by the old. The oral tradition distrusted writing, manuscript culture was contemptuous of printing, book culture hated the press, that "slag-heap of hellish passions," as one nineteenth century scholar called it. A father, protesting to a Boston newspaper about crime and scandal, said he would rather see his children "in their graves while pure in innocence, than dwelling with pleasure upon these reports, which have grown so bold."

What really disturbed book-oriented people wasn't the sensationalism of the newspaper, but its nonlineal format, its nonlineal codifications of experience. The motto of conservative academicians became: *Hold that line!*

A new language lets us see with the fresh, sharp eyes of the child; it offers the pure joy of discovery. I was recently told a story about a Polish couple who, though long resident in Toronto, retained many of the customs of their homeland. Their son despaired of ever getting his father to buy a suit cut in style or getting his mother to take an interest in Canadian life. Then he bought them a TV set, and in a matter of months a major change took place. One evening the mother remarked that "Edith Piaf is the latest thing on Broadway," and the father appeared in "the kind of suit executives wear on TV." For years the father had passed this same suit in store windows and seen it both in advertisements and on living men, but not until he saw it on TV did it become meaningful. This same statement goes for all media: each offers a unique presentation of reality, which when new has a freshness and clarity that is extraordinarily powerful.

This is especially true of TV. We say, "We have a radio" but "We have television"—as if something had happened to us. It's no longer "The skin you love to touch" but "The Nylon that loves to touch you." We don't watch TV; it watches us: it guides us. Magazines and newspapers no longer convey "information" but offer ways of seeing things. They have abandoned realism as too easy: they substitute themselves for realism. *Life* is totally advertisements: its articles package and sell emotions and ideas just as its paid ads sell commodities.

Several years ago, a group of us at the University of Toronto undertook the following experiment: 136 students were divided, on the basis of their over-all academic standing of the previous year, into four equal groups who either (1) heard and saw a lecture delivered in a TV studio, (2) heard and saw this same lecture on a TV screen, (3) heard it over the radio, or (4) read it in manuscript. Thus there were, in the CBC studios, four controlled groups who simultaneously received a single lecture and then immediately wrote an identical examination to test both understanding and retention of content. Later the experiment was repeated, using three similar groups; this time the same lecture was (1) delivered in a classroom, (2) presented as a film (using the kinescope) in a small theatre, and (3) again read in print. The actual mechanics of the experiment were relatively simple, but the problem of writing the script for the lecture led to a consideration of the resources and limitations of the dramatic forms involved.

It immediately became apparent that no matter how the script was written and the show produced, it would be slanted in various ways for and against each of the media involved; no show could be produced that did not contain these biases, and the only real common denominator was the simultaneity of presentation. For each communication channel codifies reality differently and thus influences, to a surprising degree, the content of the message communicated. A medium is not simply an envelope that carries any letter; it is itself a major part of that message. We therefore decided not to exploit the full resources of any one medium, but to try to chart a middle-of-the-road course between all of them.

The lecture that was finally produced dealt with linguistic codifications of reality and metaphysical concepts underlying grammatical systems. It was chosen because it concerned a field in which few students could be expected to have prior knowledge; moreover, it offered opportunities for the use of gesture. The cameras moved throughout the lecture, and took close-ups where relevant. No other visual aids were used, nor were shots taken of the audience while the lecture was in progress. Instead, the cameras simply focused on the speaker for twenty-seven minutes.

The first difference we found between a classroom and a TV lecture was the brevity of the latter. The classroom lecture, if not ideally, at least in practice, sets a slower pace. It's verbose, repetitive. It allows for greater elaboration and permits the lecturer to take up several *related* points. TV, however, is stripped right down; there's less time for qualifications or alternative interpretations and only time enough for *one* point. (Into twenty-seven minutes we put the meat of a two-hour classroom lecture.) The ideal TV speaker states his point and then brings out different facets of it by a variety of illustrations. But the classroom lecturer is less subtle and, to the agony of the better students, repeats and repeats his identical points in the hope, perhaps, that ultimately no student will miss them, or perhaps simply because he is dull. Teachers have had captive audiences for so long that few are equipped to compete for attention via the new media.

The next major difference noted was the abstracting role of each medium, beginning with print. Edmund M. Morgan, Harvard Law Professor, writes:

> One who forms his opinion from the reading of any record alone is prone to err, because the printed page fails to produce the impression or convey the idea which the spoken word produced or conveyed. The writer has read charges to the jury which he had previously heard delivered, and has been amazed to see an oral deliverance which indicated a strong bias appear on the printed page as an ideally impartial exposition. He has seen an appellate court solemnly declare the testimony of a witness to be especially clear and convincing which the trial judge had orally characterized as the most abject perjury.[5]

Selectivity of print and radio are perhaps obvious enough, but we are less conscious of it in TV, partly because we have already been conditioned to it by the shorthand of film. Balázs writes:

> A man hurries to a railway station to take leave of his beloved. We see him on the platform. We cannot see the train, but the questing eyes of the man show us that his beloved is already seated in the train. We see only a close-up of the man's face, we see it twitch as if startled and then strips of light and shadow, light and shadow flit across it in quickening rhythm. Then tears gather in the eyes and that ends the scene. We are expected to know what happened and today we do know, but when I first saw this film in Berlin, I did not at once understand the end of this scene. Soon, however, everyone knew what had happened: the train had started and it was the lamps in its compartment which had thrown their light on the man's face as they glided past ever faster and faster.[6]

As in a movie theater, only the screen is illuminated, and, on it, only points of immediate relevance are portrayed; everything else is eliminated. This explicitness makes TV not only personal but forceful. That's why stage hands in a TV studio watch the show over floor monitors, rather than watch the actual performance before their eyes.

The script of the lecture, timed for radio, proved too long for TV. Visual aids and gestures on TV not only allow the elimination of certain words, but require a unique script. The ideal radio delivery stresses pitch and intonation to make up for the absence of the visual. That flat, broken speech in "sidewalk interviews" is the speech of a person untrained in radio delivery.

The results of the examination showed that TV had won, followed by lecture, film, radio, and finally print. Eight months later the test was read-ministered to the bulk of the students who had taken it the first time. Again it was found that there were significant differences between the groups exposed to different media, and these differences were the same as those on the first test, save for the studio group, an uncertain group because of the chaos of the lecture conditions, which had moved from last to second place. Finally, two years later, the experiment was repeated, with major modifications, using students at Ryerson Institute. Marshall McLuhan reports:

> In this repeat performance, pains were taken to allow each medium full play of its possibilities with reference to the subject, just as in the earlier experiment each medium was neutralized as much as possible. Only the mimeograph form remained the same in each experiment. Here we added a printed form in which an imaginative typographical layout was followed. The lecturer used the blackboard and permitted discussion. Radio and TV employed dramatization, sound effects and graphics. In the examination, radio easily topped TV. Yet, as in the first experiment, both radio and TV manifested a decisive advantage over the lecture and written forms. As a conveyor both of ideas and information, TV was, in this second experiment, apparently enfeebled by the deployment of its dramatic resources, whereas radio benefited from such lavishness. "Technology is explicitness," writes Lyman Bryson. Are both radio and TV more explicit than writing or lecture? Would a greater explicitness, if inherent in these media, account for the ease with which they top other modes of performance?[7]

Announcement of the results of the first experiment evoked considerable interest. Advertising agencies circulated the results with the comment that here, at last, was scientific proof of the superiority of TV. This was unfortunate and missed the main point, for the results didn't indicate the superiority of one medium over others. They merely directed attention toward differences between them, differences so great as to be of kind rather than degree. Some CBC officials were furious, not because TV won, but because print lost.

The problem has been falsely seen as democracy *vs.* the mass media. But the mass media *are* democracy. The book itself was the first mechanical mass medium. What is really being asked, of course, is: can books' monopoly of knowledge survive the challenge of the new languages? The answer is: no. What should be asked is: what can print do better than any other medium and is that worth doing?

Notes

1. *Television Plays,* New York, Simmon and Schuster, 1955, pp. 176–78.
2. George Hoellering and T. S. Eliot, *Film of Murder in the Cathedral,* New York, Harcourt, Brace & Co., 1952, p. vi; London, Faber & Faber, 1952.
3. Béla Balázs, *Theory of Film,* New York, Roy Publishers, 1953, pp. 48, 31, 40; London, Denis Dobson, 1952.
4. "Writers and Motion Pictures," *The Atlantic Monthly,* 199, 1957, p. 69.
5. G. Louis Joughin and Edmund M. Morgan, *The Legacy of Sacco and Vanzetti,* New York, Harcourt, Brace & Co., 1948, p. 34.
6. Béla Balázs, *op. cit.,* pp. 35–36.
7. From a personal communication to the author.

4
Media Values
and Interpersonal Roles

Are you pleased when the hero in the movie or TV rides off alone to seek his destiny even though the grateful villagers have offered him wealth and security for having saved the village? Do you feel good when the woman in the soap opera gives up her job as a hospital administrator, as well as her intern lover, and returns to her husband, daughter, and home with a commitment to never stray again? Would you decide on a political career after you read and see in the news media that politicians are able to accept bribes and "feather their nests" at the taxpayer's expense? Do you expect medical doctors to be sacrificing of their personal lives and to take a deep and abiding interest in their patients? Do you try to act like Steve Martin or Carol Burnett when you are at a party? Have you ever quit listening to a radio DJ or stopped reading a magazine because you did not like the products advertised?

No matter how you answer these questions, your answers reflect in some way your values and your expectations about social and occupational roles. All of us carry around an organized set of attitudes and beliefs which constitute our value system. We apply our values (not always consciously) to persons, institutions, acts, behaviors and objects that confront us to determine how to feel, think and relate. If we see a fellow student cheating on an examination, our value system comes into play determining what we think, feel and do about the person and the act. At home our values affect how we act and react within the family setting. We might value pride or independence of thought much more highly than cooperativeness and compassion. As a consequence we react negatively to parental demands that we attend Uncle George's retirement party. If you have ever been "turned off" by a film, TV or radio program that used ethnic or racist humor, it was probably because of value conflict. If you were "turned on" by magazine ads showing a young virile man with clear blue eyes and a square jaw or a tall slender woman with long blonde hair and flawless skin, it was probably because of value congruence. In these and many other ways our value systems interact with the persons and events, including media persons and events, in our environment determining for us which feelings and responses are appropriate.

Individual and Societal Values

As individuals we use our values, not only to determine feelings, but to facilitate social relationships. Look around at your close friends and the groups and organizations to which you belong. You will find great similarities in the types of persons and things you value and they value. When you reject persons or groups because of their behavior, you are rejecting their values as well. In a way, our values are continually being tested or compared to others' values in our interpersonal relationships.

When values are held in concert through strength of numbers, or tradition,

BOY GETS GIRL. GIRL GETS MARRIAGE AND FAMILY.

FATHER GETS A NEW JOB AND A TAX CUT. MOTHER GETS A DROP IN GROCERY PRICES.

DIST. FIELD NEWSPAPER SYNDICATE

WATCH FOR:

MOVIE AMERICA

COMING SOON TO THE WHITE HOUSE!

they are said to be societal values. They govern individual behavior and set standards for that which is praised or rewarded in society. A society such as ours that values success pressures individuals to advance themselves and to seek the symbols of success. It also creates a structure that forces people to compete. It creates myths, dramas, literature and music extolling the virtues of success. Those who are successful are rewarded with praise, position, and influence; they become models for others to emulate. Some societal values become so entrenched that they are unquestioned, like individual freedom, or life, liberty and the pursuit of happiness.

Not all societal values are unquestioned nor are they all held in equal regard. As with individuals, societies have value hierarchies and sometimes the order of values change or move higher or lower on the scale. For example, many Americans are fond of saying that neighborliness or respect for others is not valued much anymore. Others claim that as technology has advanced, pride of workmanship has fallen on our scale of values while efficiency has risen. In societies where values are perpetuated primarily through the family, the school, the church and other local institutions, values tend to remain stable or to shift only slightly. Where societies are media dependent for information, socialization, and cultural projection, values systems tend to shift more rapidly. Furthermore, at any given moment, even in stable societies, values can be in conflict. For example, you may have long been taught that "honesty is the best policy" but find yourself working for a company that says loyalty to the company is more important than honesty with the customer. Or perhaps your parents place a high value on minding one's own business but your social club wants to help with a local youth rehabilitation program. How such value conflicts are resolved are a concern for both society and the individual. This concern is often reflected in battles over the content and control of the mass media.

In our nation we expect that the family and schools will not only dispense knowledge and skills, but will also inculcate the young with values. Schoolbooks like McGuffey's reader have always accompanied spelling lessons, grammar drills, history lessons, etc., with moral lessons which uphold the current value hierarchy. Where the values being perpetuated are unquestioned ones such as life and liberty, there is no problem. But when it comes to conflicting or shifting values, many people become concerned and want to control the means by which values are selected and projected. This is why community conflicts over electing schoolboard members and selecting school textbooks can arouse such bitter controversy. Those who determine school policies and the content of textbooks control the value hierarchy. Like school boards, those in control of the mass media directly influence the nation's value system. Some would want the Federal Communications Commission to act as "school board" for the electronic media. People who are concerned about television violence, about explicit sex in motion pictures, or about songs which promote drugs would have censors established to see that the public, and particularly the young, are exposed only to the correct values; or at least are not influenced by improper values. Others would have legislation passed to prevent the publication of the "wrong kinds" of literature or the showing of "improper" films. Still others would use boycotts and demonstrations to block the communication of undesirable values. In some societies, those in charge of the state take over direct control of mass media to insure that the public is exposed to only the official value hierarchy.

Mass Media Values

There is no doubt that the mass media have an important relationship to individual and societal values. We all learn values through experience and indoctrination. Beginning at about the age of two we are all continually exposed to the mass media. It follows that the media are an important source of value development. A cursory examination of media content would reveal that almost all media dramatizations are miniature morality plays in which individualism, freedom of choice, perserverance and faith in God triumphs. News presentations of foreign news are from the viewpoint of American rather than foreign values, and local news tends to stress the virtues of law and order and good citizenship. What makes the media so appealing is that they uphold our dominant value system. The mass media even go to some length to avoid taking positions where there is a strong value conflict.

The mass media are not simply mirrors reflecting societal values. They subtly, and sometimes not so subtly, shape our value hierarchy and even project values onto society. The media bring us into contact with a wide variety of people and events, providing us with the means to "cross-check" values upheld by our family, by our friends, and by our culture. This checking may reveal that values other than those we learned in our interpersonal relationships are important and we may be influenced to accept "external" values. Or we may reject them because they threaten our way of life. This is why some groups like the Amish so vigorously oppose any media inputs into their communities.

The very structure of the mass media can project values onto the whole society, values which otherwise may not have existed. For example, all the mass media are geared to presentation of material in short time segments. Television programs are generally limited to half-hour or hour-long lengths. Radio news items rarely exceed thirty seconds. Motion pictures hardly ever use more than two hours for a presentation. The time limit tends to place a great emphasis on action, movement and quick resolution. Things which are slow to evolve, which are not action oriented, and which tend to extend over a long period of time, do not get presented by the mass media. The media value action and quick resolution, and all of us are influenced. We may find that on an interpersonal basis we are looking for quick relationships, for fast resolution of interpersonal problems, and superficial encounters.

Perhaps, more subtly, the "grammars" of media (those elements and techniques which define a medium) have come to influence our values because the process of perception has been modified. For example, the use of the close-up lens in motion pictures, photography, and television has had a marked effect on our concepts of personal distance and social attractiveness. The close-up has made us more conscious of the human face. Faces with zits, dirty pores, or pockmarks are not appreciated by the close-up lens and there-fore the visual media have sought out the flawless skin, bright teeth, and clear eyes. (Dental hygiene moved up the value scale with the development of the photographic camera and popular magazine advertising.) The media rejects facial imperfections or, when they are shown, they represent vulgarity or un-healthiness. All of us are taught to value a clear complexion. We have come to value it so highly that we are willing to pour billions of dollars into the cosmetic industry.

No doubt you can think of other ways that some values have been empha-sized through the grammar of the media. Does radio sound place an empha-sis on spoken fluency, on a voice that is deep, well modulated and male? Have we come to value "voices" like that? to trust them more than other kinds of voices? to think of them as more authoritative? Has the focus of the camera made the smiling face, the cheerful countenance, an important asset? Could George Washington or Abe Lincoln have made it in a mass media world? Is that the secret to Ronald Reagan's rise to the top? Another way to put the question might be, to what degree are all of us "on camera" or speaking through the microphone when we are communicating on an inter-personal basis?

Conflicting Values

It is important to recognize that the modern mass media have also contrib-uted to the growing number of value conflicts in our society. As we men-tioned earlier, there have always been value conflicts in our social system, but the modern media are projecting some values that may be threatening to long cherished traditional values. For instance, despite almost universal de-nunciation of commercials and other advertisements, the economic needs of the mass media have managed to create a new value for us—consumerism! The frequent trip to the supermarket or the shopping center has become an important part of the life of every American. The right to buy the newest na-tionally advertised product and to discard the old, out of date, out of style but still usable item has been firmly established. A whole way of life has grown up around the American shopping center. For very young children it has replaced the playground to become a training ground for a lifetime of consumerism. (Surveys indicate that two- and three-year-old children can dis-tinguish among nationally advertised brands and can point them out on the store shelves). For teenage Americans, it has become the after-school place where all the latest products can be checked out so that one can be in style.

Media advertising has created a new value hierarchy: life, liberty and the pursuit of consumer products. Conflict arises with individuals and institutions who uphold "thrift" as an important value. It is hard to believe in saving one's money or saving energy or any of the other aspects of thrift when all the mass media make consuming not only exciting and attractive, but link it with "the American Way." The old tradition of thrift, the one that tells us to save our pennies for a rainy day, to never throw away something that could be mended or repaired, is dormant.

Another value conflict is created by our growing dependence on media to instruct us about what is important. This dependence conflicts with the more traditional value of self-reliance and independence of thought and action. In *The Lonely Crowd,* David Riesman claims that Americans have become "other directed" rather than "inner directed" or "tradition directed." Riesman suggests a connection between this shift and the mass media. Many other individuals are concerned that Americans are coming to value media experience more highly than firsthand experience, to value one-way communication more highly than two-way, interpersonal communication.

All of us have to learn which values are important, and we have to absorb them into our personalities. Parents, teachers, and peers have been the traditional source of such instruction. These sources of value instruction are now supported, and in some cases supplanted, by the mass media. The mass media have become our personal "educators." They instruct us about personal happiness and how to obtain it, success and how to achieve it, honesty and its rewards, greed and its punishment. Through advertising, dramatization, entertainment and news, we are all instructed, directly and indirectly, about the important values. The media provide us with interesting and exciting visual and auditory "lessons" about what happens when the "right" values are upheld. The media, more than interpersonal interaction, have become the testing grounds for our value systems. Is personal honesty something we value? We don't have to test it interpersonally to know where it stands in the value hierarchy. We can see and hear it tested every day through media "reality." This could be a valuable adjunct to the development of values, but as James Chesebro points out in his seven year study of television, the television portrayals do not accurately reflect the diversity and complexity of the American value system. They disproportionately dramatize a very narrow set of roles and values.

It becomes exceedingly difficult to value the role of the aged in our society if the media continually portray old people as foolish and a bother to have around. It may be impossible for women to value independence when the media portrayal "rewards" those who become housekeepers and "punishes" the single independent woman by showing her to be lonely, neurotic, bitchy or secretly waiting for the right man to come along.

Roles and Values

The mass media do not always, or even usually, uphold values directly and explicitly, rather they are implicit in the situations and characters presented.

It is mainly through media personalities and roles they enact that values are implied. The radio DJ is cool or hip; the news anchorperson is objective, not emotionally involved, serious but not overly concerned; the talk show host is convivial, nonthreatening, witty and caring; the cop-show hero is tough, independent, untrusting of others; the sit-com heroine is aggressive, talkative, easily diverted and warm-hearted. There tends to be a similarity among role types on the mass media and the values that go with each role. If the "let's not take all this too seriously" type newscaster becomes popular (i.e., attracts a large audience) then almost all the newscasters appear in this role, just as the popular sadistic cop-hero becomes the one for the other networks to imitate. In each case the role implies certain values and situations are manipulated in the media to make this type of role and its values appropriate.

Conflict exists in this situation because it reverses the fundamental relationship among role, value, and situation found in the usual interpersonal context. In face-to-face communication all of us must play a variety of roles. A student must not only fulfill the student role, but must balance the roles of son or daughter (mother or father), companion, lover, confidant, leader, follower, in all kinds of real world transactions. A teacher must be able to enact the roles of mother-father, husband-wife, disciplinarian, counselor, organizer, golfer. These roles are vital to human interaction because they represent the mutually agreed upon expectations that we hold for ourselves and for those with whom we interact. We learned from early childhood to observe role models—first parents and relatives, then teachers, and finally our peers—to learn which roles were appropriate to which situations. Through appropriate role taking we came to develop self-esteem and empathy (the ability to project oneself into the role of another). Values are inextricably bound with role modeling and role taking. The values we hold determine the appropriateness of the roles we assume and the roles we assume reenforce or negate values. Effective interpersonal communication is based on being able to enact roles which are appropriate to the situation. Our sense of self and other, our self-esteem and our ability to empathize is increased when the roles we take reflect values appropriate to the situation.

There are few problems when the media provide role models which reflect our social values and help us recognize the choices we have in selecting appropriate roles. Problems are created when media not only project role models but manufacture images which are mythic roles. When the media situation is manipulated to make it appropriate to the role, we have created for us an image of a role—a role that is always appropriate because the situation and the values have been manufactured for the role rather than vice versa. This is the difference between what Daniel J. Boorstin calls a celebrity and a hero. A hero is one who has appropriately reacted to the demands of the situation in a way that makes all of us feel that important values have been upheld. A celebrity is an image of a role and is dependent on the media to create situations and events appropriate to that role. In this case the values upheld are self-aggrandizement, popularity, and, frequently, monetary pay-off. It is Boorstin's belief, along with others, that the media have made us suspicious of role taking in our interpersonal relationships because of the confusion of image and role. There are those, also, who fear that when media images become the role models for young persons, we are bound to have an increase in alienation as more and more persons find out that these mythic roles are inappropriate for working out the day-to-day problems of interpersonal communication.

WILLIAM R. CATTON, JR.

Value Modification by the Mass Media

Does TV makes us self-indulgent and uncaring? Do motion pictures contribute to sexual immorality? Do comic books make children violent and aggressive? The fact that media controversies frequently involve questions like these suggests that we believe there is a connection between social values and mass media content. But how do the media induce, alter, or subvert our values? That question itself is shrouded in controversy.

The paper presented here was prepared by Professor William Catton for the U.S. Government Media Task Force studying the causes and prevention of violence. He claims that values are acquired through the socializing process and that the mass media are an intricate part of that process. This excerpt explains how various media socialize us, even when we use them "only for entertainment," and how they influence our acquisition of values. You should read the article in Section 1 by Lee Thayer, "On the Mass Media and Mass Communication: Notes Toward a Theory," for a wider perspective on the many ways we "use" media to gratify our needs and to clarify and reinforce our values. You might also want to examine the report of the National Commission on the Causes and Prevention of Violence. It presents a comprehensive view of our society in the 1960s and the role of the mass media as one of the significant instruments of social change.

Before turning to research data that indicate modification of values by exposure to mass media, some clarification of concepts is required.

Values may be briefly defined as conceptions of the desirable.[1] Most values can be stated in words, but for some this is difficult and even impossible. Even when people can verbalize their values, it is not clear how effective such values are as determinants of behavior. People may behave as they do because they hold certain values, but there are many other factors that shape almost any human act.

Values can sometimes be stated by the people who hold them.

Values can sometimes be inferred, even when not explicitly stated, from what people do, from rules that say what people should do, or from things people say.

From Robert K. Baker and Sandra J. Ball, editors, *Mass Media and Violence: A Report to the National Commission on the Causes and Prevention of Violence.* (Washington D.C.: United States Government Printing Office, 1969).

Values can change. Since the link between values and actions is problematic, however, a change in values does not necessarily entail changed behavior. Nor does changed behavior necessarily presuppose changed values. To be specific: a population might differ from its ancestors in the degree to which it admires certain forms of violence and the degree to which it abhors other forms, yet it might behave in the same violent ways on the same kinds of occasions as before.

Some of the ways in which behavior may change without a corresponding change in values will be examined in the Report. The present analysis simply assumes that there is such connection between values and behavior that the fact that people behave in one way instead of another can sometimes be regarded as an expression of preference, and can thus be taken as a basis for inferring their values. If people interact with each other, for example, in situations where it would be possible for them to inflict physical injury upon each other, and if they seem to strive to avoid inflicting these injuries, it might be inferred that they value the lives of others. Perhaps each values only his own safety and behaves nonviolently toward others to avoid retaliatory violence: even then, the expectation of retaliation would imply a norm enforced by sanctions. The existence and enforcement of the norm would seem to imply that the secured condition is valued. "Live and let live" is preferred to "kill or be killed."

Thus values can sometimes be inferred from norms. It will be assumed that values can be inferred from verbal expressions of preference. Patrick Henry's rhetorical question, "Is life so dear, or peace so sweet, as to be purchased at the price of chains and slavery?" was an implied expression of preference. At least on the verbal level, precarious liberty was being declared preferable to enslaved security; he was declaring the value of freedom.

It should not be assumed that values inferred from verbal expressions of preference will necessarily be congruent with values inferred from non-verbal behavior. For example, men have not always responded affirmatively to the challenge to "Put your money where your mouth is."

The process of inferring values from preferences, either verbal or nonverbal is not a simple one. If, on a certain stretch of road, we observe that most drivers of high-powered cars keep their speed under thirty miles per hour, we cannot simply infer that they value moving at a leisurely pace. More likely, they value avoidance of speeding tickets and accidents, and have seen signs indicating a twenty-five-mile-per-hour speed limit. The posted speed limit does not indicate that some legal authority assigns a negative value to speed as such; the negative value may again be attached to the risks of accident, injury, or death which would be made excessive in this congested area by speeds that would be tolerable elsewhere.

Acquisition of Values

Values are acquired in the socializing process. To the extent that the mass media are involved in socializing human personalities, there is an inherent possibility that these media can affect the way people acquire values and the kinds of values they acquire.

LaPiere speaks of a category of "fugitive" values, which people impute temporarily to certain acts or objects because of their newness. Group status is determined partly by sharing in these fugitive values. All groups assign such values.[2] For teenagers, there are slang expressions, popular songs, and hair styles. For academicians, there are intellectual fashions. For motorists, there is the value assigned to owning the latest model car. Mass media, of course, have the power to create or implement such fugitive values. This is indicated by the role of the radio disc jockey. The play he gives a particular record on the air affects its "popularity" far more than the frequency with which he, or any other private individual, plays it at home. This is why "payola" was considered scandalous, because people who have a fondness for music did not want to feel that the frequency with which a piece was played on the air was induced through monetary considerations.

There are various ways in which different media can affect or have affected values. When a new medium first comes into existence, the mere fact that some people have access to it and some do not may give one group an advantage over another. In the ancient and medieval worlds, only a select segment of the population, distinguished by status and education, constituted the reading public. Literacy was at first associated with membership in a ruling elite.[3] Now that literacy is so nearly universal in a number of lands, the ability to read no longer has that special value, although in a sense it has greater utility than ever because of the continued multiplication and diversification of written materials. Similarly, when the electronic media were new, social distinctions arose between set owners and non-owners. Quite apart from the impact of broadcast content upon audience values, set ownership had a social value that is now lacking. Both radio and television came on the scene after literacy was nearly universal in our society, and set ownership, especially of television, has now reached the same status.

The transition from non-literacy to nearly universal literacy took several thousand years. The elite status of literate people in the early centuries of that transition was not a "fugitive" value. In the United States, it took less than one generation for radios to become standard household fixtures, and the corresponding transition for television took about a decade. Since universal literacy already prevailed at the beginning of these latter two transitions, it was never possible for early access to either of these electronic media to have the powerful stratifying effect that early access to literacy had had. Early television ownership did have some kind of "fugitive" value, but this seldom gave anyone access to a fund of information from which non-owners were totally and hopelessly cut off: newspapers and other media were always available. Consequently, what mattered to the television viewer was the subtler difference between the eye-witness quality of membership in the television audience versus the quality of indirectness inherent in membership in the audiences of the printed media. The difference between membership in the viewing audience of television and in the listening audience of radio was even less, though it was great enough to stimulate the rapid adoption of television by a nation already equipped with radios.

The invention of printing increased the importance of literacy because there was more available to read. As literacy became more universal, it took on a different kind of value; the ability to read lost its aura of religious and political power. The spread of literacy provided the social context for the invention of new kinds of printed media, including the daily newspaper. A century ago relatively few people really needed to keep abreast of current events, but as newspaper publication began to make this more possible, the knowledge of current events acquired a social value (and a lack of this knowledge implied a loss of social status).

The value of being "informed" was further enhanced with the advent of radio newscasting. It was now possible not only to know what had occurred, but to be involved in it in a new way. One did not just read about the President's "State of the Union" address; it could be heard on the radio, and this gave the message a great deal more immediacy. Accordingly, the value of audible events and experiences was enhanced.

The advent of television did not reduce the number of radios, but did bring about a drastic change in radio programming. The audiovisual medium improved on some of the innovations that the sound-only medium had been performing rather well. Most drama, and a good deal of the news, were even more interesting when experienced through the audiovisual medium. Programmers soon realized that radio was at a distinct disadvantage in comparison with the sound-and-sight combination, and radio programming became largely confined to music and abbreviated news, and some special events coverage and sportscasting aimed at people only temporarily out of touch with television.

Just as radio newscasting discovered that the distinctive things it *could* do it *must* do (e.g., replay recorded excerpts of a president's speech rather than just a newcaster's descriptive summary), so the networks have found that because they *can* show interesting events, they *must*.[4] The visual aspects of the news event or a drama thus acquired new values. During a radio broadcast of a presidential address, the listener is allowed to form his own opinions about the speech and the various points in it. Television, on the other hand, must (because it can) show which senators or congressmen are or are not applauding, and must show any disturbance in the gallery, or any cabinet member who happens to be dozing during any part of the speech. Because television *can* make eyewitnesses of its audience, it *must* and must therefore go out of its way to present interesting and unusual visual aspects. There is thus an inherent tendency for television to introduce a visual bias into our value system.

Because television allows its audience to see and hear, its socializing power should be appreciably greater than that of radio, which in turn has somewhat more socializing power than most printed media. The power of visual broadcasting to change attitudes and behavior is well-illustrated in an experiment by Bandura and Menlove.[5] Children in nursery school at Stanford who were afraid of dogs showed a significant reduction in this behavior (on a test consisting of a graded series of actual acts of approach) after they had been exposed to eight three-minute films, two per day on four alternative days. The films showed a child making progressively bolder approaches to a dog. Two different treatments were tried in the experiment. One group saw a series of films which all used the same five-year-old male model and the same cocker spaniel. Another group saw a series in which the same single-model sequence was interspersed with scenes in which models of both sexes and of various ages approached different dogs in a graded series of increasing size and fearsomeness. Both groups showed significant and lasting reduction in their fear of live dogs in comparison with a control group of equally apprehensive children who were shown neutral films (Disneyland and Marineland scenes).

Television programs frequently portray actions which most viewers would have some inhibition about performing—from switching cigarette brands or using a hair color rinse for the first time, to killing an adversary. The viewing these events could be expected to reduce inhibitions to some degree, in much the same manner as the dog-approaching inhibitions of the children. Before the films were shown, the children had a negative attitude toward dogs; after seeing the films, in which approach behavior was exhibited without adverse consequences to the model, these values (as expressed in overt behavior) had been shifted in a positive direction. The children not only learned to approach the dog used in the experimental test, but their learning was generalized to include other dogs.[6]

It seems to be well established that differential vicarious reinforcement can produce differential amounts of imitative behavior. There is no reason for assuming that human actions described or depicted in the mass media will not function as models in this manner. Berelson and Salter, after performing a content analysis of a magazine fiction sample and finding majority-type Americans overrepresented among the characters and especially among the favorably portrayed ones (whereas minority members were underrepresented numerically and unfavorably treated in the stories), commented on the "presumable effects" of such images. They had not actually studied reader behavior before and after exposure to the stories, but their comments are significant in the light of subsequent experiments on observational learning. They wrote:

> These stories are probably offered and accepted purely as entertainment. Their typical effect upon readers is . . . respite . . . from daily routines and daily cares . . . but it is certainly not the only one. Many communications have other than their intended effects upon readers or listeners and this is probably such a case. . . . Readers with latent tendencies to assign the usual stereotypic descriptions to groups whom they do not know, or toward whom they are unsympathetic, or with whom they do not come in personal contact, can find support for their convenient tags, labels, and aggressions in such magazine fiction. Thus the condition and behavior of fictional characters can readily be used to "prove" that the Negroes are lazy or ignorant, the Jews sly, the Irish superstitous, the Italians criminal, and so on.
>
> The nature of these stories, then, tends to perpetuate the myth of the "100% American" by differentiating subtly and consistently between *The Americans* and the representatives of other groups.[7]

A key idea here is that people are influenced in serious ways even when they seek only entertainment (or "respite") by exposure to mass media. This was also found to be true in the case of those who listened to the radio daytime serials, or "soap operas." From a study of one hundred intensive interviews, Herzog noted three major types of soap opera listener gratification: (1) emotional release—a "chance to cry," or derivation of comfort from sensing that "other people have troubles, too"; (2) opportunities for wishful thinking—exposure to happy episodes which offset one's own problems; and (3) a chance to obtain usable advice. The third type was considered something of a surprise, and was further studied in a poll of 2,500 serial listeners who were asked whether these programs helped them deal better with their own everyday problems. Forty-one percent claimed to have been helped, 28 percent said they had not been helped, and 31 percent had not thought of it that way, did not know, or did not reply.[8]

The propensity to take advice from radio serials varied inversely with education, directly with the perceived amount of worry, and directly with the number of soap operas listened to. The kind of advice obtained consisted mainly of: (1) learning "how to take it" (acquiring what might termed "stoical values" and absorbing the conviction that "things come out all right"); (2) learning to project blame on others (because the interpersonal problems portrayed are attributable to another's character defects); and (3) acquiring ready-made formulas of behavior (e.g., don't slap your children, deprive them of something; take things calmly, don't get excited).[9]

In England, Himmelweit and his associates found that, even with regard to values that are implicitly rather than explicitly preached editorially, television does have some measurable impact on children despite their exposure to many other sources of values. The influence of television depends on repetition in dramatic form and is most possible where views are not firmly fixed. The optimal age of responsiveness varies for different topics and depends on emotional and social maturity as well as mental or chronological age. The more emotionally responsive the child is to television, the greater its influence.[10]

Notes

1. See also William R. Catton, Jr., "A Theory of Value," *American Sociological Review,* 24 (June 1959), pp. 310–317; Douglas Waples, Bernard Berelson,

and Franklyn R. Bradshaw, *What Reading Does to People* (Chicago: Univ. of Chicago Press, 1940), pp. 21–22. For a somewhat different but compatible definition, see Richard T. LaPiere, *A Theory of Social Control* (New York: McGraw-Hill, 1954), p. 133.

2. LaPiere, *Theory of Social Control*, p. 142.
3. Waples, Berelson, and Bradshaw, *What Reading Does to People*, p. 103.
4. Wilbur Schramm, Jack Lyle, and Edwin B. Parker, *Television in the Lives of Our Children* (Stanford, Calif.: Stanford Univ. Press, 1961), pp. 22–23.
5. Albert Bandura and Frances L. Menlove, "Factors Determining Vicarious Extinction of Avoidance Behavior Through Symbolic Modeling." *Journal of Personality and Social Psychology*, 8 (1968), pp. 99–108.
6. Ibid, p. 106.
7. Bernard Berelson and Patricia J. Salter, "Majority and Minority Americans: An Analysis of Magazine Fiction," *Public Opinion Quarterly*, 10 (Summer, 1946), pp. 168–190.
8. Herta Herzog, "Motivations and Gratifications of Daily Serial Listeners," reprinted from Paul Lazarsfeld and Frank Stanton (eds.), *Radio Research, 1942–1943* (New York: Duell, Sloan & Pearce, 1944) and in Wilbur Schramm (ed.), *The Process and Effects of Mass Communications* (Urbana, Ill.: Univ. of Illinois Press, 1954), pp. 50–55.
9. Ibid.
10. Hilde T. Himmelweit, A. N. Oppenheim, and Pamela Vince, *Television and the Child* (London: Oxford Univ. Press, 1958), pp. 260–261.

JAMES W. CHESEBRO

Communication, Values, and Popular Television Series—A Seven Year Assessment

This article by Professor Chesebro is based on an earlier study published in the *Journal of Popular Culture* in 1975. In that original article, Chesebro, along with Professor Caroline Hamsher, set up a framework in which to categorize popular TV series and determine the implicit values. In the present essay, Chesebro updates that earlier study, extending his examination over a seven-year period and demonstrating that his system of categories for analyzing and evaluating TV series can be applied to constantly changing network schedules.

Chesebro has provided us with a unique and very useful schema for examining popular television series. His method takes us past the usual comedic and dramatic qualities of these programs and into the underlying value systems which provide the foundations for the characterizations and plot lines. His examination clearly establishes that popular entertainment forms are communicative acts that reflect, convey, and reinforce selected values.

Our specific attitudes and everyday behaviors are typically a reflection of the values we have acquired. We assign or impose a relative worth, utility, importance, or excellence to the experiences and the phenomena we encounter. In this sense, we constantly valuate. These assessments or values determine, in part, what we will and will not endorse, reject, and do. Granted, circumstances or necessities may sometimes force us to experience or to do certain things. However, when we are able to function as "free agents" selecting among various options, it is our values which determine our particular attitudes and daily behaviors.

Given the centrality of values in the life of every human being, a key question emerges: "How do people acquire the values they employ?" Or, asked in equally valid terms, "What determines which values are employed and which values are rejected by individuals?" Cast in this fashion, the issue becomes one of *socialization,* and we are essentially asking what the primary and independent variables are which control the socialization or "humanizing" process.

This is an expanded version of an article written expressly for the first edition of *Inter/Media*. Copyright © 1978, 1982 by James W. Chesebro.

As people mature, certain social institutions have traditionally exerted an obvious and direct control over the selection of the values controlling humans. Existing evidence[1] suggests that the family, peer groups, religious training, and the educational system function as primary and independent socialization variables, exerting significant influence over the values governing people. And yet, particularly in an ever-changing world, it is appropriate to determine if new and emerging factors might not be capable of controlling the selection and utilization of human values.

Since the 1950s, critics and researchers have, in fact, sought to determine if television could be viewed as one of the relatively new factors controlling human value systems. Framed as a serious research question, the issue becomes: "Does television function as a primary and independent socialization variable, possessing the same significance in controlling value orientations as parents, friends, religion, and education?" While the question is overwhelmingly significant, the answer would appear to be—at least at first glance—an easy and quick "yes."

When first examined, television does appear to possess all of the apparent qualities which could lead one to anticipate that television viewing decisively shapes the values which govern our lives. In the average American home, the television set is on for six and three-quarters hours a day[2] (a figure that has been increasing steadily during the last decade), making television a kind of ever-present companion. While this form of television viewing is "a discontinuous experience with spurts and disconnections, and often accompanied by some other activity"[3] such as eating, the average American actually does watch television for some three hours a day.[4] Accordingly, Americans spend three-fourths of their total media time watching television[5] and "40 percent of their total leisure time with television."[6] Thus, of the primary activities in life, television is the most important for Americans after work and sleep.[7] As a matter of fact, television set owners sleep 13 percent less than nonset owners,[8] and as George Comstock reports, television "set owners also spend less time attending social gatherings away from home, listening to the radio, reading books, engaging in miscellaneous leisure activities, attending the movies, conversing, watching television away from home, and doing household tasks."[9] But, these same set owners do watch one hour a day more of television than nonset owners.[10]

This extensive use of television has led some critics to claim that television has affected all of the basic cultural values and institutions in America. Critic Robert Brustein has maintained, for example, that "television" has "not only fragmented family life; it has also been dividing the country, by generating myths, formulas and celebrities that, for all their mass appeal, are almost totally foreign to most serious-minded Americans."[11] Yet, Brustein fails to offer evidence for his claims. Like most social scientists, Brustein is unable to marshall the kind of research necessary to demonstrate that television functions as a primary and independent variable controlling cultural values and institutions. The evidence may simply not exist. As Comstock has observed, after surveying 2,500 social science research reports which sought to determine the effect of television, the "social scientists . . . have tended to reserve the conclusion that television has an important effect for instances in which there has been some large, independent impact on the average viewer, and typically they have not found one."[12] As Jeffrey Schrank has noted, "Exactly how television has influenced our psychology we don't know."[13] We are, at this point, left with Comstock's overall observation: "Television and human behavior is a topic about which there will always be question marks."[14]

Yet, despite all of this evidence, I want to maintain in this essay that there is a significant relationship between popular television series and cultural values. I am convinced that when the proper research framework is employed, a relationship between television and cultural values can be vividly demonstrated. However, there are assumptions and key terms in this thesis which should be explicitly addressed. I examine these assumptions in the conclusions of this essay, because it is initially appropriate to present the research framework and data which provide the warrants for these assumptions.

Objectives of This Study

The relationships among communication, values, and popular television series are complex; no single study is likely to reveal all of the dynamic intricacies among these three systems. In this essay, we can only begin the complex process of identifying the ways in which popular television series affect the values of viewers. This study is designed only to identify the communication strategies employed on television series to convey and to reinforce selective values. Four questions mold the analysis offered here:

1. *What patterns, types, or kinds of human relationships are portrayed in popular television series?*
2. *How are human problems and difficulties resolved in popular television series?*

3. *How have popular television series changed, particularly in the last seven years?*
4. *What particular values are reinforced by popular television series and which of these values has been predominantly emphasized in the last seven years?*

In order to answer these questions, four lines of analysis are developed. First, a system is outlined for describing and interpreting popular television series as communication systems. Some forty-two different series appeared on the air during the 1980–81 season, each with a host of different plot lines, minor characters, and ideas expressed each week. A classification system was needed to make some coherent or logical sense out of this barrage of messages. The formulation of such a system technically requires the presentation of what is called a theory of logical types, which simply allows a critic to explain the symbol-using on popular television series in the context of a systematic framework. The theoretical system outlined here produces a framework that allows the critic to view a television series as essentially one of five communication strategies. This scheme is detailed in the first section of this essay. While this classification system was developed to explain symbol-using in popular television series, the basis for the system is also explicitly identified because it can account for other major types or forms of communication in everyday situations.[15] Second, these five types of communication are illustrated from television series in the 1980–81 season. Third, this theory is employed as a grid for classifying all television series in the 1980–81 season and for identifying changes in the nature of communication patterns in these series since the 1974–75 season. Fourth, the values promoted by these television series are explicitly identified as well as which of these values has been most dramatically emphasized during the last seven years.

A Theory of Logical Types for Classifying Communicative Acts

A theory of logical types for classifying communicative acts requires rules for the formulation of such a matrix. These concerns led Herbert W. Simons to propose that generic formulations proceed along certain methodological lines:

> First, there must be a class of genres into which a particular genre can be put. . . . A second requirement for generic identification is that the categorizer must have clear rules or criteria for identifying distinguishing characteristics of a genre. . . . Third, the necessary and sufficient distinguishing features of a genre must not only be nameable but operationalizable; the categorizer must

be able to tell the observer or critic how to know a distinguishing feature when he sees it. Finally, if items of discourse are to be consistently identified as fitting within one genre or another, it follows that these items should be internally homogeneous across salient characteristics and clearly distinguishable from items comprising an alternative genre.[16]

These rules are used for the formulation of the communication matrix proposed here.

In order to generate a matrix, all communicative acts must first be examined on the same level of abstraction or be members of one "class of genres." Among communicologists, any number of approaches or classes may be selected to satisfy this first methodological requirement. Communicative acts may be viewed as manipulative *strategies;* this view has allowed the generation of a matrix in which communicative acts are classified as either consensus, confrontation, apologia, or concession strategies.[17] Or communicative acts may be viewed as responses to various types of *situations.*[18] Communicative acts might also be grouped by the apparent *purpose* for initiating the act, and thus a set of categories might include acts as attempts to persuade, to entertain, or to inform.[19] Others might group communicative acts by their similarities and differences as policy recommendations, essentially an *act*-centered matrix.[20]

An *agent*-oriented criterion is employed here for the classification of communicative acts. An agent-centered approach reflects the image orientation of our popular culture. The notion of an *image* implies that there is a presentation or staging of the self to others. While an image may conceal or distort, there is also a sense in which every person must employ one role or posture rather than another, depending upon the time, circumstances, needs, and available means which emerge during an interaction. While less contrived or more spontaneous presentations of the self may be preferred, nonetheless image creation and image manipulation are now a focal point of all complex cultures. Whether these images are created with clothing, make-up, hair arrangements, or by carefully worded policies that compromise differences, *style* is now a "god-term" of our culture. In this context, Daniel Boorstin has observed that the number of "pseudo-events" or "planned, planted, or incited" events have increased drastically.[21] Kenneth Boulding has likewise argued that there has been a "growth of images, both private and public, in individuals, in organizations, in society at large, and even with some trepidation, among the lower forms of life."[22] This constant bombardment of images may have been created, for example, by magazines such as *Playboy, Playgirl,* and *Blueboy,* which suggests that a life-style may emerge from a quasi-sexual and quasi-technological orientation, with other public forms such as television talk shows or *People* magazine reinforcing particular life-styles by virtue of their coverage of popular celebrities. In this regard, David M. Berg has noted that mass media, "particularly television," create "a higher incidence of exigencies than that reality which is experienced directly." He concluded that "media do more than merely reflect events; they also create them."[23] Thus, our decision to employ an agent-centered orientation in the formulation of a communication matrix appears appropriate, particularly given the centrality of image or character references which dominate popular television series.

Having selected an agent-centered matrix, Simons' second methodological requirement becomes relevant: a set of "clear rules or criteria for identifying distinguishing characteristics of a genre" must be employed. Northrop Frye provides a convenient set of rules for distinguishing types of central characters in fiction.[24] Because Frye's concern and the focal point of this analysis are similar, Frye's scheme is easily adapted as a mechanism for analyzing central characters on television series. In Frye's view, two variables generate and distinguish major kinds of communication systems: (1) the central character's apparent intelligence compared with that of the audience; and (2) the central character's ability to control circumstances compared with that of the audience.

These two variables produce five kinds of communication systems.

In the *ironic communication system,* the central character is both intellectually inferior and less able to control circumstances than is the audience. In the ironic communication system, the person responsible for an act lacks both the scope and the appropriate kinds of interpretive concepts and categories for assessing reality, as well as the skills necessary to mobilize or to generate the support required for concerted agreements and actions. All of us have faced this situation at one time or another, and, as a result, the act carried out did not reflect or "say" what was meant. Whenever a disparity exists between what is said or done and what is meant, irony emerges. For the central characters placed within this category, this disparity is a central and constant feature of their behavior.

In the *mimetic communication system,* the central character is "one of us," equally intelligent and equally able to control circumstances. In mimetic communication systems, all are perceived, believed, or treated as equals: a common set of symbolic perceptions, descriptions, and interpretations of reality are shared by individuals if they are members of a mimetic system; moreover, members of such a system face and deal with similar problems and situations with equal skill. For all practical purposes, human interactions cast as mimetic appear to be "slices of everyday life."

In the *leader-centered communication system,* the central character is superior in intelligence to others but only in degree by virtue of special training, personality conditioning, and so forth. However, the central character in the leader-centered communication system faces and deals with the same kinds of circumstances the audience confronts. Thus, the leader generates a configuration of symbols for acting that others find compelling, thereby creating the concerted actions necessary to deal with shared problems, situations, or questions.

In the *romantic communication system,* the central character is superior to members of the audience in degree, both in terms of intelligence and in terms of the ability to control circumstances. In romantic communication systems, the central character thus possesses a symbol system which allows her or him to account for more environmental variables in more incisive ways than others (intelligence) and to create more effective options and programs for acting upon those environmental factors than others (control of the environment).

In the *mythical communication system,* the central character is superior in kind to others both in terms of intelligence and in terms of his or her ability to control circumstances. If we view Christianity as a communication system, for example, the "word of God" is presumed to stem from a kind of superior intelligence far beyond any kind of understanding humankind may ever possess as well as being capable of producing environmental changes which no mere mortal may ever achieve. While "mystical" in nature, such symbol systems should *not* be viewed as somehow less "real" than any other mode of communication, for such systems have profoundly altered the attitudes, beliefs, and actions of massive groups of people.

These five communication systems thus constitute the basic distinguishing categories or framework for classifying television series. However, our ability to distinguish these communication systems remains incomplete, for the question emerges: "How does the critic determine the relationship between the central character and the audience?" Simons' third methodological rule for matrix formulation provides a response to this question, for it posits that systems must be *operationally discrete* as well as conceptually distinct: "the categorizer must be able to tell the observer or critic how to know a distinguishing feature when he sees it."

In order to identify operationally and systematically the unique pattern of dramatic action which characterizes each communication system, Kenneth Burke's "dramatistic process" has been employed. Burke maintains that all human dramas are carried out in four discrete stages.[25] These four stages and their concomitant critical questions are: (1) *Pollution*—"What norms are violated and cast as disruptive to the social system involved?" (2) *Guilt*—"Who or what is generally held responsible for the pollution?" (3) *Purification*—"What kinds of acts are generally initiated to eliminate the pollution and guilt?" and (4) *Redemption*—"What social system or order is created as a result of passing through the pollution, guilt, and purification stages?" This *pollution-guilt-purification-redemption* framework can be used to describe systematically behavioral differences among each of the five communication systems at each key stage of a human drama. A series of very different behaviors develops each dramatic stage of each communication system identified here. Thus, the dramatistic process allows us to detect operational differences among the five communication systems. Table 1 provides a complete conception of the behavioral matrix ultimately generated.

Surveys of popular television series carried out by this researcher for the last seven years have led to several conclusions: (1) central characters in television series engage in explicit and varied behaviors when functioning in human relations or human dramas (conflict-resolution patterns); (2) these explicit behaviors can be classified into one of the five communication systems; and (3) the central characters in each category can be grouped together because they display shared, common, or redundant patterns of action at each stage of the dramatistic process in each type of communication drama. Thus, although Table 1 is presented here as a formal deductive system, it was derived inductively based upon the behaviors of central characters on television series.

Symbolic and Dramatic Progressions in Popular Television Series

The dramatic progressions that distinguish the ironic, mimetic, leader-centered, romantic, and mythical communication systems can be illustrated by specific television series in the 1980–81 season. The ironic system is first examined and is appropriately revealed as a symbolic system by the character of Archie Bunker in *All in the Family* and *Archie Bunker's Place*.

Table 1. Types of communication dramas

Dramatistic Stages	Ironic	Mimetic	Leader-centered	Romantic	Mythical
Pollution	The central character violates major rules of the system.	Rules violated are minor and the result of accidents, the best of intentions, and/or circumstances.	Values of the central character are violated by others.	The central character identifies the significance and scope of the problem (a problem of mind, body, and spirit).	Universal problems beyond human control—unreasonable, overwhelming, and often religious/ideological—set off the drama.
Guilt	The central character is explicitly recognized as the cause of the pollution: scapegoating.	Guilt is easily admitted by agents because pollution is both insignificant and unintentional.	The central actor assumes responsibility for correcting the pollution: self-mortification.	The central character is the primary, if only, agent who identifies all of the dimensions of blame in a way that allows for correction.	Blame cannot be attached to any particular and individual agent—forces are to fault.
Purification	Characters beside the central character initiate acts to correct the pollution.	The accidents and/or circumstances are explicitly recognized; intentions are explained; forcing a reinterpretation and/or forgiveness for the pollution.	The leader mobilizes others to achieve the original ends through selective means chosen by the leader.	The more highly developed skills, intelligence, and sensitivity of the central character are combined in the unique fashion essential to produce the most desirable set of corrective acts.	Superhuman powers of the central character emerge during the corrective process.
Redemption	The central character is reestablished as the controlling force to reinitiate pollution.	The previous system can be reestablished with all characters "wiser" for the experience.	The leader's values are reestablished and explicitly recognized as controlling.	The central character is recognized overtly as the embodiment of all that's right.	A new social system is established due to unique powers of central character.

The Ironic Communication System

An ironic character may assume several forms. The ironic character may *intentionally* assume a pretense of ignorance or pretend to learn from others in order to reveal the false conceptions of others. Such ironic characters purposely use words which convey the opposite meaning of their literal meaning, typically producing an incongruity between the normal or expected results and the actual results of a sequence of events. Thus, the notion of *Socratic irony* has come to identify the agent who intentionally pretends to be stupid in order to inconspicuously force an answerer to reveal false conceptions. On the other hand, *dramatic irony* exists when the audience understands the incongruity between what is said and what is known while the characters in the interaction are unaware of the incongruity. Or, *tragic irony* may exist when an attitude of detached awareness creates an incongruity between what is and what is known.

With Archie Bunker, dramatic irony dominates. In the dramatic ironic form, the ironic character may *unintentionally* articulate and defend positions which are inconsistent with known events. In such cases, the character has unknowingly become ironic; only the audience is aware of the incongruity. Unintended ironic behaviors introduce a comic dimension into an interaction. Thus, the role of "expert," for example, is ironically portrayed if the actor mispronounces the technical terms of a discipline, misstates common understandings of a field, or employs nonverbal symbols which are inconsistent with the verbal symbols of the field of expertise. Thus, the intentions of the character, the environment in which the character exists, and the "universe of understanding" possessed by the audience, all determine the degree to which a given set of behaviors is perceived as ironic.

Typically portraying a dramatically ironic character, Archie Bunker predisposes an audience to anticipate that he will function as an ironic character in a human drama without his own knowledge. His faulty diction, misstatements of fact, and failure to interpret events as most would, all predispose most audience members to view Archie as an ironic character. Moreover, Archie is inconsistent with the environment in which he must function. He applauds the politics of Herbert Hoover, endorses outdated systems of discrimination, employs stereotypes as accurate barometers of reality, and unknowingly violates existing norms of propriety. Thus, Archie exists in a social context that he cannot appropriately respond to, adapt to, or control.

When human relationships and dramas unfolded each week on *All in the Family,* the inciting incident or pollution was typically the result of Archie's actions. Archie's "sins"—after some seven years on *All in the Family*—are almost unlimited now; he had lied to Edith, forged her signature, gambled, hurt the feelings of others, said the "unbelievable," and argued for the "impossible." At the same time, Archie was the "hero" of the series, and herein resides yet another level of irony. We anticipate that the hero of a drama will correct, not create, pollution. Yet, Archie was the "breadwinner" and the "head of the family" while simultaneously creating the pollution that generated the drama.

Others in the family attributed the responsibility for the pollution to Archie, or circumstances creating the pollution forced Archie to admit that he had erred, or he slowly realized that he had been mistaken. In a technical sense, Archie is a *scapegoat;* others blame him for the disorder. The irony of the series was thereby extended, for again the hero was held to be a central causal agent for the pollution dominating the drama.

The pollution and guilt were typically resolved or "purified" by actions of characters other than Archie. When Archie planned to file a fraudulent insurance claim after a minor fire in the bathroom, for example, it was Edith who eliminated the basis for the false insurance claim and the foundation for any criminal action against Archie. Likewise, Archie once detained a mentally retarded delivery man, knowingly jeopardizing the man's job. It was not Archie, but George the delivery man who finds himself another job. Archie's patronizing attitude toward George and all mentally retarded persons was simultaneously "corrected," for George was employed in the same job on the same loading dock as Archie. In this case, the "victim" of the drama purifies the drama. The "hero" was again cast as ironic for the incongruity between common-sense expectations of a hero and Archie's actions was reasserted.

In the final redemptive stage of the Bunker drama, a closing scene typically reestablished Archie as head of the family. The sensitivity of others, Archie's "basically good heart," and perhaps a begruding act of atonement on Archie's part provided the warrant for reestablishing Archie's status. Thus, the series closed with a final touch of irony, for Archie was now able (next week) to set off an entirely new dramatic incident.

As the character of Archie Bunker moved from *All in the Family* to *Archie Bunker's Place,* Archie's circumstances and the people he encounters are different. Archie now co-owns with Murray a bar; Archie is a "businessmen." Yet Archie continues to create the problems. He is blamed for these actions; others correct them. And, with that final touch of irony, Archie returns to the position of central agent, free to again initiate yet another drama.

However, the opening two-part show of *Archie Bunker's Place* at the beginning of the 1980–81 season deserves special mention. On one level, the show is like all of the other shows of the series. Archie fails to do what he is expected to do, and his friends are required to initiate those actions that correct the situation. The ironic form is clearly evident again. However, a noteworthy twist is introduced. It is no longer clear that Archie is a dramatically ironic character. Archie appears to possess a sense of knowledge of the disparity he creates; he appears to be, as a result, more of a tragically ironic character rather than a dramatically ironic character. Archie's actions and behaviors do not change as a result of this transformation; he continues to go through roughly the same stages we have already described in lock-step fashion. However, there is a new sense of awareness about Archie Bunker. While continuing to remain a basically ironic character, he now seems to possess a greater sense of self-awareness of the disparities and incongruities which exist in life. In the season's two-part opener in 1980–1981, for example, Edith has died unexpectedly, but Archie chooses to pretend nothing has happened rather than acknowledge his grief. Archie's friends, particularly Murray, Stephanie, and Veronica, must take those steps needed to purify the situation. Archie remains ironic in our sense of the concept, but his decision to avoid grief, in this case, has a more understandable dimension that Archie himself seems to recognize. The incongruity, then, seems an almost necessary one, or at least an understandable one, for grief is to be ignored if at all possible. Archie seems to understand this; he shifts, accordingly, from a solely·dramatically ironic character to more of a tragically ironic character. Granted, Edith's death and Archie's ability to grieve over her death do not change Archie's relative degree of intelligence or his relative ability to handle circumstances compared with the audience's, but Archie does seems to possess a greater sense of awareness in this episode than we typically associate with the character of Archie Bunker. Thus, while Archie remains ironic in terms of the behaviors that describe him as a central character during the major stages of the drama of each show, he now seems to possess greater depth, at least in the sense that he may shift back and forth from a dramatic to a tragic sense of irony. The comic continues to emerge at different moments in *Archie Bunker's Place,* but a tragic element can now be introduced into the series just as easily. This change in the nature of the series does not detract from our confidence in classifying the series as a ironic drama; it does, however, reveal the true range and depths which can be found in the use of irony itself. Irony may range from the comic to the tragic. *Archie Bunker's Place* now seems to more realistically reflect the scope of the figure of irony as we find it in other more complicated forms.

The Mimetic Communication System

Marcel Marceau has frequently been identified as the outstanding mime of the twentieth century. On an empty stage, in whiteface and dressed in black, he silently copies or imitates scenes from everyday life. The acts he portrays are intended to reflect what all of us do—the common, the ordinary, or those "slices of life" all of us experience are revealed. Thus, Marceau portrays a "man walking in the rain against the wind," a "man walking upstairs," or a "man trapped in a box." His mimetic acts closely resemble real life, but the resemblance is superficial and therefore a form of what is technically identified as "comic ridicule." While we may enjoy and laugh at the mime, the mimetic performer also allows us to identify and therefore to prepare for those moments when others may find us in an embarrassing situation, and when we must admit the humor of our own everyday actions.

The mimetic form may also be employed to disarm us and make us view other persons or products as a normal part of our everyday lives when, in fact, such representations are persuasive efforts to make us endorse "foreign" agents or objects as part of us. Thus, the politician employs the mimetic form when he proclaims in the agricultural district: "I was once a farm boy myself.[26] Or, the mimetic form is used to sell us paper towels or coffee: after being cast as "our next-door neighbors" and therefore as persons to be trusted, Rosie and Mrs. Olsen then proceed to reveal their overwhelming zeal and commitment to Bounty and Folgers. Such bandwagon techniques are grounded in the mimetic form—a dramatic imitation of life, usually but not always in a slightly exaggerated manner, designed to reinforce or to alter perceptions, attitudes, beliefs, and actions.

Moreover, the mimetic form can also be used to characterize entire patterns of human action. Such mimetic patterns attempt to cast both the "content" and the "manner" of dramas as everyday phenomena: the pattern thus minimizes the unusual and unique; it casts particular goals, values, beliefs, attitudes, concepts, actions, and manners as common or popular. Dramas operating within the constraints of this mimetic form, then, typically portray incidents as common: problems are conceived as accidents, a product of misunderstood intentions, or the results of unavoidable circumstances, all of which ultimately creates the view that the problems involved are relatively insignificant and unpremeditated; once the accidental, unintentional, or circumstantial nature of the problem is confirmed, characters typically return to their previous and established modes of action, perhaps wiser for the experience.

The popular television series Barney Miller functions as an excellent example of a mimetic communication system, and it is used here to illustrate mimetic patterns of interaction. The apparent major focus of the show selected for analysis here deals with Detective Dietrich's decision to resign from the New York Police Department, Dietrich had been sent out on a robbery call. In answering the call, Dietrich is forced to "shoot some kid" trying to hold up a liquor store. Although Dietrich says he "did what a cop has to do," he shortly thereafter resigns because "I don't feel I have the right to take the life of another human being. . . . Listen, I thought this out very carefully. I've just decided that my personal integrity and moral code is worth a hell of a lot more than any badge." However, two other plots are also involved in this show. In the second plot, a check forger, Ira Ruso, wanted in Arizona for grand theft, has turned himself in because, "I was tired of running, tired of hiding. I just want to go back and make things right." Mr. Ruso explains that, "What I did was so horrible. The guilt, the shame, they're eating away at me until I can't even sleep any more. . . . I stole $1,300. . . . I took it from nuns. See, they ran this orphanage in the desert for Indian kids. They hired me. They trusted me. Well, two days before Christmas, I took their bank accounts and stole their bus. I spent the money on liquor and prostitutes." In addition, a third plot is also evident, a mutual assault between an actor, Mr. Heath, and a playwright, Mr. Novak. Detective Harris explains that, "According to accounts from the audience at ringside, a performance of Mr. Novak's play was in process in which Mr. Heath has a part when Mr. Novak bounded on stage, and began to choke Mr. Heath because Mr. Heath refused to answer a ringing phone on stage." Mr. Heath interjects that he wasn't "motivated" to answer the phone. Mr. Novak counters by observing that actors are like "primadonnas." Mr. Novak further explains that, "This play is really my first successful effort. There's talk of taking it uptown. We're even thinking of having teeshirts made. If only there was a way of doing it without the actors." Challenging this view, Mr. Heath explains that, "all that writers ever care about is their words, their expressions, their thoughts. Actors have thoughts, too, you know. You see, the written word is merely the foundation upon which we actors build. The essence of the theater is the actor, and the essence of acting is interpretation, breathing life into stagnant ideas, molding them, until they fit each character like a finely tailored suit." All three of these plots, then, define the dramatic base for the show analyzed here.

The problems of "pollution" and "guilt" that set off the show appear extremely significant but only at the outset of the show. In the beginning, the issues appear to be Dietrich's personal integrity and moral code regarding the taking of another human life, Ruso's grand theft, and Novak and Heath's mutual assault. The issues seem compelling. However, as the show evolves, the viewer is informed that these are not really the issues at all. Rather, the actual issues turn about the intentions of the agents involved in these plots as well as the circumstances they faced. In the mimetic system, then, the pollution and guilt initially faced do appear overwhelming, but such a perspective—the viewers later find out—is a ruse and misconception of the "real" issues. Intentions and circumstances are revealed that tremendously minimize, if not eliminate, the pollution and guilt creating these plots.

It is during the purification stage that the viewer "finds out" that the problem and responsibility for the problem have been greatly overstated. Dietrich's concerns for morality and his sense of personal guilt are, for example, eliminated by a barrage of rationales provided by the other men in the squad room. Harris initially notes, "You know how Dietrich is— always keeping things all pent up inside. This letter is nothing more than his way of letting off a little steam." Miller adds that it is "normal reaction to a situation like this." Likewise, rather than accepting Dietrich's stance that the issue is one of the sanctity of human life or ethical principles which are in conflict with Dietrich's role as a police officer, Wojo argues that "what he is really saying is that the only guys who can be cops are the guys who are unprincipled, trigger-happy slobs." Later, employing irony, Wojo argues that, "Yeah, I think you should quit. I think a person with your high moral code shouldn't have to associate with people that are on our low level. . . . You think that we must be morally deficient or something." Harris then asks Dietrich, "What makes you so damned special? Somebody's got to take the responsibility. Or, maybe you don't think so." In this vein, Miller adds that Dietrich's decision "reflects on us. . . . I'm sure you can appreciate that those of us who remain behind might take a certain offense at the implication of some of the things you've said."

Moreover, Miller asks a chain of questions which imply that lack of a professional commitment to any occupation rather than personal ethics is the "real" reason Dietrich is quitting: "Weren't you a medical student?" Dietrich replies, "Yeah . . . I quit." Miller responds, "Oh, yeah, and how long did you stay in law school?" Dietrich's answer is "a couple of weeks." Miller again questions: "Teacher? Actor?" Dietrich, realizing Miller's perspective, adds, "You left out bee keeper and lumberjack—my wilderness period." Miller draws his own conclusion: "Seems to me you've had a continuing difficulty committing to anything." Dietrich affirms Miller's observation but questions the significance of the observation. Wojo provides the necessary explanation: "So maybe the high moral code and the integrity are really just an intellectual smokescreen to rationalize away the fact that you're quitting again." Harris draws the final conclusion, "You walk out of here today, you and your principles are going to be right back where you started: all dressed up and no place to go." So reinterpreted, Dietrich realizes that he misunderstood his own intentions: "You know, I don't have to sit here and listen to all of this. But, then again, I have no good reason to get up. Look, maybe everything you guys say is right, okay? But I still have to hold onto my principles. But, maybe I still have to hold onto this job."

Likewise, the dispute between the playwright and the actor is reduced to an issue of having realistic motives. The producer of the play resolves the Novak-Heath conflict. He asks, "Is this the way professional theater people behave? Of course not. If you have a disagreement, you don't attack one another during a performance. You wait 'til later and do it in a restaurant. . . . I have had it up to here with this artistic-creative-control gabbage. We are doing a play, not *Hamlet*." After the producer provides bail, he reframes the entire issue of artistic intent and asks: "Are you going to behave yourselves and start acting like adults?" The rule of thumb, observes the producer, is "not to be so sensitive. Everything you write isn't carved in stone. . . . And, you—actor—try having a little respect for the written word. The man wrote you a nice play: say some of it! All right?" The response is: "I'll try."

Similarly, Mr. Ruso's crime is placed in another perspective; we are told that the circumstances of the crime are essentially insignificant given the scope of criminal issues society should deal with. The D.A.'s office in Phoenix particularly resolves Mr. Ruso's pollution and guilt by minimizing the entirety of the drama created by Ruso—the circumstances of Ruso's crime, we are told, is simply too minor to bother with. Wojo explains to all that, "The D.A.'s office in Phoenix doesn't want to come back for Ruse. . . . They said that the nature of his crime isn't serious enough to make it worth their while to come back and get him. . . . But, if he wants to pay his own expenses back, they'll be willing to prosecute." Ruso doesn't, however, "have the money, honest!" Miller then speaks to the Arizona D.A.'s office but without effect. The conclusion is provided by Miller, "We have no reason to hold you."

In all three cases, then, intentions and circumstances are reframed to purify the pollution and guilt that set off the dramas. Accordingly, redemption requires no special action except a recognition of having "learned something" and being "somewhat wiser for the experience." Ultimately, such mimetic series imply that disagreements require only clarifications or that circumstances need only be more realistically assessed to eliminate conflict in everyday life. Such series, among many other things, reinforce the notion that the personal life is satisfying.

The Leader-Centered Communication System

As a point of departure, a common-sense notion of a leader functions as an excellent description of the leader-centered communication system. Typically, leaders are believed to be those individuals who direct others, possess authority or influence, manage the affairs of a group, and possess some heroic characteristic. This conception of a leader corresponds nicely with our previous notion of a leader as one who possesses superiority in terms of intelligence by virtue of special training, personality conditioning, and so forth, but who must deal with the same circumstances others face. More particularly, from a communication perspective, leaders dominate others in the sense that they employ a set of symbols that mobilize the responses of others; they introduce and formulate goals, tasks, and procedures; they delegate or direct actions; they integrate or pull together the efforts of other individuals; they provide transitions or interconnections among events; and they appear confident of their values—others may, in fact, treat the value judgments of leaders as factual statements.

On the television series *House Calls*, the character of Dr. Charles Michaels seems to satisfy the requirements of a leader. In the show examined here, Michaels' patient, Mr. Sam Gerbner, had been recovering from surgery. However, without apparent reason, Mr. Gerbner began to have "some problems." This reversal is the basis for Michaels' reaction and the definition of the inception of the drama.

The nature and essence of the pollution generating the drama is a direct result of Michaels' definition of the situation. The violation of Michaels' values, as a leader, defines the pollution controlling this drama. Initially, Michaels' ethical system is violated if only by virtue of his commitment to care for the physical health of his patient. In Michaels' view, Mr. Gerbner's reversal "doesn't," in Michaels' words, "make any sense. Just a few days ago, he was responding to the medication." It is with this pronouncement that the viewer knows that a problem exists. Moreover, Michaels' interaction with Mr. Gerbner reveals a psychological as well as a physical problem. Mr. Gerbner confides that he has given up: "Because it doesn't matter anymore. I lost my wife years ago. There's only the one boy, and he doesn't care about what happens to me. . . . He doesn't know I'm anywhere. And, if he does know, he couldn't come. My boy is a criminal. . . . He's not in prison, but if he shows his face around here, he will be." Michaels determines that Mr. Gerbner's physical reversal is therefore psychologically caused. To the other physicians on the staff, Michaels therefore declares that Mr. Gerbner "has lost his will to live. He is literally dying to see his son." The pollution, then, is not only defined by Michaels but comes into existence by virtue of Michaels' ability to determine the exact nature of the pollution.

The responsibility for Mr. Gerbner's condition is likewise not only determined by Michaels but also becomes a burden which Michaels assumes. Michaels initially determines that the cause of Mr. Gerbner's depression is his son, Lenny. Lenny Gerbner, we are informed by Michaels, "went underground" during the antiwar protest era, but "he was not on the FBI's 'most wanted list.' In those days, every long-haired kid who made a speech was arrested for starting a riot." Yet, Michaels doesn't "care what Lenny Gerbner did or didn't do. My only concern is his father." However, Michaels cannot unite the father and son because, as Michaels discovers, Lenny is pursued by police officer Ed Fox, who maintains his pursuit of Lenny as a personal vendetta because he lost a promotion when Lenny went underground. Michaels confronts Fox: "Your job is interfering with my job. Now, Mr. Gerbner is a very sick man. I'd appreciate it if you didn't bother him." Yet Fox will not withdraw. Sam Gerbner becomes more anxious: "Tell Fox to leave me alone. He's crazy. He never stops." Michaels, then, determines who is responsible for the problem. But, more important, despite the circumstances, Michaels decides that Mr. Gerbner's problems are his—Michaels assumes responsibility for the cause of the problem. Michaels will therefore determine and initiate those actions necessary to eliminate the pollution and guilt that have set off this drama.

The purifying acts initiated by Michaels are complex and, as we might suspect of a leader, he elicits the support of a large group of "followers" who agree to carry out his schemes. And the schemes are elaborate, requiring masterful coordination and a knack for the strange. In order to contact Lenny Gerbner, Michaels must secure a "code sentence" or elaborate password, demonstrate his authenticity with a ring from Sam Gerbner. Shortly thereafter, in order to get Lenny past police officer Fox, Ann is called upon to stall Fox, another of Michaels' colleagues poses as a patient, and Michaels and a third colleague finally sneak Lenny in to see Sam. The schemes are "do-able," but extremely complex, requiring perfect timing and a tremendous sense of originality. The entire purification process, then, is executed under the direction of Michaels. Michaels must deal with the same circumstances that anyone of us might face, but Michaels is a leader and therefore possesses the skills necessary to mobilize all of those around him to accomplish his task.

The final redemption process is, of course, the clear assertion of Michaels' values. Michaels confronts Fox. The importance of health and psychological care are cast as more important than legal prosecutions. Biological survival is aligned with Michaels while rather meaningless rationales for legal action are viewed as less than compelling. The leader, in this sense, is a kind of "rugged individualist" who can mobilize the responses of others but is ultimately responsible for the values endorsed and promoted.

The Romantic Communication System

In the romantic communication system, classical notions of romance are featured. The romantic hero or heroine is believed to be or is treated as if he or she had prodigious courage and endurance: the heroic are adventurous, idealized, and frequently mysterious; their tales are legendary, daring, and chivalrous. These classical conceptions of romance led us earlier to suggest that the central character in a romantic communication system would possess a symbol which would allow the hero or heroine to account for more environmental variables in more incisive ways than others and to create more effective programs for acting upon those environmental factors. Thus, while romantic agents are superior to others only in degree, the situations they face seem to contain almost overwhelming elements of unknown danger and risk as well as requiring remarkable levels of human power, intensity, dedication, and capacity. We almost expect that the ordinary laws of nature must be suspended if these dramas are to be successfully resolved. Clearly romantic agents must be intellectually superior to others and be capable of exercising superior control of their environment.

On the television series *Charlie's Angels,* three policewomen have left the police force because they were assigned only routine office work rather than dynamic detective work in the field. All three were at the top of their classes in the police academy—they are expert shots, capable of executing crippling karate kicks and punches, extremly bright, creative, and, as we might expect in a romance, they are glamorous, slender, and beautiful. Affectionately called his "Angels," these three women are hired as private detectives by Charlie, a powerful, mysterious, and wealthy figure who owns a detective agency designed to handle highly sensitive, complex, perilous, and demanding situations. Besides the subtle Cinderella transformation that is emphasized at the beginning of the series each week, the requirements of each show thus persistently call for a dynamic team of heroines capable of simultaneously resolving dramas laced with intricate psychological, explosive situational, and physically exacting dimensions.

In one show of the series, "Pretty Angels All in a Row," Kelly and Kris vie to be "Miss Chrysanthemum" while Sabrina and Bosley play television reporters when the Angels infiltrate a beauty contest being ravaged by terrorism. However, the necessity for all of these covert actions and even the existence of terrorism is unknown until the Angels begin their investigation.

Initially, the pollution detected by the coordinators of the beauty pageant is perceived only as an attempt to undermine and to destroy the pageant. Mr. Paul, master of ceremonies for the tournament, notes that the contestants are "dropping out left and right" and that the pageant starts "tomorrow and we only have nine girls left" out of the original fifty-six. However, during the Angels' briefing, Charlie sees the pollution as potentially more complex and dangerous, for he believes that the attempt to frighten a contestant with a tarantula constitutes a more serious issue. As the Angels investigate the situation, they confirm Charlie's speculation, and they find, in fact, that attempted murder, kidnapping, bribery, conspiracy, and blackmail are also part of the "problem." Thus, while others were unable to identify the "full scope" of the problem, the Angels were able to do so. In addition, only the Angels are able to determine that unsuspected psychological motivations also permeate the scene. Thus, when a gunshot misses Kris by only three feet, only the Angels are able to determine that perhaps the gunmen "did not really want to kill her," especially given particular circumstantial evidence. Moreover, when a sandbag is intentionally cut from the ceiling of the pageant hall and just misses the contestants by feet, Sabrina knowingly asks, "Was that sandbag supposed to scare someone or kill someone?" Moreover, after Millicent, one of the pageant judges, is assaulted and kidnapped, Kris pointedly alerts us that the scene has changed: "Up till now everything's been done only to scare everyone." Thus, the Angels reveal a controlling problem more profound and more extensive than anyone else had suspected. Not only are the kinds of crimes involved more extensive, but the psychological motivations for these crimes are understood and revealed only by the Angels.

Similarly, until the Angels enter the case, virtually no one connected with the pageant has any idea who is responsible for the terrorism or for what reasons. Sabrina, by virtue of her undercover role, is able to spot the most likely suspects, trail them to their car, sneak into the trunk of their car without the suspects' knowledge, overhear their telephone call to their boss C. J., and before her hiding spot is detected, Sabrina is first able to locate the suspects' hideout. Thus, at least one of the Angels is able to reveal the entire "web of guilt" that leads to a boss—C. J. is a millionaire stockbroker who hopes to have his daughter Billy Jo crowned "Miss Chrysanthemum" so that she can model in his corporation's commercials on television. Before the Angels' investigation, no one within the drama had ever heard of or been aware of C. J.'s existence.

Having identified the "real" pollution and the "true" scope of guilt, the unique powers of the Angels enable them to purify the drama. They are able to function as undercover beauty contestants only because of their glamour and beauty, positions that allowed them to literally jump the suspects from the stage by surprise. Moreover, their karate experience allows the Angels to "make short work" of the suspects: they are "flattened in less than a minute." Likewise, from Sabrina's undercover role, she is able to trace as well as disarm the suspects because of her extensive knowledge of firearms acquired at the police academy.

Having purified the drama, the criminals are jailed, Billy Jo is disqualified from the contest, and C. J. is apprehended as an accessory to the crimes. Moreover, Kris and Kelly are redeemed as "beauties," for we are informed that Charlie had instructed the judges that they were only "substitute noncontestants" in the contest. The show closes with all of the Angels smiling. All conditions of the romantic drama have been satisfied.

The Mythical Communication System

A myth is a fabricated, invented, or imagined story of historical events in which universal struggles concerning Truth, Beauty, and Patriotism are depicted. In an almost sacred or timeless order (ritual or dream), a hero or heroine embarks upon a long, unknown, and difficult journey in order to retrieve a "precious object" that is guarded by unusually powerful counteragents. In the process of completing the quest, the hero or heroine displays superhuman powers, thereby creating a myth, fantasy, illusion, or vision. Thus, Jason's quest for the golden fleece and Superman's demand for law and order constitute myths. Both Jason and Superman face universal problems beyond the responsibility of any particular human force. The resolution of these problems requires "superhuman" powers employed toward the formulation of a new social system.

On *The Incredible Hulk,* David Banner, hero of the series, appears to meet the requirements of a mythical hero. Dr. David Banner was a physician and scientist, searching for a way to tap into the hidden strengths that all humans have. His research program is interrupted by an accidental dose of gamma radiation, which altered his body chemistry. And now, when David Banner grows angry or outraged, a startling metamorphosis occurs. A kind of lycanthropic transformation occurs, and Banner's eyes first take on a fluorescent blue-green glow, his skins turns to a pea-green hue, he grows a good foot in height, and he develops the muscles of Mr. Universe. During this transformation, his clothes are ripped away, and a half-naked green ape-like creature stands before us. Beyond the fact that technology is responsible for this transformation much as it was responsible for the changes created in *The Six Million Dollar Man, New York Times* critic Carly Rivers also notes that as, "The camera zeroes in on Bixby's chest, and one watches in fascination as the fabric stretches taut to the breaking point" and as "the sound of rending of garments and a huge, pea-green torso breaks through," it is difficult to miss "the erotic potential of the whole thing" and what is "the height of 'Beefcake Camp.' "[27] Perhaps even contributing to the sexual appeal of the series, the creature is driven by rage and pursued by an investigative reporter. With a touch of understatement, Banner at one point tells this investigative reporter who is unaware that Banner is the creature, "Mr. McGee, don't make me angry. You wouldn't like me when I'm angry." Indeed, when the creature does emerge, in the arresting detail of slow motion, whole rooms and even buildings can be destroyed, diesel trucks traveling 60 miles per hour have been stopped dead and overturned, and people may be thrown, beaten, and crushed against walls. Yet, throughout all of this chaos, only those identified as "evil" face the wrath of the incredible hulk; the "good" are protected and saved by the hulk. The creature is, however, wanted for a murder that he didn't commit. Furthermore, David Banner is believed to be dead. And, we are told at the beginning of each show of the series that Banner "must let the world believe that he is dead until he can find a way to control the raging spirit that dwells within him."

In one show, Banner enters New York City's world of high fashion by way of the "behind-the-scene" setting of Manhattan's garment district. At first, the problems faced by Sam, Banner's employer and owner of a struggling garment factory, appear common enough, not the kinds of universal issues associated with mythical heroes as they deal with pollution. Sam does face real economic problems but not the universal problems of Truth, Beauty, and Patriotism. He owes $12,683.12 for six months of invoices for fabric; his employees are quitting because they have not been paid; and Sam needs $15,000 for his daughter Liz for her fashion show. However, even these issues are not inherent, for Banner explains that at Liz's fashion show, "she'll be showing all of her original designs and there'll be models and buyers from stores all over the country and I'm sure that after that there'll be more than enough orders to cover Sam's debts." Moreover, Sam's indebtness is not intentional. As Banner informs his co-worker Solly, "Sam was nice enough to give me a job." Solly responds, "Sam's a good man. He's got a good heart." In even greater detail, Liz later explains that Sam "is not a businessman. Sometimes I think he just doesn't understand money or want to. Sam believes he should be treated the way he treats other people, with trust. Like family." Finally, to insure that the problems do not appear insoluble, David Banner is cast as Sam's solution. A fabric buyer notes of Banner to Sam, "This fellow makes sense, Sam. You should let him do your talking all the time. Save you a lot of grief." Later, Sam himself observes, "David's got a good head on his shoulders, you know what I mean? Just the kind of guy I'd like to see take over this business after I'm gone." Sam may, then, be incompetent in terms of economics but he is not unethical nor are the problems he faces beyond control. As Banner says, "Sam's only crime is giving too much."

However, pollution does escalate—slowly but surely—to a universal level. Sam decides to borrow money to pay for Liz's fashion show and in the process, in order to secure his loan, lies and claims that Banner—already perceived by all at this point in the drama as bright, capable, and a good businessman—is a partner in the fashion show venture. Besides involving Banner unfairly, Sam's loan opens up a host of more universal problems. Sam borrows the needed money from loan sharks who are not above using strong-arm tactics, arson, and even murder to secure their payments. But even more universal issues are involved. The loan sharks represent "generations of crime." The loan shark's son is taking over the "business" just as his father took over the business from his father: generations of criminal injustice must be broken. Moreover, these loan sharks would destroy the "American way" of competing in the capitalistic system. Liz's fashion show is cast as an exemplar of capitalistic values involving a kind of "pioneer morality," designed to secure achievement and success, change and progress, equality of opportunity, effort and optimism, and material comfort. For the loan sharks to interfere with this venture is therefore an attack upon the "American way of life" itself. Finally, the kinship system between Sam and Liz is threatened by the loan sharks, thereby endangering the more universal value of loyalty and patriotism as well as the necessary support which should exist between father and offspring. The issues to be resolved, then, are universal.

Yet, guilt is not easily assigned for these conditions. Sam might be blamed by virtue of his inept business practices, but we are told that his only crime is he gives too much to others. Besides, Sam cannot be held responsible for the existence of generations of gangsters, the tactics of these gangsters, or their decision to challenge the "American economy" and kinship systems. In a sense, even the gangsters themselves are not responsible for the particular situation they create. Generations of conditioning have established the perspective and tactics they are bound by. At best, the system as a whole is to be blamed for allowing such agents to exist for as long as they have. At the same time, little can be gained at this moment in the drama by blaming "the system." Blame is not attached, as a result, to any particular and individual agent. Larger societal forces are at fault. Rather than dwelling upon the frame of guilt, the action of the show pays deference to the issue but moves rather quickly to the question of purifying the pollution.

David Banner's supernatural powers as the hulk are needed to correct the situation. These powers are "incredible," and not to be found in other "mere mortals." Moreover, this purifying solution by the supernatural is unpredictable in the sense that we do not know when or exactly how the hulk will engage his powers to eliminate the pollution and the societally caused factors responsible for the pollution. Even David Banner cannot predict when he will become angry enough to make the transformation into the hulk. In the particular case of the hulk's "contest" with the loan sharks, the hulk physically prevents both the son and the father from stopping the fashion show; the loan sharks' criminal activities are publicly revealed and we are led to believe they will be arrested. The hulk then runs so rapidly to the warehouse to prevent the arsonist from "torching it" that we can see the hulk only by the marvels of the slow motion camera. Arriving just before the match is struck, the hulk hangs the arsonist from a hook and releases Liz from the cage she was imprisoned in, where she surely would have died had not the hulk stopped the arsonist. The hulk's supernatural powers thus come into play at each of these purifying moments as well as his "supernatural" sense of what good and evil are.

The show concludes by suggesting that a new social system can now emerge. Redemption can include a reaffirmation of a "crime-free" environment, a reinvigorated belief in the American system of capitalism, and a renewed opportunity for the American family to function as a support system. These values are provincial but, as we shall see, they are an important feature of the value orientation provided by all stages of the mythical communication system.

Popular Television Series as Communication Systems, 1980–81 and 1974–75

Having defined and illustrated the communication matrix proposed here, the 1980–81 television series are now appropriately classified into the matrix. Table 2 provides the results of such a classification; the 1974–75 television series have also been similarly classified because this contrast plays a central role in the analysis which follows. Moreover, once the nature of this classification system is understood, there is reason to believe that others are likely to classify these popular television series into the same categories of this matrix.[28]

During the last seven years, popular television series have undergone changes in their communicative emphasis. Table 3 details these changes on a year-by-year basis. Table 4 provides a compilation of these changes, highlighting the changes from 1974–75 to 1980–81.

Using Tables 3 and 4 as our base, we can come to four major conclusions. First, not all communication systems are equally represented and emphasized over time. Ironic and mythical communication systems have

Table 2. Television series—a seven year comparison*

Communication System	1974–1975 Season	1980–1981 Season
Ironic	"All in the Family"	"Archie Bunker's Place"
	"The Texas Wheeler"	"The Jeffersons"
	"Sanford and Son"	"Three's Company"**
Mimetic	"The New Land"	"Love Boat"
	"Friends and Lovers"	"WKRP in Cincinnati"
	"The Mary Tyler Moore Show"	"Six O'Clock Follies"
		"Good Time Harry"
	"The Bob Newhart Show"	"Happy Days"
	"Apple's Way"	"Laverne & Shirley"
	"Rhoda"	"Taxi"
	"Happy Days"	"Mork & Mindy"
	"Good Times"	"Angie"
	"That's My Mama"	"Benson"
	"Little House on the Prairie"	"Alice"
	"The Odd Couple"	"Flo"
	"Paper Moon"	"Little House on the Prairie"
	"Chico and the Man"	"Ladies' Man"
		"Too Close for Comfort"
		"Eight Is Enough"
		"Barney Miller"
		"It's A Living"
		"I'm A Big Girl Now"
		"One Day At A Time"
		"Diff'rent Strokes"
		"Facts of Life"
		"Bosom Buddies"
Leader	"Emergency"	"BJ and the Bear"
	"Nakia"	"M*A*S*H"
	"The Rookies"	"Dukes of Hazzard"
	"Maude"	"Vega$"
	"Born Free"	"Lou Grant"
	"Adam-12"	"White Shadow"
	"Lucas Tanner"	"House Calls"
	"Movin' On"	"Enos"
	"The Rockford Files"	"Trapper John, MD"
	"Mannix"	
	"Gunsmoke"	
	"Cannon"	
	"Streets of San Francisco"	
	"Kodiak"	
	"Police Woman"	
	"Get Christie Love"	
	"M*A*S*H"	
	"Barnaby Jones'	

Communication System	1974–1975 Season	1980–1981 Season
Romantic	"Kung Fu"	"Quincy"
	"Kojak"	"Hart to Hart"
	"Medical Center"	"Charlie's Angels"
	"Marcus Welby, M.D."	"The Waltons"
	"Hawaii Five-O"	
	"Manhunter"	
	"Petrocelli"	
	"Harry O"	
	"The Waltons"	
	"Ironside"	
Mythical	"Six Million Dollar Man"	"Buck Rogers in the 25th
	"The Night Stalker"	Century"
	"Planet of the Apes"	"Fantasy Island" **
		"Incredible Hulk"

* "Television series" was defined as being: prime time (8–11 P.M. E.S.T.), national network productions of a dramatic nature (conflict-resolution patterns, excluding sports, news specials, regularly scheduled news programs, and documentaries) in which a single character or team of central characters appear weekly (which would exclude variety shows, movies, made-for-TV movies, specials, and semidocumentaries). While 1974–1975 season series seldom changed during the season, the "data base" beginning with the 1977–1978 season changed continually. Some critics claimed that by the midpoint of the 1977–1978 season, the equivalent of three different sets of "seasons" had already been created by the networks. Almost 50% of all new series had been replaced by "newer" series by the midpoint of the 1977–1978 season and by the end of this season, many of the replacements had been replaced by "newer" series. The same condition existed during the 1980–1981 season. Consequently, I decided that seasons would be defined as those series listed by *TV Guide* for the first week of the season. The 1974–1975 season was those series listed September 7–13, 1974, the 1977–1978 season those listed September 10–16, 1977. This technique provided a uniform method of defining each season until the 1980–1981 season. During the 1980–1981 season, the actor's strike and the miniseries "Shogun" generated a list of only 21 series. As a result, it was decided to randomly select three other weeks to supplement the list of series to be classified for 1980–1981; these three weeks were October 25–31, 1980, November 8–14, 1980, and November 22–28, 1980. When these three additional weeks were added to the original "first week of the season," an additional 21 series were "picked up." In addition, only episodic series are included in this definition of a series, for the soap opera form does not necesarily resolve all of the issues in its open-ended time format.

** It is possible for a series to shift from one category to another at any time. Most series, however, "work out" a format for the series, and, as a result, most series remain within one category as long as they are on the air. From the 1979–1980 to the 1980–1981 season, one series did shift categories. "Fantasy Island" had originally been classified as a romantic communication system, because each of the fantasies created for the "guests" coming to the island were humanly constructed. During the 1980–1981 season, however, the fantasies are created as a result of magic, often generating "unreal" transformation (e.g., a puppet becomes a human being or characters are transported back in time to a different century) or encounters (e.g., the devil is physically and directly encountered, a contest between good and evil is portrayed, and the devil loses the battle). In addition, during the 1980–1981 season, "Three's Company" lost a major central character (e.g., Crissy played by Suzanne Sommers); the series underwent a transformation from a mimetic to an ironic series with Jack Tripper or Joyce becoming the central character in different shows of the series in predominantly ironic forms.

Table 3. Changes in the communication patterns of television series

Communication System	1974–1975		1975–1976		1976–1977		1977 1978	
	N	%	N	%	N	%	N	%
Ironic	3	6%	4	7%	3	5%	3	5%
Mimetic	13	28%	23	40%	25	45%	27	48%
Leader	18	38%	22	39%	17	31%	12	21%
Romantic	10	21%	5	9%	7	13%	10	18%
Mythical	3	6%	3	5%	3	5%	4	7%
Total *	47	99%	57	100%	55	99%	56	99%

Communication System	1978–1979		1979–1980		1980–1981	
	N	%	N	%	N	%
Ironic	2	4%	6	10%	3	7%
Mimetic	21	47%	23	41%	23	55%
Leader	10	22%	9	16%	9	21%
Romantic	9	20%	16	29%	4	10%
Mythical	3	7%	2	4%	3	7%
Total *	45	100%	56	100%	42	100%

* Rounding off accounts for differences above and below 100%.

been consistently underrepresented during the last seven years, each accounting for as little as 4 percent of all television series in some years and only 10 percent at their highest peak of popularity. Yet, overall, both ironic and mythical communication systems are a relatively constant and stable part of television options. Moreover, the series in these two categories—"Archie Bunker's Place," "The Jeffersons," "Three's Company," "Buck Rogers in the 25th Century," "Fantasy Island," and "The Incredible Hulk"—are some of the most popular series on television.

Insofar as the ironic series have been successful modes of communication, and insofar as the ironic form reflects "the rhetoric of the loser," viewers apparently find such explorations and modes of interaction significant. The ironic form apparently, then, functions as a temporary corrective, creating the opportunity to enjoy a moment of cynicism in which the central and controlling characters in life are cast as the cause of the problems that "minor," surrounding characters must correct.

On the other hand, and perhaps balancing the excesses of the ironic form, the mythical communication system provides an opportunity for viewers to fantasize and escape from life's realities. While the mythical form is relatively stable as a percentage of all television series—ranging only from 4 percent at its lowest to 7 percent at its highest peak—nonetheless, the mythical form constantly introduces novelty into television's prime-time hours. Human bionics and technological innovations ("The Six Million Dollar Man" and "The Bionic Woman"), animal intelligence ("Planet of the Apes"), the occult ("The Night Stalker"), the future ("Buck Rogers in the 25th Century"), human transformations ("The Incredible Hulk"), and wish fulfillment ("Fantasy Island") have all constituted dimensions of the popular mythology in these series.

Thus, the ironic and the mythical forms do function as important modes of communication on television. However, the fact that these systems of interaction are underrepresented compared with the other categories may

Table 4. Changes in the communication patterns of television series

Communication System	1974–1975 Season		1980–1981 Season		% Shift from the 1974–1975 to the 1980–1981 Season
Ironic	3	6%	3	7%	+ 1%
Mimetic	13	28%	23	55%	+27%
Leader	18	38%	9	21%	−17%
Romantic	10	21%	4	10%	−11%
Mythical	3	6%	3	7%	− 1%

indicate that while people do need a sense of the cynical and the godly, pragmatically life cannot be controlled by these modes of interaction.

Second, the mimetic form has become the dominant mode of communication on popular television series. While controlling over one-quarter of the series seven years ago, the mimetic form is now employed as the controlling mode of presentation on over half of current television series. Moreover, with the exception of one year, the mimetic form has consistently increased in importance every year during the last seven years.

The increasing use of the mimetic form coincides with national changes in popular self-conceptions among Americans. The Gallup poll organization, on a rather irregular basis, has asked a random sample of all Americans how "satisfied" they are with their "personal life" during the last seven years. When asked at four different points[29] during the last seven years, Americans expressed the following degrees of satisfaction:

August 1974	35 percent satisfaction
February 1978	57 percent satisfaction
February 1979	77 percent satisfaction
July 1979	73 percent satisfaction

While we cannot determine, given available data, if this sense of personal satisfaction has been consistently increasing at a stable rate during the last seven years, we do know that when Gallup's latest poll results are compared with his 1974 survey, an additional 38 percent of the population have found their personal lives satisfying. Likewise, mimetic television series have increased 27 percent during this same period. A correlation seems evident. However, we have no way of determining if the correlation is causal in either direction. We do not know if popular television series only *reflect* the growing sense of personal satisfaction in the life of Americans or if these series *cause* such satisfaction by virtue of the "happily ever after" attitudes conveyed by mimetic television series. Regardless of whether or not this causal issue can ever be resolved, it is sufficient to know that the changing rate of mimetic television series has thus far been an accurate barometer of personal satisfaction in America.

Third, in contrast to the mimetic form, leader-centered series have sharply declined as a mode of dramatic presentation on popular television series. With the exception of this last season, leader-centered dramas have consistently declined as a percentage of all television series. During the last seven years, these series have declined some 17 percent as a total percentage of all series.

The decline in leader-centered series coincides with our understanding of the changes in the popular conception of the nation's leaders and institutions. Gallup poll data have noted an increasing distrust of the nation's institutions during the last seven years.[30] When a random sample of Americans were asked by Gallup if they had "confidence" in the U.S. Congress, the results were as follows:

1973	42 percent confident
1975	40 percent confident
1977	40 percent confident
1979	34 percent confident

It is clear that not even a majority of Americans have confidence in the U.S. Congress. Moreover, from 1973 to 1979 (the latest available data), the percentage of Americans having confidence in the U.S. Congress has declined 8 percent. Similarly, when Gallup asked a random sample of Americans if they approved of the way the U.S. Congress was handling its job,[31] only 29 percent—less than one-third of the country—believed that the Congress was doing its job in August of 1975. By June of 1979 (the latest available data), the percentage had declined to 19 percent. Ten percent fewer Americans approve of the way the U.S. Congress is handling its job. The direction and rate of these popular trends coincides with the decline of 17 percent in leader-centered television series. Again, as is true of the mimetic trends, we cannot determine from these data if the decline in leader-centered television series is a reflection or a cause of the declining confidence and approval Americans have of the nation's leaders and institutions.

Fourth and finally, Tables 3 and 4 indicate that romantic television series have declined some 11 percent from 1974–75 to 1980–81. However, this decline has been neither persistent nor stable. These series are extremely volatile, shifting up and down by as much as 8 percent on the average from one year to the next. Accordingly, while the 19 percent decline from 1979–80 to 1980–81 is the most significant change recorded for these series in the last seven years and may be a sign that a major trend is about to "take off," nonetheless, the volatile nature of this form of communication requires that we be extremely guarded in offering any assessment of the long-term direction and rate of change of romantic communication systems on television. At the same time, we can claim that the romantic frame of reference is extremely volatile, changing drastically from year to year, and this observation is itself an important conclusion.

In this regard, the volatile nature of romantic television series coincides with the nation's sporadic and rapidly shifting periods of idealism. The "Camelot" era established by John F. Kennedy collapsed in one day with an assassin's bullet; the landslide election that put Richard Nixon in the White House in 1972 collasped in three months in 1974. To cast anyone as a romantic figure is a risky business. The ever-present "eye" of the media, for example, exposes the slighest blemish and mistake. Every nation must celebrate its ideals, but in an ever-changing nation-state, it is unclear what person, institution, policy, or action can sustain such glorification. The United States appears to be desperately searching for its ideals, rapidly shifting from one ideal to another, seeking a sense of permanence in a world of ever-increasing rates of change. Romantic television series reflect, or perhaps cause, this neurotic quest for a humanly attainable vision and goal for the nation.

When all five types of communicative drama on television are examined as a whole, then, it is clear that television is a part of the culture, not an independent force operating outside of the nation's ongoing experiences. The media are not a "fourth branch of government" functioning as an independent check and balance on the rest of society. The media are instruments shaped by the cultural agents that create them, at least until the media begin to function as independent reinforcement systems controlling the agents who create them. In either role, the media are a product or producer of the culture controlling social action. At the same time, these popular television series have a dramatic affect upon the value system of Americans.

Popular Television Series as Value Systems

At the outset of this essay, a value was defined as a standard of worth, utility, importance, and excellence that controls specific attitudes and daily behaviors; values are the basis for endorsing or rejecting experiences and phenomena encountered in everyday interactions. While retaining this general conception of a value, it is appropriate at this juncture to recognize that values can be conceived in at least two different ways. First, a value can be a manifest standard, explicitly identifiable in behavior or in the context of language using. Or, second, values can be viewed as more amphorous orientations that implicitly govern a host of human actions indirectly; in this case, the nature of the controlling values may only be evident after the fact when a wide range of activities have been "summed up" in an effort to determine the regulating principle of selectivity controlling how and why apparently diverse choices are actually constrained and consistent. These two conceptions of a value are not necessarily inconsistent, but we can explore the relationship between popular television series and values in greater depth by using both views of a value.

Values as Specific Behavioral and Content Standards

In describing the value system controlling America between 1940 and 1952, Edward D. Steele and W. Charles Redding discovered that some eighteen values were precise enough to be viewed as manifest behaviors or content in speeches. They concluded that:

> In spite of the hazards, however, it has been found that it is possible to cast many cultural values in a form precise enough to be perceived within the "content" of a speech, and that a reasonable quantitative "content-analysis" can be executed. What we are discussing, therefore, in this paper is not some shadowy, intuitive guess. The concepts of culture and cultural values (premises) are, indeed, intellectual abstractions, but they refer to real behavior.[32]

Adopting such a behavioral concept of a value, Gerald R. Miller reports that "every communicative act involves, of necessity, a value judgment."[33] Even entertainment, itself a special type of communication but nonetheless communication, is deeply embedded in the process of making evaluations. As Comstock concluded, after examining available social science research on television programming, "entertainment programs can maintain or alter behavior."[34] Such a conclusion gains even more credibility when it is recognized that producers of popular television series admit that they selectively dramatize certain values rather than other. While entertaining their viewers, these producers also appear to be functioning as persuaders who intentionally emphasize certain values discriminately. While each might promote a different value, virtually all of the major producers are overtly aware that their series dramatize certain values to the exclusion of others.[35] In producing *The Waltons,* for example, Lee Rich has reasoned that, "the success of this series is because of what is going on in the country today, the loss of values. Many people see ethical qualities in this family that they hope they can get back to."[36] In this context, Richard D. Heffner has aptly argued that television series may appropriately be viewed as "subtle persuaders." As he has put it, "Television, the newest and far more prevalent form of fiction, is even more profoundly influential in our lives—not in terms of the stories it tells, but more importantly, the values it portrays."[37]

Treating each of the five communication dramas as forms of subtle persuasion, and relying upon the manifest content defining each of these dramas, the following sets of "equations" emerge:

Ironic Communication = Existentialism
Mimetic Communication = Individualism
Leader-Centered Communication = Authority
Romantic Communication = Idealism
Mythical Communication = Theology

The primary value associated with each of these communication systems was initially explored by Northrop Frye when he first defined each category. His conception functions as our point of departure as we consider the nature of each of these equations one at a time.

In equating ironic communication with an existential value orientation, we should first note that irony is characterized by a sense of disparity or inconsistency. The ironic figure says one thing but means another. The ironic character may (Socratic irony) or may not (dramatic irony) intend to create the disparity, but the disparity or inconsistency is a minimum condition for irony to exist. Moreover, for irony to exist, an "audience" must be aware of the disparity—the disparity is not "announced" in the ironic form itself but relies upon the discerning "eye" of the audience. In this sense, the ironic figure is "out of control" while the "knowing audience" functions as an "inner group" which knows the "real" meaning behind the baffling exterior of the disparity.

Second, the tragic ironic character possesses a sense of being randomly set aside or isolated from the rest of society. As Frye has noted, the ironic character "is innocent in the sense that what happens to him is far greater than anything he has done provokes, like the mountaineer whose shout brings down the avalanche."[38] This "sense of arbitrariness," continues Frye, "casts the victim as having been unlucky, selected at random or by lot, and no more deserving of what happens to him than anyone else would be. If there is a reason for choosing him for catastrophe, it is an inadequate reason, and raises more objections that it answers."[39] Even if the ironic character is comic, the audience still possesses the sense that the ironic figure (even if he or she created the catastrophe) is "innocent," for who would want disaster to befall Archie Bunker, George Jefferson, or Jack Tripper. In such cases, the needs or conditioning of these ironic characters "forces" them to create the disparities. The audience is aware, then, of the source or motive of the inconsistency. Nonetheless, there remains a sense in which the ironic character is isolated from society, particularly when other characters in the series are aware of the discrepancy and must correct the disparity. In such cases, the realism of the act itself stands out regardless of the intent of the ironic figure. What happened—a true sense of realism—controls, not what is intended. In more tragic forms, when the ironic character senses the isolation, "melancholy," perhaps to the point "where the individual is so isolated as to feel his existence a living death"[40] can emerge. In more comic forms, the ironic character experiences the isolation by virtue of his or her sense of embarrassment, stupidity, or desire to ignore the inconsistency. In either case, this sense of isolation scapegoats the ironic character.

Third, the ironic act is completely objective. As we have already noted, the arbitrariness of the catastrophe faced by the ironic character is part of the audience's response. Technically, the ironic form itself makes no such statement. The form itself is, in this sense, completely objective. Socrates, for example, "pretends to know nothing, even that he is ironic. Complete objectivity and suppression of all explicit moral judgments are essential to his method." Thus, concludes Frye, "pity and fear are not raised in ironic art: they are reflected to the reader from that art."[41] In our culture, this sense of an ironic objectivity emerges when it becomes the norm to believe that human actions cannot be evaluated as good or bad; evaluative assessments are avoided: actions are viewed only as mere acts, devoid of any moral implication. As Frye aptly observes in terms of literature, "In our day an ironic provincialism, which looks everywhere in literature for complete objectivity, suspension of moral judgments, concerntrating on pure verbal craftsmanship, and similar virtues, is in the ascendant."[42] In its extreme form, then, the ironic form actually "passes through a dead center of complete realism, a pure mime representing human life without comment and without imposing any sort of dramatic form beyond what is required for simple exhibition."[43]

The joining of the sense of disparity, isolation, arbitrariness, and objectivity creates the existential quality. For our purposes here, existentialism can be conceived as a philosophy that is centered upon the analysis of existence and of the way the human being finds himself or herself existing in the world, that regards human existence as not exhaustively describable or understandable in scientific terms, and that stresses freedom and responsibility of the individual, the irreducible uniqueness of an ethical or religious situation, and usually the isolation and subjective experiences (such as anxiety, guilt, dread, and anguish) of the individual. This philosophical view carries with it, then, a profound sense of the ironic which easily lends itself toward the use of satire, parody, ridicule, burlesque, and even the casting of paradoxes, potentially functioning as a rationalizing value for the political tactics of the radical revolutionary who, feeling isolated and removed, finds it "natural" to invoke violence in the name of peace.

In equating the mimetic communication system with individualism, the equation gains power insofar as everyday life is captured or our own personal experiences are portrayed. The emphasis here is upon the routine drama of everyday interactions. Accordingly, the visions of the gods, the extraordinary personality, symbols of authority, and the cynical are diminished—the life of "Everyman" and "Everywoman" are highlighted. The unique and esoteric features of the personal life emerge. In this context, Frye has observed that mimetic forms "deal with an intensely individual society."[44] Accordingly, the appeal of the mimetic residues in pathos. "Pathos," in Frye's words, "presents its hero as isolated by a weakness which appeals to our sympathy because it is on our own level of experience."[45] Frye concludes his train of thought by noting that, "The root idea of pathos is the exclusion of an individual on our own level from a social group to which he is trying to belong. Hence the central tradition of sophisticated pathos is the study of the isolated mind."[46]

When the entire social system is cast as mimetic, one has the sense of a world of diverse and unique individuals, each proclaiming his or her own identity. As Frye has aptly put it, "mimic wars" are "made out of 'points of view.' "[47] Accordingly, the mimetic television series seem to have little in common if lifestyles are emphasized. Life in Cincinnati at WKRP has little to do with the issues plaguing Laverne and Shirley and is far removed from what Flo faces at the Yellow Rose, which is, of course, completely distinct from Barney Miller's world. Yet these series do find a common and unifying theme; they all emphasize the individuality of each central character. We are drawn to these unique worlds out of curiosity, because we want to see what others like us are dealing with and how they are dealing with it, and perhaps because there is a style for dealing with everyday life that can be recognized, if not modified and used. In this sense, the appeal of a style emphasizes the means, agency, pragmatics, and conventions of life. To focus upon a particular style, to examine it in detail, and to allow one style to characterize all, are ways of knowing that are technically identified as synecdoche and metonymy. But, we need not emphasize such serious overtones here, for the mimetic is profoundly individualistic and therefore avoids the common "groupthink" required for political action. In fact, the effort to achieve social identification with others is, in many ways in these series, cast as a comic but enjoyable experience.

In sharp contrast, the leader-centered communication system places symbols of authority, influence, and power over others as necessary, effective, and useful modes for human interaction. Authority can be viewed as a set of skills, resources, and so forth that allows one to control. Or, authority can be viewed as a relationship in which one agent's behavior causes or is allowed to cause another's behavior. In either case, those in authority examine the situation or scene, consider the materials available and the material outcomes of decisions, and attempt to develop and secure support for an idiom that will allow all to move "logically" from one issue to the next in proper syllogistic order until the solution emerges. Others may have to be coached to accept certain percepts—a form of the didactic—if the necessary concerted actions are to be taken. The goals, aims, or solutions toward which these steps are taken may require the use of metaphors. In the end, the voice of the political liberal can function as a model for such modes of authority. Thus, Hawkeye, Lou Grant, and Trapper John are individuals, but they also wield authority, authority directed toward a liberal end.

The romantic communication system, as an idealistic value system, highlights the extraordinary features of the almost unbelievable personality—those few geniuses among us are emphasized in this form. In Frye's words, romance is a "rhetoric of personal greatness"[48] which looks "everywhere for genius and evidences of great personality."[49] This romantic character, beyond being "an extraordinary person," also "creates his own world," exists "in a state of pantheistic rapport with nature"[50] and lives with "adventure."[51] The quest defines the universal pattern of the romantic figure. As Frye has put it:

> The complete form of the romance is clearly the successful quest, and such a completed form has three main stages: the stage of the perilous journey and the preliminary minor adventures; the crucial struggle, usually some kind of battle in which either the hero or his foe, or both, must die; and the exaltation of the hero.[52]

A complete understanding of the quest is very likely to take the form of a proverb, "a secular or purely human oracle" whose "wisdom is the tried and tested way" with the accompanying "virtues" of "prudence and moderation."[53] As is true of proverbs, they are often designed to create a state of the mind in which one's initial predisposition leads to yet another and then to another until the final state of mind adheres to a quality quite different from the original predisposition. Burke has identified such symbolic forms as qualitative.[54] Before leaving the romantic form, however, we should also note its implicit class and political emphasis. As Frye has noted, "The social affinities of the romance, with its grave idealizing of heroism and purity, are with the aristocracy."[55] More directly, Frye observes that, "In every age the ruling social or intellectual class tends to project its ideals in some form of romance, where the virtuous heroes and beautiful heroine represent the ideals and the villains the threats to their ascendancy."[56] Frye argues that this class bias accounts for the character of chivalric romance in the Middle Ages, aristocratic romance in the Renaissance, bourgeois romance since the eighteenth century, and revolutionary romance in contemporary Russia. While there is a sense in which the "commoner" identifies with the struggles of the romantic hero or heroine, the conservative appeal of the romantic system may be more than an accidental feature of the form, for inherent within the romantic scheme is an essential belief in a superiority of some to many by virtue of genius or extraordinary personality. Such characteristics are not learned or acquired—the romantic hero or heroine is "born, not made," and protected and insulated by the social institution they have created. Despite this political dimension, nonetheless, the romantic frame of reference inspires, idealizes, and offers hope. "Hart to Hart" introduces us to the world of the millionaire; "Quincy" reveals the power of technology and specialization; "The Waltons" symbolize the full power of humanism.

As we shift to our final mode of communication, the mythical system, a theological value scheme emerges. Theologies are associated with the class of religious communities, but the essence of a theology is its reliance upon some kind of god or divinity. Whatever the divinity, its will is assumed to create and to regulate the natural, human, and ethical laws controlling all human beings. Such systems are easily transformed into fate-control systems: one's purpose in life is externally imposed. In rather blunt terms, Frye argues that, "Mythology projects itself as theology."[57] As a form of theology, a myth can therefore carry with it the sense that a commandment, a parable, an aphorism, or a prophesy is involved in the meaning of the myth. As an "inspired" oracle, for example, the future may be foretold. Thus, the myth functions, in Frye's words, "near or at the conceivable limits of desire."[58] It does not, however, "mean that it necessarily presents its world as attained or attainable by human beings."[59] Nonetheless, by virtue of the divine purpose and mysticism associated with myth, human actions are compelled. Moreover, the divine purpose will repeat itself as a form in virtually all dimensions of human and natural experience—the divine will is cast as "everywhere," permeating and reflected in all things, and is therefore commonly identified as a repetitive form. When used for political ends, the divinely inspired leader is cast as inspired directly by a god—he or she is superb and godlike, if not supremely good. Under such conditions, democracy is unnecessary, for who would use a popular vote to determine the good when the word of a god is immediately available through the divinely inspired leader. Such reasoning is reactionary in essence and often destructive in practice. Yet the mythical scheme need not possess such negative connotations. On "Fantasy Island," wishes—even the most impossible—come true. On "Buck Rogers in the 25th Century," time travel provides a world of adventure and excitement. Likewise, the green incredible hulk destroys only evil and protects the good. A mythical framework does, however, determine the good and the evil; others must abide by the values contained in the myth.

Values as Orientations Integrating Diverse Human Actions

While values can be perceived as specific standards evident in particular behaviors and the content of speech, values can also be usefully viewed as orientations implicitly constraining a host of diverse human actions. Employed in this sense, a value is a form of consciousness, philosophy of life, or unifying life-purpose. In this context, Burke has advanced these four propositions as interrelated dimensions of an orientation:

> (a) There is a sense of relationships, developed by the contingencies of experience; (b) this sense of relationships is our orientation; (c) our orientation largely involves matters of expectancy, and affects our choice of means with reference to the future; (d) in the human sphere, the subject of expectancy and the judgment as to what is proper in conduct is largely bound up with the subject of motives, for if we know *why* people do as they do, we feel that we know *what* to expect of them and of ourselves, and we shape our decisions and judgments and policies to take such expectancies into account.[60]

When values are cast as orientations, we expect consistent linkages among a person's motives, philosophy, method for developing conceptions, sense of power or politics, language, and aesthetics. While people are never completely consistent, we do expect—if others are to be predictable in any way and if we are to understand what particular acts mean to them—that they roughly adhere to a unifying theme or value in their various life activities.

As we shift from the sense that values are manifest in certain behaviors and in speech content to the notion that a value is an orientation, our definition of each communication system as a value system does not change. The ironic continues, for example, to be viewed as basically an existential value system. However, seeing values as orientations alters the ease with which we can expect to detect or to identify an overall and controlling principle. The nature of the controlling value may only be evident after the fact when a wide range of activities have been "summed up." As critics, at this "summing up" moment, we can err, imposing our own understandings rather than another's upon certain acts, or we can highlight a different feature of an event than someone else does, or we can link two events that others might not link together. We can err in any number of ways. Accordingly, I have found it useful to be as overt and conscious as possible when specifying the particular substantive and strategic variables associated with each of the five types of communication dramas. While not adding any additional features to the nature of each communication system beyond what I have already suggested, I have found Table 5 to be a scheme that usefully specifies all of the interrelationships we have discussed earlier. Table 5 overtly identifies the motivation, dramatistic philosophy, type of formal progression, political position, and rhetorical and poetic figures associated with the value orientation of each of the five communication systems. You may find it useful to view this table as a summary of our previous discussion. In addition, for those who wish to explore the relationships posited in this table in greater depth, a host of relevant essays are available.[61] I would recommend, if you are so moved, a careful examination of the citations provided in note 61 at the end of this essay. Finally, a word of caution: the linkages provided in Table 5 are intended to describe only popular television series; at this point, I would make no claim as to the applicability of this scheme as an appropriate description or interpretation to any other type of symbolic action. I anticipate that this scheme, while only a speculation, would have to be altered to describe any other form of symbolic behavior adequately. In other words, I am convinced that the interrelationships provided in Table 5 account for the central value orientations of popular television series but that the features defining these value orientations may only be accidental features—if they exist at all—of other human constructions. I am, however, currently attempting to determine if these interrelationships adequately account for the nature of popular music and popular films. It seems to me that only extensive analysis and research can determine if the scheme is applicable to other symbolic activities.

Conclusions

We have come a long way in this essay. Mass media issues, methodological frameworks, complex and detailed data, and the entire question of value and cultural orientations have all converged here. Our conclusions therefore both summarize as well as posit overall conceptions regarding the meanings of this study. These summarizing and conceptual observations are cast as ten conclusions. The first six conclusions deal with substantive relationships among communication, values, and popular television series. The last four conclusions consider methodological issues that possess heuristic potentialities for future research.

1. *Television has altered the structure, processes, priorities, and preferences of Americans.* The issue is not *if* television is altering or will alter the basic nature of American life. The issue is *how* television has already changed the American lifestyle. Television viewing is now the primary activity of the average American after work and sleep.[63] In addition, television has significantly reduced the time spent in social gatherings and in live human conversations.[64] Television has, indeed, altered the behavior of the typical American. Moreover, when given alternative choices, Americans prefer to watch television. Of sixteen options such as being home with friends or being with friends and relatives or dining out or going to the movies, Americans rank "watching television" as their "favorite way of spending an evening": watching television was not only the most preferred activity, it was twice as popular as the second ranked activity and as popular as the second, third, and fourth ranked items combined.[65] The primary priority and preference of Americans is to watch television. Rather than being with other human beings, television is now the preferred companion of Americans both in practice and by choice.

2. *Television creates persuasive messages as well as reinforcing its own persuasive messages.* As Heffner has so aptly put it, television "combines the traditional two steps of impactful communications: statement and reinforcement."[66] In terms of the creation of persuasive messages, Comstock observes, after underscoring the demonstrated effectiveness of television advertisers, that "television can be persuasive when its messages are designed to be."[67] We have already demonstrated that the producers of pop-

Table 5. Substantive and strategic variables associated with the value orientation of each of the five communication dramas

Substantive and/or Strategic emphasis	Ironic	Mimetic	Leader	Romantic	Mythical
Value orientation	Existentialism	Individualism	Authority	Idealism	Theology
Motivation	Act	Agency	Scene	Agent	Purpose
Dramatic philosophy	Realism	Pragmatism and nominalism	Materialism	Idealism	Mysticism
Formal progression	Minor form: Paradox	Conventional	Syllogistic	Qualitative	Repetitive
Political position	Extremist	Apolitical or apathetic	Liberal	Conservative	Reactionary
Typical rhetrorical figure	Dialectic, parody, and ridicule	Pathos, synecdoche, and metonymy	Metaphor	Quest, epic, proverb, and allegory	Parable
Poetic category	Satire and burlesque	Humor, ode, and comedy	Didactic	Epic and elergy	Grotesque

ular television series design their series to be persuasive and that these series selectively dramatize certain values rather than others. However, the persuasive effectiveness of television is clearest in the area of violent television programs and adolescent aggressiveness, where "the majority of television research"[68] has been carried out. After considering "the most justifiable interpretation of the total array to findings" in this area, Comstock concludes that there is "a positive correlation among young persons between aggressiveness and the amount of violent television viewed."[69] Accordingly, the meaning of such popular television series as "The Incredible Hulk" and "Buck Rogers in the 25th Century" must be reconsidered. In addition, once such a correlation is established, all subsequent violent television programs reinforce this relationship by virtue of the number of shows in each of these series, if nothing else. Television can therefore be demonstrated to be persuasive. By virtue of its use of repetition, television also reinforces the persuasive messages it conveys.

3. *Popular television series are a barometer of national trends in America.* Given the polls provided by organizations such as Gallup, the data provided in this study indicate that the changes in the five communication systems described herein parallel the level, direction, and rate of changes in popular American attitudes in the areas circumscribed by these systems. These poll-systems correlations suggest that: (a) major changes in popular television series signify basic transformations in American life; (b) television is a reflection and product of the culture, not an agency which exists outside of the ongoing social, economic, personal, and political systems; and (c) if poll organizations do not provide more regular, consistent, or periodic accounts of shifting American attitudes in the areas considered in this study, it may be necessary and appropriate to utilize the kind of data provided in this study as a barometer of national trends in America.

4. *During the last seven years, popular television series have increasingly dramatized an amoral mode of human interaction.* Television is a symbolic universe which possesses an overall identity. Currently, amoral human interactions are announced and promoted by popular television series. The rise in mimetic television series, signifying a profound increase in individualism, tends to reduce the social system to diverse points of view. At the same time, insofar as leader-centered systems of communication decline, symbols of authority, power, and influence can no longer transcend and unify competing and divergent individual perspectives. Likewise, when the idealism associated with the romantic mode of communication fluctuates quickly and unpredictably, societal aims and goals cannot

function as a unifying and enduring base for concerted actions. Moreover, the cynical perspective and the theological frame of reference linked with the ironic and mythical communication systems are drastically underrepresented when compared with the volume of mimetic systems by roughly a three-to-one ratio. Accordingly, popular television series—probably unconsciously—have dramatized the uniqueness of individualism without the needed corresponding social corrective that generates cultural coherence along certain unifying principles. We are left with a tower of Babel wherein respect for individuality overwhelmingly ignores the societal principles essential for concerted human action.

5. *Television is a secondary socialization variable affecting role-specific behavior.* As we implied at the outset of this essay, primary socialization is a process of internalizing the nature of both objective and social realities as conceived by significant others. These significant others are significant or primary socialization variables because they control what and how a child abstracts from specific roles and specific attitudes to roles and attitudes in general. In contrast, "secondary socialization is," in the words of Peter L. Berger and Thomas Luckman, "the acquisition of role-specific knowledge, the roles being directly or indirectly rooted in the division of labor." [70]

While primary socialization variables always exist, it is possible for any single primary variable to diminish in its significance as new variables emerge. As Berger and Luckman note, "the development of modern education" is "the best illustration" of "secondary socialization taking place under the auspices of specialized agencies" and generating "the resultant decline in the position of the family with regard to secondary socialization." [71] When primary socialization variables undergo such transformations, the cause of these changes is generally a realignment of relevant language sources. Berger and Luckman argue, in fact, that, "language constitutes both the most important content and the most important instrument of socialization." [72]

With these premises in mind, it is tempting to claim that television is an emerging primary socialization agency. After all, television is a language source. Children employ this source at the stage when they are learning to abstract. Moreover, given the available data on violent television programs and aggressive behaviors in adolescents, children do seem to use television directly as a language source. Yet the case is incomplete. Television viewing is a passive activity and it has yet to be determined, for example, that television creates a highly charged emotional attachment for a child. As

Berger and Luckman suggest, "there is good reason to believe that without such emotional attachment to the significant others the learning process would be difficult if not impossible." [73] As a result, we are left with the conclusion that television is a secondary socialization variable. Nonetheless, if television can generate adolescent aggression under certain cases, the consequences of television as a secondary socialization variable are enormous. Finally, we need also recognize that in a "multiple causation" era, it may be virtually impossible to conclusively prove that any single language source is a primary and independent socialization variable.

6. *The media of the popular culture may be treated as systems or patterns of communication equal in power to the contributions of the "high" culture.* The approach taken by this essay sets it apart from the concerns of most critics. Typically, the fine arts and major political events attract the notice of critics. From one perspective, however, such traditional critics operate from a *high culture bias*—the one-of-a-kind, rare, and unique receive attention. This essay has implicitly suggested that phenomena viewed daily by millions of people throughout the entire year should be of equal concern.

7. *Longitudinal studies of television are both feasible and desirable.* Critical assessments of television series have typically been "one-shot affairs." While this seven-year assessment is not conclusive by itself, it does suggest that research designs may be structured to allow for "follow-up" or longitudinal results. Herbert J. Gans has critically observed that, "all the studies measure . . . short-range impact occurring weeks or months after media exposure, and do not report on the long-range effects of living in a society where media use takes up so much time. There are thus significant omissions in the available evidence, mainly" because "long-range effects are difficult to study empirically." [74] However, as the methodological procedure employed here has suggested, sufficiently flexible categories may be designed for such longitudinal studies by emphasizing the patterns of symbolic interaction and the concomitant communicative values reinforced by the national networks during prime-time viewing.

8. *The behavioral implications of television viewing remain to be determined.* While this study has established a relationship between the attitudes of television viewers and the communication systems and values of popular television series, it was not designed to determine the behavioral implications of this relationship. Naturalistic field studies are required.

9. *Films and made-for-TV movies should be included in the matrix employed in this study.* This study examined only national network prime-

time television series. Films and made-for-TV movies as well as mini-series were excluded.[75] My examination of these longer forms has indicated that they may be different in kind from the half-hour and hour television series. Beyond the fact that central characters are not as easily identified and that villains occupy a much more important role in defining the nature of the plot line, longer forms also have a tendency to shift categories as an inherent part of the plot line (e.g., the "commoner" or mimetic character who becomes a king or romantic figure). Nonetheless, our preliminary analyses suggest that it may be possible to modify the matrix described in this study so that such longer forms could be included in the results reported. If such a modification can be executed, it would be possible to eliminate the "national network bias" that has also controlled this study. Neil Hickey reports that national network programs during prime time now account for only 90 percent of the viewing audience and that by the 1984–1985 season, network programs will account for only 85 percent of television viewers.[76] The influence of cable television should be accounted for in these reports. Home Box Office, Entertainment and Sports Programming Network, USA, and Satellite Program Network provide—beyond their emphasis on sports, how-to-do it programs, cultural events, and interviews—a host of films which attract television viewers. If a modification can be made in the method outlined in this study, such viewing habits could be included within this study.

10. *Communication studies should consider the contributions that other disciplines can provide in the study of popular television series.* I am not proposing a general "call" for the kind of interdisciplinary approaches that seem to dilute the power that a single discipline's perspective can generate. Rather I would underscore the increasing usefulness that a structural analysis has provided in this study. Accordingly, the methodological contributions of disciplines such as structural anthropology seem to be directly relevant in a study such as this one. I have, in fact, been tempted to consider what a merger of the disciplines of communication and structural anthropology might produce. Are subdisciplines such as *anthropological communication* and *symbolic anthropology* feasible if such mergers emphasized common methodological assumptions? Certainly, perspectives and objects of study will make a difference, but links on a methodological level may produce significant implications.

Television may always, as Comstock has forecasted, leave us with question marks. But we do know a great deal about television and its effects and meanings as a communication system, value system, and activity in

America. Television has drastically altered the lifestyle of the average American. This observation itself is extremely profound information. But this study also adds new information to the corpus of understandings we possess about television. Overall, this study demonstrates that modes of entertainment such as popular television series are also communication systems which reflect, convey, and reinforce selective values that are manifest in the national trends that dominate the United States. In particular, this study demonstrates that a relationship does exist between the attitudes of television viewers and the communication system and values of popular television series. Moreover, during the last seven years, television series have emphasized mimetic modes of communication with the focus upon individuality and diverse points of view without a corresponding attention upon needed unifying societal principles. Finally, the long-term perspective of seven years adopted in this study suggests that television does exert multiple and diverse effects upon the United States' culture and lifestyles. We need, as a result, to continually keep track of this "one-eyed monster" or cyclops.

Notes

1. See Jack Dennis, ed., *Socialization to Politics* (New York: John Wiley, 1973).
2. George Comstock, "Television and Its Viewers: What Social Science Sees," in *Mass Communication Review Yearbook*, volume 1, ed. by G. Cleveland Wilhoit and Harold de Bock (Beverly Hills, California: Sage, 1980), p. 502.
3. Comstock, p. 499.
4. Comstock, p. 502.
5. Comstock, p. 500.
6. Comstock, p. 500.
7. Comstock, p. 500.
8. Comstock, p. 500.
9. Comstock, p. 500.
10. Comstock, p. 500.
11. Robert Brustein, "For Those Who Have No Interest in Television," *New York Times Book Review*, April 12, 1981, p. 3.
12. Comstock, p. 503.
13. Jeffrey Schrank, *Snap, Crackle, and Popular Taste: The Illusion of Free Choice in America* (New York: Delta, 1977), p. 25.
14. Comstock, p. 491.
15. See, e.g., James W. Chesebro, Jay E. Nachman, and Andrew Yannelli, "Popular Music as a Mode of Communication: A Twenty-Five Year Assessment and a Ten Year Projection, 1955–1989," 91 manuscript pages, versions read at the 1979 Speech Communication Association convention, the 1979 Speech

Communication Association of Pennsylvania convention, and the 1980 National Popular Culture Association convention.

16. Herbert W. Simons, "A Conceptual Framework for Identifying Rhetorical Genres," Central States Speech Association convention paper, April 1975, p. 2. While Simons' guidelines control the formulation of this generic system, the specific method employed here is content analysis: the content of television series is examined and persistent or repeating behavioral patterns found in these series are isolated and classified into the five-part communication drama system. However, this use of content analysis avoids the typical reason for rejecting content analysis as a data selection and data classification technique; traditionally, content analyses have isolated the smallest bit or unit of information and classified these bits into schemes without any regard for the context from which these bits were extracted. The use I am making of content analysis preserves the context from which bits are classified as well as the progression of the form from which these bits were extracted.

17. See, e.g., James W. Chesebro and Caroline D. Hamsher, "The Concession Speech: The MacArthur-Agnew Analog," *Speaker and Gavel,* 11 (January 1974), 39–51.

18. For a general conception of a *rhetorical situation,* see Lloyd F. Bitzer, "The Rhetorical Situation," *Philosophy & Rhetoric,* 1 (January 1968), 1–14.

19. See, e.g., John F. Wilson and Carroll C. Arnold, *Dimensions of Public Communication* (Boston: Allyn and Bacon, 1976), pp. 132–147.

20. For a general conception of this approach, see: Ernest J. Wrage, "Public Address: A Study in Social and Intellectual History," *Quarterly Journal of Speech,* 33 (December 1947), 451–457.

21. Daniel Boorstin, *The Image: A Guide to Pseudo-Events in America* (rpt. 1961; New York: Harper and Row, 1964), p. 11.

22. Kenneth B. Boulding, *The Image: Knowledge in Life and Society* (rpt. 1956; Ann Arbor, Michigan: Ann Arbor Paperbacks/University of Michigan Press, 1966), p. 18.

23. David M. Berg, "Rhetoric, Reality, and Mass Media," *Quarterly Journal of Speech,* 58 (October 1972), 255–257.

24. Northrop Frye, *Anatomy of Criticism* (Princeton, New Jersey: Princeton University Press, 1957), especially pp. 33–34. I am using Frye's categories in a rather "pure" form, although I realize the degree to which Frye underscores the interrelationships among the five categories. I have not emphasized these interrelationships simply because the nature of popular television series does not seem to require the recognition of such complexities. Frye's emphasis upon the categories' interrelationships emerges when he begins to apply his system to rather sophisticated and complex, not to mention much longer, literary forms. Popular television series are, on a comparative basis, much simpler forms that adhere to the more "basic" or "pure" nature of the categories as Frye theoretically describes them. The popular television series "Mork & Mindy" would constitute, at best, the only exception, for Mork is an alien from outer space with powers not possessed by humans. At the same time, Mork is cast as a mimetic character on the series. Yet because Mork seldom

makes use of his special powers to resolve the conflicts that emerge during the show, I have classified him as predominantly a mimetic character. I would grant, however, that with this one series, one might generate insight into the nature of the series by considering the series to be one which transcends the mimetic-mythical distinction.

25. Kenneth Burke, *The Rhetoric of Religion: Studies in Logology* (rpt. 1961; Berkeley, California: University of California Press, 1970), especially pp. 4–5. I have rather drastically adapted Burke's conception in reducing his seven moments to four and in employing the behavioral emphasis that I have.

26. See: Kenneth Burke, *A Grammar of Motives and a Rhetoric of Motives* (rpt. 1945 and 1950; Cleveland, Ohio: Meridian/World, 1962) for an extension of this concept of "identification" as a theoretical foundation for this discussion. For other relevant discussions of the mimetic form on popular television series, see Robert Sklar, "TV: The Persuasive Medium," *Popular Culture* (Del Mar, California: Printers, Inc., 1977), especially p. 18, and Lance Morrow, "Blacks on TV: A Disturbing Image," *Time*, 111 (March 27, 1978), 101. Moreover, at the outset of this analysis of mimetic communication systems, it should be noted that the selection of *Barney Miller* is a particularly useful illustration of mimetic communication from a critic's perspective, because it introduces issues that "test" the ability of the irony-mime-leader-romance-myth framework to deal with complexities in several ways. First, rather than having the one major plotline found in most series, *Barney Miller* typically involves two or three minor and independent plotlines unified only by virtue of the fact that the "crimes" occurred in the Twelfth Precinct and because the style of the officers of the Twelfth Precinct is employed as a common solution to these diverse plots. From a critic's perspective, each of these plots can be examined independently in terms of the framework on Table 1, or a critic might focus upon the overall style used to handle the diverse plots and attempt to classify this "overall style." Regardless of which approach is employed, the series appears to be mimetic. Second, rather than having the one major character found in most series, the central character on *Barney Miller* can be defined in at least two different ways. Generally, each show features or emphasizes one of the regular characters on the series—a typically "minor" character is elevated to a major character for one show and then returns to the role of a minor character in other shows of the series. Accordingly, from a critic's perspective, it would seem defensible to highlight this one character in classifying the series. Yet, a second possibility exists—all of the characters could be viewed as one collective hero by virtue of their joint solutions to a single problem even though each contribution by each character could vary from show to show in terms of its overall significance. Apparently, the actors on the series tend to adopt such a view. As Ron Carey, who plays uniformed patrolman Officer Levitt on the series has put it, "There's no single star of *Barney Miller*" (see Ben Pesta, "Cross Lou Costello with a Trappist monk, put him in blues . . ." *TV Guide*, 29 [May 23–29, 1981], 21–22 and 24, particularly 22). Regardless of which approach to central characters is employed, the series continues to be mimetic. Third and finally, the series is intriguing from a critic's perspective, because there is apparently one leader on the series, the character of Captain Barney

Miller, and yet the series is classified here as a mimetic series. Formally, Captain Miller only appears to function as the leader of the men in the squad room. Granted, he does set the roster of duties for the other men; the other men always "report in" to Captain Miller; Captain Miller "disciplines" the other men for infractions of the rules; and Captain Miller deals with city officials and other "higher ups" during "crises." However, in terms of the drama of human interaction, all of the men of the squad room are equals, each contributing to the comic and the tragic dimensions of each plotline, and each of these contributions comes from their unique experiences and everyday conditioning. Our analysis of Detective Dietrich's resignation illustrates the point. Thus, Captain Miller may, at best, provide the context for a dramatic resolution, but the resolution itself may emerge from any one or all of the members of the squad room. Each officer brings his own "sense of understanding" to these problems—no one of the men emerges as a consistent dramatic leader in dealing with the diverse range of problems found in the Twelfth Precinct.

27. Caryl Rivers, "And Now, for the Women in the Audience," *New York Times,* March 19, 1978, Section 2, p. 33.

28. During the last seven years, multiple reliability tests of this classification scheme have been carried out under various testing conditions. In April of 1978, for example, ten Ph.D. candidates, trained in the use of the method, in the Department of Speech at Temple University classified nine randomly selected series. The nine series represented all five of the communication dramas (two series for each type except for the one series that represented the ironic). Using a standard of perfect agreement, the percentage of graduate students unknowingly agreeing with my prior and independent classification ranged from 66 percent to 100 percent for each type of communication, with an overall reliability agreement of 84.4 percent. For details regarding this test, see: James W. Chesebro, "Communication, Values and Popular Television Series—A Four Year Assessment," in *Inter/Media: Interpersonal Communication in a Media World,* ed. by Gary Gumpert and Robert Cathcart (New York: Oxford University Press, 1979), pp. 558–559.

More recently, in April 1981, ten undergraduate students in a "Communication in Popular Culture" course at Temple University were asked to use Table 1—as provided in this essay—as a basis for classifying 38 of the 42 series in the 1980–81 season (the four series added from the week of November 22–28, 1980, had yet to be included in this study at this time). Students were given no examples of how to classify a television series and no explanation of Table 1. Overall, students unknowingly agreed with my classification of series 72.4 percent of the time. In terms of each of the types of communication dramas, the following agreement was obtained:

Type of Drama	Agreement
Ironic	100%
Mimetic	79%
Leader-Centered	61%
Romantic	78%
Mythical	89%

29. See Tom Wicker, "The Satisfaction Boom," *New York Times*, February 19, 1978, Section 4, p. 17. Also *Gallup Opinion Index*, Report 164, p. 3 and Report 169, p. 28.

30. See *Gallup Opinion Index*, Report 166, p. 1.

31. See *Gallup Opinion Index*, Reports 122 (p. 13), 144 (p. 5), 148 (p. 20), and 167 (p. 5). Similar results are available in terms of the courts. See Tom Goldstein, "Survey Finds Most People Uninformed on Courts," *New York Times*, March 19, 1978, Section 1, p. 20.

32. See: "The American Value System: Premises for Persuasion," *Western Speech*, 26 (Spring 1962), 178.

33. Gerald R. Miller, *An Introduction to Speech Communication*, 2nd ed. (Indianapolis, Indiana: Bobbs-Merrill, 1972), p. 10.

34. Comstock, p. 495.

35. For one overview of the intentions of these producers, see Bill Davidson, "Forecast for Fall: Warm and Human," *TV Guide*, 22 (February 16, 1974), 5–8 and 10.

36. Quoted in Edith Efron, "What Makes a Hit?" *TV Guide*, 22 (April 27, 1974), 2–4 and 6–7, particularly 3.

37. Richard D. Heffner, "Television: The Subtle Persuader," *TV Guide*, 21 (September 15, 1973), 25–26.

38. Frye, p. 41.

39. Frye, p. 41.

40. Frye, p. 29.

41. Frye, p. 40.

42. Frye, p. 62.

43. Frye, p. 285.

44. Frye, p. 59.

45. Frye, p. 38.

46. Frye, p. 39.

47. Frye, p. 347.

48. Frye, p. 60.

49. Frye, p. 62.

50. Frye, p. 59.

51. Frye, p. 186.

52. Frye, p. 187.

53. Frye, p. 298.

54. Kenneth Burke, *Counter-Statement* (rpt. 1931; Berkeley, California: University of California Press, 1968), pp. 124–128.

55. Frye, p. 306.

56. Frye, p. 186.

57. Frye, p. 64. For an alternative, but complementary, conception of myth that contrasts it to ideology and utopia, see Willard A. Mullins, "On the Concept of Ideology in Political Science," *American Political Science Review*, 66 (June 1972), 498–510.

58. Frye, p. 136.

59. Frye, p. 136.

60. Burke, *Permanence and Change,* p. 18.

61. For a discussion of the philosophical/value orientation of each communication system, see Frye. For a discussion of the central motivational feature of each system, see Kenneth Burke, *A Grammar of Motives and A Rhetoric of Motives* (rpt. 1945 and 1950; Cleveland, Ohio: Meridian Books, 1962), pp. xvii and 128. For a discussion of the various forms of progression, see Burke, *Counter-Statement,* pp. 124–128. For a discussion of the relationship between Burke's pentad and the political positions, see Bernard L. Brock, "A Definition of the Four Political Positions and A Description of their Rhetorical Characteristics," unpublished Ph.D. dissertation, Northwestern University, 1965. For a description of the rhetorical figures listed here, see Frye. For a description of these poetic categories, see Kenneth Burke, *Attitudes Toward History* (rpt. 1937; Boston: Beacon Press, 1961), pp. 35–36, 39, 41–44, 49, 55–60, and 75).

63. See the previous analysis in the introduction to this essay as well as the footnote references.

64. See the previous analysis in the introduction to this essay as well as the footnote references.

65. *Gallup Opinion Index,* Report No. 146, pp. 14–15.

66. Heffner, 25–26.

67. Comstock, p. 495.

68. Comstock, p. 495.

69. Comstock, p. 496.

70. Peter L. Berger and Thomas Luckman, *The Social Construction of Reality: A Treatise in the Sociology of Knowledge* (rpt. 1966; New York: Anchor, 1967), p. 138.

71. Berger and Luckman, p. 147.

72. Berger and Luckman, p. 133.

73. Berger and Luckman, p. 131.

74. Herbert J. Gans, "The Critiques of Mass Culture," in *Mass Media and Mass Man,* edited by Alan Casty, 2nd ed. (New York: Rinehart and Winston, 1973), pp. 55–56.

75. For six years from 1974–1975 through 1979–1980, series dominated the national networks' prime-time premiere weeks. With the 1980–1981 season, however, film (including made-for-TV-movies and mini-series) became the number one type of program broadcast by the national networks.

	1980–81	1979–80	1974–75
Percentage of Series	38.8%	38.8%	68.2%
Percentage of Films	44.4%	36.5%	23.8%
Percentage of "Other"	16.8%	24.7%	7.9%
Total *	100.0%	100.0%	99.9%

* Rounding off accounts for differences above and below 100.0%.

76. Neil Hickey, "Can the Networks Survive?" *TV Guide,* 29 (March 21, 1981), 7.

JAMES M. CURTIS

Rock 'n' Roll and Rock—And Now What?

Applying Marshall McLuhan's proposition that media structures historical processes, James M. Curtis relates rock to the events of the 1960s and 1970s—youth, rebellion, drugs, and alienation. He describes the intricate relationship of popular music, social change, and societal values. In addition, he relates recording technology to musical and cultural fashion. His conclusion is that "country and western" music has replaced rock, reflecting the new mood of our society. Whatever direction popular music now takes, it is apparent that it is an important medium for relating people to the social system.

> *We come after.*
> —*George Steiner*

George Steiner[1] means, "We come after totalitarianism and must somehow learn to live with that fact." We also come after modernism and must somehow learn to live with that fact as well. For the contemporary theorist, working with the relationship between modernism and postmodernism offers a most stimulating challenge, as Leslie Fiedler suggests:

> Almost all living readers and writers are aware of a fact which they have no adequate words to express, not in English certainly, not even in American. We are living, have been living for two decades—and have become acutely conscious of the fact since 1955—through the death throes of Modernism and the birth pangs of Post-Modernism. The kind of literature which had arrogated to itself the name Modern (with the presumption that it represented the ultimate advance in sensibility and form, that beyond it newness was not possible), and whose moment of triumph lasted from a point just before World War I until one just after World War II, is *dead,* i.e., belongs to history not actuality. In the field of the novel, this means that the age of Proust, Mann, and Joyce is over: just as in verse that of T. S. Eliot, Paul Valéry, Montale and Seferis is done with. Obviously, *this* fact has not remained secret: and some critics have, indeed, been attempting to deal with its implications. But they have been trying to do it in a language and with methods which are singularly inappropriate, since both method and language were invented by the defunct Modernists themselves to apologize for their own work and the work of their preferred literary ancestors (John Donne, for instance, or the *symbolistes*); and to ed-

ucate an audience capable of responding to them. Naturally, this will not do at all.[2]

The general acceptance of modernist art has resulted in its taking on the stature of a kind of classicism; the rebels have become the academy. Art that no longer threatens may retain its beauty, but it belongs to the past: we must understand it in order to incorporate the past, yet we can understand the present only by responding to the images and experiences of the present.

While postmodernism has a definite continuity with modernism, it differs from it in at least three ways: (1) the substitution of process for the modernist opposition of space and time; (2) a conscious emphasis on binarism; and (3) the formative experience of popular culture. This [essay] . . . will draw on all three of these characteristics, but especially the last one, in analyzing the music that created the post-modernist sensibility in the fifties and sixties.

Although both McLuhan (in *Understanding Media*) and Ong (in *Romance, Rhetoric, and Technology*) have done some work with popular music, I want to write about it here not because they have, but because doing so means merging my personal and professional motivations. Elvis Presley and the Beatles have meant a lot to me; moreover, their lingering presence in my consciousness had made me unable to use paradigms that make a dichotomy between popular and high culture.

This book has emphasized the holistic nature of the nonlinear paradigm in general and of McLuhan's work in particular; I want to conclude it with the discussion of rock 'n' roll because I believe that any contemporary paradigm that makes holistic claims must have the capacity to deal seriously and, above all, without condescension with popular culture as an aspect of social process. If, as McLuhan believes, media structure historical processes, then they structure all aspects of those processes and thus popular culture. If the analyst who works with a holistic paradigm disdains popular culture, then he or she simply has not internalized the paradigm.[3] While dichotomies do remain in postmodernism, the serious analyst can and will minimize them.

One can use a genuinely rich nonlinear paradigm on a great variety of materials. The paradigm is, ideally, indifferent to the material on which one uses it. Therefore, I wish to show here that since modernism and post-modernism both came into existence as manifestations of implosion, the sociological patterns and recurring motifs that I found in the modernist material of the preceding chapter have analogues in postmodernist phenomena. In addition to demonstrating further the power of the paradigm, these analyses will suggest the pervasive continuity between modernism and postmodernism.

In working with popular culture, an emphasis on the concept of function has a great advantage because it tends to preclude, or at least make difficult, value judgments of the kind which reject popular culture as undignified, or unworthy of serious injury. To take a simplistic example, a car must have both pistons and wheels. It makes no sense to prefer pistons to wheels, or wheels to pistons; they simply have different functions. To apply the concept of function in comparing historical processes, however, one must work in a more abstract way; one must compare, not specific phenomena, but the similar function of different phenomena in the respective periods. One therefore asks, not "Is this good or bad?" but "What role in the given historical process did phenomenon X have?"

Thus, if we notice that Picasso's painting sometimes refers to African masks, and Roy Lichtenstein's painting to comics, we may conclude that primitivism functioned for modernism as popular culture functions for postmodernism. (Similarly, one could compare the role of folk music in the work of Bartók and Stravinsky to the role of blues music in the development of rock 'n' roll.) The cool structures of primitivism and popular culture have offered artists a vocabulary with which they could express implosion, and they have offered theorists ample justification for their principles—Worringer used primitivism as McLuhan used popular culture. The analogy also calls our attention to the fact that any period of implosion can only resolve dichotomies gradually, and never all at once. Thus, primitivism and popular culture in their respective periods have both had the effect of resolving the dichotomy high culture–low culture.

The period and general aesthetics of modernism, art nouveau, and cubism correspond roughly to the two postmodernist periods of popular music, rock 'n' roll (which lasted from 1955 to 1964), and rock (which lasted from 1964 to 1970). Artists who had grown up, respectively, with art nouveau and rock 'n' roll used these styles in their early work, and then destroyed them by creating cubism and rock. When Bob Dylan began playing the electric guitar, it marked the changeover from rock 'n' roll to rock and shocked many of his fans, just as Picasso shocked Matisse and even Braque when he painted *Les Demoiselles d'Avignon*.

Media complexes structured these four interrelated processes in various ways. If art nouveau expressed the age of the telephone, and cubism the age of the radio, rock 'n' roll expressed the natural association of two hybrid media, the automobile and the AM radio. In turn, stereophonic sound—a binary experience—gave rise to rock, and long-playing albums and FM radio became the creative media. Each period perceived the previous one as literate in various ways, and at the beginning of each new period, the major artists of the previous one suffered a certain disorientation.

But at this point something McLuhan's critics liked to notice becomes relevant; McLuahn *wrote* about orality; he used print to discuss demise of print (or so it seemed in the sixties). I find myself expressing a similar contradiction in that I am using the print of a university press to discuss music, and worse yet—popular music. "Worse yet," because popular music expresses the contradiction of our age in a greatly amplified way. On one hand, popular music has structured the perception and consciousness of many of us; we have shared it, and it has thus become a paradigm. On the other hand, and a powerful hand it is, popular music comes from big business, and thus conforms to the structure of other types of Big Business In America. Although the musicians themelves have little to do with literacy, their lawyers and record companies emphatically have a great deal to do with literacy.

This situation affects our lives only if we wish to *write* about the music, and reproduce the words in print; I attempted to do so, and rapidly found out that musical revolutionaries (or their lawyers at least) still consider the songs private property and want to make as much money from them as they can. Thus, the nominal subject of this chapter, the tension between orality and literacy in popular music, structures it as well; I have used the quotes for which I could get permission and have simply referred to some of the songs that have meant the most to me, and to America.

Specific analysis may begin by noticing the striking similarity in the sociology of postmodernism and that of modernism. Just as most modernists came from areas of residual orality, virtually all the musicians who created rock 'n' roll came from the most oral part of the United States, the South. Elvis Presley was born in Mississippi, and Jerry Lee Lewis in Tennessee. Possibly even more significant are the Southern blacks: Fats Domino (Louisiana), Little Richard and Ray Charles (Georgia), and Chuck Berry (who moved to Missouri at an early age). These Southerners shared a good deal, not only early poverty, but also the extremely important tradition of communal singing in small Southern churches.

Elvis began singing in church, and recorded several albums of hymns.

The very title of Ray Charles's hit of the fifties, "Hallelujah, I Just Love Her So" suggests a secular hymn. Virtually all black singers—Aretha Franklin, Dionne Warwicke, and even Chuck Berry—got their starts by singing in church, and those with ears attuned to the sound of gospel choirs can detect its echoes in their work. But here the paradox arises, for the very opportunities of mobility that television made possible meant fragmentation. Gospel singing in small Southern churches has a very tribal quality, and is certainly not art in the Renaissance sense. But "Hallelujah, I Just Love Her So" has turned gospel singing into art in just this sense. Thus the very fact that oral peoples can respond creatively to implosion means that they also experience fragmentation.

This dual process of fragmentation and implosion accounts for the disorientation and consequent violence—both physical and verbal—in the behavior of many blacks. (I am assuming, of course, that social oppression in all its forms occurs as a manifestation of fragmentation.) Among rock 'n' roll musicians, Little Richard shows this vacillation between religion and art most distinctly. When the engine of a plane on which he was flying (1961) caught fire, he made a vow to return to the ministry if he survived. He did survive and kept the vow, but began performing again in 1969.

The position of blacks thus resembles that of Jews in the earlier part of the twentieth century. In both cases, artistic success meant the renunciation of some integral aspects of the cultural heritage that made the success possible in the first place. Because fragmentation had begun earlier for Jews, we find them associated in American media history with radio (David Sarnoff and William Paley) and movies (Louis Mayer, Samuel Goldwyn, Adolph Zukor, and many others). However, with the important exceptions of Bob Dylan and Paul Simon, Jews did not have particular importance in rock 'n' roll, or in rock. Yet when we think of the way Irving Berlin, George and Ira Gershwin, Jerome Kern, and Richard Rodgers dominated American popular music in the first half of the twentieth century, Dylan and Simon seem isolated by comparison. What happened was that poor Southerners experienced fragmentation after World War II, as Jews had done after emigrating to America. This new music so speeded up the social process that it became general; I doubt that one can find significant patterns in the sociology of rock.

In the fifties, songs typically used the media which formed rock 'n' roll: a 45-rpm record over an AM radio in a car. Carl Belz, in *The Story of Rock*, discusses the changeover from the 78 rpm record to the 45 rpm record in very McLuhanesque terms.

While its speed was slower, in all of its other features the 45 constituted a speeding-up process. This was true for everyone connected with the record: manufacturers, distributors, shop owners, disk jockeys, and individual buyers. . . . The lightness of 45, coupled with their doughnut shape and the large spindle of 45 players, also produced faster, easier listening. The "search" for the small hole in the center of the 78 was eliminated, and a listener could quickly skim through a large group of records, playing or rejecting them at a moment's notice. The process of playing records therefore became more casual, and there was a more immediate relationship between listener and record than had been possible with the heavy and breakable 78s.[4]

After television began to create a new orality, radio stations that played 45-rpm records could, and did, serve as a tribal drum by speeding up the pace and diction that the announcers used. These media changes naturally accompanied changes in singers and the songs they sang.

"It's got a good beat. You can dance to it." This cliché from the fifties sums up the crucial change that rock 'n' roll represents. In the new orality, people wanted to hear the tribal drum, not the lush melodies of previous popular music. "Melody, the *melos modos,* 'the road round,' is a continuous, connected, and repetitive structure that is not used in the 'cool' art of the Orient" (p. vi). Literate people disliked the new music because of the total physical involvement of dancing that the beat implied. The beat also made the words largely irrelevant, as at the beginning of Little Richard's "Tutti Frutti": "A wop bop a loo bop a lop bam boom." Actually, this extreme style continued the experiments of futurist poets with purely associative sounds. Russian poets called this style "trans-sense language." But of all the groups and performers of the fifties, from Bill Haley and the Comets to Elvis Presley, no single performer made more characteristic records than Chuck Berry.

Chuck Berry's career as a hitmaker coincided almost exactly with the period of rock 'n' roll, and his style remains essentially unchanged. He had an extraordinary capacity to create verbal icons in a universally accessible style. For example, he sensed the oral structure of the new music when he sang in "Johnny B. Goode":

> He never learned to read or write so well,/ But he could play a guitar just like ringing a bell.

Two of his best songs, "Roll Over, Beethoven," and "Brown-Eyed Handsome Man," articulate a reaction against literacy. Great tension still existed between popular and high culture (and hence gave rise to many comedy routines on television), and "Roll Over, Beethoven," which singles out music's great individualist, asserts the power of the new rhythmic music. A joke about the Venus de Milo in "Brown-Eyed Handsome Man" expresses the same tension, and even has a precedent in modernism. Berry's witticism gives a verbal equivalent to Duchamp's mustachioed Mona Lisa, "L.H.O.O.Q." The two men were using different means to express a common distaste for the high-definition, representational art of classical antiquity and the Renaissance.[5] In "Maybelline," Berry created a three-minute Populist epic, in which the hero-narrator, who drives a Ford, the car of the common man, catches Maybelline, who has gone for a ride in his rival's Cadillac.

Television turned high school, the primary institution for inculcating literacy, into an art form. Although the film *Blackboard Jungle* first made this apparent, no one wrote better high school songs than Chuck Berry, with "School Days," "Sweet Little Sixteen," and "Anthony Boy." The great popularity of high school songs, and or pseudo-religious songs—such as "Teen Angel" and "My Prayer"—and Chuck Berry's patriotic "Back in the U.S.A." illustrate the manner in which the content of each medium is another medium. Before television, the experience of high school, the sentimentality of American religion, and patriotism, were everyone's water. After television, they became art forms.

The great significance of high school songs and their rapid disappearance (the Beach Boys' early hit "Be True to Your School" was probably the last one) demonstrates the manner in which media process the changes in institutional relationships. Teenagers continued to go to proms, and get excited about Friday night football games, of course, but they did so with the sense of participation in the large society that made more high school songs unnecessary. (The song "High School U.S.A."—and the Beach Boys' variant "Surfin' U.S.A."—made the connection between the individual place, and the nation as a whole, in a very direct way.)

Television began to make people aware of their interrelationships, and in May 1954—just after the number of television sets in America surpassed that of radios—the Supreme Court found that separate schools for blacks and whites could not also be equal. Thus began a tension between fragmentation and implosion in American politics which, to some extent, ended with the resignation of President Nixon. However, it took three years for the tension between the centralizing power of the federal government and the supposedly autonomous power of the states to reach a breaking point.

In 1957, President Eisenhower created the Civil Rights Division, which played a crucial role in the social change of the sixties, and integrated Central High School, in Little Rock, Arkansas, by sending federal troops to that tense city. In doing so, Eisenhower was enforcing centralization by breaking down local autonomy, which the representatives of linear tribalism had hardened into a dogma for its own sake. Essentially, the civil rights movement meant centralization as long as it lasted in its classical form. But soon after the passage of the civil rights bill in 1964, many of the attitudes that had seemed so pure and good began to smack of paternalism, i.e., literacy. Militant black groups who wanted autonomy, not centralization, began to appear. This meant that a new medium had changed the now familiar, comfortable relationships of the fifties. For the young, anyhow, that medium was stereophonic sound, which Columbia Records first marketed in 1958.

Stereo meant a change from the 45-rpm record to the long-playing album, and the media complex of the fifties. Mick Jagger sensed this when he sneered at that complex in "Satisfaction":

When I'm driving in my car, / And a man comes on the radio / Telling me more and more / 'Bout some useless information / Supposed to defy my imagination. . . .

People began to perceive the car radio, the tribal drum of the fifties, as part of the literate, commercial culture they wished to reject. The very music of the fifties, with its tight stanzas, neat rhymes, and uniform beat began to seem as dull as a crew cut. By 1968 Frank Zappa, the Marcel Duchamp of rock, could say, "It is laughable now to think of that dull thud on the second and fourth [beat] as lewd and pulsating."[6] Yet by 1968, people like Zappa had forgotten the controversy that attended the birth of rock 'n' roll.

Although this chapter deals mainly with music, two problems of the late sixties, university riots and the use of drugs are so important and so much a part of rock that they deserve a few comments. If high school appeared as an art form in the fifties, it also seemed permanent and inevitable. Juvenile delinquents (to use a phrase of the time), turned to violence mostly out of despair, as in *Blackboard Jungle* and *Rebel Without a Cause*. In the sixties, people saw that popular action could bring about some change, however partial and gradual. This knowledge made the nihilism of the fifties passé, and attempts to change, not destroy, the literate, highly centralized university structure followed. Given the intensity of the times, violence ensued, as at Columbia University in the spring of 1968.

Speaking of violence, the war in Vietnam has the same kind of meaning for postmodernism that World War I had for modernism. Both wars evoked protest (artistic and political) and interest in pacifism, and generated a cultural malaise, a sense of the loss of innocence, which found expression in a spate of brilliant art works in the years following their uneasy termination.

In the middle and late sixties, many musicians and others began taking LSD, yet no one seems to have noticed that they were actually taking advantage of its therapeutic value. (That drugs subsequently became an end in themselves does not alter the validity of this statement.) Bernard Rimland's *Infantile Autism* makes it possible to integrate the use of LSD, current neurological theory, and McLuhan's theory of media. As we know, the lack of awareness of others, the obsessively literal thought, and inability to comprehend wholes, which characterize the autistic child, represent extreme forms of literate or linear thought. Rimland opposed autism to schizophrenia, which we can interpret here as an extreme form of oral, nonlinear thought.

> Differences in the symptomatology of early infantile autism and schizophrenia appear to reflect differences in the manner in which stimuli are associated with memory. Our hypothesis is that in autism necessary neural connections are made with extreme difficulty and only the strongest and most relevant impulses traverse the pathways, while in schizophrenia associations are made *too* freely, sometimes almost randomly. Stated differently, in autism it seems that the mental associations made by the afflicted child are exceedingly limited, that he has access only to highly specific fragments of memory. The schizophrenic child, in contrast, appears to be pathologically *unrestrained by relevance in making associations.*[7]

Now if the creative musicians of the sixties began to feel their literacy as undesirable, this meant that they sensed their inability to make associations. People like Ken Kesey, who began using LSD very early, knew of its therapeutic value in helping to make these associations. To cite Rimland again:

> LSD-25, which produces schizophrenia-like symptoms in normal persons, exerts an *excitant* effect on the reticular formation and a heightened awareness of sensory stimuli. . . . LSD may prove useful in facilitating reticular formation. In other words, LSD or a similar drug may have a normalizing effect on autistic children.[8]

In the sixties, "mind" came to mean "literacy"; "blowing your mind" meant using LSD to blow open channels of association that literacy had closed.

(A "heavy metal" group from Detroit, the MC5, called their theme song "Kick Out the Jams.")

Acid trips affected many forms of expression in the sixties, of course, but not quite in the way that most people have assumed. People usually think that the musicians took acid, and then wrote down what they saw and/or experienced. But this attitude, like so many other interpretations of popular culture, simply continues the premises of nineteenth-century realism, which state that the artist reproduces that which is "out there" in some sense. (The shift from an external to an internal landscape in no way implies a change in paradigm.) One can interpret acid-inspired rock as an interaction of tradition and cultural process by saying that acid made people more sensitive to European surrealism and decadence and that the artists could therefore draw on this tradition, which had become acceptable— i.e., no longer perceived as belonging to high culture—to their listeners. Dylan's perceptions in his music, for instance, have definite affinities with surrealism (see the liner notes to his album *Desire* for a highly significant reference to Rimbaud), as did Jim Morrison, who knew modern poetry well. Surrealism created some biographical precedents for the artists, also.

In several ways, the best example one can cite is Alfred Jarry, who found his *lycée,* and especially the man who taught Newtonian physics, intensely alienating. The physics teacher became a crucial figure in his principal work, the play *Ubu Roi* (1896). Jarry tried to liberate himself from his literacy through alcohol and eventually drank himself to death—more or less deliberately. Brian Epstein, Brian Jones, Jimi Hendrix, and Janis Joplin did much the same thing, with the difference that they combined alcohol and drugs. Jim Morrison, lead singer and songwriter for the strongly expressionist group The Doors, resembled Jarry not merely in that both were alcoholics; both burnt themselves out at an early age in an attempt to alter the distinctions between life and theater. Jarry and Morrison both died primarily because they had no desire to live any longer.

And Elvis had no desire to live any longer, either. When one of the greatest performers in American history dies a nonviolent death at the age of forty-two, it is such an extraordinary event that I wish to insert a few comments on it here. One can say that Elvis died because he couldn't think of anything to do except drive one of his Stutz Bearcats around Memphis at night. That is to say, he had an instructively American kind of greatness.

When people write about Elvis, they often begin by commenting on a haunting photograph of Elvis and his parents that someone took in 1937, when Elvis was two years old. Greil Marcus, in his brilliant—really incomparable—book *Mystery Train: Images of America in Rock 'n' Roll Music,* calls the faces of Elvis's parents "vacant," and they are that. But they also have a familiar quality. We know them well, because we have seen their likes before. James Agee and Walker Evans spent most of the summer of 1936 in northern Alabama, less than a hundred miles from Tupelo, doing the fieldwork for what became *Let Us Now Praise Famous Men.* And Evans, in now-famous photographs recorded just the painful, hopeless faces that Elvis's parents have. Their faces have little in common with those of the folks who live in those big white houses with tall columns which figure so prominently in Southern myths. In the Delta, where those houses do exist, the well-to-do whites drank mint juleps and become social climbers. Significantly, the Mississippi Delta has produced many great black artists—like Robert Johnson—but no great white artists.

Elvis's Mississippi, Tupelo, a trading center for the rural areas of the northeast part of the state, had little in common with the Delta, even though the Delta was only about eighty miles away. For Tupelo is located in the hill country, and it was simply not profitable to own slaves there. In fact, Winston County, Alabama, where Agee and Evans spent some of their time, actually seceded from the Confederacy; the hill people there decided that this was a rich folks' war, and that the rich folks could fight it themselves. Thus it happened that the hill country of the South became, and stayed, poor, protestant, and puritan. As such, it produced the vacant faces of Elvis's parents, and the shapeless clothing they wear. One looks in vain for a relationship between the adults' sadness (they look defeated as only poor Southerners can look, and Evans taught us to see their dignity in this defeat), and the boy's smile. This tension between the parents and the child really means a tension between the inadequacy of Tupelo as an environment and the boy's still undeveloped talent. Elvis lived in Tupelo for thirteen years, and I suggest that during those thirteen years that tension created his indomitable ambition, which we never understood before Marcus's book. The pain and hurt of being a poor Southern boy in those bare hills gave power to the jaunty, yet visceral assertiveness that made Elvis a censored sensation on the Ed Sullivan Show eighteen years after the photograph was taken.

I sensed something of the pent-up drive the only time I saw Elvis perform in person. He came back to Tupelo in October of 1956 to do two shows after he had finished making *Love Me Tender.* (Rumor had it that Natalie Wood had made the shirts he wore.) But, mostly, I remember the National Guard. The day Elvis came to town, there was a National

Guardsman standing on every street corner downtown, and each one held a rifle with a fixed bayonet. I had never seen soldiers hold rifles like that before, and they seemed disturbing; I didn't know it then, but they anticipated the soldiers who would integrate Central High School in Little Rock the next fall. For the agitation Elvis evoked manifested the same energy of social change as that of the other upheavals in the South that coincided with his career.

The very orality that Elvis embodied was being fragmented by the process whose energy made him famous; as the rest of the country became more oral, the South became more literate. During his campaign, Jimmy Carter accurately commented that he could never have become a candidate for president if it had not been for Martin Luther King. King's work gave great impetus to the fragmentation of local power structures in the South. The fragmentation of those power structures necessarily preceded the merger of Southern politics into national politics. (Incidentally, King used the rhythms of Southern protestantism for political purposes as Elvis used them for artistic purposes. Somehow, Southern protestantism becomes communicable outside the South only in nonreligious forms.)

Elvis changed the way people dressed and sang and felt about their bodies, and he could do so because of the extraordinary openness and permeability that literacy has produced in American society. That openness means that American society can absorb and commercialize anything—and it absorbed and commercialized Elvis. Once Elvis had gotten out of Tupelo—metaphorically speaking—and had become rich and famous as few people have ever been, he became great and irrelevant in equal measure. Elvis agreed to become a product, and products do not confront pain and despair. His movies expressed the mindless optimism which his life, and voice, and body, negated at every instant.

Elvis's first big record for Sun, "That's All Right," expressed the anger and hostility between the sexes that intense change evokes, and "Heartbreak Hotel" gave a surrealistic image of our loneliness in a fragmented society. Although Elvis believed in what he was, he never believed in what he could do, and never wanted to find out. Thus, his later records never took chances, and he had to rely on other people's words in an age when performers wrote their own songs. And when he performed, he never chose songs which resonate within the heart of darkness at the center of the American dream, such as Bruce Springsteen's "Born to Run." As a result, in his last years he resembled a dynamo that generated great power but couldn't transmit it. His body became blocked—it eloquently expressed the way his greatness was blocked—and the energy turned in on him, and killed him.

The house in which Elvis was born is now a monument, of course, and forms part of Elvis Presley Park in East Tupelo, that part of town which was always on the other side of the tracks. I don't suppose that the people of Tupelo meant it this way, but Elvis's birthplace stands near the intersection of Presley and Berry Streets. The unconscious reference to the greatest performer of the fifties and the greatest songwriter of the fifties stands there unnoticed, as a suggestion of the South's role in unifying American music.

But a unity seeks to enlarge itself, and the new electric environment of the sixties made people want to learn from other parts of the world, and when the Beatles and the Beach Boys went to India to meditate, reporters found this startling and newsworthy. Because of the ever-present distinction between art and entertainment, no one stopped to think that these performers went to India for reasons similar to those which caused Rilke to go to Russia, and caused Gide and Klee to go to Tunisia. In fact, in visiting the East and taking an interest in nonlinear thought patterns, the musicians were doing what a large number of other European artists had done, because rock music continued the same process that began with modernism.

The Beatles began this, of course, with *Sergeant Pepper's Lonely Hearts Club Band*, but they recorded their masterpiece in 1968: *The Beatles*. This album uses as an art form the 45-rpm record that the Beatles first encountered as an American product with the work of American artists like Chuck Berry and Elvis Presley. As one listens to this album again and again, one realizes that the United States itself, as the most literate country in the world, becomes an art form. Of this great album, I can only discuss the first song, "Back in the U.S.S.R.," because of the way it uses the 45-rpm record.

"Back in the U.S.S.R." begins with a demonstration of the stereo effect when a jet plane passes from left to right. This emphasizes the difference between the album's style and that of the monophonic 45. The Beatles recall the fifties with the standard rock 'n' roll complement of guitars and drums, and closely paraphrase Chuck Berry's "Back in the U.S.A." of course, but with the crucial difference that by the pun on the U.S./U.S.S.R. they convey the similarity of tribal linearity and linear tribalism. They beautifully express these similarities when they adopt the Beach Boys' falsetto style. Moreover, the second verse specifically refers to Brian Wilson's classic "California Girls"; Lennon–McCartney wittily substitute the Ukraine, in southern Russia, for southern California. The Beach Boys appear here because, more than that of any group before the rise of acid rock, the Beach Boys' music represented a way of life—the American devotion to life, liberty, and the pursuit of happiness. By combining innocent hedonism with complex counterpoint, the Beach Boys expressed the American myth as very few artists in our society ever have, and the fact that no individual member of the group has become a star in his own right merely emphasizes the cohesive force of that myth.

If the content of the 45-rpm record seemed foreign, its use of the recurring beat did not, because it structured a nonlinear use of language and experience. In "My Back Pages," Dylan explains that literacy (note the irony of the title) caused a dissociation of sensibility within his psyche in the past; but the chorus expresses the irrelevance of chronological, Newtonian time. In a wonderful play on words, Dylan states that implosion has brought with it a resurgence of the libido, in the Jungian sense, and thus of youth.

Rock also used some explicitly mythical concepts of the eternal return of existence, as in "Turn! Turn! Turn!" by the Byrds, whose words Pete Seeger adapted from Ecclesiastes. A little later Joni Mitchell used the image of the carousel for an explicit statement of the eternal return in "The Circle Game":

> And the seasons they go round and round/ And the painted ponies go up and down/ We're captive on the carousel of time/ We can't return we can only look/ Behind from where we came/ And go round and round and round in the circle game./

Since print can convey none of the textual qualities of rock—the tape effects, multiple dubbing, key changes, and all the rest, it seems simplest to conclude this discussion of rock with some remarks about the songwriter whose work suffers least when abstracted from the sound of the record, Bob Dylan.[9] A comment from Ong's *The Presence of the Word* gives a leading idea: "Since sound is indicative of here-and-now activity, the word as sound establishes here-and-now presence."[10] The spoken word, by its very nature, implies the presence of another who can hear it. The spoken word creates a conversation, a binary whole. The particular power of Dylan's songs comes from his ability to restore this binary quality to the word. To be sure, poets have addressed ballads to the beloved from time immemorial, but before Dylan literacy had made the address meaningless, and rendered it a lifeless convention, like the unity of time in eighteenth-century neoclassical drama. A hit of the early fifties, "Let Me Go, Lover," provides a good example of the convention for its own sake. Two aspects of Dylan's records make the difference: his obviously untrained, rasping (Riegl would have called it "tactile") voice that drew on the "talking blues" tradition, and his ability, reminiscent of Pound's, to use colloquial English for startling imagistic effects. When Dylan addresses a "you," he demands a reply, as in the famous refrain of "Ballad of a Thin Man."

A great many of Dylan's songs simply continue the tradition of ballad address in a fresher, more vivid style. Whatever their differences, "Boots of Spanish Leather," "Honey, Just Allow Me One More Chance," "It Ain't Me, Babe," and "Temporary Like Achilles" are all addressed to a girl. This strain culminates in "I'll Be Your Baby Tonight" on *John Wesley Harding,* and the mellow classics of *Nashville Skyline,* "Lay Lady Lay," "Tell Me That It Isn't True," and "Tonight I'll Be Staying Here With You." Had Dylan written only songs like these, which I call his "private" dialogue songs, he would have reinvigorated a tradition, but would not have attracted such intense feelings. His major importance comes from his two other groups of songs, his "public" dialogue songs, and his surrealist songs. The masterpieces occur as a fusion of the two groups.

In discussing Dylan's public-dialogue songs, one should keep in mind two of Eliot's statements that Dylan has always implicitly understood, and that his admirers have rarely understood: "In writing himself, the great poet writes his time," and "The emotion of art is impersonal." As a comment in the liner notes to *The Freewheelin' Bob Dylan* attests, Dylan knew that the great blues singers were not just "expressing themselves," as romantics usually believe. He knew that they were using the discipline of a tradition—just as Picasso had known that the makers of African masks were not indulging in an "aesthetic operation." Because of his consciousness of the impersonal quality of what he was doing, he could adopt the pose of the bard who voiced the feelings of the tribe to threatening outsiders. Love, past or present, appears in his private-dialogue songs; hate, or at best, distaste, appears in the public dialogue, or protest, songs such as "The Times They Are A Changin' " and "Blowin' in the Wind." Yet Dylan's supreme achievements occur when he uses this public dialogue in a surrealistic way.

One of the songs on *Highway 61 Revisited,* "Desolation Row," absolutely demands a few special comments. "Row" suggests the sequential nature of print, of course, and the phrase "Desolation Row" images print as what Eliot and Mumford called a wasteland. As usual, Dylan's images of violence in "Desolation Row" evoke associations with literacy. To put the matter far less forcefully than Dylan did, in this song the representatives of literacy want to keep people from escaping to Desolation Row because an awareness of the desolation of literacy implies a rejection of it.

The sixties ended quite abruptly, on the afternoon of 6 December 1969, at the Rolling Stones' free concert at Altamont, California, when the Hell's Angels stomped a black man to death while Mick Jagger was singing "Under My Thumb." The chaos of that afternoon eventually forced people to confront the inadequacies of their belief in flower power and the love generation. After Altamont, the sixties seemed literate, and hence naive, just as the seventies eventually will. The energy of implosion then became more diffuse, and the Beatles ceased to function as a whole that was greater than the sum of its parts. When the energy of the process no longer operated through them, the Beatles, and the members of the other groups that broke up, simply became talented professional musicians. John Lennon even said in an interview about a year after Altamont:

> The dream is over. It's just the same, only I'm thirty, and a lot of people have got long hair. That's what it is, man, nothing happened except that we grew up, we did our thing—just like they were telling us.[11]

All the creative movements of the twentieth century have had a self-liquidating quality. Their ability to bring about revolutions in sensibility presupposes a certain tension between the artist and the public. As the work communicates between the artist and the public, it eases this tension, and thus liquidates its own rationale.

Don McLean's "American Pie" became the most important song of the early seventies precisely because it turned the fifties and sixties into an art form. (The movie *American Graffiti* and the television show "Happy Days" have had an analogous function, yet neither has elicited a musical response as intense as "Killing Me Softly," Roberta Flack's response to "American Pie.") "American Pie" has one characteristic feature of the poetry of traditional oral societies—formulas. The formulas of "American Pie" come from the only viable cultural tradition that America can have—a tradition of artifacts and images that have found widespread acceptance.

"American Pie" really amounts to a formulaic history of the period 1955–1970; its references range from Marty Robbins and a fifties hit by the Monotones called "The Book of Love" to Altamont. The song, with its nonlinear syntax, would simply make no sense to anyone who did not know rock 'n' roll—and rock. While Eliot and other modernists used formulas, they proceeded rather differently. By incorporating the whole of world literature as a "simultaneous order" of formulas, they made demands on their audience that necessarily limited it. Whatever their other problems, songwriters of today do not have this one, for they can validly assume that records, radio, and concerts have made the music of the fifties and sixties part of the consciousness of the audience. (In addition to "American Pie," hear also Rick Nelson's "Garden Party," with its references to Chuck Berry, and Elton John's "Crocodile Rock," which uses the melody of Paul Anka's "Diana" in the chorus.)

This use of formulas, which constantly recurs in the brilliant prose of *Rolling Stone* as well, expresses a shared, tribal consciousness we didn't have before The Beatles. For all the cultural significance of formulas, however, we find it difficult to institutionalize them, and as a result lyrics have played a relatively insignificant role in the work of the four most creative groups of the early seventies: the Allman Brothers and Santana from the United States, and Pink Floyd and Yes from Great Britain.

The phenomenal success of the film *Love Story* signaled to many people a "Return to Romance," as *Time* called its cover story on Ali McGraw. Actually, *Love Story* may have defined the most general process of the seventies: a synthesis of literacy and the new orality. A culture can change only so rapidly, and after the period of intense implosion in the sixties, literate structures such as love stories seem comforting to many. (Hear the hit by Paul McCartney and Wings, "Silly Love Songs.") An analysis of country and western music, which has replaced rock as the most meaningful American idiom,[12] might well elicit this ambivalence. Country and western music has generally expressed fragmentation by turning rural life into an art form, but television has recently cooled it off.

Someone has said, "Times which are interesting to read about are not pleasant to live through." Certainly, we cannot expect tranquillity as a characteristic of implosion, and this fact has created great problems for popular culture, which usually accedes to its audience's demand for affirmation—for obsessive cheerfulness and the happy ending—above all. In the sixties, popular music at its best offered catharsis, not overt affirmation, and thus achieved extraordinary power and meaning. But catharsis can occur only after a genuine confrontation with pain, and in the more diffuse situation that came into being in the late sixties, we cannot assume that we can achieve catharsis through media experiences that we can all share. It may help to keep in mind these lines from John Fogerty's "Bad Moon Rising":

> Hope you've got your things together/ Hope that you are quite prepared to die/ Looks like we in for nasty weather/ One eye is taken for an eye./

Notes

1. George Steiner, *Language and Silence*, p. ix.
2. Leslie Fiedler, "Cross the Border, Close the Gap," in *The Collected Essays of Leslie Fiedler*, pp. 461–62. Fiedler's emphasis.
3. I consider it a serious shortcoming of French structuralism that it has not generally dealt with popular culture. The lack of interest in popular culture on the part of French critics contrasts strikingly with the attitudes of French artists. One thinks, for instance, of the distinctly pop sensibility which Michel Butor expresses in *Mobile* as well as in other works. French critics no doubt neglect popular culture for analogous reasons to those which make them neglect technology. Their implicit assumptions about what a Parisian intellectual should, and should not, do demonstrate the inertial force of French nationalism in an international age. See my "Marshall McLuhan and French Stucturalism, *Boundary*, 2 (Fall 1972), pp. 134–36.
4. Carl Belz, *The Story of Rock*, p. 5.
5. Cf., Bob Dylan's subsequent comment on the demise of perspective in painting in "Visions of Johanna."
6. Frank Zappa, "The Oracle Has It All Psyched Out," p. 86.
7. Bernard Rimland, *Infantile Autism: The Syndrome and Its Implications for a Neural Theory of Behavior*, p. 165. Rimland's emphasis.
8. Ibid., p. 169.
9. Cf. Dave Van Ronk's testimony that Dylan owed a conscious debt to modernism: "When he [Dylan] had a place of his own, I went up there and on the bookshelf was a volume of French poets from Nerval to almost the present. I think it ended at Apollinaire, and it included Rimbaud, and it was all well-thumbed with passages underlined and notes in the margins." Quoted in Anthony Scaduto, "Bob Dylan: An Intimate Biography. Part I," *Rolling Stone*, p. 39.
10. Walter J. Ong, S. J., *The Presence of the Word*, p. 113.
11. Quoted in *Rolling Stone*, 4 February 1971, p. 37.
12. The polyphonically structured film *Nashville* makes this apparent. As Robert Altman has said, the film is not about Nashville, but about America. (I suggest that insofar as the film is "about" anything, it is "about" power: what people will do to get it, and what it does to them after they get it.) Rock musicians could not now present sufficiently general meaning for the current stage of America's process.

Women's Magazines: Marry, Don't Work

Professor Tuchman, in this excerpt from her recent book *Hearth and Home: Images of Women in the Mass Media,* looks at the way so-called "women's magazines" present sex roles for women. She views the popular magazine medium as creating narrow, stereotyped roles for women, primarily to satisfy advertisers who sell products to women. Her concern is that these roles, repeated in all media, become models which women are compelled to follow. She does, however, find hope in the fact that some magazines are responsive to the changing roles of liberated women.

What changes have you noticed in women's roles on TV, in magazines, on the radio? Do you agree with Tuchman that most media portrayals of women place a higher value on the role of housewife and mother than other roles?

Read "Dissociation in a Hero: Superman and the Divided Self," by Arthur Asa Berger and "Double Play and Replay: Living Out There in Television Land" by Ron Commings for some thoughts about how male roles are influenced by the mass media.

As the American girl grows to womanhood, she, like her counterpart elsewhere in industrialized nations, has magazines available designed especially for her use. Some, like *Seventeen,* whose readers tend to be young adolescents, instruct on contemporary fashions and dating styles. Others, like *Cosmopolitan* and *Redbook,* teach about survival as a young woman—whether as a single woman hunting a mate in the city or a young married coping with hearth and home.

This section reviews portrayals of sex roles in women's magazines, seeking to learn how often they too promulgate stereotypes about the role their female readers may take—how much they too engage in the symbolic annihilation of women by limiting and trivializing them. Unfortunately, our analyses of images of women in magazines cannot be as extensive as our discussion of television. Because of researchers' past neglect of women's issues and problems, few published materials are available for review.

Like the television programs just discussed, from the earliest content

From Gaye Tuchman, Arlene Kaplan Daniels and James Benet, editors, *Hearth & Home: Images of Women in the Mass Media.* (New York: Oxford University Press, 1978). Copyright © 1978 by Oxford University Press, Inc. Reprinted by permission.

538

analyses of magazine fiction (Johns-Heine and Gerth, 1949) to analyses of magazine fiction published in the early 1970s, researchers have found an emphasis on hearth and home and a denigration of the working woman. The ideal woman, according to these magazines, is passive and dependent. Her fate and her happiness rest with a man, not with participation in the labor force. There are two exceptions to this generalization: (1) The female characters in magazines aimed at working-class women are a bit more spirited than their middle-class sisters. (2) In the mid-1970s, middle-class magazines seemed less hostile toward working women. Using the reflection of hypothesis, particularly its emphasis upon attracting readers to sell advertisements, we will seek to explain the general rule and these interesting exceptions to it.

Like other media, women's magazines are interested in building their audience or readership. For a magazine, attracting more readers is *indirectly* profitable. Each additional reader does not increase the magazine's profit margin by buying a copy or taking out a subscription, because the cost of publication and distribution per copy far exceeds the price of the individual copy—whether it is purchased on the newsstand, in a supermarket, or through subscription. Instead a magazine realizes its profit by selling advertisements and charging its advertisers a rate adjusted to its known circulation. Appealing to advertisers, the magazine specifies known demographic characteristics of its readership. For instance, a magazine may inform the manufacturer of a product intended for housewives that a vast proportion of its readership are homemakers, while another magazine may appeal to the producer of merchandise for young working women by lauding its readership as members of that target group. Women's magazines differentiate themselves from one another by specifying their intended readers, as well as the size of their mass circulation. Additionally, they all compete with other media to draw advertisers. (For example, *Life* and *Look* folded because their advertisers could reach a larger group of potential buyers at a lower price per person through television commercials.) Both daytime television and women's magazines present potential advertisers with particularly appealing audiences, because women are the primary purchasers of goods intended for the home.

Historically, middle-class women have been less likely to be members of the labor force than lower-class women. At the turn of the century, those married women who worked were invariably from working-class families that required an additional income to assure adequate food, clothing, and shelter (Oppenheimer, 1970). The importance of this economic impetus for working is indicated by the general adherence of working-class families to more traditional definitions of male and female sex roles (Rubin, 1976). Although middle-class families subscribe to a more flexible ideology of sex roles than working-class families, both groups of women tend to insist that the man should be the breadwinner. The fiction in women's magazines reflects this ideology.

Particularly in the middle-class magazines, fiction depicts women "as creatures . . . defined by the men in their lives" (Franzwa, 1974a, p. 106; see also Franzwa, 1974b, 1975). Studying a random sample of issues of *Ladies' Home Journal, McCall's,* and *Good Housekeeping* between the years 1940 and 1970, Helen Franzwa found four roles for women: "single and looking for a husband, housewife-mother, spinster, and widowed or divorced—soon to remarry." All the women were defined by the men in their lives, or by their absence. Flora (1971) confirms this finding in her study of middle-class (*Redbook* and *Cosmopolitan*) and working-class (*True Story* and *Modern Romances*) fiction. Female dependence and passivity are lauded; on the rare occasions that male dependence is portrayed, it is seen as undesirable.

As might be expected of characterizations that define women in terms of men, American magazine fiction denigrates the working woman. Franzwa says that work is shown to play "a distinctly secondary part in women's lives. When work is portrayed as important to them, there is a concomitant disintegration of their lives" (1974a, p. 106). Of the 155 major female characters depicted in Franzwa's sample of magazine stories, only 65, or 41 percent, were employed outside the home. Seven of the 65 held high-status positions. Of these seven, only two were married. Three others were "spinsters" whose "failure to marry was of far greater importance to the story-line than their apparent success in their careers" (pp. 106–7). One single woman with a high status career was lauded: She gave up her career to marry.

From 1940 through 1950, Franzwa found, working mothers and working wives were condemned. Instead, the magazines emphasized that husbands should support their spouses. One story summary symbolizes the magazines' viewpoint: "In a 1940 story, a young couple realized that they couldn't live on his salary. She offered to work; he replied, 'I don't think that's so good. I know some fellows whose wives work and they might just as well not be married'" (p. 108). Magazines after 1950 are even less positive about work. In 1955, 1960, 1965, and 1970 not one married woman who worked appeared in the stories Franzwa sampled. (Franzwa selected stories from magazines using five-year intervals to enhance the possibility of finding changes.)

Since middle-class American wives are less likely to be employed than their working-class counterparts, this finding makes sociological sense. Editors and writers may believe that readers of middle-class magazines, who are less likely to be employed, are also more likely to buy magazines approving this life-style. More likely to work and to be in families either economically insecure or facing downward mobility, working-class women might be expected to applaud effective women. For them, female dependence might be an undesirable trait. Their magazines could be expected to cater to such preferences, especially since those preferences flow from the readers' life situations. Such, indeed, are Flora's findings, presented in Table 1.

Table 1. Female dependence and ineffectuality by class, by percentage of stories *

	Working Class	Middle Class	Total
Female Dependence			
Undesirable	22	18	20
Desirable	30	51	41
Neutral	48	31	40
Female ineffectuality			
Undesirable	38	18	28
Desirable	4	33	19
Neutral	58	49	53

* Adapted from Flora (1971).

However, this pattern does not mean that the literature for the working-class woman avoids defining women in terms of men. All the women in middle-class magazines dropped from the labor force when they had a man present; only six percent of the women in the working-class fiction continued to work when they had a man and children. And Flora explained that for both groups "The plot of the majority of stories centered upon the female achieving the proper dependent status, either by marrying or manipulating existing dependency relationships to reaffirm the heroine's subordinate position. The male support—monetary, social, and psychological—which the heroine gains was generally seen as well worth any independence or selfhood given up in the process" (1971, p. 441).

Such differences as do exist between working-class and middle-class magazines remain interesting, though. For they indicate how much more the women's magazines may be responsive to their audience than television can be. Because it is the dominant mass medium, television is designed to appeal to hundreds of millions of people. In 1970, the circulation of *True Story* was "only" 5,347,000, and of *Redbook*, a "mere" 8,173,000. Drawing a smaller audience and by definition, one more specialized, the women's magazines can be more responsive to changes in the position of women in American society. If a magazine believes its audience is changing, it may alter the content to maintain its readership. The contradictions inherent in being women's magazines may free them to respond to change.

A woman's magazine is sex-typed in a way that is not true of men's magazines (Davis, 1976). *Esquire* and *Playboy* are for men, but the content of these magazines, is, broadly speaking, American culture. Both men's magazines feature stories by major American writers, directed toward all sophisticated Americans, not merely to men. Both feature articles on the state of male culture as American culture or of male politics as American politics. Women's magazines are designed in opposition to these "male magazines." For instance, "sports" are women's sports or news of women breaking into "men's sports." A clear distinction is drawn between what is "male" and what is "female."

Paradoxically, though, this very limitation can be turned to an advantage. Addressing women, women's magazines may suppose that some in their audience are concerned about changes in the status of women and the greater participation of women in the labor force. As early as 1966, before the growth of the modern women's movement, women who were graduated from high school or college assumed they would work until the birth of their first child. Clarke and Espositio (1966) found that magazines published in the 1950s and addressed to these women (*Glamour, Mademoiselle,* and *Cosmopolitan*) stressed the joys of achievement and power when describing working roles for women and identifying desirable jobs. Magazines addressed to working women were optimistic about these women's ability to combine work and home, a message that women who felt that they should or must work would be receptive to. Indeed, in 1958 Marya and David Hatch criticized *Mademoiselle, Glamour,* and *Charm* as "unduly optimistic" in their "evaluation of physical and emotional strains upon working women." Combining work and family responsibilities may be very difficult, particularly in working-class homes, since working class husbands refuse to help with housework (Rubin, 1976). But even working-class women prefer work outside the home to housework (Rubin, 1976, Vanek, forthcoming) since it broadens their horizons. Wanting to please and to attract a special audience of working women, magazine editors and writers may be freed to be somewhat responsive to new conditions, even as these same writers and editors feature stereotyped sex roles in other sections of their magazines.

Additional evidence of the albeit limited responsiveness of women's magazines to the changing status of women in the labor force is provided by their treatment of sex-role stereotypes since the advent of the women's movement. The modern women's movement is usually said to begin in the mid-1960s with the founding of the National Organization for Women. The data is of consequence for the study of sex roles in women's magazines because of Betty Friedan's involvement in the National Organization for Women. Her book, *The Feminine Mystique*, published in 1963, provided much of the ideology for the young movement. And, its analysis of sexism ("the problem with no name") was based in part on an analysis of the portrayal of sex roles in women's magazines. In an undated manuscript cited in Busby (1975), Stolz and her colleagues compared the image of women in magazines before and after the advent of the women's movement. Like others, they found no changes between 1940 and 1972. However, a time lag ("culture lag") is probably operating since nonmaterial conditions (ideas and attitudes) change more slowly than do material conditions (such as participation in the labor force).

Several very recent studies affirm that women's magazines may be introducing new conceptions of women's sex roles that are more conducive to supporting the increased participation of women in the labor force. Butler and Paisley [1] note that at the instigation of an editor of *Redbook*, twenty-eight women's magazines published articles on the arguments for and against the Equal Rights Amendment, a constitutional change prompted by the women's movement and the increased participation of women in the labor force. Franzwa's impression of the women's magazines she had analyzed earlier is that they revealed more sympathy with working women in 1975. [2] Sheila Silver (1976) indicates that a "gentle support" for the aims of the women's movement and a "quiet concern" for working women may now be found in *McCall's*. By the terms "gentle support" and "quiet concern," she means to indicate that the magazine approves equal pay for equal work and other movement aims, although it does not approve of the women's movement itself. That magazine and others, such as the *Ladies' Home Journal*, continue to concentrate upon helping women as housewives: They still provide advice on hearth and home. The women's magazines continue to assume that every woman will marry, bear children and "make a home." They do not assume that every woman will work some time in her life.

In sum, the image of women in the women's magazines is more responsive to change than is television's symbolic annihilation and rigid typecasting of women. The sex roles presented are less stereotyped, but a woman's role is still limited. A female child is always an eventual mother, not a future productive participant in the labor force.

Notes

1. Matilda Butler and William Paisley. Personal communication, Fall 1976.
2. 1976, personal communication.

VIRGINIA KIDD

Happily Ever After and Other Relationship Styles: Advice on Interpersonal Relations in Popular Magazines, 1951–1973

Virginia Kidd has provided us with a most unusual approach to the study of a mass medium. She has examined twenty-four popular magazines (e.g., *American Home, Ebony, Esquire, Good Housekeeping, Time, Life, Seventeen*) over a twenty year period, tracing the derivations of particular lines of thought contained in the articles. She has found that two different "visions" or images of social relationships emerged over this period. One vision dominated the 1950s and early 60s while the other started in the 60s and assumed the dominant position in the 70s. In her article, reprinted here, she carefully examines each vision and the implications for social values and roles. Her conclusions are not optimistic. She finds that while our society is wrestling with deep problems about how humans can get closer to each other, the answers provided in popular magazines are not likely to provide useful solutions.

When you have finished reading her analysis of Vision I and Vision II, see if you can apply the same method to other mass media like television or the cinema. What do you think will happen to Vision II? Will the media create a "new" vision of social relationships in our society in the near future?

The *Reader's Digest* in November of 1972 blazed across its front cover the legend "Three Ways to Save a Marriage."[1] The *Saturday Evening Post*, November, 1953, featured the article, "So You're Not Speaking to Each Other."[2] *Seventeen* in June of 1963 pondered the question "Why Can't I Talk to My Mother?"[3] The articles fulfilling these titles lack the detailed development of scholarly treatises, but they touch upon subject matter common to communication scholarship. Quite obviously, advice on interpersonal relations is being offered in massive doses through the media of public rhetoric, and this advice reaches and potentially influences readers numbering in the multi-millions.

Such articles contribute to the development of what Ernest Bormann has termed "rhetorical visions,"[4] concise interlocking dramas which fuse into a symbolic reality of the world. The rhetorical visions thus derived provide

From the *Quarterly Journal of Speech*, vol. 61, # 1 (February 1975). Reprinted by permission of the publisher and the author.

for those who accept them an understanding of the world, motivation for behavior, and most importantly, cues for meaning to be given to various verbal and nonverbal interaction. Bormann urged critics to examine "the social relationships, the motives, the qualitative impact of that symbolic world as though it were the substance of social reality for those people who participated in the vision."[5]

Popular magazines indicate social realities readers may come to accept. Kenneth Boulding, in *The Image,* explained the process by which such rhetorical visions in the mass media assume importance:

> The burnt child receives a vigorous message from nature regarding the relationship between heat and pain. The unburnt child, however, likewise dreads the fire because it has been taught to do so by its elders who speak with the voice of authority. Probably by far the larger portion of our relational image comes with the authority of the transcript not with the authority of the experience.[6]

Mass media become the "authority of the transcript"; they provide what Walter Lippmann termed "pictures in our heads—pictures which are representations of the real world."[7] Through these representations a composite image of "reality" is constructed, a rhetorical vision which has its base not so much in "reality" as in rhetoric.

Popular magazines, reaching vast numbers of readers, are an important element in the furthering of rhetorical visions. They can be presumed both to reflect and to inspire attitudes in their readers, and while an examination of the rhetorical visions of popular journals is not a verification of the beliefs of the readers, it is an indication of popular mood.

This study examined rhetorical visions of interpersonal relations in popular magazines over the last twenty years. The twenty year time period allowed for the tracing of derivations and development of particular lines of thought while at the same time focusing on contemporary attitudes.

Journals were selected for inclusion in this study on the basis of two criteria: (1) Inclusion in the *Reader's Guide to Periodical Literature.* The *Reader's Guide* has traditionally offered access to the popular journals, indexing the major large circulation magazines and excluding specialized periodicals. As such, it provided a useful cross-section of the popular visions as presented in contemporary journals. Magazines not included in the Guide for the entire twenty years were examined only during the years of inclusion in the *Guide.* (2) Having a circulation of over 1,000,000. This dividing point allowed a broad enough circulation for each magazine to have a significant influence on the "mass culture" and at the same time included a large enough number of magazines to supply the information needed.[8] A random selection of ten percent of all articles dealing with human relations in these journals for two year periods between 1951 and 1973 was analyzed.

Two rhetorical visions describing interpersonal relations were evidenced in the popular journals from 1951 to 1973. Vision I dominated the journals in the 1950s and early 1960s and continues to be operative today. Vision II is newer, appearing sporadically in the early sixties, gaining impetus in the late sixties and assuming a major position in the last few years. Each vision included explanations for appropriate behavior in caring relationships, specific suggestions for face-to-face interaction, and provided readers models of meaning in exchanges between persons. Despite the similarities of function, the specific advice each vision proffered was unique to it.

Dramas presented in Vision I were set in a world which was relatively unchanging. Behavioral patterns were described as continually repeating, and the repetition established a pattern of normality. This standard of normality was indicated through the continually reappearing assumption that any given dramatized situation had only one correct line of action for the characters. Behavior was dramatized on a bipolar continuum. Issues were right or wrong, left or right, and behavior was acclaimed or condemned. Regular columns, such as *Better Homes and Gardens'* "What's Wrong with This Family?" and *Ladies' Home Journal's* "Can This Marriage Be Saved?" presented relationship situations in which experts revealed the right behavior to the confused participants. Journals regularly gave readers the opportunity to test their mastery of appropriate behavior through quizzes which offered as a matter of course only one correct answer to each question.

Even more revealing of the single standard was the Vision I presentation of sex roles. Females and males were expected to behave according to traditional patterns, and when one did not do so, it was not the pattern but the individual's sexuality that was at fault. Dr. Margaret Mead's report on the Arapesh culture, for instance, where males are "gentle, always cooperative rather than competitive and never aggressive," was so out of line with the Vision I image of woman as the passive homemaker and man as the aggressive breadwinner that it was entitled "Where Men Must Have Feminine Traits."[9] So pervasive was this standard as a basis for relationships that Robert Coughlan could write in *Life,* 1956, of the violation of the norm, "In New York City the 'career woman' can be seen in fullest bloom and it is not irrelevant that New York City also has the greatest concentration of psychiatrists." [10] Such an argumentative leap was permissible in Vision I because deviation from the norm literally communicated emotional problems. The dramas offered dire predictions for those who dared to violate Vision I standards. In terms of the working wife, for· example, Coughlan wrote, "She may find many satisfactions in her job, but the chances are that she, her husband and her children will suffer psychological damage, and that she will be basically an unhappy woman." [11] Through such ominous rhetoric, Vision I indicated the power of the standard it set up, and Vision I authors reinforced the rhetoric by giving the sex role standard empirical bases. Reported Dr. Clifford R. Adams in *Ladies' Home Journal,* 1957, "Generally a fourth of a wife's married happiness and a third of her husband's, depend on the sexual adjustment they make. The greater importance to the male is probably due to his greater sex drive. . . ." [12] Researching such a hypothesis might prove a challenge to scholars throughout the discipline of speech-communication, but it was no problem for Vision I authors: the standard was so well accepted that no one would question it.

Though examples of the dominance of the single standard are most readily evident in sex role relations, the standard existed in relationship situations throughout Vision I, providing the foundation on which the vision rested. The single standard gave clear meaning to behavior. Characters in Vision I dramas had only to conform to the standard of normal to communicate the specific meaning such normal behavior aroused. Violations of the standard were immediately deviant and suspect.

Given a knowable and known standard against which behavior could be monitored, authors in Vision I were able to prescribe appropriate behavior easily. Basically, Vision I drama indicated how to create an image which most closely resembled the ideal in order to have high value on the interpersonal marketplace. [13] To help readers create such an image, authors developed an elaborate catalogue of prescriptions for interpersonal communication which, if followed, would develop readers into the heroes and heroines of Vision I dramas. The "ten easy steps" genre of article grew in prominence as authors explained how simple changing Cinderella into a princess really could be.

Fundamental to Vision I's ideal interaction was that an individual should make "others" happy. Paramount among the suggestions for accomplishing this goal was the admonition, "Above all, think of the other's problems before you think of your own." [14] This putting aside of self was defined as loving behavior, and conversely thinking of self first was unloving and displayed lack of genuine concern for others.

Intertwined with what was dramatized as a genuine desire to create happiness for others was the implied promise that those who brought such kindliness would be rewarded. When *Coronet*, 1953, proclaimed the virtue of compliments, for example, the author suggested, "We may even make some of them so memorable that they will still bring pleasure to the recipients long after we've spoken them," then added pragmatically, "A compliment has greater purchasing power than money." [15] Even listening could be pursued for profit as well as friendship. *Reader's Digest*, September, 1965, showed how a listener could benefit from an otherwise dull conversation:

> There is no such thing as a worthless conversation provided you know what to listen for. The attentive listener . . . listens for what people unconciously reveal about themselves while they're talking. Thus he can derive meaning from a conversation even though the other person may be talking nonsense. [16]

The goal was not to break through the nonsense to the speaker, but rather to give the speaker the courtesy of appearing to listen while searching for personal advancement from the interchange.

An extension of "putting the other first" was an attempt to avoid any incident which might cause the other discomfort. Disagreement of conflict was seen as indicating serious relationship problems, and journals described at length alternatives to confrontive behavior. *Seventeen* explained to its readers:

> If you really want to get rid of a fellow, there are some effective ways that will avoid deeply hurt feelings or the embarrassment of constantly running into someone you've had an argument with. One way is never to make a date with him. You never make dates far in advance, you tell him, and just this week you happen to be awfully busy with lots of things. Not dates. Just "things." So he waits a week, and somehow or other, you're so busy again. In a while he'll take the hint. And meanwhile, you haven't really rejected him outright. [17]

Motivation for this behavior was generally in the best interests of the "other." Marion Hilliard, in the *Reader's Digest*, 1957, urged women to deceive their husbands deliberately during sexual intercourse. She explained, "A man can feel kinship with the gods if his wife can make him believe he can cause a flowering within her. If she doesn't feel it she must bend every effort to pretend." [18] Dr. Hilliard sanctified such manipulation of facts. It was, she wrote, "the worthiest duplicity on earth." [19]

A final Vision I criteria of ideal interaction in a relationship was simply being with others in the relationship. Vision I writers were the agents who spawned "togetherness." Acting together in mutual concerns was held up as the symbol of family solidarity; it was dramatized as uniting a family to the point that its members found in each other's company pleasure "so great you don't even *want* a night out."[20] Those who did want a night out were manifesting relationship problems.

Vision I presented a consistent, coherent picture of the world of relationships which dominated much thought between 1951 and 1970. Characters in the dramas of the time interacted through social norms which praised selflessness, absence of open confrontation, and stategic interaction as positive relationship behavior. Since individuals compared the behavior to those with whom they related to a preconceived standard in order to give meaning to behavior, meaning-giving was fairly consistent for all persons. Vision I's weakness as a communication system came when individuals did not wish to convey by their behavior what the preconceived notion demanded. Vision I offered little outlet for creativity in communication, for formulating new ways of expressing relationship messages, or for forming new ways of relating which were not prescribed by the vision. In addition, the Vision I emphasis on creating a good impression, putting genuine personal feelings aside, and living up to a predetermined standard could easily destroy honest responses betwen people as well as any beneficial change which might result from honest feedback. (One can well imagine, for instance, that moment when the wife who did not feel a flowering within as a result of her husband's lovemaking finally stabbed him through the heart with the butcher knife in a fit of frustration. Suggesting changes in his behavior seems a lot simpler.)

Beginning slowly in the early sixties and increasing steadily thereafter, a new notion of appropriate interpersonal relations evolved to challenge the dominant position previously held by Vision I. Henry Miller articulated the basic position of Vision II in a 1966 *Esquire* article: "The idea of permanence is an absurd illusion. Change is the most permanent thing you can say about the whole universe."[21] Vision II authors always assumed, and often directly asserted, that life was ever changing and so were relationships. Consequently, so was meaning. Standard preconceived meaning could no longer adequately be applied to human interaction. Meaning was therefore negotiable, and the task of Vision II dramatists was not to prescribe to readers how to match a specific standard but rather how to function in negotiation of meaning.

Articles indicated this change in philosophy in their descriptions of relationships. A discussion of marriage in *Redbook,* 1968, for example, was a far cry from the prescriptive lists of the fifties:

> Specialists who study family life now agree that it is pointless to compare real marriages with some imagined ideal. The model marriage is a myth. . . . We must begin with a basic fact. Not all marriages are alike and they cannot be measured by the same standards.[22]

Erich Fromm not only rejected the preconceived standard, but cast it as a villain in his metaphor of plant care in *McCall's,* 1967: "If I have preconceived ideas of 'what is good for the plant'—for instance, the idea that lots of water is good for everything—I will cripple or kill the plant. . . ."[23] Thus the ordered dramatic scene of Vision I, with its prescribed meanings for human relationships, was replaced in Vision II by a world in which universal conventions ought not to be applied to all relationships and indeed carried possible harmful effects when applied.

In such a setting the "we can talk it out" theme became paramount. What was once "conversation" was now the "miracle" or "magic" of communication, and authors echoed such ideas as those of John Lagemann, who wrote in the *Reader's Digest,* 1966, that "when people talk together honestly and intensely the human spirit is lifted and refreshed."[24] Characters were dramatized as coming together in unity when they established "an atmosphere of openness so that everyone feels free to discuss and express his feelings."[25] *Redbook's* monthly "Young Mother's Story" typified the attitude in a drama of marital problems resolved through communication entitled "Please Talk to Me."[26]

Conflict was included in this talking out behavior. Vision II authors dramatized burying conflict and denying disagreement as causing dissension to fester and grow. Representative of this approach was a 1972 *Redbook* article: "Unpleasant feelings, petty resentments and frustrations do not go away simply because one refuses to let them show. Rather, they can build up a deadly store of bitterness."[27]

In a world without prescribed meaning for interpersonal behavior, where individuals had to confer meaning, the individual was vital. "Being your real self," "self-fulfillment," "being more yourself" were cue words for wise, alive behavior. Often the "self" was equated with an individual's feeling. Consequently, expression of feeling was cherished in Vision II dramas and constraining such feeling was negative behavior. Obviously the self-sacrifice practiced in Vision I was antithetical to this philosophical position; it was pictured as reulting in resentment and possessiveness.

As the self increased in importance, social institutions were subordinated and lost their power to define relationships. For example, *The New York Times Magazine* in 1972 described the "the breed of marriage counselors" whose motto was "Save the spouses, rather than the marriage."[28]

Indicative of Vision II ideals was its depiction of negative behavior. The truly villanous act of Vision II dramas was the failure to become involved with others. Lee Salk, for example, advised his *McCall's* readers in 1972 that hate was not the opposite of love, "Indifference is."[29] Fromm asserted, "Suffering is not the worst thing in life—indifference is."[30] Symptoms of indifference were displayed in dramas where living, growing beings were unrecognized by the villains of the piece who treated them as "objects" rather than people. Clearly, a rhetorical vision which functions on the basis of human exchange, which demands negotiation of meaning for interpersonal relationships to progress, cannot tolerate the absence of such interaction. Building such refusal to interact into a highly negative behavior was necessary for the vision's success.

Vision II's strength as a communication system was the emphasis it placed on the communication process. In a world of change, constant movement and reassessment of values, the traditional roles and norms of community were no longer pervasive. Meaning could not be acurately conferred on words or actions by comparing them to preconceived definitions. Rather, individuals had to arrive at a consensual meaning. The resultant exchanges between individuals could at times, unfortunately, be highly confusing. Meanings had to be deciphered from a complex morass of possibilities and were subject to constant redefinition. Despite the potential confusion of the system, meaning was more flexible than in Vision I and offered participants a greater freedom of expression. As well, Vision II allowed for more direct expression. Individuals were expected to describe their reactions in relationship situations in order to negotiate meaning; such description functioned as clarifying behavior. Vision II's weakness as a communication system was its almost simplistic approach to some communication situations, ironic in a vision based so firmly in the recognition of the world as complex. Vision II equated talking about problems with resolution of problems and suggested that the only element involved in "talking it out" was a decision to talk. The authors did not dramatize problems which discussion could not resolve, did not envision human interaction made less satisfying by open revelation of feelings, and did not portray characters incapable of expressing themselves.

In order for a rhetorical vision to gain credence as a belief system, it must perform two functions (1) it must offer the potential believer some benefit for accepting the vision, some reason for believing, and (2) it must do so while adequately taking into account "reality links," the tangible events in an individual's life which exist outside the world of rhetoric. An examination of how Vision I and Vision II fulfilled these two functions indicates how Vision II gained acceptance against the once unquestioned authority of Vision I.

Vision I offered its adherents a world heirarchy which gave them significance and security. Significance was available through identification with characters in the dramas. Anyone could be the heroine or hero if she or he was willing to abide by the definitions the vision offered. Everyone was rhetorically allowed a role that could be center stage, if not immediately, then at the apex of a life of effort and careful advancement. As well, Vision I offered security. The world was taken from a state of random chaos and given pattern and thus meaning. The future was predictable and controllable. To believe in such a vision gave followers a way to understand human interaction.

Not all readers, however, were willing to identify with the characters Vision I dramas depicted. Increasingly through the sixties, groups of individuals outside the magazine world were not identifying with the traditional life styles. Women's liberation groups rejected the dramatization of women, individualists ridiculed "togetherness," "the establishment" was assaulted on multiple fronts. And in the press of these reality links, Vision I continued to offer the same rhetoric. No changes in the vision indicated the changes historically occurring outside the dramas because Vision I had no provision for change. If meanings could fluctuate, then the whole foundation of Vision I crumbled.

Vision II offered an explanation of the world for those who could no longer find identity in Vision I. Like Vision I, it offered its believers significance. Each character bore internally the promise of a wondrous identity, and the confusion of a chaotic world which so plagued Vision I was readily assimilated into the newer vision as a potential source of growth for the individual.

Vision II has not completely replaced Vision I, however, though it continues to challenge. Perhaps this lack of complete acceptance stems from its weaknesses as a rhetorical explanation with which readers could identify. The significance Vision II offered in its dramas was offered only to the strong. Unlike Vision I, Vision II did not provide identity for all. The average American was not the hero of Vision II: rather, the special person was. The vision offered no heroes of heroines who were indecisive, unable to handle difficulty, insecure, afraid or unable to speak their minds. Characters who were unable to function at an optimum level interpersonally were presented in a negative light. Individuals who believed themselves to be inadequate in some aspect would find little comfort in the vision dramas which provided no identity for weakness, no rationale for failure. In addition, Vision II did not offer the security that Vision I offered so well as a belief system. The vision authors dramatized characters who put their faith in growth, change, and the individual's ability to deal with the future, yet in so doing they lost the vast persuasive rhetoric that security offers.

Assessing the exact influence of dramas presented in popular magazines on their readers is clearly impossible. To make such an assessment, a critic would have to know to what extent readers accepted what they read in their own lives. In addition, the critic would have to separate the influence of popular magazines from all other sources of influence on magazine readers. To do either is clearly impossible.

Anyone can speculate, however, about probable reactions to the two visions and to the magazine influence. Two general observations seem particularly relevant. First, the impact of any popular journal is limited and somewhat defined by the journal's readership. With the exception of the *Reader's Digest* and *Coronet*, the magazines carrying the bulk of the articles on the interpersonal relations had predominantly female readerships.[31] The result of this readership weighting was that articles were generally slanted toward the woman reader, accenting the woman's role in the dramas presented. The extension of this journalistic slanting is that the articles taken as a whole seem to be suggesting that the woman bears a greater responsibility in human relations than does her male counterpart. Dramas in both visions featured examples of how women could resolve problems and how women could interpret behavior. The modeling process provided by these dramas left little doubt as to who bore the responsibility for solving relationship difficulties or enhancing relationships in general, and implied by the absence of modeling examples that the male's responsibility was negligible. Whether women readers believed what they read or not, they were at least sensitized to communication situations in ways that non-readers were not.

Second, the short length of magazine articles, fundamental to the journal's form, lends itself to the deception that communication in close human relationships can be attained so easily that the process can be explained in two thousand words or less with space left over for the toothpaste ad.

Both Vision I and Vision II testify to the kind of interaction to be expected in the society that creates the visions. As well, they speak to the aspirations of that society. The rhetorical visions of interpersonal relations expressed in popular magazines have at their core the belief that somehow people can be close, that some techniques tried at the right time and in the right manner, will allow individuals to reach through the barriers of human separation to feel the emotional pulse of a loved one. Popular magazine authors are attempting to help people make that contact, and the enormous readership of these journals makes them far too significant to be put aside as skeletons-in-the-closet of communication scholarship.

The massive amount of published material this survey represents attempts to deal rhetorically with the fundamental issue of human isolation. The need for such articles emphasizes one repeated comment, the despairing observation that life is somehow, at the innermost core of our most significant relationships, unsatisfying. The urgency of that issue is reflected in the prominence of such articles, in the continual popularity of potential relationship elixers which describe how individuals might reach other individuals and might go on reaching them year after year. The problem is that the elixers offered are often so inadequate. In the final analysis, the popular magazine articles, the rhetorical visions they foster, and ultimately the expectations about relationships given into the minds of believing readers through the visions, do no more than skim the surface in their approaches to human encounters. Neither vision ever confronts the awesome possibility that human separation may be unavoidable, may in fact be necessary, in some self-preserving way. All the advice of Margaret Blair Johnstone, Ann Landers, Benjamin Spock, Lee Salk, and Erich Fromm together is meaningless if isolation is the ultimate refuge of sanity.

Notes

1. Ruth Stafford Peale, "Three Ways to Mothproof a Marriage," *Reader's Digest,* Nov. 1972, pp. 105–107.
2. H. A. Smith, "So You're Not Speaking to Each Other," *Saturday Evening Post,* 7 Nov. 1953, pp. 22–23ff.
3. "Why Can't I Talk to My Mother?" *Seventeen,* June 1963, pp. 100–101ff.
4. Bormann's description of the rhetorical vision critical techniques is explained in detail in Ernest G. Borman, "Fantasy and Rhetorical Vision: The Rhetorical Criticism of Social Reality," *Quarterly Journal of Speech,* 58 (1972), pp. 396–407. Bormann uses the methodology to examine an issue in the 1972 Presidential campaign in "The Eagleton Affair. A Fantasy Theme Analysis," *Quarterly Journal of Speech,* 59 (1973), pp. 143–159. This article not only il-

luminates the issues surrounding the removal of Senator Tom Eagleton from the Democratic Presidential ticket; as well it exemplifies the rhetorical vision methodology.

5. Bormann, "Fantasy and Rhetorical Vision," p. 401.

6. Kenneth Boulding, *The Image,* Ann Arbor Paperbacks (Ann Arbor: University of Michigan Press, 1956), p. 70.

7. Cited by Rod Holmgren and William Norton, eds., *The Mass Media Book* (Englewood Cliffs, New Jersey: Prentice-Hall, Inc., 1972), p. 4.

8. Journals included in the analysis were *American Home, American Magazine, Better Homes and Gardens, Colliers, Coronet, Cosmopolitan, Ebony, Esquire, Farm Journal, Field and Stream, Good Housekeeping, Ladies' Home Journal, Life, Look, McCall's, Newsweek, New York Times Magazine, Parents Magazine, Reader's Digest, Redbook, Saturday Evening Post, Scholastic, Seventeen, Time,* and *Woman's Home Companion.*

9. Judson T. Landis and Mary G. Landis, "The U.S. Male—Is He First Class?" *Colliers,* 19 July 1952, pp. 22–23ff.

10. Robert Coughlan, "The Changing Roles in Modern Marriage," *Life,* 24 Dec. 1956, p. 110.

11. *Ibid.,* p. 116.

12. Clifford R. Adams, "We Agree On Almost Everything Except Sex," *Ladies' Home Journal,* June 1957, p. 54.

13. The metaphor of the marketplace was common to Vision I. Ernest Havermann in *Reader's Digest* and *Life,* 1961, cited sociologist Clifford Kirkpatrick, who "feels that courtship can best be regarded as essentially a bargaining process; you go looking in the open market for the best possible mate to whom your own qualities entitle you." "Modern Courtship: The Great Illusion?" *Reader's Digest,* Dec. 1961, p. 82. Even Rosalind Russell got into the act, explaining in *Reader's Digest,* 1959 that "the girl who shops carefully, for a husband or a dress, generally gets better value. . . ." "I'm Glad I didn't Marry Young," *Reader's Digest,* Feb. 1959, p. 75.

14. Lynn Mighell and Marjorie Holmes, "What's Your Paycheck Doing to Your Marriage?" *Better Homes and Gardens,* March 1954, p. 65.

15. Helen Colton, "Making Friends with Compliments," *Coronet,* July 1953, p. 108.

16. J. N. Miller, "Art of Intelligent Listening" *Reader's Digest,* Sept. 1965, p. 85.

17. Jimmy Wescott, "Good-by, My Love," *Seventeen,* May 1963, p. 22.

18. Marion Hilliard, "The Act of Love—Woman's Greatest Challenge," *Reader's Digest,* June 1957, p. 45.

19. *Ibid.*

20. Marjorie Holmes, "Can Husband and Wife Be Friends?" *Better Homes and Gardens,* Oct. 1953, p. 194.

21. David Dury, "Sex Goes Public, A Talk with Henry Miller," *Esquire,* May 1966, p. 121.

22. Wells Goodrich with Robert J. Levin, "What Makes a Marriage Succeed," *Redbook,* Dec. 1968, p. 44.

23. Erich Fromm, "Do We Still Love Life?" *McCall's,* Aug. 1967, p. 108.

24. John Kord Lagemann, "Conversation Can Nourish Your Life," *Reader's Digest,* June 1966, pp. 131–132.
25. Lee Salk, "You and Your Family," *McCall's,* Nov. 1972, p. 68.
26. "Please Talk to Me," *Redbook,* April 1972, pp. 28ff.
27. *Ibid.,* p. 34.
28. M. W. Lear, "Save the Spouses Rather than the Marriage," *New York Times Magazine,* 13 Aug. 1972, pp. 12–13ff.
29. Lee Salk, "You and Your Family," *McCall's,* Sept. 1972, p. 64.
30. Fromm, "Do We Still Love Life?" p. 110.
31. The journals carrying the heaviest proportion of articles about interpersonal relationships were *Cosmopolitan, Ladies' Home Journal, McCall's, Parents Magazine, Reader's Digest, Redbook, Seventeen* and, while they were in publication, *Coronet* and *Woman's Home Companion.*

ARTHUR ASA BERGER

Dissociation in a Hero:
Superman and the Divided Self

This is an excerpt from *The Comic Stripped American* by Arthur Asa Berger. The book examines the interrelationships of comic strips and American society. In this selection Berger focuses on the superhero—Superman. Berger does not see Superman as the all-powerful individualist that some associate with this comic strip character. Rather, Berger sees him as a reflection of American values faithfully mirroring popular attitudes and beliefs. He even sees our hero's double identity (Clark Kent/Superman) as a reflection of a split personality in American culture. Superman is a fantasy, but one which is indicative of the American value system. Are comic strips influential in reshaping or subverting societal values?

Even Superman is in for a change. In future issues he will come to feel that he is a stranger in an imperfect world, the editors say. Surveying ant-like hordes of human beings from a skyscraper, he muses in one forthcoming issue, "For the first time in many years, I feel that I'm alone."

"Superman was created in the Depression as an icon, a Nietzsche superman," says Carmine Infantino, editorial director of National Comics. "At that time, people needed a perfect being. But now they want someone they can relate to. Like kids today, the new Superman will suffer from an inability to belong."

RICHARD J. HOWE, *The Wall Street Journal,* April 15, 1970

Comic-book cultists are fascinated by how the superheroes were born and developed. The saga of how Superman traveled from the doomed planet Krypton to Earth aboard a rocket and was discovered by kindly old Jonathan and Martha Kent is, of course, as familiar to cultists as the legend of Washington and the cherry tree.

They also know the original Superman did not possess x-ray vision or superhearing, and that his ineffectual alter-image pitched a fumbling pass at Lois Lane on page 11 of the summer 1939 issue of Superman's magazine (He: "Why is it you always avoid me at the office?" She [looking away]: "Please, Clark! I've been scribbling sob stories all day long. Don't ask me to dish out another"). The cool, unapproachable Miss Lane, of course, was hung up on Clark Kent's hidden self—the indigo-haired Man of Steel—right from the first issue (She: "But when will I see you again?" He [looking away]: "Who knows? Perhaps tomorrow—perhaps never").

Newsweek, February 15, 1965 (p. 89)

In recent years Superman has been changing. As Jules Feiffer described it in "Pop Sociology" (*New York Herald Tribune,* January 9, 1966), the changes have been quite significant:

> In my day Superman was the total individualist, unfettered by either the laws of gravity or the courts of justice. Today's Superman has, like the rest of us, *responsibilities.* He has two emasculating girl reporters competing with each other to see whose life he has to save more often. He has a hero-worshiping cub reporter he has to look after. He even has Batman and Robin (and a host of other masked, caped and leotarded heroes) suddenly dropping in on short visits from rival comic books, expecting to be looked after, expecting to be taken care of. So, married or not, Superman's a family man, loaded with other people's demands, other people's problems. Is it any wonder that these days he often has his weaknesses, his failures—that, in a recent issue, he lost a fight to a *girl?* One difference between our idealism in the thirties and our cynicism in the sixties is that, today, we even allow our Supermen to turn impotent.

When we discarded our old legacy of rugged individualism and self-sufficiency, we also abandoned the view that a heroic superpowerful individual might solve all our problems with some magnificent gesture.

But what is important about Superman is not that he is changing; most of the comic book superheroes are becoming more "relevant" and are involved with social problems such as racism and war and reflect various psychological difficulties. It is what Superman represents, as a symbol, *before* he started changing that I am most interested in; and it is his symbolic significance that is most important, I feel, for our purposes.

Though he may have been a relatively simple-minded hero in the old days before he became socially conscious, *as a symbolic figure he presents many difficulties.* This is because his symbolic significance has many different dimensions. For example, the notion of a superman, a strong, heroic figure who transcends ordinary man, has obvious Oedipal interpretations. The desire of young boys to rid themselves of their fathers coupled with their need for the knowledge and protection of their fathers is very closely realized in the role Superman plays in his adventures.

Superman also is a superego figure, a symbol of conscience. He is pledged to be a champion of the oppressed and to help people in need. In the course of his activities he often must fight with evil, and his triumphs can be seen, from a Freudian perspective, as representing the dominance of a highly developed superego. (The superego is defined as "a major sector of the psyche that is only partly conscious and that aids in character formation by reflecting parental conscience and the rules of society" [*Webster's Seventh Collegiate*].) Good-guy superheroes have this function, no doubt, but Superman's fantastic powers make the super ego's dominance most apparent. Dick Tracy, a rather morbid and perhaps pathological figure, also represents a highly developed superego, but he is, at least, human and vulnerable. Superman, possessing all kinds of superpowers, cannot be denied!

The very fact that Superman has such prodigious powers presents a problem to his writers. They are forced to create various extraordinary challenges for Superman, so there can be some question about the resolution of the various adventures. In some ways he must be humanized, so that he does not merely wipe out his antagonists. Kryptonite, the fragments of the planet where Superman was born before he was sent to earth, thus make it conceivable that he will be foiled, though all comic book readers know that their heroes will ultimately triumph.

The use of a substance that makes superior aliens vulnerable is common in science fiction and can be found in H. G. Wells's *The War of the Worlds*. In that story, harmless germs kill the superior aliens from Mars (who represent a certain type of villain, the bug-eyed monsters). These monsters, with "minds that are to our minds as ours are to those of the beasts that perish," are similar in power to Superman, except that he is good and identifies with mankind. The question that Wells brings up is: How do we (earthlings) relate to superior and hostile aliens? How do we deal with them? The answer he offers in his particular story is not hopeful. However, by using the device of the weakening or destructive substance he is able to resolve the dilemma and find a way for mankind to survive in the face of powers beyond comprehension.

We have, to this point, been discussing Superman from a psychological standpoint—as a figure representing the superego who must, somehow, be diminished and humanized so there can be suspense and a question about how his adventures will be resolved. But he may also be analyzed from a sociological and political standpoint. After all, there is something strange about a democratic, equalitarian society having a hero who represents values that are antithetical to our basic beliefs, and which have been associated with Nazi Germany, in particular, and European elitist culture in general.

There is a fairly close relationship, generally, between a society and its heroes; if a hero does not espouse values that are meaningful to his readers, there seems little likelihood that he will be popular. The term "super" means over, above, higher in quantity, quality, or degree, all of which conflict with the American equalitarian ethos. I believe the answer to this dilemma lies in Superman's qualities and character. He is, despite his awesome powers, rather ordinary—so much so that he poses as a spectacled nonentity of a reporter in order to avoid publicity and maintain some kind of privacy.

His superiority lies in his powers, and though he possesses great physical attributes and abilities, they are always at the service of his fellow man. He is not, by any means, an aristocrat who values "breeding" and has a sense of superiority. What Emerson said about Napoleon, an everyman with superhuman capacities, can also be said of Superman; he is "the idol of the common men because he had in transcendent degree the qualities and powers of common men" ("Napoleon, Man of the World").

Thus a difference in degree (of power) has not led to a difference in kind (sense of superiority). It might even be said that Superman is rather shy and quite bland. In a society which will not tolerate pretensions, which has no hereditary aristocarcy, even Superman is forced to present himself as a supreme democrat. He is an ordinary person who just happens to be the strongest man in the world. *Webster's Seventh Collegiate* defines a superman as "a superior man that according to Nietzsche has learned to forgo fleeting pleasures and attain happiness and dominance through the exercise of creative power." This is very close to the basic middle-class American pattern of deferred gratification—you give up minor pleasures of the moment for better pleasures later. In many respects Superman is a middle-class square!

The problem that Superman faces is that, as a superior man in a society which is stridently equalitarian, he must disguise himself, lest people be envious and cause difficulties. In the tale of his origin this is made evident. A scientist from the doomed planet Krypton sends his infant child to earth, where it is discovered by an elderly couple, the Kents. They place him in an orphanage and later adopt him. In the fifth frame of the origin tale (which takes only two pages), Mr. Kent says to young Clark: "Now listen to me, Clark! This great strength of yours—you've got to hide it from people or they'll be scared of you!"

And Mrs. Kent adds: "But when the proper time comes, you must use it to assist humanity."

As he grows older, his powers develop. After his foster-parents die, we find the following:

> Clark decided he must turn his titanic strength into channels that would benefit mankind. And so was created—Superman, champion of the oppressed, the physical marvel who had sworn to devote his existence to helping those in need.

The language almost has a Biblical ring, with the use of the passive tense in "And so was created." This suggests that his origin has a mythical dimension, and perhaps a sacred one. The Biblical parallel is furthered by the similarity between the way Moses and Superman were found.

Superman is different from many other comic book superheroes in that his true identity is Superman and Clark Kent is a disguise. When dangerous situations develop, Kent strips off his clothes and leaps into action as Superman, a caped crusader in a brilliant red and blue costume.

The matter of *identity* is one of the central problems of Superman. Underneath the mask, the persona of an incompetent reporter, is a Superman. There is some kind of schizoid split in having one person with two separate beings. As Kent, Superman is often fooled by Lois Lane; it is quite inconceivable that Superman would fall for her tricks, yet Superman and Clark Kent are the same person. It is almost as if there were two separate beings with complete dominance within their particular sphere of operations. When Superman is pretending to be Clark Kent, he actually is Clark Kent and when Superman is Superman, he bears no relation to Clark Kent, though they are one and the same being. Superman seems to be a "divided self," to use R.D. Laing's term from *The Divided Self,* except that Superman/Clark Kent does not seem to be psychotic.

There is a great deal of confusion in *Superman*. Clark Kent likes Lois Lane, who spurns him, while Lois Lane likes Superman, who in turn spurns her. We find ourselves in a situation in which a woman likes and dislikes the same man or, rather, his different identities. The only way we can explain such matters is to postulate two separate identities in the same person which are autonomous in their own particular realm.

In this respect the costumes Superman and all superheroes wear are significant. When he has his usual work suit on, and his glasses, Superman is not really Superman, so to speak. He is timid, somewhat incompetent, and terribly boring. It is only when he strips off his veneer and his suit, and emerges resplendent in his cape and leotards, that he acts like Superman. The Superclothes make the Superman; no doubt about that.

In *The Waning of the Middle Ages,* Johan Huizinga explains the significance of clothes and costumes:

> The modern male costume since the end of the eighteenth century is essentially a workman's dress. Since political progress and social perfection have stood foremost in general appreciation, and the ideal itself is sought in the highest production and most equitable distribution of goods, there is no longer any need for playing the hero or the sage. The ideal itself has become democratic. In aristocratic periods, on the other hand, to be representative of true culture means to produce by conduct, by customs, by manners, by costume, by deportment, the illusion of a heroic being. . . .
>
> But all the aristocratic aspects of the heroic being have been lost in an equalitarian society, so only the costume remains. It is the costume that counts, and Superman's costume is probably a version of the old costume of the swordsman and nobleman, brought up to date for pseudo science fiction.

Superman's lack of interest in Lois Lane correlates closely with symptoms found in schizophrenics. As Robert Waelder says in *Basic Theory of Psychoanalysis:*

> Two characteristic features of these patients—the difficulty of establishing contact with them, i.e., a deficiency in their object relations, and the fact that some, though not all of them, produce megalomanic ideas—seemed to be accountable by one single assumption, viz., that the libido had been withdrawn from the objects and concentrated upon the ego.

Waelder brings up this subject in his discussion of *narcissism.* The narcissist takes himself as an object of love, though it must be pointed out that self-love cannot be equated with self-interest; indeed, the two are often opposed to one another. The point is that a withdrawal of the libido and an element of self-love might possibly explain Superman's lack of interest in Lois Lane. As a Superman he has learned, as Nietzsche explains, to forgo fleeting pleasures—one of which may be romantic involvement with Lois Lane, members of the opposite sex in general, and perhaps everyone. After all, a Superman "deserves" a Superwoman.

In a number of ways Superman's divided self and history are significant (and perhaps even paradigmatic) for American society and culture in general. Superman has left a destructive—in this case self-destructive—place of origin for a new world where his powers make him the strongest man on earth. His history is similar to that of the Puritans, who left a corrupt old world for a blissful new one, where their spiritual powers might flower. And like Superman the Puritans labored heroically for goodness and justice, as they interpreted both.

Just as Kryptonite weakens Superman, so does contact with the corrupting old world weaken innocent Americans and destroy their moral integrity. Thomas Jefferson believed this to be the case, and the notion of America as innocent and Europe as corrupt is part of the conventional wisdom and mythology of the American mind. Superman, like the American, thus must avoid contact with the past in order to maintain his powers. With the American this has led to an antihistorical attitude, a belief in the future and repudiation of the past. We may have half the historians in the world teaching in our universities, but the basic frame of reference of the American mind is antihistorical.

We believe that when we left Europe and our fatherland, says Geoffrey Gorer in *The American People,* we escaped from time. We left institutions (such as the Roman Catholic Church, nobility, royalty) that are associated with history and escaped to the forest, where we became nature's noblemen. This nineteenth-century view of things still colors our beliefs; Americans tend to see themselves as simple people living in an arcadia. Rather than accept the fact that we live in an urbanized, bureaucratized, and industrialized society we take recourse in myths such as the notion of the self-made man who, if he has adequate will power, can realize any and all goals he sets for himself.

In this sense we all see ourselves as supermen. Beneath the facade of the bumbling, inefficient, or even rather ordinary white-collar worker is the superman, just waiting for his chance. Unfortunately, by the time the average man reaches his middle thirties, life seems to close in on him and he begins to realize that not much is likely to change, that he isn't a superman, and that heroic will power is not enough to help him realize his dreams. The tragedy is that our culture promotes fantastic expectations, which are rarely realized. Failure becomes all the more bitter, since people have no one to blame except themselves; if success is personal and individual (being essentially a function of the super will), then so is failure.

The schizoid split within Superman symbolizes a basic split within the American psyche. Americans are split like Superman, alienated from their selves and bitter about the disparity between their dreams and their achievements, between the theory that they are in control of their own lives and the reality of their powerlessness and weakness.

Superman's identity problem is very similar to ours. The American's obsession with identity is a well-known phenomenon. It is because we have no sense of the past that we have no sense of who we are. Like Superman we perform superheroic tasks, one after the other, but they do not seem to give us any sense of being. Just as Superman keeps his identity hidden, so do we hide ours by repudiating the past. And various Americanizing institutions, such as the schools, have prided themselves upon their ability to erase the ethnic identities of our immigrants and turn them into quintessential Americans within a generation or so. But we took their identities away with their traditions and practices and gave them nothing in return except a few myths and pipe dreams.

Originally Superman represented a heroic force who could use his superpowers to lessen the impact of natural disasters or take direct action against criminals. As Marshall McLuhan puts it in *The Mechanical Bride:*

> The attitudes of Superman to current social problems likewise reflect the strong-arm totalitarian methods of the immature and barbaric mind. Like Daddy Warbucks in "Orphan Annie," Superman is ruthlessly efficient in carrying on a one-man crusade against crooks and anti-social forces. In neither case is there any appeal to the process of law. Justice is represented as an affair of personal strength alone. Any appraisal of the political tendencies of "Superman" (and also its many relatives in the comic-book world of violent adventure known as the "Squinky" division of entertainment) would have to include an admission that today the dreams of youths and adults alike seem to embody a mounting impatience with the laborious processes of civilized life and a restless eagerness to embrace violent solutions.

Superman, as an individualist, could not be expected to bother with red tape and delays and all the judicial processes which exist. Better a super bash in the teeth, which is quick and also allows readers to assuage their desire for vengeance and relieve themselves of aggressive feelings.

What has happened, ironically, is that instead of America becoming a society full of individual supermen (and the various manifestations of this concept such as the rugged individualist, the self-made man, the tycoon, etc.) just the opposite has occurred. The nineteenth-century notion postulated no society itself, so to speak; just a collection of supermen who happen to live in the same territory. Instead, what has happened is that America seems to be a society full of powerless weaklings, while the state has taken on the superpowers. We have a superstate with prodigious powers, while as individuals we feel feeble and unable to control our own destinies.

In the *Superman* comics, Krypton was introduced to facilitate plots but also for another reason, which is not apparent. We have a fear of power that is out of control, and Kryptonite helps us to relieve the anxiety caused by the presence of a power that cannot be controlled. But in present-day America there seems to be no moral equivalent of Kryptonite to curb the powers of a superstate that seems to be out of control.

JAMES LULL

The Social Uses of Television

Do we watch TV as individuals or as members of a family? Is the TV an essential part of modern family living? James Lull provides evidence that television
viewing is an elaborate ritual involving individual and family needs. Based on
findings from systematic participant observation, Lull presents a typology of
the social uses of TV and reveals the importance of television viewing to family relationships. Compare this essay with those of Messaris, Faber *et al.*, and
Bliese. Do you find a pattern that establishes that TV is a member of the
family? How do other media like radio, records, and magazines affect family
relationships? Is the pattern different or similar?

Mass Media as Social Resources

Social actors can be thought to actively employ the tools of communication in order to purposively construct their social realities. Symbolic interactionism (Blumer, 1969), language-action (Frentz & Farrell, 1976), and
communicative constructivism (Delia, 1977) are, to varying degrees, contemporary derivatives of the social constructivist position. The uses and
gratifications paradigm in mass communication is another manifestation
of the constructivist view. Adherents to this perspective posit that individuals selectively use mass media in order to satisfy their human needs. In
Katz' words, "this is the research tradition which asks not what the media
do to people, but what people do with the media" (Katz, 1977). According
to the modern conception, "uses" of media are observable evidences of the
audience's control over the receptive instruments of mass communication.

Less obvious social uses of television, many of which are embedded in
the taken-for-granted communicative substance which surrounds the viewing experience, generally have not been examined. However, the recent
tradition of ethnomethodology, wherein the assumptive world of social
interaction is itself treated as a phenomenon (Garfinkel, 1967; Zimmerman & Pollner, 1970; Mehan & Wood, 1975; Zimmerman, 1978), provides a perspective to disclose additional insights into the nature of human
communication, including interpersonal uses of the mass media.[1] Common

social instances of media consumption can be viewed as delicate and situated accomplishments created by the persons involved.

In the study of human communication, specimens of language, occasions for talk, and the structural properties of interaction patterns can all be identified among available resources for the accomplishment of such interpersonal objectives as the creation of communicative displays which attest to the social competency of an interlocutor or to the correct fulfillment of role incumbencies (Hymes, 1964; Philipsen, 1975). These resources are so central to daily living that verbal strategies are even known to be utilized together with a host of other communicative provisions in order for a social member to display gender effectively (Garfinkel & Stoller, 1967).

Mass media can also be viewed as important and uniquely employed social resources in interpersonal communication systems. They are handy expedients which can be exploited by individuals, coalitions, and family units to serve their personal needs, create practical relationships, and engage the social world. Television and other mass media, rarely mentioned as vital forces in the construction or maintenance of interpersonal relations, can now be seen to play central roles in the methods which families and other social units employ to interact normatively. The interpersonal uses one makes of the mass media constitute the construction of a particular subset of actions which find many practical applications in the home environment. One approach to documenting these behaviors is participant-observational research, which leads to ethnographies of mass communication.

The Ethnographic Method in the Study of Media Audience Behavior

In mass communication research, the most fundamental aspects of human interaction—those distinct and detailed events which social actors create *in their own terms and on their own grounds* in order to make the substance of their ordinary routines meaningful—are seldom taken into account by researchers. The rough edges, special cases, and subtle peculiarities of the social world are sometimes ignored in order to facilitate cleanliness, parsimony, and predictive strength in mathematically induced designs and theories.

Participant observational strategies offer alternatives to the methods which are commonly employed. The use of participant observation for documentation of intensive naturalistic case studies in mass communication allows for theory building which binds together conceptual communicative elements, messages linkages, and exchanges by social actors as holistic units-in-interaction (Blumer, 1969). The family, television's primary audience, is a natural unit for this kind of analysis. Through ethnographic inquiry, the researcher can study actual communication contexts and ways in which media experiences enter the lives of family members.

• • •

The ethnography of mass communication is meant to be a sustained, microscopic, inductive examination of the natural interactional communications which connect human beings to the mass media and to each other. From data generated by ethnographic inquiries with this purpose, and by means of a review of the contributions made by other researchers to the uses and gratifications literature, a beginning typology of the social uses of television has been constructed and is presented in the next major section of this paper. Evidence presented in support of the typology derives from a review of the major findings in the uses and gratifications literature and from ethnographic data collected at the University of Wisconsin and the University of California.

More than 200 families, representing blue-collar, white-collar, and farm types, were studied during the past three years at these locations. They were contacted through social agencies such as girls' clubs, boys' clubs, community nursery schools, university resources, and religious groups. In the variety of studies, families have been randomly selected from mailing lists, telephone lists, or members present at general meetings attended by the researcher. The acceptance rate for families contacted was about 30 percent. This figure is less when "normal" families only (two parents present) are used (Bechtel et al., 1972). Observational periods ranged from two to seven days per family.[2] Observers studied these groups from mid-afternoon until bedtime. Intensive independent interviewing of each family member followed the last day of observation in each case. Following the writing of the reports, family members were asked to read and confirm the validity of the observations.

Families at first were given only a general introduction to the purpose of the research. They were told that the observers were students in communication who were interested in "family life." It was not possible to reveal the researchers' particular interests since that knowledge probably would have influenced families' media activities during the observational period. Debriefing followed the collection of all data.

Observers' procedures for data gathering were standardized as much as possible from family to family. Each observer maintained a preprinted log on which the ongoing behavior of families was documented throughout the day. Since they were known to the families only as students, the observers took most of their notes in the guise of "homework" chores conducted while they sat in the living rooms or television-viewing areas of the homes. In this way, observers were able to take many notes on the premises and record the details of interpersonal interaction and media use as they occurred. A reconstruction of daily behavior was made by each observer after returning home following the observation periods each night.

Observers took part in the routines of the families for the duration of the observation period. They ate with the families, performed household chores with them, played with the children, and took part in group entertainment, particularly television watching. Families were told from the beginning that in no case should they change their routines in order to accommodate the observer.

Observers looked for regularity in communicative acts reflected in the interpersonal roles and relationships associated with the use of mass media. Particular interactional behaviors such as dominance strategies and talk patterns were noted. Interpersonal behaviors involving mass media, such as the dynamics of the television program selection process and the viewing experience, were other primary areas for observation.

A full accounting of the data collected in studies such as this is not well suited for journal reports because of the lengthy analyses which typify ethnographic research. Family communication is so vivid, detailed, and theoretically intriguing under naturalistic conditions that the alert ethnographer becomes seemingly inundated by pertinent observations. Henry, in his accounts of five mentally disturbed families (Henry, 1965), used about 100 pages of text to discuss each family. Lewis discussed the behavior of five Mexican families in 300 pages (Lewis, 1959) and required nearly 700 pages to present a single Puerto Rican extended family (Lewis, 1965). Other classic ethnographies of neighborhoods, gangs, and cultures, have also been reported in book-length form (Gans, 1962; Liebow, 1967; Whyte, 1943; Anderson, 1923). Ethnographic data presented in support of the following typology is, necessarily, a distillation of the findings.

The Social Uses Typology

A previous attempt to organize audience uses of the mass media into a descriptive typology has been made by McQuail, Blumer, and Brown

(1972). Their category system is arranged into four components: (1) diversion—the use of television and other media for escaping routines and problems, emotional release; (2) personal relationships—social utility, companionship; (3) personal identity—personal reference, reality exploration, value reinforcement; (4) surveillance.

In the following paragraphs, an accounting for the primary social uses, opposed to the personal uses implicit in much of the McQuail et al. schema, is presented. It is somewhat arbitrary to distinguish between the personal and interpersonal uses of television, however, the inventory and explication of the uses of television described here focus directly on their communicative value as social resources.

Social uses of television in the home are of two primary types: structural and relational (Figure 1). The focus of this section will be on the latter category, but by a brief discussion of the former is helpful in clarifying the different uses of the medium. Examples which illustrate components of the typology are by no means thought to be exhaustive of the individual categories. The evidence presented here is meant to provide an introductory agenda of behaviors which can be classified according to the factors which are described.

Structural Uses of Television

Television is employed as an *environmental resource* in order to create a flow of constant background noise which moves to the foreground when individuals or groups desire. It is a companion for accomplishing household chores and routines. It contributes to the overall social environment by rendering a constant and predictable assortment of sounds and pictures which instantly creates an apparently busy atmosphere. The activated television set guarantees its users a nonstop backdrop of verbal communication against which they can construct their interpersonal exchanges. Of course, it always serves its timeless environmental function as a source of entertainment for the family.

Second, television has the structural characteristic of being a *behavioral regulator*. Television punctuates time and family activity such as mealtime, bedtime, choretime, homework periods, and a host of related activities and duties. Patterns of talk are affected by viewing routines. External family communication is similarly regulated by television. Taking part in community projects, recreational activities, or outside entertainment are directly influenced by the scheduling of television programs.

<u>Structural</u>

Environmental (background noise; companionship; entertainment)

Regulative (punctuation of time and activity; talk patterns)

<u>Relational</u>

Communication Facilitation (experience illustration; common ground; conversational entrance; anxiety reduction; agenda for talk; value clarification)

Affiliation/Avoidance (physical, verbal contact/neglect; family solidarity; family relaxant; conflict reduction; relationship maintenance)

Social Learning (decision-making; behavior modeling; problem solving; value transmission; legitimization; information dissemination; substitute schooling)

Competence/Dominance (role enactment; role reinforcement; substitute role portrayal; intellectual validation; authority exercise; gatekeeping; argument facilitation)

Figure 1. Social Uses of Television

Television viewing takes place in social units other than families. Viewing in various settings can be free and selective, as it is in college dormitories, or it can be parceled out as a reward granted by the proper authorities. Children in nursery schools are allowed to watch television after they pick up their toys. Girls in a California reform school can view only when their rooms pass inspection and when they complete their evening chores. Television in a retirement home is an attractive alternative to sitting alone in a private room. Under all these conditions, television viewing contributes to the structuring of the day. There is a time for viewing. That time is often related to other responsibilities and activities in which the individual is involved.

Relational Uses of Television
The ways in which audience members use television to create practical social arrangements can be organized into a behavioral typology of four major divisions. While the exclusivity of the categories is not absolute, an argument for the internal validity of the components of the schema described below will be made. Further, the order of presentation of the four relational functions (communication facilitation, affiliation/avoidance, so-

cial learning, competence/dominance) is made sequentially in order to demonstrate the relative complexity of the constructs.

Communication Facilitation

Television's characters, stories, and themes are employed by viewers as abundant illustrators which facilitate conversations. Children, for example, use television programs and characters as primary known-in-common referents in order to clarify issues they discuss. Television examples are used by children to explain to each other, and to their parents and teachers, those real-world experiences, emotions, and beliefs which are difficult to make interpersonally transparent in attempts at verbal communication.

A child often uses television in order to enter an adult conversation. When a child is ignored during conversations held by adults, he or she can gain entry to the discussion by using a television example which illustrates a point being made by one of the adult interactants. If participants in the conversation are familiar with the television example, the child has introduced a common referent in order to gain access to the conversation from which he or she was otherwise left out.

The viewing experience itself can be facilitative. Conversational discomfort is sometimes reduced when the television is turned on and in view of the interactants. The uneasiness of prolonged eye contact is lessened since the television set ably attracts attention during lulls in conversation. Also, the program being watched creates an immediate agenda for talk where there may otherwise be none.

The medium is used as a convenient resource for entertaining outside guests in the home. To turn on the set when guests arrive is to introduce instant common ground. Strangers in the home may then indulge in "television talk"—verbal responses to television programs which allow audience members to discuss topics of common experience which probably have little personal importance. Television viewing under these circumstances provides an opportunity for abundant talk with little substance— an exercise in conversational form for the interlocutors. In this way, viewers become better acquainted but invest minimal personal risk. Television also helps some family members clarify interpersonally their attitudes and values, especially in recent years since the medium has presented more controversial programming.

Affiliation/Avoidance

A fundamental social use of television is its potential as a resource for the construction of desired opportunities for interpersonal contact or avoidance. One uses and gratifications researcher believes that this is the primary social use of the medium (Nordenstreng, 1970). The proxemic nature of audience positioning in front of the television set is often used to advantage by young children who desire to engage physically or verbally their admired older siblings. Some adults orchestrate rare moments of physical contact in front of the television screen, an intimacy which need not be accompanied by conversation. An entertainment medium, however defined, is useful for this purpose. In one family which was observed, the husband and wife touched each other only twice during the seven-day period. The first time the man playfully grabbed his wife and seated her on his lap while his daughter, acting as a kind of medium, told a humorous story about something that had happened at school that day. The other occasion for physical contact during the week took place one night while the couple watched television. The man was a hard-working laborer who nearly always fell asleep when he watched television at night. He dozed as he sat in a recliner rocking chair with his shoes off. He snored loudly with his mouth open. His wife, who had been sitting on the floor in the same room, pushed herself along the floor until she was close to his chair. She leaned back until her head rested against his bare feet and smiled as she created this rare moment of "intimacy."

Television viewing is a convenient family behavior which is accomplished *together*. The medium is used to provide opportunities for family members or friends to communally experience entertainment or informational programming. A feeling of family solidarity is sometimes achieved through television-induced laughter, sorrow, anger, or intellectual stimulation (Katz & Foulkes, 1962). Confirmation of the family as a unit of interdependent personalities is made by the attempts of viewers to predict consensually the outcomes of television shows while they watch or by the creation of on-going discussions of the details or implications of the televised stories. Audience members also use television as a family relaxant whereby group viewing promotes family harmony by reducing interpersonal discord, at least during the viewing period.

Television can lessen the demand for the manufacture of talk and the exchange of thought by providing a sustaining focus for attention which can be employed as a kind of social distractor, rendering less intense the communicative formalities which might otherwise be expected. Since television is used by the viewer as a focus for attention, creating "parallel" rather than interactive viewing patterns, it also becomes a resource for escape—not just from the personal problems or responsibilities of the individual viewer, but from the social environment (Walters and Stone, 1975).

Anthropologist Edmund Carpenter (1972) reported that a U.S. Army official in Germany recently blamed the high divorce rate among his troops on the lack of an English-language television station in the area where they live. The officer said, "That means a soldier and his wife have got to talk to each other in the evenings and they suddenly discover that they really don't like each other" (Carpenter, 1972, p. 10). A blue-collar family which was observed said it was grateful for television since it occupies so much of the grandparents' time in the evening, thereby keeping them away from their home which is located just three doors away. This young couple preferred not to be bothered by their parents. Television limits unwanted visits.

Television functions as a social resource in a unique way which helps married couples maintain satisfactory relationships. Unlike print media which transmit bits of information, television can provoke a vicarious, evanescent fantasy world which serves for some the psychological purpose of a desirable, if temporary, occupation of an alternative reality.

Psychological transformations triggered by program viewing become resources put to use by the inventive social actor. An example is revealed in the case of a farm woman who 15 years ago resigned her premed scholarship to a major midwestern university, married her high-school boyfriend, and attended vocational school in order to become a medical secretary. Her first child was born one year following her marriage, causing her to quit her job at the medical office.

The *only* television shows watched by this woman during the research period were programs which featured settings and themes directly related to the medical profession ("Marcus Welby, M.D.," "Medical Center," "Medical Story"). When these programs were aired, she engaged in a continual and intense commentary about the nature of the story, particularly as it related to medical considerations. She remarked about the appropriateness of operating-room procedures. She evaluated the work of subordinates and always referred to the doctors by their formal titles. She praised medical work well done and found fault with mistakes made by the staff. The Caesarean section of quintuplets during one melodrama fascinated her as she remarked instructively about the importance of quickly trimming "all five cords."

During an interview probe following a week-long observation period conducted by the researcher, the woman said:

> I've always been interested in anything medical, in anything to do with the
> medical field. So, that's what I like . . . I usually find that their (medical)

information is pretty accurate for their diagnosis of disease and so forth . . . so, I enjoy it because I worked around a lot of that and it just kinda' keeps me in the business. I guess.

Her husband appeared to recognize the desirability of using television as a fantasy stimulant for his wife. Although his wife knew full well what times her favorites were televised, he reminded her of these and encouraged her to watch. He even changed the television channel from "Monday Night Football" in order to insure that she watched a medical program which was presented by a competing network at the same time. His encouragement of her participation in the dream world which their marriage and child raising denied her may have helped him dismiss whatever guilt he harbored for having been, in part, responsible for curtailing her vocational opportunities.

Social Learning
Television is widely regarded as a resource for learning (Lyle, 1972). Of special interest here are the social uses made of the many opportunities for learning from television. Much information for daily living is available from the electronic media. Obvious examples are the consumer and political spot messages which provide an agenda for decision making, actions which have important implications for the society, the family unit, and the individual (Schiller, 1973; Mander, 1977). But more subtle learning experiences have been noted as well. Early studies of the soap operas demonstrated that these melodramas provide practical suggestions for social interaction which are widely imitated by audience members (Lazarsfeld & Stanton, 1949; Herzog, 1944). These imitations may be useful in the solving of family problems which bear resemblance to difficulties resolved in television dramas. At the very least, television provides an abundance of role models which audience members find socially useful.

Parents encourage their children to watch television game shows, public television, or network specials as substitute school experiences. Themes and values implicit in television programs are used by the parents to educate their children about the topics being presented in accord with their own view of the world. In this way, the value system of the parent is transmitted to the child and attitudes already in place are reinforced (Katzman, 1972).

Scholarly research on how individuals learn from the mass media, then pass the information along in predictable interpersonal diffusion patterns, dates back more than 30 years (Lazarsfeld, Berelson, & Gaudet, 1948;

Merton, 1949; Berelson, Lazarsfeld, & McPhee, 1954; Katz & Lazarsfeld, 1962). The two-step flow and the multistep flow theories implied that opinion leaders, who are heavy media consumers in their areas of expertise, learn much about their specialities from television and other media. These informational experts then transmit their knowledge to a network of human acquaintances.

In accomplishing the information-dissemination task, opinion leaders use information from the media to not only educate their friends, acquaintances, or coworkers, but also to assert themselves as valued members of society. The opinion leader uses television and other media to help create and then fulfill an interpersonal role which may have the effect of demonstrating competence.

Competence/Dominance

There are a variety of ways in which television provides unique opportunities for the demonstration of competence by means of family role fulfillment. The regulation of childrens' television viewing by a parent is one means for accomplishing this objective. For those adults who desire to supervise closely or restrict the flow of unwanted external information into the home, the methodical and authoriative regulating of television viewing is useful as an occasion for the undertaking of a gatekeeping function. In doing so, the parent, often the mother, makes observable to the children and spouse a correct role-determined and rule-governed action which confirms the individual as a "good parent" or "good mother." Successful enactment of the television regulatory function directs media experiences of the children into forms which are consistent with the parents' moral perspective. Simultaneously, the parent asserts an expected jurisdictional act which confirms proper performance of a particular family role.

The symbolic portrayal of roles by television characters may confirm similar roles which are undertaken by audience members. When behavior by an actor or actress on television resembles the way in which the viewer behaves under similar circumstances, the experience may be useful to the viewer as a means for demonstrating role competence to the other audience members. Similarly, a family member may use television in order to learn acceptable role behavior, then imitate this behavior in a way which results in acceptance of the role enactment by other family members.

The role of a missing parent can be played by a television character. It is convenient in some single-parent families for the adult who is present to encourage the watching of particular television programs where a favored image of the missing parent is regularly presented. Implicitly, the role of the lone parent can be preserved or clarified as the substitute parent's complementary actions are portrayed on the screen.

Some viewers capitalize on the one-way nature of television by verbally assaulting the characters, newscasters, or commercials. One man who was observed constantly disagreed out loud with the evening news reports on television. He clarified the reports and chided the announcer for not knowing the "real facts." Vocal criticisms of programs or commercial announcements also serve as ways for viewers to reassure one another that, despite the fact that they are now watching, they know how *bad* television is, a self-promoting evaluation.

In another case, a housewife who majored in French in college repeatedly corrected the poor pronunciation of French words uttered by an American actor who attempted to masquerade as a Frenchman. Gans, in a study of poor Italian families in Boston, found that his subjects received attention from other viewers when they noticed that activities on the screen were technically unfeasible or when they pointed out "anachronisms or mistakes [that] appear in the plot" (Gans, 1962, p. 194).

A television viewer may or may not use the medium to demonstrate competence for purposes of dominating other family members. But, cases in which this occurs are numerous in ethnographic research. For instance, family members often use television as a validator of contested information, thereby demonstrating intellectual competence. In one family, for example, the capture and arrest of William and Emily Harris of the Symbionese Liberation Army was a topic of conversation at the dinner table on the evening the couple was apprehended in San Francisco. There were conflicting reports among family members as to whether or not Patty Hearst had also been captured. The highly authoritarian father had heard an early report on radio that only the Harrises had been arrested. He had not learned the later news that Hearst had been taken into the custody of police as well. His wife and daughter *both* told him that they had heard on the car radio that Hearst had been arrested too. He arrogantly denied the validity of their reports and said that the family could find out the "true situation" by watching the news on television. The husband later was embarrassed to discover on the news that Hearst had indeed been apprehended, a turn of events which falsified his version of the incident. "See," his wife said emphatically when the news was revealed. "We were right! I told you that Patty Hearst had been caught and you wouldn't believe me." The medium had confirmed her and disconfirmed him on the issue. A few minutes later television provided an opportunity for him to recapture his dominant position. During a commercial message, he voiced an opinion about some attribute of the product which was being promoted. His wife disagreed. Seconds later the television announcer on the commercial gave information which supported the husband. He quickly and defiantly turned to his wife and said, "I don't talk much. But when I do you should listen."

Men, women, boys, and girls use television to communicate to each other attitudes toward the appropriateness of male and female behavior with respect to sex roles. Teenaged boys were observed shouting criticism at the female detectives on the program "Charlie's Angels" with their sisters in the room. The program provided an opportunity for the boys to vocalize their negative feelings about the qualifications of the television actresses for doing "men's work." Similarly, adolescent girls competed to correctly identify wardrobe fashions of various historical periods during a program which featured this topic. The girls tried to identify the periods before the announcer on the program did so. Correct identification gave status to the girl who guessed right, validating her as a relative expert on women's fashions and placing her in an esteemed position in the eyes of her peers.

Interpersonal dominance strategies involve television in other ways. Television viewing in many homes is authoritatively granted or taken away as a reward or punishment. Adults and children argue to decide who will watch what programs, thereby creating an opportunity for the airing of personal differences. For family members who are angered by each other, television viewing (the program decision-making process or the viewing experience) provides incessant opportunities for argument, provoking possible dominance struggles among family members.

More subtle uses of the medium are made by some viewers to influence other audience members. In one case, a married couple watched a television program in which the lead actor passionately embraced a young woman. The husband at home asked his wife during this scene if the two on the screen were married. She answered, "Do they look married to you?" They both laughed quietly without taking their eyes off the screen. By coorienting and commenting on the television program, these family members spoke to each other indirectly, but made their positions about relational matters clearly known.

Conclusions

Although the natural television audience, the family, has been identified in social theorizing as a "unit of interacting personalities" since the work of

Burgess (1926), the study of various family processes as they occur at home has seldom been tried. Further, researchers who study family behavior today have recognized that "communication is increasingly emphasized as both the keystone of family interaction and the key to understanding family dynamics" (Anderson & Carter, 1974, p. 111). Hopefully, this paper has helped demonstrate that the methods which individuals construct, using television and other media, constitute important subsets of unique and useful communicative behaviors which are central to family life. . . .

Notes

1. Ethnomethodology is, in a general sense, a manner for conducting social research since it is a way of thinking about social structure and process. But, the term is intended to direct researchers to observation and interpretation of the social "methods" of their subjects as the substance for analysis, particularly routine behaviors which are often overlooked. The "method" in "ethnomethodology" refers to the ways in which people construct their social realities, not to a research strategy.

2. For family research, a one-week-long observation period per family is most efficient. Henry (1965, pp. xv–xxiii) makes a convincing argument for this length of observation. Certainly some additional data would be gathered in a longer stay, but the researcher must utilize the time wisely in order to maximize sample size while simultaneously retrieving the most valuable data.

PAUL MESSARIS

Parents, Children, and Television

This essay, like many others, is concerned with the effects of television on children, but what is different is the consideration of the role of parent within child-medium interaction. Paul Messaris deals with some intriguing issues such as the role of television in shaping our perceptions of reality and the role of parents in shaping our perceptions of television reality. Think of your early childhood experiences with this medium. How did you learn to distinguish the make-believe from the real, the commercial from the program, the drama from the news? Can you remember at what age? Are you still sometimes unsure? Did your parents use television characters and situations to teach you about the "real" world? Professor Messaris tells us the answers given by mothers to these and similar questions.

One of the things that make the effects of television on children so complicated to study is the fact that children don't respond to television in a social vacuum.[1] A child's social relationships—in particular, the relationship between parents and children—can influence the child's response to television in a variety of ways. For example, parents' opinions about violence have been found to make a difference in children's reactions to violence on TV. On the other hand, relationships between parents and children may themselves be influenced in several ways by television. In particular, as we will see below, situations and issues that a child has been exposed to on television can become important topics of parent-child discussions. In view of these complications, perhaps the most adequate way to summarize the situation is to say that what a child gets out of his or her relationship with TV depends on a broader set of relationships including not just the medium and the child but also, at the very least, the child's parents. The aim of this chapter is to investigate some consequences of the parent-child-television relationship.

This investigation will be divided into two parts, corresponding to two kinds of things children may learn as a result of their joint relationship with television and their parents: on the one hand, how to perceive the world; on the other hand, how to behave toward it. More specifically, our

This article was written expressly for the present volume. Copyright © 1982 by Paul Messaris.

first concern will be with the various ways in which parents and television together may contribute to a child's developing stock of knowledge about the real world and, in particular, the child's sense of the nature of society and social relationships. Second, we will sift through some of the evidence on a question that many writers about television have examined: To what extent can children's imitation of violence or other kinds of behavior seen on TV be influenced by their parents?

In addition to drawing on past research where appropriate, our discussion of these issues will be based to a great extent on a recent study whose aim was to find out what kinds of things parents and children talk about in reference to television.[2] The study consisted of a series of exploratory, open-ended interviews with mothers of grade-school-age and younger children. A total of 119 mothers were interviewed, all of them residents of the Philadelphia area. Each interviewee was asked some thirty questions about various kinds of TV-related talk. For example: "Do you ever tell your children that something on TV is unrealistic, that things wouldn't happen like that in real life?" "Do your children ever ask you to explain something they didn't understand in a TV program?" "Do you ever find it convenient to use an example from TV to teach your children how they should act— or how not to act?" Whenever a mother said that a particular kind of discussion had occurred in her own family, our interviewers would ask for detailed examples of the incidents in question. In an exploratory study like this one, the examples themselves are what counts, of course, rather than the initial "yes" or "no." Several of these examples will be used to flesh out the discussion that follows.

Parents, TV, and Children's Perceptions of Reality

Through television, a child can be exposed to a constant stream of images about things outside his or her own experience. It is often assumed that these images make important contributions to children's notions of what the world is like. However—contrary to popular assumptions—the learning process involved here may rarely be simply a matter of believing everything one sees. Rather, it seems that parents are often crucially involved in this learning process and that children themselves actively rely on parents in using material from television to construct a picture of the real world. There are at least three important ways in which parents may contribute to their children's formation of television-based world-views: First, parents may have to teach a child the distinction between various categories of

programming—e.g., fantasy, "realistic" fiction, news, documentaries, etc.—
each of which has a different kind of relationship to the real world. Second,
once a child has learned this general distinction, parents may be called
upon to perform a more specific task: since there is wide variation within
program types in the degree to which any one program accurately reflects
some aspect of reality, parents may play the role of validators of specific
portrayals. Finally, a parent may supplement information provided on television, by giving the child background data, pointing out connections between events, and so forth. We will examine each of these three possibilities separately.

Categories of Programming and Their Relationship to Reality

One of the mothers in our interviews described the following problem:
Her five-year-old son had noticed that actors who "die" in one TV program often "come back to life" in other programs, commercials, or reruns.
So, when one of the family's dogs was killed in a fight, the son wanted to
know when the dog was going to come back. By her own account, this
mother had found it very difficult to clear up her child's confusion. The
reason for this difficulty may perhaps be clear: merely telling the child that
in real life people or animals don't return from the dead could not have
been enough to "set him straight" on all aspects of his misconception of
the situation. Unless a child already knows that there is such a thing as a
distinction between "real life" and "fiction," the statement that a particular event doesn't occur in real life must be meaningless. Learning this distinction itself, then, may be a prerequisite to any discussion of whether
something observed on TV can occur in real life or not. But there is also
another aspect to this child's confusion. As the example makes clear, the
child did not understand the distinction between one program and the next
or between fiction, commercials, etc. Consequently, a blanket statement
about the difference between "fiction" and "reality" would also have been
bound to mislead him, since it is more than likely that he would have had
no notion of which aspects of TV are fictional and which are not.

The general point that this example should make clear is that a child's
mastery of the relationship between TV and reality must begin with the
formation of categories: one kind of program must be distinguished from
another, and, for each type, the appropriate distinction between its contents and reality must be learned. How does this learning occur? On the
one hand, the child's general cognitive development appears to play a role.[3]
On the other hand, the specific intervention of parents—or older siblings,
when they are available—also seems to be a crucial part of this process.

From our interviews with mothers, it is possible to derive a rough estimate of the stages that children go through in learning about these matters. There are obviously many distinctions to be learned, but all of these can be subsumed under two overriding principles, namely, that TV as a whole is distinct from reality and that TV programming itself can be subdivided into various categories. Our interviews indicate that these two general principles are frequently learned in connection with the following more specific distinctions: first, an initial distinction between the "fantasy" part of TV and the real world; second, within TV, a distinction between fictional and "reality" programming (news, documentaries, etc.).

The first of these distinctions appears to be the earliest one that parents try to impress on their children, and the reasons for its urgency are clear: first, parents are often anxious about the possibility that a child will hurt himself or herself by trying to imitate some of the impossible feats shown in "superhero" programs or cartoons. For example, one mother told us that she was repeatedly trying to impress on her children (ages two and five) that, "in real life, you could never run over someone with a car and they bounce back up, you know, after being flattened like a pancake." Another made the following familiar point: "I'm always telling him that Spiderman and Superman can't fly because I don't want him leaping out of any windows on me. 'If your daddy can't do it, it can't be done!' " (The child in this case was a five-year-old). A second reason for parents' concern over the TV-reality distinction is the frequent need to soothe children's fears of monsters, vampires, and other nonexistent creatures. In the following case, for example, a mother explains how she and her husband tried to deal with her six-year-old son's fear of the Wicked Witch's cackle in "The Wizard of Oz," which the child had seen on TV:

> So what we would do is cackle. You know, try to, uh, show that it's—it's just, um, a play put on or an act, that there aren't any witches, you know, around, that *I* can cackle and make myself look like a witch just like she can. You know, we try to deal with it that way.

The crucial lesson that a child presumably derives from such discussions is that the things shown on TV are of a different kind from the rest of his or her experience. Much remains to be learned, of course, about the precise nature of the relationship between these two realms, but this basic distinction seems to be the starting point for all subsequent learning. However, a second essential building block is also necessary for this kind of learning, namely, the notion that TV programming itself is divided into various categories. From our interviewees' accounts, it appears that the way in which this second notion is introduced is frequently as a partial "retraction" of the lesson that children derive from the kinds of discussions cited above. In other words, what seems to happen is that children are often left with the impression that *all* of TV is fantasy or fiction, so that the first step toward distinctions between programming types is the realization that some of TV is not fictional at all. This situation is illustrated in the following example of a mother's reminiscence about an event that occurred when her oldest child was about six or seven and her youngest about two or three:

> I remember during the Viet Nam war getting very upset: We were watching television, the news, while we were eating dinner. And they were showing the children and women dead in the village and I—I started crying, and I couldn't eat my dinner. And the kids got very upset. It wasn't the thing to watch at dinnertime, actually. . . . I explained to them that everything that you see on television isn't make-believe. The news is real. And . . . it hit cold to them that this was real that they were looking at. And it upset them terribly.

In ways like this, then, children learn that there are different categories of TV programming, each with its own relationship to the real world. Many specific distinctions have to be constructed on the basis of this general principle; and, in view of the subtlety of some of them (for example, "docudrama" vs. "regular" drama vs. documentary; "live" broadcasts vs. videotapes[4]), it is probably safe to say that at some point many parents are themselves faced with situations that they don't fully comprehend.

The Accuracy and Representativeness of TV Portrayals of Reality

Once a child has grasped the basic notion of a distinction among categories of programs, a different kind of problem presents itself to him or her. This is the problem of the degree to which a specific program or portrayal is accurate or representative in its depiction of reality. In other words, the issue is no longer one of constructing categories but, instead, that of judging specific items within any one category. For example, a child may want to know whether conditions under slavery were really as bad as shown on "Roots"; whether big-city life is really as dangerous as it seems to be on various police shows; and so forth. According to the mothers in our interviews, questions of this sort are a frequent topic of parent-child discussions. By providing answers to such questions, parents may play a significant role in their children's use of television as an instrument for exploring the nature of the real world.

As one might expect, children seem particularly likely to ask their parents questions about images that have troubled them in some way. Portrayals of evil characters, of human or animal suffering, of various kinds of dangers were often mentioned by our interviewees as topics of children's questions. However, the things that children found disturbing weren't always negative in themselves. Quite frequently, children also seemed threatened by images of wealth or happiness that contradicted their own circumstances in life. In cases like these, too, parents would be asked to comment about the accuracy of the troubling image. We will look at some instances of this kind of situation first, before discussing how parents deal with more negative portrayals.

Many observers have pointed out that the population of the "television world" tends to be wealthier than its real-life "counterpart"[5] and that less well-to-do TV viewers, in particular, may be confronted with a considerable disparity between their own life-styles and what they see on the screen.[6] Furthermore, aside from the issue of wealth, the quality of parent-child relationships in many family shows—especially the calm rationality of parents—can also be enviably different from the real-life home environment of many younger viewers. Accordingly, many of our interviewees described instances in which they had felt the need to emphasize to their children that such images are exaggerations and that one shouldn't expect real life to be as glamorous, pleasant, etc. For example, one mother described her reaction to hearing her eleven-year-old daughter wish for a life and a job like that of the "bionic woman":

> I do remember then going into a discussion of, you know, things always being pretty nice and the jobs on TV always being famous and adventurous and that, and I told them that, you know, that that just is not so all the time. Everything looks glamorous on TV, but in real life it's not like that every day.

The program our interviewees mentioned most often in this vein was "The Brady Bunch," which was being shown in reruns every weekday afternoon during the period in which these interviews were being conducted. These are some of the things mothers said about this program:

> You know, like the Brady Bunch . . . it's so, uh, gingerbready, that show, you know. They don't make—really make it real, you know. Everything is like fluffed over, like Ozzie and Harriet. The father's always in a suit and the mother's always dressed up with her hair done. I mean, who does their housecleaning like that, you know? And you try to point out to them that that's not really real life.

> Their rec room was so clean. There were never any dishes in the sink. You never see anybody vacuuming. You never see anybody wearing old clothes, jeans, and a sweatshirt.

What seems to be happening in these cases, then, is an attempt by mothers to dampen possible unrealistic expectations that a program might create for a child, although a touch of resentment also appears to be operating here, particularly in the "Brady Bunch" examples. Both of these ingredients are apparent in mothers' comments about how their children respond to programs like "The Brady Bunch": "I think that at one point he must have felt very deprived because he wasn't living in a house like the Brady Bunch." "The children seem to feel that that's reality and what they're living in is somehow a mistake." Whether these perceptions on the part of the mothers are accurate or not is, of course, an open question, although mothers did say that their children ask them such things as "How come you don't solve things like Mrs. Brady?" or complain that "Mrs. Brady wouldn't do it like that." In other words, mothers who tell their children that portrayals like that of the "Brady Bunch" are exaggerated or false may be doing more than protecting their children from painful disillusionment with reality. They may also be protecting their own families from the strain that can be caused by a child's resentment.[7]

We can now turn to cases in which parents and children confront the darker side of the world of television: portrayals of evil and crime, suffering and danger. Here, too, mothers' comments to their children about these troubling visions contained a clear element of protectiveness. In these cases, however, this protectiveness typically led to confirmation, rather than negation, of the accuracy of the images in question. In other words, in apparent attempts to warn their children about the dangers of the real world—or, at least, that aspect of it that appears on TV—mothers would typically tell their children that TV's troubling portrayals of a cruel and dangerous reality were true. In both of the examples that follow, the children were entering adolescence:

> Well, when you see, uh, if you'll excuse the expression, a real bastard, um, you know, uh, I guess something like—like that fellow on "Dallas," not that they watch it, uh, "Well, can people really be that rotten and mean?" And, uh, they've seen it on television and it is true. It does happen. Yeah, we've referred to that. People do get murdered.

> Like these, this thing they had on the runaway kids: We had a big discussion about that because I told him that, you know, the kids, like, they do run away, they do get in trouble, and, you know, they do get in things like this white slavery stuff. You know, I said they do abuse them and all, you know, like we've had a good discussion about that. . . . Well, he wanted to know if it was really true there, you know, if that does really happen to kids. . . . I told him that stuff is true, that, you know, boys, they do get into, you know—or

they sell their bodies. I said, I call that white slavery that you have to do things for other people, you know, with sex and all. I says, it's not like you're clean-ing, you know, it's that kind of thing. I said, and this stuff really does happen when kids run away.

As this second example shows, warnings of this kind may also contain implicit statements about the advantages of one's own family life. This element is present more explicitly in the following example, from the mother of a ten-year-old girl:

They had a special on child abuse and, uh, I let them watch it, you know, and—I mean, this really sounds terrible, but, like, I told her, I said, "You are really lucky, 'cause there are parents that treat their children like that." You know, so I mean, I have done things like that, which probably sounds cruel to you.

In other words, these comments also seem to have the double element which we saw in parents' dealings with "positive" programs like "The Brady Bunch": On the one hand, the parents appear to be trying to make sure that their children will develop adequate images of the good and bad sides of the outside world. At the same time, however, the parents also appear to be concerned with strengthening their own families, either by playing down a threatening difference between TV and their own circum-stances or by playing up a difference which is to their advantage.

Parental Supplementation of TV Information

TV programming is typically designed to be compatible with even the most impoverished stock of information on the part of the viewer. Nevertheless, younger TV viewers are bound to encounter situations with unfamiliar premises from time to time. When that does happen, parents are likely to be the ones turned to for an account of the "background" information that the child doesn't have—although older brothers or sisters are also pressed into this kind of service. In our interviews with mothers, this kind of TV-related discussion—providing supplementary information—turned out to have been a very common experience. Four-fifths of the mothers described detailed incidents of this sort.

The kinds of information that mothers said they had provided in con-nection with TV varied widely, but it is possible to make a rough distinc-tion between two general categories: on the one hand, information that all—or almost all—people acquire as they grow up; and, on the other hand, more "specialized" information, either of a "scholarly" kind (histor-ical, scientific, etc.) or having to do with specific occupations, ethnic groups,

etc. The first of these two categories includes such issues as human reproduction (where babies come from, how they are born), death, sex (and
rape, adultery, prostitution, venereal disease, etc.), marriage and divorce,
illness and drug addiction, delinquency and crime, etc. For example, one
mother told us that, when a program on childbirth had been shown on
television, her seven-year-old daughter had watched it with her and "she
literally asked me everything from beginning to end about the show." Another mother remembered that, after her children had seen a funeral on
television, "they wanted to know, you know, 'Does everybody die? When
do they die?' " and she had to "explain it all to them." A third mother
told us that her children had assumed, because of the prevalence of divorced parents on TV shows, that divorce is a standard part of marriage
and wanted to know when their own parents were going to get divorced.

Naturally, parents vary in the degree to which they are willing to answer
questions on some of these topics, especially when sex is somehow involved. Whereas one mother told us that her ten-year-old daughter's questions about sex on TV were always answered fully ("We don't hide anything or hold anything back"), another described the following "non-
answer" to a sex-related question:

> Once he saw a comic show and there was a line that said something like, "Sex
> is like peanuts. Once you start eating them you can't stop." And everyone
> laughed. . . . He repeated it a couple of times . . . "peanuts . . ." and he
> asked me, "What does that really mean?" And I said, "I can't really explain
> it but it's as being though something you start and it's hard to stop. It's like
> when you start eating a cracker. Sometimes you want to keep eating some
> crackers." But that's as far as it went.

What difference does it make how a parent answers this kind of question?
More generally, what is the consequence of children's questions and parents' answers on these "adult" topics?[8] At first blush, it might seem that,
to the extent that parents do in fact give their children full details on such
topics, they are "speeding up" the children's entry into the informational
world of adulthood. From this point of view, one could say that television,
by injecting these "adult" topics into parent-child discussions, is causing
children to "grow up" before their time.[9] However, one should be cau-
tious in drawing such a conclusion. Once children are in school, information (and misinformation) on sex and other "adult" topics can be transmitted "horizontally" among children of the same age, so that any one
child's reliance on information from "above" (parents, older siblings,
"adult" media) is lessened considerably. In this kind of situation, a par-

ent's refusal to deal with a certain topic at home may be of little consequence to the child's stock of information on that topic. This situation is
illustrated in the following quotation from our interviews:

> I told her that it was something I didn't think she was old enough to under-
> stand or really comprehend. And I said, there is so much in some of these sex
> movies . . . the shame of it is they leave nothing to the imagination. I think
> it's a mystery that should be left a mystery to some people. Leave a little bit
> to be desired. They show everything. I just said I didn't think at that time she
> was old enough. She thought I was ridiculous. She said she understands and
> other children have seen it and her friends watch this and that. . . .

In cases of this sort, then, television and the parent may not be important
sources of information on a particular issue. This is not to say, of course,
that the nature of the interaction between parent and child is a trivial
matter in such cases. As the above example suggests ("She thought I was
ridiculous"), such interactions can have important consequences for the
parent-child relationship itself.

Aside from asking TV-inspired questions about "adult" topics, children
also question their parents about matters that are unfamiliar in a different
way: distant times and places, unencountered religious practices or ethnic
groups, scientific principles and findings. For example:

> I was watching "Dr. Zhivago" and my eleven-year-old son was with me, and
> he was discussing—he wanted to know how they could do certain things, uh,
> take over their houses in Russia and capture him and take him to the army,
> and I had to explain to him the difference in cultures, and what democracy is
> and what communism is, and he understood what I was telling him.

Other mothers described discussions of such things as the American Western migration (in connection with "Little House on the Prairie"), the economic system of the South under slavery (in connection with "Roots"), the
meaning of the Jewish Seder (in connection with "Holocaust"), etc.

This kind of parental involvement in children's television viewing is often
encouraged by people concerned with the educational potential of television. Experiments in which an adult watches television with a group of
children and supplies interpretive commentary suggest that children absorb
televised information better under such circumstances than when they are
viewing alone.[10] But the benefits to the child of this kind of behavior may
extend far beyond the specific information gleaned from a particular program or set of parental comments. It can be argued that, when a parent
responds positively to a child's request for this kind of "specialized" information about a TV program, two "lessons" are being conveyed to the

child: in addition to gaining the specific information requested, the child is also being reinforced in his or her use of TV as a "springboard" for the intellectual mastery of new areas of knowledge. Indeed, this reinforcement can probably occur even if the parent does not have the information herself, so long as the child's intellectual curiosity is rewarded. A good example of this in our interviews was the case of a mother who watches "Nova" with her grade-school son and helps him dig through the encyclopedia for explanations of things which neither of them may have understood. To the extent that it successfully reinforces a child's tendencies for intellectual exploration, parental behavior of this kind must have far greater consequences for a child's view of the world than any specific item of knowledge would be likely to have. What this behavior can cultivate in the child is a view of the world as a realm to be conquered through the exercise of one's mind. Few particular aspects of reality can be more important than this general view.

Research in progress by several scholars indicates that the kind of TV-related behavior described above is most likely to be found, not surprisingly, in families in which there is a more general tendency to support intellectual flexibility and an uncompromising pursuit of knowledge.[11] Related work by other researchers has also supported a connection between this kind of family environment and a more information-seeking (rather than entertainment-oriented) approach to television.[12] It is also worth noting that sociologists concerned with the ultimate consequences of this general style of parental behavior have argued that it is particularly likely to facilitate achievement in children's later lives, since the pursuit of intellectual mastery is an adaptive trait in a society which places high value on professional occupations.[13] However, these broader implications of the behavior we are examining here are mere speculation at this point.

Parents, TV, and Children's Behavioral Learning

Do children learn to behave in one way or another by imitating what they see on television? This question has occupied communication researchers for some twenty years. Most of this research has dealt with the imitation of aggression, although investigators have increasingly been looking at the subject of "prosocial" behavior too: helping other people, sharing things, etc. The most common interpretation of all of this research is that television can indeed—at least in principle—affect children's behavior, although the actual extent of this effect may not always be large and is, in any case, difficult to measure. As for the possible influence of parents on children's responses to TV, the consensus seems to be that parents can modify or block the effects of TV if they make an active effort to that end,[14] but that otherwise children are "at the mercy" of the medium. In the following discussion, however, a somewhat different position will be presented.[15] What will be argued here is that the common view of these matters may have got things the wrong way around: In other words, it may be the case that imitation doesn't occur at all unless parents (or other people) have previously encouraged a child—knowingly or not—to engage in the kind of behavior being imitated. According to this position, then, parental involvement is a prerequisite for imitation, rather than simply a possible modifier of its occurrence. Although this position certainly represents a minority view, there is much evidence that points in its direction.

In examining this position, we will be drawing primarily on findings from past research, rather than on the interviews that we have used up to this point. In particular, because of the considerable detail that has been covered in research on aggression, we will focus our discussion on that aspect of imitation, with the understanding that what is said about aggression should be taken to apply, in many respects, to other kinds of behavior as well. The starting point in any discussion of visually mediated aggression is usually the work of Albert Bandura and his colleagues.[16] In a series of experiments beginning in the early 1960s, these investigators demonstrated that children who have seen a small-screen, TV-like film of a man assaulting a Bobo doll in various ways are more likely to do the same kinds of things to a Bobo doll themselves than children who haven't seen the film. The conclusion that is usually drawn from these experiments is that the children learned the aggressive behavior from the film. In other words, it is concluded on the basis of this kind of evidence that children can pick up behavioral patterns purely from visual presentations. The implication, of course, is that, unless parents intervene, children who watch a lot of violence on TV may turn into violent people themselves.

One of the reasons for the stir caused by findings of this sort is that they seem to go against a long- and widely-held psychological principle according to which children cannot learn new forms of behavior unless their environment actively reinforces what they are learning.[17] The experiments described above appear to contradict this principle, since the children in the experiments seem to be learning to be aggressive without any environmental reinforcement: a TV or movie screen cannot respond to them, no matter what they do. However, this contradiction may be an illusion. To begin with, we must remember that the children who participated in these experiments obviously had past histories, which would have included their parents' responses to previous aggression on their own part. To what extent did these past experiences with aggression influence their behavior in the experimental setting? Many violence researchers would argue that such previous influence couldn't be operating in the experiments, because the kinds of aggression that children were being tested on (lassoing a Bobo doll with a hula-hoop, for example) were too unlikely to have occurred in a child's previous experience. But this argument is less impregnable than it may sound: it could well be that the learning of one kind of aggression carries over into another kind too—in other words, that what one learns is "aggression" in general. It is worth pointing out, for example, that in experiments in which children were tested on forms of aggression that were deliberately different from what they had seen on TV, strong relationships between exposure and subsequent aggression were found all the same.[18] In order to find out what role prior experience could have played in these experiments, then, we must go to studies that have examined these things directly.

One set of studies has looked at the connection between a child's past history of aggressiveness and his response to aggressive TV in an experimental setting. These studies did not examine the role of parents in the children's previous experiences with aggression, but it is probably safe to assume that, where parents did exist, they were an important source of influence in the development of the child's aggressive tendencies.[19] In any case, what these studies show is that a child's pre-existing aggressive tendencies appear to make a considerable difference to the child's response to an aggressive TV "diet." The less aggressive a child was initially, the less likely he was to respond aggressively to the televised aggression—and, in fact, in some cases the less aggressive children didn't respond aggressively at all.[20] What this tells us, in other words, is that previous environmental reinforcement does indeed seem to be necessary for imitation, and that the movies or TV programs used in these experiments were probably triggering behavior that had already been learned, rather than teaching children something new.

As to the role of parents in the development of the tendencies that a violent TV program can then operate upon, several studies provide relevant evidence. Each of these studies has looked at the influence of family environment on the relationship between adolescents' real-life aggressiveness and their real-life exposure to aggressiveness on TV. In each case, what has been found is that this relationship becomes weaker or stronger depending on various aspects of parental behavior: for example, how strongly parents emphasize nonaggression,[21] how clear a picture they have conveyed to their children of their stance on aggression,[22] what kinds of means (aggressive or otherwise) they use to discipline their children,[23] and so forth. These studies give us grounds for concluding, therefore, that children's aggressive responses to violence on TV depend on tendencies developed in the course of a child's interactions with his or her parents.

More generally, the thrust of this whole argument has been that parents are probably much more intimately involved in their children's imitative responses to TV than most people think. Whereas the typical assumption is that parents influence their children's imitations only when they make a deliberate effort to do so, the position outlined above is that prior parental reinforcement of behavior may be indispensable to subsequent imitation from TV, regardless of any deliberate parental intervention in the child's experience with TV itself. In other words, even if a parent's behavior toward the child is never explicitly concerned with television, a child's imitation of television may depend crucially on previous parental influence on the child's behavior. It goes without saying, of course, that these conclusions are tentative, since the findings we have examined were concerned exclusively with aggressive behavior and since, moreover, the amount of space available to us has not permitted us to examine possible counterarguments[24] in detail.

Nothing that has been said so far should be taken to imply that parents cannot—or do not—control their children's behavioral responses to TV through deliberate intervention as well—in other words, through comments, advice, etc., referring directly to TV, as opposed to the more general kind of influence we have examined above. Our own interviews with parents yielded numerous examples of attempted control of this sort. Among other things, parents described warning their children not to imitate the behavior of "the Fonz" (in this parent's words, "he's such a creep!"); the fictional character played by Gary Coleman ("that little guy Gary Coleman is just . . . he's rude. I don't care what anybody says, but if any kid ever talked to me the way he did, he'd be wearing his teeth on the back of his head"); the nose-picking teenagers in "Saturday Night Live" ("you're trying to teach children not to do it and they make a joke out of it"); or the phrase "Watch it, sucker!" from "Sanford and Son." On the other hand, many parents also described instances in which they had encouraged imitation, rather than the opposite. For example, one mother told us that she often used characters from "Romper Room" as behavioral models for her three-year-old daughter:

> If she'll stick out her tongue or spit, I'll tell her, "Now, do the children in Miss Nancy's classroom spit and stick out their tongues?" . . . Um, I use that a lot with my middle one because on "Romper Room" they're all good. They're all goodies.

Another mother described a long pep talk aimed at getting her son to imitate the hard work which must have been involved in the achievements of a certain winter Olympics champion:

> These people were not born, uh, jumping off cliffs and mountains and, uh, on skates and what have you. A lot of hard work, a lot of desire, a lot of push, and that's the end result.

How effective is this kind of advice in encouraging or discouraging children's imitations of TV? The question has been studied systematically in a pair of related experiments.[25] In these experiments, an adult member of the experimental team would sit with a child during the screening of a violent film and would make either disapproving comments ("He shouldn't do that"; "That's wrong"; "That's awful"), approving comments ("Boy, look at him go"; "He sure is a tough guy"; "That's really something"), or no comments at all. The victim in these films was a Bobo doll, shown being hit with a hammer, kicked around, etc. After the screening, the child would be allowed to play in a room containing, among other things, a Bobo doll and various likely weapons. The object of the experiments, of course, was to determine if the adult's comments had any influence on the child's imitative aggression. The findings turned out to depend on the children's age. With younger children (five-year-olds), the adult's comments seemed to make a difference only if the adult stayed with the child in the playroom during the period in which imitation was being measured. With older children (ten-year-olds), however, the influence persisted even after the departure of the adult "commentator." In both age groups, the direction of the influence was what one would expect: the adult's approving comments appeared to encourage imitation, while the disapproving comments discouraged it.

 These results suggest fairly clearly that parental control of imitation through direct involvement in a child's TV viewing is feasible. In view of the rudimentary "commentary" used in these experiments, it should be added that there is some indirect evidence that more extensive attempts to reason with a child are also effective means of controlling responses to TV in the parents' absence, whereas authority-based commands are not.[26] It need hardly be added, of course, that a fool-proof way of preventing imitation is to block exposure in the first place. Although studies have indicated that parents do not generally exercise much direct control over their children's program choices,[27] some specific programs are exceptions to the rule. For example, many of the mothers in our interviews told us that they prevented their children from watching "Three's Company" because of its presentation of cohabitation and, in one mother's view, the fact that "it's promoting gaiety." To the extent that parents succeed in preventing their children's exposure to such material, they are also by definition precluding the possibility of imitation.

Summary

The aim of this chapter has been to show that parents may play a crucial role in determining what children learn from television. Two aspects of learning were examined: first, the development of the child's perceptions of reality; second, behavioral learning through imitation. With regard to the first of these, the following points were made: (1) Parental instruction appears to be a vital ingredient in the process by which children come to grips with the distinction between categories of programming and with the relationship of each category to the real world. (2) By conforming or denying the accuracy of specific programs or portrayals, parents may add a filter of their own to the world-view that a child extracts from television. (3) Since parents are often called upon to supplement the information provided in a television program, the final lesson that a child extracts from the viewing experience may be a joint product of what was shown on the screen and what was provided by the parent. With regard to children's behavioral learning through the imitation of things seen on television, the following argument was made: there is considerable evidence in favor of the notion that children's imitation of visual images does not occur at all unless the behavior in question has already been reinforced by parents (or other people with whom a child has had a substantial history of interaction). Consequently, previous parental encouragement or discouragement of a certain kind of behavior may crucially determine whether that behavior will be imitated when a child observes it on TV. This encouragement or discouragement may be made with explicit reference to TV, but it need not be explicit to be effective. Both with regard to the perception of reality and with regard to overt behavior, then, what a child learns from television may in fact be a product of the broader relationship among medium, child, and parent.[28]

Notes

1. For other perspectives on this general point, see Steven H. Chaffee, "The Interpersonal Context of Mass Communication," in *Current Perspectives in Mass Communication Research,* eds. F. G. Kline and P. J. Tichenor (Beverly Hills: Sage Publications, 1972), pp. 95–120; J. A. Anderson, P. J. Traudt, S. R. Acker, T. P. Meyer, and T. R. Donohue, "An Ethnological Approach to a Study of Televiewing in Family Settings," Paper presented to the Western Speech Communication Association, Los Angeles, 1979; James Lull, "The Social Uses of Television," *Human Communication Research,* 6:197–209 (1980), reprinted in this volume.

2. For further details on this study, see Paul Messaris and Sari Thomas, "Social-Class Differences in Mother-Child Discussions about Television," Paper presented to the Speech Communication Association, Anaheim, 1981.

3. Leona Jaglom and Howard Gardner, "Decoding the Worlds of Television," *Studies in Visual Communication,* 7(1):33–47 (Winter 1981). See also D. B. Wackman and E. Wartella, "A Review of Cognitive Developmental Theory and Research and the Implications for Research on Children's Responses to Television," *Communication Research,* 4:203–224 (1977).

4. For a discussion of some of the complexities involved here, see Gary Gumpert, "The Ambiguity of Perception," *Et cetera,* 34 (June 1977), reprinted in this volume.

5. B. S. Greenberg, K. W. Simmons, L. Hogan, and C. K. Atkin, "The Demography of Fictional TV Characters," in *Life on Television,* ed. B. S. Greenberg (Norwood, N.J.: Ablex, 1980), pp. 35–46.

6. T. R. Donohue, T. P. Meyer, and L. L. Henke, "Black and White Children: Perceptions of TV Commercials," *Journal of Marketing,* October 1978:34–40.

7. On these points, see also Dennis Kerr, "Family Discussions about Depictions of Families on Television," Paper presented to the Conference on Culture and Communication, Philadelphia, 1981.

8. For another point of view on these issues, see Catherine E. Kirkland, "Televised Portrayals of Sexual Topics as the Basis of Parent-Child Interaction," Paper presented to the Conference on Culture and Communication, Philadelphia, 1981.

9. Joshua Meyrowitz, "Television and the Obliteration of Childhood," Paper presented to the Conference on Culture and Communication, Philadelphia, 1981.

10. C. Corder-Bolz and S. L. O'Bryant, "Can People Affect Television? Teacher vs. Program," *Journal of Communication,* 28(1):97–103 (1978); C. Corder-Bolz, "Mediation: The Role of Significant Others," *Journal of Communica-*

tion, 30(3):106–118 (1980). See also W. Andrew Collins, Brian L. Sobol, and Sally Westby, "Effects of Adult Commentary on Children's Comprehension and Inferences about a Televised Aggressive Portrayal," *Child Development*, 52:158–163 (1981).

11. Carla Sarett, "Socialization Patterns and Children's Television- and Film-Related Play," Ph.D. Dissertation, University of Pennsylvania, 1981; Avishai Soudack, "Social Class and Parent-Child Television-Related Interaction," M. A. Thesis, Annenberg School of Communications, University of Pennsylvania, 1981.

12. Steven H. Chaffee, Jack M. McLeod, and Charles K. Atkin, "Parental Influences on Adolescent Media Use," in *Mass Communications and Youth*, eds. F. G. Kline and P. Clarke (Beverly Hills: Sage Publications, 1971). See also James Lull, "Family Communication Patterns and the Social Uses of Television," *Communication Research*, 7:319–334 (1980).

13. M. L. Kohn, *Class and Conformity* (Chicago: The University of Chicago Press, 1977).

14. A. D. Leifer, N. J. Gordon, and S. B. Graves, "Children's Television: More than Mere Entertainment," *Harvard Educational Review*, 44:213–245 (1974).

15. The author has made the same argument in Paul Messaris, "Family Processes and the Social Functions of Television," Paper presented to the Conference on Culture and Communication, Philadelphia, 1981.

16. For an overview, see Albert Bandura, "Social-Learning Theory of Identificatory Processes," in *Handbook of Socialization Theory and Research*, ed. D. A. Goslin (Chicago: Rand McNally, 1969).

17. B. F. Skinner, *Science and Human Behavior* (New York: The Free Press, 1953); J. L. Gewirtz, "Mechanisms of Social Learning: Some Roles of Stimulation and Behavior in Early Human Development," in Goslin, *op. cit.*

18. R. M. Liebert and R. A. Baron, "Short-term Effects of Televised Aggression on Children's Aggressive Behavior," in *Television and Social Behavior*, Vol. 2, eds. J. P. Murray, E. A. Rubinstein, and G. A. Comstock (Washington, D.C.: U.S. Government Printing Office, 1972).

19. Michael E. Roloff and Bradley S. Greenberg, "TV, Peer, and Parent Models for Prosocial and Antisocial Conflict Behaviors," *Human Communication Research*, 6:340–351 (Summer 1980).

20. C. K. Friedrich and A. H. Stein, "Aggressive and Prosocial Television Programs and the Natural Behavior of Preschool Children," *Monographs of the Society for Research in Child Development*, 38(4), Serial No. 151 (1973); R. D. Parke, L. Berkowitz, J. P. Leyens, S. West, and R. J. Sebastian, "Some Effects of Violent and Nonviolent Movies on the Behavior of Juvenile Delinquents," in *Advances in Experimental Social Psychology*, Vol. 10, ed. L. Berkowitz (New York: Academic Press, 1977).

21. Jack M. McLeod, Charles K. Atkin, and Steven H. Chaffee, "Adolescents, Parents, and Television Use: Adolescent Self-Report from Maryland and Wisconsin Samples," in *Television and Social Behavior*, Vol. 3, eds. G. A. Comstock and E. A. Rubinstein (Washington, D.C.: U.S. Government Printing Office,

1972); Jack M. McLeod, Charles K. Atkin, and Steven H. Chaffee, "Adolescents, Parents, and Television Use: Self-Report and Other-Report Measures from the Wisconsin Sample," *Ibid.*

22. J. R. Dominick and B. S. Greenberg, "Attitudes toward Violence: The Interaction of Television Exposure, Family Attitudes, and Social Class," in G. A. Comstock and E. A. Rubinstein, *op. cit.*

23. F. Korzenny, B. S. Greenberg, and C. K. Atkin, "Styles of Parental Disciplinary Practices as a Mediator of Children's Learning from Antisocial Television Portrayals," in *Communication Yearbook 3,* ed. D. Nimmo (New Brunswick, N.J.: Transaction Books, 1979).

24. R. M. Liebert, L. A. Cohen, C. Joyce, S. Murrel, L. Nisonoff, and S. Sonnenschein, "Effects of Television: Predispositions Revisited," *Journal of Communication, 27*(3):217–221 (1977).

25. D. J. Hicks, "Effects of Co-observer's Sanctions and Adult Presence on Imitative Aggression" *Child Development, 39*:303–309 (1968); J. E. Grusec, "Effects of Co-observer Evaluations on Imitation: A Developmental Study," *Developmental Psychology, 8*:141 (1973).

26. V. K. Prasad, T. R. Rao, and A. A. Sheikh, "Can People Affect Television? Mother vs. Commercial," *Journal of Communication, 28*(1):91–96 (1978).

27. P. J. Mohr, "Parental Guidance of Children's Viewing of Evening Television Programs," *Journal of Broadcasting, 23*:213–228 (1979).

28. For a discussion of other aspects of this issue, see Paul Messaris and Carla Sarett, "On the Consequences of Television-Related Parent-Child Interaction," *Human Communication Research, 7*:226–244 (Spring 1981).

RONALD J. FABER, JANE D. BROWN, and JACK M. McLEOD

Coming of Age in the Global Village: Television and Adolescence

Adolescence is a period of intense cognitive development, of preoccupation with future roles, and of struggles with sexual relationships. It is also a time of increased freedom of choice of media involvement. These factors, according to the authors of this essay, make adolescents' use of television a particularly important area of study. Although there is much public concern over the effects of television on very young children, little has been done to study adolescent use of the medium.

The subject of this essay is adolescent crises and tasks and the role of television in their resolution. What is discussed tells us much about how the mass media in general and television in particular affect the way individuals resolve issues related to their life stage.

Julie is a junior in high school. She is planning to take the college entrance examinations in a couple of weeks and has been studying hard in preparation for them. She becomes nervous, however, and grows increasingly unsure of her ability to score high enough to get into college. Her mother Ann, her sister Barbara, and the building superintendent Schneider are looking through college catalogues suggesting schools and potential majors for Julie. However, for Julie this only increases her fear of failing and she finally threatens them that maybe she won't go to college at all. This threat leads to an argument over the advantages and disadvantages of a college education. During the argument Julie accuses her mother of trying to run her life. She says she hasn't had time to decide what she wants to do for herself. Eventually both Julie and her mother give in a little and Julie decides to take the exams to avoid closing any options, yet does not make a commitment that she will go to college as her mother desires.

Each week, about 40 million television viewers tune in to view an episode of "One Day at a Time," from which this storyline was taken. Each week they witness the interpersonal drama (and comedy) of a three-person household made up of a young divorced woman and her two adolescent

Reprinted from Ronald J. Faber, Jane D. Brown, and Jack M. McLeod, "Coming of Age in the Global Village: Television and Adolescence," pp. 215–249 in *Children Communicating: Media and Development of Thought, Speech, Understanding*, Ellen Wartella, ed., © 1979 Sage Publications, Inc.

daughters. This show, and numerous other top rated programs like it, frequently focuses on the difficult and painful problems people face in their own lives. These shows, designed primarily as entertainment, have dramatized such serious problems as death, running away from home, falling in love for the first time, and coping with the stigma of a physical handicap. Do all viewers "take away" the same information and perceptions from this viewing experience? What is it they learn from watching such shows?

In this [essay] . . . we will argue that different viewers learn different things from such portrayals of life issues. We will develop a model of assessing mass media effects which suggests that the critical factor lies not just in how the program focuses on the problem, but rather in where the individual viewer is in relation to the problem. For example, an adolescent watching the episode of "One Day at a Time" just described may focus on how Julie deals with resolving the dilemma of future educational and career choices. The adolescent might also learn more about the specific kinds of educational options Julie is considering, as well as the arguments in favor of or against going to college. On the other hand, a mother of adolescent children would probably be more interested in the dilemma Julie's mother faces: how to persuade her daughter to take the tests and not limit her future options. However, another mother whose children are grown up and is considering what to do with the rest of her life may be most sensitive to the arguments for going to college or going to work even though they are discussed by an adolescent in the television presentation. A younger viewer might be expected to find Julie's problem interesting in that it points to issues they will soon have to grapple with themselves. Perhaps yet another viewer is currently involved in an argument with his or her own parents about an entirely different topic. This viewer might be most sensitive to Julie's discussion tactics as an example of strategies that might be used with his or her own parents.

These differences in perspective or issue salience brought with the viewer to the specific content will affect what that viewer takes away from his or her exposure. A number of other factors will intervene in the process of learning from television portrayals about life issues. Some of these factors will be discussed as important to an understanding of individual differences in media effects. A viewer who has had little personal experience with a range of occupations, for example, may more readily accept the television portrayal of various occupations, while a viewer who has had personal experience with persons in the occupation will compare the television portrayal with his or her prior understanding of the occupation. An individual's ability to think abstractly or to understand the underlying roles being portrayed will also affect what is learned from the presentation. The direction and pattern of influence of other socialization agents will also influence how an individual perceives specific media portrayals.

Before describing in more detail how these factors are interrelated, we will examine the issue of central concern here: how the resolution of developmental tasks may be related to media exposure. It is our intent here to develop a research model which may account for individual differences in mass media effects. The basis of the model is that we cannot assume that the media audience is similarly motivated to attend to the same attributes of particular presentations. The audience differs on a number of factors, but a critical difference is their current set of life issues. These life issues or tasks may be linked to various stages of human development. We argue that, if we can assess the salience of these life tasks at any one point in time, we will be able to predict which aspects of the media presentation will be attended to and will affect subsequent levels of knowledge, values, and behaviors of that individual.

Although any life stage can be examined similarly, we will focus here on the adolescent life stage for three reasons. First, a number of adolescent researchers and theorists (Havighurst, 1972; Erikson, 1968) have clearly specified certain developmental tasks which most adolescents are faced with between the ages of 12 and 22. These tasks include such things as choosing an occupation and other future roles, learning how to interact with the opposite sex, developing a sex-role identity, and achieving independence from the family. Second, adolescence is a period of increased activity oriented toward gathering information about the future. Such activity should increase the importance of television as an important source of information. Third, adolescents are generally in the final stage of cognitive development, unlike younger children whose thought processes are still progressing. Thus, the behavior of adolescents is less a function of what they *can* do and more a matter of what they *actually* do. They are also a more active audience than younger children because they have more control over how their individual needs for information will be satisfied. Thus, we might expect adolescents to understand more complex portrayals and perhaps even seek out such portrayals since they are relevant to their own lives.

Developmental Task Resolution Strategies

The central elements of the research model described here are what we have called internal constraints. These are factors which are generated within the individual and are directly related to the specific tasks of the life stage. As the individual grows older and faces critical life decisions, he or she may adopt different strategies for dealing with the resolution of these life conflicts, e.g., what job to choose, what sort of political ideology to adhere to. The strategies a person develops for coping with these decisions vary along two dimensions. First, persons differ in the degree to which they have made a commitment to or personal investment in particular alternatives (choosing to be a doctor rather than a lawyer or nurse). Second, individuals differ in the degree to which this commitment (or lack of commitment) is based on active exploration of the range of alternatives. These dimensions are derived from Erikson's (1968) argument that firm commitments which are preceded by periods of crisis or consideration of alternative options are necessary conditions of successful decision-making regarding life tasks. Marcia (1966) has based a program of research on Erikson's theory. He has labeled these two dimensions of decision-making "commitment" and "crisis." By dichotomizing the dimensions, he has developed a four-fold typology which may be thought of as four different strategies of life task/conflict resolution (see Figure 1). Presence or absence of crisis and the extent of commitment in any life task serves to define the decision strategy.

The *achievement* strategy is one in which the individual has experienced a crisis period and has invested in or commited him or herself to a partic-

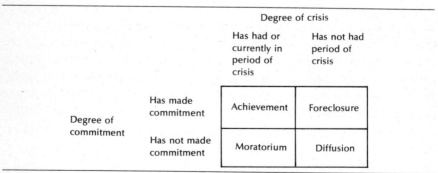

Figure 1. Developmental task resolution strategies adapted from Marcia's (1966) conceptualization of Erikson's criteria for successful adolescent development

ular choice. The *moratorium* strategy refers to those individuals who are currently engaged in decision-making, but have not yet been able to make a commitment. Individuals who adopt a *foreclosure* strategy have not experienced a crisis but have firm, often parentally or externally imposed or determined commitments. Those with a *diffusion* strategy have almost no strategy at all. The diffusion individual is not currently involved in trying to make a decision and has not made a commitment to any alternative, unlike the foreclosure who has made a commitment, but, similarly, has not experienced crisis.

An individual may be characterized by different strategies depending on what life task is being examined. For instance, an adolescent may have successfully made a commitment to being a lawyer after many days of looking at alternative occupational choices. The person would be labeled as in an achievement strategy—having made a commitment after experiencing a crisis. At the same time, he or she may have adopted a diffusion strategy for dealing with the problem of autonomy from his or her parents. The adolescent is either comfortable in the current situation or not yet ready to cope with the anxiety of examining alternatives.

Marcia (1976) has found that decision-making strategies may also change in a rather logical sequence culminating in the achievement strategy. In a longitudinal study he found some evidence for a progression from the diffusion or foreclosure strategy to the achievement strategy through moratorium. Thus, as an adolescent moves into a period of actively seeking alternatives from which to choose (crisis) and begins to make tentative commitments (commitment), he or she moves out of the passive strategy of diffusion into moratorium. As the individual begins to firm up those commitments and narrow them down to particular, finite choices, he or she moves into the achievement strategy. The individual who begins with a foreclosure strategy (at adolescence, generally simply accepting the parents' commitments) might be pushed into a moratorium strategy by the critical change toward seeking alternatives. He or she might then conceivably get frightened by too many alternatives and either resort to the diffusion strategy or retreat back to the original foreclosure strategy. He or she could also, however, cope with the moratorium strategy of exploration of alternatives and move in the direction of adopting an achievement strategy.

Adolescent Developmental Tasks

A review of the literature on adolescent development indicates that these crises or tasks which an adolescent may be dealing with can be condensed and synthesized into five distinct areas. These tasks, in the chronological order that they are usually encountered during adolescence, are: (1) accepting changes in one's body and developing a positive body image; (2) developing more completely defined sex roles and learning about cross-sex relationships; (3) beginning to achieve economic and emotional independence (freedom from authority); (4) preparing for future occupational and family roles; and (5) developing civic competence. It is our belief that television, while not the sole socializing agent, can contribute to the way an individual resolves each of these tasks. Furthermore, we feel that Marcia's categories of decision strategies can be applied to each of the tasks to help determine what information from television will be most important to an adolescent using different decision strategies.

Body Image

The beginning of adolescence is usually defined by the onset of puberty and the development of changes in body shape (Campbell, 1969; Douvan and Gould, 1966). For girls, physical changes generally start around 10 years of age and last until 12½. For boys, the growth spurt usually starts to develop around 12 and these changes continue until approximately 14½ (Matteson, 1975; Tanner, 1964; Douvan and Gould, 1966).

These physical changes in early adolescence have been shown to affect also adolescents' attitudes toward themselves and their peers. Adolescents are highly self-conscious about their looks. Frazier and Lisonbee (1971) found that 50% of male and 82% of female adolescents were concerned about some aspect of their facial appearance. Jones and Bayley (1950) found that two-thirds of the adolescents they interviewed expressed a desire to change some component of their physique.

Physical attractiveness also seems to be an important factor in acceptance by peers during early adolescence. Research has shown that most young adolescents rate physical attractiveness as more important than similarity of ideas in choosing friends of either sex (Gronlund and Anderson, 1957; Cavior and Dokecki, 1973). These physical and attitudinal changes combine to form the first major task of adolescence—the development of a positive body image.

Entertainment television may play an important role in helping adolescents work through this task. Preadolescents and those people first entering adolescence have neither resolved nor thought much about their own concept of beauty or attractiveness. In Marcia's terms, these adolescents may be labeled as in diffusion in regard to their body image. For these people, television may serve as an informational device for learning what society's standards of beauty and attractiveness are. Television provides many examples of the ideal male and female bodies (for example, "Charlie's Angels" a show starring three beautiful women detectives who solve cases at the direction of their unseen boss Charlie. "The Six Million Dollar Man" and the "Bionic Woman" both shows starring physically attractive persons who have superior bionic powers which they use to solve crimes and avert disasters). These characters, representing the extreme stereotypes of masculine and feminine beauty, are often placed in action-adventure programs. Thus, not only are these characters beautiful, but they also display excellent control over their bodies.

Situation comedies may also be useful to adolescents who are concerned with learning society's values of beauty. Situation comedies are more likely to provide both ideal and nonideal types. For example, "Happy Days," a comedy set in the 1950s and centered around a middle-class American family, shows both the ideal (Fonzie) and the average (Richie, Potsie, and Ralph). "Welcome Back Kotter," a show about a high school teacher's relationship with his class of ne'er-do-wells, provides an even greater range of examples from Vinnie Barbarino (the ideal type) to Arnold Horshack. Thus, adolescents in diffusion may learn both the ideals and the range of acceptable body types from television.

Adolescents who are already concerned with their appearance, but who have not yet decided on how they can make the most of what they have, can be described as being in moratorium. These adolescents already know what society's values are and are concerned with living up to these values or learning to accept themselves as they are. For these adolescents, television may serve to provide a different type of information. These teenagers may pay particular attention to specific attributes of a wide range of characters. For example, the hair styles of the women on "Charlie's Angels," and "Bionic Woman," and other characters may be compared and contrasted by these adolescents to determine which they think are the best styles and/or which would most suit them. The same thing may also be done for other attributes of attractiveness such as make-up, clothes, physical builds, and walking styles. Thus, adolescents in moratorium are likely to use television to compare specific options they have open to them and to help decide which specific characteristics will most benefit themselves.

Foreclosure and achievement adolescents have already determined how they plan to resolve this task. For these young people, television may be useful only insofar as it presents characters who exhibit the particular style the adolescent has chosen for him or herself. These characters may be attended to in order to learn more detailed information. For example, an adolescent who views himself as very similar to Vinnie Barbarino may adopt some of Vinnie's mannerisms or copy his walk. These adolescents may pick up some of the more subtle information about body image, such as the importance of self-confidence in attractiveness, from a specific character. However, characters who do not fit with the adolescent's own self image are likely to be ignored or ridiculed, especially among foreclosure adolescents.

Sex Roles

Although evidence shows that much sex-role learning has already occurred before adolescence, this is the stage during which increased awareness of the biological determinants of sex differentiated behavior and increased interaction with age mates of both sexes leads to increased pressure to conform to sex "appropriate" behaviors. Nonstereotypical sex role behaviors are frequently accepted prior to adolescence on the ground that "this is just a stage which the individual will grow out of." If the person still wants to pursue these nontraditional behaviors into adolescence, however, they will often face ridicule from peers. This may be especially true for boys because they generally seek support from the full peer group while girls typically seek out a few close friends for support.

We assume that foreclosure is the most typical strategy for the sex role task in adolescence. Learning from parents, peers, and the media all combine to push the average adolescent toward sex-stereotyped roles before the adolescent or preadolescent has made any attempt to consider alternative forms. These adolescents will probably reject or ridicule television portrayals of nontraditional behaviors. While the vast majority of television content reinforces stereotyped behaviors, adolescents who are considering alternative roles may find their greatest (if not their only) source of support from those few, sensitively handled, nonstereotypical portrayals in the media.

Recent research on the concept of androgyny, or the blending of roles based on gender, suggests that sex roles are not a unidimensional construct. Individuals adopt patterns of behavior which are typically associated with their own gender along with attributes which have been traditionally associated with the opposite sex. Societal norms are slowly shifting toward greater acceptance of androgynous behaviors by both males and females. It appears that a greater degree of sensitivity in men and assertiveness in women, for example, is now acceptable.

These changes in societal norms may be encountered in the media before they are found among peers or parents. It is also now more acceptable for men to cry in some situations and for women to be less helpless and more athletic. Even a character who embodies the macho male toughness as much as the Fonz is now able to cry when his best friend is seriously injured. Action-adventure programs with female leads such as "Charlie's Angels" and "Wonder Woman" show women as competent and successful in difficult and dangerous situations. Women's sports have also gained greater respectability and wider television coverage. These programs may encourage women to continue in sports when they previously may have been discouraged by those around them. Television is even showing that women can compete with men in sports with programs like "Challenge of the Sexes" in which both male and female television stars compete in a variety of sports events. These shows may provide support for those adolescents currently considering what their options are as well as change the expectations and norms for younger viewers.

Another area of sex role learning which occurs during pre- and early adolescence is in regard to cross-sex relationships. Dunphy (1963), using participant observation, found that peer groups move from unisex groups to heterosexual cliques during adolescence. Those adolescents who are still in unisex peer groups and have not yet begun to date may be characterized as in diffusion on this task. These adolescents are aware that they will begin to date at some point and may be engaged in anticipatory socialization to prepare for this occurrence. Matteson (1975) has proposed that cross-sex behaviors are learned via the media before adolescence. During adolescence when sexual feelings begin to emerge, adolescents may express these feelings in the ways they have seen them portrayed on television and in films.

What an adolescent will attend to during cross-sex encounters on television may differ depending on the adolescent's own prior experiences. Preadolescents who have not started to date may be most concerned with how their same sex characters are expected to act, what one does on a date, or what the sexual expectations are. Adolescents closer to beginning to date may be more concerned with specific strategies for getting dates. Entertainment television may provide examples for these adolescents. For example, strategies for asking someone out on a date have been explored in "James at 15" (the story of a young boy's adolescence), "Happy Days," and "Wecome Back Kotter." The appropriateness of girls asking boys for dates has been discussed on "Laverne and Shirley" (two young working-class women on their own in the 1950s), and "One Day at a Time." More subtle (and traditional) ways for girls to attract boys have been portrayed on "One Day at a Time," "Laverne and Shirley," "Three's Company" (two single women who have a male roommate), and "Rhoda" (single, now divorced woman on her own in New York City). Ways for women to turn down dates they do not want have also been shown on several of these shows. These portrayals may be the only way for adolescents to learn these strategies other than by trial and error. This may be especially true among males where one may feel compelled to pretend to have more experience than one does in order to obtain status within the peer group.

Television can also provide useful information to those adolescents who have already begun dating. These adolescents may use entertainment television programs to reinforce the behaviors they have already learned. Gerson (1966) found that while adolescents' use of media for norm acquisition about dating behavior is more common (42.4% report doing this sometimes or more frequently), media use for reinforcement was also fairly common (35.2%). Not surprisingly, nondaters in Gerson's study used media almost solely for acquiring norms and strategies, while those adolescents already dating reported greater usage of media for reinforcement.

Another way in which television's portrayal of cross-sex interactions can help adolescents involved in dating is by allowing them a glimpse of what life is like for the opposite sex. Girls who watch "Happy Days" or "James at 16" (the same adolescent boys one year older), for example, may be able to gain a greater understanding of the fears boys may experience in getting up the courage to ask a girl out. Similarly, boys watching shows like "One Day at a Time" may gain greater insights into adolescent girls' fears and expectations. Research studies have found that adolescent males stress eroticism over romanticism while adolescent females stress romanticism first (Ehrmann, 1959). Entertainment television may enlighten viewers of each sex about the values of the opposite sex. One episode of "One Day at a Time" recently centered around an adolescent girl's decision over which type of boy was more important to her; an attractive and popular boy who was interested in her only as a sex object versus a less physically desirable boy who was more sincere and cared for her as a person. Shows like this may help adolescents recognize these values and priorities in themselves and those around them.

Independence

Another task of adolescence is to begin to achieve emotional and economic independence from one's family. Three factors combine to make this task somewhat easier. First, strong peer groups exist during this period. During adolescence, the values of the peer group may for the first time begin to conflict with those of the family, thus giving the adolescent an alternative viewpoint (Bowerman and Kinch, 1959). Second, the adolescent is given greater opportunity to spend time outside of the home, making family relations less crucial. This also acts to prepare the adolescent for the future emotional break from home. However, studies have generally shown that adolescents use peer group norms for less important decisions such as clothing styles and music tastes, while the family's influence is still stronger for more important and long range decisions (Kandel and Lesser, 1969; Brittain, 1969). The final contributing factor is the acquisition of part-time or summer employment. These jobs make the first dent in the adolescent's economic dependence on the family.

Television may act as an anticipatory socialization agent for this task. Initially, adolescents in diffusion may be attracted to strong, independent characters who appear to have control over their own lives and successfully defy authority figures. However, as this task gains salience for adolescents and they become more concerned with actually making a break from their parents (greater crisis), the type of portrayal which is most likely to influence them changes. At this stage adolescents may attend to young adult characters on television who have or are in the process of making a break from their families. Shows like "Laverne and Shirley," "Busting Loose," and "Three's Company" show young adults out on their own for the first time, and the problems they experience.

Some programs have portrayed the difficulties in leaving home and shown the more negative aspects of life on one's own within individual episodes. The "Waltons" (a show which portrays an extended family in rural Virginia during the Depression) showed the difficulties of the oldest son's attempt to break from home to go to college. An episode of "Happy Days" depicted Richie leaving home to live with his older brother so that he could have more freedom. "One Day at a Time" ran a four-part episode where Julie ran off to live with her boyfriend. In the last two examples, the episodes ended with the major characters returning home after discovering the problems of life on their own. This may be functional in keeping those viewers who are not yet prepared from making the break from home too soon, or it can be dysfunctional in reducing the adolescent's confidence in his or her own ability to "make it" away from the family. Either way, these shows can alert the adolescent to potential problems in making the separation, as well as provide those adolescents who have already decided with specific strategies for making the break from home.

Autonomy in decision-making is also a recurrent theme on many family dramas and situation comedies. These presentations may alert the diffusion and some foreclosure adolescents to the impending task of making a separation from parental influence. For adolescents with other decision strategies, these programs may provide specific arguments and strategies they can use to gain greater decisional autonomy from their parents. However, these shows may provide the greatest benefit to those adolescents who watch them with their parents. These programs may lead to discussions of autonomy within the context of the viewer's own family. These discussions can be brought up in a less threatening and argumentative atmosphere than might have occurred without the televised presentation. These programs and/or the ensuing discussions may also serve to alert parents to the fact that their children are growing up.

Future Roles

During adolescence the individual is expected to begin preparing for the roles he or she will take on in adulthood. One of the most important future roles the adolescent will assume is the occupational role. While some search and thought about occupations occurs in childhood, there are usually large increases on both the crisis and commitment dimensions during later adolescence in regard to occupations (Ginzberg et al., 1951).

The process of occupational choice can be divided into three distinct stages. In the first stage, the individual searches through all of the possible options. Television presentations can affect this stage of the process in two ways. Normally adolescents cannot view or even know about all the potential occupations available in a modern industrial society. Technology and societal fads can invent new jobs overnight. Many potential occupations remain unknown to the majority of the population. The media can expose some of these possibilities to the adolescent. McLuhan first suggested such a sequence when he described television as serving as a global village, showing people the options they cannot come into contact with in their own lives. Even though television has been criticized for portraying only a limited range of occupations, this range may still be broader, or at least different from, those occupations the adolescent comes in contact with in his or her own environment.

Current programs on television are also beginning to present a wider range of occupational alternatives than have existed in the past. Previously, entertainment television has been characterized as presenting only a few possibilities (primary doctors, lawyers, and police officers) primarily at the upper end of the occupational status categories (DeFleur, 1964). While these occupations are still prevalent, there is now a wider range of characters in less prestigious occupations such as garage mechanic (Fonzie), maintenance man (Schnieder on "One Day at a Time"), waitress ("Alice"), and factory workers ("Laverne and Shirley"). The middle range of occupational status positions is also represented by characters such as Archie Bunker (bar owner on "All in the Family"), Howard Cunningham on "Happy Days" and Walter on "Maude" (store owners), the characters on the "Mary Tyler Moore" show and "Lou Grant" (television and newspaper reporters, editors, and producers), Rhoda and Julie on "One Day at a Time" (designers), and Ann Romano on "One Day at a Time," Julia and Maria on "On Our Own," and J.J. on "Good Times" (various jobs in advertising). This list represents only major characters on long running series. The number of occupations represented by characters appearing on just one episode of a program is even greater. At this stage of occupational decision, where the adolescent is merely looking at the possible options, these one-shot appearances are just as important as characters in recurring roles.

The way in which an occupation is presented may also affect whether or not it will be considered as an option. Traditional portrayals, in terms of sex appropriateness, may cause an adolescent to close out options, while nontraditional portrayals may increase the possibilities a person will consider. For example, the depiction of Jack on "Three's Company" as studying to be a chef, or of Angie Dickinson as a police officer in the show "Police Woman," may lead adolescents to consider sex-stereotyped jobs as open to both sexes. Additionally, if an occupation is consistently shown as being dull or undesirable, it is not likely to get much consideration. DeFleur and DeFleur (1967), for example, found that children (6–13 years old) appear able to learn the prestige of various occupations from television. High television viewers were much closer to matching the status ratings parents and experts gave for occupations highly visable on television than less frequent viewers. However, at this first stage of occupational choice, the individual is more interested in what occupations are available rather than focusing on the merits of any particular job.

The second stage of occupational choice involves narrowing down all of the potential choices to those which are most desirable. Media presentations can affect this decision process. Adolescents are generally in the formal stage of logical operations. According to Piaget, one aspect of formal operations is the ability to think in terms of abstract, hypothetical reasoning (Piaget, 1972). The individual can now integrate different pieces of information in new ways. Therefore, adolescents should be able to extract different portrayals of an occupation and mentally put them together to provide increased knowledge of the differing rewards and requirements of each job. The degree to which the individual perceives televised portrayals of these occupations as realistic will obviously play an important part in determining whether this televised information is used to narrow the possibilities. If occupational portrayals are viewed as realistic, this should result in the elimination of some of the possibilities and the enhancement of others.

The last stage in the occupational decision-making process is to narrow the alternatives even further until a final decision is made. This is the process of moving from moratorium to achievement. This requires more specific information about the rewards, routines, and requisites of each occupation, as well as an awareness of the individual's own goals and values. Because televised portrayals rarely go into extensive depth in presenting occupations, it is unlikely that television will have a very large impact at this stage. However, it is possible that some televised portrayals may aid adolescents at this stage as well as those adolescents who have already made an occupational decision (foreclosure and achievement). For these people, subtle variations in their considerations may be influential.

The brother of one of our colleagues provides an example of how these subtle considerations may work. This particular adolescent had already decided that he wanted to become a chef. Upon watching an episode of "Love Boat," a comedy about short-term relationships evolving on short ocean cruises, he realized for the first time that chefs would be needed on ocean liners. Thus, he could combine his choice of vocation with his enjoyment of boats by seeking this type of employment. This possibility may never have occurred to him without his viewing of this program. This additional information may not seem very important to us, but could prove crucial to his future happiness.

Civic Competence

The final task of adolescence is the development of civic competence, a minimally informed participation in the affairs of the community. While this area, like most of the others already discussed, has its foundations in childhood, change continues through late adolescence when the legal age of voting becomes imminent and community issues become more pertinent. Not only are these changes manifested by the accumulation of specific pieces of political knowledge, but later adolescence shows a difference in the frames of reference used to evaluate political action. Our political socialization research, utilizing the category system of Adelson and O'Neil (1966), found that 16 year olds compared to those three years younger saw problems of community conflict in rather different terms: they were more likely to consider future implications rather than just the present situation; they used impersonal as well as personal standards; they viewed the whole problem beyond its parts; they concentrated on the positive aspects of the situation rather than simply the negative facets; and they more often invoked a force of principle in analyzing conflict. All these attributes should affect the intake of television content.

Along with the growth in civic competence, older adolescents also begin to use the public affairs content of the media more (Jennings and Niemi, 1974; McLeod and Brown, 1976). There is also a growing awareness that the media may play an important role in developing political competence. Public affairs media use has been linked to the learning of specific information by adolescents during election campaigns (Chaffee et al., 1970), and our research also suggests that use of this type of content may develop more mature political frames of reference as well.

Information about politics and our legal system can also be gathered by watching entertainment television. Certainly the fact that most adolescents know that a person being arrested must be read their rights is a direct result of watching police programs on television. Most adolescents have never been in court yet they can pick up some information about the workings of the judicial system from shows like the "Tony Randall Show" where the main character plays a judge. However, entertainment television programs may be dysfunctional in this area by providing a distorted view of the judicial system for the sake of dramatic presentation.

Civic competence also includes developing one's own morals and values. Erikson, Marcia, and Kohlberg all discuss the period of adolescence as an important point in developing these values. Kohlberg's work (1976) in moral development shows that as a person moves through the moral judgment stages there is a change in who they consider when making a moral decision. There is a movement from an egocentric orientation to a consideration of relevant others, to a societal orientation, and finally to a prior-to-society orientation.

At the beginning of adolescence individuals are usually at stages two or three in Kohlberg's hierarchy. These stages are concerned with what relevant other people will think of the individual. At stage three, for example, people determine what is morally right on the basis of what friends and peers will think. Stage four is the beginning of a societal orientation. Here, morality is based on what the law says is right. At the end of adolescence some people may reach stage five. This stage is based on a social contract philosophy. Rules and laws are seen as necessary for a smooth running society, but they are also seen as arbitrary and changeable. There is an awareness that certain principles may be more important than specific laws. This is the first stage of the prior-to-society orientation.

Kohlberg has found that most American adults never go beyond stages three or four. Additionally, the longer a person remains at a given stage the less likely he or she is to go beyond that stage. Thus, if people are going to reach the more principled levels (stages five and six), they generally do so at the end of adolescence or early adulthood.

Entertainment television presentations of the reasoning behind the action in decision-making situations can help or hinder social development. Kohlberg and Turiel state that stage growth occurs when a person begins to see the flaws in his or her own reasoning. This causes cognitive disequilibrium, which eventually produces stage change. Lorimer (1971) has shown that exposure to films can produce these changes. He used two experimental conditions. In one, subjects were taught how to reason through dilemmas and were given opportunities to try. The second group saw the movie "Fail-Safe" and two weeks later held an informal discussion about it. A control group was also used. In a 10-day posttest the instruction group showed the greatest amount of stage increase. However, on a 50-day posttest most of these subjects reverted back to their original stage. The film group, on the other hand, had a smaller increase on the 10-day posttest, but showed even greater increase on the 50-day posttest. Puzzled by these results, Lorimer reinterviewed several of the subjects. They indicated that the training group considered the instruction like school work—something to be memorized, regurgitated, and then forgotten. Subjects who saw the movie, however, were confronted with alternative forms of reasoning which they compared to their own decisions. This led to actual disequilibrium which, in turn, led to true stage growth. Therefore, it seems that some television presentations, coupled with interpersonal communication, can lead to stage change. However, given the current television content and the time constraints for presenting decisions in depth, it seems probable that stage growth beyond the conventional level (stages three and four) is more likely to be inhibited than enhanced. Nonetheless, the present trend toward mini-series like "Roots" and "Rich Man, Poor Man" and more feature-length televised movies may allow for greater depth in presentations which could contain the type of content necessary to stimulate stage growth.

Aside from an overall moral orientation, specific values are also undergoing examination during adolescence. These specific values appear in many individual episodes of the current television shows. "One Day at a Time," "What's Happening" (three adolescent black boys), and "Happy Days" have explored the issue of cheating in school. Lying or keeping silent to protect a friend has been dealt with on "James at 15," "One Day at a Time," and "Good Times" (a show depicting the life of an urban black family). Doing or not doing things which are against one's personal values for the sake of acceptance by peers has frequently been shown on shows like "James at 15," "Good Times," and "Eight is Enough" (a family of eight children and their parents). These are just a few of the possible examples. These programs may help adolescents to think about and clarify their own values and ethics, and eventually help them to achieve their own sense of morality.

External Constraints

Until this point we have argued that the stage of resolution and the content of the task currently being resolved by individuals will affect what kinds of effects television presentations will have on their audiences. We have generally assumed that, except for the stage of resolution of the specific task, adolescents are similar in how they will perceive television shows. But even adolescents in similar resolution stages probably do not perceive the same portrayals similarly. At least three kinds of factors intervene or serve as constraints on the linkage between developmental task resolution and the effect of exposure to television. Adolescents differ in terms of prior relevant experience with the content matter, cognitive and social abilities, and social-cultural norms. We have labeled these factors external constraints because they are external to the task resolution process. We will describe each set of external constraints in turn.

Experiential Constraints

Varying amounts and diversity of personal experience provide individuals with more or less information with which to evaluate media portrayals in relation to their own perceptions of social reality. These evaluations will play a part in determining the extent to which an individual uses media to help resolve the various life cycle tasks. Pingree (1978), for example, found that when children were told that actresses in television commercials actually hold jobs they represented in the commercials, the children showed less stereotypical attitudes than other children exposed to the same commercials.

Amount of experience is an important variable since we hypothesize that television will have a greater effect when individuals do not have personal experiences to use as a yardstick, to measure the accuracy of the television portrayal. Noble (1976) describes television as a necessary extension for learning for modern man. In village societies all potential options are available for observation within a person's everyday encounters. However, due to the complexity of modern industrial societies, many alternatives now lie outside an individual's normal experiences. Thus, television may help to provide information about these unobservable possibilities. We would expect, for example, that urban adolescents who have had relatively little opportunity to be exposed to occupations located primarily in rural areas, such as farming or taking care of animals, would attend to portrayals of such activities in a less judgmental way than rural adolescents who have had the opportunity to observe such activities first-hand.

Cognitive and Social Ability Constraints

Adolescents differ developmentally in terms of both cognitive and social skills. We have already discussed briefly how cognitive variables may limit what adolescents can take away from media exposure. These cognitive variables are important during adolescence in at least two ways. First, adolescents who have achieved a higher level of reasoning (formal operations), and thus the ability to think abstractly, would be expected to be able to take parts of different portrayals across different shows and mentally manipulate and integrate them in different applications in their own lives. Adolescents who have not achieved this more abstract reasoning ability would be less likely to be able to assimilate diverse portrayals and thus in a qualitative sense would be learning quite different things from their exposure to television. We would expect, for example, that adolescents who have not achieved formal operations would be less likely to move into the moratorium or achievement stages of task resolution since they lack the ability to integrate different pieces of information into a coherent pattern. Pre-formal-operations adolescents might be expected to accept more readily the full role portrayal rather than only certain aspects or attributes of the portrayed role.

Second, cognitive variables are important in that they serve as a constraint on an adolescent's orientation toward the future. Concrete operational individuals have been found to be primarily limited to a "here and now" orientation, rooted in the present. The development of formal operations, on the other hand, allows the person to move beyond the present to a more future planning orientation. With the onset of formal operations, the adolescent is able to project him or herself into the future and speculate what different roles might be like. Until this time television portrayals may not seem relevant except in a very specific, short-term sense. However, in relation to some of the tasks, such as body image and interpersonal relations, the ability for future projection may not be as important as with some of the other tasks such as the development of civic competence and the selection of occupational roles, which require consideration of future, relatively unpredictable situations.

Social skills or role-taking ability may also act as a constraint on learning from the media. Generally, role-taking, or the ability to put oneself mentally in the place of the other, has been found to change with age (Selman, 1971; Flavell et al., 1968). To comprehend fully the demands and constraints on a television character, that viewer must be able to place him or herself in the character's position. This sort of comprehension is not possible until higher stages of role-taking ability have been reached. Generally, the study of role-taking has been concerned with the understanding of only one relevant constraint on another's viewpoint. However, the process of role-taking can also involve understanding multiple roles which have conflicting demands. The few studies which have investigated conflicting role presentations have found that the ability to cope with the conflicting information changes during adolescence. Gollin (1958), for example, studying how children of different ages resolve inconsistencies in role portrayals (i.e., the character is helpful in one situation and nasty in another), found that younger children (10½ year olds) focused on only one of the behaviors in describing the character. Viewers who were 13½ years old mentioned both the good and bad aspects of the behaviors, but still used only one of them in describing the character's personality. Subjects who were 16½ years old, however, were able to discuss both behaviors and to attribute motivations to account for both of them. These results have implications for both interpersonal interactions and for what an adolescent can and will comprehend in media presentations.

Persons with higher levels of role-taking ability may also be more likely to comprehend the difference between attributes of an individual character and the attributes of the role that character occupies. This is a crucial aspect of gathering accurate information about sex, occupational, and familial roles. For example, one must be able to discriminate between attributes which are due to Kojak's personality and those which are general attributes of all police officers. This ability to separate attributes allows the viewer to determine more appropriately how he or she might "fit in" to a given role. For example, in making choices about occupational roles, the adolescent must be able to match his or her own values, abilities, interests, desires, and so forth with attributes of the occupation such as the potential rewards, the requirements for entrance to the occupational category, and the various routines of the job. Without higher levels of role-taking ability, this process of objective comparison is not possible.

Societal and Cultural Constraints

Factors in the adolescent's environment may also influence to what extent media are used in task resolution and which aspects of media presentations are found relevant. Previous research on such variables as social class, family communication patterns, and degree of peer group integration has found that these factors influence both the pattern of media use and the kinds of effects exposure has on the individual.

For example, a large number of studies have found a positive relationship between an adolescent's social class standing and his or her occupational aspirations and expectations (Leifer and Lesser, 1976; Wylie, 1963). Social class has also been found to be related to patterns of media use. Greenberg and Dominick (1969) found that blacks and adolescents from lower social class backgrounds watch more television than adolescents from higher social strata. Lower income adolescents have also been found to perceive television as being more like real life than adolescents from higher income families.

A series of studies (summarized in McLeod and Chaffee, 1972) have shown that the patterns of communication emphasized in the family influence the adolescent's subsequent usage of the mass media. These studies have shown, for example, that adolescents who have been constrained by the need to maintain harmony in interpersonal communication situations are the heaviest users of television and spend the most time with entertainment rather than public affairs–oriented content on television. This suggests that adolescents learn patterns of communication from the interpersonal situation which they may then generalize to the mass communication situation as well. It also suggests that they may approach the mass communication situation with compensatory motives. For example, adolescents in families that emphasize the maintainence of harmony and discourage the exploration of controversial issues have been found to use entertainment television as a source of aggression. Here then, they may be able to find an outlet for those repressed desires they are not allowed to express in their family environment. Thus, we might expect that adolescents who approach the viewing situation with different motives as well as different communication expectations will attend to different aspects of the media content and will learn different things from the exposure.

The cultural context of the adolescent can influence the relationship between media exposure and task resolution in still another way. Television, or the media environment, is only one of a variety of sources of information about the larger social environment. As adolescents grapple with the tasks of their life stage, they are influenced not only by their parents, their teachers, and perhaps their church, but also by their age mates. Although most research on the influence of peers during asolescence suggests that parents retain their status as the more influential socialization agent, other research suggests that regardless of influence, simply the process of being involved with the peer group is an important part of adolescence. Johnstone (1974) found, for example, that adolescents who aspired to be accepted as members of specific peer groups, but were not fully integrated with the chosen group, were the heaviest viewers of television. Horrocks (1965:20) writes: "In addition to providing emotional bulwarks for the adolescent in the form of security, prestige and so on, the peer group has the further function of acting as a proving ground—a place to test oneself, to try things out, and to learn to cope with others."

Perhaps when the adolescent does not have the "security" of the peer group in which to test these things out, he or she may turn to another kind of proving ground—that of the world of television. Perhaps with television the adolescent may find learning about interpersonal relationships less threatening than in the peer group, which may ridicule or ostracize the adolescent for deviant "testing out" behaviors. Thus, we would expect to find greater use of the media for learning about things which are threatening or taboo in the peer group, as well as greater use of the media by adolescents who are not well-assimilated in the peer group with which they desire to be associated. Although somewhat less likely, adolescents may also use television as a third standard of comparison when the values proposed by their parents and friends are in conflict.

In sum, a number of other factors operate as constraints on the relationship between the adolescent and his or her use of television in the resolution of life tasks. We have discussed some which we consider most relevant. As more research in conducted on the use of television by adolescents other constraints will certainly emerge. At this point, however, these are some of the other factors which should be taken into account. The full research model we have been describing here is diagrammed in Figure 2.

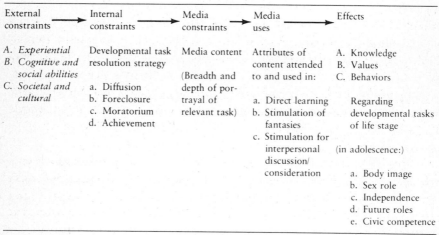

External constraints	Internal constraints	Media constraints	Media uses	Effects
A. *Experiential* B. *Cognitive and social abilities* C. *Societal and cultural*	Developmental task resolution strategy a. Diffusion b. Foreclosure c. Moratorium d. Achievement	Media content (Breadth and depth of portrayal of relevant task)	Attributes of content attended to and used in: a. Direct learning b. Stimulation of fantasies c. Stimulation for interpersonal discussion/ consideration	A. Knowledge B. Values C. Behaviors Regarding developmental tasks of life stage (in adolescence:) a. Body image b. Sex role c. Independence d. Future roles e. Civic competence

Figure 2. Model of life-span developmental approach to mass media uses and effects

Media Constraints

We have discussed the first two sets of constraints (internal and external) diagrammed in the model. A third set of constraints, those within the media content per se, remain. Obviously, media can be a factor in adolescent development only if portrayals relevant to life tasks are available. In our previous discussion we have provided anecdotal evidence which suggests that, at least on prime time entertainment television of recent seasons, issues centered on adolescent tasks have been portrayed. Existing content analyses of television unfortunately do not provide us with adequate information regarding the extent and diversity of such portrayals. We do not know, for example, how often and in what way issues relevant to the resolution of the task of achieving independence from the family are presented. However, we do know that, although a variety of occupations are portrayed on television, television characters are most likely to be in professional occupations and women are underrepresented in occupational roles of any kind (DeFleur, 1964). We also know that a great deal of television content is devoted to the analysis of interpersonal relationships as well as the discussion of public affairs, which suggests that television is a potential source of learning about such tasks as developing a sex role and civic competence, but also that such portrayals may be highly stereotypical or inaccurate, thus serving to limit options.

We also know, however, that television has begun to explore more taboo subjects (masturbation on "Mary Hartman, Mary Hartman"), alternative lifestyles (homosexual marriage, also on "Mary Hartman"; transsexualism on "Medical Center"), and nontraditional occupations (female lawyers and police officers). These presentations may broaden the range of options perceived by adolescents. In fact the media may play its most important role in presenting information about nontraditional lifestyles and options because these may be the most threatening topics for an adolescent to bring up in interpersonal communication. Their only source of information about these possibilities may be media presentations.

Television presentations may be an important factor in the resolution of life tasks for still another reason. Television presents a strong visual image of the outcomes of different problems and resolution strategies. Janis (1980) and Abelson (1976) argue that when a person has a particularly strong visual image of an upcoming event or outcome, it will exert an inordinately strong influence on their decision-making regarding that event. This visual image is called a script. Janis believes that people can easily develop personal scripts from television, because the vivid visual image is presented there for the individual. Repetition of a specific image can add to its likelihood of being adopted as a personal script. If television can facilitate the development of personal scripts, and these scripts do influence decision-making, then media content may be of central importance in resolving many of our developmental tasks.

Media Uses

The three types of constraints just discussed are expected to influence media usage. Media uses are defined here as the specific content attended to and recalled, as well as the ways in which such content is used in the process of resolving specific life tasks. We have hypothesized three ways in which television content can be used in the process of task resolution.

First, television content may be used for direct learning of information relevant to the task. Adolescents may learn directly from media presentations about societal norms and ideals of female beauty, for example, from watching televised beauty pageants or commercials for beauty products. Direct learning is likely to be most important to people who feel that their considerations about a task are likely to be ridiculed or rejected in an interpersonal communication situation. For example, adolescents who mature physically earlier than their age mates may feel embarrassed about discussing the changes in their bodies with parents or peers. Similarly, an adolescent who is considering a nontraditional sex role or occupation which does not conform to peer or parental expectations may be highly fearful of discussing these topics. Therefore, much of their learning about such topics may come from the media, which is a less threatening source of information.

Second, the media can affect the resolution of life tasks through the stimulation of fantasies. Singer (1973) has found that day-dreaming is most frequent during adolescence. Adolescent fantasies tend to focus on romance, sex, achievement, and the future. Adults, on the other hand, tend to fantasize about more concrete, real life situations (e.g., where to spend a vacation, job promotions). Because adolescents are day-dreaming about future possibilities, media content relevant to the tasks of their life stage may act as a springboard for these fantasies.

Third, media content may serve as a stimulus for interpersonal discussion and consideration of options relevant to the issues of adolescence. Television has been found to be a topic of conversation in interpersonal communication between adolescents and their parents and friends (Foley, 1968; Lyle and Hoffman, 1972). Television presentations may help to raise subjects which might otherwise be hard to bring up. It may also be less threatening to discuss these issues in terms of the television character rather than as directly relevant to one's own self.

Media Effects

Finally, the model predicts that each of the constraint sets as well as the uses made of the media content (generation of fantasies, interpersonal communication, direct learning) will affect knowledge, values, and behaviors regarding each of the life tasks. We hypothesize that adolescents will gain information about the task area, will learn and apply new values, and finally will exhibit patterns of behavior based, at least in part, on observation of media presentations. Changes in knowledge should occur all during the task-resolution process. Changes in basic values and behaviors are more likely to occur at the point of reaching stable achievement on the task, although some exhibition of different behaviors may occur during periods of experimentation with various options (e.g., wearing make-up for a period of time to see what it looks like because women on television wear make-up).

We have presented a rather speculative look at how the mass media in general and television content in particular may affect how individuals resolve issues related to their stage in the life cycle. The focus has been on the adolescent life stage as an example of how this model may be applied. We believe this model provides a useful framework for a better understanding of the effects of the mass media on individuals.

NANCY WOOD BLIESE

Media in the Rocking Chair: Media Uses and Functions Among the Elderly

Have you thought about getting old? Do you picture the aged "you" surrounded by family and friends or alone in a room with a television set? It cannot be denied that we all age and that an increasing proportion of our society falls into the "aged" category each year. The United States Census Bureau states, in its latest report, that the number of Americans sixty-five years of age and older doubled between 1950 and 1980. Nancy Bliese has been involved in ongoing research on the elderly and their changing cognitive and communicative patterns. This essay presents her findings on how the elderly use the media.

After reading the essay, reflect upon your image of the elderly and evaluate your present media patterns. Are your media uses different than those of the elderly interviewed in this study? In what ways do you expect your media involvement to change as you join the ranks of the elderly?

Irma watches a lot of television. Her "friends" are the hosts of game and talk shows and the characters on soap operas. She writes long letters to her favorites, speaking to them as though the friendship were a mutual and longstanding one, and speaks to her acquaintances of these people at great length and using a familiar tone. One might say she has lost touch with reality. Sarah, on the other hand, has little time for television. She usually watches one or two programs a day, which she chooses for their informative or cultural enrichment characteristics. She says that she is too busy to bother watching "trash" programs, and she is right. She has a very busy schedule of volunteer work during the day and her evenings are spent catching up on correspondence with friends, doing necessary housework, engaging in her hobby of needlepoint, or curling up with a good book. Both of these women are real, though their names have been changed to protect their identities. One of them is forty-two years old, the other is eighty-four. Which is which?

If you guessed that Sarah is the elderly person, you chose correctly. Yet Irma more nearly fits our stereotypes about elderly persons and their uses of media. As you read this article, you will find out more about the myths and realities surrounding media use by elderly persons. The myths come from a number of sources including the media themselves and, unfortunately, some scholarly literature. The realities come from interviews with 214 individuals over age seventy and from twelve panel interviews with groups of eight to thirteen men and women over age sixty-five. The sample includes persons from both urban and rural environments, from all levels of the socioeconomic spectrum, and from several different cultural backgrounds. It also includes both homebound elderly and persons who are able to get about freely. It does not include any persons living in nursing homes, because the small proportion of the elderly population living in nursing homes (about 5 to 10 percent) is not representative of the elderly population in general.

Defining Media

Defining mediated communication is a problem. Just as Gumpert and Cathcart say that, "Every type of human communication . . . is still basically an interpersonal communicative act,"[1] it is equally possible to define every human communication act as being mediated. It is probably more appropriate to speak of degrees of mediation than to draw a black-and-white distinction between mediated and unmediated communication. Even a face-to-face interaction between two people, probably the most unmediated form of communication, is affected by such physical factors as distance and ambient noise levels. The more removed the source from the receiver and the smaller the possibilities for feedback, the greater the amount of mediation.[2]

Rather than pursue an exact definition of mediated communication, an exercise with a high probability of failure, let us instead talk about the behaviors that were surveyed and the relationships among them. In the individual interviews the respondents were asked about a wide range of communication activities including face-to-face interaction, attendance at meetings, use of radio and television, use of the telephone and citizen's band radio, and use of both printed and personal written communications such as books, magazines, newspapers, and personal cards and letters. In the panel (or group) interviews, most of the time was spent on uses of mass media such as television, radio, and various print media. The results of these interviews, as you will see, show that some of the popular beliefs about the uses and functions of media among elderly persons are true, some are questionable, and some are plainly wrong.

Old People and the Media

The first thing that we learned about old people and the media is that making generalizations is almost impossible. The elderly differ widely in their uses of media and in the functions that those uses serve. Some older persons, like Sarah, are so busy that they do not have much time for television or other media use; others, especially the homebound, use media to fill time. The range of types of media used, functions of those uses, and amount of usage seems to be very similar to the range for all adults over age thirty-five. While the variety is about the same, the intensity or amount of uses varies considerably from that of younger adults and the distribution of use is different. (For example, older people tend to read fewer newspapers because more of them have problems of either eyesight or budget that limit this activity.)

The interviews indicate that there are several categories of media usage. The functions served by the categories are the same as those for the general population, but a particular function may take on more or less importance as a person ages. The categories are not listed in order of importance. You must also understand that they were derived from the answers to open-ended interview questions rather than being given as a checklist. The latter method might have been an easier way to gather data, but it could have left out some important uses that would not have occurred to us in creating the questionnaire. The ten functions, each of which will be discussed individually, are:

(1) To supplement or substitute for interpersonal interactions
(2) To gather content for interpersonal interactions
(3) To form and/or reinforce self-perceptions and to gather information about societal perceptions of various groups of people
(4) To learn appropriate behaviors (including age-appropriate ones)
(5) For intellectual stimulation and challenge (e.g., game shows)
(6) As a less costly substitute for other media (e.g., television news instead of a newspaper)
(7) For networking and mutual support
(8) For self-improvement (e.g., exercise programs, language lessons)
(9) For entertainment
(10) For "company" and safety.

Below we define each of these functions and talk about their relative importance to the elderly.

To supplement or substitute for interpersonal interaction. Two of the most individious hypotheses regarding use of media by the elderly are the disengagement hypothesis[3] and the substitution hypothesis[4] The disengagement hypothesis holds that it is inevitable that older persons will desire to disassociate themselves from increasingly larger portions of their environments. The consequence of this desire for disengagement is withdrawal from both social interaction and exposure to other sources of stimulation, including the media. Fortunately, even before the present study was done the disengagement hypothesis had come into considerable question.[5] Our study shows these doubts to have been valid. Not one of our subjects *desired* disengagement, though a few had even become "de facto" disengaged because of psychological trauma. All of these people wished that they had the ability to interact with others.

Disengagement implies lack of psychological ability to interact. Isolation implies lack of others with whom to interact. Many of our subjects were isolated to some degree. In fact, some could be classified as quite isolated (one to two face-to-face interactions per month). Both they and the disengaged subjects partially confirmed the substitution hypothesis. This hypothesis says that older persons will tend to substitute mass media communication for interpersonal communication when the latter is unavailable or extremely difficult. Eighty-nine percent of our subjects engaged in substitution all or part of the time. Forty percent used substitution occasionally (during illness, when friends or relatives were away); 32 percent used it moderately (to compensate for loneliness created by the deaths and moves of friends and relatives rather than making new friends); and 17 percent used it extensively (mass media were almost a total replacement for interpersonal contact). Most of this last group were homebound; however, most of the homebound persons in our sample used substitution only occasionally or moderately. In other words, most of the homebound persons dealt with their situations by having friends come in or by visiting on the telephone. If the telephone is classified as a substitution, which it is not in the original literature on the hypothesis, then all of our subjects used substitution to some degree. However, as we will see later, it seems more appropriate to treat telephoning separately.

Several studies have indicated that substitution increases life satisfaction.[6] While it is probably true that persons who use substitution are more satisfied than those who use absolutely none, it is also true that 93 percent of our subjects who found themselves forced to substitute mass media communication for interpersonal communication were moderately to extremely dissatisfied with the substitution. Their attitudes are summarized by one homebound woman, age ninety-three, who said: "I watch a lot of television and listen to the radio because I have no one to talk to. All my friends are dead and the relatives I have left don't care. But every time I turn the set on it reminds me that I have no one and that is very depressing. Sometimes I don't bother because I don't want to be reminded of my situation." [7] When we measured life satisfaction in a subsample of two groups of homebound persons that were matched for amount of face-to-face and telephone contact, we did not find a significant correlation between amount of mass media use and satisfaction. Thus, our conclusion is that while it is certainly true that mass media use is substituted for direct interpersonal interaction, the substitution is far from satisfying.

To gather content for interpersonal interactions. This was a rather surprising use of media. It did not occur to us before beginning the interviews. However, 43 percent of our sample volunteered that they used television, radio, and newspapers in this way. Both specific and general information-gathering were used. About 29 percent of the sample mentioned watching specific programs that their friends also watched so that they could use the program as a topic of conversation. Forty percent also mentioned general information-gathering (e.g., "I like to keep up with the news so I won't seem stupid."). The total is more than 43 percent because many people engaged in both specific and general information-gathering.

Self and societal perceptions. There is considerable literature that shows that television is an important influence on our perceptions of ourselves and on our understanding of societal stereotypes and opinions. [8] Though no one in the sample mentioned watching television or using any other medium intentionally for this purpose, almost everyone mentioned the impact of media portrayals on their own behaviors and opinions. Many also mentioned a great deal of irritation at the negatively stereotypic portrayals of older persons in both electronic and print media. They were particularly displeased by the portrayals of older people in commercials and print advertisements. One man, age eighty-four, said: "To see the ads on TV these days a body would think that old folks spend all their time worrying about constipation, loose dentures, and arthritis. And look at that old geezer on the [name deleted] lemonade commercial! They make him out to be deaf and stupid, besides. The whole thing gives old people a bad name." 9 In the panel interviews we talked about whether media portrayals affected the participants' views of themselves and their reactions toward others. Everyone agreed that with few exceptions the effect on their own self-images was negative, something to be overcome. When asked what they would like to see more of in the media, the second choice (after less sex and violence) was more programs specifically for and about old people and more realistic portrayals of the elderly in other programming. In general, both the panels and the individual interviewees felt that the negative stereotype of the elderly presented in the media reflected a societal opinion that older people were useless, infirm, crochety, senile, and a burden. Unless evidence to the contrary is given, most feel that younger people have such attitudes toward them as individuals and behave accordingly. This may lead to a sort of self-fulfilling prophecy in which escalating degrees of negative feelings are displayed between the generations.

Learning appropriate behaviors. This function is related to those discussed in the previous section. Whenever we are called upon to learn new roles, we gather information from a variety of sources. The media, both print and electronic, certainly serve this function for older persons. Seventy-three percent of the respondents said that they follow advice given in the print and electronic media regarding appropriate role behavior (e.g. how to be a good mother-in-law), etiquette, and relations toward others. The problem with following such advice is that the youth-oriented bias mentioned in the previous section may lead to inappropriate behavior and/or interpersonal discomfort. Even though senior citizens find this situation obnoxious, they may follow the models or advice given for lack of more appropriate options.

Intellectual stimulation and challenge. This was another surprising finding. Seventy-six percent of the respondents said that they watch game shows requiring skill or memory in order to challenge themselves. In other words, they play against the players. In general, they find harder games more desirable and prefer not to watch games in which the primary element is luck. They believe that engaging in the mental exercise provided by difficult games preserves intellectual functions. Thirty-eight percent of the sample also work crosswords, acrostics, or other word games at least twice a month for the same reason. Still others work mathematical puzzles, play postal chess, or see Shakespeare to "keep the brain working." There is a very great fear among older people of losing their mental faculties. There is no scientific evidence to indicate that any of the activities mentioned serve a prophylactic function, but there is a widespread belief among the elderly that they do.

As a less costly substitute for other media. One thing that elderly persons have in common with young people is that both groups usually have to function on relatively strict budgets. Among the economies mentioned, the most common was "waiting until the movie comes on television." For the older person in the city this action serves a double function—economy and safety. However, this particular economy is practiced in rural areas with approximately the same frequency as it is in the city. In addition, 56 percent of the sample said that television and the very inexpensive or free entertainments provided by senior centers, religious groups, museums, and the like constituted their *only* forms of entertainment. Other economies included using television and radio news as a cheaper substitute for a daily newspaper, watching public television instead of going to a live performance ("Live from Lincoln Center" appears to be quite popular), writing letters instead of telephoning, and (mostly in the city) taking advantage of free films offered by various groups. There is often an effort to economize even on those media for which one pays by exchanging printed matter with friends, taking advantage of senior citizen discounts, and using libraries and public reading rooms instead of buying books and newspapers.

For networking and mutual support. Though the telephone is a less immediate form of communication than face-to-face conversation, it plays an important role in the lives of the elderly. Unlike substitution of mass media for interpersonal communication that most of the people surveyed found to be unsatisfactory, 97 percent thought that telephone conversations were as good as or better than face-to-face interaction. Eighty-eight percent of the sample participated in some form of formal or informal telephone networking system designed to check to see whether people are in good health. One of these involved no actual interaction. If the person picked up the telephone after three rings and immediately hung up, that was the signal that all was well. Most of the networks involve extensive communication among the members. Thus they serve the functions of friendship and support as well as giving the reassurance that someone will check regularly to see that each person is alive and well. Though there has been no previous research to document whether telephone conversations serve the same functions as personal visits in maintaining cognitive function and psychological health, there is good reason to suppose that they would, at least if supplemented with occasional personal visits.[10] The primary ingredients necessary to maintaining cognitive function and psychological health are feedback and emotional support. Both of these functions are served by the telephone. As mentioned earlier, some older people actually prefer telephone visits to personal ones because telephone conversations do not require dressing, house-cleaning, getting out of bed, or providing refreshments. There is also less feeling of obligation because a telephone call is perceived as requiring less effort on the part of the caller than a personal visit. Of course, no one indicated a desire to completely replace personal interactions with telephone visits, but almost everyone felt that a telephone call was as good or better than a visit in many cases. Everyone interviewed indicated that the telephone was crucial to feeling secure and independent and it appeared that almost everyone would give up nearly every other convenience and necessity before giving up the telephone if economy measures were necessary. In fact, such is the fear among the elderly that they will become ill out of reach of the telephone that those who are able to afford it have one in each room or a cordless portable model. One popular device is a battery-operated medallion that will ring "911" when a button is pressed.

For self-improvement. Our culture instills in us the value of constant self-improvement. This is no less true among elderly persons than among other groups. In fact, they may have a greater need to engage in activities that lead to self-improvement because they do not have the excuse of too much work to assuage their guilt. Almost everyone in the sample engaged in hobby, volunteer, self-improvement or other "work." Twenty-one percent of the sample used television or radio self-improvement programs for purposes of maintaining health (mainly exercise programs) or learning something (cooking, a language, carpentry, gardening). Thirty-nine percent used print media for systematic learning or self-improvement. A part of this thirty-nine per cent overlaps the 21 percent who used television and radio, but a total of 51 percent of the entire sample used identifiable media sources for self-improvement of some sort. In addition, a large number of people—about 62 percent of the sample—regularly listened to phonograph or tape recordings of music or other materials for purposes of learning something or improving themselves in some way and 12 percent of the sample had made a telephone call to a tape-recorded medical information library in the previous year.

For entertainment. Everyone in the sample used media for entertainment at rates which ranged from twice per week to almost constantly. From the participation figures given by the subjects, it seems reasonable to believe that some of what was listed as "pure entertainment" had already been listed elsewhere (gathering content for interpersonal interactions, self-improvement, etc.) by the coders because some of the busier subjects seem to have had no room for sleeping and eating in their schedules. This category was originally meant to reflect recreational communication, but it seems to have been contaminated along the way. Despite this problem in coding, it seems reasonable to conclude that elderly people, like everyone else, spend a certain amount of time using the media recreationally. For the same reasons that differences occur among younger adults—cultural values, time taken by other activities, psychological needs, and so on—there is a wide range in recreational activity levels.

For "company" and safety. All of our subjects lived alone in their own homes or apartments. Thus it is not surprising that, like younger people, many of them play the television, radio, or phonograph so that they will not seem so "alone" in the house. Fifty-four percent of the sample used the media for "company" at least part of the time. We have not been able to find any corresponding data for younger adults, but the fact that most who used media in this way said that they had either done it all their lives or at times when they had been alone would lead us to believe that such usage by younger people would be similar. For some reason, 34 percent of our sample (some overlap with the "company" figures) also believed that having the television or radio on gave them an additional measure of safety from intruders when they were in the house alone. Police have indicated to us that while additional protection from intruders is afforded by playing a radio or television when one is away because it makes the dwelling seem to be occupied, there is no extra protection if someone is already in the house.[11] Perhaps the sounds make these people (mostly women) feel less alone, or perhaps they have misunderstood the police advice about home protection, but for some reason they feel safer if the television or radio is playing.

Content Preferences of Older Persons

Although the kinds of media use by older people are similar to uses found among younger groups, their content preferences are markedly different. Nearly everyone in our sample felt that there was too much explicit sexual activity (some of what they defined as explicit is defined as innuendo by others) and too many "dirty" jokes on prime time television and in films. Ninety-four percent of the sample expressed disapproval of such television programs as "Three's Company," "Charlie's Angels," "Mork and Mindy," "M.A.S.H.," and other popular programs. Many of them watched the soap operas but tended to think that they had "gone downhill since they started to get dirty." Approximately 15 percent refused to watch soap operas any longer, though they had been ardent fans at one time, because of the increased explicitness and sexuality. They tended to prefer dramas with little sex or violence and bland humor such as "Little House on the Prairie" or "The Waltons." Lawrence Welk's musical show was also a great favorite. In short, the older audience is much more conservative about sex and somewhat more conservative about violence than the younger generation.

Conclusions

The catalogue of media uses and functions is the same for both older and younger adults. The primary differences occur in the relative importance of the various uses and in preferred content for such media as radio, television, and films. But to describe the similarities and differences in use between older and younger generations is not to tell the whole story. The media serve as a source of both the substance and the form of our interpersonal interactions. Our only other models are our own and others' real-life interactions. It would be very tidy if the media and real-life models did not interact. But they do. Each modifies the other in innumerable and not easily definable ways.

We cannot blame the media for our dread of growing old. That dread has led many persons to risk life and limb in search of a "Fountain of Youth." We can ask the media to present old age realistically—neither ignoring it, nor debasing it, nor glorifying it. We can also ask the media to serve the needs of the older population more adequately than they are now doing. Currently most prime-time programming has been aimed at the magical eighteen to thirty-four-year age group, which advertisers are only now beginning to realize is rapidly shrinking in both numbers and monetary resources.[12] As the older groups grow in numbers and monetary resources, advertisers may begin to listen to their demands and the balance may be restored. Then the media and real-life interactions may become reasonably similar in substance and form. At least one can hope.

Notes

1. Gary Gumpert and Robert Cathcart, eds., *Inter/Media: Interpersonal Communication in a Media World.* New York: Oxford University Press, 1979, p. 154.

2. The idea of degrees of mediation is suggested by many perceptual psychologists; see Fritz Heider, *The Psychology of Interpersonal Relations,* New York: John Wiley, 1957; and by media specialists; see Wilbur Schramm, "Channels and Audiences," in Ithiel de Sola Pool, et al., eds., *Handbook of Communication,* Chicago: Rand McNally, 1973.

3. E. Cumming and W. E. Henry, *Growing Old.* New York: Basic Books, 1961.

4. M. J. Graney and E. E. Graney, "Communications Activity Substitutions in Aging," *Journal of Communication,* 1974, 24(4), 88–96.

5. There are many problems with disengagement theory. Several articles surrounding the issue appear in L. R. Goulet and P. B. Baltes, eds., *Life Span Developmental Psychology: Research and Theory,* New York: Academic Press, 1970.

6. M. J. Graney, "Happiness and Social Participation in Aging," *Journal of Gerontology,* 1975, *30,* 701–706.

7. Interview with subject #17336, October, 1980, New York, N.Y.

8. For a good review of this literature see Melvin DeFleur and Edward Dennis, *Understanding Media,* Chicago: Scott-Foresman, 1981.

9. Interview with subject #22748, December, 1980, New York, N.Y.

10. The same interviews that served as the basis for the study reported here also included a number of tests of cognitive functioning and questions about direct interpersonal communication levels. The results of these questions indicate that cognitive functioning level and psychological well-being are strongly associated with levels of feedback and support.

11. Personal communication, Senior Citizen Protection Program, New York City Police Department, May, 1981.

12. "Oldsters Grow More Numerous," *Active Aging,* Wichita, Kansas: Wichita State University, May, 1981, p. 4.

Postscript

It is interesting to speculate about the future, to try to imagine what life will be like in the year 2001. Will we really be able to travel from galaxy to galaxy as easily as we fly to London or Honolulu? Will we be able to see and talk with anyone, at any time, anywhere in this world with the simple flip of a switch? Will humanlike computers do most of our thinking and work for us? It's fun to think about the kind of technical hardware that will be available to us twenty years from now: there seems to be no limit, considering what we have seen developed in the last twenty years. One thing we can be sure of is that all these technological innovations will even further speed up and extend our reliance on the mass media of communication.

A little more difficult to imagine and maybe more frightening than fun is what will we be like as persons in the twenty-first century? How will we relate to each other when our mediated face-to-face interactions can be carried on everywhere, all at once, with almost everyone in the world? What will happen to our sense of self as we become more cut off from immediate personal sensory perception and become almost totally dependent on mediated sensing? What will happen to feelings of love and intimacy when there is no more privacy? What will happen to our relationships with doctors and teachers, when diagnosing and instructing will be done through computers? We don't know the answers to these questions, but they can't be ignored and they won't go away because we cannot escape the fact that all of our lives and all of our relationships are intricately intertwined with the technology and the media which surround us.

We end this volume with a look into the future. Jon Bradshaw calls his article "A Science Fiction Story That's All True." He traces the development of future media and gives his interpretation of what we will be like when that future takes shape. Although lighthearted, Bradshaw is warning us that the future will bring about drastic changes in all of us, some of which may not be to our liking.

No matter what you think our future may be, bright or gloomy, remember that most of the predictions made in 1882 about the twentieth century didn't work out the way the futurists said they would. Whether we are better off now or worse off than we were then is debatable. What is not debatable is that we do live in a media world and all our interpersonal relationships are part of that world.

JON BRADSHAW

The Shape of Media Things to Come
(A Science-Fiction Story That's All True)

This is no place to begin. There is no *real* place to begin. Confronted with infinity, with this wonderfully unreal world we have made, it is difficult to conjure up beginnings. Impossible, really. I'll try to recall a few of the less pedestrian memories, but it was all so long ago and the records of the period are sketchy and incomplete.

It is probably best to begin in the middle 1970s. There was an exaggerated concern then that man was becoming plastic, that his best instincts had been somehow pirated, that he had become, in a quaint word of the time, homogenized. Ridiculous, really, in light of what happened later. But an ecology movement had begun. People, usually the young, gorged themselves on natural foods, grew plants and vegetables, jogged, hiked, camped out, and spoke religiously of the environment. Everyone talked about . . . the soil. It was, I imagine, escapist and fun and gave many otherwise uneducable youths something essentially harmless to do.

But while this movement reeled clumsily backward toward communes and the land, a separate revolution was taking place—accelerating more quickly than anyone could have known then. During the early seventies, world communications were still imperfect, primitive even, little more than common gadgetry. People *communicated*—at least that was what it was called—but with considerable delay and at inconvenient distances. In 1976 people still drove automobiles; they read newspapers, magazines, and books; they traveled to cinemas and listened to stereo systems that were little more than crude machines. They communicated on walkie-talkies and plodded between the earth and the moon on cramped spaceships. They watched an audio-visual contraption called "television," listened to pictureless "radio," and had just begun to toy with the computer in their homes. As the seventies drew to a close, the more affluent members of the society became obsessed with "electronics."

From *New York,* April 19, 1976. Reprinted by permission of the publisher and the author.

The so-called media room was created in the home and it was stocked with the sophisticated gimmickry of the period. Such rooms had something called the Advent screen, a seven-foot-diagonal television screen, its images projected from an ugly box which dominated the room. There were video-tape casettes with which one recorded television programs, and audiotape decks that played music through huge speakers, in order to give a kind of sense-around sound. There were video disks containing current films, and luminous video art occupied the walls.

Throughout the rest of the home, communications systems were hooked up to a Touch-tone telephone system—the dual-tone multifrequency phone, or D.T.M.F., as it was known. This ancient transmission device enabled its owner to check a bank account, order prescriptions, shop for food, and verify credit cards automatically, without leaving home. The so-called code-a-phone could take messages and be accessed remotely in order to retrieve those messages taken in the owner's absence. A telephonic call-forwarding device rerouted incoming calls. A device called speedcalling connected one instantly, to other cities across the world. And add-on conference calls enabled one to plug in three or four callers simultaneously. The telephone could be programmed to wake you up; on cold days, it could pre-ignite the car engine and heater and turn on the heating in your country home. It could, in fact, be made to control all electrical functions in the home—the oven, the doors, lights, radios, television sets, and air conditioning.

Despite the simplicity of these devices, more and more people were becoming, in a phrase of the time, "communications freaks." A huge industry proliferated around them. Automobiles, personal transportation modules, were equipped with telephones and television. Wireless citizen-band radios were an automobile necessity—for highway emergencies and traffic updates. Homes were fitted with video intercoms and video security systems. Wireless telephones and wireless headsets came into general use. Picture phones were available but they were in black and white and were employed, for the most part, in executive conference rooms. There were video tennis matches and hockey games, and video chess games preprogrammed by experts. Many homes contained video synthesizers and colorizers, enabling a child to draw psychedelic pictures on the television screen. Telephonic photostat machines transmitted written words and pictures across the world.

The technology was unsophisticated, but widespread. Already, the functional illiterate of the time was the person who couldn't type, because one *had* to type to work a computer. Due to the digital clock, this was the last generation to know the difference between clockwise and counterclockwise. One early computer device was the DIVA—data input, voice answer—but it was soon replaced by audio computers which translated words into functions. During the late seventies, the stored-program computerized telephone systems, which were replacing the outdated electromechanical telephone exchanges, were obsolete on installation, due to improvements in circuitry and miniaturization. A low form of early computer talk, FORTRAN, was being taught in the universities, and elementary schools were teaching computer logic. A new slang sprang up, employing such words as "phase," "out of phase," "interphase," "biofeedback," "biofeed-forward," and, when referring to human malfunctions, "gigo" (garbage in, garbage out). The media room was being transformed from an entertainment center to a kind of communications command post. Yet the underlying technology remained at a childish level.

Experts and technocrats were strangely ignorant of the direction technology would eventually take. Since computerized equipment was simply too expensive for the mass of home users, it took many years for a market to be created. And, as elementary as it now sounds, it was the backwardness of communications which produced the major dilemmas of the period—for example, pollution, the preference for living in vertical spaces, the widespread lack of food that led to war and other forms of profiteering, and the obstinate addiction to the old-fashioned wheel.

In retrospect, man's lack of ingenuity is almost unbelievable, and I must continually remind myself that in those dark times he was little more than a barbaric child. The chief characteristics of that culture, particularly the American culture, were immediacy, impact, and sensation. In electronic terms the culture was merely self-indulgent. The future meant instant gratification, which is what instant photographs and videotapes were all about. It was not until copper wires had been replaced with broad-band optical fibers that communications became somewhat more refined. Broad-band optical fibers, activated and enforced by laser propulsion, meant that their users could link up with central information services in order to hear what they wished to hear instead of what someone else wanted them to hear. For example, a universal television retrieval system came into being, attached to the telephone. Wired to a home computer terminal, the system contained a constantly updated encyclopedia of information available to anyone with the ability to press a button. Security systems became computerized and could detect and isolate burglaries instantaneously. All shopping was performed through the computer-telex and all mail and newspapers were now effected through computer-television.

The large TV screen, modern so short a time before, was replaced with a three-dimensional wraparound wallscreen. Even middle-class homes were glutted with voice-activated typewriters, picture phones, hologram-projection machines, and laser burglar alarms set not to kill but to stun. The well-to-do sported decorative computer watches on their wrists and laser scanners in their libraries. Most homes were solar powered. Videophiles had become videomaniacs.

The home had now become a total environment—the ultimate cocoon—and life, its bemused inhabitants believed, was terribly modern. More important, and for the first time, an intimate dialogue had been initiated between man and the machine. The computer had eliminated the merely mechanical. All essentially mechanical movements, in fact, were becoming obsolete, although they had not yet been taken, as you will see, to their purely logical conclusions.

Almost no one "traveled" anymore. More and more business was conducted from the home. Students were educated in the home; and as an alternative to the horrors of enforced holidays, the three-dimensional wraparound screen allowed one to *be* in, say, the South of France, and the sound-around system made soft Mediterranean noises. The wraparound screen also enabled one to link up with live concerts, sporting events, or any other public function. Computer units had become micro-miniaturized, operating on a less-input, more-output ratio. The computer, or Central Processing Unit as it came to be known, controlled everything. The demand for communication between computers was filled by the laser. The portable C.P.U., worn as a watch, was a peripheral device linked by matching light frequencies to the main C.P.U., and it provided a time-divisional highway along which multiplexed information was transmitted. The tiny device functioned as a calculator, watch, telephone, and memory bank. You didn't have to know what you wanted from the C.P.U.; it calculated that for you. It always knew what you wanted because it knew you.

In the home itself, manual lighting had been replaced by glow walls, which stored light by day and emitted it by night. The kitchen had become redundant. In its place, each home was equipped with a photosynthesis module that provided highly enriched liquids for human nourishment. There was no longer any need for old-fashioned "foods." Curiously, to begin with there were grudging complaints that life would never be the same without "cheeseburgers" or "Château Lafite '39," but it soon ceased to be a problem. No one could remember what they had tasted like.

The art world, too, had been revolutionized. Homes of the period were decorated with multiflex neon sculptures, frozen-light murals, and dancing three-dimensional laser paintings. Some homes had image walls on which one could project computerized portraits in color.

No one actually wrote anymore. Books had long since disappeared. As for newspapers and magazines, in the late seventies they were already hopelessly archaic. With the introduction of the new photonic systems, information was now being transmitted by light, almost always when one was asleep, so that on waking one had already "read" the "newspaper."

The computer had become self-evolving, self-sustaining. It performed its own maintenance as well as physical repair. Unlike men, it never required a doctor. Functioning in seconds, it soon sped to microseconds, to milliseconds, and then to nanoseconds, and continued to accelerate.

Computers were used to build computers, of course. Only another computer, in fact, could provide the degree of accuracy necessary to breed a further generation of computers. It was learned that just as human families have generic traits, so do computers. As a result, new breeds of computers came into being, their birth made possible by a much improved generic program.

Although world communications had evolved considerably, one major flaw remained which impeded progress for many years. In pure computer-communicative terms, man had always been beamed into his environment. It was not until man learned to beam the environment into *him* that real progress, as we understand it today, was possible. As early as 1976, scientists experimented with computers that had no external monitor—brain-implanted computers—but they were crude gimcracks.

As everyone now knows, the evolutionary process began to accelerate. All essentially mechanical movements, whether those of machines or of man himself, became slowly obsolete and man, in time, arrived at a new definition of himself. It is interesting to note that man, who had never been as advanced as the computer, relinquished his mechanical grasp of life only after the computer had compelled him to evolve or die.

Given the old dilemmas of environmental pollution, the rising decibel level, and the constant exposure to the new visual age, there had been a steady erosion of purely human senses. The swift advances in computerized communications only hastened the inevitable. The sense of taste was the first sense to disappear, then smell, then touch, and almost immediately thereafter, hearing. Speech had always been a highly mechanical form of communication, tiresome and time-consuming. As long ago as 1984, the spoken vocabulary had dwindled to a few hundred words. I have always been surprised that the spoken word lasted as long as it did, that it had not disappeared with the introduction of the telepathic computer, which permitted one to "talk" in a more direct and efficient manner. Once the telepathic computer—worn as a watch and linked directly to the nervous system—became fashionable, speech was no longer necessary. The new language created instant communication, instant comprehension.

The same electronic potentials that in the old days were used to program the computer were now employed to load the core of the brain, and they could initiate queries to the computer. At first, "speech" was known as "data input" and ultimately was reduced to logic format for purposes of communicating with more sophisticated beings—as computers were now called. They revolutionized the home, of course. Spaces were equipped with ultrasonic mood systems, especially sensitized to their inhabitants, so that intimate communication was possible on every level without people having to move from one room to another.

New thresholds demanded new anatomies. The human body itself, long an awkward weight to cart around, had become little more than a vexatious bore. The crude mechanical functions for which it had been created—hunting, walking, eating, reproducing—were antiquated now. Sex, for example—if history is to be believed—was considered an amiable pursuit, but it never could have been more than a vulgar form of communication. Fortunately it was much improved upon. Once it became a telepathic act, intercourse was purer, more perfect, and, most important, more efficient.

The last of the crude senses to atrophy was sight. Given what seems, even to such a cynic as myself, the really extraordinary developments in cosmic technology, it was soon no longer necessary to open the eyes. Why bother? Entire universes were available when the eyes were shut. It was the last of the old sensory barriers to be overcome.

It is difficult and not a little tedious to catalog the complicated advances that have taken place since then. And I've said much too much already. Suffice it to say that one occupies infinity. And I've not left this particular space for twenty years or more. There is no longer any "time," at least as you would comprehend it, so it is difficult to be precise. There are no "people" as such. There is no "sign of life." Consider it another way. As you must know, the source of all life is light, and we have simply, if I may use so complex a term, become light again. And it amuses me, you understand, to use this primitive form of communication in order to tell you so.

Bibliography

MICHAEL SCHUDSON   **The Ideal of Conversation in the Study of Mass Media**

Chaffee, S. H. (1967) "The public view of the media as carriers of information between school and community." Journalism Q. 44 (Winter): 732.

Dewey, J. (1948) Reconstruction in Philosophy. Boston: Beacon Press.

—— (1920) "Americanism and localism." The Dial 68 (June): 686.

Duvignaud, J. (1970) Change at Shebika. New York: Random House.

Emery, E. (1972) The Press and America. Englewood Cliffs: Prentice-Hall.

Iwanska, A. (1958) Good fortune: second chance community. Washington Agricultural Experiment Stations State College of Washington, Bull. 589 (June): 29.

Juergens, G. (1966) Joseph Pulitzer and the New York World. Princeton: Princeton Univ. Press.

Keenan, E. (1974) "Norm-makers, norm-breakers: uses of speech by men and women in a Malagasy community," pp. 125–143 in R. Bauman and J. Sherzer (eds.) Explorations in the ethnography of speaking. Cambridge: Cambridge Univ. Press.

Marshall, L. (1968) "Sharing, talking and giving: relief of social tension among IKung bushmen," pp. 179–184 in J. A. Fishman, Readings in the sociology of language. Hague: Mouton.

Mead, G. H. (1926) "The nature of aesthetic experience." International J. of Ethics 36 (July): 382–393.

Park, R. (1923) "The natural history of the newspaper." Amer. J. of Sociology 29 (November): 273–289.

Pinter, H. (1962) "A Slight Ache," in Three plays. New York: Grove.

Reisman, K. (1974) "Contrapuntal conversations in an Antiguan village," p. 115 in R. Bauman and J. Sherzer (eds.) Explorations in the ethnography of speaking. Cambridge: Cambridge Univ. Press.

Schudson, M. (1978) Discovering the news. New York: Basic Books.

Sennett, R. (1977) The fall of public man. New York: Alfred A. Knopf.

GERALD R. MILLER   **A Neglected Connection: Mass Media Exposure and Interpersonal Communication Competency**

Berger, C. R., Gardner, R. R., Parks, M. R., Schulman, L., and Miller, G. R. (1976) "Interpersonal epistemology and interpersonal communication." In

G. R. Miller (Ed.), Explorations in interpersonal communication. Beverly Hills, Calif.: Sage Publications.

Blumer, J. G., and Katz, E. (Eds.). (1974) The uses of mass communication: Current perspectives on gratifications research. Beverly Hills, Calif.: Sage Publications.

Bundens, R. W. (1980) The effects of type of information, dogmatism, and sex of dyad on predictive accuracy. Unpublished masters thesis, Michigan State University.

deTurck, M. A., and Miller, G. R. (1981) A scale for measuring propensity for psychological-level prediction. Unpublished paper, Michigan State University.

Katz, E., and Lazarsfeld, P. F. (1955) Personal influence. Glencoe, Ill.: The Free Press of Glencoe.

Katz, E., Gurevitch, M., and Haas, H. (1973) "On the use of mass media for important things." American Sociological Review 38: 164–181.

Kelly, G. A. (1955) The psychology of personal constructs. Vol. 1. New York: W. W. Norton.

Lazarsfeld, P. F., Berelson, B. R., and Gaudet, H. (1944) The people's choice. New York: Duell, Sloan and Pearce.

McLuhan, N. (1964) Understanding media: The extensions of man. New York: McGraw-Hill.

Miller, G. R. (1977) "Communication in the third 100 years: Can humanity and technology coexist peacefully?" Centennial Review 21: 176–193.

Miller, G. R., and Steinberg, M. (1975) Between people: A new analysis of interpersonal communication. Chicago: Science Research Associates.

Miller, G. R., and Sunnafrank, M. (1982) "All is for one, but one is not for all: A conceptual perspective of interpersonal communication." In F. E. X. Dance (Ed.) Human communication theory. New York: Harper & Row.

Nordenstreng, K. (1970) "Comments on gratifications research in broadcasting." Public Opinion Quarterly, 34: 130–132.

WILBUR SCHRAMM **Channels and Audiences**

Allport, F. H. (1955) Theories of Perception and the Concept of Structure. New York: Wiley.

Allport, Gordon W., and L. J. Postman. (1945) "The basic psychology of rumor." Transactions of the New York Academy of Science (second series) 8:61–81.

Asher, J. J. (1961) Sensory Interrelationships in the Automated Teaching of Foreign Languages. Washington, D.C.: U.S. Office of Education.

Bauer, R. A. (1964) "The obstinate audience." American Psychologist 19 (No. 5):319–328.

Baxter, W. S. (1960) "The mass media and young people." Journal of Broadcasting 5:49–58.

Berelson, Bernard. (1949) The Library's Public. New York: Columbia University Press.

Berelson, Bernard; P. F. Lazarsfeld: and W. N. McPhee. (1954) Voting: A Study of

Opinion Formation in a Presidential Campaign. Chicago: University of Chicago Press.

Berelson, Bernard, and G. A. Steiner. (1964) Human Behavior: An Inventory of Research Findings. New York: Harcourt, Brace and World.

Berlo, David K. (1960) The Process of Communication. New York: Holt, Rinehart and Winston.

Blumer, Herbert. (1946) "The crowd, the public, and the mass," in Alfred McClung Lee, Jr. (ed.), New Outline of the Principles of Sociology. New York: Barnes and Noble.

Broadbent, D. E. (1958) Perception and Communication. New York: Pergamon Press.

Canadian Daily Newspaper Publishers Association. (1963) Report of a Study on the Daily Newspaper in Canada and Its Reading Publics (September-October, 1962). Toronto: Canadian Daily Newspaper Publishers Association.

Cantril, Hadley, and Gordon W. Allport. (1935) The Psychology of Radio. New York: Harper.

Carey, J. W. (1967) "Harold Adams Innis and Marshall McLuhan." The Antioch Review 27 (No. 1):5–39.

DeFleur, M. L. (1966) Theories of Mass Communication. New York: McKay.

Deutschmann, P. J. (1957) "The sign-situation classification of human communication." Journal of Communication 7 (No. 2):63–73.

Feigenbaum, E. A., and H. A. Simon. (1961) "Brief notes on the EPAM theory of verbal learning." Pp. 333–335 in C. N. Cofer and Barbara S. Musgrave (eds.), Verbal Behavior and Verbal Learning. New York: McGraw-Hill.

Festinger, Leon, and John W. Thibaut. (1951) "Interpersonal communication in small groups." Journal of Abnormal and Social Psychology 46:92–99.

Freedman, J. L., and D. O. Sears. (1965) "Selective exposure." Pp. 58–97 in Leonard Berkowitz (ed.), Advances in Experimental Social Psychology. Volume 2. New York: Academic Press.

Fujiwara, N. (1969) "Televiewing of Japanese people." Studies of Broadcasting 7:55–104.

Geiger, Kent, and Robert Sokol. (1959) "Social norms in television-watching." American Journal of Sociology 65 (September):174–181.

Handel, Leo A. (1950) Hollywood Looks at Its Audience: A Report of Film Audience Research. Urbana: University of Illinois Press.

Hartman, F. R. (1961) "Single and multiple channel communication: A review of research and a proposed model." AV Communication Review 9 (No. 6):235–262.

Hovland, Carl I. (ed.). (1957) The Order of Presentation in Persuasion. New Haven: Yale University Press.

Hovland, Carl I.; I. L. Janis; and H. H. Kelley. (1953) Communication and Persuasion. New Haven: Yale University Press.

Hovland, Carl I.; A. A. Lumsdaine; and F. D. Sheffield. (1949) Experiments on Mass Communication. Princeton: Princeton University Press.

Hsia, H. J. (1968) "On channel effectiveness." AV Communication Review 16 (No. 3):245–267.

Innis, H. A. (1950) Empire and Communications. London: Oxford University Press.

—— (1951) The Bias of Communication. Toronto: University of Toronto Press.

Jacobson, Homer. (1950) "The information capacity of the human ear." Science 112:143–144.

—— (1951a) "The information capacity of the human eye." Science 113:292–293.

—— (1951b) "Information and the human ear." Journal of the Acoustical Society of America 23:463–471.

Katz, Elihu, and P. F. Lazarsfeld. (1955) Personal Influence: The Part Played by People in the Flow of Mass Communications. Glencoe, Illinois: Free Press.

Kendall, P. L., and K. M. Wolf. (1949) "Deviant case analysis in the Mr. Biggott study." Pp. 152–179 in P. F. Lazarsfeld and F. N. Stanton (eds.), Communication Research, 1948–49. New York: Harper and Row.

Klapper, J. T. (1960) The Effects of Mass Communication. New York: Free Press of Glencoe.

Lasswell, H. D. (1927) Propaganda Technique in the World War. New York: Knopf.

—— (1948) "The structure and function of communications," in Lyman Bryson (ed.), The Communication of Ideas. New York: Harper.

Lasswell, H. D., and Dorothy Blumenstock. (1939) World Revolutionary Propaganda: A Chicago Study. Chicago: University of Chicago Press.

Lazarsfeld, P. F. (1940) Radio and the Printed Page. New York: Duell, Sloan and Pearce.

—— (1948) Radio Listening in America. New York: Prentice-Hall.

Lazarsfeld, P. F., and P. L. Kendall. (1948) "The communication behavior of the average American." Pp. 1–17 in Radio Listening in America: Report on a Survey Conducted by the National Opinion Research Center of the University of Chicago. New York: Prentice-Hall.

Lazarsfeld, P. F., and R. K. Merton. (1948) "Mass communication, popular taste, and organized social action," in Lyman Bryson (ed.), The Communication of Ideas. New York: Harper.

Lewin, K. (1953) "Studies in group decision," in Dorwin Cartwright and A. F. Zander (eds.), Group Dynamics. Evanston, Illinois: Row Peterson.

Link, H. C., and H. A. Hopf. (1946) People and Books. New York: Book Industry Committee, Book Manufacturers' Institute.

McLuhan, Marshall. (1962) The Gutenberg Galaxy. Toronto: University of Toronto Press.

—— (1964) Understanding Media. New York: McGraw-Hill.

May, M. A., and A. A. Lumsdaine. (1958) Learning from Films. New Haven: Yale University Press.

Merrill, I. R. (1961) "Broadcast viewing and listening by children." Public Opinion Quarterly 25 (No. 2):263–276.

Miller, G. A. (1956) "The magical number seven, plus or minus two: Some limits on our capacity for processing information." Psychological Review 63:81–97.

Nebylitsyn, V. D. (1961) "Individual differences in the strength and sensitivity of both visual and auditory analysers." Pp. 52–74 in Neil O'Connor (ed.), Recent Soviet Psychology. Translation by Ruth Kisch [and others]. New York: Liveright.

Newsprint Information Committee. (1961) A National Study of Newspaper Reading—March, April, 1961. Prepared for Newsprint Information Committee. New York: Audits and Surveys Company.

Osgood, C. E. (1953) Experimental Psychology. New York: Oxford University Press.

Pierce, J. R., and J. E. Karlin. (1957) "Reading rates and the information rate of a human channel." Bell System Technical Journal 36:497–516.

Politz, Alfred. (1947) The Readers of the Saturday Evening Post. Prepared by Alfred Politz Research, Inc. Philadelphia: Curtis Publishing Company.

Riley, Matilda W. (1969) Aging and Society. Volume 2. New York: Russell Sage.

Samuelson, M.; R. F. Carter; and W. L. Ruggels. (1963) "Education, available time, and use of mass media." Journalism Quarterly 40 (No. 4):491–496.

Schneider, Louis, and Sverre Lysgaard. (1953) "Deferred gratification pattern." American Sociological Review 18 (April):142–149.

Schramm, Wilbur. (1954) "How communication works." Pp. 3–26 in Wilbur Schramm (ed.), The Process and Effects of Mass Communication. Urbana: University of Illinois Press.

Schramm, Wilbur; Jack Lyle; and E. B. Parker (1961) Television in the Lives of Our Children. Stanford, California: Stanford University Press.

Schramm, Wilbur; Jack Lyle; and Ithiel deS. Pool. (1963) The People Look at Educational Television. Stanford, California: Stanford University Press.

Schramm, Wilbur, and D. M. White. (1949) "Age, education, economic status: Factors in newspaper reading." Journalism Quarterly 29 (No. 2):149–159.

Steiner, G. A. (1963) The People Look at Television. New York: Knopf.

Stephenson, W. P. (1967) The Play Theory of Mass Communication. Chicago: University of Chicago Press.

Tada, T. (1969) "Image-cognition: A developmental approach." Studies of Broadcasting 8:105–174.

Travers, R. M. W. (1964) "The transmission of information to human receivers." AV Communication Review 12:373–385.

Travers, R. M. W., and J. J. Bosco. (1967) "Direct measures of the human information channel capacity." Pp. 273–274 in Proceedings of the 75th Annual Convention [Washington, D.C., September 1–5]. Washington, D.C.: American Psychological Association.

Wade, Serena, and Wilbur Schramm. (1969) "Mass media as sources of public affairs, science, and health knowledge." Public Opinion Quarterly 33:197–209.

Waples, Douglas; Bernard Berelson; and F. R. Bradshaw. (1940) What Reading Does to People. Chicago: University of Chicago Press.

Westley, B. H., and W. J. Severin. (1964) "A profile of the daily newspaper nonreader." Journalism Quarterly 41 (No. 1):45–50.

Whorf, B. L. (1956) Language, Thought, and Reality. Edited by J. B. Carroll. New York: Wiley.

Zimmerman, Claire, and R. A. Bauer. (1956) "The effect of an audience upon what is remembered." Public Opinion Quarterly 20:238–248.

S. J. BALL-ROKEACH AND MELVIN L. DeFLEUR
A Dependency Model of Mass Media Effects

Altman, I. and D. Taylor. (1973) Social Penetration. New York: Holt, Rinehart and Winston.

Ball-Rokeach, S. (1973) "From pervasive ambiguity to a definition of the situation." Sociometry 36, 3:378–389.

Blumler, J. and E. Katz [eds.]. (1974) The Use of Communications. Sage Annual Reviews of Communication Research, Vol. III. Beverly Hills, Calif.: Sage.

Cooley, C. (1909) Social Organizations. New York: Scribner's.

Durkheim, E. (1951) Suicide (trans. by J. Spaulding and G. Simpson). Glencoe, Ill.: Free Press.

———— (1933) The Division of Labor in Society (trans. by G. Simpson). New York: Macmillan.

Hyman, H. (1973) "Mass communication and socialization." Public Opinion Q. 37, 4:524–540.

Klapp, O. (1972) Currents of Unrest. New York: Holt, Rinehart and Winston.

Larsen, O. (1964) "Social effects of mass communication," in R. Faris (ed.) Handbook of Modern Sociology. Chicago: Rand McNally.

Lerner, D. (1969) "Managing communications for modernization: A developmental approach," in A. Rose (ed.) Politics, Personality, and Social Science in the Twentieth Century. Chicago: Univ. of Chicago Press.

———— (1959) The Passing of Traditional Society. New York: Free Press.

Marx, K. (1961) Economic and Philosophic Manuscripts of 1844. Moscow: Foreign Languages Publ. House.

McLeod, J., L. Becker and J. Byrnes. (1974) "Another look at the agenda-setting function of the press." Communication Research 1, 2:131–166.

Mead, G. (1934) Mind, Self and Society. Chicago: Univ. of Chicago Press.

Merton, R. (1946) The Social Psychology of a War Bond Drive. New York: Harper.

Rokeach, M. (1973) The Nature of Human Values. New York: Free Press.

Rosenthal, A. (1964) Thirty-Eight Witnesses. New York: McGraw Hill.

Seymour-Ure, C. (1974) The Political Impact of Mass Media. Beverly Hills, Calif.: Sage.

Sheatsley, P. and J. Feldman. (1969) "The assassination of President Kennedy," pp. 259–283 in R. Evans (eds.) Readings In Collective Behavior. Chicago: Rand McNally.

Stein, A. and L. Friedrich. (1971) "Television content and young children's behavior," pp. 202–313 in Television and Social Behavior, Vol. 11. Washington, D.C.: Government Printing Office.

Weiss, W. (1969) "Effects of the mass media of communication," pp. 77–195 in G. Lindzey and E. Aronson (eds.) Handbook of Social Psychology (vol. 5, 2nd ed.). Reading, Mass.: Addison-Wesley.

Wertham, F. (1954) Seduction of the Innocent. New York: Holt, Rinehart and Winston.

Wright, C. (1974) "Functional analysis and mass communication revisited," pp. 197–212 in J. Blumier and E. Katz (ed.). The Uses of Mass Communications. Sage Annual Reviews of Communications Research, Vol. III. Beverly Hills, Calif.: Sage.

Wright, C. (1959) Mass Communication. New York: Random House.

KARL ERIK ROSENGREN AND SWEN WINDAHL   **Mass Media Consumption as a Functional Alternative**

Blumler, J. G., Brown, J. R., and McQuail, D. (1970) The Social Origins of the Gratifications Associated with Television Viewing. Mimeo.

Brown, J. S. (1968) "Acquired drives." International Encyclopedia of the Social Sciences, vol. 4. New York: Macmillan.

Dysinger, W. S., and Rucknick, C. A. (1933) The Emotional Responses of Children to the Motion Picture Situation. New York: Macmillan.

Emmett, B. P. (1968) "A new role for research in broadcasting." Public Opinion Question 32: 654–65.

Horton, D., and Wohl, R. R. (1956) "Mass communication and para-social interaction." Psychiatry 19: 215–29.

Lundberg, D., and Hultén, O. (1968) Individen och Massmedia, Stockholm: Nordstedt & Soner. (in Swedish)

Noredenstreng, K. (1969) "Consumption of mass media in Finland." Gazette 15: 249–259.

Merton, R. K. (1963) Social theory and social structure. New York: Free Press, pp. 34 ff.

Theodorson, G. A., and Theordorson, A. G. (1970) A Modern Dictionary of Sociology. London: Methuen.

Turner, M. A. (1958) News-reading behavior and social adjustment, Journalism Question 35: 199–204.

Zetterberg, H. L. (1965) On theory and verification in sociology. Bedminster Press, pp. 72 ff.

SHERRY TURKLE   **Computer as Rorschach**

Armer, P. (1963) "Attitudes towards intelligent machines." In Computers and thought, edited by Edward A. Feigenbaum and Julian Feldman. New York: McGraw-Hill.

Neisser, U. (1966) "Computers as tools and as metaphors." In The social impact of cybernetics, edited by Charles Dechert. Notre Dame, Indiana: The University of Notre Dame Press.

Weizenbaum, T. (1976) Computer power and human reason: from judgment to calculation. San Francisco: W. H. Freeman and Co..

GAYE TUCHMAN   **Women's Magazines: Marry, Don't Work**

Busby, Linda J. (1975) "Sex-role research on the mass media." Journal of Communication, 25(4):107–31.

Clarke, P. and V. Espositio. (1966). "A study of occupational advice for women in magazines." Journalism Quarterly. 43:477–85.

Davis, Margaret. (1976) "The *Ladies' Home Journal* and *Esquire:* A comparison." Unpublished manuscript. Stanford University, Department of Sociology.

Flora, Cornelia. (1971) "The passive female: Her comparative image by class and culture in women's magazine fiction." Journal of Marriage and the Family. 33(August):435–44.

Franzwa, Helen. (1974a) "Working women in fact and fiction." Journal of Communication. 24(2):104–9.

———— (1974b) "Pronatalism in women's magazine fiction." In Ellen Peale and Judith Senderowitz (eds.), Pronatalism: The Myth of Motherhood and Apple Pie. New York: Thomas Y. Crowell, pp. 68–77.

———— (1975) "Female roles in women's magazine fiction, 1940–1970." In R. K. Unger and F. L. Denmark (eds.), Woman: Dependent or Independent Variable. New York: Psychological Dimensions, pp. 42–53.

Johns-Heine, P. and H. Gerth. (1949) "Values in mass periodical fiction, 1921–1940." Public Opinion Quarterly. 13(Spring):105–13.

Oppenheimer, Valerie Kincaid. (1970) The Female Labor Force in the United States: Demographic and Economic Factors Governing Its Growth and Changing Composition. Population Monograph Series No. 5. Berkeley: University of California, Institute of International Studies.

Rubin, Lillian. (1976) Worlds of Pain. Life in the Working-Class Family. New York: Basic Books.

Silver, Sheila. (1976) "Then and now—content analysis of *McCall's* magazine." Paper presented at the annual meeting of Association for Education in Journalism. College Park, Maryland, August.

Vanek, Joann. (Forthcoming) Married Women and the Work Day: Time Trends. Baltimore, Md.: Johns Hopkins University Press, chap. 4.

JAMES LULL   **The Social Uses of Television**

Anderson, N. (1923) The hobo. Chicago: University of Chicago Press.

Anderson, R. E., and Carter, I. E. (1974) Human behavior in the social environment. Chicago: Aldine.

Bechtel, R., Achelpohl, C., and Akers, R. (1972) "Correlates between observed behavior and questionnaire responses on television viewing." In E. A. Rubinstein, G. A. Comstock, and J. P. Murray (Eds.), Television and social behavior, 4: Television in day-to-day life: Patterns of use. Washington, D.C.: Government Printing Office, 274–344.

Berelson, B. Lazarsfeld, P., and McPhee, W. N. (1954) Voting: A study of opinion formation in a presidential campaign. Chicago: University of Chicago Press.

Blumer, H. (1969) Symbolic interactionism. Englewood Cliffs, N.J.: Prentice-Hall.

Bruyn, S. (1966) The human perspective in sociology: The methodology of participant observation. Englewood Cliffs, N.J. Prentice-Hall.

Burgess, E. W. (1926) "The family as a unit of interacting personalities." The Family, 1, 3–9.

Carpenter, E. (1972) Oh! What a blow that phantom gave me. New York: Holt, Rinehart and Winston.

Cicourel, A. V. (1974) Theory and method in a study of Argentine fertility. New York: Wiley.

Delia, J. G. (1977) "Contructivism and the study of human communication." Quarterly Journal of Speech, 1, 66–83.

Frentz, T. S., and Farrell, T. B. (1976) "Language-action: A paradigm for communication." Quarterly Journal of Speech, 4, 333–349.

Gans, H. J. (1962) The urban villagers. New York: Free Press.

Garfinkel, H. (1967) Studies in ethnomethodology. Englewood Cliffs, N.J.: Prentice-Hall.

Garfinkel, H., and Stoller, R. J. (1967) "Passing and the managed achievement of sex status in an 'intersexed' person—part 1." In H. Garfinkel, Studies in ethnomethodology. Englewood Cliffs, N.J.: Prentice-Hall.

Glaser, B. G., and Strauss, A. L. (1967) The discovery of grounded theory: Strategies for qualitative research. Chicago: Aldine.

Henry, J. (1965) Pathways to madness. New York: Vintage Books.

Herzog, H. (1944) "What do we really know about daytime serial listeners?" In P. Lazarsfeld and F. N. Stanton (Eds.), Radio research: 1942–43. New York: Duell, Sloan, and Pearce.

Hymes, D. (1964) "Toward ethnographies of communication." American Anthropologist, 6, part 2.

Katz, E. (1951) "The two step flow of communication: An up-to-date report on an hypothesis." Public Opinion Quarterly, 1, 61–78.

Katz, E., and Lazarsfeld, P. (1962) Personal influence: The part played by people in the flow of mass communications. Glencoe, Ill.: Free Press.

Katz, E., and Foulkes, D. (1962) "On the use of mass media as 'escape.'" Public Opinion Quarterly, 4, 377–388.

Katz, E., Blumler, J. G., and Gurevitch, M. (1974) "Uses of mass communication by the individual." In W. P. Davision and F. T. C. Yu (Eds.), Mass communication research. New York: Praeger.

Katz, E. (1977) Looking for trouble: Social research on broadcasting. Lecture given to the British Broadcasting Corporation, London.

Katzman, N. (1972) "Television soap operas: What's been going on anyway?" Public Opinion Quarterly, 1972, 2, 200–212.

Lazarsfeld, P., Berelson, B., and Gaudet, H. (1948) The people's choice. New York: Columbia University Press.

Lazarsfeld, P., and Stanton, F. N. (Eds.). (1949) Communications research: 1948–1949. New York: Harper.

Lewis, O. (1959) Five families. New York: Basic Books.

Lewis, O. (1965) La Vida. New York: Random House.

Liebow, E. (1967) Tally's corner. Little, Brown and Company.

Lull, J. (1976) Mass media and family communication: An ethnography of audience behavior. Doctoral dissertation, University of Wisconsin-Madison.

Lull, J. (1978) "Choosing television programs by family vote." Communication Quarterly 26: 53–57.

Lyle, J. (1972) "Learning from television." In E. A. Rubinstein, G. A. Comstock, and J. P. Murray (Eds.), Television and social behavior, 4: Television in day-to-day life: Patterns of use. Washington, D.C.: Government Printing Office, 19–21.

McQuail, D., Blumler, J. G., and Brown, J. R. (1972) "The television audience: A revised perspective." In D. McQuail (Ed.), Sociology of mass communication. Harmondsworth, England: Penguin Books, 135–165.

Mander, J. (1977) Four arguments for the elimination of televison. New York: Morrow.

Mehan, H., and Wood, H. (1975) The reality of ethnomethodology. New York: Wiley.

Merton, R. K. (1949) "Patterns of influence." In P. Lazarsfeld and F. Stanton (Eds.), Communications research: 1948–1949. New York: Harper.

Nordenstreng, K. (1970) "Comments on 'gratification research' in broadcasting." Public Opinion Quarterly, 2, 130–132.

Philipsen, G. F. (1975) "Speaking like a man in teamsterville: Culture patterns of role enactment in an urban neighborhood." Quarterly Journal of Speech 1: 13–22.

Schiller, H. I. (1973) The mind managers. Boston: Beacon Press.

Walter, J. K., and Stone, V. A. (1975) "Television and family communication." Journal of Broadcasting 4: 409–414.

Whyte, W. F. (1943) Street corner society. University of Chicago Press.

Zimmerman, D. H., and Pollner, M. (1970) "The everyday world as a phenomenon." In J. D. Douglas (Ed.), Understanding everyday life. Chicago: Aldine.

Zimmerman, D. H. (1978) "Ethnomethodology." The American Sociologist 1: 6–15.

RONALD J. FABER, JANE D. BROWN, AND JACK M. MCLEOD **Coming of Age in the Global Village: Television and Adolescence**

Abelson, R. (1976) "Script processing in attitude formation and decision making." In J. Carroll and A. Payne (eds.), Cognition and social behavior. Hillsdale, N.J.: Lawrence Erlbaum.

Adelson, J., and O'Neil, R. (1966) "Growth of political ideas in adolescence: The sense of community." Journal of Personality and Social Psychology, 4:295–306.

Bowerman, C., and Kinch, J. (1959) "Changes in family and peer orientation of children between the fourth and tenth grade." Social Forces, 37:206–211.

Brittain, C. (1969) "Adolescent choices and parent-peer cross-pressures." In R. Grinder (ed.), Studies in adolescence. Toronto: Macmillan.

Campbell, E. (1969) "Adolescent socialization." In D. Goslin (ed.), Handbook of socialization theory and research. Chicago: Rand-McNally.

Cavior, N., and Dokecki, P. R. (1973) "Physical attractiveness, perceived attitude similarity, and academic achievement as contributors to interpersonal attraction among adolescents." Developmental Psychology, 9:44–54.

Chaffee, S., Ward, S., and Tipton, L. (1970) "Mass communication and political socialization." Journalism Quarterly, 47:647–659, 666.

DeFleur, M. (1964) "Occupational roles as portrayed on television." Public Opinion Quarterly, 28:57–74.

―――― and DeFleur, L. (1967) "The relative contribution of television as a learning source for children's occupational knowledge." American Sociological Review, 32(5):777–789.

Douvan, E., and Gould, M. (1966) "Modal patterns in American adolescence." In M. Hoffman and L. Hoffman (eds.), Review of child developmental research, Vol. II. New York: Russell Sage Foundation.

Dunphy, D. (1963) "The social structure of urban adolescent peer groups." Sociometry, 26:230–246.

Ehrmann, W. W. (1959) Premarital dating behavior. New York: Holt, Rinehart and Winston.

Erikson, L. H. (1968) Identity: Youth and crisis. New York: Norton.

Flavell, J., Botkin, P., Fry, C., Wright, J., and Jarvis, P. (1968) The development of role-taking and communication skills in children. New York: Wiley.

Foley, J. (1968) "A functional analysis of television viewing." Unpublished Ph.D. dissertation, University of Iowa.

Frazier, A., and Lisonbee, L. K. (1971) "Adolescent concerns with physique." In R. Muuss (ed.), Adolescent behavior and society: A book of readings. New York: Random House.

Gerson, W. (1966) "Mass media socialization behavior: Negro-white differences." Social Forces, 45:40–50.

Ginzberg, E., Ginsburg, S. W., Axelrad, S., and Herma, J. L. (1951) Occupational choice: An approach to a general theory. New York: Columbia University Press.

Gollin, E. (1958) "Organizational characteristics of social judgment: A developmental investigation." Journal of Personality, 26:139–154.

Greenberg, B., and Dominick, J. (1969) "Racial and social class differences in teenager's use of television." Journal of Broadcasting, 12:331–344.

Gronlund, N., and Anderson, L. (1957) "Personality characteristics of socially accepted, socially neglected and socially rejected junior high school pupils." Educational Administration and Supervision, 43:329–338.

Havighurst, R. (1972) Developmental tasks and education. New York: Longmans, Green.

Horrocks, J. (1965) "Adolescent attitudes and goals." In M. Sherif and C. Sherif (eds.), Problems of youth. Chicago: Aldine.

Janis, I. (1980) "The influence of television on personal decision making." In S. Withey and R. Abeles (eds.), Television and social behavior. Hillsdale, N.J.: Lawrence Erlbaum.

Jennings, M., and Miemi, R. (1974) The political character of adolescence: The influence of families and schools. Princeton, N.J.: Princeton University Press.

Johnstone, J. (1974) "Social integration and mass media use among adolescents: A case study." In J. Blumler and E. Katz (eds.), The uses of mass communications: Current perspectives on gratifications research. Beverly Hills, Cal.: Sage.

Jones, M. C., and Bayley, N. (1950) "Physical maturing among boys as related to behavior." Journal of Educational Psychology, 41:129–148.

Kandel, D., and Lesser, G. (1969) "Parental and peer influence on educational plans of adolescents." American Sociological Review, 34:212–222.

Kohlberg, L. (1976) "Stages and moralization: The cognitive-developmental approach." In T. Lickona (ed.), Moral development and behavior: Theory, research and social issues. New York: Holt, Rinehart and Winston.

Leifer, A., and Lesser, G. (1976) The development of career awareness in young children. Washington, D.C.: National Institute of Education Papers in Education and Work: Number one, H.E.W.

Lorimer, R. (1971) "Change in development of moral judgments in adolescence: The effect of a structured exposition versus a film and discussion." Canadian Journal of Behavioral Science, 3(1):1–10.

Lyle, J., and Hoffman, H. (1972) "Children's use of television and other media." In E. Rubinstein, G. Comstock, and J. Murray (eds.), Television and social behavior, Vol. IV, Television in day-to-day life: Patterns of use. Washington, D.C.: U.S. Government Printing Office.

Marcia, J. (1966) "Development and validation of ego identity status." Journal of Personality and Social Psychology, 3:551–558.

——— (1976) "Identity six years after: A follow-up study." Journal of Youth and Adolescence, 5:145–160.

Matteson, D. (1975) Adolescence today: Sex roles and the search for identity. Homewood, Ill.: Dorsey.

McLeod, J., and Brown, J. (1976) "The family environment and adolescent television use." In R. Brown (eds.), Children and television. Beverly Hills, Cal.: Sage.

McLeod, J., and Chaffee, S. H. (1972) "The construction of social reality." In J. Tedeschi (ed.), The social influence process. Chicago: Aldine-Atherton.

Noble, G. (1976) Children in front of the small screen. Beverly Hills, Cal.: Sage.

Piaget, J. (1972) "Intellectual evolution from adolescence to adulthood." Human Development, 15:1–12.

Pingree, S. (1978) "The effects of nonsexist television commercials and perceptions of reality on children's attitudes about women." Psychology of Women Quarterly, 2:262–277.